MW01015133

To John Bell
I hope this can pass muster
with a Carleton-educated scholar!
Best wishes
James P. Gannon

Irish Rebels
CONFEDERATE TIGERS

The 6th Louisiana Volunteers, 1861-1865

James P. Gannon

Savas Publishing Company
1475 S. Bascom Avenue, Suite 204
Campbell, CA 95008

Manufactured in the United States of America.

Irish Rebels, Confederate Tigers:
The 6th Louisiana Volunteers, 1861-1865

Includes bibliographical references, index, and appendices.

Savas Publishing
1475 S. Bascom Avenue, Suite 204
Campbell, California 95008
(408) 879-9073

Printing Number:
10 9 8 7 6 5 4 3 2 1

ISBN: 1-882810-16-3
First hardcover edition

This book is printed on 50-lb., acid-free stock.

The paper in this book meets or exceeds the guidlines for permanence and durability of the Committee on Production Guidelines for Book Longevity of the Council on Library Resources.

To the Irish Confederates
of New Orleans,
especially Dennis Cavanaugh,
and to all the men of the
6th Louisiana Volunteers.

Pvt. Reddick W. Sibley, Company A, 6th Louisiana, in uniform early in the war. Sibley was captured during the Chancellorsville Campaign near Fredericksburg and severely wounded at Second Winchester, where he lost his leg. *United States Military History Institute, Carlisle, PA*

Table of Contents

Cartography

Photographs & Illustrations

Preface

On March 13, 1865, in the trenches near Petersburg, Virginia, Maj. William H. Manning responded to an order to write a brief history of his infantry regiment, the 6th Louisiana Volunteers. His few remaining men slouched in the muddy trenches that surrounded besieged Petersburg, where Gen. Robert E. Lee's ill-clothed and hungry Army of Northern Virginia was desperately trying to hold out against Gen. Ulysses S. Grant's larger and more powerful Army of the Potomac.

Exhausted and discouraged, the 27-year-old major took up his pen. With no records to guide him, he reconstructed from memory a brief account of the war record of his depleted but proud regiment. He opened his memo with the regiment's organization at Camp Moore, Louisiana, on June 2, 1861, then moved on to record the names of its original commanding officers. It was a roll call of the dead: Col. Isaac Seymour, the prominent New Orleans newspaper editor who had volunteered at age 56, only to be killed at the Battle of Gaines's Mill; Col. Henry Strong, a native of Ireland like so many in the regiment, shot from his white horse at the Battle of Sharpsburg; Maj. Arthur McArthur, killed in the Louisiana Brigade's spectacular charge in the First Battle of Winchester.

With pride tempered by sadness, Manning recorded the memorable campaigns of the previous four years: with the legendary "Stonewall" Jackson in the Shenandoah Valley in 1862; under the revered Robert E. Lee in Maryland in 1862 and Gettysburg in 1863; with Jubal Early in the Valley and at the very gates of Washington in 1864. "In fact," Manning writes, "there has not been any great event in the History of the Army of Northern Virginia in which this Regiment has not rendered Material Service."

And then he turned to the reality faced by the 6th Louisiana at that moment:

> Originally over one thousand men strong, it has been reduced by the fortunes of war to a mere skeleton of its former numerical strength. More than three hundred of the rank and file of this command attested their devotion to the Cause in which they embarked by surrendering

their lives in its behalf. Hundreds of its brave men, maimed and crippled, scattered broadcast throughout the land, bear on their persons living evidences of duty and fidelity to their Country, while the few surviving brave and true men who are still left to do battle in a Just Cause exhibit still the same stern devotion which actuated them in the outstart of the war."[1]

Less than a month after Major Manning wrote his brief narrative, the march of the 6th Louisiana, begun with 916 jubilant volunteers in New Orleans four years earlier, ended with 55 exhausted and forlorn survivors at the small Virginia crossroads of Appomattox Court House.

The story of the 6th Louisiana is like that of so many other regiments of the Confederate Army: a story of hope and despair, of bravery and cowardice, of glory and disgrace, of heroes and deserters. What makes it different from most others is the nature and the background of the men themselves. The 6th Louisiana had a special ethnic character that set it apart from other regiments of the Confederate Army. It was a regiment dominated by Irish Catholic immigrants. Roughly half of its rank and file listed Ireland as their birthplace, and many more were American-born sons of Irish immigrants.

Theirs was the longest march to America's great Civil War—a journey from Ireland, awash in poverty and famine, to the battle fields of Virginia. Driven from their homeland, they found themselves caught up in the epic struggle of their adopted country, which had split in two.

Just as the Irish immigrants in New York, Boston, Philadelphia and other Northern cities rallied to the Union cause, the Irish who poured into New Orleans in the 15 years before the Civil War embraced the cause of the Confederacy with typical Irish loyalty and passion. Though less numerous—and destined to be far less famous—than their countrymen who fought for the Union in the fabled Irish Brigade, these Irish rebels wrote an equally stirring story fighting for the Confederacy. They are the Civil War's forgotten Irish sons—the Confederate Irish.

The Confederate Irish were far outnumbered by their countrymen in the Northern states when war broke out in 1861. More than a million immigrants from Ireland flooded America's shores from the mid-1840s to the mid-1850s as a result of Ireland's disastrous potato famine, and the vast majority of these refugees settled in the North. But many landed at Southern ports or found their way south, so that in 1860, the Irish were the largest white ethnic group in the Confederacy, numbering nearly 85,000. When war came, Irishmen both orth and south answered the

call to arms. While some 150,000 Irish immigrants in the more populous Northern states eventually served in the Union Army, an estimated 30,000 Irish-born Southerners fought for the Confederate army, and Irish units were raised in eight of the eleven states of the Confederacy.[2]

The 6th Louisiana was by no means the only Irish unit fighting for the South. The Confederate Army included scores of heavily-Irish units, from companies to regiments, that often bore colorful names with Celtic flavor: Savannah produced the Irish Jasper Greens, two companies of the 1st Georgia Volunteers; the Emerald Guards, a company of the 8th Alabama Infantry, were Irishmen from Mobile; Charleston produced the Emerald Light Infantry and the Old Irish Volunteers of the 1st South Carolina regiment. The 10th Tennessee infantry regiment from Nashville was largely Irish, while the 1st Virginia infantry regiment included Irish immigrants from Richmond.

No state produced as many Irish Confederates as Louisiana, and no city as many as New Orleans, which in 1860 was home to more immigrants from Ireland than any other place in the South. Several thousand Irish fought in Louisiana regiments during the war. They were scattered throughout the ranks in many regiments and concentrated in a few, most notably the 6th Louisiana. The 6th's roster reads something like a Dublin phone book. This was the regiment, after all, that included 16 Murphys, nine Murrays, eight Sullivans, seven O'Neills, seven Ryans, a half-dozen each of the Fitzgeralds and the Collins', and at least 54 "Micks," that is, names beginning with "Mc," from McCauley and McCormick to McGee and McMahon. An officer shouting, "Private Murphy!" might have found a dozen men snapping to attention.

The Irishmen of the 6th Louisiana, for the most part, were common laborers: dock workers, riverboat crewmen, carpenters, bricklayers, blacksmiths, wagon drivers, sailors. Some were store clerks, printers, policemen, barkeepers or butchers. They were the urban underclass of their day—working-class immigrants of little or no formal education, packed into New Orleans' poorest river-front neighborhoods, competing for jobs with the city's free blacks and slaves, scrambling to grab the bottom rung on the social and economic ladder in a city whose establishment regarded them as the lowest order of humanity.

Given their background and education, the Irish of the regiment left little written record of their war experiences. The Irish-born officers who would have been best able to tell the story of the 6th Louisiana, including Cols. Henry B. Strong and William Monaghan, died leading their men in battle. No history of the regiment has ever been written in the 130 years since the war ended. Except for scattered fragments here and there, the 6th Louisiana and its story slid into obscurity, while the exploits of hundreds of other regiments, North and South, were recorded and glorified.

In the years shortly after the war ended in 1865, a brief article appeared in one of New Orleans' newspapers and was clipped and pasted in the family scrapbook of William J. Seymour, the son of the first commander of the 6th Louisiana, Col. Isaac Gurdon Seymour. The article recalled that three successive field commanders of the regiment—Colonels Seymour, Strong and William Monaghan—died leading the 6th Louisiana in combat. The writer lamented the fact that very little had ever been recorded of the history of this regiment, and asked: "Will the state of Louisiana let the days pass, and her dead heroes be forgotten, and the names and deeds left out of the history of the times that tried men's souls. . .? Let us hope that the historian will appear in time."[3]

My goal in researching and writing this work is to be that long-awaited historian. I began researching the Irish of New Orleans without any such intention. I began simply out of personal curiosity about a man named Dennis Cavanaugh, brother of my great-grandfather Patrick Cavanaugh. Along with that great wave of Irish immigration, Patrick and Dennis arrived in New Orleans in the 1850s. Patrick was destined to become a prosperous pioneer farmer in Minnesota, after taking a Mississippi riverboat as far north as he could go before the outbreak of the Civil War. His brother Dennis was destined to become a Confederate soldier and to die an old man in New Orleans' Confederate Soldiers' Home five decades after the war ended. Looking into Dennis' sad and lonely life, I became intrigued with the story of the Irish Confederates, so long ignored by historians. Though Dennis did not serve in the 6th Louisiana (he enlisted in a combined infantry-artillery-cavalry outfit called Miles' Legion and later served in the 1st Louisiana Heavy Artillery), I decided to focus on the 6th Louisiana because it was the most thoroughly Irish of all the Louisiana regiments—and because its story was so worth telling.

In referring to the 6th Louisiana as an "Irish regiment," I do not intend to overlook the fact that a large minority of its soldiers were non-Irish—German and other immigrants, native Louisianians and Mississippians, and transplanted Northerners as well. Just as Maj. Gen. Richard Taylor thought of the regiment as his "Irishmen" and wrote of their peculiarly Celtic traits, I too refer in this work to Seymour's Irishmen, or the "Irish regiment." This of course is not a slight to the non-Irish of the 6th Louisiana, but rather a recognition of the special characteristic that made this regiment stand out among others, even earning it the nickname of the South's "Irish Brigade." I have tried in this work to give due credit to all the officers and men of the 6th Louisiana, Irish and otherwise, while maintaining a special focus on the Irish personality of the regiment.

It has taken too long for history to give recognition to the Confederate Irish. For the men of the 6th Louisiana, this is their story.

James P. Gannon
Castleton, Virginia. February 1998.

ACKNOWLEDGMENTS

A great many people assisted in producing this book. One of the rewards of my research was the opportunity to meet and to learn from so many helpful historians, archivists, librarians, scholars and Civil War buffs. There are more than I can acknowledge and thank in this space, but special appreciation must be expressed to the many who went out of their way to aid a newcomer aspiring to the ranks of Civil War historians.

The historians of the National Park Service's battlefield parks were uniformly helpful and friendly. I owe special thanks to the following: Robert K.Krick of Fredericksburg & Spotsylvania National Battlefield Park; his son Robert E.L. Krick of the Richmond National Battlefield Park; Ted Alexander at Antietam, Cathy S. Beeler at Monocacy, Chris Calkins at Petersburg, Scott Hartwig at Gettysburg, Keith Bohannon at Fredericksburg, Ray Brown and Chris Bryce at Manassas. For their generous guidance, suggestion of sources, explanations of battles and strategy, and their willingness to wade through early drafts of chapters and offer advice and corrections, I am in their debt.

In New Orleans, the helpful staff of the Special Collections department of Howard-Tilton Memorial Library at Tulane University guided me to the critical manuscripts and 6th Louisiana records without which this work would have been impossible. To Wilbur E. Meneray and his patient staff, especially Courtney Page, I offer thanks for their assistance over a three-year period. Sherrie S. Pugh, librarian at the Jackson

Barracks Library of the Louisiana Office of the Adjutant General, went above and beyond the call of duty in digging out musty military records relating to the 6th Louisiana and related subjects. Patricia Ricci and her staff at the Confederate Memorial Hall in New Orleans provided similar help.

Many other archivists and librarians helped build the story in these pages. Michael Musick, military historian at the National Archives in Washington, D.C., dug out records and steered me to critical materials stored there. Robert Cox and his staff at the William L. Clements Library at the University of Michigan, Ann Arbor, provided important documents on Isaac and William Seymour. Others who provided similar help included Jeanette Kling at the Louisiana State Archives in Baton Rouge, David Madden at the United States Civil War Center at Louisiana State University, Dr. Richard Sommers of the U.S. Military History Institute at Carlisle Barracks, Pa., Mary Ison of the Division of Prints and Photographs of the Library of Congress in Washington, and John M. Coski at the Museum of the Confederacy in Richmond, Va. Among those who helped me most often were the local librarians at the Culpeper (Va.) Public Library, especially Ann Robson, and the Rappahannock County Library, where I camped for much of my reading and research.

Other writers and scholars were generous in sharing their knowledge and expertise, including Terry Jones, Clark "Bud" Hall, Joseph W.A. Whitehorne, N. Wayne Cosby, Thomas W. Brooks, Michael D. Jones, Ed Gleeson, Mike Kane, Kerby Miller, David Gleason and Charles Laverty. Arthur Bergeron Jr., historian at Pamplin Park Civil War Site in Petersburg, Va., not only provided research help on Louisiana military units but generously reviewed and critiqued my manuscript, as did Terry Johnston of the University of South Carolina. Their expertise saved me from many errors and filled gaps in my research. The errors and omissions that remain are my own.

Special thanks go to several descendants of 6th Louisiana men who shared family documents, lore and photographs of their ancestors with me. These included George W. Gervais (Col. Isaac Seymour), William Calloway (Capt. Allen M. Calloway), James Trahern Micklem, Sr. (Cpl. William E. Trahern) and Joyce Watkins (Pvt. George Zeller).

I want to thank my friend Richard Willing, a font of inspiration and enthusiasm as well as a scholar of all things Irish and the Civil War, for his unflagging support and help. He would have made a fabulous officer for the 6th Louisiana. I would also like to thank Monalisa DiAngelo,

Dave Fox and Susan Gladding of Prussia Graphics of Santa Clara, CA for excellent work in producing this book. Of course, this work would never have materialized without the encouragement and unstinting support of my publisher and chief editor, Ted Savas, who saw something worthwhile at the beginning, and turned an amateur's effort into a polished book.

Finally, there is a debt of the heart to my wife Joan, who understood and encouraged this labor of love, and to that distant figure who inspired it all, Dennis Cavanaugh of New Orleans, my own Irish Rebel ancestor. I cannot overstate the appreciation I have gained for the courage, honor and endurance of the Civil War soldier, especially those Irish immigrants who willingly donned the Confederate gray, and who inspired me to tell their story of sacrifice and service. We shall not see their like again.

Introduction

"Spoilin' for a fight with old Abe"
— *Daily Delta*, April 19, 1861.

On April 28, 1861, two weeks after Confederate guns had fired the first shots of the Civil War against Fort Sumter, a notice appeared in the *Daily Picayune*, one of New Orleans' leading newspapers. The notice was a call to arms aimed at the thousands of Irish immigrants of the city:

> The roll for the formation of Company B, Irish Brigade, will be opened on Monday, the 29th inst., at 10 o'clock A.M., at the Olive Branch Coffee House, corner Erato and Tchoupitoulas streets, the undersigned will be present every day and evening until the roll shall be filled up, when the members will elect their officers. Prompt action is now expected of every Irishman in the present crisis. [signed] Wm. Monaghan.[1]

Whether the selection of the Olive Branch Coffee House as a site to recruit for war was an expression of William Monaghan's Irish sense of ironic humor is uncertain, but there is no doubt that he was a true son of the auld sod. Born in Ireland, he worked in New Orleans before the war as a notary public, a position requiring education and a literacy level that many of his fellow immigrants lacked. He was a man marked for leadership, and would in time rise to command the Confederate regiment sometimes called the South's "Irish Brigade." Exactly what impelled him to recruit a company of his fellow countrymen to fight for the Confederate cause is not known, but his evident pro-Southern sentiments were widespread and enthusiastically held among many of the Irish living in New Orleans.

In the weeks leading up to the crisis at Fort Sumter, the Crescent City was gripped with war fever. Cannon boomed and church bells rang on January 26, 1861, when word arrived that the state secessionist convention at Baton Rouge had voted Louisiana out of the Union. Crowds gathered in the streets, business houses closed, militia companies paraded in gala uniforms and fired 100-gun salutes to independence. For weeks following, the city's newspapers crackled with belligerent rhetoric against the North and were full of notices of new military companies forming and holding drills. The news from Fort Sumter heated this patriotic pot to a boil, rallying the city's men to respond to President Jefferson Davis' April 16 call for 32,000 men to the service of the Confederate States of America, 5,000 of whom were to come from Louisiana.[2]

In New Orleans, the largest city in the South and a booming port of commerce at the mouth of America's greatest river, the call to arms was heard by a population more diverse than any other throughout the Confederacy—and perhaps the whole continental nation. The great port at the mouth of the Mississippi River was the melting pot of the South. Despite its history as a French and later Spanish colony and its Creole and Cajun culture, New Orleans in 1861 was home to more Irish immigrants than any other place in the South. The city was more than four times as large as Richmond, Virginia, and was more like New York and Boston in respect to its polyglot ethnic makeup than it was to the Confederate capital-to-be. At the outbreak of the Civil War, New Orleans was packed with more Irish and German immigrants than Richmond, Charleston, Memphis, Mobile, Savannah and Montgomery combined.[3]

The 1860 census found 24,398 Irish-born residents in New Orleans, some of whom had arrived as early as the 1830s and had risen to prominent positions in the city as merchants, bankers or hotel-keepers. More had arrived in the 1840s, attracted to jobs digging the swampy city's canals and laying its railroads, or working as longshoremen or wagon drivers on the city's bustling wharves and levees. But the great tidal wave of Irish immigration came in the early 1850s as a result of Ireland's historic calamity, the Potato Famine of 1845-49. This national disaster devastated the staple of the Irish peasant's diet and triggered massive emigration of destitute, hopeless, rural Irish refugees to America. More than a quarter of a million immigrants—mostly Irish but also including thousands of Germans, Italians and others—flooded New Orleans between 1850 and 1855. Most of them moved on, up the great river to the new frontiers of the Mississippi Valley, but thousands settled in the Crescent City, where jobs were plentiful and wages were good—at least by the standards of a people fleeing poverty.[4]

The Irish who landed at New Orleans in the 1840s and 1850s arrived as an odd by-product of the trans-Atlantic cotton trade. The ships that carried Dixie's cotton from New Orleans to England landed and unloaded at Liverpool. Eager to fill their empty holds for the return trip to America, owners of these ships offered the cheapest passage to America, attracting thousands of famine Irish. It was "bricks or Irishmen for ballast," in a popular saying of that day, and the desperate Irish willingly packed themselves into the dreary vessels as their only hope of reaching America.[5]

Living in tenements and shantytowns such as the city's "Irish Channel" neighborhood, and working as common laborers, most of these famine Irish had spent only a few years in New Orleans before the clouds of war gathered in late 1860. They competed for work with New Orleans' large population of free blacks, and often accepted jobs—such as digging canals through the steamy, malarial swamps that surrounded the city—slave-owners would not risk assigning to their valuable slaves. The Irish were plentiful, strong, desperate and expendable, and these qualities that made them useful as cheap labor would also serve well in the bloody work of war to come.[6]

New Orleans' newly-arrived Irish ranked at the very bottom of the social order, regarded by the city's better classes as uneducated, drunken, brawling social misfits who bred epidemic disease and destitute children. They arrived in "coffin ships" ridden with illness and filth, and easily fell victim to tropical New Orleans' frequent epidemics of cholera, malaria and yellow fever. When 12,000 New Orleanians—one third of them Irish—died of yellow fever in the summer of 1853, the epidemic was widely blamed on the influx of these sickly people who lived in shantytowns, boarding-houses, and even shacks abandoned by Negroes. Against the thinly-veiled contempt of the natives and upper classes of the city, these clannish Celts huddled together in their Catholic churches, political clubs, neighborhood saloons, and budding labor unions, hoping to eventually be accepted as true Americans and loyal Southerners.[7]

The coming of war in 1861 provided the Irish an opportunity to display their patriotism and loyalty. Eager to prove themselves every bit as worthy and brave as the sons of the South's ruling classes, New Orleans' Irish immigrants rallied to the Confederate flag. By donning a Confederate soldier's uniform, they would take on the cloak of loyal sons of the South and show skeptical Southerners that they were not foreigners but new Americans. Like most volunteers, they also were attracted to the adventure and excitement of the bloodless pageantry that preceded the real war, as well as the promise of steady pay. The city's recruiting offices quickly filled with excited and willing Irish volunteers. The *Daily Delta* reported that all foreign-born residents of New Orleans were eager soldiers, adding, "As for our Irish citizens—whew!—they are 'spiling' for a fight' with old Abe."[8]

Other newspapers of the city hailed the turnout of Irish volunteers and praised those leading the effort. On May 24, the *Daily Picayune* carried a salute to "The Irish Brigade":

> This fine body of men will compare with any yet raised in our city, and is attached to the 6th Regiment of Louisiana Volunteers. Mr. Michael O'Connor has been greatly instrumental in raising this corps, and justly deserves the title of 'Father of the Brigade.' He has been one of our best citizens, and for the past sixteen years an exempt fireman.

O'Connor, a New Orleans store-keeper, would accompany the regiment to the battlefront in Virginia as the 6th Louisiana's sutler, the itinerant merchant who supplied soldiers with food, clothing and other goods. O'Connor evidently served in the patron or godfather role assumed at that time by leading citizens such as bankers, businessmen or planters, who helped organize and outfit particular companies.[9]

The recruitment notice for William Monaghan's "Irish Brigade" company was just one of many such appeals aimed at the city's ethnics. It appears that there was some thought of creating a Louisiana Irish Brigade—that is, three or four regiments totaling 3,000 to 4,000 men—judging from the widespread use of the term in newspaper recruiting notices. The same day that Monaghan's notice appeared in the *Daily Picayune*, another notice in that newspaper declared that "Company A, Irish Brigade" would meet for drill that evening at its headquarters at 64 St. Charles Street. The notice was signed by "S. L. James, Captain"—the same Samuel L. James elected major of the 6th Louisiana the following month.

Another notice in the Sunday *Delta* of May 19, appearing under the heading "The Irish Brigade," argued that the Southern Irish were at least as eager as Irish immigrants in the Northern states to sign up to fight for their side. "They may boast in the North of their 79th Regiment, and their Billy Mulligan Rangers, said to be Irishmen to the backbone," read the notice, "but we can vouch for 4,000 Irishmen in this city, ready and willing to enter the Brigade and fight for the South to the cannon's mouth; and as evidence we call attention to the advertisement of Company 'C' Irish Brigade, Capt. McCann."[10]

If a full Irish brigade actually was contemplated, it failed to materialize. Instead, the various companies of Irish volunteers raised in New Orleans were assigned to different Louisiana regiments, several of which had a strong Irish composition. No state in the Confederacy had as many regiments boasting an Irish character as did Louisiana. The 1st Louisiana Volunteers included companies composed mostly of immigrants and bearing such Irish names as the Emmet Guards and Montgomery Guards. The 7th Louisiana Volunteers were more than one-third Irish-born and included a company from Donaldsonville, the Irish Volunteers, which was 92 percent Irish. The notorious Louisiana Tigers of Maj. Roberdeau Wheat's 1st Special Battalion—who would earn a reputation for rowdy behavior even before they won fame as a fierce fighting unit on the battlefield of Manassas—were mainly New Orleans "wharf rats," the rough, Irish dock workers who loved a good brawl as much as they loved a jug of whiskey. The polyglot 10th Louisiana Volunteers eventually fielded five companies dominated by Irish immigrants, although Germans, Italians, Polish, French, Scotsmen, Russians and other nationalities were represented.[11]

The 6th Louisiana was the most thoroughly Irish regiment of them all. Seven of its ten companies were recruited in New Orleans, primarily among the city's immigrants. Of the 980 men of the 6th Louisiana whose birthplace is recorded, at least 468 were born in Ireland. Another 100 men, undoubtedly sons of immigrants, bore common Irish surnames. From this it appears that close to 60 percent of regiment was Irish by birth or ancestry. The 6th's foreign flavor was enhanced by at least 123 German immigrants and 73 others born abroad—Englishmen, Frenchmen, Scots, Canadians—even a scattering from Norway, Sweden, Holland, Mexico and Cuba. In total, about two-thirds of the 6th Louisiana's soldiers whose birthplaces are recorded were foreign-born.[12]

By April 1861, hundreds of New Orleans' citizens had responded to the call to arms, joining independent military companies that were awaiting muster into Confederate service. The Metairie Race Course outside the city became the first camp for these soldiers-to-be. By early May, some 3,000 volunteers had overwhelmed the boggy grounds of the race course, which was dubbed Camp Walker. It was located in a swampy area infested with mosquitoes and lacked good drinking water. Louisiana Governor Thomas Overton Moore, fearing an epidemic, ordered that a better camp be found away from the city to serve as the state's main assembly point for the thousands more that would be called to war.

Irish lads recruited in New Orleans by Capt. Samuel L. James were the first to arrive at the new camp and helped lay it out in a woods along the railroad line that ran north to Jackson, Mississippi. James, a New Orleans civil engineer of Irish parentage, and his Company A, Irish Brigade, took the New Orleans, Jackson and Great Northern railroad 78 miles north of the city to the station at Tangipahoa to help select the site and prepare it for the influx of troops. About a mile north of the station, in the piney woods near the Mississippi border, they laid out an expansive camp along Beaver Creek and the Tangipahoa River. The new grounds, named Camp Moore, offered well-drained camping sites and plenty of clean water. Within days, the railroad began carrying thousands of volunteers to the new camp for brief drilling before being sent to war.[13]

The various companies that would form the 6th Louisiana began arriving at Camp Moore by mid-May. It's not known just how the companies were selected and assigned to different regiments, but it appears that the seven companies from New Orleans that were dominated by immigrants were chosen to form the nucleus of the 6th Louisiana, giving it its strong ethnic character. Three companies assigned to the regiment were overwhelmingly Irish. In Capt. Henry Strong's Calhoun Guards, which became Company B of the 6th Louisiana, 89 of the original 105 officers and men were born in Ireland. In William Monaghan's "Irish Brigade" company, which became Company F, 93 of the 102 original volunteers were Irish-born. In the other "Irish Brigade" company of Captain James, which became company I, 80 of the 90 original volunteers were Irish-born. In addition, Irish recruits made up about half of the Violet Guards, which became Company K; and a third or more of the Orleans Rifles, which became Company H, and the Mercer Guards, Company E. In contrast, more than half of the Pemberton Rangers, which became Company G, were Prussians, Bavarians and others from New Orleans' Germanic community.

To fill out the regiment, three companies recruited far from New Orleans were added. Louisianians dominated the St. Landry Light Guards, recruited in St. Landry Parish, which became Company C; the Tensas Rifles, volunteers from the parish of that name, included a diverse mix of native Louisianians, Mississippians, Irishmen and others, and became Company D; the Union and Sabine Rifles, recruited from those two parishes and destined to be the 6th Louisiana's Company A, probably was made up mostly of native Louisianians, though birthplaces for its men are not recorded. Overall, however, men born in Louisiana accounted for only about 17 percent of those whose birthplaces are known—163 men out of 980 total.[14]

The 6th Louisiana was organized at Camp Moore on June 2 as the men of the 10 assembled companies elected the officers that would command them. Isaac G. Seymour was selected as colonel, Louis Lay as lieutenant colonel, and Samel L. James as major. The man they chose as their colonel was a distinguished, white-haired New Orleans newspaper editor of social prominence, Ivy League education and strong military background. At age 56, Seymour was much older than the men he was to lead, who were mostly in their twenties, though some teenagers and a few graybeards over 40 also were in the ranks. The aging colonel, descended from an old Connecticut family, was born in Savannah, Georgia, in October 1804. He graduated with honors from Yale University in 1825 and soon moved to Macon to practice law. But he found lawyer's work distasteful and turned to publishing, becoming editor of the *Georgia Messenger* in Macon, a position he held for 17 years before moving to New Orleans in 1848. There he became the editor of the *Commercial Bulletin*, the city's major business newspaper, and a figure of social and political influence in the South's pre-eminent business center.[15]

Besides publishing, Seymour had one other great passion. He was, a long-time colleague wrote, "enthusiastically fond of military life." In 1836, he commanded a company of volunteers in the war against the Seminoles in Florida, serving under General Winfield Scott. He led a battalion of cavalry under Scott again in the war against Mexico in 1846-47, during which such young officers as Robert E. Lee and Ulysses S. Grant began building their military reputations. A New Orleans newspaper described Seymour as "an experienced soldier, an accomplished tactician and strict disciplinarian" whose fatherly oversight and rigid drilling of the 6th Louisiana "soon made that regiment one of the most efficient in the service."[16]

As an editor with family ties to the North and a former officer in the U.S. Army, Seymour was no secessionist. "He was a strong and persistent friend of the Union, and had a peculiar attachment to its flag, having braved danger and death under its folds, and having had two of his ancestors killed outright in battling for its defence," a New Orleans newspaper commented. "He believed that the wrongs of the South could be more readily redressed and its rights more certainly secured in the Union than out of it. But when the people of the State of his birth and that of his adoption resolved to secede, he thought it was his duty to range himself on the side of his native South, and though advanced in years and somewhat shattered in health, promptly proffered his sword to the Governor of Louisiana, as did many others who held like opinions."[17]

Despite his anti-secession sentiments, his age and his business responsibilities in New Orleans, Seymour found the lure of one more military adventure too much to resist. Entrusting his newspaper duties to his son William, he volunteered for service in the Confederate army. His distinguished military record made him an obvious choice to lead the 6th Louisiana.

At Camp Moore, the men who were to serve under Colonel Seymour began adjusting to life as soldiers. Private George Zeller, a 24-year-old butcher of German ancestry, wrote home on May 25: "We have a very nice cool place here, plenty of good water to drink but have to walk about a have [half] a mile for it. Dear Mother, we have to get up at 5 o'-clock in the morning and answer to our name, breakfast at 6 o'clock, Dinner at 1 o'clock, supper at 6 o'clock and to bed at nine o'clock at night. Nobody is allowed out of their tents after nine o'clock at night."[18]

Though most of the men remained healthy, some fell ill at Camp Moore, where the first fatality among the ten companies occurred. "The Irish Brigade buried one of their corporals this evening, who came to his death from a fit of apoplexy, or something like it," reported the May 19 *Sunday Delta*, without naming the unlucky soldier. "He ate very heartily and went bathing right after, and the water here being very cold, the blood rushed to his head and after walking five paces from the river, he fell dead." The newspaper rather heartlessly blamed the death on "carelessness by the deceased," and added, "In other respects the place is healthy, and superior to Camp Walker."[19]

The 6th Louisiana was mustered into Confederate service on June 4 and immediately received orders to leave for Virginia, where the first major battle of the war was expected. Half the regiment boarded the trains on June 9 and the rest two days later, bound for the "seat of war." "The Regiment left Camp Moore on the 9th [and] 11th of June and arrived at Manassas Jct. on the 14th and 16th June," recorded George P. Ring, first lieutenant of Company K, in his wartime diary. Ring would return home after the war, but more than a third of the men who boarded the trains with him would never see Louisiana again.[20]

Chapter One:

To the Front: VIRGINIA

"Nothing is needed. . .but a good fight."
— *Capt. William H. Manning, Company K*

As the summer of 1861 began the Confederate Army of the Potomac, commanded by New Orleans' own Brig. Gen. Pierre G. T. Beauregard, was stationed near the strategic railroad crossing of Manassas Junction, some 20 miles west of Washington. After arriving at Manassas, the 6th Louisiana went into camp several miles to the east at Fairfax Station, along the Orange & Alexandria Railroad, confident that Beauregard's army soon would meet and crush Brig. Gen. Irvin McDowell's Federal army in a short and glorious war. On June 20, Beauregard organized his 19 regiments into six brigades. The 6th Louisiana was placed with two Alabama regiments in a brigade commanded by Brig. Gen. Richard S. Ewell, a 44-year-old West Point graduate.[1]

Colonel Seymour relished these early days of camp life. Though he admitted to being "in the dark" as to the army's strategic plans, he wrote a friend at the War Department in Richmond that "I am very comfortably fixed. I have large tents decently furnished and my bedspread and pillows. . . .My mess is a very good one and I spread as good a table as Mrs. Lincoln. . .although we have no table cloth and drink the very best kind of Java out of tin cups. . . .My health is excellent and I am enjoying camp life to my full satisfaction."[2]

The silver-haired colonel, who was twice the age of the average enlisted man, was affectionately known in the regiment as "the old man." A stickler for military correctness, Seymour was like a stern but loving father to his men, known for his occasional use of a small rod or switch to mete out punishment to errant soldiers. Once when a drummer beat out the wrong call in camp the "old man" rushed out of his tent, grabbed a youthful fellow he thought was the drummer, and gave him a good whipping. When he returned to his tent, he found his orderly grinning and barely suppressing laughter. When Seymour asked what was so funny, the orderly told him that he had just beat a sergeant of Company F who looked like the drummer. The surprised colonel went looking for the fellow to apologize and invited him into his tent, where he treated him to an apple toddy. When the youth departed, the orderly again began snickering. Seymour demanded to know the reason for his renewed mirth. "You treated the drummer to an apple toddy," replied the orderly. "He looks so much like the Sergeant of Company F you whipped a while ago."[3]

For many of the Irish immigrants of the 6th Louisiana, the early days in camp compared favorably to their lives as laborers in New Orleans. "My health was never better in my life," Pvt. Nicholas Herron wrote in early July to his New Orleans cousin. "Climate is fine and cool except a few hours at noon the sun comes out as hot as it is in New Orleans. We only drill in the morning and evening."[4]

Though hunger would be their curse later in the war, many of the regiment ate better now than they had at home. "This is the poorest part of Virginia yet we enjoy ourselves very well," wrote Herron, a 21-year-old Irish-born bricklayer from New Orleans. "The farmer around here brings in milk and dried, fresh meat but they sell them very dear. We get very good rations here. . . .We have a suttler here that supplies us in everything we want in the way of clothing to be deducted from our $11 per month. . . ." The men were fit, rested and ready for action. "We are in fine trim for a good fight," Herron boasted.

Southerners were confident that when the fight came, Confederate troops were certain to defeat the Northerners. In a dispatch written from Fairfax Station on June 24, 1861, the war correspondent of the *Daily True Delta* informed New Orleans readers that "all Virginia is now on a formidable footing of war." The sprawling Confederate army camp around Manassas seemed "bewildering," he wrote. "The whole country around seems a continuous camp. Fortifications bristle up in every direction." The 6th Louisiana was posted closer to the enemy than any other regiment, the newspaperman wrote. "Col. Seymour's Louisiana Sixth regiment has the post of honor, being in the nearest proximity to the foe. I do not say the post of danger, for, judging from the specimens of Federal fighting heretofore exhibited, there is nothing to be feared from them, while with such men as are in the Sixth regiment, there is no such word as fail." Captains Monaghan and Joseph Hanlon, leading the two Irish Brigade companies, led a small scouting party out in advance of the Confederate lines and chased "two suspicious characters" who escaped, the correspondent added, "which shows perhaps one thing, that in the quality of running, the Lincolnites are too much for our friends in the Irish Brigade."[5]

Such boasting was the usual stuff of newspaper reports in these quiet weeks before the clash of arms, but soon the fighting qualities of the two armies would be tested for real. On July 16, General McDowell began marching toward Manassas to meet Beauregard. The Southern commander, already famous as the "hero of Sumter" for capturing the Charleston harbor fort of that name in the first clash of the war, was eager to add to his glory by smashing the Federals in the war's first major land battle. He deployed his army—some 20,000 men soon to be augmented by another 11,000 arriving by train from Winchester under Brig. Gen. Joseph E. Johnston—along the southern banks of Bull Run, a steep-banked stream twisting eastward through woods and farm fields. His thin defensive line stretched eight miles, from a stone bridge over Bull Run on the Warrenton Turnpike to the railroad bridge at Union Mills, where the Orange & Alexandria railroad crossed the stream on its way to Manassas Junction.[6]

The first clash with the Federals occurred on July 18. The 6th Louisiana was caught in an exposed position at its advance outpost at Fairfax Station. Early that morning the 6th's pickets, posted a mile or so north of the regiment's position, were driven in by the vanguard of McDowell's forces, triggering a hasty retreat of the regiment toward Beauregard's line of battle along Bull Run. "We had a very narrow escape out of Fairfax station," Private Herron wrote to his cousin. The regiment's pickets reported that the Union columns "were within two miles of us marching in three large bodies. . .so we had about 15 minutes to leave. . . .We retreated back along the rail road to Union Mills, burning the bridges as we came on." Captain Monaghan, commanding Company F, reported that his pickets were nearly captured. "My 1st Lieutenant, M[ichael] O'Connor, being officer of the picket guard, came near being cut off by the enemy with his whole guard, but by some tall walking arrived at the company as the Regt. was marching off." The regiment, after bivouacking for the night on the north side of Bull Run, crossed the stream via the railroad bridge at 6:00 a.m. on July 18, burning it after they crossed. Safely across, Monaghan's Irishmen dug rifle pits along the stream and rested on their arms.[7]

For one unlucky 6th Louisiana soldier, the hasty retreat from the regiment's advance picket post proved fatal. Making his way back toward the main Confederate line along Bull Run, Sgt. Francis X. Demaign of Company A was accidentally killed by skirmishers of a Mississippi regiment who evidently mistook him for an enemy soldier. Demaign, according to regimental records, had been cut off at his advance post near Fairfax Station on the morning of July 17, and thus may have approached the nervous Mississippians alone. He was the regiment's first battle casualty, a victim of mistaken identity rather than a martyr fallen in glorious clash with the enemy. The war that was just beginning would produce many such unlucky victims of what's now called "friendly fire."[8]

After their narrow escape, the men of the 6th Louisiana slept on their muskets alongside the Alabama regiments in Ewell's Brigade at Union Mills ford. Here they awaited McDowell's assault, which Beauregard himself expected on his right flank. They felt certain that they were in for their baptism of fire as Sunday, July 21 dawned. "We were aroused by the firing of the Yankee's large guns," Private Herron wrote. "We were fully sure that we should be in the thickest of the battle this day, but we were disappointed."[9]

McDowell, whose reconnaissance of the Confederate right on July 18 had convinced him it was too heavily defended to attack frontally, changed his strategy. After a night march of six miles the Federal commander launched a flank attack on Sunday morning on the left, far upstream from the main Confederate body. The move surprised Beauregard, who had planned to launch his own attack on the Federal left flank that very morning. Instead, McDowell had decided on exactly the same manueuver and had beaten him to the punch. Beauregard was forced to rapidly begin shifting forces to his left to try to hold back McDowell's columns advancing on his exposed flank.[10]

The attacking Union soldiers, some 13,000 strong, outnumbered the surprised Confederates, who gradually fell back to high ground around the farmhouse of a widow named Judith Henry. There, on what became known as Henry House Hill, the battle surged back and forth for hours.

A determined stand by a Virginia brigade commanded by Brig. Gen. Thomas J. Jackson gave birth to the legend of "Stonewall" Jackson, the general who would make Louisiana troops, including the Irishmen of the 6th Louisiana, famous as fighters in the months to come.

The 6th Louisiana, though, was miles from the main battle and occupied by an almost comic bit of marching to and fro, due to confusion on the part of their commanding generals and a mix-up of orders. General Beauregard's plan of attack on the morning of July 21 had called for the Confederate brigades on his right, anchored by Ewell's Brigade, to cross Bull Run and advance toward Centreville in hope of getting in McDowell's rear and cutting off his line of retreat to Washington. But Ewell, who had been ordered by Beauregard at 5:30 that morning to "hold yourself in readiness to take the offensive on Centreville at a moment's notice," never received the order to begin the attack. If such an order was sent, the courier never reached him. Instead, Ewell belatedly heard from Brig. Gen. David R. Jones, who was to join him in the advance on Centreville, that Beauregard had ordered the attack. Ewell then ordered his brigade across Bull Run, hurrying toward Centreville. Soon, however, a new order arrived from Beauregard. The Creole general was alarmed at the vigorous Federal attack on his left and ordered Ewell to fall back across Bull Run.[11]

It was a maddening situation for the 6th Louisiana. The diary of Lt. George Ring clearly conveys the frustration felt by men eager to make a mark in the first great battle of the war. "About 11 o'clock [a.m.] we received orders to make a flank movement towards the enemy's right," Ring recorded in the little leather-bound ledger book he carried with him. "But after a quick march of a mile, the order was countermanded and we were ordered to proceed to relief of our extreme left that was being hard-pressed. Making a circuit of nine miles through dust and dirt, and under a broiling sun without a drop of water, we reached the extreme left about 4-1/2 o'clock [p.m.], where we had the mortification to find that the battle had been fought and won before our arrival."[12]

Private Herron told much the same story in a letter home:

> We had to do some tall marching. We were under command of Gen. Yewell who got orders from Gen. Beauregard to march on to Centreville to outflank the enemy, but when we were within two miles of Centreville, it seems that there were some misunderstanding between Gen. Yewell and Beauregard. We got orders to right about face and march back to the battlefield. . . .The Yankees were beginning to retreat so we had not the pleasure of firing one shot at them, but it was not our fault for we were marching all day and part of the night too.[13]

Company F's Captain Monaghan filed a report brimming over with the regiment's bitter frustration over missing the battle. The regiment "first crossed Bull Run on the ruins of the railroad bridge after 7 a.m., marching toward Centreville," he wrote, "then about-faced and returned to its starting point." About 10:30 a.m. the regiment "crossed Bull Run again at the same place, marched past Union Mills on the Centreville Road until we came within 2-1/2 miles of that place," then halted and began retracing its steps back to its starting point again. After a few minutes rest, the perplexed Louisianians were ordered to march to the battlefield "where we arrived just in time to see the enemy in retreat but not near enough to get a shot at him," Monaghan reported. At dark, the frustrated men began marching back to their camp at Union mills, where they arrived at 10:00 p.m. "Thus ended the memorable 21st of July," wrote a disgusted Monaghan, "a day glorious to our sacred cause but full of bitter regrets to me and my gallant company, who, notwithstanding a march of over 25 miles, did not get a shot at the enemy. I hope for better luck next time."[14]

The 6th Louisiana's frustration was mixed with envy, too, because some of their home-state comrades, including Col. Harry Hays' 7th Louisiana Infantry and Maj. Roberdeau Wheat's 1st Louisiana Special Battalion, had fought gallantly at Manassas. Some of the envy and frustration dissipated, however, when the men of the 6th got a sobering look at the bloody field of battle, which was grotesquely littered with the corpses of Union and Confederate soldiers. "The battle field looked frightful that evening," Private Herron wrote to his cousin. "It was a sight that I will never forget and a sight that I would never care to see again."[15] Another awed member of the regiment, 2d Lt. Jeremiah Hogan of Company B, wrote to a friend that "the dead, dying and wounded lay in heaps with dead horses, arms and ammunition scattered all over the place, the wounded in agony crying for mercy and relief."[16]

In truth, the casualties of the Battle of Manassas (or Bull Run, as Northerners called it) were small by standards of the war yet to come, but the impact of the Confederate victory would loom large in the months ahead. Beauregard had rallied his army from the morning surprise of the Federal flank attack to turn the tide in the afternoon, which ultimately saw the Unionist lines crumble in the face of the Southerners' counter-attack. The Federal army's retreat had turned into a rout that sent streams of panicked soldiers scattering back toward Washington in disarray and disgrace. The shock of that defeat, and the implication that

Lincoln's troops were no match for the determined defenders of the South, cast a blanket of gloom over the North. Psychologically, the defeat temporarily paralyzed the Federals—it would be eight months later before another invasion of Virginia would be attempted—while in the long run it steeled the Union's determination and awakened Northerners to the realization that they must mobilize for a long war. For the South, the victory produced elation and false confidence that the Unionists would never match their glorious heroes on any battlefield.[17]

Soon after Manassas the Confederate Army of the Potomac was reorganized. The reorganization grouped the 6th, 7th, 8th and 9th Louisiana regiments and Wheat's Special Battalion into an all-Louisiana brigade under command of General William H. T. Walker of Georgia. It was an arrangement of promise for the Louisianians, and one that would help foster the legend of the "Louisiana Tigers." That nickname was first applied to Wheat's men and later used more generally to refer to all the Louisiana troops, reflecting their reputation as fierce fighters on the battlefield and undisciplined roughnecks in camp and on the march.[18]

The selection of a Georgian to head the Louisiana Brigade may have dismayed some officers and men of the 6th, though Colonel Seymour protested—perhaps a bit too much—that he was not disappointed to be passed over for the coveted position. "My health is very good and so is that of the Regiment," he reported in a letter to a friend written shortly after the formation of the 1st Louisiana Brigade. "As you will have heard before this, Gen. Walker was appointed to the Brigade, and I don't regret it. He is an old United States Army officer, and of large experience." But Seymour went on to hint at political intrigue and competition in the appointment. "The powers in Richmond would have given the place to Taylor, but they did not dare do it," Seymour wrote, referring to Richard Taylor, the ambitious and politically well-connected colonel in command of the 9th Louisiana Regiment. Taylor, who soon would succeed Walker in command of the Louisiana Brigade, was the son of a former president, the brother-in-law of Confederate President Jefferson Davis, and a prominent Louisiana planter descended from one of Virginia's most distinguished families.[19]

Seymour's letter was not explicit in explaining why "the powers in Richmond" did not "dare" to name Taylor to lead the brigade at this time, but clearly such an appointment would have looked political. As for his own chances for the position, Seymour commented, "I never stood a ghost of a chance for it; never expected it and of course, I am not disappointed—cause—I can not be used as a politician."

While he may not have been disappointed, Seymour still felt some frustration and concern in these early weeks of the war. Like his men, he was anxious to get into action and prove his military worth. "We are looking out for a fight this week," he wrote six weeks after the victory at Manassas. "Our troops are advancing gradually to Washington and occupying all prominent intermediate positions. We must do something soon if we expect to accomplish anything. I feel discouraged about the duration of the war. The best informed officers are of the opinion that this is to be a long, very long, war, and the idea of being kept here a long, interminable and indefinite period is disheartening."[20]

The rank-and-file soldiers were eager for the taste of battle as well. In his muster roll report at the end of October, Captain Manning, commanding Company K, wrote, "The health of my company is excellent and nothing is needed to make their position perfectly satisfactory but a good fight." But a "good fight" would not come for many months. The Confederates hoped to draw the Federal army into a decisive battle that might quickly win the war, but Lincoln and his generals, stung by McDowell's humiliating defeat at Bull Run, were in no mood to fight. There would not be another major battle in Virginia until the spring of 1862.[21]

With the prospects for battle diminishing, Colonel Seymour and his men, camped a few miles east of the Bull Run battlefield at Centreville, were settling into the routine of camp life. "We have a splendid camping grounds," Private Herron wrote to his cousin. "The mornings and evenings is getting very cold here. It is raining for the last three weeks which makes camp life very disagreeable."[22] Boredom and illness were the biggest problems for the regiment during the inactive weeks of the late summer and early fall of 1861. The restless men, tired of routine drills and camp duty, looked for diversion and often found it in a bottle of liquor, especially the hard-drinking Irishmen from New Orleans. The drinking often led to trouble. William E. Trahern, a private in Company D, the Tensas Rifles, recalled many years after the war how boredom bred trouble. "No fighting, few drills, much dissipation in the use of alcoholic spirits" was his description of this period. "Idleness, the 'Devil's workshop,' was forced upon all men in the army."[23]

The tragic consequences of idleness and alcohol were well illustrated in the accidental death of Trahern's company commander, Capt. Charles B. Tenney. "Four or five drinking Irishmen were in the habit of coming into camp late at night, and in a drunken condition, making life hideous," wrote Trahern after the war. "One night they broke the record for bachanalian revelry, and it took nearly the whole Company D to stop them." Captain Tenney tried to quiet the rowdy drunks, and feeling himself in danger, unholstered his pistol to crack the trouble-makers over the head. Suddenly, the gun discharged, "landing a bullet in his abdomen; the surgeons could not save him, and death resulted two hours later."[24]

Such rowdiness often led to brawls among the men. While these fisticuffs were normally harmless, they were occasionally injurious or even fatal. One of Captain Monaghan's Irishmen in Company F was killed on Oct. 20 as a result of such an incident. "On the 20th Pvt. James McCormack of this company was murdered by Pvt. John Travers of the Tiger Rifles, Wheat's Battalion," Monaghan wrote in his muster roll report for the period. Lt. Michael O'Connor led a squad of 10 men "in search of the murderer and arrested him at Gainesville at 2 o'clock in the morning of the 25th and brought him into camp" to await trial.[25]

Illness was a more serious problem than drunkenness and fighting in these early months of the war. By August 1861, sickness ran rampant in the regiment. Crowded together in camps with poor sanitation, exposed to the elements and to diseases for which they had no immunity, the men of the 6th Louisiana were highly susceptible to epidemics that raged through the ranks, especially that first summer in Virginia's hot, humid, bug-infested climate. The 6th Louisiana's report of sick and wounded for that month, signed by regimental surgeon P. B. McKelvey, shows that 311 men—a third of the regiment—had taken sick, and four died. The diseases ran the gamut from fevers and digestive ailments to rheumatism and paralysis. There were 101 cases of acute diarrhea, 46 of various fevers, 26 of acute bronchitis, 25 of rheumatism, and 31 of indigestion. Some of the men must have found amusement out of camp, for there were two cases of syphilis and one of gonorrhea—a problem that would grow more widespread in the future. (The regiment's illness report for April 1862, for instance, shows that 15 soldiers were treated for gonorrhea and 10 for syphilis in that month—the end of a long, idle period in camp during which the men obviously sought companionship of another sort.)[26]

Most of the illnesses were short-term (only 37 men reported absent from duty due to sickness at the end of August), but some were more serious. Even without facing the enemy, the 6th Louisiana lost seven enlisted men that month. Four died of illness: typhoid fever killed Pvt. Cornelius Sullivan of Company I; Pvt. H. B. Hedges of Company A died of gastric enteritis; Pvt. John Gold of Company G succumbed to paralysis; and an unknown ailment caused the sudden death of Private T. M. Cook of Company A. In addition, three privates were discharged due to serious illness: W. W. Walker of Company D; and Aron Friedlander and Joseph Little of Company H.[27]

"Typhoid fever is raging quite extensively in most of the camps," Pvt. Henry Handerson of the 9th Louisiana regiment wrote in a letter home from Camp Bienville, near Centreville, where the Louisiana regiments were clustered together. Some 250 men of that regiment were on the sick list at that time, he said, and about 100 had been permanently lost due to illness since leaving Louisiana.[28]

Some soldiers of the 6th Louisiana remained healthy during the first waves of contagious disease during the summer and early fall, only to succumb when the cold, wet weather of winter made camp life miserable and risky to health. In August, as many of his comrades fell ill, Cpl. George M. Lee of Union Parish wrote home to a brother-in-law that he and his brother William, both in Company A, were in fine health. "I am as fat as pork & crackers," he boasted. "Were you to see my Ambrotype now you would hardly recognize it. My hair long & disheveled and my face is as brown as a gingercake." Still, he longed for home cooking. "Tell Mother I wish she would cook me a real good country dinner & sent it to me by mail, a good peach cobler for instance it would go down faster than rain."[29]

As the weather turned cold in October, Corporal Lee's letters took on a more somber tone. Though his own health was "tolerable good," he wrote that his friend, Pvt. George W. Brantley, a comrade in Company A, had died October 1. "He has been sick for a long time and suffered much: I fear for want of propper attention." Nine days before Christmas 1861, Lee wrote that his own health was good, "but our spirits are drooping and languid, at the idea of passing off of 4 long winter months in camps, with nothing to do, nothing to love and not much to hope for." He longed to "join the family circle around the hearth stone," wondering, "Oh, will that day ever come, when the devastating tide of war shall be rolled back and peace be proclaimed throughout the land." The soldier's life is a "hard lot," but he looked forward to a furlough at the end of his initial year of service. "I have only four months and twenty days to serve, and should my life be spared I expect to see you all at the close of my term of service, but only for a short time if the war continues for I expect to be a soldier as long as the war lasts."

Though he re-enlisted for the war in early February 1862, George Lee did not see the war end. His last letter home from Virginia was dated February 3, 1862. "The weather is very cold," he wrote. "Snow has fallen today 6 inches in depth, and is still snowing tonight. We have had a big spree to-day of throwing Snow balls, and I feel none the better for it tonight. . . .Time rolls off very slowly. The time we have to stay here seems almost an age." The big snowball fight that he and his comrades had staged that day to relieve their boredom may have caused a deathly chill for the young man, for he died sixteen days later of pneumonia.[30]

For one 6th Louisiana soldier, a bout of illness provided a pleasant break from the boredom of camp life. Pvt. George Zeller wrote home in September 1861 that he "had a nice time of it" during a five-day stay in the hospital at Culpeper, and during a six-week recuperation in the care of a family living near that central Virginia town. "They were very kind to me. . . .In the morning when I got up I always went to the pond a-fishing. I use to catch catfish. . . .And we use to go a-hunting for squirrels and we killed very many of them. . . .I got acquainted with all there cousins and mighty near all the young Ladies in Culpeper. . . .They told one of the girls that I was a very handsome young man. They fell in love with me. . . .I had a great time with them."[31]

In these weeks of little military activity, the men of the 6th Louisiana rarely saw the enemy. The regiment's only active campaigning in the autumn of 1861 was a reconnaissance mission to Great Falls on the Potomac River in late September. General Walker took the brigade on this three-day expedition, which included plenty of marching, about 30 cannon shots at Federal pickets across the river, and no casualties except for blistered feet.[32]

Private Zeller was excited at his first look at the enemy. Writing home just after the march to the Potomac, Zeller told his mother that "we took six big Cannons and placed them in the woods rite acrossed from the Yankies. . . .we fired our Cannons at them and at a big store-house they had filled with things for the winter. The first shot was fired amongst the guards there at the store-house, you ought to have seen them running and hollering every which way." Zeller and his comrades were hoping to provoke a fight. "We come out in an open field and marched around so the Yankies could see us. They fired one cannon ball at us. . . .The reason we done it was to get a fight, but they would not come on the side we were. There was five thousand of Yankies and only two thousand and one hundred of us. They are to coward to come and fight us."

One reason Zeller eagerly sought a fight was an evidently common belief that the regiment would be sent home to protect New Orleans after it had been tested in battle. "We expect a fight very soon, at a moment's notice," he told his mother, sister and brother back home. "The first battle that we get into and get out safe, then our Regiment will be sent home for to protect our own City. Jeff Davis said so, and that will be very soon, for we expect it at every hour in the day and it is going to be a very big fight but I am certain that we will whip them." Zeller would never see his home again, for he was killed less than a year later at Sharpsburg.[33]

The confidence that Zeller projected in his letter home was shared throughout the regiment. Anxious for their first taste of battle, the green Louisiana soldiers were sure that it would come soon, and that they would whip the enemy. Pvt. Theodore H. Woodard of Company D wrote to his uncle in Mississippi in November, telling him of Federal troops seen crossing the Potomac toward their position in Centreville. "I expect before you receive this letter you will here of a dreadful battle here. I think we will have it in a very few days. We have Centerville heights very strongly fortified and it will take an army better than Genl. McClellan can ever bring to whip us. No fears need be apprehended as to the success of our victory, for we'll certainly be victorious." Woodard and his comrades, however, would have to wait several more months, for fighting of any consequence materialized that fall.[34]

The Georgian appointed to head the Louisiana Brigade held the honor for only nine weeks before the powers in Richmond managed to move him aside to make room for the well-connected and ambitious Richard Taylor. The Louisiana sugar planter was hardly the obvious choice for the position. He was only 36 years old, younger than the other three colonels who commanded regiments in the brigade and untested in battle. His appointment by his brother-in-law, President Davis, had all the earmarks of nepotism and political favoritism. Taylor had no military experience, whereas the men he leapfrogged—including Seymour of the 6th Louisiana, Col. Henry Kelly of the 8th and Col. Harry Hays of the 7th—had earned their credentials as soldiers. Seymour, the senior colonel of the brigade, seemed the obvious choice for leadership if a Louisianian was to be chosen, and his passing-over (for the second time in two months) surely must have been a bitter disappointment. At the time of Walker's appointment he had known that the "powers" in Richmond wanted Taylor to lead the brigade, but felt that they had not dared to make such a blatantly unjustified appointment. Now they had dared, and there was deep resentment of Taylor's appointment within the brigade's regiments. One New Orleans newspaper reported that the colonels were on the verge of resigning. Another, the daily *True Delta*, editorialized that Colonel Seymour should have had the appointment, adding, "Unfortunately, however, he is not either a relative of any of the 'grand chiefs' or a rabid politician of the Slidell stamp."[35]

Taylor later asserted that he was "seriously embarrassed" by the promotion, as if it had been unexpected. He rushed off to Richmond to confer with Davis and claimed to have asked that the promotion be revoked. Even if he did, Davis was determined to put Taylor in charge of the brigade and simply wrote the other colonels that promotions to the grade of general officer were his alone to make, for reasons "of which he alone was judge." Taylor later claimed that Davis' letter soothed the hurt feelings of the colonels and won their "hearty support" for him, an assertion which seems improbable at best.[36] Outraged over being removed from a brigade that he had spent weeks training into fighting shape, Walker abruptly resigned from the army. "I will not condescend to submit any longer to the insults and the indignities of the Executive," he informed Secretary of War Judah P. Benjamin.[37]

GENERAL RICHARD TAYLOR

Although Taylor, the brother-in-law of President Jefferson Davis, did not have any military experience when he was promoted to command the Louisiana Brigade, he quickly developed into an exceptional combat leader. Although initially despised by his men because of his strict adherence to discipline, they eventually adored him. *Generals in Gray*

Walker's replacement was a true Southern aristocrat, a large slaveowner with a keen sense of class-consciousness who felt destined by position and education to lead men. Taylor also was a man of explosive temper and ugly moods, whose staff officers soon learned to steer clear of him when he was sick or depressed, which he was often. Maj. David French Boyd, who served under Taylor as the Louisiana Brigade's commissary officer, remembered his commander as "a superb soldier and able general," who habitually suffered from rheumatism and "nervous headache" which made him "cross and irritable." Yale-educated, well-traveled and widely read, Taylor was "the most brilliant and fascinating talker that I remembered in the Southern army," Boyd recalled, but "when he was sick he was 'ugly' and we had to keep away from him."[38]

The new brigadier was also a strict disciplinarian. One of his privates in the 9th Louisiana called him "a regular martinet in the line of discipline" who "aspires to have the most orderly regiment in the service." Never was Taylor's penchant for displaying his iron rule more evident than in early December when he presided over the first executions in the Army of Northern Virginia. Two Irishmen in Wheat's Battalion—Michael O'Brien and Dennis Corkeran—were, on Taylor's orders, executed by a firing squad after having been convicted of leading a drunken attempt to free some of their comrades from the brigade guardhouse. The executions caused a sensation within the army and in the public at large. The punishment of death struck many as unjustifiably harsh for an offense involving little more than drunken rowdiness. One Northern newspaper editorialized that the executions were an example of Confederate officers' prejudice against Irish-born soldiers. There is no definitive evidence that Taylor was anti-Irish, but he had been an active participant before the war in the nativist American Party, known as the Know Nothings, a loose group united chiefly by its followers' prejudice against immigrants—especially Irish Catholics. The condemned men's commander, Major Wheat, made an impassioned plea for leniency, arguing that one of the men had risked his life by carrying the wounded Wheat from the Manassas battlefield. Taylor, however, insisted on making examples of them.[39]

No man in the army could doubt Taylor's belief in strict discipline after witnessing what Private Zeller called "an awfull scene" on December 9 at Centreville. Shortly before noon, with the entire division gathered in a three-sided square as a band played the "Death March," a wagon drove slowly to the open side of the square carrying the two condemned Tigers, who were dressed in the full Zouave uniform. A firing squad of 24 men drafted from their battalion, half of them given blanks for their muskets, stood 15 paces away from the two stakes where O'Brien and Corkeran were to be shot.

Zeller described the scene in a letter to his family:

> On the day they were to be shot, the whole Brigade had to march over there. We had to form in a square around the prisoners. When they came they were brought in a wagon to the place and the priest was with them. When they came to the place where they were to be shot they both jump out of the wagon, laughing and talking very freely. They both stood before the Genl. to here there sentence read out. After that they were led back to there stake where they were to be tide to. They both preferd to stand up to be shot but they both had to get down on there knees in front of there post and be blindfolded. . .They were blindfolded and there hands were tide behind there backs to the post. Then the company got orders to shoot a volly at them. They fired, the two poor men fell down dead. They were picked up and put in there coffin and buried at once. Most every fellow that was standing around cride."[40]

Two unruly Irish Tigers were dead, but Taylor had finally achieved absolute authority over his brigade. The aristocratic general evidently felt no qualms over the executions, which were the first in the Army of Northern Virginia. Years later, with some evident satisfaction, he wrote that the "punishment, so closely following offense, produced a marked effect."[41]

About a week before Christmas, the brigade moved to Camp Carondelet, four miles from Manassas, to settle in for the winter. On December 20, Private Herron wrote home to tell of the move: "The brigade is after falling back near Manassas while we are going into winter quarters. We have commenced to build them on yesterday. Every nine men is to build their own house. We will have them finished in a week. We will have no more moving now until winter is over." To protect themselves against Virginia's cold and wet winter, the Louisianians went into the woods and felled trees, which were cut into logs and chinked and daubed with clay to make a reasonably comfortable, though cramped, log cabin.[42]

"It generally snows all day and rains all night which makes the roads impassible," Herron wrote a few weeks later. "The Yankee soldiers I do not believe are as comfortable as what we are at present for we have our fine log houses to live in and but very little duty to do." Though well-housed, the men felt deprived of some favorite foodstuffs. "We are getting no sugar or coffee," the private complained. "Coffee is an article we do not expect but I think they ought to give us some sugar. I suppose it is getting dear like everything else."[43]

Although they learned to live without such luxuries as coffee and sugar, adjusting to the cold Virginia winter was hard for men used to New Orleans' climate. "We have snow here a foot deep and it is very cold here," Private Zeller wrote to his family in early January 1862. "We are living in our new house. We had to cut down trees to build them with and we had to plaster them with mud and we had to cut down small branches four our bed to lay on." To celebrate moving into the log hut, Zeller and his mess-mates threw a little New Year's party. "We brought buckets, pepper, sugar. . .a gallon of whiskey, five dozen eggs, six pounds of sugar, and then we made two buckets full of egg-nog. We stayed up most all night drinking and a-singing." Asking his sister to send him some clothing, he added, "If you do send them, pack them in a box and don't forget to put in two or three bottles of whiskey if you can afford it, and pack it so the bottles won't break. . .and mark the box Clothing."[44]

Evidently, Zeller got his wish, for in his next letter home he reported that he shared the whiskey with his friends and "we all got so tight drinking to your health that some of us went to bed and next we were put in the guard house and didn't get out until next morning." Perhaps this frolic taught Zeller a lesson, for he vowed to reform. "Dear Mother," he confessed, "to tell the truth the whole mess did get tight from the liquor but I have made up my mind not to drink any more, for I have done without a very long time. You may all take my word for it, as long as I am out here in Virginia."[45]

The uneventful winter encampment ended abruptly in early March 1862. During the winter, the Confederate commander at Manassas, Gen. Joseph E. Johnston, had become convinced that he could not hold his position in the face of an amply equipped and numerically superior Federal army concentrated around Washington, only two days' march away. After the defeat at Bull Run, Lincoln had replaced the luckless McDowell with Maj. Gen. George B. McClellan, who soon displayed his superb organizing and training talents by whipping the discouraged Union soldiers into a cohesive fighting force of more than 100,000 men, now dubbed the Army of the Potomac.

Johnston's army of 40,000 Confederates around Manassas, meanwhile, was being threatened by massive departures of 12-month soldiers whose terms of enlistment ended in April and May 1862. To induce them to re-enlist for the war, the Confederate government in December had passed the "Furlough and Bounty Act," which promised a bounty of $50 and a furlough of 60 days to those who re-enlisted. Awaiting a possible

Federal attack, Johnston feared that furloughs by the thousands could riddle his army's ranks and that many other men would decide against re-enlisting. The Confederate commander believed it impossible to hold his lines in Northern Virginia against a larger army. McClellan, he reasoned, could advance in such force on Richmond and by so many routes that it was folly to try to hold the line along Bull Run and the Occoquan River to the Potomac. Anticipating a spring offensive by McCellan, Johnson decided to take up a new defensive position farther South. When Johnston learned on May 5 of "unusual activity" among the Federal troops, he issued orders for his forces to fall back to the line of the Rappahannock River, a more defensible position 25 miles south of Manassas.[46]

The sudden retreat was a ragged, messy affair, made all the more depressing by the chilly rain and muddy roads. On March 8, the Louisianians received orders to pack their belongings and be prepared to move out the following day. Soldiers tried to stuff a winter's accumulation of belongings into bulging knapsacks, agonizing over what to leave behind. Taylor's Brigade was among the last of the army to pull out from its camp near Manassas. The Louisianians torched their cherished winter huts and set off on a miserable march in a downpour that turned the roads to soup. The 6th Louisiana, serving as rear guard, marched at the end of the long columns. Trudging along, Seymour's Irishmen saw clothing, boots, pots and pans and other equipment littering the roadside, the leavings of weary soldiers seeking to lighten their heavy loads as they marched. By daylight most men carried little more than the clothes on their backs. In his haste to retire, Johnston abandoned tons of equipment, foodstuffs, and personal items which could not be hauled away on the overburdened single-track railroad.[47]

The retreat stunned and disappointed the men of the 6th Louisiana. "I fear this evacuation of Manassas will have a very bad moral effect on our cause in the South & West. . .& how the Yankees will exult over the 'Rebels' running away. . . ," wrote Pvt. Ben Hubert of Company E to his sweetheart.[48] "There has been a great change taken place here since Col. Seymour gave us orders last Monday to pack up our knapsacks," Private Herron wrote. "There is great excitement among the men to no (sic) what is gone to be done. Everything [is] going away from Manassas." Herron complained, "It will be very hard on us to leave our fine house now and go and lay out on the cold ground, after all of our trouble in building them."[49]

Within days Private Herron and his 6th Louisiana comrades were living as miserably as he feared. After slogging down roads turned into mud sloughs by incessant March rains, the regiment camped near Rappahannock Station, a train stop on the river of that name. "Our brigade has stopped here for a few days & then I think we will move on to the vicinity of Gordonsville where I hope we will be able to procure more comfortable Quarters than we have here," Private Hubert wrote on March 17. "The weather is terribly disagreeable—raining almost constantly, and the troops are without tents. . . .I have been sleeping on the damp ground for several nights with no protection but a tent fly & fear that the exposure will cause a relapse of my sickness. . .the weather, our falling back, and everything disagreeable combined has given everyone the 'blue devils.'"[50]

As they camped along the swollen Rappahannock, the discouraged and rain-soaked Confederates of the 6th Louisiana realized that the comforts of their winter camp were behind them. Ahead lay a spring campaign that would finally test their endurance, their courage and their fighting skills.

Chapter Two

Service With Stonewall Jackson:
THE SHENANDOAH VALLEY

"They were as steady as clocks as chirpy as crickets."
— *Maj. Gen. Richard Taylor*

Early spring of 1862 found the men of the 6th Louisiana camped along the Rappahannock River, eager for action but unsure when and where it would come. On St. Patrick's Day, March 17, as Seymour's Irishmen celebrated their national saint's day, General McClellan was loading his Union army of 100,000 men onto boats in the Potomac River to embark on his campaign to capture Richmond. Many of the Louisiana troops believed that they soon would be moving east to defend the Confederate capital, unaware that their baptism of fire actually awaited them in the Shenandoah Valley, across the Blue Ridge Mountains to the west.

Stonewall Jackson's legendary Valley Campaign of 1862 would become, in many ways, the happiest chapter of the war for the men of the 6th Louisiana. They would look back upon it later as the best of times—when the regiment was whole, healthy, and full of fight, proud to be marching under a leader that many in the regiment considered the most daring and imaginative Confederate general. They would remember this campaign as a springtime of victories, a time when the vision of ultimate triumph of the Confederate cause was not an impossible dream.

Unaware of what was to come, the Louisianians settled into their new camp on the south bank of the Rappahannock, picketing the river as the army's rear guard. Except for Ewell's Division, to which the Louisiana Brigade was assigned, General Johnston's army had retreated 20 miles further south across the Rapidan River to camp near Orange Court House. The 6th Louisiana spent an uneventful and rainy month along the

Rappahannock until April 18, when it marched with the division to rejoin the rest of the army across the Rapidan at a camp near Gordonsville. There it would remain only 10 days before marching west to the Shenandoah Valley.[1]

The valley was the military domain of Maj. Gen. Thomas J. Jackson, the hero of Manassas who had been selected the previous October to command a newly created Valley District with its own army, to operate under General Joe Johnston's overall command. The creation of the separate Valley Army and the selection of the aggressive Jackson to lead it reflected the strategic importance of the rich Shenandoah Valley to the Confederate cause. Lying between the Blue Ridge Mountains on the east and the Allegheny Mountains to the west, the valley was and is today a rich and bountiful land of farms, forests and towns stretching some 150 miles from the Potomac River on the north to the James River on the south. Its importance in the 1860s lay in its geography, its fertility, and its utility as a corridor for invasion.

The valley is bounded on each side by the green, richly forested ridges of the two mountain ranges that frame it. The rolling valley floor below is the lush breadbasket of Virginia, whose rich limestone soil and favorable climate supported farms raising livestock, wheat, corn and other food crops critical to the needs of the Confederate army. An army operating in the valley could live off the land, while the products of its many grist mills, slaughterhouses, orchards and farms were vital to sustenance of Confederate troops elsewhere.

The Confederate government considered it critically important to hold the Shenandoah, not only because the valley provisioned its armies, but because it provided a natural invasion route either north or south. Viewed from the south, the valley pointed northeast like a spear aimed at the heart of the Union, allowing a Confederate army to march unseen behind its mountain screens to a point north of Washington, D.C., and within easy striking distance of Philadelphia and Baltimore. Viewed from the north, the valley would permit an invading Union army to march up (southwest) to a point below and behind Richmond and the Confederate armies defending it. This invasion corridor was enhanced by the 125-mile-long Valley Turnpike, a good road that ran from the Potomac River south through Winchester, Harrisonburg and other towns to Staunton, an important railhead at the southern end of the corridor. So crucial was the Shenandoah that General Jackson, perhaps the Confederacy's ablest student of military geography, believed that "if the Valley is lost, Virginia is lost."[2] Jackson was sent to the valley not only to try to hold that strategic region but to prevent the Federal forces there from moving east to join McClellan's expedition against Richmond. McClellan hoped to augment his large army on the peninsula east of Richmond with the 20,000 men under Maj. Gen. Nathaniel Banks operating in the Shenandoah Valley.

It was toward this crucible of war that the 6th Louisiana marched from Gordonsville on April 28. The main body of Johnston's army had moved east to meet McClellan's thrust up the peninsula toward the Confederate capital. Ewell's Division of 8,000 men, including Taylor's Louisianians, had remained at Gordonsville under orders to stay east of the Blue Ridge, available either to hurry east to join Johnston or west to aid Jackson, who had been operating in the valley since the previous December. Late in April Jackson ordered Ewell to move west to help defeat the Union forces arraying against him.

GEN. THOMAS J. "STONEWALL" JACKSON

It was under Jackson's demanding eye that the men of the 6th Louisiana experienced their first combat at Winchester in May 1862. The fighting prowess of the Louisianians helped create the Jackson mystique. His death later in 1863 was taken hard by his Shenandoah Valley veterans. *Generals in Gray*

The men of the 6th Louisiana were not happy with their new division commander. Richard Stoddert Ewell, recently promoted to major general, was a 45-year-old West Point graduate who had spent two decades as a cavalryman on the frontier before the war. His striking oddities of appearance and personality included a bald head, bright, bulging eyes, a noticeable lisp and a strange habit of cocking his head to one side when he spoke in his high pitched voice, often uttering profanities. Taylor thought he bore "a striking resemblance to a woodcock." Lieutenant Ring noted in his diary that the men in the regiment referred to their old brigadier as "Dirty Dick."[3] "We are all exceedingly dissatisfied with our division commander, Gen. Ewell, who is very eccentric and seems half the time not to know what he is doing," Colonel Seymour wrote to his son. "The consequence is we are pretty much engaged in undoing one day what we have done the previous one.

Marching and counter-marching his men, getting no nearer the enemy."[3] Seymour and his men would hold a higher opinion of Ewell in the weeks to come, when they understood that the unpredictable and sometimes inexplicable movements of the Confederate forces reflected both conflicting orders received by Ewell and the eccentric brilliance of his superior. General Jackson, who shared his plans with no one, held a strategic vision that was inscrutable to his subordinates, but when revealed in execution, struck awe in its beholders.[4]

By the time the Louisianians marched to meet him, Jackson had fought one battle against a portion of Nathaniel Banks' army at Kernstown, near Winchester, on March 23. Jackson's small Valley Army, then numbering no more than 3,000 effective fighters, had been bloodied severely at Kernstown by Maj. Gen. James G. Shields' division in what was a poorly-fought tactical defeat for the Confederates. The battle was a strategic victory for Jackson, however, for it convinced Federal authorities to keep Banks' larger army in the Valley to deal with the aggressive Confederate instead of shifting him east of the Blue Ridge to add to the mounting pressure on Richmond.[5]

Marching with Taylor's Brigade, the 6th Louisiana crossed the Blue Ridge Mountains on April 30 at Swift Run Gap, one of several passes where roads cut across the wooded peaks to the valley below. It was dogwood blossom time in Virginia, and as the winter-weary soldiers caught their first glimpses of the Shenandoah's wheat fields, sparkling streams and budding orchards, the promise of spring must have lifted their spirits. Descending the western slope of the Blue Ridge they spied the valley's most striking feature. Massanutten Mountain, which runs for 50 miles like a giant wooded spine down the center of the valley, splitting it in two. Through the main valley west of Massanutten flows the North Fork of the Shenandoah River, and through the narrower valley east of the mountain (called the Luray valley) runs the South Fork. The two rivers, which flow north, become one at the town of Front Royal, where the 6th Louisiana would receive its baptism of fire. But that was more than three weeks in the future. The regiment settled down along the South Fork of the river, at a place called Conrad's Store, to await further orders from Jackson.[6]

It was there, at Camp Bragg, that the 6th Louisiana faced a crisis of leadership when Colonel Seymour stunned the men with a sudden announcement that he planned to resign his command. The old colonel's decision came as the regiment was preparing for a reorganization and re-election of officers as required under the new law that extended the enlistments

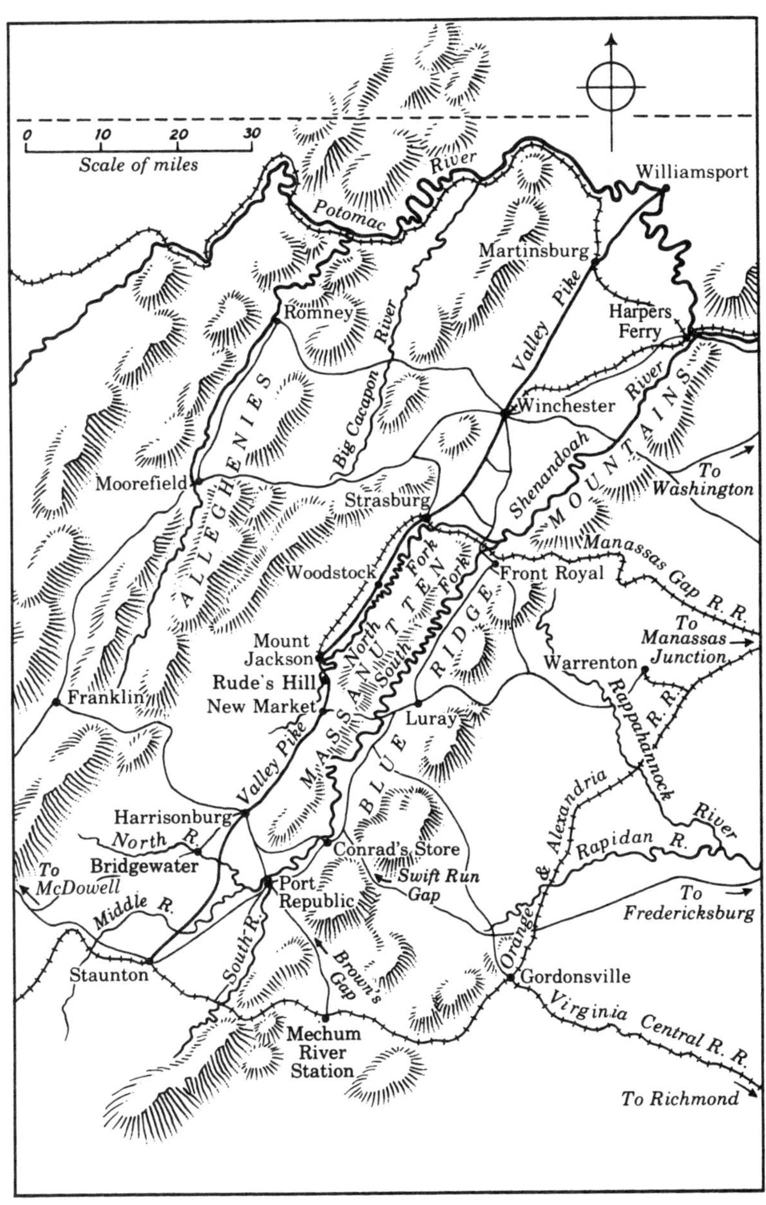
0 10 20 30
Scale of miles
Potomac
River
Williamsport
Martinsburg
Romney
River
Big Cacapon
Valley Pike
Harpers Ferry
Winchester
Shenandoah River
MOUNTAINS
To Washington
ALLEGHENIES
Moorefield
Strasburg
Woodstock
North Fork
South Fork
MASSANUTTEN
Front Royal
Manassas Gap R. R.
BLUE RIDGE
To Manassas Junction
Warrenton
Mount Jackson
Rude's Hill
New Market
Franklin
Luray
Rappahannock R. R.
Rappahannock
River
Valley Pike
Harrisonburg
North R.
Bridgewater
Conrad's Store
Swift Run Gap
Orange & Alexandria
Rapidan R.
To McDowell
Middle R.
Port Republic
South R.
To Fredericksburg
Staunton
Brown's Gap
Gordonsville
Virginia Central R. R.
Mechum River Station
To Richmond

of 12-month men for the duration of the war. The 6th Louisiana's leader was in a poor frame of mind at this time. Unhappy with his division commander, General Ewell, and disappointed at being passed over for brigadier in favor of an inexperienced in-law of the Confederate president, he was also bitterly disillusioned with some of his own subordinate officers, whose behavior disgusted him. "I am not pleased at all with my present fortunes," Seymour wrote in a letter from Camp Bragg to his son William. "I am attached to my regiment, and I like the men, and the feeling is reciprocated, but with a number of my officers I am utterly disgusted. Some dozen or so of them are low, vulgar fellows and habitual whiskey drinkers," he explained. "I cannot have any respect for them but rather feel a loathing for them, and I cannot conceal this feeling and they well know my opinions of them."[7]

Seymour had publicly rebuked these officers (whom he did not name) on dress parade one day because he felt they set such a bad example for the men. "I told them in the plainest language that it was not the commission [that] made the gentleman, but on the contrary, commissions often by accident fell into the hands of those where were not and never could become gentlemen." If he could find a way to resign "with propriety," he would do so, he told his son. "I am getting tired and want some rest. Since my dunking in the creek when my horse fell with me, I have had rheumatism in my shoulder, which when I am wet, and which is most of the time, is very painful." His rheumatism, he thought, might provide "a good way and not an ungraceful one to get rid of my command."[8]

The regiment's election of officers was set for May 9. On the evening before the election, Seymour appeared in full dress uniform before the entire regiment and bid them adieu, refusing to stand for re-election without disclosing his reasons. According to one newspaper account, some of his rough-hewn soldiers "wept like babies" at the news before attempting to change their colonel's mind. Borrowing a band from a neighboring regiment, they marched to Seymour's tent and serenaded him. The colonel emerged, touched by the gesture but unmoved, to say he would leave in the morning. The men dispersed "in deep silence."[9]

The next morning "the 6th Louisiana was drawn up in line as if on dress parade, no officer near them, all perfectly orderly." A petition signed by all of the first sergeants of the companies and addressed to General Taylor was read, imploring the brigade commander to persuade Seymour to stand for re-election.[10] A separate petition, addressed to General Ewell, begged the division commander to intercede, explaining that "some difficulty has arisen between the company officers and our colonel." This petition credited the colonel for "the immense amount of labor he has extended on us, to render us proficient in drill and all that constitutes good soldiers," and added that "you cannot wonder at our feeling for him a love, almost if not quite filial." Expressing a fear that "the petty aspirations of subordinate officers" were driving their beloved colonel from his command, the petition asked Ewell to use his "authority or influence to save us from the consequences of an error so fatal." It was signed simply, "The members of the 6th Regt. La. Vols."[11]

The outpouring of sentiment from the rank and file evidently changed Seymour's mind, for he soon consented to stand for re-election. When his re-election was announced to the assembled regiment "such shouting as now took place can hardly be imagined," a New Orleans paper reported. The election kept Seymour in command but brought in new officers under him. Irish-born Henry Strong, captain of the Calhoun Guards, was elected lieutenant colonel to fill a vacancy created the previous February when Louis Lay resigned. Arthur McArthur, captain of the Union and Sabine Rifles, was elected major, displacing George W. Christy, who had held the rank briefly following the resignation of Samuel L. James.[12]

With its crisis of leadership a thing of the past, the regiment remained camped near Conrad's Store for another 10 days while General Ewell awaited orders from Jackson, who had stormed off on another of his mysterious expeditions. This time Jackson marched deep into the Alleghenies, west of the Shenandoah Valley, to defeat Union Brig. Gen. R. H. Milroy's division at McDowell on May 8. Milroy commanded the advance element of a Federal Army under Maj. Gen. John C. Fremont, which was operating in the western Virginia mountains and in a position to join with Banks in the valley. For several days Jackson's army, now expanded to over 10,000 men with the addition of Brig. Gen. Edward Johnson's brigades, chased Fremont's men deep into the Alleghenies, effectively removing another threat to the Shenandoah Valley.[13]

When Jackson returned to the Valley, General Ewell rode off to meet him at Mt. Solon, near Harrisonburg. The subordinate was confused by the conflicting orders he had received from Jackson, Joe Johnston, and the authorities in Richmond. The frustrated Ewell was being pulled in several directions, unsure whether to join Jackson, chase Banks' army, or march east to help Johnston defend Richmond, all of which had been urged upon him by conflicting superiors. His May 18 meeting with Jackson clarified matters. He would join Jackson in an attack on Banks' army, which six days earlier had been weakened by the departure of General Shields' 10,000-man division. Shields was marching over the Blue Ridge to Fredericksburg to add his division's weight to the Federal pressure on Richmond. This was what Jackson was in the valley to prevent, so the situation called for immediate and dramatic action.[14]

The morning after the Jackson-Ewell meeting, the 6th Louisiana marched out of its camp at Conrad's Store with the rest of Taylor's Brigade, taking a route that skirted around the southern end of Massanutten Mountain and pointed west toward the Valley Pike, where Jackson already had his army on the march. Taylor's men separated from the rest of Ewell's Division, which marched north on the east side of Massanutten toward Luray, where it would later meet the army. Marching rapidly, the Louisianians caught up with Jackson on May 20. Thousands of Jackson's men had gathered on both sides of the Valley Pike to watch the Louisianians march into camp, Taylor recalled later. "Over three thousand strong, neat in fresh clothing of gray with white gaiters, bands playing at the head of their regiments, not a straggler but every man in his place, stepping jauntily as if on parade. . .the brigade moved down the broad, smooth pike and wheeled on to its camping ground." Taylor may have romanticized this picture in hindsight, but a Georgia private who was there was equally impressed with the scene: "Then, here come General Dick Taylor's Louisiana Brigade, over three thousand strong. Each man, every inch a soldier, was perfectly uniformed. . . .The blue-gray uniforms of the officers were brilliant with gold lace, their rakish slouch hats adorned with tassels and plumes. Behold a military pageant, beautiful and memorable. . . .It was the most picturesque and inspiring martial sight that came under my eyes during four years of service."[15] After weeks of waiting the 6th Louisiana was finally part of Stonewall Jackson's army.

The Louisianians marched with Jackson to New Market, then turned east over the only road across Massanutten to link up with Ewell's waiting forces at White House Bridge on the South Fork of the Shenandoah, just west of Luray. Now, with his forces finally concentrated, Jackson's Valley Army was a formidable fighting force—between 16,000 and 17,000 men, including Col. Turner Ashby's Virginia cavalry and eleven batteries containing 48 guns.[16]

On Thursday, May 22, Jackson marched his army north from Luray along the South Fork of the Shenandoah River with Ewell's Division in advance, stopping for the night within ten miles of the town of Front Royal. The small town was nestled at the base of the Blue Ridge at a point where the two forks of the Shenandoah joined, only 12 miles east of Strasburg.

There, Banks' reduced army of less than 7,000 men was dug in, expecting an assault by Jackson from the south, on the Valley Pike. Banks had no idea Jackson was then on his left flank, threatening to swoop into his rear and cut off the Federals' line of retreat down the valley toward Winchester and the Potomac River. That was Jackson's plan, once he eliminated whatever Union force held Front Royal.[17]

A small Federal garrison of less than 1,000 men, commanded by Col. John R. Kenly of the 1st Maryland Infantry, held the small town. Kenly's defenders included nine companies of his own regiment (one was on detached duty) totaling 900 men, two companies of the 29th Pennsylvania regiment of infantry, and a section of artillery consisting of two 10-pounder rifled guns. That force would be enough to drive off marauding cavalry, but was grossly overmatched by the army Jackson was about to bring to bear against it.[18]

The next day was a memorable one for the 6th Louisiana, for it brought the regiment its baptism of fire. "On the 23rd of May 1862, we for the first time had the pleasure of being exposed to the fire of the enemy," Lieutenant Ring wrote in his diary. At daybreak the advance of Jackson's column moved out, led by the Confederate 1st Maryland regiment—who would face their home-state brothers in blue when the fighting began—and followed by Taylor's Louisiana Brigade. As the column approached the wooded heights overlooking Front Royal, Jackson diverted it off the main road to a twisting, narrow path on the right (aptly named, then and now, the Snake Road) which connected to the Gooney Manor road, which in turn led into town. Jackson's approach avoided the Federal pickets guarding the main road and achieved nearly total surprise in his attack. The Confederate column did not encounter any enemy pickets until it was within about 1-1/2 miles of Front Royal. There, a light skirmish fire broke out about 2:00 p.m. and the Federal pickets guarding the road began scrambling back to their comrades in town.[19]

The Louisiana troops, including Seymour's Irishmen, were given a leading role in the attack. Jackson ordered the assault led by the 1st Maryland regiment, followed by Wheat's Louisiana Tiger battalion, with the rest of Taylor's Brigade in immediate support. These troops "pushed forward in gallant style," in Jackson's words, charging the Federals, who put up "a spirited resistance." The two retreating companies of Federal pickets joined one other company of fellow Marylanders stationed in town, some of them firing from windows of the courthouse and a hospital nearby. "As soon as the enemy discovered us, he opened fire upon us," Lieutenant Ring noted in his journal. Colonel Kenly's other six companies of Maryland infantry were posted on a hill northeast of town near the river, along with his artillery, which soon found the range on the attacking Confederates. Major Wheat's Louisiana Tigers and Col. Bradley T. Johnson's Confederate Maryland regiment swept through the town's streets, followed closely by the 6th Louisiana and the rest of Taylor's command. The attackers drove Kenly's town guards back to their colonel's position on the hill by the river.[20]

A Front Royal townsman, Charles Eckhardt, saw the Confederates marching into town as artillery shells whistled over his house. Hustling home from the courthouse at the center of town, where he saw the first Union prisoners being rounded up, Eckhardt encountered some of the Louisianians. "A part of the brigade of General Taylor stood in battle order behind my house, the Yankee battery firing at them," Eckhardt recorded in his diary. "But soon they marched through the town, hot for the fight and eager in pursuit." Some of the Louisiana men paused briefly at the Eckhardt home for something to eat or drink, while other ecstatic citizens of Front Royal, including 19-year-old Lucy Buck, stood out on their porches or in their yards cheering and passing out cold drinks to the hot, thirsty attackers. Young Miss Buck joyfully scribbled in her diary that the hated Northerners "scampered out of town like a flock of sheep" accompanied by some fleeing Negro slaves. "Leaning out of the back window we saw them, contrabands and Yankees together, tearing wildly by," as the young woman jeered at them.[21]

As the Confederate infantry moved out into the open fields beyond the town, Federal artillery pounded them without effective Confederate response, for the only guns Jackson had immediately available were unable to match the range. The Federal guns would have to be silenced. Jackson ordered Taylor to send three regiments forward into the open area to support the now-stalled attack of the Tigers and Marylanders. One of the regiments was to sweep around to the west and north to attack the guns in flank. Taylor deployed the 7th, 8th and 9th Louisiana behind Johnson's Marylanders and called on the 6th Louisiana to attack the guns. "Our Regiment was ordered to execute a flank movement and attempt the capture of the battery," Lieutenant Ring recalled. Colonel Seymour's men filed off to the left through a patch of woods along the South Fork of the river to outflank the Federal artillery from the west. Though the excited Irishmen hurried toward the booming of the Federal cannon, anticipating a glorious attack, they never got the chance to rush the battery. "Before we could reach it," Ring wrote with some disappointment, "it was withdrawn."[22]

While the 6th Louisiana had been moving toward his guns, Colonel Kenly had wisely concluded his position was untenable. The Federal commander had managed to hold the hilltop for more than two hours. He had sent a courier to Banks, alerting his superior to the attack, attempting to buy time to allow Banks to organize a retreat from Strasburg northward to Winchester, to avoid being flanked by Jackson. Unbeknownst to Kenly, the precious time gained by his courageous stand was squandered by Banks, who misjudged the action at Front Royal as nothing more than a cavalry raid. About 4:30 p.m., the plucky Federal colonel saw a regiment of Confederate cavalry rapidly advancing on his right rear between the two forks of the river. These horsemen were some of Turner Ashby's Southern troopers, who were returning from cutting the railroad and telegraph between Front Royal and Strasburg. The approaching cavalry threatened to cut off the Unionists' line of retreat. Colonel Kenly's back was to the rivers, and his only escape was over some bridges behind him, a wooden wagon bridge and a railroad bridge over the nearer stream, the South Fork, and the Winchester Turnpike bridge over the North Fork, about a mile beyond. The Federal commander had to retreat or be surrounded.[23]

Kenly hurried his defenders over the bridges, which he then ordered burned. Once safely across he posted his two guns on a prominent ridge known as Guard Hill, which commanded the approach to the structures. He also arrayed his infantry on the near slopes to fire on the Confederates if they attempted to cross. Under fire from this new Federal position, Taylor brought his Louisiana Brigade forward to the riverbank. It is not clear whether the 6th Louisiana had rejoined the brigade at this time from its flanking maneuver toward the first Federal position. In any case, Taylor called on the 8th Louisiana to charge under fire across the railroad bridge, during which, he later wrote, "several men fell to disappear in the dark water beneath," turbulent and swollen from recent rains. Smoke and flames rising from the wagon bridge nearby caught Taylor's attention, and he ordered the rest of his men to brave the fire and storm across. Many of the obliging soldiers were scorched or had hands burned fighting the flames. By the time the Louisianians reached the far bank, Colonel Kenly had pulled his men from Guard Hill and the Federals were "in full flight to Winchester."[24]

The final phase of the five-hour battle of Front Royal was played out some five miles north of town along the Winchester pike, near a hamlet called Cedarville. There, Colonel Kenly decided to make a last stand. He had barely deployed his men and two guns in an orchard on the east side of the pike when he was quickly attacked and surrounded by Confederate cavalrymen. The horse riders rode through the panicked Federals, hacking with sabers and firing pistols. Several Unionists fell wounded in the action, Colonel Kenly among them. The final charge was made by Colonel T. S. Flournoy's 6th Virginia Cavalry and involved only some 250 horsemen, but so vigorous was the attack that one Federal officer estimated their numbers at 3,000.[25]

The final blow was delivered entirely by Flournoy's cavalry, though much of Jackson's infantry, including the 6th Louisiana, took part in the pursuit. Lieutenant Ring's diary notes that the regiment chased the fleeing bluecoats "for four miles beyond the town." Despite all the fighting and chasing, the 6th did not suffer any casualties. Taylor reported that Wheat's Tigers lost one killed and six wounded, and the 7th Louisiana had one killed and one wounded. Jackson's total casualties numbered only 26 men.[26]

Colonel Kenly's Federal force, however, was virtually destroyed. More than 700 of his men were captured while 32 were killed and 122 were wounded. Only about 130 officers and men remained of the 1,063 Federals who defended Front Royal before the attack. Jackson's men captured both of Kenly's rifled guns plus tons of supplies left in Front Royal storehouses and along the Winchester pike, which was littered with wrecked and burning wagons. For the 6th Louisiana, Front Royal offered a bloodless baptism of fire and the pleasure of watching the Union forces flee in hasty panic. For Jackson, the victory yielded not only hundreds of prisoners and trainloads of supplies, but significant tactical advantages. "The enemy's flank was [now] turned," he later reported, "and the road opened to Winchester." Jackson now set his sights on destroying Nathaniel Banks' army.[27]

Dug in at Strasburg, Banks was slow to react to the news of fighting at Front Royal. The political general doubted the reports and could not believe that Jackson's whole army—which he thought was still south of him—was on his eastern flank. By 9:00 a.m. on Saturday, May 24, however, the Federal commander realized his peril and began marching his whole command to the north, deciding, "to enter the lists with the enemy in a race for the possession of Winchester," as he later reported. Jackson, who had begun a parallel march northward on the Front Royal-Winchester turnpike at dawn, received his first report of Banks' movement about 11:00 a.m., at which time he decided to divide his army to advance upon the retreating Federals from two directions. He ordered General Ewell to stay on the turnpike to Winchester with one brigade plus the Maryland regiment and two batteries, while he took the rest of the command, including Taylor's

Louisianians, via Cedarville to a road that cut west and joined the Valley Pike at Middletown. His aim was to catch Banks' army while it was strung out along the pike and split it in two at Middletown, 13 miles south of Winchester.[28]

The men of the 6th Louisiana resumed their march about noon up the winding and hilly road toward Middletown. Unaware that it would be another 12 hours or more before the relentless Jackson would allow them to eat or rest, they trudged along the rough, forested road through a light rain. Jackson led the column with Ashby's cavalry, some artillery, and Wheat's Louisiana Tigers in the van. It was about 3:30 p.m. when the sound of cannon up ahead alerted Colonel Seymour's men that Jackson's artillerists had found a target at Middletown.[29]

Stretched out before Jackson on the macadam turnpike below were Federal wagon trains, ambulances, and cavalry hemmed in between two stone fences that ran along the sides of the pike. The first salvo from the Confederate guns clogged the road with wrecked wagons and dead horses, panicking the trapped Union column. No Federal artillery or infantry were in sight as Jackson's guns and volleys from Wheat's Tigers chewed up the Union column mercilessly.[30]

General Taylor, upon hearing the cannonade ahead, spurred the rest of his Louisianians to a double-quick to join in the action. After additional rounds from the batteries and volleys from Taylor's infantry, the turnpike "presented a most appalling spectacle of carnage and destruction," in Jackson's words. "The road was literally obstructed with the mingled and confused mass of struggling and dying horses and riders," he reported. By the time Taylor came upon the scene, Wheat's Tigers were running amuck around the Federal wagons, loaded with goods much coveted by the hungry and ill-equipped Confederates. "The gentle Tigers were looting right merrily, diving in and out of wagons with the activity of rabbits in a warren," Taylor recalled. "But this occupation was abandoned on my approach, and in a moment they were in line, looking as solemn and virtuous as deacons at a funeral."[31]

The attack cut the retreating Union column in two, but Jackson had no way of knowing whether Banks' main body was still to his south or had already passed Middletown and was escaping northward. Before long artillery shells from Union guns flew toward Middletown from the south. Jackson ordered Taylor to advance his brigade toward the enemy visible in that direction and attack. The Federals, cut off from their main column, were retreating along a road heading west from the turnpike, and on reaching a crest overlooking that highway they unlimbered their guns. Taylor drew up the Louisiana Brigade in line of battle. "The brigade was rapidly formed and marched straight upon them, when their guns opened," he recalled years later. One shell knocked over several men of the 7th Louisiana, and another exploded almost underneath Taylor's horse, but neither horse nor rider were scratched. It soon became clear that the body of Federals to the south was merely Banks' rear guard, which fled west into the mountains after lobbing a few shells at the Louisianians. As they disappeared, Taylor turned his regiments north to catch up with Jackson, still in pursuit of the fleeing Banks.[32]

The men of the 6th Louisiana had a special reason to be proud of the action at Middletown. Two of its companies, A and B, each captured a Federal battle flag, a fact that Taylor proudly noted in his official report. There was no time to savor any glory yet, however, for Jackson was intent on reaching Winchester before Banks could fortify on the hills south and west of town—even if it meant marching all night. It almost did. Lieutenant Ring recorded the day as a grueling one marked by frequent skirmishing as the Confederates pressed the Union rear guard for 10 miles toward Winchester. "Driving them before us, we kept up a scorching fight all day and night," he recalled, "only halting for a few hours after midnight." After more than 18 hours of marching and fighting, the weary Louisianians dropped to the ground three miles south of Winchester to snatch some brief but desperately needed sleep.[33]

The first light of Sunday, May 25, revealed that Banks' army indeed had managed to occupy the hills overlooking the Valley Pike. While General Banks spent the night comfortably in town, Brig. Gen. Alpheus S. Williams, commanding the Federal 1st Division, deployed his two infantry brigades to meet the Confederate threat from separate directions—Jackson on the Valley Pike to the south of town, and Ewell on the Front Royal road from the southeast. Williams posted one brigade of about 2,000 infantry and six guns to cover the Front Royal road, and another of 2,100 men, plus six cannon and five companies of cavalry, on hills overlooking the Valley Pike.[34]

Three miles down the pike near Kernstown, the 6th Louisiana members had managed only two or three hours sleep before being roused out of their slumber about 5:00 a.m. They were on the road to Winchester early that Sunday morning when the first sounds of cannon and musketry echoed across the valley. It was not yet 6:00 a.m. The rolling sound of battle came from the east, where Ewell opened the action with an attack up the road from Front Royal, meeting stiff resistance from the Federals well posted behind stone walls on the slopes near the road. Up ahead of the Louisianians, Jackson began deploying his troops. He ordered Brig. Gen. Charles S. Winder, commanding the Stonewall Brigade, to occupy the southernmost hill commanding the Valley Pike, which the Virginians accomplished against little resistance. But Winder's men soon came under destructive fire from Union artillery posted on a higher ridge to their northwest. As Jackson fed two additional brigades into line on Winder's left, he sent a courier to General Taylor to hurry forward his Louisianans.[35] Taylor galloped up to find Jackson by the Valley Pike. Pointing to the ridge to the left where the Federal cannon belched destruction upon the Confederate line, Jackson said simply, "You must carry it." It was a typical Jackson order: direct, simple, unmistakable.[36]

Taylor, with a few moments to spare before all his troops arrived, rode out to inspect the ground of the contemplated attack. A small stream called Abraham's Creek flowed through the little valley at the base of the ridge. The creek bed ran northwesterly from the Valley Pike behind Winder's position toward the enemy's right wing. A march of a mile along the creek would bring the Louisianians to the foot of the ridge below the Union guns on the Federal right flank. The ascent was a steep one across a thicket of low trees, outcropping stone, and two fences. On the summit Federal infantry crouched behind a stone wall. It was a scene designed to strike fear into a soldier's heart. "I felt an anxiety amounting to pain for the brigade to acquit itself handsomely, and this feeling was shared by every man it," Taylor recalled later.[37]

There was even greater anxiety along the Federal line on the ridge, where Col. George H. Gordon, commanding a brigade of four regiments, watched the Louisianians file to his right, partly concealed by the woods along Abraham's Creek. To meet this flanking maneuver, Gordon extended his line to the west, hustling the 29th Pennsylvania and the 27th Indiana regiments to his right along the ridge, where they would be in position to oppose the regiments seen marching along the creek valley below.[38]

As the Louisianians filed to the west, they came under fire of the six guns posted on the ridge above, as Taylor and Jackson trotted alongside the column. Noticing some of his men ducking their heads and dodging as the shells exploded nearby, killing and wounding at least a few, Taylor bellowed at them, "What the hell are you dodging for? If there is any more of it, you will be halted under this fire for one hour!" If he thought such bravado would impress his commanding general, Taylor was mistaken, for the straight-laced Jackson instead seemed shocked by the brigadier's intemperate outburst. The army commander placed his hand on Taylor's shoulder and admonished him, "I am afraid you are a wicked fellow." With that, the general turned back toward Winder's position to watch Taylor's attack unfold.[39]

Partially screened by the ridge and the morning fog, the long line of nearly 3,000 Louisianians stepped out behind Taylor. In a steady walk the brigade began the ascent just as the sun rose over the ridge. "It was a lovely Sabbath morning," recalled Taylor, who was struck by the sight of a bluebird fluttering by with a worm in its beak, as smoke from the guns above made spirals in the air. Halfway up the hill the 6th Louisiana and its sister regiments broke into full view of both armies, and hundreds of eyes turned to watch the daring spectacle. "The enemy poured grape and musketry into Taylor's line as soon as it came in sight," recalled a private in the 21st Virginia regiment.[40]

The Louisiana general rode in front of his brigade, sword in hand, occasionally turning his horse or twisting in his saddle to check his line's progress. "They marched up the hill in perfect order, not firing a shot!" the Virginian remembered. From over the top of the ridge, a body of Federal cavalrymen charged the left of the advancing Louisiana line. Col. Harry Kelly's 8th regiment repelled them with a single volley. At that moment, Taylor shouted "Charge!" and the Louisianians leapt forward. The 6th Louisiana "went at it with a cheer that made the Yankees shake," recalled one of its officers. According to Taylor, Colonel Seymour ran toward the enemy waving his sword in one hand and his cap in the other, his long silver locks streaming behind him. He turned toward his excited Irishmen and yelled, "Steady men! Dress to the right!" On the ridge, Colonel Gordon's Federals discharged "a destructive fire of musketry," but the Confederates confidently rushed on, "little shaken by our fire," as he reported later. Fearing that his brigade would soon be overwhelmed, Gordon prepared to give the order to withdraw. The 27th Indiana began melting away to the rear before he could order an evacuation, and other regiments in the line quickly followed the Hoosiers. The Federal right wing was collapsing as the Louisianians surged toward the top. "The brigade, with cadanced step and eyes on the foe, swept grandly over copse and ledge and fence, to crown the heights from which the enemy had melted away," Taylor proudly recalled years after.[41]

From the door of a house near the Union position, a Winchester wife was watching the bloody drama unfold:

> I could see. . .the hillside covered with Federal troops, a long line of

> blue forms lying down just behind its crest, on the top of which just in their front a battery spouted flame at the lines which were slowly advancing to the top. Suddenly I saw a long, even line of gray caps above the crest of the hill, then appeared the gray forms that wore them, with the battleflag floating over their heads! The cannon ceased suddenly, and as the crouching forms that had been lying behind the cannon rose to their feet they were greeted by a volley from their assailants.[42]

Veterans of the Valley Army later claimed the charge of the Louisiana Brigade was one of the most spectacular of the war. "Moving as if on parade, with alert bearing, rhythmic steps, eyes on the foe, they swept smoothly over ledge and fence to possess the heights. . ." recalled a Georgia private watching from Ewell's position to the east. "Warm-hearted Dick Ewell cheered until he was hoarse" as he led his own troops forward after the Louisiana Brigade's breakthrough. "I have rarely seen a more beautiful charge," wrote Henry Kyd Douglas, one of Jackson's staff officers. "This full brigade, with a line of bayonets bright in that morning sun, its formation straight and compact, its tread quick and easy as it pushed on through the clover and up the hill, was a sight to delight a veteran." Jackson himself, who was spare with words of praise, called the Louisianians' charge a "gallant advance." According to his report, the brigade "Steadily, and in fine order, mount[ed] the hill, and there fronting the enemy, where he stood in greatest strength, the whole line magnificently swept down the declivity and across the field, driving back the Federal troops and bearing down all opposition before it."[43]

Jackson, watching the spectacular success of the Louisianians' charge and the collapse of the Federal right wing, grew uncommonly excited. "Order forward the whole line, the battle's won," he shouted to his aide Henry Douglas. The other brigades along the turnpike surged ahead, and Ewell's men to the east also swept toward the town, pursuing the retreating bluecoats. As some of Taylor's and Winder's troops ran past Jackson, he raised his battered gray cap aloft and cried out, "Very good! Now let's holler!" A deafening Rebel yell went up from the whole line, echoing through the valley and signaling to the citizens of Winchester that they were about to be delivered from Federal occupation.[44]

The Federal troops falling back into the town preserved their order at first, but the retreat became increasingly confused and disorderly as they passed through the city streets, which were full of deliriously happy citizens who cheered the victors and harassed the vanquished. Lieutenant Ring described the moments of the Federal collapse in his diary: "Away they go and away we follow, every man striving to see who shall be 'in at the death' first. We chased them clean through the streets of Winchester and for five miles beyond when the cavalry relieved us and we were allowed to throw ourselves down for a much needed rest." Writing to his wife Virginia after the battle, the 6th Louisiana officer fairly glowed with pride. General Jackson told Taylor "that he never saw or read of such a charge as was made by us at Winchester, and I am proud to say that I was as near the front of the line as anyone else. I was within ten feet of our colors all through the charge," he explained, and "the Virginia troops in this army say that we beat anybody they ever saw at a charge, and now they say we can stand as long under a murderous fire as any troops in the world." Ring confessed that he had experienced "a narrow escape" at Winchester when "a ball passed through my straw hat and another struck the heel of my boot."[45]

Others in the 6th Louisiana were not so lucky. Among the five men of the regiment killed was Major Arthur McArthur, who "died while leading the charge on the heights." McArthur was a Connecticut-born planter's son from Union Parish, Louisiana. He began the war as captain of Company A, the Union and Sabine Rifles, and had been elected major only a few weeks before he was killed. Like McArthur, most of the regiment's killed and wounded fell during the charge up the hill. In addition to the killed, 39 others were wounded and three more were listed as missing.[46]

Ring considered the loss of McArthur a grave one. Another company officer, Capt. Joseph Hanlon, the commander of Company I, was "severely wounded and now [is] a prisoner in the enemy's hands," Ring informed his wife in a letter home. Hanlon had been shot though the body and would never fully recover, though he would return to the regiment through a prisoner exchange by early August.[47]

General Taylor singled out one member of the 6th Louisiana for special praise in his official report. While serving Taylor as a mounted orderly, Private Henry B. Richardson went out on reconnaissance and brought back "important information of the enemy's position and movements" during the battle at Winchester. In recognition of his "valuable services," Taylor recommended Richardson be promoted to lieutenant, a recommendation endorsed by General Ewell, who noted, "I am aware of the invaluable services rendered by him on various occasions."[48]

A week of fighting under Jackson had instilled a new sense of confidence and pride in the men of the 6th Louisiana. They had been tested on the march and in battle, and had been found not only capable but, at times, heroic. The victory at Winchester provided a huge psychological lift to soldiers who had waited nearly a year to meet the enemy in battle. The regiment also developed great admiration and affection for the bold Jackson, even though they were often baffled by his strategy and exhausted by his demands on the march. "If God spares me safely through the danger of the campaign, it will be something to boast of hereafter, that I was one of Stonewall Jackson's Army of Occupation," wrote Lieutenant Ring, offering a glimpse into the early development of the Jackson mystique then spreading amongst his men. "I had rather be a private in such an army than a field officer in any other Army. Jackson is perfectly idolized by this army, especially this Brigade, and he is as much pleased with us as we are with him."[49]

Though they admired Jackson, they were also acutely aware of the hardships that his style of generalship demanded. Explaining Jackson's relentless activity to his wife, one officer wrote, "I think this regiment who was so anxious for active service and plenty of fighting have got a little more than they wished for, as we have not had three consecutive days in one camp for the last four weeks, sometimes not getting more than four hours sleep after marching from 20 to 25 miles a day." A week later, Lieutenant Ring wished he could tell his wife "all we have gone through in the past month, not only in the fighting but in the marching line. You cannot think, darling, how much we have suffered," he explained. "One meal a day and that only bread and meat, from five to six hours sleep and two-thirds of the time it rains every night. When it did not it was very cold and our sleep did us little good. Were it not for the oilcloths we captured from the enemy, I do not know what we would have done as a good many times our wagons did not catch us in time to get our blankets."[50]

The shine of military life was beginning to dull a bit. Still, Ring felt fine and even reported that upon weighing himself "I find that I am heavier than I was when I left home a year ago." The time would come when Ring would look back at these weeks in the Valley with Jackson (and those meals of bread and meat) as the best of times. In days ahead, the 6th Louisiana would consider such a meal, a pair of shoes and a blanket to be long-forgotten luxuries.[51]

Jackson's campaign thus far had been a resounding success. His victories at Front Royal on May 23 and Winchester two days later disrupted Federal plans to open a second front in the drive on Richmond. General McDowell was preparing to march his 40,000-man column south from Fredericksburg to join McClellan's army east of the Confederate capital when the first word of Jackson's capture of Front Royal reached Washington a few hours after the fighting ended. Washington's consternation was increased by erroneous reports from a Federal commander east of Front Royal that Jackson's army was marching toward Centreville, which would threaten the Northern capital. Reacting to the alarming news, President Lincoln decided to rally Federal forces to go after Jackson's Valley Army. On May 24, as Jackson pounced upon Banks' rear guard at Middletown, Lincoln ordered General Fremont with his 15,000 men to advance from the Allegheny Mountains west of the Shenandoah Valley to Harrisonburg. From there Fremont could march down the Valley (north) behind Jackson to relieve Banks. That same afternoon, Lincoln ordered General McDowell to forgo his plans to march upon Richmond (scheduled to begin May 26) and lead two of his four divisions—about 20,000 men—to the Shenandoah to destroy Jackson. McDowell called the order a "crushing blow," for it deprived McClellan of the added force that could have finally collapsed Richmond's strained defenses. "If the enemy can succeed so readily in disconcerting all our plans by alarming us first at one point, then at another, he will paralyze a large force with a very small one," McDowell accurately complained to Washington. Unfortunately for the Federals, no one heeded this sage advice.[52]

McDowell's complaint rather neatly summarized Jackson's mission in the Valley—to paralyze a larger Federal force with his smaller one, thus relieving Richmond. The alteration of Union plans signaled that the Valley Army had succeeded beyond even the fondest of Confederate hopes. When Lincoln issued the change of orders to Fremont and McDowell, "the Valley Army won its Valley Campaign," in the judgment of Robert Tanner, a scholar of Jackson's 1862 operations in the Shenandoah.[53]

Such might be the judgment of history, but in the days following Jackson's capture of Winchester much fighting and marching remained to be performed. Lincoln's orders, while disrupting McClellan's plans for the siege of Richmond, substantially increased the peril of the Army of the Valley by threatening to trap it in a deadly triangle formed by Banks on the north, Fremont moving from the west, and McDowell's two divisions marching from the east. If Jackson could be encircled by these three converging forces, numbering 50,000 men, his Army of the Valley could be wiped out.

As Lincoln was putting these forces into play, Banks' army had retreated north across the Potomac River and was regrouping near Harpers Ferry, a strategic town located at the confluence of the Potomac and Shenandoah rivers. It had suffered more than 3,000 casualties, most of them prisoners, in the three days of fighting against Jackson. In contrast, the Southerners had lost barely 400 wounded and killed. While Banks regrouped and Jackson pushed elements of his army as far north as the heights overlooking Harpers Ferry, McDowell's force was marching from the east toward Front Royal. His advance division, commanded by General James Shields, an Irish-born veteran of the Mexican War, easily recaptured Front Royal on May 30, prying loose the 12th Georgia regiment posted there. Meanwhile, word from cavalry scouts reached Jackson that Fremont's army was on the march via roads that would bring it into the Shenandoah Valley at Strasburg, rather than Harrisonburg. With Shields at Front Royal, only 12 miles east of Strasburg, Jackson was threatened by a pincer movement which could cut off his only viable line of retreat up the Valley Pike to Strasburg, 18 miles south of Winchester.[54]

By noon on Friday, May 30, Jackson decided he must retreat south to avoid the trap. He ordered his entire army to march for Winchester except for Winder's Stonewall Brigade, which remained skirmishing near Harpers Ferry to screen the withdrawal. The Louisiana Brigade was camped several miles to the east of Winchester, guarding the Valley Army's flank near Berryville. General Taylor received orders on Saturday, May 31, to "move through Winchester, clear the town of stragglers and continue to Strasburg," as he later recalled. The 6th Louisiana, along with the rest of the brigade, marched 30 miles on that very hot Saturday, retreating through the city that they had helped liberate only a week before, reaching Strasburg after dark. Jackson was busy there forwarding his enormous stockpile of captured Union supplies, in a wagon train that stretched eight miles along the Valley Pike. His goal was the safe haven of Staunton, 74 miles south.[55]

Sitting around a campfire that night, Jackson told Taylor that Fremont's army was only three miles to the west. It must be attacked and defeated the next morning, he explained. In an unusually talkative mood, Jackson revealed that Shields' Federal division was marching south, up the Luray valley, which runs parallel with the main valley across Massanutten Mountain. From Luray, Shields could strike west across Massanutten Gap to descend upon Jackson at New Market, or he could continue marching and swing around the base of the mountain to attack near Harrisonburg, 17 miles farther south. Either maneuver might enable Shields to link up with Fremont's force in a joint attack on Jackson's long, slow column, encumbered by the lumbering train of captured goods. Jackson's best hope was to prevent Fremont and Banks from converging against him. Ewell's Division, he decided, would hold off Fremont in the morning in the foothills just west of Strasburg, while Jackson took the wagon trains south before Shields could cross Massanutten and cut the Valley Pike.[56]

At sunrise on June 1, Ewell deployed his division four miles northwest of Strasburg to challenge Fremont's army, which had reached the wooded hills along the road from Wardensville. Soon cannon fire boomed from the timber and skirmishing broke out along the opposing lines. The 6th Louisiana was with Taylor's Brigade in reserve to the rear of Ewell's line as the cannonading continued for some time. As the morning hours ticked away, Ewell became impatient for action and puzzled at Fremont's lack of aggressiveness. He was constrained, however, by Jackson's orders to simply hold off Fremont and not seek battle. The division commander summoned Taylor, who suggested that the Louisiana Brigade might be moved to the extreme right of the Confederate position to feel out the enemy's left flank. "Do so," responded Ewell eagerly. "That may stir them up, and I am sick of this fiddling about."[57]

The Louisianians followed their brigadier to the far right of Ewell's line where a wounded Mississippi colonel told Taylor that he had just tested the Federal left flank and driven the enemy back. That sounded promising, so Taylor put his regiments in motion. "The brigade moved forward until the enemy was reached, when, wheeling to the left, it walked down his line," he wrote years later. The Louisianians rolled up the Federal flank in what their commander called "a walkover." In Taylor's words, "Sheep would have made as much resistance as we met. Men decamped without firing or threw down their arms and surrendered, and it was so easy that I began to think of traps."

But there were no traps. Fremont's jumpy fugitives simply gave way, and the only casualties suffered by the Louisianians were caused by Confederate skirmishers mistakenly targeting Taylor's men as they moved down the Union line. The Confederates took some prisoners, whom Taylor later said were Germans who spoke no English. They were the immigrant soldiers of Brig. Gen. Louis Blenker's division, composed of Germans and other recent refugees of Europe from New York and Pennsylvania, who displayed far less appetite for fighting than did Seymour's Irishmen. Both Taylor and Ewell were tempted to pursue Blenker's discouraged troops, but they reluctantly resisted the urge. Jackson did not want a battle. He just needed to keep Fremont at bay, and the action had accomplished that purpose. Fremont mistakenly thought he had been attacked by 15,000 men, with 8,000 more coming up, and hesitated to press forward after the skirmish.[58]

Jackson pushed the rest of his army south along the Valley Pike during Fremont's feeble sparring with Ewell's Division. Late that day, the commanding general personally gave Taylor orders to position his brigade facing west on the hills above the turnpike south of Strasburg and hold in position there to guard against any further advance by Fremont. As darkness fell, the Louisianians lay down to rest. Under orders not to light campfires, the men munched cold rations and rested. Taylor couldn't sleep, and after some hours of restlessness decided to investigate the sound of firing coming from the north. To his dismay, he discovered an enemy cavalry force pushing his way. He immediately ordered his sleepy brigade to break camp and get moving on the pike, which was done amid much stumbling and swearing. From the 6th Louisiana, which was positioned at the tail of his column, Taylor selected two companies to stay with him as a rear guard.[59]

Taylor was glad to have the Irishmen with him that night, which he later claimed was so black that "owls could not have found their way across the fields." Out of this pitch blackness rode a gang of Federal horsemen who crashed into Taylor's little force, knocking down some of the Irishmen and severely bruising one. The cavalry had charged a detachment of Confederate cavalry, driving it into the startled Louisianians. "There was a little pistol-shooting and sabre-hacking," Taylor recorded, but no serious casualties. The general dismounted and marched with the men of the 6th Louisiana, occasionally wheeling them around to fire their muskets in an attempt to keep the Union horsemen at bay. Most of the Federal troopers' shots sailed over the heads of the Confederate guard, but the riders "were bold and enterprising, and well led, often charging up close to the bayonets." Taylor remarked on this to the men, "whereupon the Irishmen answered, 'Devil thank 'em for that same.'"[60]

The disconcerting affair revealed the best qualities of the 6th Louisiana's Irishmen to Taylor, who was impressed by their good humor and their Celtic appetite for a good fight. "It was a fine night intirely for divarsion," one of the Irishmen told his general. Taylor hardly agreed with that sentiment, but he was pleased with the pluck of his New Orleans Irish. "They were steady as clocks and chirpy as crickets, indulging in many a jest whenever the attentions of our friends in the rear were slackened," he recalled later. Taylor's men had heard that General Shields was in the vicinity, "and knew him to be an Irishman by birth, and that he had Irish regiments with him," the Louisiana general wrote. When he confirmed that a fight with Shields' division was likely soon, one of the 6th Louisiana Irishmen remarked, "Them Germans is poor creatures, but Shields' boys will be after fighting." To this Taylor responded that he was sure that "my 'boys' could match Shields's any day," which brought forth "loud assurance from half a hundred Tipperary throats: 'You may bet your life on that, sor.'" During the night, Taylor suggested relieving the Irishmen as the rear guard, but they hooted down the suggestion, saying, "We are the boys to see it out."[61]

That night of rear-guard fighting, marching, and jesting in the pitch blackness along the Valley pike bonded the aristocratic Louisiana general to his Irish foot soldiers as never before. "My heart has warmed to an Irishman since that night," he wrote years later. If Taylor ever held any prejudice against the immigrant Irish, as was charged by a Northern newspaper after his summary execution of two of Wheat's Irish-born Tigers the previous December, it must have dissolved along the retreat from Strasburg. Indeed, after the war he wrote of the 6th Louisiana with admiration and affection. The regiment, he wrote, "was composed of Irishmen, stout, hardy fellows, turbulent in camp and requiring a strong hand, but responding to kindness and justice, and ready to follow their officers to the death." It was the finest tribute to the Louisiana Irish Confederates ever penned, and all the more significant since it came from a patrician planter whose views of immigrant Americans were generally condescending.[62]

Though Taylor was impressed by the Irishmen's behavior, the regiment suffered a significant loss in numbers during this retreat up the Valley. At least 52 men were captured about June 2 in the vicinity of Strasburg and Woodstock, perhaps during that night of fighting and retreating. Most of those captured were Irishmen and Germans, including Captain Monaghan of Company F, one of the highest-ranking Irishmen of the 6th Louisiana. Monaghan remained a prisoner until he was exchanged early in August, but most of the others captured in this action escaped the rest of the war by taking the oath of allegiance to the United States to win their release from prison. With Monaghan's capture, the regiment had lost both captains of its "Irish Brigade" companies, as the wounded Captain Hanlon had fallen into enemy hands after the battle at Winchester.[63]

The 6th Louisiana's rear-guard duty ended shortly after sunup June 2 when it was relieved by the Stonewall Brigade. The Virginians took up the work of keeping the pursuing enemy at bay while the Louisianians, after only an hour's rest, resumed the march down the Valley Pike. It was now June in Virginia. The summer climate blends exhausting heat and humidity with sudden, drenching thunderstorms. For men on the march with knapsack and musket, with little protection from a searing sun during the day and a chilling rain at night, Virginia's summer was an enemy which could only be endured, not defeated.

"The day was uncommonly hot, the sun like fire, and water scarce along the road, and our men suffered greatly," Taylor recalled. At one point when the Federals pressed in on Winder's men, Taylor drew up his brigade on a knoll. "The position was good, my battery was at hand, and our men were so fatigued that we debated whether it was not more comfortable to fight than to retreat." As it turned out, they did not debate the question for long, for Ashby's cavalry came up and drove the Union forces back. Shortly thereafter, the day's heat was broken by a raging thunderstorm that drenched the weary troops and swelled the streams in the Valley.[64]

Like his brigade commander, Lieutenant Ring also found the weather, marching and hunger hard to endure. On June 7, he headed one of his letters "Camp Hungry" (it is unclear whether this was Ring's own wry joke or whether the regiment actually called one of their overnight camping places by this name). "I have passed through some exciting times" he informed his wife, "have marched over two hundred miles, been in three battles and through the mercy of God still unharmed and well, only a good deal fagged out with the hard marches and bad weather." He added that "we have not had three consecutive days in one camp for the last four weeks, sometimes not getting more than four hours sleep after marching from 20 to 25 miles a day."[65]

The pace at which Jackson drove his army caused widespread straggling, as worn-out men dropped by the roadside to rest, unable or unwilling to keep up the relentless march. "We have lost out of this Brigade during our retreat from Winchester nearly three hundred men by their straggling behind," Ring observed. "We have eighteen missing in our company alone."[66] There was an understandable reason behind Jackson's frenetic pace, however, as his army was being pursued by Fremont on the Valley Pike while Shields pressed south through the Luray Valley, on the other side of Massanutten Mountain. If the Federal forces combined against him, Jackson would face overwhelming odds and likely defeat. He had to keep moving and find a way to defeat them one by one.

On June 5, the Valley Army reached Harrisonburg, where it left the Valley Pike by turning east toward the village of Port Republic, nestled at the base of the Blue Ridge at the junction of two streams, the North River and the South River. The two waterways joined at the little town to form the South Fork of the Shenandoah River. A covered wooden bridge spanned the North River, the larger of the two streams, and a ford crossed the South

River, but after the recent thunderstorms the swift-flowing currents made the ford of little use to infantry. Ashby's cavalry had destroyed all the bridges to the north to prevent Shields from crossing the Shenandoah to join Fremont, leaving the bridge at Port Republic the only avenue for such a junction. It became clear to Jackson that the fighting that he had delayed thus far with his rapid march and burning of bridges was almost certain to occur in the vicinity of Port Republic, when Shields would be in his front and Fremont closing in on the rear.[67]

A similar thought occurred to Lieutenant Ring as he and the men of the 6th Louisiana enjoyed a rare day of rest on Saturday, June 7—their first in 15 days since the storming of Front Royal. Writing from the camp of the Louisiana Brigade near the village of Cross Keys, seven miles west of Port Republic, Ring told his wife that "we are within five miles of the enemy and are lying upon our arms expecting to be called up at any moment either to retreat or fight." Though he noted that "no one knows anything of Stonewall Jackson's ideas," the young lieutenant displayed a good understanding of the Valley Army's situation and prospects. "We have come thus far in awful quick time with a pretty large force on each side and in our rear, trying to cut us off," Ring told his wife. "I think however we are all right now as we have the Shenandoah River to protect our flanks and I suppose we will fight Fremont who is behind us, today or tomorrow." Ring's supposition proved correct, for the Southerners would indeed "fight Fremont" on the morrow, June 8, at Cross Keys.[68]

What Ring could not foresee was that the Cross Keys battle would be but one of a pair of sharp clashes, the second occurring a day later at Port Republic.

Chapter Three

The 'Hell Spot': PORT REPUBLIC

"They cheered and screamed like lunatics.
they fought like demons. they died like fanatics."
— *Post-war newspaper account of the Battle of Port Republic*

Sunday, June 8, dawned "bright, warm, calm and peaceful," in the words of Jackson's staff aide, Henry Kyd Douglas. "The absolute quiet of it, after so many of noisy activity was unnatural, but it was most welcome." Jackson, a religious man who preferred not to fight on Sunday (though he seemed destined to do so often, as at Winchester), issued orders that the troops would spend the day in camp and chaplains would hold services.[1]

There was a special reason for religious observance that day. Two days earlier, as his rear guard engaged in a hot skirmish with Fremont's advance, Jackson's dashing cavalry commander, Turner Ashby, had been killed near Harrisonburg. Jackson was grieved by the loss and a gloom fell over the army. Lieutenant Ring wrote his wife that it was "a loss that this army can little afford," because Ashby was "a mainstay of this Army and the greatest dread of the Yankees of all our Army."[2]

As it turned out there would be no rest or religion that day. The peace of the morning was suddenly dissolved in the unexpected boom of cannon as the town of Port Republic came under artillery fire about 8:30 a.m. Jackson, headquartered on the western end of town in the spacious home of Dr. George W. Kemper, had only three companies of infantry—fewer than 100 men—and an artillery battery with him in the village, along with the army's huge wagon train. The rest of his men were across the North River, camping on the hills opposite town, or as far away as

Cross Keys, where Ewell's Division (including the 6th Louisiana) protected Jackson's rear. Though Jackson had ordered elements of Ashby's now-leaderless cavalry to guard the northern approaches to Port Republic and warn of any sign of Shields' division from that direction, the demoralized Confederate troopers failed in that mission and allowed Shields' advance—a brigade led by Col. Samuel S. Carroll—to slip by them during the night. By daylight Carroll had placed his four artillery pieces in position to shell the town and the bridge over North River, and readied his 150 cavalrymen for a dash upon the lightly-defended position. His four regiments of infantry waited nearby to support the advance.[3]

When the cannon opened fire, Jackson made a dash for the North River bridge, galloping down the town's main street trailed by two of his staff aides and thundering across the wooden span even as cannon fire sent splinters flying around him. By this time Federal cavalry raiders were splashing across the river and charging into town, and the Confederate army commander came within a hair's breadth of being captured.[4]

As Jackson was dispatching a regiment of infantry to confront the Federals, Ewell's Division at Cross Keys came under attack by a portion of Fremont's army, which had marched east that morning from Harrisonburg. The surprise assault at Port Republic "had hardly been repulsed before Ewell was seriously engaged with Fremont, moving on the opposite side of the river," recalled Jackson. As the cautious Federal commander approached Cross Keys, a tiny settlement along the road from Harrisonburg to Port Republic, his army of 10,500 outnumbered Ewell's blocking force of about 5,000. Fremont, however, did not take advantage of his numerical strength. Of his 24 infantry regiments, only five were sent forward in the attack. Worse still, the unfortunate regiments were Blenker's Germans, the "sheep" so easily driven by the Louisiana Brigade's "walkover" near Strasburg eight days earlier.[5]

Blenker's "sheep" walked to the slaughter. Ewell had smartly positioned his infantry and artillery along a commanding ridge overlooking an open meadow watered by Mill Creek. His left and right flanks were-carefully concealed in heavy woods along the ridge, which was bisected by the road to Port Republic. After initial skirmishing and a heavy duel of artillery, the Federal attack was delivered against the Confederate right flank, where Brig. Gen. Isaac Trimble's Brigade lay in ambush in the woods, unseen until it unleashed a devastating volley at close range on the unsuspecting New Yorkers and Pennsylvanians of Brig. Gen. Julius Stahel's brigade. Stahel's leading regiment, the 8th New York, walked into a hail of flying lead from 1,500 muskets discharged simultaneously. The volley dissolved the attack in a bloody repulse and sent the stunned Federals retreating for cover.[6]

At the outset of the action at Cross Keys, the 6th Louisiana was posted in the center of Ewell's line with the rest of Taylor's Brigade. Before Fremont's ill-fated attack unfolded, though, the Louisiana Brigade received orders from General Jackson to rush to Port Republic. Shaken by the surprise raid of Colonel Carroll's guns and cavalry and the possibility of a general attack by Shields, Jackson sent orders to Ewell to send his "best Brigade to Port Republic." Ewell responded by relaying the order to Taylor, whose Louisianians by that time had earned the reputation as Jackson's shock troops, the hammer to be swung into action whenever a hard blow was needed. Taylor, who in retrospect called Fremont's attack at Cross Keys "feeble in the extreme," received Jackson's message about 9:00 a.m., when a staff officer "in hot haste" galloped up with the order to "march my brigade double-quick to Port Republic." The Louisiana regiments, he wrote, "started on the run, for such a message from Jackson meant business."[7]

The business, however, did not turn out to be what the Louisianians expected, which was a sharp fight. Just as at First Manassas, the men of the 6th Louisiana were caught up in another back-and-forth marching exercise rather than a battle. After a rapid march of two miles toward Port Republic, the Louisiana Brigade received orders to halt. Soon Jackson rode up and explained that he had called for Taylor due to the raid of the Federal cavalry into the riverside town, which had since been driven off. The Confederate commander ordered the Louisianians to about-face and head back to Cross Keys to support Ewell.[8]

The brigade reached the battlefield about 2:00 p.m., after the bloody repulse of Stahel's brigade. Ewell, still worried that Fremont's superior numbers might yet be brought to bear, used the Louisiana regiments to shore up each of his flanks. Dividing the brigade, he dispatched the 7th and 8th Louisiana regiments to the far left, while the 6th Louisiana filed off to the right along with the 9th Louisiana and Wheat's Tigers. Colonel Seymour led his weary foot soldiers to Trimble's sector of the battlefield, where the 8th New York had met its slaughter. There they halted near a small church known as Mill Creek church or the Dunkard church, where one of Trimble's regiments, the 21st Georgia, was resting after the hot engagement. A Georgia captain who watched as the Louisianians arrived remembered the scene years later:

> The Louisiana Brigade marched up in quick line, by the flank, each fours in perfect line, arms at 'right shoulder shift.' The 6th Louisiana was near us. Their old Colonel, Isaac Seymour, a martial man with long, silvery locks, whirled his horse and gave the command: 'Battalion Halt. Front! Right Dress!' Every rifle was quickly brought to 'Shoulder Arms' and the alignment perfected without a wobble. At the command 'Order Arms" the rifles of 800 men struck the ground as one man. 'Fix Bayonets. Stack Arms! Break Ranks!'"[9]

This display of drill-parade precision was followed by a scene that contributed to the reputation of the Louisiana soldiers generally, and the Irishmen of the 6th Louisiana specifically, as ill-disciplined scoundrels. As soon as they broke ranks, many of the New Orleans men set to looting the dead Federals, a pasttime which shocked the 21st Georgia onlookers. One of Seymour's Irishmen, while bent over the body of a dead rifleman of the 8th New York, remarked to the wide-eyed Georgian watching the gruesome spectacle: "This fellow will not need his watch where he has gone, as time is nothing there, and the burial corps will soon get everything that's left. These dom non-combatants get too much already, and they don't fight for it." The looter remarked to the Georgia captain that while "these German bounty men" were poor fighters, "Shields' boys" (which he mistakenly assumed were Irishmen) would prove to be more worthy foes.[10]

For the rest of the afternoon the Louisiana regiments played a passive role as reserves, "not actually in action on this day," as Taylor reported, but "much exposed to the enemy's shell" which caused several casualties. While the regiment never got into the battle, it suffered under the artillery fire and recorded the brigade's only fatality at Cross Keys. The unlucky recipient of the flying metal was a Bavarian immigrant from New Orleans, Pvt. Cornelius Schmidt of the mostly-German Pemberton Rangers, who was killed by an exploding shell.[11]

The battle had gone badly for Fremont and his Federals. Trimble's Confederates, after ambushing Stahel's unlucky Germans, pursued the retreating Unionists for a mile, bending back Fremont's line on his left. This drained what little fight remained in the Federal commander, who showed little initiative for the rest of the day. Late in the afternoon, the aggressive Trimble tried to persuade Taylor to join him in an assault against the bloodied Federals, who had retreated to a woods a mile away. The more prudent Louisiana general saw little advantage in Trimble's scheme. Besides, the Louisiana Brigade was weary from its marching and counter-marching and needed rest and food—in hindsight a wise decision on its commander's part considering the crucial role his men would have to play the following day. Taylor left Trimble to stew about his attack plans while he reassembled his divided brigade near the Mill Creek church, where the 6th Louisiana and her sister regiments went into bivouac.[12]

As darkness fell over the Shenandoah Valley that Sunday night, Ewell's Confederates rested victorious at Cross Keys. Jackson, who allowed his able division commander to fight his own battle while he remained back at Port Republic, determined that when Monday dawned, he would attack Shields.

At daylight on Monday the men of the regiment left their camp at Mill Creek Church and marched seven miles to Port Republic. The rolling lush farmland glistened with dew in the rising sun and the Louisianians were struck with the beauty of the valley. One of them described the scene in rapturous prose:

> The limpid waters of the Shenandoah softly murmured along the base of the majestic Blue Ridge. . . .The rich wheat fields waved their nodding plume to the music of the soft, sighing winds that played so gently through them, while the peaks of the Blue Ridge rose in their towering height from the deep blue mist which enveloped them. . .all nature hushed and still, its peaceful tranquillity shortly to be disturbed by the fierce conflict of arms.[13]

The brigade crossed the wooden bridge over the North River and passed through the village between the waters to the South River, where a temporary bridge had been constructed overnight by Jackson's engineers. It was a rickety affair made of a half-dozen wagons strung together and topped with narrow planks. "The bridge improvised for the occasion was a frail structure," one Louisianian recalled, "built on wagon wheels, and was only capable of allowing the troops to make the passage in single file." It would prove to be a serious bottleneck that prevented Jackson from quickly amassing his forces when the battle began.[14]

The Louisianians were not the first to cross the wobbly wagon bridge. About sunrise four of the five regiments of Winder's Stonewall Brigade began threading their way across the narrow, poorly secured planks. It was slow going from the start. As the planks loosened and shifted under the boots of hundreds of tramping Virginians, the structure weakened. The bridge slowed Jackson's deployment to an agonizing trickle. Unbeknownst to Winder's men, they—together with one of the Louisiana regiments—would pay a dear price for this poor engineering feat.[15]

The order in which the Louisianians and their commander crossed the wagon bridge would have fateful consequences. The first regiment to cross was the 8th Louisiana, commanded by Col. Henry B. Kelly, who had orders from General Taylor to move down the road and halt to give time to the other regiments to cross and form upon his. After Kelly's men crossed, Col. Leroy Stafford marched his 9th Louisiana over the wobbly footbridge, followed by Major Wheat's battalion of Tigers, and Colonel Seymour's 6th Louisiana. Last to cross was the 7th Louisiana, led by Col. Harry Hays. General Taylor rode somewhere near the rear of the column as it crossed the South River.[16]

Taylor's regiments halted by the side of the road to eat breakfast, which within moments was interrupted by a rising din of small arms fire and cannon. The time was about 7:30 a.m. Colonel Kelly, at the head of the brigade's column, recalled that his men had just stacked arms and broken ranks when artillery was heard down the valley below Port Republic. As the cannon echoed, one of Jackson's aides galloped up and gave Kelly orders to advance at once and report to the commanding general. The 8th Louisiana commander rushed his regiment forward, followed in turn by the others of the brigade. Their breakfast disrupted, the regiments "sprang into ranks, formed column and marched," Taylor remembered, while he mounted his horse and galloped a mile ahead to discover what was happening.[17]

As the Louisiana general dashed down the road toward the sound of the guns, the battle was unfolding on terrain that decidedly favored the Federals, who had bivouacked in the area the previous night. About a mile northeast of the town of Port Republic, an open level plain about three-quarters of a mile wide stretched between the river and the wooded foothills of the Blue Ridge, which rose abruptly from the plain. The road on which the Confederates advanced angled away from the town through the open fields for a mile and then for two miles skirted along the edge of the wooded foothills that rose steeply on the right. Between the road and the river, the ripening wheat fields were traversed by two parallel farm lanes nearly a mile apart, and between the two lanes ran a wooden rail fence dividing the farm of the widow Evaline Baugher from that of neighbor John Lewis. The approaching battle would be largely fought within the little quadrangle of roughly three-quarters of a mile square between the two farm lanes. The key to victory or defeat, however, was a piece of prominent geography just outside this box, an elevated shelf cut into the forested foothill to the right of the road known as "the Coaling."[18]

General Taylor's attention was drawn to the elevated plateau as he galloped toward the battle, for it was belching smoke and iron from six Federal cannon strategically situated there. The Coaling, named for an old hearth built there to make charcoal from the timber of the surrounding hills, loomed over the road and the open fields below so that the cannon were "sweeping every inch of the plain" where the battle was developing, Taylor recalled. The guns stood immediately above and behind Lewiston, as the Lewis family residence was called, where the Federal troops camped the night before and now were deploying to meet the Confederates approaching on the road and through the fields.[19]

Two Union brigades totaling eight infantry regiments, supported by a cavalry regiment and 16 pieces of artillery, were moving into position to confront the Confederates' slowly-developing challenge. Colonel Carroll's four Federal infantry regiments and horsemen, who had participated in the surprise raid on Port Republic the morning before, were joined by a brigade of four Ohio regiments led by Brig. Gen. Erastus B. Tyler, who was in command of the Federal forces. This body of Federals comprised Shields' advance, but the Irish-born major general himself was not on the field at Port Republic. He had been fooled into holding half his force near Luray by a false report that a large Confederate force was approaching from the east. Tyler's 3,000 men were deployed in line of battle in a strong position along the Lewis farm lane, their right flank protected by the swollen South Fork, their left flank anchored on the mountainside, where the admirably-sited Coaling guns commanded the entire field and the road on which the Confederates approached. Several of these Union regiments had helped defeat Jackson at Kernstown, and Tyler had watched the legendary Stonewall retreat from that field. "The position was strong, and the men who held it were of different calibre from Blenker's Germans, and the leaders of stauncher stuff than Fremont," as military historian G. F. R. Henderson aptly noted.[20]

Against these hard men in a strong position Jackson was feeding in his forces as fast as they arrived, which was not fast enough. Initially, the battle opened with 3,000 Federals opposed by only 600 Confederate infantry on the plain. There, two of Winder's regiments—the 5th and 27th Virginia—were suffering under punishing fire, while two others—the 2nd and 4th Virginia—had been sent by Jackson through the woods and up the hills to try to flank the guns on the Coaling. The battle was going badly by the time General Taylor galloped forward to find Jackson, who was at the front with his old Stonewall Brigade.[21]

Taylor was alarmed by what he saw as he spied Jackson just down the road. "Federal lines, their right touching the river, were advancing steadily, with banners flying and arms gleaming in the sun," he wrote. Winder's "small force was suffering cruelly, and its skirmishers were driven in on their thin supporting line. As my Irishmen predicted, 'Shields' boys were after fighting.'" Ewell's Division was slowly oozing itself through the wagon-bridge bottleneck, but the Louisiana general feared that Winder's bloodied force would be driven back on them before they could come to the rescue.[22]

Weighted by these worries, Taylor pulled up abreast of his commanding general. "Jackson was on the road, a little in advance of his line, where the fire was hottest, with reins on his horse's neck, seemingly in prayer," according to the Louisianian. Seeing his subordinate, Jackson exclaimed, "Delightful excitement." Taylor replied that he was pleased to learn the general was enjoying himself, but added that "such fun" might give him indigestion if that six-gun battery on the mountainside was not soon silenced. The Confederate commander had already concluded that capturing the Coaling guns held the key to victory, but his first effort to do so was coming to naught, for the two Virginia regiments sent on that mission before Taylor arrived were thrashing about in the woods after being driven back by the cannon and supporting infantry fire.[23]

Though the battle was going badly for his small force on the open plain, Jackson chose to use the Louisiana Brigade to attack the Coaling guns rather than to shore up Winder's wavering line. He had come to rely on Taylor's men, who had carried the day at Winchester and proved their mettle up and down the Valley, as his favorite shock troops. Here was another assignment that was critical to victory or defeat. Jackson pointed up the mountain at the guns and ordered Taylor to attack them—but to leave just one regiment behind to reinforce Winder's struggling foot soldiers on the plain.[24]

Though Taylor's post-war account implies that the Louisiana brigadier led his entire brigade through the woods and up the hill to the Coaling, the majority of his men were already struggling uphill toward the guns when Taylor met with Jackson. Taylor's advance regiment, Colonel Kelly's 8th Louisiana, had hurried down the road after being summoned by Jackson's aide, and after coming under the fire of the Coaling guns, had filed off to the right of the road into the field adjoining the woods. Kelly's men were followed by Stafford's 9th Louisiana. Leaving Stafford in charge of the two regiments, Kelly had ridden off to request orders from Jackson when he encountered Major Wheat of the Tiger battalion. Wheat had just seen Jackson, who had given him orders to advance. With Wheat's Tigers joining his two-regiment command, Kelly led three-fifths of the Louisiana Brigade into the woods toward the Coaling.[25]

While Kelly and his force clawed their way up the mountain through the laurel thicket, Taylor released the 7th Louisiana from the tail of his column to join the battle on the plain. That left the brigadier in command of only the 6th Louisiana as he moved to carry out Jackson's order and catch up to the rest of his brigade. Again in the company of Seymour's Irishmen, whose bravery on this day would deeply impress him, Taylor had an advantage that Kelly and his men lacked—the help of an experienced guide. While Kelly's force groped blindly toward the sound of the guns, Taylor and the 6th Louisiana were led on a somewhat longer but easier route by Jed Hotchkiss, Jackson's map maker, who knew the area well. Colonel Seymour and his regiment followed Hotchkiss and Taylor into the woods, where they found an obscure mountain road used by timber-cutters for hauling wood to the Coaling. As Taylor rode with Hotchkiss up this path, his guide explained that the road would come to a gorge just opposite the elevated plateau where the Federal guns rested. That would put the Louisianians on roughly the same elevation as the guns, but separated from them by a ravine which would have to be crossed during the attack.[26]

The forest path allowed for fairly rapid movement, enabling Seymour's men to cover a somewhat longer route in the time that Kelly's detachment struggled uphill through the undergrowth for about three-quarters of a mile. Despite the obstacles and difficult terrain, the 8th Louisiana colonel advanced his force in line of battle, uncertain when he might come face-to-face with infantry guarding the Federal guns. The 6th Louisiana advanced up the mountain road in column, but at some point near the top it left the path and also deployed into line, with skirmishers in front, advancing cautiously. The 8th Louisiana colonel was "within a few paces of the crest of the hill overlooking the Deep Run ravine, and commanding, at close range, the ground upon which the Federal batteries stood, when Gen. Taylor came up with the 6th Louisiana and took command of the movement," Kelly wrote.[27]

At this point the 6th Louisiana was well to the right of Kelly's line and higher up the slope of the hill. Taylor decided to reposition Seymour's men down the slope, probably to better align with the position of the Federal guns. The six cannon, it turned out, were not all clustered close together on the Coaling, but spread downward along the slope almost to the road below. The six pieces were from three batteries. Capt. Joseph Clark of the 4th U.S. Artillery had two Parrott rifles on the far Federal left, on the Coaling itself. To his right, one 12-pounder howitzer from Capt. Lucius Robinson's 1st Ohio Light Artillery (Battery L) stood between the Coaling and the road. Three additional guns, at least two of them rifled, from Capt. James Huntington's 1st Ohio Light Artillery (Battery H), were near the road just below the Coaling, some 70 feet lower in elevation. The 6th Louisiana worked its way down the mountain slope to a position facing Huntington's guns. Seymour's men marched across the rear of the other regiments and extended the brigade line down toward the open ground on the left. According to historian Robert K. Krick, the 6th Louisiana enjoyed the least cover and faced the heaviest combat risk of the attacking force. "The fortunes of war, compounded by geography," explains Krick, "threw the 6th Louisiana onto ground where it would lose almost as many men killed as the other three units combined."[28]

Seymour's regiment now anchored the far left of the Louisiana attack formation. Wheat's Tigers lined up just to the right of the 6th Louisiana, then came the 9th Louisiana in the center of the line and finally Kelly's 8th Louisiana, which occupied the highest ground on the far right. The 6th Louisiana was still shuffling into line when loud cheers from the Union soldiers on the plain below indicated that the tide of battle was turning against the Southerners. The formation of the line "had scarcely been completed when loud and prolonged cheers, rendered in that measured term peculiar only to the enemy, were heard on the left, announcing his success," one Louisianian recalled. At the sound of the yelling, "we well knew that the battle was going disastrously against us in the lowlands," Colonel Kelly recalled. Out on those cannon-swept wheat fields Winder's Virginia regiments, bolstered by the 7th Louisiana, had boldly attacked the strong Federal line which still outnumbered them two-to-one. The Confederate attackers sustained horrendous casual-

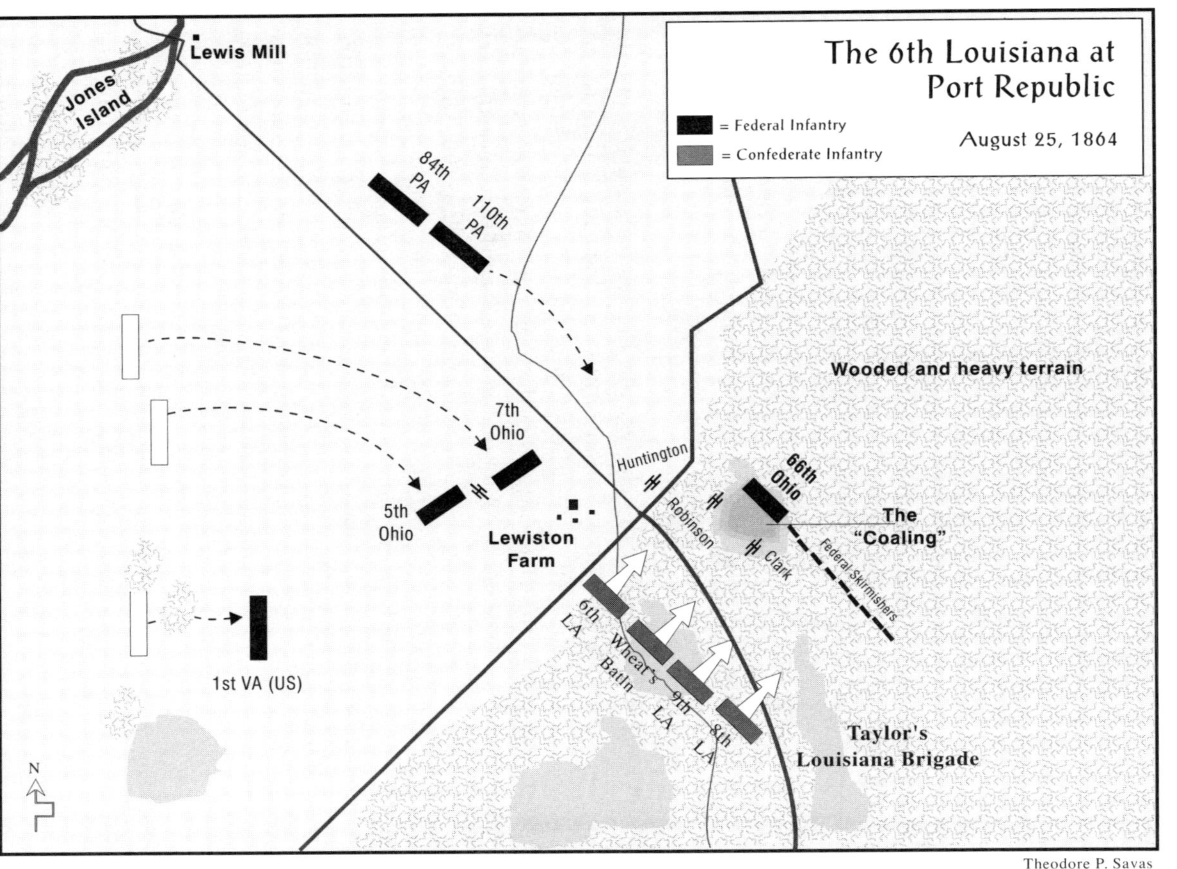

Theodore P. Savas

ties—the 7th Louisiana carried fewer than 400 men into the battle and lost nearly half of them—and fell back in disarray as the Union regiments surged across the plain with a loud cheer in pursuit. The rout of Jackson's men on the open fields made the attack on the Coaling by the Louisianians a do-or-die affair. On the wooded hillside, one participant recalled, "the Louisianians waited with breathless anxiety," knowing that the battle depended upon what they must do now. "It was rather an anxious moment, demanding instant action," Taylor remembered.[29]

As the Louisiana brigadier steeled himself for the charge, a courier came crashing through the woods with a message from a desperate General Winder begging Taylor to attack. The Virginians were on the verge of defeat in the fields below. "The order was rapidly passed along the line, 'prepare for the charge,'" recalled one participant. "The suspense of those few moments was terrible." From Seymour's Irishmen down the slope to Kelly's Creoles and Cajuns far up the hillside overlooking the ravine, the 1,700 men of Louisiana fixed bayonets and whispered final prayers.[30]

When Taylor ordered the charge, the Louisianians burst from the dense forest undergrowth with that protracted, high-pitched battle-cry known as the Rebel yell. "The wild spirit of the men found vent in one loud, prolonged yell, which ran along the entire line like an electric current," wrote a Louisianian. "Who that has ever heard that unearthly yell will forget it? The preface to a charge, it was always the certain index of success, the spontaneous outburst of the soul." The screaming assault exploded upon the Federal gunners and their thin infantry support as a stunning surprise. The attack was "sudden and unexpected," admitted General Tyler after the battle. Its surprise was enhanced by the terrain and the dense forest. "The thick undergrowth prevented our seeing them until they were quite near us," reported Captain Clark, the commander of the smoking guns parked high on the Coaling.[31]

The Federals recovered quickly, however, and began swinging the muzzles of their cannon toward the onrushing Confederates as riflemen of the 66th Ohio regiment, posted in the woods behind and above the guns, unleashed a leaden hail on the attackers. The ravine crossed by the Louisianians was narrowest and steepest at the top of the hillside, while near the bottom it was flatter and more open. The result was that Kelly and his 8th Louisiana had a shorter distance to traverse to reach the guns than did Seymour. The 6th Louisiana not only had to cover more terrain but was also completely exposed to a destructive fire. Clark's guns at the top of the Coaling could not depress their muzzles steeply enough to bear on Kelly's men, but Captain Huntington's three pieces on the lower slope near the road found ready targets in the men of the 6th Louisiana and Wheat's battalion as the Southerners charged directly toward them. Huntington, fearing just such an attack, had stacked canister in front of his guns, and now his men frantically began pouring the shotgun-like blasts into the screaming figures dashing through the smoke toward them.[32]

"On the Louisianians dashed, regardless of the terrific fire of canister," penned one attacker. "Emerging from the woods, they came in full view of the enemy; a sharp fire of musketry from the right is poured into the line, but its only effect is to accelerate the speed of the men in their impetuous charge." Kelly and his men charged down and then up the steep ravine and reached the guns first—in what seemed to the 8th Louisiana colonel "like a flash." For the 6th Louisiana, the only flash was that of Huntington's cannon, which tore gaps in Seymour's line as his men sprinted across the open ground near the Lewis house. In the hail of lead and iron, men were dropping left and right. One of them was a private in the 6th Louisiana's Tensas Rifles named William E. Cochran. The 20-year-old Mississippi-born farmer from St. Joseph, Louisiana, took a shot in the head that fractured his skull but miraculously did not penetrate into his brain. While he would live to be discharged in August, many of the men falling along the advancing line were not so lucky. The 6th Louisiana's dash was more prolonged and deadly than its sister regiments, but in a few moments all four units were swirling about the cannon in one of the most savage hand-to-hand encounters of the war. All organization was lost, with officers and men of the three regiments and the battalion converging into one mingling mob of frenzied fighting men.[33]

"It was not war on that spot. It was a pandemonium of cheers, shouts, shrieks and groans, lighted by the flames from the cannon and musket—blotched by fragments of men thrown high into trees by the shells," in the words of a post-war newspaper account of the assault. "In every great battle of the war there was a hell-spot. At Port Republic, it was on the mountain side."[34] Vicious hand-to-hand fighting marked the collision, as the Federal gunners resisted savagely and bravely, with men on both sides employing bayonets, knives, clubs, and bare hands. "Men ceased to be men. They cheered and screamed like lunatics—they fought like demons—they died like fanatics," reported one newspaper account.

This is a modern photograph of the "Coaling" at Port Republic. *Christopher Gannon*

"To lose the guns was to lose the battle. To capture them was to win it." In General Taylor's words, "the fighting in and around the battery was hand to hand, and many fell from bayonet wounds. Even the artillery men used their rammers in a way not laid down in the Manual, and died at their guns. As Conan said to the devil, 'Twas claw for claw.'" Up to this point in the war the Louisianians had not met such die-hard resistance from any Federals. "The cannoniers fought with their pieces to the last; no words can to justice to their heroism," one of them wrote in a postwar tribute.[35]

After a brief but bloody struggle Taylor's fighters overwhelmed their opponents and captured the six pieces. Their initial success was helped by an ill-timed move by the Federal commander when General Tyler shifted two Pennsylvania regiments from a supporting position near the Coaling guns to the plain below. The transfer took place just before the Louisianians attacked. Only the 66th Ohio was left in support of the artillery, but that circumstance was soon to change. The Louisianians "were rejoicing and shouting" over capturing the six guns, Colonel Kelly recounted, when a strong Federal counter-attack burst upon their celebration. "Suddenly a scathing fire of canister was poured into them by a section of Clark's Battery, which had been rapidly brought over from the Federal right to within two hundred yards of the position of the captured guns," according to the 8th Louisiana commander. At the same time Tyler pulled the 5th and 7th Ohio regiments from his line on the plain and wheeled them to their left and rear to assault the Confederates packed around the captured guns. The disorganized Louisianians found themselves under a withering fire of musketry and canister from the rallying Unionists.[36]

When the 9th Louisiana's lieutenant colonel, William "Big" Peck (who stood 6'6" and weighed 300 pounds), saw Tyler's Ohio regiments approaching, he yelled at the men to kill the artillery horses so that the enemy could not move the guns. A slaughterhouse scene followed. The Louisianians slashed the horses' throats and shot them point blank in the head as the Federals surged upon them. It was pandemonium as the bleeding horses thrashed and bucked in their death throes among Union and Confederate soldiers hacking at each other with bayonets, clubbing each other with muskets, shooting in all directions amid curses, bellowing animals, and flying blood. "It was a sickening sight," one witness said, "men in gray and those in blue piled up in front of and around the guns and with the horses dying and the blood of men and beasts flowing almost in a stream."[37]

Some of the excited Confederates on the Coaling who saw the Federal troops falling back from their lines on the plain below assumed that the move signaled a retreat from the battlefield. "Another yell burst from the Louisianians" as they cheered the Federal withdrawal, one witness reported, but their celebration was premature. Instead of retreating, the blue line wheeled to the right and came straight at the surprised celebrants. The disorganized Louisianians milling about the guns could not withstand the Federal counter-attack and fell back in small groups to the wooded hillside and the grounds about the Lewis house, just below the Coaling. The Union forces had possession of their guns again, but could not move them for lack of horses. Colonel Kelly rallied part of the Louisiana Brigade around Lewiston, directing musket fire on the Federals from doors and windows of the big brick house, but "the enemy soon swarmed into the orchard and the grounds about the building in such numbers as to render it necessary to withdraw from it to avoid capture." Kelly and his fighters retreated to the woods along the Port Republic road near the Deep Run ravine, where he found General Taylor and "a body of officers and men still without formation, except a short line with the colors of the 6th Louisiana." From this position and around

Seymour's knot of men, Taylor and Kelly organized a second attack on the Coaling.[38]

The second charge on the bloody plateau, claims historian Robert Krick, "probably cost Taylor's regiments as dearly as the first." Indeed, contemporary accounts portray the second attack in terms as bloody as the first. "They re-form under a terrific fire and rush with an impetus which even the hand of death cannot stop," reported one newspaper account. "They reach the guns again, and again men shoot, stab, cut, hack—aye! they grapple and roll under the wheels of cannon so hot that they would almost blister. . . .For a second time the Federals are pressed back, and for the second time the guns speak under Confederate hands." But the Confederates' second success on the Coaling did not last any longer than the first, for General Tyler's determined Ohioans once again rallied and drove the Louisiana regiments from the guns. "Panting like dogs—faces begrimed—nine-tenths of them bareheaded—the Federal wave rolls back on the guns, and now there is a grapple such as no other battle ever furnished." The fierce fighting on the mountainside attracted the attention of both Unionists and Confederates on the plain below. "They hear this pandemonium of shrieks and screams on the mountainside and they halt," a newspaper article reported. "It is a sound ten times more horrible than the whistle of grape or the hiss of canister. Men cease firing to look up. They can see nothing for the smoke, but what they hear is a sound like that of hungry tigers turned loose to tear each other to death."[39]

The thinning ranks of the Louisianians were beaten back from the guns a second time. A short lull in the fighting followed as both sides had exhausted themselves. While the bloodied Confederates contemplated the grim necessity of a third attack, more Union reinforcements were seen coming up toward the Coaling. General Taylor watched them with growing unease. The Federals "had counter-marched. . .and came into full view of our situation," he recalled. "Wheeling to the right, with colors advanced, like a solid wall he marched straight upon us. There seemed nothing left but to set our backs to the mountain and die hard."[40]

At this grim moment General Ewell came "crashing through the underwood," in Taylor's words. His arrival "produced the effect of a reinforcement, and was welcomed with cheers." With the enemy falling back from the plain below, easing the pressure on Ewell's front, the aggressive old cavalry soldier rushed to aid the hard-pressed Taylor, bringing fragments of two of his regiments, the 44th and 58th Virginia, with him.

"The remnants of the two regiments reached General Taylor at the moment when. . .fresh troops of the enemy had driven him from the battery he had captured," Ewell reported after the battle. The major general and his few reinforcements provided the spark the weary Louisiana fighters needed to launch their third and final assault on the Federal guns. According to one soldier's account, when Ewell arrived on the scene he asked, "What troops are these?" Told they were the Louisiana Brigade, their division commander responded: "Men, you know me. We must go back to that battery." The Louisianians would never deny the old general his wish. "The men rose to their feet, a shout—the death knell of the enemy—burst spontaneous from the line, and without further orders they again dashed forward to the battery, over the ground already strewn with their dead comrades." This was the last "desperate rally," in which even his drummer-boys joined, that Taylor portrayed in his memoirs as the climax of the four-hour struggle at Port Republic.[41]

The third assault captured the Federal guns for good, except for one piece that Captain Huntington's gunners managed to drag off by hand. The Louisianians' success on the Coaling had turned the tide of the battle on the plain by forcing General Tyler to rush troops to the rear to counter the Confederate attack on the mountainside. With the Federal line wavering and falling back through the fields, Jackson's men on the plain were finally able to rally and drive forward. Though they could not know it at the time, the Federal commander had issued orders to organize a retreat after Taylor's men captured the Coaling guns for the first time. "From the instant the batteries were first taken by the Louisiana infantry the battle was lost, irretrievably, to the Federal forces," Colonel Kelly of the 8th Louisiana wrote in retrospect, "and what, up to that moment, was a disastrous defeat to the Confederate arms, was changed to certain victory."[42]

As the Federals retreated up the road toward Conrad's Store, the Louisianians turned the captured guns on them, with Ewell pitching in as a gunner. Jackson rode up "with intense light in his eyes," as Taylor remembered, and grabbed the Louisianian's hand, saying that his brigade would keep the captured cannon. "I thought the men would go mad with cheering, especially the Irishmen," the brigadier recalled. "A huge fellow, with one eye closed and half his whiskers burned by powder, was riding cockhorse on a gun, and catching my attention, yelled out, 'We told you to bet on your boys.'"[43]

For the "boys" of the 6th Louisiana, Port Republic became the deadliest battle of the entire war. Official returns place the regiment's casualties at 66 men: 11 killed and 55 wounded. A regimental casualty list, however, lists the names of 18 men killed (including mortally wounded). The regiment's compiled service records, though, show 23 men killed and mortally wounded. Based on either of these figures, no other single battle produced as many fatalities for the 6th Louisiana in four years of war. The names of the killed and mortally wounded give witness to the Irish character of the 6th Louisiana. It was the Foleys and Gallaghers and Mullens who gave the regiment's Port Republic casualty list the flavor of a guest book at an Irish wake. Of the 20 dead whose birthplaces are known, 12 were born in Ireland, three were immigrants from Germany and two were natives of states in the North. Only three were native Louisianians. Most of the dead were privates, but the Germans in Company G, the Pemberton Rangers, lost their commander, Capt. Isaac A. Smith, who was killed instantly on the battlefield.[44]

~~~~~~

The 6th Louisiana's Losses at Port Republic

Killed in Action

Name	Company	Birthplace
Pvt. John F. Croake	F	Ireland
Pvt. Christian Euth	G	Germany
Sgt. Daniel A. Fitch	C	Louisiana
Pvt. Daniel Fitzpatrick	B	Ireland
Pvt. Declon Foley	I	Ireland
Pvt. James Gallagher	K	Ireland
Pvt. Thomas Gallagher	F	Ireland
Pvt. Michael Martin	G	Germany
Pvt. Daniel Mullen	G	Ireland
Pvt. Michael Murray	F	Ireland
Pvt. James Noonan	K	Ireland
Pvt. John F. Smith	F	Ireland
Capt. Isaac A. Smith	G	unknown
~~~~~~

Mortally Wounded

Lt. Thomas P. Farrar	D	Louisiana
Pvt. William Flood	I	Ireland
Pvt. John Fox	B	Ireland
Pvt. H.K. Goldsby	A	unknown
Pvt. Thomas Kane	F	Ireland
Pvt. John McCormick	F	New York
Cpl. George Montgomery	A	unknown
Pvt. Conrad Spoonhamer	G	Germany
Pvt. John Wade	C	Louisiana
Pvt. Thomas Windsor	H	Ohio

~~~~~~

Port Republic was costly not only for the 6th Louisiana but for Taylor's Brigade as a whole. Official returns reported 288 casualties—33 dead and 255 wounded. Robert Krick, in his exhaustive study of the battle, lists 53 dead or mortally wounded, 270 wounded, and 27 missing, for a total brigade loss of 350. That is a casualty rate of about 17 percent of the roughly 2,100 engaged. Krick calculates total Confederate losses at 1,263 killed, wounded and missing, and total Federal casualties at 1,103, with both figures considerably higher than official returns.[45]

Witnesses who saw the Coaling battle site immediately after the fight said it was one of the most gruesome scenes of the war. "I have never seen so many dead and wounded in the same limited space," wrote Taylor in his postwar memoirs. In his battle report, which credited Colonel Seymour and his other regimental commanders and their men "with the most determined gallantry," the Louisiana general claimed that men "of each of the regiments engaged in the charge were found dead under the guns of the captured battery." The horror of the scene was accentuated by the sight of dozens of slaughtered horses mingled among the bodies of the Union and Confederate fighters. The Coaling was "covered with dead horses," recalled a member of Jackson's Rockbridge Artillery. "I think there must have been eighty or ninety on less than an acre; one I noticed standing almost upright, perfectly lifeless, supported by a fallen tree." Other witnesses saw dead men frozen in the positions of the final instant of their lives.[46]
~~~~~~

With their awful sacrifice the soldiers of the Louisiana Brigade won the battle and solidified their reputation as Jackson's best fighters. As a result they received the recognition due them. Nine days after the battle, the *Richmond Whig*, which usually reserved its highest praise for Virginia's soldiers, lauded the Louisiana Brigade in glowing rhetoric:

> This brigade. . .has crowned the Pelican flag with undying glory. It did splendid work at Winchester, excellent at Cross Keys, and virtually won the battle at Lewiston [Port Republic]. Old Stonewall told them as much, and presented them with the 6 pieces they captured. . . .The world produces no better fighters than the Louisianians—few, very few, so good. . . .When a thing is to be done that nobody else dares do or can do, it is the very thing Louisianians insist upon doing, and always do it. The fact is, there is a little touch of the very devil in the Louisianians—as some people on the other side of the Potomac will discover, one of these fine days.[47]

General Ewell was no less generous in his praise of the Louisianians in his report on Port Republic. "To General Taylor and his brigade belongs the honor of deciding two battles—that of Winchester and this one." Jackson gratefully praised Taylor and his men, as well he should have, for the Louisianians saved his Virginia troops on the plain below from an impending disaster that loomed out of Jackson's own impetuous initiation of battle before his forces were concentrated. "While Winder's command was in this critical condition," he wrote, "the gallant and successful attack of General Taylor on the Federal left and rear diverted attention from the front, and led to a concentration of their force upon him." The Louisiana Brigade's attack on the Coaling saved Jackson from ending his Valley Campaign with a defeat instead of the glorious victory that went far to engrave his name in history.[48]

In fact, as the brigade's modern historian, Terry Jones, has pointed out, the Louisianians played a critical role in the success of the entire Valley Campaign: "Taylor's men saved the crucial bridge at Front Royal, cut the Federal column at Middletown, pushed the enemy out of Winchester, and broke the Union flank at Port Republic." Jackson recognized as much himself in recommending, the day after Port Republic, that Taylor be promoted to major general.[49]

The men of the 6th shared in the pride and glory of the campaign. It was just five days after Port Republic that Lieutenant Ring wrote that he would "rather be a private" in Stonewall Jackson's ranks "than a field officer in any other Army." He was proud of the bravery of his own company as well. "In our trip up and down the Valley," he wrote his wife, "the Violet Guards have lost in killed, wounded and missing, twenty-four men. So you see darling, I don't command a lot of cowards. Only one man in this crowd has as yet shown the white feathers and we are going to give him one more trial, if he fails again he will be drummed out of the service." Ring rather neatly summed up the remarkable campaign that was just ended: "Since we have formed a junction with Jackson's Army, we have marched from the Shenandoah River to the Potomac and back, fighting on the trip five pitched battles besides any quantity of skirmishes. All this has been done within a month. . ."[50]

In that remarkable month the 6th Louisiana's Irishmen had won the respect and affection of their brigade commander. General Taylor's biographer, T. Michael Parrish, observed that:

> More than any other soldiers in this brigade, these New Orleans Irishmen of Isaac Seymour's Sixth Louisiana had indeed become Taylor's 'boys.' They had joined him for a wild and jovial night of action during the retreat up the Valley pike; here at Port Republic they had received his personal guidance during the flanking movement so that he would be certain to have them when he attacked the battery; and they suffered the most casualties in his brigade. . . .In his memoirs Taylor described them with admiration and affection.[51]

That admiration and affection is evident in an observation that Taylor made about his 6th regiment Celtic fighters, which also points out a great irony about the Irish: "Strange people, these Irish! Fighting everyone's battles, and cheerfully taking the hot end of the poker, they are only found wanting when engaged in what they believe to be their national cause." It was true: the Irish had never been as successful fighting for Ireland's independence as they had for so many other causes, from Britain's colonial wars to the American Civil War.[52]

As they withdrew from the Port Republic battlefield on the evening of June 9, the exhausted survivors of the 6th Louisiana carried their own pride in the regiment's accomplishments and the respect of their superiors with them. They had played a key role in one of the most strategically successful military campaigns in history. They had helped Jackson to tie up a much larger Union army in the Shenandoah Valley and prompted Lincoln to withhold substantial forces McClellan insisted he needed in his offensive against Richmond. They had participated in a campaign that ensured the survival of the Valley as the breadbasket of the Confederacy, and had dealt a telling blow to Federal morale. It was a shining moment for the Confederacy as well as for the Irish rebels from New Orleans. In 20 days they had marched more than 250 miles and fought the enemy five times.

They contemplated these remarkable days as they trudged up the Blue Ridge that night to camp under a cold rain atop the mountain at Brown's Gap. There they met their supply wagons, which had been sent on ahead, and finally had their first chance to eat since that interrupted breakfast some 18 hours earlier. In the darkness, they lay down in the rain to sleep.[53]

Chapter Four

To the Peninsula:
THE SEVEN DAYS' BATTLES

"A perfect hailstorm of bullets greated our advance."

— Private Handerson on Gaines' Mill

Throughout Jackson's Valley Campaign the men of the 6th Louisiana were nagged by a growing worry: the fate of their families and friends back in Louisiana. Since February, when the U. S. Navy under Admiral David G. Farragut began assembling a formidable fleet of warships near the mouth of the Mississippi River, New Orleans had known that an assault was coming. In winter camp and later on the march into the Valley, the New Orleanians of the 6th heard about the threat to their city in letters from home.

"It is often rumored here that the Yankees have taken New Orleans," Private Herron wrote to his cousin in mid-February. "I suppose they will make an attack some fine morning, but I hope they will not be so successful as at Roanoke Island. I suppose that there are plenty of Sunday soldiers to protect it against any force that will be brought against it."[1]

Sunday soldiers was an apt description of the pitiful military force left in New Orleans. The city had been stripped of manpower, as most men of prime military age had already enlisted and gone to the Confederate armies in Virginia or Tennessee. Only about 3,000 militiamen were left to defend the city. One observer described them as "merchants, bankers, underwriters, judges, real-estate owners and capitalists" with gray or bald heads who "had done no harder muscular work than carve roasts and turkeys these twenty, thirty, forty years."[2]

Still, New Orleans maintained an unshakable faith that Farragut and his gunboats would never approach the city because they would be unable to pass two formidable forts, Forts Jackson and St. Philip, located 75 miles down river. Garrisoned by about 1,100 men, the two stone forts, one on each side of the Mississippi, could bring to bear nearly 150 guns against any ship attempting to pass upstream. It was almost universally believed in New Orleans that no wooden ship would ever get by the forts.[3]

Farragut proved otherwise. In the black of night on April 24 his deep-water fleet ran by the forts after a furious exchange of fire. On April 25, the Federal fleet appeared at the levee in New Orleans, whose sky was black with smoke from burning cotton bales and warehouses set fire by Confederate orders. Within days, New Orleans was ruled by Maj. Gen. Benjamin F. Butler and the 15,000 Union troops brought to shore by Farragut's fleet. One of the Confederacy's most important cities fell without a fight.[4]

The loss of New Orleans was a strategic catastrophe which gave the North control of the mouth of the Mississippi River and threatened to split the Confederacy in two. For the soldiers of Louisiana, so far from home in Virginia, the city's capture was a bitter and mortifying personal blow. "Everybody seems very gloomy in the Louisiana Brigade since the disheartening intelligence from N. Orleans has been received, and curses 'not loud but deep' are freely bestowed upon Genl. Lavel [Mansfield Lovell] who commanded the city," the 6th Louisiana's Pvt. Ben Hubert wrote from the Shenandoah Valley to his sweetheart in Charlottesville, Virginia.

> Everything looks more & more gloomy each day that passes, for we are constantly hearing of defeats and reverses but seldom of a victory. I heard General Ewell remark this morning that he thought Va. would be evacuated by our army within less than two months & everyone is fearing that Richmond will be taken ere long by means of their gunboats. The 'night' is becoming darker & darker for our confederacy but yet no one ever thinks of giving up the Struggle, not if we are driven back in the interior by superior numbers & have to adopt a guerrilla mode of warfare.[5]

"We are grieved beyond measure at the loss of New Orleans," Colonel Seymour wrote to his 30-year-old son William, "but we are humiliated the most at the little or no resistance made by the city." The colonel was beside himself with worry about his son, whom he had left behind to manage his newspaper, largely because William had volunteered as an aide to Confederate Brig. Gen. Johnson K. Duncan, who commanded the defenses of New Orleans. William was present at Fort Jackson during

Farragut's furious bombardment of the forts, and Colonel Seymour wasn't sure his son had survived.

"I write you under the influence of the most painful emotions I ever experienced," the elder Seymour wrote. "We are homeless and wanderers on the face of the earth. . . .I have your condition and destiny about my whole mind, and all else is a minor consideration. Whether you are a prisoner, and was everyone sacrificed with the fort, or whether you escaped and have found refuge somewhere in the interior, I am unable to form even a conjecture." In fact, William Seymour was among the Confederate soldiers who surrendered to Federal forces on April 28, 1862; he was paroled and had returned to his newspaper.[6]

Colonel Seymour's anguish about home and family was shared by many of his men. Most of them had scant information about conditions in New Orleans or the fate of their loved ones and their property. The thought of hated Northerners taking over their homes and belongings was hard to bear. "I suppose the Yankees are in possession of all our effects and that my library and other fixings have been all confiscated or destroyed by the vandals," Colonel Seymour fumed in his May 2 letter to William.

The Federal occupation of New Orleans stirred up anger among the men of the 6th Louisiana. From the Shenandoah Valley, Lieutenant Ring wrote home to express his joy at receiving a letter from his wife Virginia, indicating that she and their children, who had fled to Montgomery, Alabama, were safe and well. "As long as you are thus blessed, my dear wife, I am happy," Ring wrote, "feeling at the same time to the depths of my heart how very uncomfortably you are situated, still as long as God gives you and the children good health and safety from the vile hordes of our enemies, we have every cause to be thankful."[7]

Feeling lonely, Private Ben Hubert appealed for more letters from his sweetheart Letitia Bailey, whom he had met when the regiment marched through Charlottesville in June 1861. "I have no one to love & no one to love me except my Letitia, for my old home and friends are now under the rule of the accursed Yankees, & I cannot even have the consolation of hearing from my dear relatives," pined the homesick private. "My mother and sisters were not living in N.O. at the time of its capture so I have at least the consolation of knowing that they are safe, & I verily believe I should have had to desert if I knew they had been in the city at the time it was taken!"[8]

General Butler, who quickly earned the nickname of "Beast," managed to rub salt in the wounds of the worried soldiers from Louisiana with his iron-fisted rule of New Orleans and his penchant for insult, including his infamous "woman order" of May 15. Any female who persisted in the then-frequent practice of insulting Federal soldiers, Butler decreed, "shall be regarded and held liable to be treated as a woman of the town plying her avocation." That was the worst sort of slur upon the women of New Orleans, who were much revered by their absent fighting men, and it fed the bitterness that was growing in the hearts of the 6th Louisiana troops as they completed the Valley campaign with Jackson. They knew that New Orleans was lost and occupied, and they were frustrated that they could do nothing about it. Soon, however, it would be time to face a challenge that they could do something about: rescuing Richmond, the Confederate capital, from the same impending fate.[9]

After the Battle of Port Republic, the exhausted men of the 6th Louisiana had a chance to rest for the first time in weeks. Following that first rainy night on the mountain top at Brown's Gap, the regiment "remained there two days and nights, when we returned to the vicinity of Port Republic where we were allowed the much required rest after our arduous campaign," Lieutenant Ring's diary relates. For nearly a week, the men relaxed, nursed sore feet and muscles, and recovered their strength as they camped along the tranquil river in a wide, tree-shaded valley. For once, there were no Unionists to harass them or disturb their peace at their camp near Weyer's Cave. As the regiment and the rest of the Louisiana Brigade recuperated, however, General Taylor sank into "a great weariness and depression," as he later described it. The brigade commander had heard nothing from his family since New Orleans had fallen, and was worried sick. He took a short leave and traveled by train for Richmond, where he found letters from his wife waiting, somewhat easing his anxiety. He soon heard hints of major battles to come around Richmond, and hurried back to his command.[10]

Taylor's exhaustion and depression would play a fateful role in shaping the final days of the 6th Louisiana's beloved old Colonel Seymour. On June 17, Seymour's men received orders to march out of the Shenandoah Valley to the east, where the colonel's last days as a soldier would play out in the series of battles around Richmond that came to be known as The Seven Days'.

General George B. McClellan's Peninsula Campaign, designed to take Richmond from the east, was moving toward its climax in June 1862. By early April, a Federal flotilla of 389 vessels had landed a Union army totaling 121,500 men, nearly 15,000 animals, 44 artillery batteries and

1,224 wagons at Fort Monroe, 75 miles southeast of Richmond. By late May, McClellan's army had slowly fought and marched its way west against Johnston's retreating Confederates to within sight of Richmond's church spires.[11] McClellan deployed his army astride the Chickahominy River, a sluggish stream that flowed within a few miles of Richmond and spread out in places into swamp land tangled with trees, vines, and undergrowth. Three of McClellan's five corps were north of the Chickahominy, and two corps were deployed to the south, on the Richmond side of the river. At the end of May, a botched offensive by Johnston against the two Federal corps south of the Chickahominy at Seven Pines and Fair Oaks cost the Confederates more than 6,000 casualties, including Johnston himself, who was severely wounded and disabled from command. On June 1, President Davis named his personal military adviser, General Robert E. Lee, to command the Confederate forces defending Richmond. The aggressive Lee, a 55-year-old West Point graduate and highly regarded soldier from the "old Army," renamed his forces the Army of Northern Virginia. Determined to strike rather than passively sit by and await the move of his enemy, Lee set about formulating plans for an offensive to cripple McClellan's army. Jackson's Valley Army, including the Louisiana Brigade, was tagged to play a significant part in the forthcoming struggle.[12]

Lee sent Jackson orders on June 16 to transfer his army to Richmond. The next day, the 6th Louisiana began the march with Taylor's Brigade across the Blue Ridge towards Gordonsville. Jackson took unusual pains to shroud his movement in secrecy. The men had no idea where they were going, but there was much speculation that the column would turn northeast and fall upon McDowell's corps at Fredericksburg, then perhaps continue to Washington. For part of the journey the weary troops were shuttled forward on cars of the Viginia Central Railroad, which would pick up the rear of Jackson's column and carry it to the front, then return again to the rear for more troops, a leapfrog shuttle that provided some relief to the marchers.[13]

By rail and foot Jackson's veterans moved eastward, reaching Ashland, some 12 miles north of Richmond, on the evening of June 25. There the men camped and were ordered to cook three day's rations, a sign they were going into action. All was not well in the Louisiana Brigade's camp, for General Taylor had taken seriously ill. All day on the 25th the brigade commander suffered from what he called "severe pains in the head and loins." The next morning he was unable to mount his horse. With growing paralysis in his limbs, Taylor was left behind in a vacant house in Ashland when the brigade resumed its march on June 26.[14]

The command of the brigade passed to its senior colonel, Isaac Seymour. Though his military experience stretched back as far as the Seminole Wars in Florida in the 1830s, the silver-haired commander of the 6th Louisiana had never held such high military responsibility before. At the age of 57, he was two years older than General Lee and one of the oldest officers in the Confederate army. The former newspaper editor's abiding passion for military life had led him toward this historic opportunity, and with the brigade about to go into a battle that might determine the fate of Richmond, the old soldier's moment of destiny had finally arrived.

Col. Isaac G. Seymour

A New Orleans newspaper editor took command of the 6th Louisiana Volunteers at the age of 56. Well-educated and sporting distinguished silvery side whiskers and flowing locks, Seymour led the regiment for one year. The beloved colonel was in temporary command of the Louisiana Brigade at Gaines' Mill, where he was killed in action. His loss was a bitter blow to his men. *Schoff Civil War Collection, William L. Clements Library, University of Michigan.*

Mounted on his big mare, which he once described as so "full of life and spirit" that it made him "the best mounted officer in the brigade," Seymour led the Louisianians eastward from Ashland and then southward about 12 miles to Pole Green Church, near Hundley's Corner. The march, with Ewell's Division in the van of Jackson's command, used up most of the day by the time Ewell's skirmishers encountered a Federal cavalry picket near the church. The Union horsemen were driven off after a brief skirmish and the column halted for the night. As the Louisianians settled into their bivouac around the church, the rumble of cannon fire in the distance told of a battle already underway. "The sound of artillery upon our right indicated that the ball had already opened," recalled one Louisiana soldier. Yet no order came to march to the sound of the guns, even though three hours of daylight remained.[15]

If it struck the 6th Louisiana's fighting Irish as curious that General Jackson would ignore a nearby battle and go into camp at such an early hour, they kept such doubts to themselves. But it was strange, and it was the first clear sign that their commanding general was not behaving like the aggressive victor of the Valley. In the previous month, Jackson had driven himself to the point of exhaustion in a campaign that allowed him little rest and no relief from constant stress. While his army moved toward Ashland, he had spent two sleepless nights (June 22/23 and 23/24) on horseback on all-night rides to and from a conference with General Lee. By the 26th, Jackson was suffering from what a later age would call stress fatigue—an advanced state of exhaustion that impairs judgment.[16]

When Jackson went into camp that evening at Hundley's Corner, he had already missed his first appointment for battle. In his meeting with Lee three days earlier, the Confederate commander had revealed his plan for attacking McClellan's army, which was astride the Chickahominy River just east of Richmond. While most of the Union army by then was south of the Chickahominy, its right wing was aligned north of it. This isolated wing, consisting of Brig. Gen. Fitz John Porter's V Corps, was Lee's target. If the Union right flank could be turned and driven, Lee believed, McClellan's railroad supply line on the peninsula would be threatened or cut, and his divisions south of the Chickahominy would be compelled either to retreat or come out of their entrenchments to give battle in the open. Lee assigned the crucial task of turning the Federal right to Jackson, who was to move beyond Porter's flank and rear. The divisions of Maj. Gens. James Longstreet, Ambrose Powell Hill and Daniel Harvey Hill were to cross the Chickahominy to assault Porter's front. This would give Lee some 50,000 men with which to overwhelm Porter's three divisions of about 25,000 men. Leaving the divisions of Maj. Gens. John Magruder and Benjamin Huger on the defensive line before Richmond, the Confederate commander gambled that one third of his total force could hold McClellan's army in position south of the river while he employed two thirds of his strength to destroy Porter's corps.[17]

Porter's men were dug into a strong position behind Beaver Dam Creek, near the village of Mechanicsville. Lee's plan called for Jackson to begin his march at 3:00 a.m. on Thursday, June 26, and to get into position to assault Porter's right flank and rear or cause him to fall back. A.

P. Hill would wait until he could confirm Jackson's approach, then cross the bridge to Mechanicsville to begin an assault on the Federal lines at Beaver Dam Creek, followed by Longstreet and D. H. Hill. Jackson's uncharacteristic slowness that day frustrated Lee's plan. His sluggish march began late and proceeded slowly, and when he failed to show up by 3:00 p.m., the impetuous A. P. Hill decided to open the attack on his own. The confused and uncoordinated Confederate assault went forward without Jackson's brigades. It was Hill's attack that the Louisiana men heard as they went into camp at Hundley's Corner that afternoon. They were less than three miles from the battle and desperately needed, but Jackson retired for the night and failed to send any communication of his whereabouts.[18]

The Battle of Mechanicsville, or Beaver Dam Creek, was a tactical disaster for the Confederates. Hill's poorly coordinated attacks against Porter's strong position were easily hurled back, and he suffered nearly 1,500 casualties against just 361 for the Federals. Jackson's flanking maneuver, the key to Lee's battle plan, had failed. Lee was not even sure where Jackson was that afternoon.[19]

Despite his victory, Porter abandoned his position along Beaver Dam Creek early the following morning. General McClellan, wrote one observer, discovering that "Jackson was really approaching in large force," decided that the Porter's V Corps' position could not be held in view of Jackson's threat to its right flank. The North's "Young Napoleon" had already decided upon a "change of base" which would shift the entire Union army south to a position on the James River, where it would enjoy the protection of Federal gunboats. McClellan ordered Porter's corps to withdraw to a position to protect the bridges over the Chickahominy needed for the army's retreat toward the James. Porter's divisions began pulling out of their entrenchments during the early morning of Friday, June 27, and were still on the move as daylight arrived.[20]

The men of the 6th Louisiana awoke that morning unaware that they had completely missed the first of what would be known as the Seven Days' Battles. They were ordered to take the front of Ewell's column as skirmishers. Moving out from the camp near Hundley's Corner, the regiment, now under command of Lieutenant Colonel Henry Strong, engaged in light skirmishing with Porter's rear guard as it pulled back. Years afterward, one of the regiment's New Orleans Irishmen remembered the two days leading up to the Battle of Gaines' Mill. "The first day at Richmond we did little more than follow the enemy," wrote Lt.

Blayney T. Walshe, referring to the June 26 march. "The forenoon of the second day we were engaged in light skirmishing, often going in at one end of their camp as they [Porter's rear guard] left at the other." Walshe, a 23-year-old native of County Wexford, Ireland, would see plenty of action later in the day as he led Company I in the desperate fight of that afternoon.[21]

After a two mile march south, Jackson's column reached a crossroads marked by the Walnut Grove Church. There, General Lee at last found his wayward subordinate, and the two conferred privately in the church yard. Despite the mix-ups and reverses of the previous day, Lee was determined to renew the attack on Porter's corps. By 11:00 a.m. Jackson had his orders, but for a second consecutive day he would be late in arriving to the battlefield. Jackson's lack of familiarity with the confusing tangle of roads through the wooded and swampy terrain, and a misunderstanding with his guide, led to a time-consuming detour after Jackson discovered he was on the wrong road. The six-mile roundabout march cost about three hours' delay.[22]

The march that Friday was slow and cautious, according to a 9th Louisiana soldier. "During almost the whole day [we] marched through and by deserted camps strewn with the debris of our departed foes," Pvt. Henry Handerson wrote. "Thousands upon thousands of letters were scattered over the ground, and for hours as we marched slowly and cautiously forward we amused ourselves with reading these records of private life and relations." One who was not in such a carefree mood was Major Wheat of the Tiger battalion. Handerson saw Wheat and the 9th Louisiana's Col. Leroy Stafford riding together at the head of the regiment. Wheat seemed "subdued and almost sad," and Handerson was surprised to hear this hard-bitten soldier of fortune speaking of his past life, of his mother and old-time friends. Wheat, who had earlier that day suffered a premonition of his own death, tearfully told Col. Leroy Stafford and others he was sure to die that day, and asked them to bury him on the battlefield where he fell.[23]

That battlefield was now within earshot. By 2:00 p.m. the Louisianians could hear the rattle of musketry as they approached New Cold Harbor. Although no enemy could be seen, the sounds of a battle well in progress emerged from a dense woods ahead. Lieutenant Walshe remembered the sense of urgency that arose then, as the Louisianians picked up the pace and "marched rapidly" forward.[24]

What the Louisianians could not see through those tangled woods was one of the most formidable defensive positions that they would face in the war. Porter had selected his ground well and deployed his troops effectively. His crescent-shaped defensive line ran for a mile and three-quarters parallel to a boggy creek called Boatswain's Swamp. The sluggish stream ran through a deep wooded ravine which separated the Confederates from their enemy. The ravine rose steeply to a high plateau, on which the Federal corps commander posted his formidable batteries, totaling 96 guns, to cover every approach. On the steep forested slopes above the stream, two of Porter's three divisions dug in behind makeshift breastworks of logs and knapsacks, positioned in three separate lines down the slope, so that the artillery above could fire over their heads to the approaching Confederates. Brig. Gen. George W. Morell's division of three brigades was on the Federal left, linking to Brig. Gen. George Sykes division composed entirely of U.S. regulars, also in three brigades, on the right. On the crest of the hill, Brig. Gen. George A. McCall's division, the Pennsylvania Reserves, stood ready to feed fresh regiments into the line wherever needed.[25]

The Confederates facing this formidable position could approach through woods on their left, but on the center and right the ground was generally open pasture or cultivated fields, where the attackers would be exposed not only to Porter's batteries but to McClellan's long-range guns across the Chickahominy, immediately in Porter's rear. The Southerners would have to cross these open fields under fire, descend the steep ravine through woods tangled with vines and underbrush, then wade through a knee-deep stream made more difficult by felled trees, only to begin a long, steep climb against three lines of entrenched riflemen to the open crest of a ridge bristling with cannon and reserve infantry.[26]

By the time Ewell's Division marched into sight at the head of Jackson's column on the road to Old Cold Harbor, A. P. Hill's brigades were being severely punished by Porter's artillery and dug-in infantry, which could barely be seen through the woods and smoke. Hill had marched on the road from Mechanicsville, first encountering resistance about noon from a Union regiment posted to dispute his crossing of Powhite Creek at Gaines' Mill, half a mile from New Cold Harbor. He delayed attacking Porter's main force until Longstreet arrived about 2:30 p.m., and then unleashed his brigades, one after another, against the nearly impregnable Federal position. "These brave men had done all that any soldiers could do," he reported, in their "desperate but unavail-

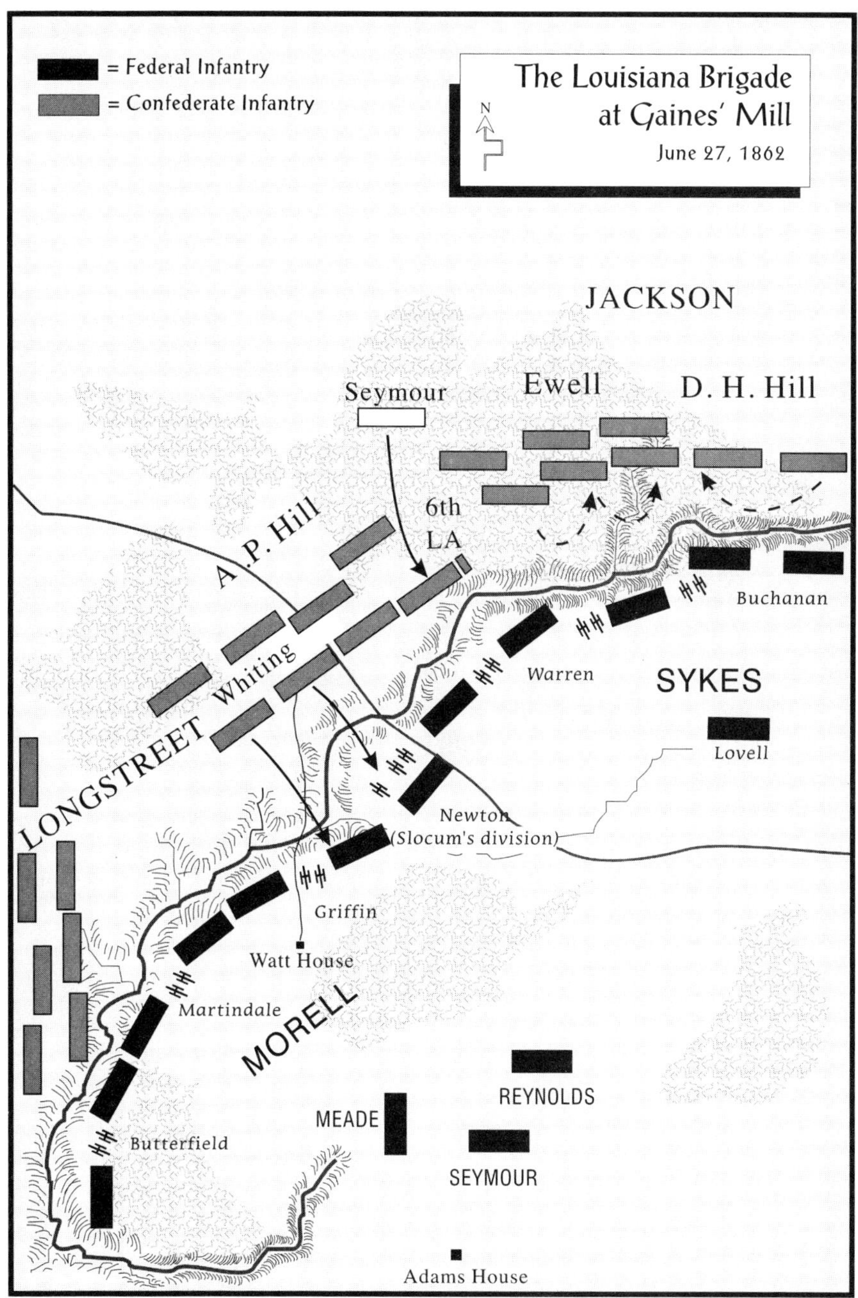

Theodore P. Savas

ing attempts" to break Porter's line. After two hours without support, his bloodied regiments were barely hanging on in the face of accurate and stubborn fire by the confident Northerners.[27]

Even while Hill's regiments were suffering terribly, Lee initially held back Longstreet, waiting for the arrival of Jackson which "was momentarily expected." But "momentarily" stretched on and on, with no sign of Jackson. Finally at about 4:00 p.m., Lee ordered Longstreet to mount a diversionary "feint" on the Federal left, which Longstreet soon converted into a full-scale assault. The battle was in full roar by the time Ewell approached with his division, including the Louisiana Brigade. Ewell was nearing the field when Col. Walter Taylor of Lee's staff, desperately searching for reinforcements, galloped up and ordered him to "hurry up my division as rapidly as possible."[28]

According to the 6th Louisiana's Lieutenant Walshe, "The necessity for prompt action was so great that we were hurriedly formed in line of battle in an open common, and were rapidly marched under a terrific fire from the artillery as well as the infantry." The Louisiana Brigade, with Colonel Seymour in command, was formed up in the open fields to the right of a road leading from New Cold Harbor down through the wooded ravine to the McGehee house on top of the ridge, which was occupied by the Federals. Behind Seymour's men, Isaac Trimble's Brigade formed a second line, ready to support the Louisianans.[29]

Seated on his large and spirited mare, Colonel Seymour ordered the brigade forward as shells exploded in the open field around them. The four regiments and Wheat's battalion descended the slope toward Boatswain's Swamp as men began to pitch over dead and wounded from the fire of unseen skirmishers posted behind trees across the stream. "When we were near enough," Lieutenant Walshe wrote, "a charge was ordered, and we soon reached a creek, the crossing of which was difficult, as the enemy had felled timber to impede our progress." As they waded across the knee-deep water, the 9th Louisiana's Private Handerson still could not see the enemy "though the occasional whiz of a bullet assured us that the foe was not far distant." Once the Louisianians climbed out of the creek and began ascending the hill, however, "a perfect hailstorm of bullets greeted our advance," according to Handerson, who wrote to his family after the battle that "the intensity of the fire far exceeded all that we had experienced in the Valley."[30]

The Louisianians were advancing toward the center of the Union position, where the right wing of Morell's division poured deadly volleys of lead from the three lines of riflemen on the slope. It was, in the words of General Trimble, "a perfect sheet of fire." Louisiana casualties multiplied rapidly as they struggled to advance against this deadly hailstorm from above. "Four of my companions fell dead, and four severely wounded, within ten steps of me in the short space of fifteen minutes, while I escaped with a bullet hole in my hat," Private Handerson wrote.[31]

Lieutenant Walshe also suffered the same deadly experience once he and his comrades crawled up out of the marshy creek. "In the swamp we were, in a measure, protected, and we received the order to commence firing," wrote Walshe. "This we did, advancing through the water, up the slope on the opposite side, where the Federal troops were stationed on a commanding hill. Many of our brigade, officers and men, fell killed or wounded at this point. . . ." The casualties included Walshe himself, who took a shot in the leg as the charge of the brigade bogged down. "Many of us were wounded, and all within a space of thirty yards, and that was as far as the brigade went."[32]

As the assault bogged down in the swampy thickets, Colonel Seymour, while desperately trying to rally his men, was shot from his horse. One minie ball entered his head, while another pierced his body. He died within minutes, in the first battle in which he led the brigade. About the same time, Major Wheat of the Tiger battalion also was killed, eerily fulfilling his premonition. Private Handerson of the 9th Louisiana witnessed Wheat's lonely death: "Just then, a little to my left and perhaps ten paces in advance of our line, I noticed Major Wheat picking his way slowly and carefully through the dense underbrush, quiet and determined, apparently, but uttering no word and followed by none of his own, or, indeed, any other command. A moment more and he fell motionless, seemingly without a groan or struggle, and I knew that his restless career was ended."[33]

The situation for the Louisiana survivors was growing more desperate by the minute. They were pinned down under a deadly crossfire from an enemy they could hardly see. Movement in either direction was virtually impossible. The confused Confederates looked around for leadership and found none. Taylor was absent, Seymour and Wheat were dead. Stafford, who was to inherit command, had not yet taken charge, for he was ignorant of Seymour's death, according to Handerson. "Now was the critical moment when a voice of authority to guide our uncertain steps and a bold officer to lead us forward would have been worth to us a victory," the 9th Louisiana soldier wrote later. "But none such appeared."

Lieutenant Walshe, bleeding from his wounded leg, helped others of the 6th Louisiana drag the body of their beloved old colonel back down the slope toward the protection of the creek banks. Many other Louisianians, now leaderless, confused and dispirited, began stumbling and crawling back down the hill toward Boatswain's Swamp. Despair swept the ranks of Wheat's Tigers. One of them, scrambling back down the slope, told an officer who tried to stop him: "They have killed the old Major, and I am going home. I wouldn't fight for Jesus Christ now!"[34]

The attack of the Louisiana Brigade, so irresistible in the battles in the Valley, had sunk miserably into the boggy lowlands of Boatswain's Swamp. There, tenderly protecting the limp body of the brave old man who had led them from New Orleans to this bloody ravine, Lieutenant Walshe and his comrades became mere spectators to the climax of the five-hour battle. Walshe described the closing scenes in his vivid account:

> We had moved down the hill, and were crossing the water, when a fresh brigade advanced, and we lay down alongside the body of Col. Seymour, in the running water, behind some of the fallen timber. We lay there while this brigade advanced, firing. I was told it was Hood's brigade, and the fire given by them and returned by the enemy was terrific, making the water in which we lay spurt up like it does in a very heavy rain. We lay there between the fires of friend and foe for fully half an hour, when the Confederate yell was heard, and we knew that the position had been carried.[35]

The charge of Brig. Gen. John B. Hood's Brigade in the center of the Union line, along with assaults by other brigades on the right and left, finally pierced the Federal defenses at dusk. Hood personally led his 4th Texas regiment in the charge, which swept down the ravine and across the creek close to the position where the Louisiana Brigade had been pinned down for two hours. Private Handerson of the 9th Louisiana wrote that he witnessed Hood's charge shortly after "the [Louisiana Brigade's] whole line retreated slowly down the hill" to the bottom of the ravine. According to Handerson, "At this moment with a shout and a rush appeared the brigade of Hood's gallant Texans sweeping by and over us and disappearing like a vision in the underbrush and smoke. One deafening yell, one rattling volley and the victory was won."[36]

Private Handerson's romantic notion notwithstanding, other Confederate units had taken a hand in earning the bloody victory. Though Hood's Texans were widely credited with the first breakthrough, nearly simultaneous attacks by D. H. Hill on the Confederate left and Longstreet on the right contributed to a sudden and widespread collapse of the Federal position. The repeated, hammering assaults of the Confederates all afternoon—from A. P. Hill's opening attacks through the Louisiana Brigade's fruitless attempt and down to the final charge by Hood and others—had steadily weakened the Federal defenses and used up Porter's reserves until the exhausted defenders gave way. Though Porter kept feeding in fresh regiments all afternoon, using McCall's Pennsylvanians plus a division from the Federal VI Corps that was rushed over the Chickamoniny as reinforcement, the pressure was overwhelming. "For each regiment thrown into action there seemed to be two or three fresh regiments brought up by the enemy," he lamented in his report. The final Confederate assault came "just as darkness was covering everything from view [when] the enemy massed his fresh regiments on the right and left and threw them in with overpowering force against our thinned and wearied battalions."[37]

Porter's defensive front simply unraveled as his beaten men pulled back up the hill. They were able briefly to rally around the canister-belching cannon rushed forward to stave off the Confederate onslaught. The pressure of the Southern advance and confusion caused by a sudden charge of Federal cavalry, which panicked some of the Union troops, caused another panic and a general retreat to the bridges over the Chickahominy was underway. Darkness and Confederate exhaustion ruled out any significant pursuit.[38]

The costly Battle of Gaines' Mill was a major victory for General Lee. It precipitated the strategic retreat of McClellan's army as the Union commander abandoned his hope of taking Richmond. Despite the Confederate victory, the day did not end happily for the men of the 6th Louisiana, whose leader was dead and whose ranks were again thinned. The regiment lost eight killed and 39 wounded. The 6th's 47 casualties exceeded those of any other regiment in the brigade, which ranged from 19 lost in the 9th Louisiana to 44 in the 8th. The Louisiana Brigade as a whole lost 32 dead and 142 wounded in a battle that severely depleted the ranks of the Army of Northern Virginia. The Confederate dead and wounded, nearly 7,900, totaled almost twice those of Porter's command, though the nearly 3,000 Union soldiers captured made the overall casualty figures only narrowly in the Federals' favor.[39]

Beyond the sorrow over lost comrades, the Louisianians came out of the June 27 battle without the personal pride and satisfaction they had come to savor in their heady victories in the Valley, where the brigade won honors and glory. Their attack had failed, and they knew it. There was no dishonor in this, for the effort had been gallantly attempted. Indeed, brigade after brigade had suffered the same fate in that death trap at the bottom of the ravine. But there was no glory in it, either.

How had the 6th Louisiana and the other units under Colonel Seymour fought that day? The assessments of their superiors and various historians present a mixed picture. General Ewell, in his report, painted a picture of bravery which ended tragically. "These troops were attacked in front and flank by superior numbers and were for hours without reinforcements," he wrote, referring to both Seymour's and Trimble's brigades. "The Louisiana Brigade," he added, "having sustained a very severe loss in field officers, besides suffering in rank and file, was driven off the field, but the line was held by part of Trimble's Brigade. . . ." General Jackson's report, written six months after Ewell's and obviously derived from the latter's account, generally uses the same language but softens the verdict by reporting that the Louisiana Brigade "was drawn from the field," suggesting an orderly withdrawal.[40]

A postwar memoir by Capt. James C. Nisbet of the 21st Georgia Infantry, Trimble's Brigade, supports the notion that the Louisianians were not "driven" from the field but withdrew in orderly fashion after being pinned down and severely cut up. The Louisiana Brigade "after a gallant charge failed to carry the position and were compelled to retire," Nisbet wrote. When Trimble's Brigade was ordered into the fight, he continued, "We met the Louisiana Brigade coming out in good order. One said, 'Boys, you are mighty good, but that's hell in there.'"[41]

Virginia historian Clifford Dowdey, who wrote a book on the Seven Days' Battles, contended that the Louisiana Brigade "broke to the rear in a rush," a judgment which seems unsupported by most evidence. "This break," Dowdey concluded, was "the only blight on the history of the brigade." A more recent study of these battles by Stephen Sears blames Colonel Seymour for the Louisiana Brigade's failure at Gaines' Mill. "The Louisianians were under the command that day of their senior colonel, Isaac Seymour, in place of the ill Richard Taylor," wrote Sears, "and under Seymour's inexperienced hand they soon became confused in the woods and boggy thickets of Boatswain's Swamp."[42]

It was not Seymour's inexperience but rather the deadly nature of the terrain and the tactical advantages held by the dug-in Union defenders that blunted the Louisianians attack at Gaines' Mill. There is no good reason to believe the outcome would have been any different if General Taylor had been at the head of the charge. Taylor himself seemed to believe that if he had been there, he would have been killed rather than Seymour. The absent brigade commander, who had dragged himself from his sickbed when he heard the sound of battle and rode to the field in an ambulance, was despondent when he learned that Seymour had sacrificed himself doing Taylor's job. "I had a wretched feeling of guilt, especially about Seymour, who led the brigade and died in my place," wrote Taylor in his memoirs. "Brave old Seymour! I can see him now, mounting the hill at Winchester, on foot, with sword and cap in hand, his thin gray locks streaming, turning to his sturdy Irishmen with 'Steady, men! dress to the right!' Georgia has been fertile of worthies, but will produce none more deserving than Col. Seymour." Seymour, he added, was "a man of culture, respected by all."[43]

At home in New Orleans, Seymour's newspaper initially published a denial that he had been killed. It was more than a month later when the *Commercial Bulletin* acknowledged the truth: "We are deeply pained to learn from indisputable authority, that the report of the death of Col. Seymour is correct." The lengthy obituary went on, in florid nineteenth century style, to eulogize the former editor as the epitome of Southern manhood. The Yale-educated ex-editor had "few or no enemies," and struck all who knew him as a "genial Southern gentleman," considerate of others and graceful in his manners and expression. Unlike those whose youthful ardor and ambition drove them to seek glory in the military, the newspaper added, Seymour was merely a patriot in the twilight of his life, whose "motive that carried him to the field was simply duty. . . .It was duty that placed him in the front of danger at the battle of the Chickahominy; and, in fine, it was on the altar of duty that he offered up his life."[44] This praise of his own father by William Seymour brought about his arrest and imprisonment for two and one-half months by General Butler. The obituary defied the Union commander's censorship order banning such pro-Confederate commentary.[45]

After the Battle of Gaines' Mill, the men of the 6th Louisiana mourned their losses and reorganized themselves. The severely wounded Lieutenant Walshe recalled being taken to a field hospital, where several operating tables were busy with the grisly work of non-stop amputations. "A hasty examination was made of myself and Sergt. O'Reilly of the Sixth, and it was decided that my foot must come off, and that O'Reilly was mortally wounded," wrote Walshe. "So I was given immediate attention, while an opiate was administered to my comrade." But the feisty New Orleans Irishman was not about to part with his foot or his friend so easily. "I protested against the amputation of my foot and insisted upon being sent to a Louisiana hospital. My request was granted, and a few days later O'Reilly and I were sent to the Louisiana hospital at Richmond; his life and my foot were saved."[46]

At the Louisiana Hospital, one of several organized and supported by individual Confederate states, Walshe and his companion probably were cared for by the most famous woman associated with the 6th Louisiana, Mary S. Hill. The Irish-born nurse from New Orleans volunteered for medical duty in Virginia after her brother, Samuel Hill, joined the regiment at the start of the war. In order to be near her brother, she sometimes accompanied the regiment in the field. At the time of the Seven Days' Battles she was in charge of the Louisiana Hospital in Richmond. She was "looked upon with reverence" by the soldiers and earned the name "Florence Nightingale of the Army of Northern Virginia."[47]

Colonel Seymour's death opened avenues of promotion for his subordinates. Lt. Col. Henry B. Strong was promoted to colonel and assumed command of the regiment. Maj. Nathaniel G. Offutt rose to lieutenant colonel, a move which was not applauded by many in the regiment. There was talk in the ranks that the major had been less than brave in recent battles, hanging back out of danger when the brigade attacked at Port Republic and again at Gaines' Mill. These grumblings would boil into a crisis in the weeks after the Seven Days' Battles, but for now the men watched in dismay as Offutt advanced up the chain of command. A more popular officer promoted at this time was William Monaghan, in command of Company F, one of the two "Irish Brigade" companies. He was bumped up to major in absentia, for he remained a prisoner and would not return to the regiment for another several weeks following his exchange at Aiken's Landing near Richmond on August 5.[48]

For the first time in the war the Irishmen of the regiment had one of their own as their colonel. Henry B. Strong was a 40-year-old Irish-born clerk from New Orleans when he enlisted only a year earlier. Now he had his chance to show what an Irishman could do in leading the regiment. Offutt, a 31-year-old planter's son from St. Landry parish, was not Irish, but Monaghan was, which gave the field officers of the 6th Louisiana a strong Celtic cast. There was no time for the Irish to celebrate, though, for the battles against McClellan were far from over.

After Gaines' Mill, General McClellan began in earnest his withdrawal southward toward the James River, having mistakenly convinced himself that he was outnumbered by the Confederates and having lost hope of taking Richmond. It was a movement of enormous difficulty and presented the Confederates with several opportunities to strike crippling blows against the Federal army while it was in motion. Unfortunately, these possibilities were bungled by Lee and several of his subordinates, including Jackson, who continued to dawdle and display a strange lack of initiative. In General Taylor's words, "from Cold Harbor [Gaines' Mill] to Malvern Hill, inclusive, there was nothing but a series of blunders, one after another, and all huge."[49]

By the morning of June 28 it was clear that Porter's defeated corps had escaped over the Chickahominy to rejoin the rest of McClellan's army. Lee and his generals were left to ponder McClellan's next move. He might yet fight to maintain his supply line via the York River Railroad, which now was threatened by Lee's forces north of the river, or he could abandon that line of supply and withdraw southward to a new base on the James River. Because Lee did not know that McClellan had already chosen the latter course, the Confederate commander ordered his cavalry and Ewell's Division to advance along the north bank of the Chickahominy to the railroad line at Dispatch Station. There, Ewell's men, including the Louisiana regiments, spent the day tearing up the railroad tracks after discovering that the Federals had burned the station and its stores as well as the railroad bridge over the Chickahominy—clear signs that McClellan was abandoning his old supply line and his base at White House Landing on the Pamunkey River.[50]

The 6th Louisiana and the rest of Taylor's Brigade did not take part in the battles which developed over the next two days as the Confederates pursued the Union army in its retreat toward the James River. Their unexpected respite was largely the result of General Jackson's lethargic actions, which kept his troops from playing the important role Lee had planned for them. On Sunday, June 29, the men of the 6th Louisianians heard the sounds of battle from across the Chickahominy. The Louisiana Brigade, which General Taylor had rejoined to assume command, was just across the river from Savage's Station, a stop on the York River railroad. That afternoon, "a great noise of battle came—artillery, small arms, shouts," according to Taylor. The engagement was the Battle of Savage's Station, in which John B. Magruder's Division suffered severe losses attacking the rear corps of

McClellan's retreating army—without the support Lee had expected from Jackson's command. Lee had ordered Jackson to cross the river at Grapevine bridge, from which position he could have fallen on the Federal flank. Jackson, however, instead spent the day rebuilding the damaged bridge and did not cross to aid the embattled Magruder, who decided to unleash his attack alone.[51]

The Louisiana Brigade crossed the Chickahominy late that Sunday and bivouacked on bottom ground along the river that turned into a swamp in that night's heavy rain. On Monday the 30th, the Louisianians again were distant listeners as the Confederate divisions of Longstreet and A. P. Hill fought the bloody battle of Frayser's Farm, near Glendale. Lee had expected Jackson to bring his divisions into the battle, but again Jackson failed to play his part. Instead, he spent the day bombarding Federal troops who held the bridge crossing White Oak Swamp. The conqueror of the Valley deployed artillery but never asked his infantry to force a crossing, which the Federal commander opposing him later admitted could have been done at a lightly-defended ford a mile away. The 6th Louisiana and the rest of Taylor's brigade idled away the day as Longstreet's and Hill's men fought a bloody battle scarcely a rifle-shot away. Jackson reported that the sounds of battle made him "eager to press forward," but he claimed that the marshy ground, the destruction of the bridge, and the strength of the Federals defending the crossing, prevented his doing so. Lee lamented this lack of cooperation in his report, contending that the battle at Glendale "would have proved most disastrous to the enemy" had Jackson and others carried out their orders.[52]

Glendale (Fraser's Farm) offered the last good opportunity for Lee to catch McClellan's Army of the Potomac in motion. By Tuesday July 1, the Federal commander had his army deployed on Malvern Hill about one mile north of the James River. This new position was 150 feet high and flanked by deep ravines, which meant it would have to be attacked frontally and uphill across open fields. The narrowness of the front between the ravines—only 875 yards at one point—created a bottleneck that funneled the attacking forces into a virtual tunnel under the mouths of Federal cannon. McClellan massed his artillery on Malvern Hill, dozens of guns arranged in a crescent to sweep the plain below. To the north, northwest, and northeast—the directions from which the Confederates would approach—its fields of shocked wheat declined gradually to the edge of a woods through which ran a marshy stream, Western Run.[53]

"Malvern Hill was a desperate position to attack in front," General Taylor wrote after the war. His was an opinion widely shared among the Confederates that July 1. Lee himself called Malvern Hill a "position of great natural strength," and described it in his report with words which convey the perilous nature of the attack he planned. The open ground below the cannon-studded crest, Lee wrote, "was completely swept by the fire of his [the enemy's] infantry and artillery. To reach this open ground, our troops had to advance through a broken and thickly wooded country, traversed nearly throughout its whole extent by a swamp passable at but few places and difficult at those. The whole was within range of the batteries on the heights and the gunboats in the river, under whose incessant fire our movements had to be executed."[54]

To some Confederate commanders the attack appeared suicidal. The usually aggressive Jackson opposed attacking, preferring instead a flanking maneuver to turn the Federal right. General D. H. Hill, who had been given a description of Malvern Hill's superb military value by a local citizen, urged Lee to forego the attack. Longstreet, however, persuaded Lee that by posting artillery to create a crossfire on the Union batteries, the hill could be stormed successfully. Lee, frustrated by the failures of the previous days and desperate to seize one last chance to cripple McClellan's army, agreed.[55]

The 6th Louisiana approached the Malvern Hill battlefield from the north, along the Willis Church Road. The route carried the regiment past Glendale, where the stifling hot morning air was already rank with the stench of dead bodies from the previous day's carnage. The Louisianians trudged along the dusty road in Jackson's long column, whose van neared the vicinity of Malvern Hill around noon. All morning the men had heard guns ahead, and by the time the Louisiana Brigade reached Willis Church, a mile north of Malvern Hill, the shelling had grown heavy. The clouds of dust raised by the march attracted the fire of the Union artillery, which sent shells screaming toward the Confederate column. To avoid the peril, the column swerved off the road to the left into a pine forest on the Poindexter farm, where the Louisiana Brigade lay down in line. General Taylor, again feeling ill, turned the command over to Colonel Stafford. The 6th Louisiana, still mourning Seymour's loss, was under the untried command of Lieutenant Colonel Strong.[56]

From their prone position in the pine woods, the Louisianians could not see the Federals above them on Malvern Hill. The narrow front of the strong Union position allowed room for only two divisions along the line facing toward the approaching Confederates. There, General Porter, in command at Malvern Hill as he had been at Gaines' Mill, deployed Morell's division and the division of Brig. Gen. Darius Couch of the Union IV Corps. Morell's three brigades were on the Federal left, while Couch's three brigades formed the right—some 17,800 infantrymen posted in a gentle arc, with sharpshooters posted in advance of the line. Eight batteries of field artillery totaling 37 guns were unlimbered to sweep the open approaches. Their formidable firepower would prove more deadly than the infantry's.[57]

Colonel Strong and his men spent much of that hot afternoon under the fire of Porter's cannon while Lee slowly deployed for the assault. It was a long and restless wait, according to Ewell's aide, Capt. G. Campbell Brown: "As they lay for hours in reserve they were exposed to a cannonade the violence of which rendered rest impossible, and every now & then one of their number was stricken down." The Confederate deployment went slowly due to the thick woods, swampy ground and the difficulty of communication between commanders. It was not until 4:00 p.m that the line of battle was formed. Jackson, on the Confederate left, formed his line with the division of General William H. C. Whiting on the left and D. H. Hill's Division on the right. Most of Ewell's Division was held in reserve, but when Whiting maneuvered his division forward, he found a gap between his right and Hill's left. He called for a brigade to fill it, and Stafford's Louisianians were sent forward to complete the Confederate front. Stafford described the brigade's position as "a ravine near the enemy's batteries," where the Louisianians anxiously awaited the order to attack while the cannons above roared.[58]

The Confederate attack which finally moved out against the heights was a disjointed and sloppy affair marred by confusing orders, miscommunication, and a general lack of coordination. Individual brigades made gallant charges, in piecemeal fashion, against the nearly impregnable Federal position and were thrown back with great loss. "It wasn't war, it was murder," exclaimed North Carolinian D. H. Hill, who entered the battle with 6,500 men and left 2,000 behind.[59]

During these futile assaults by Hill's brigades and others to their right, the Louisianians hugged the ground as the sun set and dusk crept across the smoky battlefield. The brigade had been detached from Ewell's

Division and put under the command of Whiting. The confused situation was ripe for a mix-up, for the brigade was under an untested commander in Colonel Stafford, who was unsure of its role in a battle few generals grasped. Amid the chaos the Louisiana troops were fed into the maelstrom by mistake. In the gathering twilight, they undertook an attack that was never meant to happen.

Late in the day, "a heavy fire opened just in front of us, where Stafford was posted," wrote Captain Brown, who saw the events unfold from Ewell's position behind the Confederate line. "We at first supposed the enemy attacking, but soon found Stafford had advanced on them—a movement which we could not explain, as Whiting's line, with which he was to co-operate, was stationary." The Louisiana regiments were charging a Federal battery on their own and without support. Why? "At dusk an order was brought. . .to charge forward on the battery," explained Stafford in his report. "This order was given by an officer unknown to myself or any of the officers of my command." Captain Brown said later that the mysterious officer probably was one of General Whiting's aides. "A staff officer apparently of Gen'l Whiting's had in an excited manner ridden up to one or two of the left reg'ts. [of Stafford's Brigade] & inquired why they didn't charge with the troops on the left—& had ordered them to charge. Expecting such an order, they had obeyed it & the command passed from reg't. to reg't. along the whole brigade."[60]

The unintended command to charge swept down the line, from regiment to regiment, from right to left. Not everyone in the brigade heard it, however. Only three of Stafford's regiments—the 6th, 7th and 8th Louisiana—responded to the directive and charged toward the Federal battery above the ravine. The 9th Louisiana, anchoring the far left of the brigade's line, did not move. "It now being night, this order was not heard or properly understood by the Ninth Louisiana, and no advance was made by that command," Stafford wrote. Private Handerson of the 9th Louisiana was asleep when the order to charge was given. He didn't realize a charge had been made until he awoke in the dark and discovered only a few of his comrades remained about him. "The left of the line failed to receive the order, nor in the darkness of the swampy glade did they notice for some time the advance on the right," he wrote. "We, who occupied the extreme left of the line and were probably sleeping, heard nothing of the movement and were left in our places."[61]

The accidental charge in which the 6th Louisiana participated was as costly as it was pointless. Dashing into the gathering darkness toward the muzzle flashes of the Federal cannon, the Louisianians charged up the hill as deadly fire from above tore gaps in their ranks. "The result of their isolated attack was a sharp, short fight and a speedy repulse," Captain Brown declared. The assault was over "in a half hour or less," he thought, but "not until they had silenced & very nearly captured a battery that stood in advance of the enemy's main line." The attack was courageous but futile, coming at the end of a battle which was lost before it began.

The price of the wasted effort was high, especially for the 6th Louisiana. Official returns show that the regiment lost nine killed—the most fatalities of any of the three regiments involved. Another 27 Louisianians were wounded. The regiment's immigrant character clearly shows through in the list of Malvern Hill fatalities, for six of the killed or mortally wounded were Irish-born, one was German, one English, and one Swedish. "The charge resulted in the loss of some valuable lives," Stafford reported, in a tone suggesting that he didn't think it was worth the loss. The brigade as a whole suffered 111 casualties. In Brown's view, "the whole affair was over so soon & the uselessness of the attack so evident at once, that fewer lives were lost than might have been expected." Brown believed much of the plunging Federal fire went over the heads of the onrushing Louisiana regiments.[62]

The 6th Louisiana's charge at Malvern Hill also generated new controversy in the regiment concerning the behavior of Lieutenant Colonel Offutt. The common talk in the ranks had it that the lieutenant colonel had lurked behind a large tree, feigning a wound, and had been carried off by the ambulance corps. This was the third report of Offutt's cowardice in the face of the enemy, and resentment began to boil among the men and some of the company captains. When Offutt returned to the regiment the day after the battle with no evidence of having suffered any wound, the disgusted officers began to consider what steps they might take to remove the lieutenant colonel from command. When they had a chance to act, they would make their move against him.[63]

The Battle of Malvern Hill stands out as an example of the futility of infantry charging uphill against massed artillery supported by infantry. Years after the war, survivors of the slaughter spoke with awe of the carnage caused by the Federal artillery. D. H. Hill asserted that more than half the Confederate casualties in the battle were caused by field artillery, which he believed was "unprecedented" in warfare. Lee's Army of Northern Virginia lost 869 dead, 4,241 wounded and 540 missing. The

Confederates' 5,650 casualties were almost twice the Federal losses of 3,007.[64]

Despite his stunning and easily won defensive victory, McClellan pulled his forces back from Malvern Hill during the night to the safety of Harrison's Landing on the James River, where his gunboats offered protection from another attack. The retrograde movement, which effectively ended the Seven Days' Battles, surprised and chagrined many of his officers and men. McClellan had failed in his grand objective of taking Richmond, but had saved his army to fight another day. Lee had succeeded in defending Richmond but was frustrated by his failure to inflict a decisive blow on the enemy. "Under ordinary circumstances the Federal Army should have been destroyed," the disappointed Confederate commanding general reported.[65]

As dreams of destroying the Federals in a decisive victory dissolved, the men of the 6th Louisiana may have realized that the war would drag on much longer than any of them had ever imagined.

Chapter Five

Back to Northern Virginia: SECOND MANASSAS & CHANTILLY

"I saw the whole army. . . .become an ungovernable mob."
— *Father James B. Sheeran, Louisiana chaplain*

After the Battle of Malvern Hill, the 6th Louisiana moved with Ewell's Division on July 3 to follow McClellan's army to its new James River stronghold at Harrison's Landing, near a plantation called Westover. Ewell's wet and weary foot soldiers, drenched by a thunderstorm the previous day, slogged through the mud toward the new Federal position in no mood for the battle which they assumed would soon follow. Though Ewell pushed skirmishers forward far enough to engage their Union counterparts, an order quickly came from Jackson to halt the advance. Lee had concluded that his soldiers were too worn out and the Federal position too strong to attack. In his diary, Lieutenant Ring gave no hint of the relief that the 6th Louisiana must have felt at this reprieve, but wrote in a triumphant tone: "Continuing our pursuit of our flying foes, we only halted when we had run them into their holes at Westover on the James River."[1]

The regiment remained in front of Harrison's Landing until July 8, when Lee began to pull his army back to Richmond. By then the Confederate commander had correctly surmised that McClellan was unlikely to resume his campaign against the Confederacy's capital. The 6th Louisiana joined the pullback to Richmond, where it arrived on July 10. Writing from the Confederate capital, Ben Hubert was "most heartily glad to get out of the Chickahominy Swamps," but was unimpressed with the city. "Richmond itself is of course the dullest place in the

Confederacy—full of sick & wounded soldiers and busy men who are 'too good' to fight for the Southern Confederacy but indulge in all manner of good wishes for its welfare, always taking care tho to keep out of harm's way for fear they might get hurt!"[2]

In Richmond the regiment boarded the Virginia Central Railroad for Gordonsville, from which it marched to camp on ground it had occupied previously, now named Camp Wheat in honor of the slain commander of the Tiger battalion. The Seven Days' Battles had so devastated the Army of Northern Virginia, which suffered nearly 20,000 casualties, that Lee had to reorganize his forces. Several Louisiana regiments were shuffled in this reorganization. The 9th Louisiana was taken out of Taylor's Louisiana Brigade, and the 5th and 14th Louisiana Volunteers were added to it. Wheat's Special Battalion, leaderless and decimated in battle, was disbanded and its men dispersed to various Louisiana regiments, including the 6th. The reorganization also resulted in the creation of a second Louisiana Brigade, comprised of the 1st, 2nd, 9th, 10th and 15th Louisiana regiments, and the 1st Battalion, Louisiana Zouaves. The 1st Louisiana Brigade in Ewell's Division, consisting of the 5th, 6th, 7th, 8th and 14th Louisiana regiments, also lost its commander, General Taylor, who was promoted to major general and transferred west to a command in the Trans-Mississippi Department. Taking his place as the new brigadier general was the former colonel of the 7th Louisiana, Harry T. Hays, a hard-drinking and hard-fighting 42-year-old veteran of the Mexican War. Hays, though, was still recovering from a wound received at Port Republic, so the brigade was temporarily led by Col. Henry Forno of the 5th Louisiana, a former New Orleans police chief.[3]

The reorganization of the Louisiana units brought to Hays' Brigade a Catholic priest, the Rev. James B. Sheeran, who was chaplain of the 14th Louisiana. Born in Ireland, Father Sheeran served at the Redemptorist Church in New Orleans in 1861, volunteering to become a Confederate chaplain when the war broke out. He apparently was the first Catholic chaplain to serve with Ewell's Division, and his appearance in camp in early August 1862 must have been a consolation to many of the Irish Catholics of the 6th Louisiana, despite their reputation for irreverence and weaknesses of the flesh. Fortunately for historians, the priest kept a diary during his war service from 1862 to 1865, recording his observations of life in camp, on the march and in battle. After being warmly welcomed by General Ewell, who "expressed much pleasure at having a Catholic chaplain in his division," Father Sheeran spent his first days in camp hearing confessions, celebrating Mass and distributing Holy Communion to the Catholic troops, who were numerous in the Louisiana regiments. As an Irish-born, fervently pro-Southern cleric from New Orleans, he would have been a kindred spirit, indeed, for Colonel Strong's Irishmen.[4]

The 6th Louisiana moved west to Gordonsville as part of a new campaign opened by General Jackson under Lee's orders to meet the threat of a Federal advance from that direction. While McClellan remained inactive east of Richmond, Union Maj. Gen. John Pope began moving his newly organized Army of Virginia towards Gordonsville and its vital railroad junction. Pope had been appointed by President Lincoln in late June to unite under his command the three formerly independent armies under John Fremont (who resigned rather than serve under Pope) now commanded by German-born Maj. Gen. Franz Sigel; Nathaniel Banks (whom Jackson had defeated in the Valley); and Irvin McDowell's corps. These columns formed the basis of three corps of the Pope's Army of Virginia, which totaled about 47,000 men. Pope's seven divisions were scattered over a wide area, from Fredericksburg in the east to Sperryville along the Blue Ridge in the west.[5]

REV. JAMES B. SHEERAN

Dressed in priestly garb and hat, Reverend Sheeran was chaplain to the 14th Louisiana Infantry, but ministered to the other Louisiana regiments in Lee's Army of Northern Virginia, including the many Catholics in the 6th Louisiana. Born in Ireland, Father Sheeran was a transplanted Northerner who became a rabid Southern partisan in New Orleans. His war diary provides valuable insight into the life and attitudes of the Louisiana Confederates. *Tulane University Library*

Jackson, resting his troops in the vicinity of Gordonsville, where the Virginia Central and Orange & Alexandria roads met, looked for an opportunity to strike at some part of Pope's army before the whole concentrated against him. Lee reinforced Jackson in late July by dispatching A. P. Hill's Light Division to Gordonsville, doubling Jackson's command to about 24,000 men. Though the Confederates remained outnumbered, Pope could be dealt a blow if the Confederates could pounce on some portion of his army before he managed to unite his scattered forces.[6]

The opportunity arrived in early August when Pope sent Banks' two divisions into Culpeper County. The Confederates marched north and the clash came about 5:00 p.m. on August 9 at Cedar Mountain, eight miles south of Culpeper Court House. There, in a little valley cut by a stream called Cedar Run, Banks threw his 8,000 men against Jackson before the Confederate commander had all his strength on the field. For more than an hour after their attack that blistering hot afternoon, the Federals had the advantage, breaking behind the Southerners' left flank. The Union assault severely punished Early's Brigade of Ewell's Division and Jackson's old division under Charles Winder, who was killed. The tide turned against the Northerners, however, when A. P. Hill's fresh brigades counter-attacked near sundown, driving Banks' men back toward Culpeper Court House.[7]

Colonel Forno's Louisianans were spectators to most of the action at Cedar Mountain. The 6th Louisiana was deployed with the rest of the brigade under cover of woods on the northwest slope of the mountain, some 200 feet above the far right of the Confederate lines, where they could see the fighting below them. The regiment was under command of Capt. William H. Manning, as both Colonel Strong and Lieutenant Colonel Offutt were absent sick, and Major Monaghan had not yet returned from his stay in a Federal prison. Manning and his men crouched in the woods as batteries posted by Ewell pounded the Federals from their advantageous elevation, taking counter-battery fire in return. The regiment was under shelling of the Federal artillery during the afternoon but remained inactive until nearly dark. At that point, as Jackson pressed the attack all along the line, Ewell personally led the Louisiana regiments down upon the field from their perch on the slope of the mountain, "under a heavy fire from the enemy's artillery," as he later reported. The Federals "hastily abandoned the field" as the Confederates surged forward, and Ewell continued the pursuit until dark, when it became impossible to tell friend from foe. The 6th Louisiana suffered only one casualty at Cedar Mountain when Pvt. Henry R. Kelly of Company E was wounded by a shell fragment.[8]

Relieved that for once they had no dead comrades to bury after a battle, the 6th Louisiana remained near the foot of Cedar Mountain for two days as the opposing armies cared for their wounded and buried the dead under a flag of truce. While the Federals had lost nearly 2,400 casualties, only about a third of Pope's Army of Virginia had been engaged. The 1,400 Confederate casualties stood as grim evidence that Banks' Federals had fought hard and bravely before being driven from the field by superior numbers. Numerical superiority swung in Pope's favor, however, when the balance of his divisions arrived at Culpeper. Jackson prudently pulled back to Gordonsville during the night of Aug. 11-12, prompting the bombastic General Pope to declare his August 9 defeat "only the first of a series of victories which shall make the Army of Virginia famous in the land."[9]

The Army of Virginia would be become famous, or perhaps infamous, in the next four weeks as Pope blundered though a series of defeats rather than victories. As the 6th Louisiana and the rest of Jackson's force retired 20 miles south to Gordonsville for what would become four days of rest, the strategic situation in Virginia was changing dramatically. Lincoln's new general-in-chief, Maj. Gen. Henry W. Halleck, had reached the conclusion that McClellan's Peninsula Campaign was hopeless, and on August 3 ordered the Army of the Potomac to leave its James River stronghold to join forces with Pope in Northern Virginia. McClellan protested this decision to no avail, then delayed embarking his troops until August 14. When General Lee became aware of McClellan's transfer of troops, he began shifting the bulk of the Army of Northern Virginia, which was still deployed defensively around Richmond, by rail to Gordonsville to unite with Jackson. Using interior lines, Lee's aim was to smash Pope's army before it could be reinforced by the divisions being transported by ship on the long, slow route from the James River to Chesapeake Bay, and then up the Potomac River to a landing point south of the Federal capital.[10]

General Pope, learning of Lee's move to Gordonsville, pulled his Army of Virginia back across the Rappahannock River, which provided a defensible line. After several days of probing and artillery dueling across the river, the Confederate commander decided on a daring plan: he would launch Jackson on a sweeping thrust in Pope's rear to cut his communications with Washington and capture his supply trains. The bold but dangerous maneuver relied on Stonewall's penchant for speed and stealth to prevent his force from being trapped by a larger Federal army, now being gradually reinforced by McClellan's divisions.[11]

Jackson's divisions (or "wing" or "corps," for the army was not officially organized into corps until the fall of 1862) moved up the south bank of the Rappahannock River, reaching the village of Jeffersonton on August 24. There, the men were ordered to cook three days' rations and prepare for hard marching. Quartermaster and commissary wagons were parked to be left behind when the march began next dawn. No one in Jackson's army, not even generals commanding his three divisions, had any idea where they were heading. Pope didn't even know Jackson was on the move.[12]

The men of the 6th Louisiana were among the first to move at dawn on August 25. Ewell's was the advance division on the march, with the Louisiana Brigade under Colonel Forno in front, followed by the brigades of Brigadier Generals Trimble, Lawton and Early. Their banners flapping in a breeze sweeping down from the Blue Ridge Mountains, the soldiers of the 6th Louisiana marched briskly north, crossing the Rappahannock River at Hinson's Mill Ford, four miles north of Waterloo Bridge on the turnpike from Sperryville to Warrenton, where most of Pope's army was concentrated.

The march was a rapid, clockwise flanking maneuver which covered nearly 60 miles in two days—a hard stretch even by Jackson's standards. The Louisiana men set a rapid pace, marching 26 miles the first day under a hot August sun, passing through the villages of Amissville and Orleans before halting near midnight at Salem, on the Manassas Gap Railroad. At dawn the next day Jackson's men made a sharp right turn to the east, facing into the rising sun as they tramped the railroad line through the steep, rocky cleft in the Bull Run mountains known as Thoroughfare Gap, then continued down on to the wide plain below, where tempting cornfields yielded a supplement to their meager rations. The miles-long column snaked through Haymarket and Gainesville in the afternoon heat in the direction of the Orange & Alexandria Railroad, the Federal army's main link to its supply depot at Manassas Junction and to Washington.[13]

Jackson, having swept around and behind Pope's army, now moved to sever its communications and supply line. With the Louisiana Brigade still in the van, Jackson directed his column south from Gainesville to the small rail stop at Bristoe Station, four miles southwest of the junction. After an exhausting, dusty march of 30 miles, Colonel Strong's weary men of the 6th Louisiana approached Bristoe Station about sunset. A Confederate cavalry detachment swept down on the station just ahead of them, scattering a small force of Federals posted there. The Louisianians double-quicked in the direction of the action and managed to capture a handful of Union soldiers. As Strong's Irishmen stood panting and sweating, they heard the sounds of a train approaching from the direction of Warrenton, on its way toward Manassas and Washington.[14]

"All were now waiting with the most intense anxiety," Father Sheeran, the Louisiana chaplain, wrote in his diary, "when suddenly the whistle of a locomotive in the direction of Warrenton was heard in the distance." The Louisianians feared that the train would be packed with Federal infantry. Colonel Forno quickly deployed two regiments to greet it with a deadly salute. "Our regiment in conjunction with the 5th Louisiana was ordered to form a line of battle parallel to the Rail Road and fire into the trains then approaching, and supposed to contain troops" Lieutenant Ring's diary relates. As the train neared the station, the engineer realized that something was amiss and poured on the steam, running rapidly past the two regiments as they fired their muskets. The train of empty passenger cars "made the escape pretty well, bored however by the shower of musket balls," in Father Sheeran's words.[15]

The escaping train was one of several that earlier that day had hauled some of McClellan's brigades, just off the boats from the Peninsula, from Alexandria to Warrenton to join Pope. This was only the first of several trains planning to dead-head back to Alexandria that evening to pick up more troops. The Confederates, however, had other plans for them. Father Sheeran reported that General Jackson personally helped some of his Louisianians pile debris on the tracks near the station. "He now walked slowly along the lines and in a low voice told the boys not to waste their ammunition for he had everything fixed," the priest wrote. Soon the whistle of another approaching train was heard. As it roared down upon them at a high speed, the excited Tigers forgot his instructions and "poured a volley of musketry into her boiler, causing the steam to go in every direction," according to Sheeran. The perforated and hissing locomotive hit the barricade on the tracks, jumped the rails, and plunged down a ravine into the mud, all to the excited cheers of the onlooking Confederates. To add to their delight, the priest noted, the locomotive was named "Abe Lincoln."[16]

As the Louisianians inspected the wrecked train, the headlight of yet another was seen in the distance. A quick-thinking Georgian who was an old railroad hand jumped into the cab of the derailed locomotive and blew the "all clear" signal, while another Confederate smashed the red warning lights on the back of the wrecked train. The unsuspecting engineer steamed into the station and smashed his chain of cars into the rear cars of the derailed train, his own train folding up like an accordion. The Confederates now had Pope's railroad thoroughly blocked. When a fourth train approached, the Louisianians anticipated more fun, but this time the engineer stopped short of the station, saw the trouble ahead, and threw his engine into reverse, backpedaling in panic to Warrenton to spread the alarm of the Confederate raid on Bristoe Station.[17]

The attack on the trains was sure to alert Pope to the presence of Confederates in his rear, and would undoubtedly provoke a counter-strike in the morning. It was dark, probably past 9:00 p.m., but Jackson was determined not to lose any time in capturing the Federal supply depot at Manassas Junction, which he had heard was piled high with "stores of great value." He sent General Trimble with two regiments plus Jeb Stuart's cavalry five miles up the railroad to capture the great prize, which they did against minor resistance from a small Federal garrison there. The rest of Jackson's command bivouacked for the night at Bristoe Station, arms at the ready.[18]

Back in Warrenton, General Pope was trying to figure out what was happening down the tracks toward Manassas. At first he had no idea that the trouble at Bristoe Station was more than an insignificant raid, for he ordered only a single regiment be put on a train to investigate the trouble. As the night wore on he received additional intelligence that a large Confederate force had slipped between his army and Washington. The regiment that drew the assignment to check out the situation at Bristoe Station was the 72nd New York Infantry, part of the Excelsior Brigade of Maj. Gen. Joseph Hooker's division, just transferred from the Peninsula. The New Yorkers, temporarily under command of Capt. Harman J. Bliss, neared the station just before daylight on August 27 to find the scene bathed in the light of burning rail cars and swarming with Confederates who were forming into lines of battle.[19]

As Captain Bliss watched with a growing sense of dread, the 6th Louisiana was forming up for what would turn out to be both a memorable and bloody day for the regiment. General Ewell, preparing for an expected counter-strike by the Federals, had ordered his three brigades to defend the station against an advance from the west or north. Forno's Louisianians were ordered to advance north of the railroad, while Brig. Gen. Alexander R. Lawton's Georgia regiments were deployed south of it, both brigades facing west toward Warrenton. This was the activity Captain Bliss of the 72nd New York witnessed from down the track, near the train which had carried his men there. He quickly concluded his most prudent course was to get his men back on the train and back to Warrenton Junction as quickly as possible. Before he could round up all his men to reboard the cars, however, Forno's Louisianians discovered his presence as they advanced down the track with the 60th Georgia regiment and a piece of artillery. A few well-placed shots from the cannon did some damage to the train, but Bliss hurried his men aboard and escaped down the track. He sent a telegraph to Pope warning that Confederates were at Bristoe "in very heavy force."[20]

After Captain Bliss' train backtracked toward Warrenton, Forno ordered Colonel Strong to take the 6th Louisiana forward about two miles to Kettle Run, a small stream bridged by the railroad, and establish a picket line there to watch for the enemy. The 8th Louisiana accompanied Strong's men as far as the railroad bridge, which they were ordered to destroy. The 6th Louisiana, with orders to conduct a fighting retreat if the enemy appeared in force, advanced about a mile beyond the bridge. Under a broiling August sun, Strong's skirmishers edged forward. They were aware they represented the spearhead of Ewell's force, and thus occupied the most exposed position should Pope's army advance. For several hours they waited and watched nervously while the 8th Louisiana behind them tore at the tracks and prepared to burn the bridge.[21]

It was around 2:00 p.m. when Colonel Strong and his men saw heavy columns of Federal infantry with artillery advancing from Warrenton Junction. "We discovered the enemy approaching in force and Col. Strong was ordered to fall back, skirmishing as he went," Lieutenant Ring's diary notes. The 6th Louisiana, along with the 8th Louisiana, retreated to a woods some 300 yards in front of the rest of Forno's Brigade. There the two Louisiana regiments and the 60th Georgia made a stand against the advancing Federal columns, which consisted of two brigades from Hooker's division. Lieutenant Ring described the action:

> Taking a position in front of a fence line with an open field of about three hundred yards' width before us, we calmly awaited the approach of the enemy. General Hooker's division, or part of it, emerged from the woods and with a yell attempted a charge upon our line, but before they had passed half across the field were met by a murderous fire from our ranks that caused them to halt and after a few volleys to fall back in utter confusion.[22]

General Early watched the Federal attack from his position to the right of the Louisiana regiments. "As soon as the enemy came in range," Early reported, "our artillery from its several positions opened on him, as did the Sixth and Eighth Louisiana and Sixtieth Georgia Regiments. By this combined fire two columns of the enemy of not less than a brigade each were driven. . . ." The bluecoats that attacked across that open field were New York and New Jersey men of Col. Joseph B. Carr's brigade, in the lead of Hooker's column. On encountering the Louisiana skirmishers, Carr formed his line with the 2nd New York and 5th and 8th New Jersey regiments and charged into the open field, while General Hooker himself led the 6th and 7th New Jersey Volunteers on a flanking move to the left. When Carr led this three regiments forward, the Louisianians waited until the Federals were within 60 yards before letting loose with a devastating volley. The stunned Unionists dashed for cover in a small ravine in the middle of the field, where they were pinned down for more than an hour in a close-range fight with the Louisiana and Georgia riflemen.[23]

The 6th and 8th Louisiana regiments were taking casualties and running low on ammunition as the engagement dragged on. A second Union battle line consisting of Col. Nelson Taylor's Excelsior Brigade, moved in behind Carr's men. Forno rushed forward the 5th Louisiana to bolster his two regiments. As the weight of the Federal attack increased, a Union battery opened fire on the center of the Confederate line, where the Louisianians stood. By 4:00 p.m. it was clear to Jubal Early that the enemy's force "was much larger than ours" and that the Federals appeared to be moving to a ridge on the Confederate right, threatening to cut off the Confederate line of retreat across Broad Run, a stream two miles to the rear. Ewell was operating under orders from Jackson to delay Pope's advance as long as he could, but to fall back to the main body at Manassas Junction if hard-pressed. Faced with some 5,000 of Hooker's men, Ewell ordered a withdrawal.[24]

Disengaging from an enemy while under fire, without provoking a sudden charge, was a delicate task. Ewell ordered Early to cover the retreat with his brigade. Lawton's Georgians pulled back first. The Louisianians slowly and carefully edged back in their wake, firing as they withdrew. There was no running or panic. Early, withdrawing from a pine wood where his men had been posted, covered the retreat by forming "successive lines of battle," regiment by regiment, as he pulled back. The Federal pursuit was timidly conducted and stopped when it reached the position formerly held by the Georgians and Louisianians. By 6:00 p.m., one half-hour before sunset, Ewell's Division had successfully pulled back across Broad Run, a strong stream two miles east of Bristoe Station, where Hooker's men had halted.[25]

Colonel Forno was pleased with the action of the 6th and 8th Louisiana at Bristoe Station, also called the Battle of Kettle Run. "The duty was performed to my entire satisfaction," he claimed, "these two regiments successfully repulsing two brigades of the enemy until their ammunition was expended, when I ordered up the 5th Regiment (Maj. B. Menger commanding) to support them. . . .After a few discharges from the latter regiment, the whole retired in as good order as if on parade."[26]

By all accounts the 6th Louisiana performed ably in the engagement, as did the other regiments engaged at Bristoe Station. Colonel Strong's men, however, had borne the brunt of Hooker's attack in their exposed position and thus once again held the dubious honor of suffering the most casualties in the brigade. The regiment lost 10 killed and 25 wounded, a toll roughly equal to the regiment's losses at Gaines' Mill and Malvern Hill. By contrast, the 5th Louisiana had five killed and the 8th Louisiana one, with fewer wounded as well in each of those regiments. The 6th Louisiana's dead included five Irish and four German-born soldiers.[27]

While the 6th Louisiana had been fighting, most of Jackson's men had been reveling and feasting at Pope's expense at Manassas Junction. Leaving Ewell's Division at Bristoe that morning, Jackson had taken his other two divisions to discover what Trimble and Stuart had captured at the junction the night before. The Federal army had established a huge supply base at the rail junction where the Orange and Alexandria Railroad linked with the Manassas Gap line. The ragged, famished Confederates could scarcely believe their eyes when they came upon the massive Union storehouses. In Jackson's own words, "It was vast in quantity and of great value, comprising 50,000 pounds of bacon, 1,000 barrels of corned beef, 2,000 barrels of salt pork, 2,000 barrels of flour, quartermaster's, ordnance and sutler's stores deposited in buildings and filling two trains of cars." After driving off a Federal brigade dispatched on trains that morning from Alexandria to Manassas Junction, the Confederate commander permitted his hungry soldiers to run loose and plunder the Federal larder. The delighted rebels stuffed their stomachs and their haversacks with all they could handle, including undreamed-of luxuries such as canned fruits, lobster, boxes of cigars and tins of coffee.[28]

This bacchanal was still in progress when the bloodied and weary men of the 6th Louisiana, who had been living off scanty rations and roasted corn, trudged into Manassas Junction with Ewell's Division after the battle at Bristoe Station. Though they arrived late, the Louisiana men found a mile-long supply train still untouched. Their Catholic chaplain, Father Sheeran, described the scene:

> Just imagine about 6,000 men hungry and almost naked, let loose on some million dollars worth of biscuit, cheese, ham, bacon, messpork, coffee, sugar, tea, fruit, brandy, wine, whiskey, oysters; coats, pants, shirts, caps, boots, shoes, socks, blankets, tents, etc. etc. Here you would see a crowd enter a car with their old Confed. grays and in a few moments come out dressed in Yankee uniforms; some as cavalry; some as infantry; some as artillerists; others dressed in the splendid uniforms of Federal officers. . . .I have often read of the sacking of cities by a victorious army but never did I hear of a railroad train being sacked. I viewed this scene for almost two hours with the most intense anxiety. I saw the whole army become what appeared to me an ungovernable mob, drunk, some few with liquor but the others with excitement.[29]

After eating their fill and taking all they could carry, the Confederates burned the rest of Pope's mountain of supplies. As warehouses, rail cars, and wagons went up in flames, the night sky glowed while the sound of exploding ammunition and the smell of thousands of pounds of sizzling bacon carried away on the breeze. The fires were seen 10 miles away.[30]

Though Jackson had severed Pope's communications and destroyed his vast store of goods, he wasn't satisfied. He wanted to land a crippling blow upon Pope's army, and sought a place where he could lie in wait to pounce, one where he could be joined as soon as possible by James Longstreet's divisions, which were following the route through Thoroughfare Gap earlier utilized by Jackson. The place that fit Jackson's needs was on the northwest edge of the Manassas battlefield, where Jackson had earned such distinction 13 months earlier, near the little community of Groveton, overlooking the turnpike from Warrenton to Alexandria.

After feasting and helping burn the supply depot at Manassas Junction, the footsore soldiers of the 6th Louisiana managed only a brief sleep. "About midnight we were roused up," Lieutenant Ring wrote in his diary, as Ewell's Division formed in column to march east toward Centreville. "By daylight [we] had marched to our old camp Bienville near Centreville where we rested a couple of hours and again resumed the march across the Stone Bridge to the old battlefield of Manassas," Ring penned. It was a strange, nighttime march, first heading east, then halting, then turning about face to march west. Neither the men nor their officers in the regiment had any idea where the mysterious Jackson was taking them. This time, even Jackson didn't know where they were headed. The secretive Confederate commander hadn't told Ewell where to march, but simply to follow A. P. Hill's Division. Due to a confused guide who misunderstood Jackson's orders, Hill had marched east to Centreville. Jackson had intended Hill and Ewell to march directly north on the Manassas-Sudley road to Groveton, where he planned to give battle when Pope's forces eventually moved east on the Warrenton Turnpike, as he was sure they must. But Hill's and Ewell's divisions mistakenly wandered east during the night before Jackson learned of their detour and sent messengers to turn them around. The mix-up delayed Jackson's concentration of forces at Groveton by several hours, but was to pay off unexpectedly by convincing Pope that Jackson had moved east to Centreville, where the confident Federal commander expected to trap him.[31]

After making its U-turn at Centreville, the Louisiana Brigade marched west across the old Bull Run battlefield to a patch of woods just north of the little community of Groveton, where Jackson was setting up his ambush. The Confederates would wait here, concealed in the woods, to pounce upon the unsuspecting Federal troops as they marched east on the turnpike from Gainesville and Warrenton in their search of the elusive Stonewall. The Louisiana regiments took position in the woods behind the brigade of General Early, who had been directed by Ewell to take command of both his own brigade and Forno's Louisianans.[32]

Late in the afternoon of August 28, the Union division of Brig. Gen. Rufus King was marching down the pike from Gainesville, unaware of the Confederate trap. As the Louisianians rested in the woods in reserve, Jackson's division under William B. Taliaferro, together with two of Ewell's brigades under Alexander Lawton and Isaac Trimble, marched out to confront the surprised Federals. Their attack fell mainly on the Union brigade of Brig. Gen. John Gibbon, whose Midwestern farm boys from Wisconsin and Indiana stood and fought with "obstinate determination," as Jackson later reported. The horrific standup fight which followed had the combatants blasting away at one another at a range of 80 yards or less in an open field. Dusk settled over the bloody scene as men fell out of the lines crippled and killed. The battle dragged on into the darkness past 9:00 p.m. with both sides stubbornly slugging it out, aiming mainly at the muzzle flashes from their opponents' muskets. Just before dark General Early was ordered to advance his brigade and Forno's Louisianians to the front. By the time they stumbled though the woods in the gloom and smoke, however, the bloodied Unionists withdrew from the field.[33]

Both sides suffered severe casualties in the twilight battle at Brawner's Farm (Groveton). One of the more serious, as far as the Confederates were concerned, was a shot which split open the knee of General Ewell. The painful wound necessitated the amputation of his leg the following day. The quirky but dependable division commander was much beloved by the men of the 6th Louisiana, who initially had viewed him with some skepticism. As Lieutenant Ring noted in his diary, "we were deprived of our gallant Gen. R. Ewell, who by this time had had his fancy title of Dirty Dick changed by the men to the more flattering one of Fighting Dick, who had become endeared and beloved by every man of his command." General Lawton, who led the Georgia brigade in Ewell's Division, succeeded the wounded major general in command.[34]

What would the morning bring? Jackson knew that his attack at Groveton revealed his location to the bewildered Pope, and now his 24,000 men faced potentially twice that number or more if Pope could bring all of his troops to bear. Could Stonewall hold out long enough to give Lee and Longstreet time to arrive on the battlefield from Gainesville, after passing through Thoroughfare Gap? Longstreet had reached the mountain pass while the Battle at Groveton raged during the evening of August 28, but his advance would not reach the battlefield until late on the morning on the 29th. Holding out until Longstreet's 30,000 men arrived was critical to both Jackson's survival and Confederate success.

After the sharp fight on August 28, the Louisiana Brigade slept on its arms along an unfinished railroad bed which ran through the woods north of Groveton. Here, along the protecting embankments of the railroad cut, Jackson determined to form his line of battle to fend off the inevitable attacks he believed would be launched the following day on Friday, August 29. The line, a mile and a quarter long, was anchored on the left near Sudley Church by A. P. Hill's Division. The center of the position was held by Ewell's (Lawton's) Division, while Jackson's former division, now commanded by Brig. Gen. William E. Starke in place of the wounded William Taliaferro, deployed on the right near the Warrenton Turnpike.[35]

Jackson was concerned about the danger of a Federal force from Manassas moving upon his right flank. To watch in that direction he ordered Early to take his own and Forno's Louisiana Brigade to a ridge west of the railroad cut overlooking the turnpike. There the 6th Louisiana was posted under cover of woods as the morning action opened. The Louisianians formed the extreme right of the Confederate position, bent back a bit from the main line along the railroad grade, reaching out a hand to connect with Longstreet when he arrived.[36]

The day's assaults on Jackson's front along the unfinished railroad came in a series of vigorous but disjointed attacks by various Union brigades, reflecting Pope's lack of a coherent battle plan. Jackson had the advantage of a strong defensive position in the woods along the railroad embankment, which gave his men cover. The attacking Federals fought ferociously, breaking Jackson's line on three separate occasions, but were thrown back each time because Pope failed to follow up these momentary successes with supporting troops which could have turned the breakthroughs into a disaster for Jackson's hard-pressed troops.

The men of the 6th Louisiana, a mile or so behind Jackson's front line, were watching the Warrenton turnpike and could only have heard the opening of the morning's fighting from a distance. They had no chance to see the hard-fighting men of Alabama, Georgia and North Carolina in Trimble's brigade throw back the ineptly orchestrated first assault against Jackson's center by the Ohioans and West Virginians of Brig. Gen. Robert H. Milroy's brigade. Milroy lost almost one-quarter of his command in the futile assault.[37]

About the time Milroy was being repulsed, between 10:00 and 11:00 a.m., the Louisianians saw the advance elements of Longstreet's column marching down the pike from Gainesville. The arrival of "Old Pete's" fifteen brigades in five divisions would reunite the two wings of Lee's army and all but eliminate the overwhelming advantage of numbers Pope had briefly enjoyed against Jackson. The Union army commander had no idea Longstreet was even in the vicinity, and his failure to foresee and prevent this conjunction of Confederate forces would seal the Union army's fate at Second Manassas.

Longstreet's men moved into position on Jackson's right, south of the Warrenton Pike. Lee was eager to launch an attack. Longstreet, however, advised against it because he was concerned about reports that a large body of the enemy was advancing toward his position from the direction of Manassas Junction. If true, the approaching enemy would be on his own flank and rear if he attacked the Federals confronting Jackson. Lee grudgingly agreed to hold off, which meant that Jackson's men would continue to bear the brunt of the Federal attacks alone.[38]

And the attacks kept coming. They were delivered one after another, primarily against the Confederate left held by Hill's embattled brigades. The veteran Light Division absorbed a bloody pounding and held on grimly. In early afternoon following Longstreet's arrival, the 6th Louisiana, along with the rest of Forno's and Early's brigades, moved to the left toward the action, taking up a supporting position on the slopes of Stony Ridge, about 400 yards behind the rest of Ewell's (Lawton's) Division in the center, along the railroad cut. It was here that a wandering Virginia private, lost from his command, fell in with the Louisiana men, who so impressed him with their colorful diversity that the soldier recorded his impressions after the war. "The command was as unlike my own as it was possible to conceive," the young Virginian marveled. "Such a congress of nations only the cosmopolitan Crescent City could have sent forth, and the tongues of Babel seemed resurrected in its speech; English, German, French and Spanish, all were represented, to say nothing of Doric brogue and local 'gumbo.' There was, moreover," he added, "a vehemence of utterance and gesture, curiously at variance with the reticence of our Virginians." The Louisianians rather shocked the straight-laced Virginian with their card-playing as they awaited orders to join the fight, especially when the New Orleans gamblers dealt a hand to determine which of them would run across a bullet-swept field to fill their canteens at a nearby spring.[39]

There would be no more time for resting or card-playing during the remainder of this bloody day. Pope's successive assaults against Hill's rock-like line finally pulled the 6th Louisiana and Forno's other regiments into the swirling tide of battle. At more than one point during that afternoon it appeared that the onrushing Federal waves might wash away Jackson's rapidly-thinning defensive line. One such near-disaster came about when an attack was launched around 3:00 p.m. by one of General Hooker's brigades, commanded by Brig. Gen. Cuvier Grover. A second Federal thrust involving a brigade led by Col. James Nagle, of Maj. Gen. Jesse L. Reno's division of the Federal IX Corps, nearly broke Jackson's line an hour later. There is considerable confusion and dispute over which of these attacks drew the counter-thrust by Forno's

Louisianians. Official reports penned by the participants are, unfortunately, less than precise in citing Forno's movements, and the interpretations of historians are divided. The preponderance of evidence suggests that it was Grover's attack against Hill which prompted Jackson to throw Forno's Brigade into the battle.

By mid-afternoon, the Louisianians were on Early's right, forming the reserve line behind Lawton's two other brigades in the center of Jackson's defense. Around 3:00 p.m., responding to orders from his division commander, Grover, a 34-year-old West Pointer, formed his five regiments in two lines and advanced into an open field in front of the center of Jackson's lines, where Lawton's men stood ready. Looking over the ground, Grover was reluctant to order his five regiments, only about 1,500 men, to charge over this open ground upon the hidden Confederates, for that already had been tried to no avail by Milroy's men. Upon reconnoitering, Grover decided to shift his brigade to his right, where he saw the unfinished railroad line disappear into the woods about 300 yards distant. The timber would conceal his attackers until they closed upon the Confederate line, whereupon Grover would order a bayonet charge. Grover's rightward shift, entirely across Lawton's front, moved his New England and Pennsylvania regiments over to face A. P. Hill's brigades.[40]

Grover's decision proved to be a fortuitous move for the Federals. The lateral shift brought Grover's regiments in front of troops already wearied by earlier attacks, and put part of his force directly opposite a gap of 125 to 175 yards that stretched between two of Hill's brigades—those of Brig. Gens. Edward L. Thomas and Maxcy Gregg. Gregg's South Carolinians held the extreme left of the Confederate line, with Thomas' Georgians to their right, beyond the gap that Hill and his brigadiers somehow had failed to close. To make matters worse for Hill's men, the woods in their front concealed all movement and rendered artillery virtually useless. Grover's attack would be upon them, and flowing into the gap between them, almost before Hill's two brigades knew what hit them.[41]

Grover ordered his troops to wait until they closed upon the Confederates before firing a volley and charging with the bayonet. Spurring his horse forward, he shouted, "Charge!" With a cheer, his men crashed through the woods to the railroad embankment, overran the startled Confederates, and chased fleeing gray-clad troops through the forest. "Many of the enemy were bayoneted in their tracks, others struck

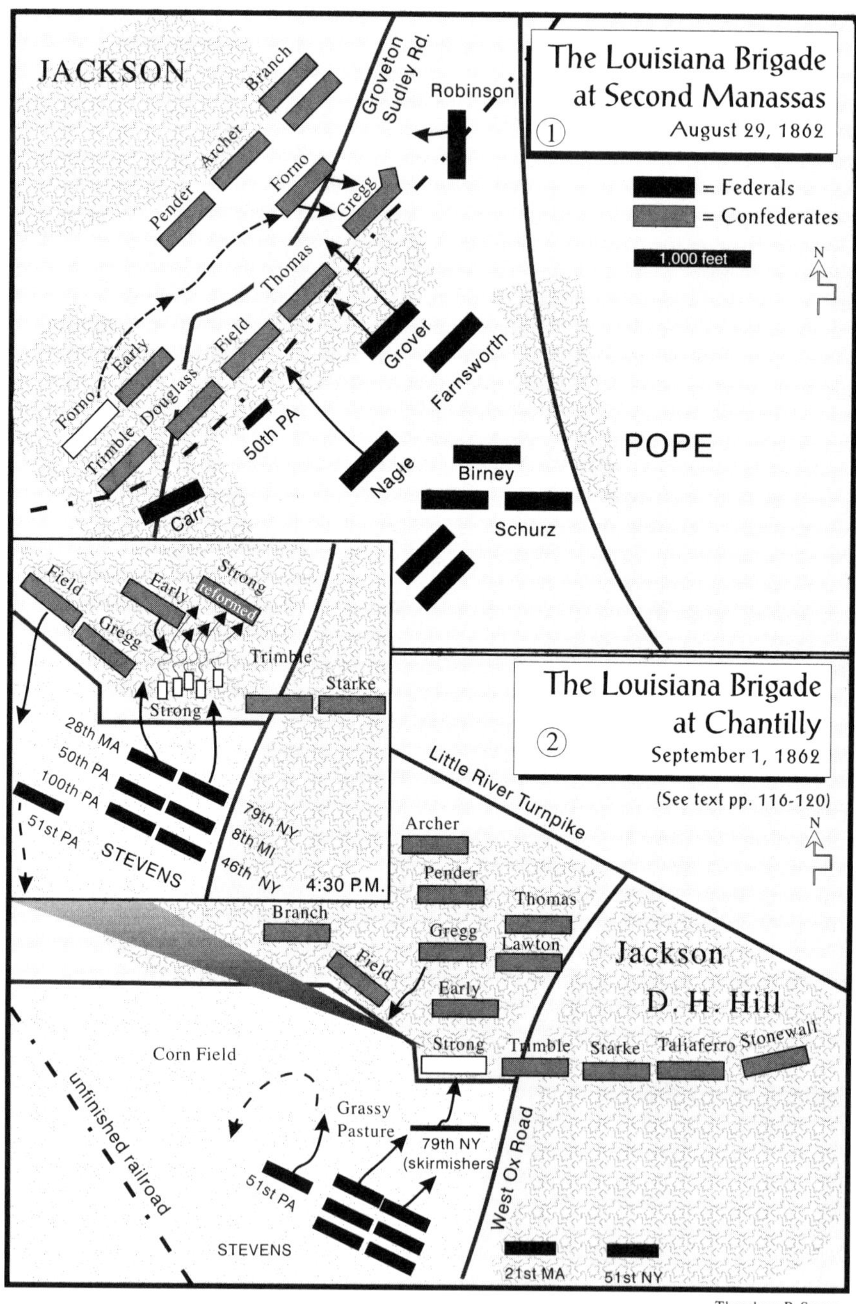

Theodore P. Savas

down with the buts of pieces, and onward pressed our line," Grover wrote in his report. The clash was "a short, sharp, and obstinate hand-to-hand conflict with bayonets and clubbed muskets." Grover's breakthrough, greatly aided by the gap in Hill's line, pushed back Thomas' brigade and threatened to cut off Gregg's South Carolinians from the rest of Jackson's force. The breakthrough might have proved decisive if Grover had received the support he expected, but reinforcements failed to arrive and his relatively small force was isolated in a pocket along Jackson's line. Hill sent in his reserves and rallied his front-line men, catching Grover's regiments in a destructive crossfire that decimated their ranks and drove them back. In about 30 minutes, Grover's brigade lost 486 of its 1,500 men.[42]

It was about this time, at the high-water mark of Grover's penetration, that the Louisiana Brigade was rushed to aid Hill. Moving from its position behind Lawton's line, the 6th Louisiana hurried to the left with Forno and his other regiments, except for the 8th Louisiana, which was somewhere in the rear gathering ammunition. It is probable that their leftward movement brought the Louisianians in behind Maxcy Gregg's hard-pressed South Carolinians, who had their hands full trying to drive back Grover's regiments. Unfortunately, Forno's official report, written five months after the battle, is sketchy and unspecific as to the place of his counterthrust, though it does pinpoint the time. "At 3:30 p.m. on the 29th was ordered to advance my brigade by General Jackson," penned Forno in his clipped style, "and soon after engaged the enemy, and after driving them with great slaughter retained the ground previously occupied by them."[43]

General Early, in a more detailed report, explained that "about 3:30 p.m. Colonel Forno was ordered to advance to the front by General Jackson to the support of one of A. P. Hill's brigades, and he advanced to the railroad and drove the enemy from it and took position on it with his brigade." Early did not specify which of Hill's brigades the Louisianians went to support, but both Jackson and General Lee reported that it was Gregg's. "General Hill reports that six separate and distinct assaults were thus met and repulsed by his division, assisted by Hays' brigade, Colonel Forno commanding," wrote Jackson in his report. He also noted that Gregg's Brigade was the most exposed and had nearly exhausted its ammunition. "About 4 o'clock it had been assisted by Hays' brigade (Colonel Forno)." General Lee added: "General Gregg, who was most exposed, was re-inforced by Hays' brigade, under Colonel Forno, and successfully and gallantly resisted the attacks of the enemy until the ammunition of this brigade being exhausted and all his field officers but two killed or wounded, it was relieved, after several hours of fighting, by Early's brigade and the Eighth Louisiana regiment."[44]

The only direct testimony from the ranks of the 6th Louisiana on the Second Manassas battle is found in Lieutenant Ring's diary, which offers scant detail. After spending the morning hours of the 29th on the extreme right, awaiting Longstreet's arrival, Ring reported, the regiment moved to a new position [behind Lawton's Brigade in the center] "and remained there until two o'clock p.m. when we were ordered to the front and our Brigade turned over to the command of Gen. A. P. Hill, who ordered us into the hottest of the fight immediately." Ring provided no further details.[45]

General Hill could have cleared up any possible confusion over where and when the Louisianians came to his aid, but his report also is devoid of much detail. "The evident intention of the enemy this day was to turn our left and overwhelm Jackson's corps before Longstreet came up," explained Hill, "and to accomplish this the most persistent and furious onsets were made by column after column of infantry, accompanied by numerous batteries of artillery. Soon my reserves were all in, and up to 6 o'clock, my division, assisted by the Louisiana Brigade of General Hays, commanded by Colonel Forno, with a heroic courage and obstinacy almost beyond parallel, had met and repulsed six distinct and separate assaults, a portion of the time the majority of the men being without a cartridge."[46]

Historian John Hennessy, who has written the most exhaustive account of Second Manassas, links Forno's advance to the later attack of Nagle's brigade, which came at 4:00 p.m. or after. Nagle's attack was directed against Lawton's Division, in the center, and the brigade of Brig. Gen. Charles Field, of Hill's Division, immediately to Lawton's left. After Nagle's attack broke the Confederate line in this sector, Hennessy wrote, "Lawton ordered Forno's brigade to move quickly to Field's support." While this is possible, it seems inconsistent with the time cited by Forno and Early, and by Jackson's and Lee's statements that the Louisianians went to the aid of Gregg's Brigade, not Field's. In any event, Nagle's initially-successful assault also sputtered out for lack of support, at a cost of another 500 Federal casualties.[47]

After Nagle's failure, Pope tried one more time to break Jackson's line on the left, where Hill's bone-weary men were barely hanging on. This last major assault, about 5:00 p.m., came close to swamping Gregg's and Thomas' defenders until Jackson sent Early with his brigade, plus the 8th Louisiana (which had just come back from its ammunition-gathering) in the nick of time. The long day ended with Jackson's weary men firmly in position along the unfinished railroad, with hundreds of Federal dead and wounded sprawled before them, the human wreckage of Pope's uncoordinated attacks.[48]

It was just after Early's successful counter-attack that the Louisianians lost their brigade commander. About 6:00 p.m., as activity on the front slackened, Colonel Forno was seriously wounded by a Union bullet and taken to the rear. Lieutenant Ring recorded the sad event in his diary, noting that the 6th Louisiana's Colonel Strong assumed command in Forno's place. Now, for the second time this year, the 6th Louisiana provided the commander of the brigade, albeit temporarily. For Henry Strong, the chance to command the famed Louisiana Tigers would be tragically brief.[49]

The elevation of the Irish-born Strong to command the brigade—the first time the Tigers had been led by an immigrant—put the 6th Louisiana under command of Maj. William Monaghan, another Irishman. The major, only recently returned after two months as a prisoner of war, impressed Lieutenant Ring with his dash and daring. "Maj. Monaghan commanded the regiment during the rest of the engagement in the most gallant manner," penned the young diariest, "leading a dashing charge on his splendid gray stallion, which with his own strikingly commanding person made him a conspicuous mark for the enemy's fire."[50]

If Monaghan was a conspicuous target, however, he had the luck of the Irish, for he emerged from the battle unscathed. Many others in the regiment were not so fortunate. As the Louisianians hung on to their position in Hill's sector along the railroad embankment for the rest of the afternoon and evening, the close combat with bayonets and fierce musketry took a tragic toll. The regiment lost seven killed, six of whom were Irishmen, and 13 wounded in the fighting of August 29.[51]

Combined with the 35 casualties at Bristoe Station, the regiment had lost 55 men in two days. It is uncertain exactly how many men the regiment carried into these battles, but a muster roll report dated August 31, the day after the fighting ended at Manassas, showed 374 men present for duty out of an aggregate on the regimental rolls of 780. Adding back the casualties, it would appear the 6th Louisiana went into the fights with an effective strength of some 425, and lost about 13 percent in the two days of fighting on August 27 and 29.[52]

As darkness ended the fighting along the unfinished railroad, the Louisianians, exhausted and out of ammunition, were sent to the rear to replenish their cartridge boxes. According to Lieutenant Ring, the 6th moved two miles to the rear to Jackson's ammunition trains, where the regiment spent the night. Along with the rest of the brigade, it remained in the rear in reserve much of the next day as the three-day battle reached its decisive climax. There is little record of the regiment's activities on Saturday, August 30. "We were relieved and sent back two miles to the rear," wrote Ring, "where we remained until the next day at two o'clock [p.m.] when we were ordered to the front to support Gen. Hill's batteries." In his report on the battle, General Early stated simply that, on August 30, "Hays' brigade had gone to the rear to get ammunition, and did not return."[53]

Colonel Strong of the 6th Louisiana commanded the brigade on the third day of battle, but it is impossible to determine whether his inexperience in command contributed to the absence of the 1st Louisiana brigade at the front as the climax approached. Probably Strong was simply waiting for orders, which did not come until early in the afternoon. An undated and unsigned account of the 1st Louisiana Brigade's actions at Second Manassas, which appears to have been written by one of the brigade's members after the war, claims that after the brigade fell "back to renew our supply of ammunition, the Brigade remained unemployed [on August 30] until 3 o'clock p.m., when Col. H. Strong of the 6th, who had assumed command, received orders from Gen. Lawton, commanding division, to join him. Before reaching him, Col. Strong was halted by Gen. A.P. Hill, who ordered him to support his batteries then engaged on the extreme left of our Army." Pressed into service around Hill's guns, the men of the 6th Louisiana and the other regiments of the brigade spent the afternoon on the far left of Jackson's line as Generals Lee and Longstreet orchestrated the decisive blow against Pope from the other end of the line.[54]

Pope had been convinced from the outset of the battle that he would overwhelm Jackson before Longstreet arrived. On the morning of the 30th, still ignoring evidence of Longstreet's arrival, Pope believed that Jackson's army had begun to retreat toward Thoroughfare Gap. Misled by the pullback of some Confederate troops who had mistakenly taken position during the night well in advance of Jackson's line, Pope about noon on the 30th ordered his army in "pursuit" of what he insisted was a retreating and beaten foe. The Federal "pursuit" once again ran into the fierce resistance of Jackson's determined troops along the railroad embankment. Once again Union assaults bent and threatened to break that line, but the Confederates grimly held on. At one point, the hard-pressed 2nd Louisiana Brigade, commanded by Brig. Gen. William Starke, ran short of ammunition and resorted to throwing rocks at the startled Union attackers.[55]

It wasn't the rock-shower but rather the full weight of Longstreet's Corps which finally proved decisive on the afternoon of August 30. Longstreet's artillery, posted on high ground to the right of Jackson, poured a deadly enfilading fire into the left flank of the Union assault. As the attack stalled, Longstreet unleashed his five divisions in a thundering counter-attack that collapsed the Union left and drove Pope's army back a mile to the east on Henry Hill, the scene of the Confederate defense that had earned Jackson his nickname thirteen months earlier.[56]

That night Pope decided to retreat to the fortifications at Centreville—the same ones, ironically that the men of the 6th Louisiana had helped construct when camped there a year earlier. Once again, as in the first battle of Manassas, the disheartened Union soldiers withdrew across Bull Run toward Centreville, having absorbed a brutal pounding by an enemy that their commanding general had insisted was defeated and in retreat.

As evening darkened, a drizzling rain began to fall, just as it had after the first battle in July 1861. The victorious Confederates lay down to sleep on the wet ground, littered with the awful slaughter of thousands. More than 3,000 dead and 15,000 wounded were strewn on the battlefield amid the debris of war. Jackson had lost nearly 4,000 men, Longstreet more than 4,700, but the Confederate losses were dwarfed by Pope's gory toll of 16,000 casualties.[57]

It was the biggest and bloodiest battle of the war so far, and it left both victors and vanquished exhausted. The 6th Louisiana bivouacked that night in the rain on the extreme left of the Confederate position, near Sudley Church, where the regiment had been ordered to remain in support of A.P. Hill's batteries. After a week of exhausting action which included more than 80 miles of marching and four days of fighting with little chance to rest or eat, the Irishmen collapsed into a fitful sleep.[58]

General Lee, however, was not satisfied with what he called "a signal victory." He saw one last chance to destroy Pope's army. Rather than attack the strongly fortified Federal position at Centreville, Lee again called on Jackson for a flanking maneuver to sweep around Pope's right and get between the Union Army and Washington, cutting off its line of retreat. On Sunday morning, August 31, Jackson's three divisions wearily began shifting north, crossing Bull Run and shuffling in the rain down a muddy country road to reach the Little River Turnpike, which slanted southeast toward Fairfax Court House and intersected Pope's line of retreat long Warrenton Turnpike at the village of Germantown, a few miles east of Centreville. The pace of the march was slow, reflecting the muddy condition of the roads, the fatigue of the men and an unusual tolerance on the part of Jackson, who stopped the march after dark, having moved only eight miles. Jackson's troops rested that night along Little River Turnpike.[59]

By mid-morning on September 1, Pope had received enough intelligence of Jackson's flank march to order a strong force to meet the Confederates on Little River Turnpike while the rest of the Union army began a wholesale retreat to Fairfax Court House, from which Pope could easily fall back to the defenses around Washington. As the Louisianians advanced slowly down the turnpike that afternoon, the Federal IX Corps led by Brigadier General Isaac I. Stevens (replacing the ill Maj. Gen. Jesse Reno) marched north from Centreville to engage them. The opposing forces were on a course to collide two miles east of an old mansion named Chantilly, at a ridge known as Ox Hill. The clash would prove to be a humiliating and damaging fight for the proud Irishmen of the 6th Louisiana.[60]

Jackson moved his column slowly to allow Longstreet's Corps, a half-day's march behind him, to close within supporting distance. The approach to Ox Hill was cautious. About the time the column passed the old Chantilly estate, Ewell's Division was placed in two columns, one marching on each side of the road, with the artillery in the road. In this arrangement, Trimble's Brigade and the Louisiana Brigade (under Colonel Strong) advanced south of the Little River Turnpike, while the brigades of Lawton and Early marched north of the road. About 4:00 p.m., the parallel columns reached Ox Hill, where the Ox Road, running north and south, crosses Little River Turnpike about two miles east of Germantown, where Pope was concentrating his forces to block Jackson. Here the Confederate commander, having received reports of Union forces moving eastward from Centreville, placed his artillery on high ground north of the Little River Turnpike and deployed his three divisions in line south of the turnpike, astride Ox Road.[61]

Dark thunderclouds boiled high in the sky over the wary Confederates as they moved into position in the woods and fields south of the pike. Jackson's Division under General Starke, which had led the column's march, filed off to the east to form the left of the Confederate line. Next Ewell's Division, under Lawton, took position in the center, while Hill's Light Division extended westward to form the right of the Confederate line. The position taken by the Louisiana regiments under Colonel Strong was near the edge of a woods facing a grassy field of perhaps 30 acres, bordered on the west by a cornfield of roughly the same size. The 6th Louisiana faced the open grassy pasture, which provided a good field of fire should the enemy approach from the south, as expected. The Louisianians' line stretched from near the Ox Road westward to almost the northeast corner of the cornfield. It connected on the left with Trimble's Brigade, which was astride Ox Road extending eastward, and on the right with Field's Brigade of A. P. Hill's division, in the woods north of the cornfield. Behind Colonel Strong and his Louisiana regiments, Early's Brigade deployed in close support, with Lawton's Georgians further to the rear and to the left, behind Trimble. With his line deployed, Jackson waited for Longstreet and Lee to come up.[62]

But the Federals were not about to allow Jackson time to wait. While the Confederates were deploying along the edge of the woods, General Stevens advanced his 1st Division of the IX Corps into the fields to the south. After some initial skirmishing, the Union line moved forward toward the woods. It was about 4:30 p.m. when the blue line swept across the grassy field toward the Louisianians. The advance coincided with a blackening sky whipped by a southwest wind that blew toward the Confederates. It was obvious a thunderstorm was about to break as the Federals came within musket range of their unseen enemy. Suddenly the dark woods spat thousands of darts of flame as the Confederates let go a single volley of musket fire. The fire, which came mainly from the Louisianians and Field's Virginians, staggered Stevens' lead regiments, including the 79th New York "Highlanders," a regiment composed mainly of Scottish immigrants whose advance faltered halfway across the grassy field in front of the Irishmen of the 6th Louisiana.[63]

As a Federal battery posted behind the advancing line sent shells screaming into the woods, the heavens boomed and flashed with thunder and lightening of their own. A drenching downpour pelted directly into the faces of the Southern troops, driven by the gusty wind. For the next two hours the battle and the storm raged simultaneously, soaking the troops, obscuring visibility and generally confusing the whole affair. The full meaning of the phrase "fog of war" became painfully clear during this dark and memorable collision, as the two sides groped for each other in the blinding storm amid confusing movements of troops and animals. The nearly simultaneous breaking of the storm and the attack of Stevens' leading regiments caught the Confederates in the midst of deploying additional brigades through the woods. Initially, a slight gap existed between the left of Field's Brigade and the right of Strong's Louisianians, and as the battle opened, Gregg's Brigade of Hill's Division was moving up to fill the gap, while two other brigades from Hill's Division marched through the woods to take up positions of support. With these brigades milling about them as the battle opened, Strong's Louisianians were not fully settled and ready for action.[64]

At about 5:00 p.m., General Stevens, after deploying other brigades into action, moved to the front of his lead brigade to rally the 79th New York, a regiment he had once commanded. Stevens found his son, Capt. Hazard Stevens, lying wounded by the initial Southern volley that had stalled the Highlanders' advance. After speaking briefly to his son, the general rushed forward and took the regiment's standard from a fallen color-bearer. Ignoring the protests of his Scotsmen against such a rash move, Stevens personally led the regiment forward, waving the flag and shouting, "Forward my Highlanders, follow your general." The Federal line surged ahead with other regiments conforming to the movement of the 79th New York, which dashed through the rain toward the woods and Strong's Louisiana regiments.[65]

Soaked by the lashing storm, many of the Confederates found that wet powder prevented their muskets from firing as the attack broke upon them. But others somehow managed to keep up a brutal fire, dropping Federals in the grassy field and adjacent cornfield. One of those to fall directly in front of the Louisianians was General Stevens, whose brain was pierced by a bullet which killed him instantly. Still, his inspired Scotsmen dashed on, crashing into the woods and driving back the Louisiana regiments in some disorder. Fighting marked by the Celtic fury of clashing Scotsmen and Irishmen raged along the entire line of woods as Union attackers fell upon the Confederates in a hand-to-hand brawl under thundering skies.[66]

The 6th Louisiana, commanded by Major Monaghan, was positioned to receive the brunt of the 79th New York's attack. As the Unionists surged into the woods, Monaghan fell wounded and the regiment reeled in confusion under the assault. According to one contemporary account, the 6th Louisiana fell back after "being thrown into confusion by the loss of its gallant commander, Maj. Wm. Monaghan," while the 7th Louisiana also fell back after "being cut off from the rest of the Brigade by Trimble's Brigade." Strong's Louisiana regiments were driven some distance into the woods, but there they soon rallied and returned to the front for the rest of the battle.[67]

The confusion and brief rout of the Louisiana Brigade was caused not only by the violence of the 79th New York's assault, but also by an ill-timed maneuver on Colonel Strong's part. When the Highlanders first advanced into the field, the Louisiana Brigade was not in the best position to receive the attack, and during the brief interval before General Stevens led its renewed advance with sacrificial valor, Strong had begun to realign his regiments. Inexperienced in handling the brigade, Strong somehow maneuvered the command in such a way that it presented no front to the enemy when Stevens' yelling men came crashing into the woods. At least that is the explanation, and the blame, as set forth in the official report filed by General Early.[68]

As Monaghan and his 6th Louisiana and the rest of Strong's brigade were driven back into the woods by the Federal attack, the Louisianians became entangled with three regiments of Early's Brigade, which was just then moving eastward in response to an urgent request for support from General Starke, on the left of the Confederate line. The Louisianians had "fallen back in confusion and passed through these [Virginia] regiments, followed by the enemy, just as my orders were being carried out," Early reported after the battle. The rain and the thick woods prevented Early from seeing the confusion, but when he marched the rest of his brigade back to the scene, he claimed that "the enemy had been successfully repulsed by my three regiments," the 13th, 25th and 31st Virginia.[69]

Early pinned the blame for this tangle of Confederates in the woods squarely on Colonel Strong, whom he later labeled as "entirely inexperienced in the management of a brigade." The Louisiana Brigade fell back in confusion, he reported, because of "an attempt by the officer in command, Colonel Strong, to change its position when the enemy were advancing, and that his want of sufficient skill in the command of a brigade caused him to get it confused, so that it could present no front, and it therefore had to fall back."[70]

Others placed the blame elsewhere. Father Sheeran, the Louisiana chaplain, claimed that a Georgia regiment "broke and retreated," triggering panic after "some Greenhorn, acting as Adjutant" came running down the line screaming that three heavy columns of Yankees were about to flank Strong's brigade. The false alarm "caused a panic among some of our regiments," precipitating the Georgians' pullout and the general retreat.[71]

Lieutenant Ring, in the midst of the battle, saw it differently, implicitly blaming General Lawton for failing to provide support when the Louisianians came under attack. "Our division being badly handled," Ring wrote in his diary, "our brigade had to bear the brunt of the battle unsupported for two hours. Our regiment after fighting against desperate odds for two hours fell back in confusion when Maj. Monaghan was wounded." Ring added that the 6th Louisiana rallied and went back into the fight under command of Capt. William H. Manning of the Violet Guards, Ring's company.[72]

Confusion and mistake were a hallmark of this fight, variously called the Battle of Chantilly or Ox Hill. Near the end of the affair, Union Maj. Gen. Philip Kearny inadvertently rode into the Confederate line. In the rain and the dark, Kearny did not know the troops about him were Southerners, and they did not know immediately that he was a Federal officer. When Kearny spoke to them, they realized he was the enemy and demanded his surrender. Kearny instead wheeled and spurred his horse to escape and was fatally shot from behind. In two and a half days at Manassas, no general officer had been killed, but at Chantilly, two promising Union generals—Kearny and Stevens—were lost.[73]

The indecisive battle sputtered out in the darkness and the rain after more than two confusing hours. The Federals pulled back and resumed their retreat toward Washington, confident they had stopped Jackson in his effort to trap them while in retreat. The Confederates remained on the battlefield for the night amid an eerie scene. "We camped on the field, sleeping side by side with the dead of both armies," one survivor remembered. "It was very dark; occasionally the moon would come from under a cloud and show the upturned faces of the dead, eyes wide open seeming to look you in the face."[74]

The stormy affair at Chantilly proved to be a humiliating episode for Colonel Strong and his comrades in the 6th Louisiana, whether or not he was to blame. It was certainly an inauspicious debut as a brigade commander. Given the blunt condemnation written in Early's official report, it is likely that the general confronted Strong in person and issued the kind of tongue-lashing for which the irascible, profane Virginian was famous. The consequences of the battle were bloody and demoralizing for the whole brigade, which suffered the highest casualties in Jackson's command—33 dead, 99 wounded and three missing. Once again, the 6th Louisiana took the heaviest losses in the brigade, with nine dead and 32 wounded.[75]

The Battle of Chantilly, which ended the Virginia campaign that had begun when Jackson was sent to Gordonsville on July 13, climaxed a deadly week for the 6th Louisiana. In just six days, the regiment had fought three battles—Bristoe Station, Manassas and Chantilly—and had lost 26 killed and 69 wounded. These 95 casualties reduced the effective strength of the regiment by roughly 20 percent. In the large scheme of the war, Chantilly was a minor engagement, but for the 6th Louisiana, it produced more casualties than Gaines' Mill, Malvern Hill, and Second Manassas. The battle also put a psychological damper on what had been a brilliant and victorious campaign by Lee's Army of Northern Virginia, which had swept the Federal army out of Virginia and opened the road North.[76]

Chapter Six

Raiding North: BLOODY SHARPSBURG

"We stood there about half an hour and found ourselves all cut to pieces."

— Lieutenant George P. Ring, Company K

The Battle of Chantilly ended a long spring-summer campaign that had forged the 6th Louisiana into a battle-hardened fighting unit. The string of battles and marches had also exhausted the men and depleted their ranks. In four months, since the beginning of Jackson's Valley Campaign, they had marched hundreds of miles in Virginia's heat and fought the enemy in ten battles and numerous skirmishes. They had survived on scanty rations and whatever they could scavenge from fields and orchards, wearing out their clothes, shoes, and equipment in the process. As autumn approached, the regiment was worn down to less than half its springtime strength.

Losses tell the story. The 6th Louisiana had suffered more than 300 casualties since entering the Shenandoah Valley four months earlier. Official records evidence 60 killed in action and 207 wounded in that period—numbers that understate true casualties. At least several dozen more were taken prisoner in various engagements. Most of these would return to the regiment after being paroled and exchanged, but others would decide they had seen enough of war and take the oath of allegiance to the United States, a signed promise they would fight no more and would not return to any Confederate state during the war. The summer's toll is reflected in the regiment's muster rolls for July-August 1862. The rolls show an aggregate strength of 780 officers and men—all those nominally in the regiment, present or absent. The number actually present for duty at the end of August, however, was only 374. The rest were sick or wounded, detailed to other duty, taken prisoner, on leave for various reasons or absent without leave—a growing problem for the 6th Louisiana as well as Lee's army as a whole.[1]

The hard marching that General Jackson demanded of his men led to a severe problem of straggling, as some men fell out of the ranks exhausted and unable to keep up. Others took advantage of opportunities to scour the countryside for provisions or to loot the dead on battlefields, falling behind as the regiment moved on. The growing problem of widespread absences without leave went beyond these temporary slackers to a deeper danger for Lee's whole army—desertion.

There had been deserters from the very beginning of the war. A few men, including Irish-born Phillip Duggan of Company F, deserted the regiment after a taste of training camp, drifting back to New Orleans even before the 6th Louisiana left for Virginia. Pvt. James Brady, a 25-year-old New Orleans Irishman enrolled in Company D, the Tensas Rifles, is recorded as having deserted on June 11, 1861, about the time the men were boarding the trains to Virginia. Three German-born men from Company G—a sergeant, a corporal and a private—deserted en route to Virginia as the train carrying the 6th Louisiana stopped in Knoxville, Tennessee. There also had been a few deserters from the regiment's camps during the fall of 1861 and the following winter.[2]

An unnamed 6th Louisiana deserter left camp at Centreville on Christmas Day, 1861, found his way into Union lines, and gave Federal officers good estimates of Confederate strength around Manassas. He also gave Federal authorities what may have been their first word of the "Quaker guns" that became infamous after the Confederate forces abandoned their fortifications in March 1862. The deserter told the Federals that "logs shaped like guns, the outer ends painted black, are put into position to appear like the guns from the outside," and that the informant knew this to be true "having helped to make and place in position those mock guns." Allen Pinkerton, the private detective who served the Union army as a top intelligence agent, reported the information provided by this 6th Louisiana deserter to General McClellan, claiming that it was worthy of belief.[3]

The desertion problem grew more serious as the campaign of 1862 wore on. Muster rolls for the late spring and summer period show a growing number of men absent without leave. The roll for Company F, one of the nearly all-Irish companies, showed only 32 of its 93 officers and men present for duty at the end of August; 31 were listed as sick, 19 as AWOL. The next muster roll, for September and October, listed 19 men as deserters.

Company B, Henrys Strong's recruits from New Orleans, listed 17 men as deserters during July and August of 1862. The names of the deserters were typically Irish and German, with a few common American names. Muster rolls for the end of August show only 17 of 66 men present for duty in Company D; 28 of 56 in the German-dominated Company G; the Pemberton Rangers; 19 of 65 men of Company H, the Orleans Rifles; 43 of the 81 men in Company K, the Violet Guards. Of course, illness, detached duty, straggling and other causes contributed to the thinned ranks of the regiment at this time. But it is clear that the AWOL problem was a growing one, and not just for the 6th Louisiana.

General Lee worried that the problem of straggling and desertion was so severe that it would undermine the success of his movement north of the Potomac River. In a letter to President Davis written from Hagerstown, Maryland four days before the Battle of Sharpsburg, Lee confessed, "One great embarrassment is the reduction of our ranks by straggling, which it seems impossible to prevent with our present regimental officers. Our ranks are very much diminished—I fear from a third to one-half of the original numbers—though I have reason to hope that our casualties in battles will not exceed 5,000 men."[4]

A week later, following the bloody battle that produced more than double the losses that Lee had optimistically projected, the Confederate commander wrote again to Davis to report that his army was "greatly paralyzed" by the increasing problem of stragglers. "I have taken every means in my power from the beginning to correct this evil, which has increased instead of diminished," Lee complained. "A great many men belonging to the Army never entered Maryland at all; many returned after getting there, while others who crossed the river kept aloof." Lee appealed to Davis for "some immediate legislation" to crack down on soldiers gone AWOL, "which ought to be construed into desertion in face of the enemy" subject to "the most summary punishment," presumably including execution. Lee would eventually discover that the problem would worsen rather than improve as the war dragged on, regardless of penalties or threats.[5]

The worsening problem of desertion and straggling can be at least understood, if not excused, by considering the relentless demands and physical suffering the war imposed on the weary soldiers. The Army of Northern Virginia was an ill-fed, poorly-shod, ragged and weakened army by September of 1862. Even as he planned his bold thrust across the Potomac, General Lee admitted to President Davis that the army was not well equipped for the move he was planning to make. "It lacks much of the material of war, is feeble in transportation, the animals being much reduced, and the men are poorly provided with clothes, and in thousands of instances are destitute of shoes," the Confederate commander wrote on September 3. Ironically, the army's destitute condition was one argument in favor of raiding the rich countryside of Maryland and Pennsylvania, where forage for the horses, food, clothing, and shoes for the men would be easily obtainable; war-ravaged northern Virginia could no longer provision the army.[6]

Despite these obvious drawbacks, Lee felt the time had come to carry the war to the North. The Federal army, discouraged and disorganized after its defeat at Manassas, was once again in turmoil, reorganizing a second time under General McClellan, whom Lincoln called back to command to replace the disgraced John Pope. Richmond was no longer at risk. A raid north would threaten Washington and panic the North, possibly increasing public sentiment in favor of making peace with the Confederacy. A victory in the North might induce England and France to recognize the Confederate government. Lee also believed—mistakenly, as it turned out—that Marylanders were ready to throw off the "oppression" of the Federal government and would welcome "liberation" by the Confederate army. Merely waiting for McClellan to reorganize the Federal army and mount a new offensive against either Lee or the Southern capital was far less attractive a strategy than carrying the war to the enemy while he was weakened by recent defeat. And so the die was cast: the Rebels would cross the Potomac for the first time.[7]

The battle-weary men of the 6th Louisiana had no such lofty strategic thoughts on their minds as they slept, under a hard rain, on the Chantilly battlefield on the night of September 1-2. They began to get some hint of the future, however, the next morning. Lieutenant Ring's diary records that "at daylight we were ordered to cook rations and prepare for more long marches." The jaded soldiers cooked and rested that day as Lee laid plans for the invasion. There was not much to cook. By this time, as Lee had admitted, the Confederates were running short of virtually everything an army needed—food, blankets, clothing, and forage for the horses. This would become the ongoing story of the Army of Northern Virginia for the rest of the war, as shortages made life miserable for the Confederate soldier.

The situation that faced Jackson's men as September 1862 began is described by General Early in his memoirs. "Provisions were now very scarce," Early wrote, "as the supply in the wagons with which we had started was exhausted. The rations obtained by Jackson's command from the enemy's stores at Manassas, which were confined to what could be brought off in haversacks, were also exhausted, and on this day [September 2] boiled fresh beef, without salt or bread, was issued to my brigade, which with an ear or two of green corn roasted by the fire, constituted also my own supply of food at this time." Early added, "I will here say that green Indian corn and boiled beef without salt are better than no food at all by a good deal, but they constitute a very weakening diet for troops on a long march, as they produce diarrhea."[8]

Whatever their diet or digestive conditions, the men of the 6th Louisiana took up the march again on September 3, moving northwest along the Georgetown-Leesburg Pike. They reached Leesburg on the following day, and camped there that night. By the following morning, as the long Confederate column marched toward White's Ford on the Potomac River, the Louisianians realized they were about to cross over into Maryland. "The greater number of our men were enthusiastic, expected that the Marylanders would flock to our standard by the thousands, and that thus recruited we would carry the war into the enemy's country," the Louisiana chaplain, Father Sheeran, wrote in his journal. In his own diary, the 6th Louisiana's Lieutenant Ring wrote that on "Sept. 5, 1862, we crossed the Potomac and at last set foot upon Yankee soil," reflecting the satisfaction of taking the war to the enemy. The troops waded waist-deep across the wide Potomac at the ford which lies about seven miles north of Leesburg. It was an historic moment for the Confederates, who had waited so long to give the comfortable Northerners a taste of war.[9]

The march along the green and rolling countryside of Maryland brought the regiment to the Baltimore & Ohio Railroad, along which it moved toward the city of Frederick. The Confederates were struck with the beauty and richness of the rolling Maryland terrain, which so starkly contrasted with the war-wasted fields of Virginia. Father Sheeran recorded the thoughts that must have been shared by many of his comrades in the Louisiana regiments: "The numerous cornfields growing abundant crops, the well stocked pasture ground, the numerous and beautiful orchards whose trees were groaning under the weight of delicious fruit, the granaries and barnyards thronged with poultry and swine presented a pleasing contrast with the desolate fields and plundered habitations of North Eastern Virginia. Here evidently," he concluded, "the people had only heard of the war, without having realized any of its sad ravages." During the march, the priest noted, "the people flocked to the roads to see us," but the reception wasn't as enthusiastic as some of the Tigers optimistically had expected. "Among the crowds we saw some friendly countenances," Father Sheeran recorded, "but the greater number looked upon us with seeming indifference."[10]

The Louisiana men finally got a chance for a good rest when Ewell's Division stopped to camp for three days at Monocacy Junction, on the railroad south of Frederick. There, along the banks of the little Monocacy River, they guarded the bridges over the stream and the roads approaching from Washington, D.C., 35 miles to the southeast. The 6th Louisiana men could not have known, of course, that this very place, so peaceful then, would be the scene of a battle for those among them still alive two years later. During their stay along the Monocacy, some of the officers and men took the opportunity to visit Frederick, where they thronged the barber shop, bought new shirts, and enjoyed a generally friendly reception from the townspeople, who waved to them from windows, doors, and balconies. For one soldier of the 6th Louisiana, however, the stay along the Monocacy proved fatal. On September 8, Pvt. Thomas Riley, a 27-year-old Irishman in Company D, was accidentally killed as the Confederates blew up a bridge over the river.[11]

The move into Maryland forced McClellan to begin moving part of his forces out of Washington to meet Lee's threat. As usual, McClellan moved slowly and cautiously. As his advance crept northwest toward Frederick, Lee moved to solve another problem—the existence of a Federal garrison of nearly 12,000 men at Harpers Ferry, some 15 miles south and west of Frederick. Such a large enemy force in his rear threatened Lee's line of communications and had to be eliminated. Once again, Lee turned to Jackson and his "foot cavalry" for the assignment: capture or destroy the Federal force at Harpers Ferry and then march rapidly to rejoin the rest of the army with Lee.[12]

On the morning of September 10, the 6th Louisiana with the rest of Ewell's Division began a long, counter-clockwise march into western Maryland, back across the Potomac River at Williamsport, and through Martinsburg to the Federal stronghold at Harpers Ferry. The town rested in a beautiful spot at the confluence of the Potomac and Shenandoah Rivers, completely surrounded by steep hills that commanded the low-lying river town. The roundabout march across Maryland and back into Virginia brought Jackson's troops in behind Harpers Ferry from the west, while other Confederate divisions under Maj. Gen. Lafayette McLaws and Brig. Gen. John Walker took up positions on the heights overlooking the town—McLaws on Maryland Heights across the Potomac, and Walker on Loudoun Heights on the Virginia side.[13]

By September 14, the Confederates had the Federal forces surrounded, looking up at enemy cannon on all the heights commanding their position. Jackson unleashed a storm of cannon fire from three sides on the 14th. Ewell's Division, including the Louisiana Brigade, was deployed in line of battle and preparing to assault the Union forces on the morrow. The Federals realized their position was hopeless, however, and before the assault got underway on September 15, the white flag of surrender appeared over the Federal fortress, drawing very "hearty and sincere cheers" from Ewell's men, who were thus spared an attack over difficult and hilly ground.[14]

"God seems to smile on our cause, judging from the general success of our arms in all quarters," Lieutenant Ring exulted in a letter to his wife written on the day of the Federal surrender. As a result of the surrender, "We have on our hands now between 9 and 11 thousand men, the same quantity of splendid arms, with a magnificent park of cannon. All this was taken without the loss of a man on our side as none of our infantry were engaged. We were not in this fight except as spectators."[15]

Nor did the men of the 6th Louisiana ever set foot in Harpers Ferry, for Jackson cordoned off the town to prevent looting. "A strict guard has been placed upon the town to secure the spoils from the soldiers," Ring told his wife. Jackson knew his men well and was taking no chances. His success at Harpers Ferry was complete: besides capturing 11,000 Federals, the Confederates took possession of 73 pieces of artillery, some 13,000 small arms and other critical supplies.[16]

While the outcome was a happy one for the Confederates, two weeks of hard marching had worn out the troops and left hundreds of stragglers along Jackson's long, circuitous route. In three and a half days, Jackson's men had marched over 60 miles, crossing two mountain ranges and forded the Potomac. The weather had been intensely hot and the roads dusty. Jackson's corps, which numbered over 22,000 men at Cedar Mountain in early August, should have numbered nearly 17,000 at this time, subtracting the losses in fighting against Pope; in reality, only some 11,500 effectives remained. Many never crossed the Potomac into

Maryland, and many more fell behind or deserted once they reached Northern soil. Regiments were shrinking daily as barefoot, discouraged, weary men dropped behind. Father Sheeran, riding the route from Harpers Ferry to Sharpsburg on the day after the Louisiana Brigade marched it, was shocked at what he saw. "The country was literally crowded with stragglers," he scribbled in his journal. "Some of the men excited my sympathy, for they looked sick and broken-down but others again I looked upon with contempt, for they evidently were professional stragglers. Some of them even threw their guns in the fence corners." Many officers, he noted with some disdain, were among the stragglers.[17]

Lieutenant Ring reflected the growing desperation of the officers of the 6th Louisiana in a letter to his wife from Harpers Ferry. "I hope to goodness that this Brigade will be left to guard this place and to recruit the ranks. We had only one hundred and ten men in the regiment to go into action with eleven officers. General Hays just came from Winchester to take command," he added, "and I hope he will inaugurate some system to keep our men in the ranks." Hays, who had been recovering from his wounds at Port Republic in June, rejoined the Louisiana Brigade on September 14. From then on, it would be known as Hays' Brigade. With Hays' return, Colonel Strong resumed command of the shrunken 6th Louisiana as Jackson moved to rejoin the rest of Lee's army.[18]

BRIG. GEN. HARRY HAYS

A veteran of the Mexican War, Hays was colonel of the 7th Louisiana Infantry before being promoted to lead the Louisiana Brigade. His Port Republic wound kept him out of action for several months, and a later wound at Spotsylvania effectively ended his career. He was an outstanding brigade commander. *National Archives*

Lieutenant Ring correctly guessed the next move would be to the north, across the Potomac. "I suppose the next step, now that we have got the enemy clean out of Virginia, will be an advance on the nice state of Pennsylvania and give the barbarous Dutchmen of hers a taste of the horrors they have inflicted upon the citizens of the Valley." But he did not look upon the prospect with enthusiasm, hoping instead to get a leave of absence, "as I am completely tired out with our constant marching." Jackson's roundabout maneuvering was almost too much for his men to bear. Ring's exasperation is clear in his letter home: "Since the 1st Sept., after having fought every day for ten days we have made a circuit through western Maryland and are now here almost where we started from," he wrote. "It is too much as the state of our ranks show, and if Jackson keeps on at it, there will soon be no army for him to command. I have only 11 men for duty now out of 112 four months ago, and I am most confoundedly disgusted at the idea of all the time being captain of a corporal's guard." One company of the 6th Louisiana had only four men present—two officers commanding two men, Ring added.[19]

While the capture of Harpers Ferry was indeed a bloodless spectator sport for the 6th Louisiana, the Irish Tigers and their comrades were about to be called to a battle remembered today as the bloodiest single day of the Civil War. On the evening of September 15, General Lawton, in command of Ewell's Division, was ordered by Jackson to march the division towards Shepherdstown on the Potomac. As the gray column moved out that evening, General Hays led the Louisiana Brigade down the road to Boteler's Ford, where it bivouacked for the night. At dawn the next day, the men again waded across the wide river and marched about three miles to a small Maryland village none of them had ever heard of: Sharpsburg.[20]

Lee was already present with the balance of the army and had assumed a defensive position west of Antietam Creek, which meandered through farmland and woods just east of Sharpsburg. McClellan's forces had caught up with the rear guard of Lee's army on September 14 at South Mountain, where a sharp engagement was fought before the Confederates withdrew to take a stand behind the Antietam, inviting a battle that would determine the fate of Lee's campaign into Maryland.

The 6th Louisiana arrived on the scene on the evening of September 16, the sound of skirmishing and sporadic cannon fire serving to foretell the blood and thunder that would come with the dawn. The regiment, depleted by casualties, straggling and desertion, probably numbered little more than 100 men. Indeed, the entire Louisiana Brigade was no larger than a regiment, as Hays could count only 550 effectives as he arrived at Sharpsburg. The tired Louisianians lay down in a woods that bordered a turnpike running north from Sharpsburg to Hagerstown, just behind a plain, whitewashed building that looked like a schoolhouse but was in fact a church of a German pacifist sect called the Dunkards, or Dunkers.[21]

About a mile to the north, Federal divisions were massing in the woods to attack at daylight on Wednesday, September 17. Three divisions of the Federal I Corps, commanded by the same General Joe Hooker whose troops fought the Louisianians at Bristoe Station, had crossed the Antietam on the afternoon of September 16. Hooker's 13,000 men bedded down in the woods just north of the Confederates as a drizzling rain fell on the anxious soldiers of both armies. In the darkness, occasional shots rang out between the opposing skirmish lines, which in places were so closely spaced the pickets could hear each other moving about. At midnight, the Federal XII Corps, under command of Maj. Gen. Joseph Mansfield, with two divisions of some 10,000 men, crossed the Antietam and went into camp about a mile behind Hooker. The rest of McClellan's army, which totaled more than 70,000 men, remained east of Antietam Creek.[22]

As September 17 dawned, Lee had no more than 26,000 fighting men available to face this massive Federal force. A. P. Hill's Light Division had been left behind to parole prisoners and secure spoils at Harpers Ferry, and two divisions under General McLaws were still on the march toward Sharpsburg. Even when they arrived, Lee would have no more than about 35,000 infantry at his command—barely half the Union strength. The Confederate commander deployed his available men a mile east of the town of Sharpsburg in a battle line stretching some four miles long. Jackson's command formed the left of the Confederate line. Formed largely along the Hagerstown Pike and massed in the woods behind it, "Old Jack's" veterans stretched southward to Longstreet's command, which formed the Confederate right. The Confederate line was stretched thin, with few reserves, though it hardly seemed so to General McClellan, who judged it to be at least twice its actual strength.[23]

Hooker, with his three divisions poised in the woods north of the Confederate left, spearheaded the Federal attack. As the first gray light of dawn appeared, between 5:30 and 6:00 a.m., Hooker ordered his brigades forward. His objective was the high ground around the Dunker

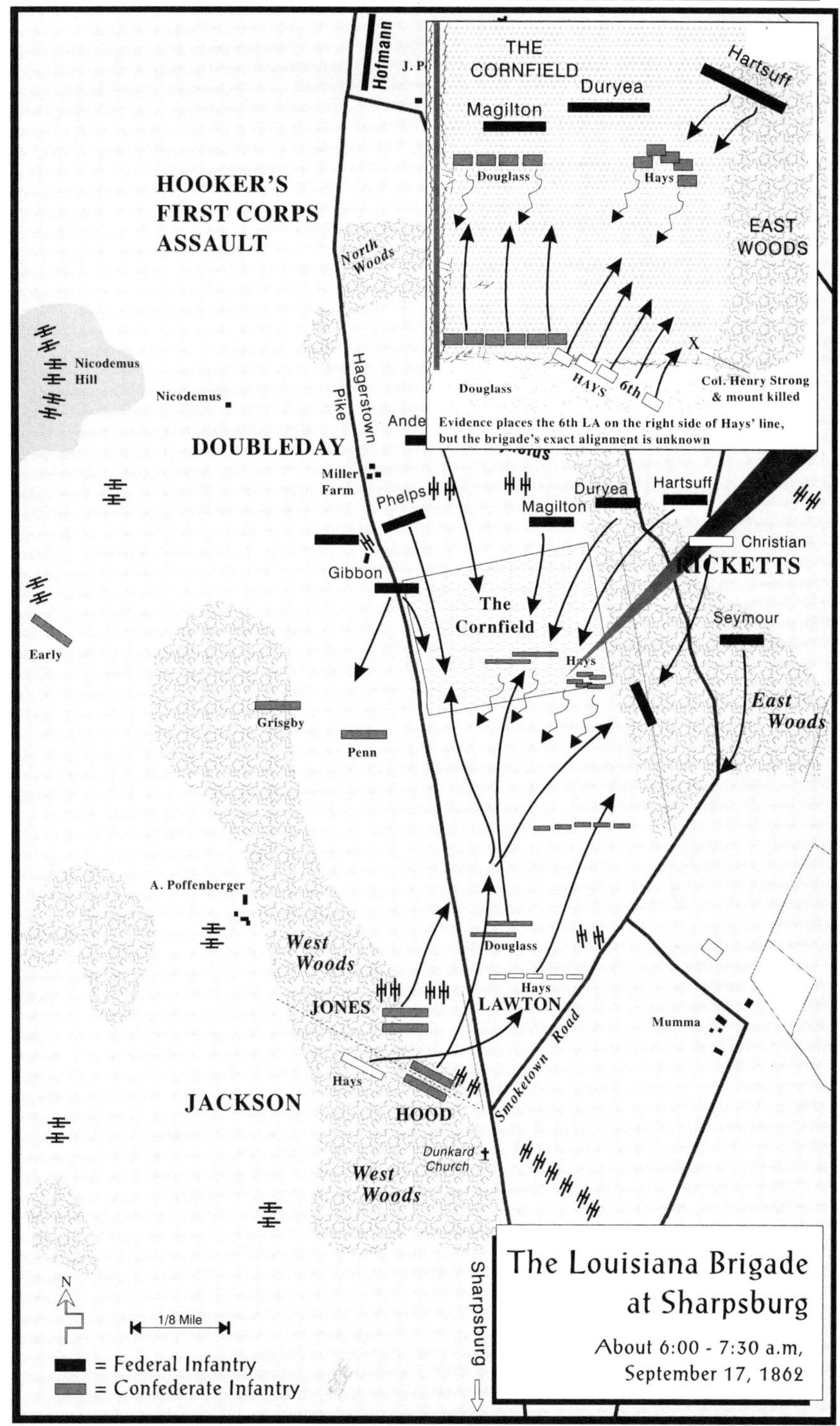

Theodore P. Savas

Church, three-quarters of a mile in front of the North Woods, where the Federals stepped off. This patch of forest occupied by the Union troops stood at the apex of a large terrain triangle. To Hooker's left, at the eastern base of the triangle, stood another patch of trees that would become known as the East Woods, while to his right was the West Woods and the little white church facing the Hagerstown Pike. In between lay David Miller's farm and its lush green cornfield of about 30 acres.[24]

The Federal line advanced warily through the morning mist across the fields of Joseph Poffenberger's and David Miller's farms. Just south of Miller's house and orchard lay the cornfield, the stalks leafy and tall, almost ready for harvest. The cornfield was bordered on the east by woods, and on the south by an open field, where two Confederate brigades—Lawton's and Trimble's, lie in line of battle, muskets ready. Some of the Southerners stood concealed in the tall corn. After the battle, General Hooker recorded a passage that painted a vivid picture of the scene that morning: "We had not proceeded far before I discovered that a heavy force of the enemy had taken possession of a corn-field. . .in my immediate front, and from the sun's rays falling on their bayonets projecting above the corn could see that the field was filled with the enemy, with arms in their hands, standing apparently at 'support arms.'"[25]

The 6th Louisiana was viewing the same scene from across the turnpike from the cornfield with Hays' Brigade. As Hooker's men advanced, a deafening artillery duel split open the stillness of the morning. After the Union corps commander saw the Southerners waiting in the tall corn, he called up six batteries, totaling 36 guns, and arrayed them on the northern edge of the cornfield, where they opened with a deadly storm of canister. Four batteries of Confederate artillery, stationed on a plateau near the small church, blasted the oncoming Union men with shot and shell, while Jeb Stuart's horse artillery poured fire into the Federal flank from a hill northwest of the church. In addition to Hooker's cannon, long-range rifled guns of McClellan's reserve artillery across Antietam Creek blasted the open fields with an enfilading fire that killed and maimed scores of Confederates before they had fired a shot.[26]

Hooker, awed by the carnage wrought by his artillery, remembered that "in the time I am writing, every stalk of corn in the northern and greater part of the field was cut as closely as could have been done with a knife, and the slain lay in rows precisely as they had stood in their ranks a few moments before. It was never my fortune to witness a more bloody, dismal battlefield."[27] The devastation was no less for Hooker's advancing regiments. Into this crossfire of cannon the Northerners marched, out of the woods and into the cornfield toward the Confederates of Lawton's and Trimble's brigades. When they came within sight, the Southerners rose up and poured musket fire into their ranks, as cannons roared on all sides. The opposing lines stood 250 yards apart, firing as fast as they could reload, with each side taking heavy casualties. Lawton, looking to reinforce his two hard-pressed brigades, turned to Hays and ordered the Louisianians across the turnpike to back up his old brigade of Georgians, now commanded by Col. Marcellus Douglass. "We were ordered out into a ploughed field and told to lie down in a line of battle," Lieutenant Ring wrote to his wife three days later. "We were about three hundred yards behind a Georgia brigade." As the lieutenant remembered it, "We lay in that position with a fire from three Yankee batteries and one from a battery of our own answering, firing over our head, besides a fire of Infantry on the Brigade in front of us." In all the hard fighting Ring had experienced, he had never seen or heard such an artillery barrage. "I thought, darling, that I had heard at Malvern Hill heavy cannonading, but I was mistaken," he told his wife. "That half hour that we were lying in that field taught me to the contrary."[28]

While waiting to be ordered forward, the 6th Louisiana began suffering casualties. Still, no order to advance was forthcoming. The Georgians in front of them were being decimated, and those still standing were running out of ammunition. Colonel Douglass desperately called for General Hays to come to his aid. The Louisiana Brigade, with about 550 men present and ready, advanced into the maelstrom. Colonel Strong, riding his conspicuous white horse, led the 6th. Hays ordered the Louisianians to begin firing as they reached Douglass' line, then pushed the Tigers 150 yards further into the cornfield toward the East Woods under a devastating fire from enemy batteries that tore huge gaps in his wavering line. The Louisiana men collided with the Federal brigade of Brig. Gen. George Hartsuff, who already had been wounded and replaced by Col. Richard Coulter. The onrushing Louisianians drove Coulter's regiments—New Yorkers, Pennsylvanians and Massachusetts men—to the edge of the East Woods, where they rallied and hung on.[29]

"We had a good many killed & wounded before we got up, which we did when the Geo. Brigade got out of ammunition," Ring remembered. "We advanced some three hundred and fifty yards and then commenced firing upon the enemy who were in front of a wood about two hundred yards off, protected by a battery. We stood there about a half an hour and found ourselves cut all to pieces." They had charged into the cornfield, a killing ground that was to become legendary that day. It was a perfect hornets' nest of flying lead—musket balls, solid shot and canister, flying shrapnel. The field was a confusing swirl of death, shrouded in thick smoke from the cannon fire and musket volleys, and from a burning house just south of the cornfield. The combatants could barely see each other. "Just in front of us a house was burning," wrote a man in the 83rd New York, one of Coulter's regiments, to his family. "The fire and smoke, flashing of muskets and whizzing of bullets, yells of men, etc., were perfectly horrible." Men fell dead and wounded by scores, then by hundreds, as the minutes slowly ticked by.[30]

The lethal fire seemed especially devastating for the officers of the 6th Louisiana. Colonel Strong, mounted on his big, white horse, presented a conspicuous target and was among the first to fall. The Irish-born colonel "was killed while bravely leading his men in the charge," according to Lieutenant Ring. Strong and his horse, also hit, died where they fell in the cornfield near the East Woods. Seeing Strong go down, Lieutenant Ring rushed to his side and was himself wounded. "I was struck with a ball on the knee joint while I was kneeling by Col. Strong's body, securing his valuables," he wrote to his wife. "I got another ball on my arm and two on my sword in my hand, so you see I have cause to thank God that he has protected me in this great battle."[31]

Ring's wounds proved slight, but several other officers in the regiment were not so lucky. Captain Allen M. Callaway, commanding Company A, was killed along with his next in command, Lt. Micajah Little. Lieutenant George Lynne, commanding Company E, also fell mortally wounded. As the men of the regiment slugged it out with the Federals on the edge of the cornfield, their officers were dropping all around them. "Our Regiment went in with twelve officers, and five of them [were] killed and the remainder wounded," Ring told his wife. Another conspicuous target was the regimental color sergeant, John Heil, a German immigrant from New Orleans. Heil was killed carrying the 6th Louisiana flag across Miller's devastated cornfield. Another young German, Pvt. George Zeller of Company K, whose letters to his mother revealed a boyish enthusiasm over his life as a soldier, was shot in the stomach and would die the following day.[32]

The Louisiana Brigade held on at the edge of the cornfield only briefly until Hays yelled for his men to retreat to the Dunker Church. As they pulled back, the Federals stormed forward, one officer stopping to pick

This photo looks east across a section of cornfield and into the East Woods. On the morning of September 17, 1862, Hays' Louisiana Brigade, including the 6th Louisiana, attacked north toward the Miller cornfield from near the Smoketown Road (from right to left across the ground depicted in this image). The brigade was shattered and the Louisianians were slaughtered by the score. The 6th Louisiana lost almost 50% of its strength in about twenty minutes of combat, and its leader, Colonel Henry B. Strong, was killed in action. *Christopher Gannon*

up one of Colonel Strong's gloves to wave triumphantly over his head. As the Louisianians retreated to the safety of the church, Brig. Gen. John B. Hood's Texas Brigade charged into the field to take their place, driving the Federals back. At the church, the Louisiana general "gathered together the remnant of my brigade." It was a brigade in name only, for it numbered barely 200 men. The fragment of the 6th Louisiana which joined Hays at the church was a nearly leaderless band of bloodied soldiers. The battle was only an hour old, and the hour barely past 7:00 a.m., but the leadership of the 6th Louisiana was devastated and its ranks riddled. With its colonel on the field dead and other senior officers absent sick or wounded, command of the regiment passed to Capt. H. Bain Ritchie, a farmer from Big Cane who led Company C, the St. Landry Light Guards.[33] Ritchie collected the handful of men from his regiment to rally around Hays behind the church. After some time to rest and bind up minor wounds—Lieutenant Ring guessed the hour to be about noon—General Hays gamely led his men back onto the battlefield.

Colonel Henry B. Strong (inset), the commander of the 6th Louisiana, was killed at Sharpsburg. This large, white horse was photographed after the battle frozen in death in a strikingly life-like pose near the southwest corner of the East Woods. Careful research by historian William A. Frassanito determined it was Strong's mount. *Library of Congress*

They made it to the edge of the woods, where General Hood and his men were found hugging the ground under a "very severe" artillery fire. It was about this time that Captain Ritchie was killed, his temporary command of the 6th Louisiana ending quickly. Hays decided to hold his survivors where they were rather than risk more losses by either attack or retreat. "We remained in the front exposed to frequent shelling from the enemy until 5 o'clock p.m. when we fell back to a less exposed position," recorded Lieutenant Ring.[34]

The Louisiana Brigade was shattered in that awful morning on the field. Of the 550 men that Hays led into battle, 323 were killed or wounded—a casualty rate approaching an astonishing 60 percent. Hartsuff's brigade, which faced the Louisianians, fared nearly as badly. The 12th Massachusetts regiment, one of those colliding with the Louisianians, took 334 men into the battle and lost 224 of them, earning it the awful honor of suffering the highest casualty rate—67 percent—of any Federal regiment on this bloodiest day of the war.[35]

The 6th Louisiana suffered 11 killed and 41 wounded, about half the men who went into action. Five of its officers were dead, including the second colonel of the regiment to be killed within three months. Eight other officers were wounded. The toll of officers killed in the 6th Louisiana was more than double that of any of Hays' other four regiments. For the 6th Louisiana, the Battle of Antietam lasted barely more than an hour—that terrible hour in the cornfield.[36]

But for the two contending armies, the fight had just begun by the time Hays' Brigade withdrew to the Dunker Church. The battle would rage on with unprecedented violence and destruction, with but brief pauses, until sunset. The fighting continued near the West Woods for some time before making its way south toward a sunken farm lane near the middle of Lee's line of battle. Late in the afternoon the divisions of Maj. Gen. Ambrose Burnside's Federal IX Corps finally stormed across a stone bridge over the Antietam—one that ever after would carry his name—and drove toward Sharpsburg. Lee's army was on the verge of a spectacular disaster when A. P. Hill's timely arrival after a forced march from Harpers Ferry drove back Burnside's men and saved the day for the Confederates.[37]

Twilight fell on the bloodiest day of the war, a holocaust that produced over 23,000 American casualties. McClellan had lost over 2,100 dead and 9,500 wounded, many of whom would die in the coming days and weeks. While the Union army lost 25 percent of those who went into action, the battle cost Lee nearly a third of those engaged—more than 1,500 dead, 7,700 wounded, and 1,000 missing.[38]

Dawn of September 18 found the two battered armies holding their positions. Lee, with his back to the Potomac and his exhausted soldiers outnumbered more than two to one, was only one major blow away from disaster. But the cautious McClellan, who still had fresh divisions in reserve, did not attempt to administer a killing blow. The day passed quietly. The 6th Louisiana "remained all day within four hundred yards of the enemy's lines," Lieutenant Ring, its temporary commander, recorded in his diary. The officer corps of the regiment was so devastated that Ring, a lowly lieutenant, was in command for three days. When McClellan refused to renew the battle on the 18th, Lee saw his chance to escape across the river to Virginia. About midnight, the Confederate columns began pulling out in retreat to the Potomac, which the 6th Louisiana waded across, near Shepherdstown, at daylight on September 19.[39]

Lee's Maryland raid was over. While a tactical draw, the fight at Sharpsburg was a strategic victory for the Union. Lincoln used the occasion to issue his Emancipation Proclamation, freeing the slaves in the Rebel territory as of January 1, 1863. The Confederate commander's dream of delivering a stunning blow against the Federal army on Northern soil was now a lost hope.

But the Confederacy was not yet a lost cause, and with their determined comrades, the men of the 6th Louisiana gamely soldiered on.

Chapter Seven

A Winter and Spring of War: FREDERICKSBURG

"Those damned Louisiana fellows can steal as much as they please now!"
— *Maj. Gen. Jubal A. Early*

For several days after retreating across the Potomac, the weary men of the 6th Louisiana feared that the Union army would follow in pursuit. On September 20, when three brigades of Federal infantry crossed the river near Shepherdstown, the Louisiana Brigade was among the Confederate forces deployed to oppose them. "After a fight of a few hours near Shepherdstown we drove them back and through the river, killing and drowning a large number," Lieutenant Ring's diary relates. This fight ended "all ideas and desire for another attempt on the part of our Yankee friends to pay us another visit," Ring added with satisfaction.[1]

The repulse of this feeler sent out by McClellan helped convince him that the Confederates were still dangerous. The Union commander's subsequent decision not to pursue Lee's retreating army gave the tired Southerners a chance to rest and fill in their ranks as stragglers and wounded returned to their regiments. The northern Virginia countryside was populated by thousands of stragglers who had not crossed into Maryland, and their return after the retreat from Sharpsburg swelled the ranks of Lee's divisions. Along with the rest of Jackson's Corps, the 6th Louisiana spent nearly a month in camp at Bunker Hill, on the road between Martinsburg and Winchester, as autumn painted her colors on the wooded Blue Ridge. During this time, Lee formally reorganized the Army of Northern Virginia into two corps. The First Corps would be commanded by James Longstreet, and the Second Corps by Stonewall Jackson; both were promoted to lieutenant general. During the reorganization, the 14th Louisiana regiment was returned to the Second Louisiana Brigade, and the 9th Louisiana rejoined Hays' Brigade.[2]

The 6th Louisiana's only active duty during these autumn weeks was what Lieutenant Ring called some "civil engineering"—tearing up railroad tracks to deny their use to the enemy. Leaving their camp at Bunker Hill, the Louisianians spent several days destroying more than 20 miles of the Baltimore and Ohio railroad between Martinsburg and Harpers Ferry, which had been reoccupied by Federal troops. The regiment, along with the rest of Ewell's Division, now under command of General Early, moved across the Blue Ridge in late October to camp at Millwood, a village some 15 miles southeast of Winchester. There, the men spent several days in mid-November ripping up some 20 miles of the Manassas Gap Railroad.[3]

It was during this autumn of relative calm that a sad chapter in the regiment's history played out. Colonel Strong's death at Sharpsburg had been doubly depressing for the 6th Louisiana, for it seemed likely to result in the promotion of a man who was both unfit to command the regiment and held in low regard by the men. When Strong died, Lt. Col. Nathaniel G. Offutt was next in line to assume command, but he was probably the last man that the soldiers in the ranks wanted as their leader. In fact, Offutt was absent for the Battle at Sharpsburg, as he had been from all the regiment's actions since the battles around Richmond. Offutt, the only son of a wealthy planter from Washington, Louisiana, in St. Landry Parish, had been openly charged with cowardice in battle by officers and enlisted men in the regiment, and had been taken to a hospital in Lynchburg, Va. in August, complaining of health problems.[4]

The charges against him came in a sensational letter written July 17, 1862, by Captain Ritchie, who had succeeded Offutt in command of Company C, and Lieutenant Ring of Company K. Written from Richmond after the Seven Days' Battles, the letter boldly laid out charges of "cowardice in the face of the enemy" against their superior officer. They cited three damning examples from recent battles. At Port Republic on June 9, Ring and Ritchie wrote, "Lt. Col., then Major N. Offutt, while his regiment was engaged with the enemy, remained behind with the ambulances and was rebuked by a private soldier for so doing." Later that month at Gaines' Mill, where Colonel Seymour had been killed leading the brigade, Offutt again shrank from danger, the officers charged. "When his regiment was ordered to charge the lines of the enemy, [Offutt] remained at the foot of the hill sheltered by a tree, completely out of danger, and was there during the whole time his regiment was under fire, a space of one hour and a half, displaying a palpable instance of cowardice." Finally, they cited Malvern Hill on July 1, "when his regiment was ordered to charge the enemy's position, before they advanced one hundred yards, [Offutt] threw himself behind a large tree," pretended to be badly wounded, "and was carried to a place of safety by the ambulance corps, at which place he remained until next morning, when he rejoined his regiment, to the surprise of everyone, by which cowardly conduct he became the common talk of his men."[5]

Offutt, the officers concluded, had "completely lost all respect of the men and from that cause is totally incapacitated and unfit to command them." Besides the signatures of Ring and Ritchie, the letter carried the names of five privates and one sergeant of the regiment as "witnesses" to Offutt's conduct. It was a devastating indictment and a bold step for the men to take against a superior officer[6]

It's not known how Offutt or his superiors, including General Hays, immediately reacted to the letter. Within four weeks, however, Offutt had checked into the hospital in Lynchburg and had begun looking for a graceful exit for himself through his political connections. Lucien Dupree, a Confederate congressman from Louisiana, wrote the Secretary of War on September 13 that he had received a letter from Lieutenant Colonel Offutt "requesting me to endeavor to obtain for him some 'post' as his health has suffered much in the last sixteen months' campaign." Dupree sought to portray Offutt as a Southern patriot, noting that he was one of the first in the state to volunteer, "leaving behind all the comfort and luxury which his wealthy family were lavishing on one who is their only son." Nothing came of the ploy, and on October 5, Offutt wrote to General Hays from Lynchburg, claiming "my health will not allow me to go into the field for active service this winter," and asking that his resignation be accepted "as soon as possible." Hays quickly agreed, endorsing the request with a note that it would benefit the army. Generals Jackson and Lee approved, and Offutt's resignation was accepted November 5, closing an awkward chapter for all concerned.[7]

The departure of Offutt opened the way for Irish-born William Monaghan to take command of the 6th Louisiana. Unlike many of his foot soldiers, Major Monaghan was educated and literate. His reports and letters, in beautiful penmanship, reflect his learning and his experience as a Notary Public in pre-war New Orleans. Monaghan possessed a biting wit and sometimes wielded the pen as a rapier. In a letter recommending Pvt. Daniel Romer of Company E for a non-combat assignment, the 6th Louisiana colonel called Romer "half an idiot" who "is of no earthly use here, has never been in a fight, and has never done any duty with his company." Monaghan was also much older than most of his men and fellow officers, having enlisted at age 44. Wounded at the Battle of Chantilly, he had missed the bloody fight at Sharpsburg, but returned to the regiment shortly afterwards. With Monaghan's promotion, Joseph Hanlon became lieutenant colonel of the regiment and William Manning moved up to major. The deadly summer of 1862 had produced a wholesale turnover of the field officers of the 6th Louisiana—Seymour, Strong and McArthur were dead and Offutt disgraced and drummed out. Several new company commanders were named at this time, including George Ring, who replaced Manning as captain of the Violet Guards, Company K.[8]

By the time Monaghan became the 6th Louisiana's fourth colonel, the regiment scarcely resembled the one Colonel Seymour first led to Virginia. Thinned by casualties, sickness, desertion and detached duty, the ranks of the 6th Louisiana had dwindled to about the size of three full companies. The whole Louisiana brigade reflected the same condition. "On the 28th of November," Ring recorded, "our Brigade was reviewed by Gen. H. T. Hays and presented a very striking contrast to the one held at Camp Buchanan just seven months ago. Then our regiment numbered nearly as many men as the whole Brigade does now." The 6th's muster rolls for the end of October show only 289 men present for duty out of a nominal strength of 664. Several companies had almost disappeared. Company E, the Mercer Guards, had only a dozen men present. The Germans of Company G, the Pemberton Rangers, were down to 18 men fit for duty. Similarly, the Irishmen of Company I numbered only 21. The slaughter of officers at Sharpsburg left many companies under the command of first or second lieutenants.[9]

Colonel Monaghan found his men in poor shape to face the long cold winter that lay ahead. Many were barefoot, or nearly so; the muster roll remarks penned by officers at the end of October indicate the severest need was for shoes, though blankets, coats and other clothing also were scarce. "The Boys are shivering & huvering around their little chunk fires," wrote one Louisiana soldier. "Though as meny as black birds, we are sadly in need of clothing & Piticularly in Blankets & Shoes." So few men had footwear that by November, this soldier wrote, "our whole Army is very nearly Shoeless." In camp at Millwood, Captain Ring was impressed with the behavior of his men but upset about their uncomfortable condition. "Health of my men excellent, conduct in the difficult engagements beyond all praise," he wrote in his muster roll report. "The men are sadly in want of blankets and shoes."[10]

Monaghan's poorly-equipped soldiers were hardly prepared for a another period of long, hard marches in miserable weather, yet that was what they were in for. As November's winds and freezing rains chilled the troops, the Army of the Potomac began to move, and Lee moved in response. McClellan, after resisting Lincoln's urging that he pursue and destroy Lee's weakened army, moved his own men into Virginia east of the Blue Ridge, concentrating around Warrenton. This put the Federals in a position to drive southward toward Richmond before Lee could move his scattered forces there. The Confederate commander could not ignore this threat, and marched his own forces in the same direction.

The 6th Louisiana left its camp at Millwood on November 21, crossing the Blue Ridge with the rest of Jackson's Corps into the Shenandoah Valley, where its movement would be screened from Federal eyes by the mountains. Back in the familiar surroundings of their springtime campaign, the men again were driven at a fast, Jackson-style pace. The first day's march to Strasburg covered 28 miles, Captain Ring noted in his diary, "and keeping up that lick until the 26th November, when we halted for two days at Madison Court House, marching one hundred and fifteen miles, crossing two gaps in the Blue Ridge Mountains, in five days." General Early remembered the march years later: "The weather had now become quite cool, and our daily marches were long and rapid, and very trying to the men. On this march I saw a number of our men without shoes, and with bleeding feet wrapped in rags." The march pushed eastward, finally arriving at Fredericksburg, along the Rappahannock River, on December 1. Here the men of the 6th Louisiana went into camp in a place that would be remembered for its bitter winter weather and two major battles that would etch the name of Fredericksburg into the history of the regiment.[11]

The historic city located on the Rappahannock River was a thriving industrial and commercial center of 5,000 residents as the Civil War began. By early December 1862, most of its citizens had fled by the time the opposing armies gathered on opposite banks of the Rappahannock. The Union army was now under command of Maj. Gen. Ambrose E. Burnside, who had replaced McClellan on November 9 after Lincoln lost patience with "Little Mac's" excessive caution. Burnside moved his army to the east bank of the Rappahannock opposite Fredericksburg, prompting Lee's move to the western side of the river to oppose a crossing. The 6th Louisiana's long march from the Valley of Virginia had brought it to a place called Skinker's Neck, a shoe-shaped bend in the Rappahannock some 12 miles downriver from Fredericksburg, where Lee had dispatched Early's Division, anticipating a possible flanking move by Burnside. The Louisianians camped and picketed the river for several days, braving the cold weather and waiting for the Federals' to make the next move.[12]

Burnside showed his hand on December 11, when his engineers started laying three pontoon bridges across the river directly into the town of Fredericksburg, and three more down river a mile or two. Rather than a flank attack, the Union commander had decided to launch a frontal assault through the town to the strong positions of Lee's army on the heights above it. There, Lee had posted Longstreet's Corps on the left, immediately behind the town itself, and Jackson's Corps on the right. The Confederates enjoyed the cover of woods on the hills, facing an open field of fire across a broad flood plain that the Federal troops would be forced to cross under murderous hail of artillery and musketry. Burnside could scarcely have chosen a more perfect killing field for his luckless troops.[13]

The 6th Louisiana soldiers remained camped along the river at Skinker's Neck from December 1 to December 12, when Burnside's activity prompted orders for their march toward Fredericksburg. The regiment left Skinker's Neck about 5:00 p.m. on the 12th and marched until nearly 2:00 the next morning, according to Captain Ring. At daylight the Louisiana Brigade was moved to the extreme right of the Confederate lines, near Hamilton's Crossing, a station on the Richmond, Fredericksburg & Potomac Railroad five miles south of Fredericksburg. Its members dug into position on the wooded hill behind the railroad tracks as the Federals opened the battle. There they hunkered down under what Early called "quite a severe cannonade" from the Federal artillery arrayed along Stafford Heights on the opposite side of the river.[14]

The new general-in-chief had reorganized the Army of the Potomac into three "grand divisions," each consisting of two corps. Burnside's battle plan called for his Left Grand Division, under Maj. Gen. William B. Franklin, to assault the Confederate right, held by Jackson's Corps, while the Right and Center Grand Divisions of Maj. Gens. Edwin Sumner and Joseph Hooker took on Longstreet's Corps on the Confederate left. When the fog lifted on the morning of December 13, the men of the 6th Louisiana looked down on masses of Franklin's troops on the plain below. The all-out assault that they expected, and that Burnside thought he had ordered, never developed. A division of Pennsylvanians led by Maj. Gen. George G. Meade did make a temporary breakthrough into Jackson's lines a mile or so to the left of the Louisianians, but Franklin failed to follow up on Meade's advantage and the Pennsylvanians were driven back by a Confederate counterattack. By mid-afternoon, the 6th Louisiana moved with the rest of Hays' Brigade left toward the point of Meade's breakthrough, but the regiment remained in reserve and never became actively engaged. The shelling from the enemy's artillery, however, wounded twelve men of the 6th Louisiana and killed one—Pvt. Henry Rosenberg, one of the few Germans in the nearly all-Irish Company B.[15]

The main Federal assault was delivered against Longstreet's sector, particularly against Georgia and North Carolina troops posted behind a stone wall along a sunken road at the foot of Marye's Heights. Throughout the afternoon, one brigade after another were sent to their slaughter in one of the most courageous and hopeless assaults of the war. Burnside's disastrous Fredericksburg attack cost the Union army more than 12,500 casualties, while Confederate losses were 4,200. The Union commander reluctantly admitted defeat and withdrew his army back across the Rappahannock during the night of December 15-16. The men of the 6th Louisiana, dug in along the ridge, "were certain" that the Federals would attack again, "but to our great surprise, lo and behold, they had taken advantage of the night and were now safely back across the river," Captain Ring wrote. He couldn't resist a sarcastic footnote that the Yankees had concluded "that Fredericksburg was not a healthy locality for the safe and successful display of their fine military qualities."[16]

Ring's smug attitude toward the fighting ability of the Union troops was not warranted, as he and his comrades would discover the following spring when they would fight on this same ground. As the men of the 6th Louisiana congratulated themselves on defeating Burnside, they still faced a harsh winter in camp and a renewed Federal offensive the following spring that would prove much more costly to the regiment.

After the Battle of Fredericksburg, the two armies settled in to a frozen stalemate, facing each other across the Rappahannock River. Burnside made one abortive attempt in January to mount a flank attack on Lee's army by marching up the river, but torrential rains turned the roads into bogs that almost swallowed artillery, wagons, mules and men, making the advance impossible. After this infamous "Mud March," the disgraced Burnside was replaced as commander of the Army of the Potomac by General Joseph Hooker, a veteran of the army's operations who intended, when spring arrived, to live up to his nickname "Fighting Joe."[17]

During these cold winter weeks, the men of the 6th Louisiana were camped with the rest of Hays' Louisiana Brigade on a low range of hills near Hamilton's Crossing. The monotony of camp life was broken by occasional picket duty along the Rappahannock, where Union and Confederate soldiers were within hailing distance of each other across the 100-yard-wide river, but by mutual understanding there was no shooting as long as the armies remained stationary. The men sought relief from boredom and from the bitter cold in a bottle of whiskey when such could be scrounged, sometimes with sad results. In December a soldier in the 8th Louisiana froze to death after getting drunk and remaining outside all night.[18]

The Catholic chaplain attached to the 14th Louisiana, Father Sheeran, attended to many of the Louisiana troops and constantly fought a battle against drunkenness. In his war journal, Father Sheeran related an incident that was characteristic of his anti-drinking crusade. While riding his horse, the priest came upon "three men sitting around a miserable fire," and stopped to see who they were. "One of them attempted to come over to where I was standing, but fell on the way. I soon discovered that they were drunk and had a canteen full of whiskey." The Chaplain "shuddered when thinking of the condition of these miserable men. They were now hardly able to take care of themselves and I was satisfied if they should drink any more they would be frozen, for it was the coldest day of the season." Sheeran, well known to the men, asked the one with the canteen for a little nip of whiskey, claiming he was feeling very cold. "He looked at me with an eye of suspicion and said, 'Will you promise not to spill it?' I pledged my word that I would not." When the soldier reluctantly handed over the canteen, "I threw the canteen strap around my neck and gave spurs to my horse," riding off with the precious liquor. Initially angry, the soldiers soon "began to laugh quite heartily" at the prank of the priest, who advised them to return to camp.[19]

The winter of 1862-63 was particularly harsh for Virginia, with frequent heavy snows and freezing temperatures. "Snow nearly knee deep, weather wet, cold & disagreeable," Capt. Michael O'Connor of the 6th Louisiana's Company F wrote in his February muster roll report. O'Connor, an Irish-born storekeeper from New Orleans who succeeded William Monaghan in command of the company, also complained of the slim rations that the men subsisted on at this time. "Rations issued for the last two weeks consists of flour, one-quarter pound, bacon, one quarter-pound, sugar, three ounces for each man per day," O'Connor recorded. "Nothing else issued for some time. Notwithstanding, the men are in good health and spirits."[20]

Despite O'Connor's upbeat appraisal of health and morale, there was grumbling about the regiment's scanty diet. "The company complains of short rations, receiving only one-quarter pound of meat per day, or one and three-quarters pounds per week," an officer wrote on Company D's muster roll report. In fact, conditions among the Louisiana regiments were deplorable. Food, clothing, shoes, blankets, tents—all the bare necessities were scarce or unobtainable. The chronic lack of shoes kept some men from the ranks. In the 6th Louisiana's Company A, for example, 13 men were listed as absent for duty because they were "barefooted," according to the company's muster roll report dated December 31, 1862. General Hays' assistant adjutant general, John H. New, paints a grim picture of the brigade's condition in his inspection report for January 10, 1863, which listed discipline as "poor" in the 6th, 7th and 8th regiments, and "good" in the 5th and 9th. The 6th and 7th regiments were rated moderately good in drilling, the 9th "tolerable," the 8th "miserable" and the 5th was excused from drill for lack of shoes. The shoe shortage was severe in all the regiments.[21]

The assistant adjutant general felt so strongly about the "enormity of the suffering" in Hays' Brigade that on January 19, 1863, he wrote to John Perkins, a Louisiana representative in the Confederate Congress to seek his help. Among the 1,500 men of the brigade ready for duty, New wrote, "there are 400 totally without covering of any kind for their feet," and thus unable to march or do any effective service. "There are a large number of men who have not a single blanket," he added. "There are some without a particle of under-clothing, having neither shirts, drawers, nor socks; while overcoats, from their rarity, are objects of curiosity." He continued, "This destitution in the way of clothing, it must be remembered, is not compensated by close shelter and abundant food, for the troops have no tents and are almost totally unprovided with cooking utensils for the petty rations they receive." He did not write to complain against the government, New said, but in the hope that the congressman might be able to devise some plan for private donations or state action to relieve "the sufferings of our men."

Troops from other states were being supplied by individual contributions from home, Hays' adjutant noted, "while we of Louisiana have received nothing whatever since the fall of New Orleans." New begged understanding of his motives, saying he was sure Louisiana's representatives would work "day and night" to provide relief if they could see the sad plight of the men for themselves. "It is so sickening to move among our men in discharge of my duties as brigade inspector in preparing my official report, and see the agony they endure in this bitter cold weather, that I can refrain no longer from trying any and every expedient that holds out, however faint, a promise of bringing relief."[22]

New's heartfelt appeal had some impact. "Are the statements in this letter true?" Confederate Secretary of War James A. Seddon demanded of the army's Quartermaster General A. C. Myers. When shown New's letter, Myers "immediately sent up a special agent with 1,000 shoes, and complete suits for the brigade." A similar complaint letter from General Hays had been forwarded to General Lee "with the hope of finding out where the fault lies," Myers added. "Almost every day supplies are sent up. Yesterday, 3,000 of each article of clothing were dispatched."[23]

The men also attempted efforts of their own to relieve the shortages, including trading with the enemy. The pickets along the river were only 100 or so yards apart, close enough for shouted conversations and for arranging barter by boat. "At times quite a brisk traffic was carried on between the opposing lines," wrote William J. Seymour, the son of the late colonel of the 6th Louisiana who joined the 1st Louisiana Brigade in April 1863 as aide-de-camp (later becoming assistant adjutant general) to General Hays. "Logs were dug out and converted into miniature boats, to which ingeniously contrived sails were fitted; these little crafts were filled with tobacco and Richmond newspapers—the only articles of traffic that our poor fellows possessed. . . .The Yankees would send return cargoes of many acceptable articles, but the most eagerly sought after and highly prized were coffee and sugar, which the CS Government was too poor to supply its soldiers with."[24]

Father Sheeran participated in the cross-river commerce by sending a note asking if there were any Catholic chaplains in Hooker's army, receiving an affirmative answer from a Federal colonel. "I was much amused and indeed not a little surprised by the nautical skill displayed by our men in the construction, rigging and managing of their little craft," the priest wrote. By carefully setting sail and rudders, they could land their miniature boats almost wherever they wished on the opposite shore, he added, but the Yankees were not so skilled in such navigation, "our boys having sometimes to swim in after their ships and carry them."[25]

Contacts between the opposing pickets became cordial enough to permit occasional cross-river visits, even though such fraternization was forbidden. One of these, involving a soldier of the 6th Louisiana, became a celebrated incident that moved Captain Seymour to cite it as one that "showed the stuff of which the Confederate Army is made." In his diary, he tells the story of an unnamed private of the 6th Louisiana who was raised around Albany, N.Y., and moved to New Orleans only a couple of years before the war. While serving on picket along the Rappahannock in the spring of 1863, this transplanted Northerner discovered that a company of Yankees on the opposite bank were from his old home town of Albany, "and that several of them were old friends and acquaintances."[26]

Invited over to the Federal side for a visit, the 6th Louisiana private crossed the river to see if he could learn any news of his aged father and mother, from whom he had not heard since the war began. Instead, he was subjected to a sales pitch. "The Yankee Captain and his men used their utmost powers of persuasion to induce their visitor to desert from the Confederate Army, promising him a safe conduct to his Parents in Albany and that he should never be called on to do duty in the Federal Army; at the same time reminding him of his tattered clothing, scanty and indifferent food," Seymour related. "They spoke of the extreme privation & sufferings of a Confederate soldier and presented to him, in vivid contrast, the superior comforts and advantages of a Federal soldier."

This Yankee harangue backfired, according to Seymour:

> The ragged, half-starved 'Rebel' drew himself proudly up, his eye flashing and face all aglow with patriotic fervor, and contemptuously spurned the dishonorable offer. He told his tempters that he had oftentimes braved danger and death side by side with those dirty, ragged 'rebs' over the River, had shared with them the exposure and sufferings of the march and the privations of the Camp—was fully aware of the superior condition of the Federal troops, but that he would not desert his colors for all the gold that the Federal Government could command. He declared that he had embarked on what he considered a right-

eous cause and, if it should be the will of God, he would die fighting for it.

During the winter after the incident along the Rappahannock, Seymour pointed out, this same proud Rebel was again on picket duty along the Rapidan River "and has neither blanket nor overcoat to shield him from the sharp cutting winds as he performs his tour of picket duty in this bleak December weather."[27]

After a hard, dispiriting winter, both the weather and spirits began to improve with early signs of spring. Father Sheeran remembered being cheered by the sight of a large throng of Louisiana men gathered to attend his Easter Sunday Mass on April 5, 1863, despite an unseasonable snowstorm. "To see so many of our brave soldiers knee-deep in the snow, cheerfully awaiting the offering of the Holy Sacrifice of the Mass, was perhaps one of the most consoling sights of my life, and never did I pray more fervently for my congregation than on this occasion."[28]

Spring also brought an increase in drills and inspections, signs of preparation for a new season of war. Captain Seymour found the morale of the Louisiana troops excellent that April, as "a confident feeling pervaded the ranks that our army would be victorious whenever and wherever the battle should be joined." Lee, dug into a defensive posture along the hills overlooking Fredericksburg, waited for Hooker's move. It came in late April, with a bold Federal stroke that would force the Confederates to fight on two fronts simultaneously, with the 6th Louisiana in the thick of it.[29]

The first sign that Hooker was beginning his spring offensive appeared on Tuesday, April 28, with a bustle of activity on the Union army's side of the river. Tents were being struck, wagons assembled into line, columns of troops forming and marching in all directions. Captain Seymour rode into the town of Fredericksburg with Col. Leroy Stafford of the 9th Louisiana to check on the activity. From the steeple of the Episcopal Church, they looked on the opposite river bank to see "the hosts of the enemy, drawn up in battle array, their burnished arms glistening in the sunlight and their banners floating proudly in the breeze." The two officers rushed back to the Louisiana Brigade camp near Hamilton's Crossing, expecting to find marching orders, but Lee was biding his time in issuing any orders until the designs of the enemy became more clear.[30]

Hooker had devised a strategy designed to destroy Lee's army by trapping it between two converging forces. He would not repeat

Burnside's error by attempting a frontal assault against Lee's strong position on the heights behind the town of Fredericksburg. Instead he would divide his army of some 130,000 men into two forces. One wing, led by Hooker and composed of about two-thirds of his army, would move up the Rappahannock to cross the river well to the north and west, far behind the Confederate left flank, while the other crossed the river below Fredericksburg and pinned Lee's main body in place. It was a classic anvil and hammer plan: While Lee's Confederates were held against the anvil created by the large Federal force threatening a frontal assault, Hooker's hammer would swing down to crush the Southerners from the rear. This strategy, Hooker believed, would either force Lee to abandon his strong defenses behind the river and fight on open ground of Hooker's choosing, or squash the Confederate army, front and rear in the vicinity of Fredericksburg.[31]

The Federal commander ordered the campaign underway on April 27, when the XI and XII Corps began marching 25 miles upriver to Kelly's Ford, followed soon after by the V Corps. This right wing of the Army of the Potomac crossed the Rappahannock on the 29th and by the evening of April 30, the elated Federal commander had some 60,000 men in position around Chancellorsville, 12 miles in the rear of Lee's entrenchments on the Fredericksburg heights. Meanwhile, the three Federal corps composing Hooker's left wing—the I, III, and VI, all under command of Maj. Gen. John Sedgwick—moved into position to cross the Rappahannock facing Fredericksburg, as Union troops had done in December. One Federal division—that which was most directly visible to the Confederates on the heights—was ordered to stay in its camp so as to suggest that the Federal army remained stationary. Although Hooker's flanking maneuver was executed with some brilliance, landing a large force in Lee's rear without any resistance, the Confederate commander would not be fooled for long.[32]

For the 6th Louisiana, encamped at Hamilton's Crossing, the first signs of the new Federal offensive came in the foggy light of dawn on April 29. Heavy firing from pickets posted along the river signaled hostile activity. Under cover of a dense fog, Union troops were furiously paddling across the Rapphannock in boats about a mile below the town of Fredericksburg, at the same place where General Franklin's force crossed in the December battle. Nearly two miles farther down the river, near the Louisianians' position, a second Union assault force prepared to embark on a similar mission—to secure a bridgehead on the Confederate side that would cover the laying of pontoon bridges for the crossing of Sedgwick's divisions. As the dawn broke, the Louisianians were roused from their sleep to form ranks and move to meet the attack at the lower crossing.[33]

Captain Seymour was sitting on his horse at the head of the brigade column, ready to march, when a touching incident occurred. "An Irish woman rushed out of her hut in the camp of the 6th Regt., in demi-toilette," he recalled, "with her red shock of hair unkempt and disordered, and coming up to me, raised her long, bony arms to Heaven and fervently called upon the Almighty to cover me with His shield in the day of battle and preserve me from the hands of the enemy." Although Seymour was not taken with her appearance—"the woman was hideously ugly," he wrote—her "earnestness and solemnity in her manners. . .produced a profound impression on the minds of all who saw and heard her. She was a laundress in my Father's Regt. & revered his memory—hence her blessing on me."[34]

When the brigade arrived at the trench lines along the railroad at Hamilton's Crossing, the 6th Louisiana was ordered down to the riverbank to relieve the 13th Georgia regiment, which was disputing the Federals' crossing but running out of ammunition. Dashing across the open plain between the railroad and the riverfront, the Louisianians were under fire from the Union batteries on Stafford Heights. "Moving rapidly to the front and under a heavy fire of artillery from the opposite bank, losing several men, we arrived at our post about 7 a.m.," Captain Ring recorded. "The regiment was deployed and at a double-quick under a very hot fire of artillery and infantry, succeeded in gaining the rifle pits on the bank of the river."[35]

Captain Seymour watched the 6th Louisiana from his position nearly a mile back, along the railroad. "It marched up to the position under a galling fire from the hills on the other side of the River and took their places in the rifle pits," Seymour wrote. "The noble fellows strove manfully to hold their position and keep the enemy from effecting a crossing, and caused many a Yankee to bite the dust by their cool and well directed fire."[36]

The 6th Louisiana wasn't expected to prevent a crossing by the Federals, but merely to delay it as long as possible. For nearly two hours, Colonel Monaghan and his men held out at the water's edge, directing a harassing fire upon Federal engineers trying to lay pontoons for the bridge. The 6th Louisiana's well-directed shots finally convinced the engineers to give up the attempt. Frustrated in the effort to lay the bridge, Union Brig. Gen. Solomon Meredith, commanding the battle-hardened Iron Brigade, ordered his men to brave the Louisianians' fire and force their way across the river in boats. The 6th Wisconsin and 24th Michigan regiments, chosen to lead the assault, dashed to the water's edge, about 50 men crowding into each boat.[37]

The 6th Louisiana's marksmen dropped some of the Wisconsin and Michigan men as they ran to the boats on the opposite bank, but the rest successfully launched and began paddling and poling furiously, recalled a 6th Wisconsin veteran. While some of the men paddled, those in the front of the boats banged away with muskets at the puffs of smoke coming from the Louisianians' rifle pits on the opposite shore, Pvt. James Sullivan wrote. The "water fairly boiled" about his boat as bullets and shells splashed nearby, and the Wisconsin Irishman marveled that the boat wasn't sunk. When they reached the Confederate side, "our lads did not wait to go out over the front of the boat, but jumped over the sides into the mud and water and rushed up the sides of the hill. . . . There was a little ravine where we landed and some of our men followed up the side of it and we took the Johnnies in the rifle pits in flank and rear and we gobbled a good many of them."[38]

Sullivan and his comrades from Michigan and Wisconsin swept down on the 6th Louisianians in the rifle pits from their left, upriver. Some of Monaghan's startled soldiers were shot where they stood, while others fled to the rear, and many were swiftly surrounded and captured. As Private Sullivan claimed, a large number were "gobbled up" by the Federals, apparently because they had failed to hear the command to retreat. That is the explanation given in another account of the riverside clash that was published in an anonymous "Letter from the Sixth Louisiana" a few weeks after the affair. According to the writer, who used the pseudonym "Chester," the regiment was ordered to fall back from the riverside after holding back the Union assault long enough to allow Confederate forces time to get in line. "Unfortunately, however, some of the Sixth, on hearing the order to fall back, understood it as applying to the Georgians who they had relieved; so some of them remained at their posts fighting away, ignorant of what was going on." This was unavoidable, Chester added, as the entire regiment was strung out along the riverbank, "and it was therefore impossible, on the extreme ends of the line, to hear the command."[39]

The men who had heard the order escaped to the old Richmond Stage Road, a sunken lane about halfway between the river and the hilltop entrenchments where the rest of the brigade watched the action. There they reformed their line and soon were joined by the 5th Louisiana, sent forward in support. While they were there, according to Captain Seymour, General Jackson rode up "amid the loud cheers of our men" to urge them "to hold the road at all hazards." As the musket balls whizzed about him, Stonewall coolly studied the positions of the enemy through his binoculars, clad in a new uniform that was such a sharp contrast to his usual dingy attire that it caused much comment among his admiring foot-cavalry.[40]

Down at the riverfront, the men who hadn't heard the order to retreat were rounded up and disarmed by the enemy. Nearly one whole company, the Union and Sabine Rifles, Company A, was captured near "Pratt's House," a mansion also known as Smithfield, about two-and-a-half miles below the town. "When the enemy had finished their preparations, they crossed quickly in their pontoons and before the company was aware of their landing, they were surrounded," 2nd Lt. James Weymouth wrote. "Only three of the company escaped by running the gauntlet of a heavy fire from a full Brigade. One was killed in the attempt to escape."[41]

The fight at the river front took a heavy toll on the regiment. The unlucky soldier of Company A who was killed trying to escape was Pvt. J. D. S. Godwin. At least six others were killed as the Federals swarmed over the riverside rifle pits, or shortly thereafter. Another dozen officers and men were wounded, but the largest numerical loss to the regiment came in the extraordinary number of men captured—78 men were tallied as missing on the official brigade casualty list. Captain Ring put the loss as "a third of our whole regiment;" muster rolls of April 30 showed 275 men present for duty. Among those captured was Lt. Col. Joseph Hanlon, who just the day before had returned to the regiment following his recovery from severe wounds received at Winchester eleven months earlier. In a similar bit of ill luck, one of the severely wounded was Capt. Frank Clarke, who had returned to command Company G, the Pemberton Rangers, only five days earlier, after recuperating from serious wounds received at Sharpsburg the previous September. Clarke's wounds disabled him from further service with the 6th Louisiana.[42]

The remaining members of the 6th Louisiana deployed along the river road until dark, awaiting an assault from the Union troops which didn't materialize. Instead, the Union men seemed to be digging in along their bridgehead as if they expected to receive rather than deliver an attack. As night fell the 21st Georgia regiment relieved the weary Louisianians, who retired to the trenches alongside their brigade comrades. The next morning opened quietly. "The enemy on our side of the river were working like beavers on their fortifications," Captain Seymour observed, while across the river heavy columns of blue-clad troops marched and counter-marched, as if to confuse the Confederates about their intentions. On a hill behind the Louisiana troops, Generals Lee, Jackson, A. P. Hill and others watched the movements of the enemy, still debating where the main attack would come. The 6th Louisiana spent the day "lying idle in the entrenchments," while Sedgwick's Federals, secure in their bridgehead, showed no disposition to attack.[43]

By late in the day April 30, the inactivity of the Federals at the riverfront and numerous reports from his cavalry detailing Hooker's moves upon Chancellorsville convinced General Lee that the main Federal attack would come from his rear, rather than the front at Fredericksburg. The Confederate commander concluded that the buildup in front by Sedgwick's force was a diversion intended to hold him in place while Hooker's main body attacked from his rear. He ordered one of Jackson's four divisions, plus one brigade from McLaws' Division, to hold the position on the Fredericksburg heights, while the rest of the army advanced west to meet Hooker.[44]

Jackson assigned Early to hold the Fredericksburg line while he prepared to move his other three divisions with Lee to confront Hooker's right wing. Joined by the Mississippi brigade of Brig. Gen. William Barksdale, of McLaws' Division, Early stretched his thin force over more than seven miles of defensive works. Barksdale's Mississippians deployed on the hills immediately behind the town, while Early's brigades manned the line reaching southward along the series of ridges down to Hamilton's Crossing. Only about 11,600 Confederates were left facing Sedgwick's 25,600 Federals on the plain below. Hays' Louisiana Brigade was part of this thinly stretched defensive line. Aware of their precarious position, the outnumbered Confederates did all they could to present a menacing face and appear stronger than they were by constantly shifting units, cheering imaginary reinforcements, and lighting thousands of campfires at night.[45]

On Saturday, May 2, the 6th and 9th Louisiana were detached from the rest of the brigade and sent to Marye's Heights, which overlooked the town of Fredericksburg, to dig in alongside Barksdale's Mississippians.

That afternoon, as they watched the Federals below, the men from Louisiana could hear the distant rumble of cannon from the direction of Chancellorsville, where Lee's battle with Hooker was underway. For the most part, Sedgwick's men remained inactive, though there was some shelling and skirmish fire. The Louisianians remained alongside the Mississippi men all day and into the night, but they were roused about 2:00 on the morning of May 3 and marched back to their old post near Hamilton's Crossing, which they reached about sunrise.[46] The dwindling regiment, which numbered only about 175 active men, had barely settled down at Hamilton's Crossing about daylight when the sound of cannon fire and musketry emanating from the direction of Fredericksburg warned them of a renewed assault. More Federal troops were pouring across the river into Fredericksburg, and Sedgwick's soldiers on the river flats were shifting toward the town.

The Louisiana men were unaware that the urgency of these Federal moves were a product of Lee's success to the west. The day before, in a daring gamble, the Confederate commander had divided his army in the face of Hooker's larger force. Jackson and his three divisions were dispatched on a wide-swinging march through the Wilderness around the Federal right flank. The stealthy Stonewall's surprise attack from the west at sundown stunned the unprepared troops of Maj. Gen. Oliver O. Howard's XI Corps—many of whom were the much-maligned "Dutchmen" Jackson had routed in the Valley Campaign. Never expecting an attack from their rear, Howard's Germans were overrun and scattered, throwing Hooker's whole force on the defensive. During the night, the confused commander of the Army of the Potomac ordered Sedgwick to fight his way through the Fredericksburg defenses and march to Chancellorsville to help him fight Lee and Jackson.[47]

The sudden activity that erupted that bright and beautiful Sunday morning in Fredericksburg was the product of that urgent order. Under Hooker's instructions, Sedgwick ordered Brig. Gen. John Gibbon's division—the one that had been left in place across the Rappahannock from Fredericksburg to mask Hooker's march upriver—to cross into the town to join the drive toward Chancellorsville. Gibbon had his men across pontoon bridges by 7:00 a.m., deploying to the right of the town, while Sedgwick marched during the night to deploy his three divisions on a line reaching from the town down the range of hills occupied by Early's thin force.[48]

General Barksdale, watching the enemy buildup below his position on Marye's Heights, alerted Early and called for reinforcements. Hays' Louisianians were ordered to march at double-quick time toward the threatened Mississippians. The 6th Louisiana had scarcely caught its collective breath at Hamilton's Crossing when the weary men received orders to march back in the direction from which they had just come. Hays' Tigers began the five-mile hike to the Confederate left under a warm sun and an even warmer barrage from the Federal artillery. Halfway along the tiring, dangerous jaunt, the 6th was ordered detached to reinforce Barksdale's Mississippians while Hays took the rest of the brigade to the extreme left of the Confederate line.[49]

Colonel Monaghan's men were assigned to support a battery of the Washington Artillery of New Orleans, dug in near the foot of Lee's Hill (where the Confederate commander had headquartered in December) near the Howison house. About 10:00 a.m., Captain Ring noted in his diary, "we were ordered to occupy the trenches in front of the battery." Another 6th Louisiana soldier remembered, "On going into the trenches we found we had so large a space to cover that we were placed in one rank, with an interval of about a pace between the men." The 6th Louisiana's thin line connected on the left with the 13th Mississippi regiment, while the rest of Barksdale's men stretched further to the left on Marye's Heights and behind the stone wall, the site of the December slaughter. As the morning progressed, General Sedgwick probed the Confederate position at several points along the line. At first it seemed as though this would be a repeat of the December battle, since the first two Union assaults against the weakly defended heights faltered short of the stone wall. Unfortunately for Lee's army, history would not repeat itself.[50]

About 11:00 a.m., two large columns formed below the hills, one advancing toward Marye's Heights while the other moved up Lee's Hill. Charging with bayonets, ten picked regiments of Maj. Gen. John Newton's division stormed over the stone wall at the base of Marye's Hill and kept coming, overrunning the Mississippians in the trenches left and right. About a mile to their right, Monaghan's 6th Louisiana riflemen were loading and firing as fast as they could, too busy staving off the three columns from Brig. Gen. Albion P. Howe's division in front to notice that the Mississippians to their left had been overrun. Seeing his center broken, General Barksdale ordered the 13th and 17th Mississippi and the 6th Louisiana on his right to fall back to the crest of Lee's Hill to try

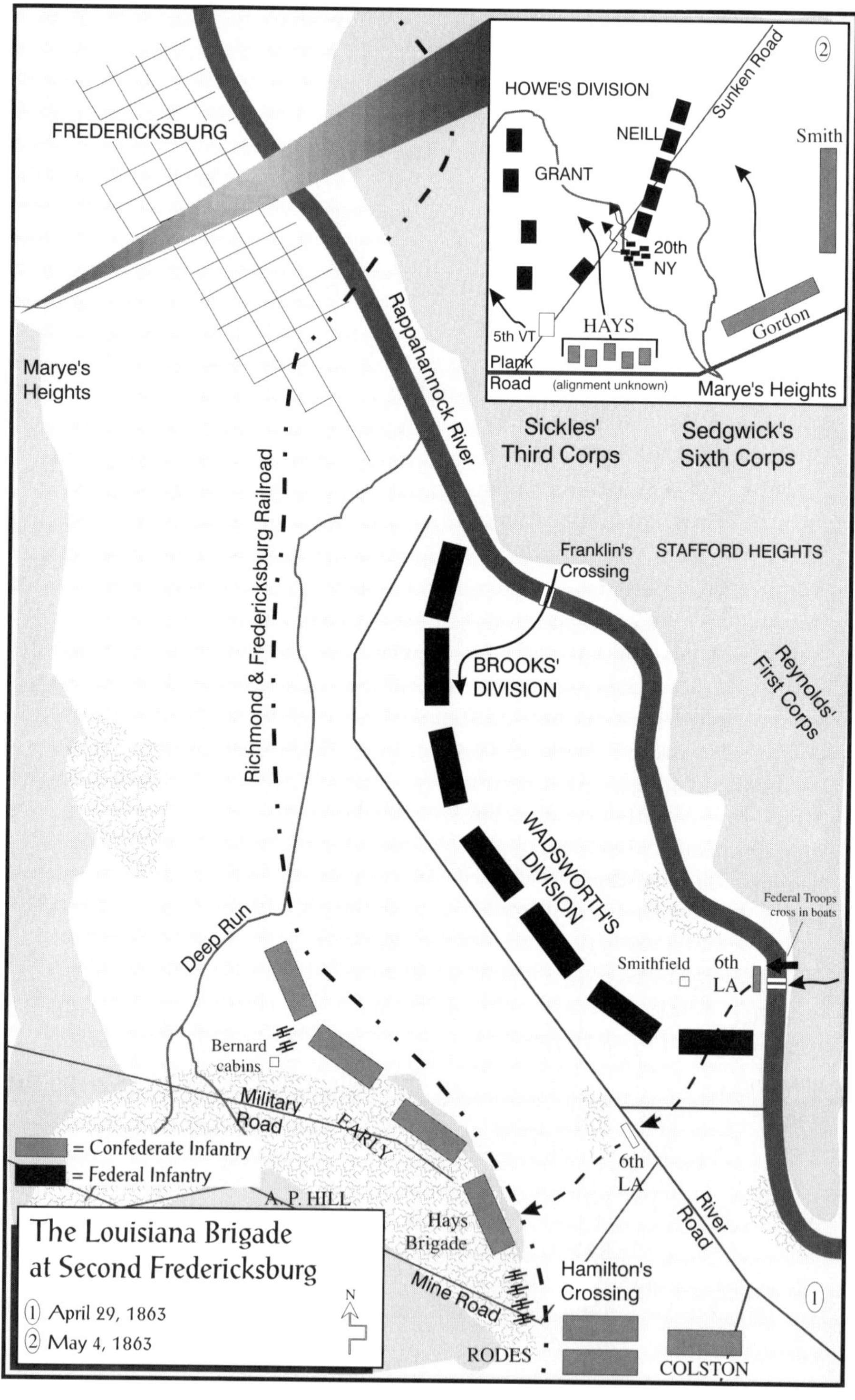

The Louisiana Brigade at Second Fredericksburg

(1) April 29, 1863

(2) May 4, 1863

to stem the Union tide. Monaghan's men began pulling up the hill, fighting alongside the Mississippians as they fell back from the advancing enemy, "resisting his approach at every step," in Barksdale's words.[51]

Captain Seymour, who watched the Federal attack from a distance on the hills to the left, where the rest of the Louisiana Brigade was posted, attributed its success to a dirty trick. Half an hour before the successful attack, Seymour wrote, the Federals sent a flag of truce to a Mississippi colonel, requesting permission to attend to their wounded in front of the Confederate line. "The unsuspecting Mississippian inexcusably permitted the flag of truce party to come within a few feet of his line," Seymour wrote. The flag-bearer was a high-ranking officer, "a shrewd, Keen, observant fellow" disguised as a lower-rank, who "quickly perceived how weak & extended our line was and that a very important ravine between Taylor's & Marye's Heights was entirely undefended. Twenty minutes after the return of the flag the enemy, who had almost his entire force in the streets of Fredericksburg, rushed up the ravine and made a dash at the Heights, which he soon captured—taking between two and three hundred of Barksdale's men, six guns and thirty-five officers and men of the Washington Artillery. . . ."[52]

Another account of the Federal attack, penned by a soldier in the 6th Louisiana, also mentioned the flag-of-truce "treachery," as did both Barksdale and Early in their official reports. This account, by the anonymous "Chester," reported that:

> during the entire morning the fight raged furiously along the line at different parts. Our brigade, the Washington Artillery and Barksdale's Mississippi brigade fought there until about 2 o'clock, when by treachery they discovered a gap in Barksdale's right, massed in his front, and after a gallant resistance on the part of the brave Mississippians, pressed through, thus flanking our heights. Nothing but the superior discipline of the two brigades ever saved them from total annihilation. We [the 6th Louisiana] were so intent watching the enemy in our front that we did not discover them on our flank and rear until it was almost too late. The brave boys of the Washington Artillery stood to their guns to cover the retreat, and actually poured two rounds of canister into the Yankee columns after the Stars and Stripes had been planted on the works.[53]

As "Chester" indicated, the 6th Louisiana was very nearly overrun, and in fact more than a dozen men in the regiment were captured. Official casualty lists for Hays' Brigade show three killed, eight wounded and 13 missing from the regiment in the fighting on May 3. In his diary, Captain Seymour wrote that, "One of our Regts., the 6th, which had been left to support the batteries on Lee's Hill, came very near being surrounded and captured, and escaped with a loss of twenty-seven men killed and wounded." (The 6th Louisiana's killed and wounded actually numbered 11, but adding the 13 captured yields a figure close to Seymour's tally.) Captain Ring made no mention of casualties in his diary, which reported simply that the enemy "made a successful attack upon Mary's Heights and after capturing this drove us out of our position and forced us to fall back some three miles."[54]

After escaping, Colonel Monaghan kept his regiment together and fell back in good order along Telegraph Road, in rear of Lee's Hill. There, the 6th Louisiana formed the core of a new defensive line patched together by Barksdale and Early to stem the Union advance. Upon learning of the disaster on Marye's Heights, Early galloped to the Telegraph Road, where he found Confederate artillery rushing to the rear. He ordered the guns halted and then found Barksdale on the ridge just behind Lee's Hill, rallying his men and skirmishing with the enemy. "Barksdale's men were rather scattered," Early wrote, "but the 6th Louisiana had retired in good order and I directed it to form a line, and Barksdale to halt and get his men in line, which he did." From there, Early's makeshift force slowly retired about two miles along the road, "taking advantage of favorable positions of the ground to make a stand until the enemy ceased to pursue." The victorious Federals eventually broke off the pursuit because Sedgwick had orders to drive west to Chancellorsville to join Hooker's forces against Lee. This he tried to do, but was stalled by stiff Confederate resistance around Salem Church, along the Orange Turnpike five miles west of Fredericksburg, about halfway to Chancellorsville.[55]

By nightfall of May 3, Lee had control of the situation near Chancellorsville. Hooker had dug himself into a defensive posture and was not showing any sign of resuming the offensive—despite his superior numbers. Turning his attention on the morning of May 4 to the Federals who had driven Early from the Fredericksburg Heights, Lee ordered the divisions of Maj. Gens. Lafayette McLaws and Richard Anderson to join Early in surrounding Sedgwick's isolated corps, hoping to destroy that wing of the Union army before it could retreat across the Rappahannock. The Confederate commander saw a chance to annihilate or capture Sedgwick, and then turn his whole army on the immobile Hooker, whose

75,000 men remained held in place by a mere 25,000 Confederates under command of cavalryman Jeb Stuart. The ubiquitous horseman had assumed command of the Second Corps after Stonewall Jackson fell wounded.[56]

General Sedgwick, after being repulsed at Salem Church, began looking for a way out of the box he found himself in on that Monday morning. At dawn, Early sent the brigade of Brig. Gen. John B. Gordon to retake Lee's Hill and Marye's Heights, which the aggressive Georgian accomplished with relative ease. Gordon's success made it impossible for Segdwick to withdraw to Fredericksburg, where he had left Gibbon's division, and forced him instead to form a defensive perimeter with his back to the Rappahannock around Scott's Ford. Anticipating an attack, he was already thinking retreat, especially after receiving a dispatch from Hooker advising him to "look well to the safety of your corps," and suggesting a withdrawal to the north side of the river. Sedgwick's three divisions, numbering about 19,000 men, deployed in a defensive rectangle anchored east and west on the river and running for a mile parallel to the Plank Road on its southern side.[57]

It took much of the day for the Confederates to move into position for the assault. "We maneuvered around until the afternoon, when, finally, we thought, we had the enemy in a trap, and anticipated a complete bagging arrangement, but we found out afterwards that the bag had a hole in it," wrote the 6th Louisiana's "Chester." By mid-afternoon, the Federal VI Corps was penned in by about 23,000 Southerners on three sides: McLaws to the west on the Confederate left, Anderson in the center, Early to the east, the Confederate right. General Lee had arrived from Chancellorsville to co-ordinate the attack, which was to begin at a signal of three guns fired in rapid succession. "Gens. Lee, Early and our brigade commanders held a council of war, whether to retake the heights by storm or not," "Chester explained. "They finally concluded that it was necessary. Gen. Lee asked who had a brigade that could do it. Gen. Hays, it is said, promptly announced that he had a brigade that would charge Hell, but I doubt it, the General being a pious man." This story may be apocryphal, though it probably reflects the eagerness of the Louisiana Brigade's commander to have his men in the thick of the fight.[58]

The afternoon was well advanced by the time Lee had all his forces in position for the attack. Early's Division was stretched out from the high ground of Marye's Heights to the deep valley of Hazel Run, in the rear of that hill and Lee's Hill. With Colonel Monaghan leading the 6th Louisiana, Hays' Brigade filed into the deep ravine formed by Hazel Run, near the Alum Springs Mill, in the center of Early's line. Gordon's Brigade of Georgians was to the right of the five Louisiana regiments, on the high ground of Marye's Heights, which Gordon had recaptured that morning. The North Carolina brigade of Brig. Gen. Robert Hoke lined up to the left of Hays, farther up the valley of the little stream. Hays divided his brigade into a left wing, composed of the 7th and 9th Louisiana, under his direct command, and a right wing, composed of the 8th, 5th and 6th Louisiana, under command of Colonel Forno of the 5th. After the line was formed, wrote one participant, "the command, 'Fix bayonets,' was given." Some Federal prisoners watching from nearby "afterwards said they know hot work was coming when they saw us obey that order."[59]

In the dark woods of the ravine, beyond the reach of the now-waning sun, the Louisianians waited anxiously for the signal to charge. They knew not what awaited them at the top of the steep hills. The Federals there were well posted to receive the anticipated attack. General Howe's Union division of nearly 6,000 men held a two-mile line on the left of Sedgwick's box, running from the river to the Plank Road. Expecting to be outnumbered and hard-pressed when the attack came, Howe had carefully examined the rolling high ground that he held and decided to deploy his regiments in two lines, plus a line of skirmishers in front. If he was unable to hold the position of his first line, Howe planned to fall back to his second line in a small skirt of woods, where he had posted his artillery. His arrangements for an orderly, planned fallback would deceive the Confederates into believing they had routed the enemy, when in fact they were approaching a stronger, concealed Federal position.[60]

It was about 5:30 p.m when the triple report of the signal guns—boom, boom, boom—sounded the attack. The 6th Louisiana's "Chester" recounted the dramatic moment: "Hays and Forno, in loud clear tones, gave the command, 'Forward, double-quick!' With a yell that sounded like a legion of 50 ton locomotives, the boys started—up, up they go without firing a gun." The heights facing the Louisianians "were steep, rugged, and very difficult to ascend. Simply climbing them was enough to exhaust men not under excitement. The enemy were on top in strong force in the rifle pits and redouts, and on Stafford Heights they had any quantity of artillery that raked us."[61]

Captain Seymour also recorded the scene: "At the order to charge, our gallant fellows rushed up the high range of Hills in their front under a heavy fire and across a broad plain raked by heavy 20 & 30 pounder batteries from Stafford Heights. Four field batteries & three lines of infantry were in our front." Once up on the open plain, the hard-charging Louisiana men encountered a deadly storm of lead and iron. "The enemy poured everything they have on us at once," remembered one of the soldiers. "Their missiles ploughed the ground in front of us as we advanced as though an earthquake were about to bury us alive. The shells bursting over our heads, and the fire from the thousands of small arms, caused such a cloud of smoke that until the men advanced further, nothing could be seen of them. I thought," he continued, "that they had been swept from the face of the earth at one blast; but hearing that unearthly yell again, I knew that they had not faltered."[62]

Private Henry Handerson of the 9th Louisiana said the crossfire of artillery and musketry "seemed to make the very air boil. Men fell on every side, and without further delay and with another shout of 'Charge!', Gen. Hays again led us forward against an enemy as yet unseen but manifestly not far off." Another Louisiana soldier said the Confederates ran into "a wall of fire on three sides; the air was fairly hissing with round shot, shell, grape, canister and minie balls."[63]

This "wall of fire" erupted first from the 5th Vermont regiment, which was posted to the south of the Plank Road in an extension of Howe's first line of defense. As the Louisianians charged across the front of the Vermont riflemen, the New Englanders "poured a terrible cross and enfilading fire into the enemy's advancing lines, creating great havoc on their ranks," claimed Col. Lewis Grant, whose other four regiments of the Vermont brigade were posted to the rear in the woods, as Howe's second line. Despite Grant's claim of wreaking havoc, the screaming Louisiana Tigers stormed by the Vermont men and slammed into the right of the first Federal line, manned by Neill's brigade. Neill's rightmost regiment, Col. Ernst von Vegesack's 20th New York, broke and fled. General Neill tried without success to rally the terrified New Yorkers, who scattered to the rear. The furious Louisiana charge certainly impressed Neill, who imagined he was being attacked by "the whole of Longstreet's Corps," as he later reported. After losing about 1,000 men, Neill pulled his brigade back in the face of what he thought were "the overpowering numbers of the enemy." It wasn't the numbers but the sheer ferocity of the Louisiana Brigade's attack that sent Neill's men flying. As "Chester" recounted it: "We gain the heights—the enemy waver—the boys close in on them; yell again, and they break; away they go to the second line, which tries to check them, but with no success. . .and they too break and run as disorderly as the first."[64]

Some of the Federal troops had dug in along a sunken farm lane that ran obliquely behind Neill's position and through the position of Grant's brigade. This old dirt road had steep banks lined with chest-high brush. The 9th Louisiana's Handerson remembered leaping the brush, not knowing what was on the other side, and being shocked to tumble headlong into Federal troops, who were just as stunned by his startling arrival. "It is hard to say which of us was most surprised, and for a moment I thought my time had come," wrote Handerson. But quickly, other Tigers were leaping into the sunken road and the Federals' threw up their arms in surrender. "Leaving them to take care of themselves, however, we clambered out of the other side of the roadway and rushed forward once more to complete our victory," Handerson recalled.[65]

General Early watched the stirring spectacle from a nearby hill. "Hays rapidly ascended the hill in front, immediately encountering the right of the enemy's front line, which he swept before him and continued his advance without a halt," Early recalled. Robert Hoke's North Carolinians also advanced swiftly. "It was a splendid sight to see the rapid and orderly advance of these two brigades, with the enemy flying before them," he wrote. Early had harshly criticized the undisciplined Tigers in the past for their habit of looting, but when he saw the charging Louisianians break through the two Federal lines, he slammed down his hat and shouted, "Those damned Louisiana fellows can steal as much as they please now!"[66]

Though the usually grumpy Early was elated with the initial assault, Hays' attack was becoming disorganized after rushing over the Federals' first line of defense. "Captains had lost their companies, and companies and regiments were so intermingled that the brigade formed simply a howling, rushing and firing mob," according to Handerson. Cols. Forno and Hays, the 6th Louisiana's "Chester" reported, "seemed to be everywhere at once — in the road, where the shelling from Stafford Heights seemed to fairly sweep everything before it, they galloped up and down, urging the men up the other side. Col. Forno's voice could be heard above the yells, carrying every command." Their horses lathered with foam, the colonels galloped to any sector where the attack seemed to be slacking from exhaustion, "and with words of cheer urged the men to keep it up, that they were driving the enemy. . . .Their actions and words infused a confidence in the men that few men have the faculty of imparting."[67]

The "fighting mob" rolled forward, excited by the sight of the Federals' backs, but the winded Louisianians were clearly nearing the limits of endurance. They rushed toward a third line of blue troops at the brow of a hill protected by an obstacle course of felled trees. This was General Howe's final line of defense, manned by Colonel Grant's Vermonters and at least six cannon. "Up we go, almost 'played out,' dragging through the limbs of trees, over logs, gullies and ditches; we gain the brow of the hill, the enemy evidently intend a desperate stand," the 6th Louisiana's "Chester" recounted. "Our boys, greatly reduced in numbers, for the first time stopped to fire; they had completely given out. . .to stand and fight was a rest truly refreshing."[68]

Grant's Green Mountain men were dug in behind breastworks of knapsacks and felled trees. The Vermont riflemen rose up and delivered a point-blank volley which staggered the Louisianians, who had already lost many of their comrades in the rear, either to exhaustion or enemy fire. "At this time," their colonel reported, "the enemy had a large force in front of our entire line, attempting with desperate vigor to force or turn it; but the Vermont regiments remained firm and unbroken, closely hugging the crest and literally presenting a wall of fire." The momentum of the attack stalled against the Vermonters' deadly wall. Some of the Louisiana soldiers hugged the turf behind small swells of ground as bullets hummed overhead and darkness crept over the smoky field, obscuring vision. To make matters worse, the Louisianians began to take fire from Hoke's North Carolina brigade behind them. The North Carolinians "mistook us for Yankees and opened a galling fire upon our rear, while the enemy engaged us in front," Captain Seymour reported. Slowly at first, and then with a rush, the Louisiana men began retreating down the hill, but many were so exhausted that they simply collapsed and were captured. The Federals rounded up hundreds of the confused and tired Louisianians in the woods, including two colonels, Leroy Stafford of the 9th Louisiana and T. D. Lewis of the 8th Louisiana, plus many other officers, though none from the 6th Louisiana. Colonel Grant claimed a brilliant victory, boasting, "A North Carolina and a Louisiana brigade must both of them have been nearly annihilated."[69]

The two brigades were hardly annihilated, but their attack ultimately failed after its spectacular initial success. Lee's hope to destroy or trap

Sedgwick's corps before it could cross the river was frustrated. While Early's men pressed their vigorous attack, Anderson's and McLaws' divisions made little progress on their fronts. Under cover of darkness, Sedgwick's three divisions retreated across Scott's Ford to the north side of the Rappahannock. Upriver, Hooker's 75,000 Federals, who had remained immobile during Sedgwick's desperate fight, followed suit a day later, escaping to safety. The opposing armies were back practically where they started, facing each other across the Rappahannock. "Everything is as it was before the campaign," wrote the 6th Louisiana's 'Chester,' "except we miss many a gallant comrade."

The fourth of May had been another bad day in a string of bad days at Fredericksburg for the 6th Louisiana. The regiment lost another six killed, 45 wounded and eight missing in the fighting on the heights. Indeed, "many a gallant comrade" had fallen at Fredericksburg. "Our regiment lost in these battles one hundred and seventy five men killed, wounded and taken prisoner," lamented Captain Ring. Official returns put the 6th Louisiana's loss at 14 killed, 68 wounded, and 99 missing—again the highest casualties in the Louisiana Brigade. Thankfully, most of the nearly 100 men captured would be exchanged within a month. The regiment's total Fredericksburg casualties, 181 men, represented nearly two-thirds of the 6th Louisiana's effective pre-battle strength of 275 men. The Louisiana Brigade lost 63 killed, 306 wounded, and about 300 captured, roughly 45 percent of the 1,500 men available for duty as the week of fighting began.[70]

The bloody week had completely used up the Louisiana men. "Exhausted we sunk upon the battlefield," wrote "Chester." "We replenished our cartridge boxes with the ammunition taken from the dead Yankees, and recruited our energies with a bountiful repast from the remnants of their eight-days' rations. Their well-packed knapsacks furnished us with clean shirts and socks, both of which we needed badly."[71]

The Chancellorsville Campaign was a decisive victory for Lee and a devastating setback, militarily and psychologically, for the North. Yet the Confederates suffered an irreparable loss with the death of the incomparable Stonewall Jackson. Wounded accidentally by his own troops after his brilliantly executed flank attack on May 2, the Southern hero clung to life for days after having his left arm amputated, but died on May 10 of pneumonia. Lee lost his best corps commander, the man he called "my right arm." Jackson's absence would be felt keenly in the army's campaigns yet to be fought. The Army of Northern Virginia went into mourning. "Never have I witnessed a more profound, heartfelt & universal sorrow as pervaded the whole army on this occasion," Captain Seymour wrote in his journal.[72]

Chapter Eight

The Second Battle: RETURN TO WINCHESTER

"The storming of those breastworks was the grandest sight my eyes ever beheld."
— *Miss Lizzie Yonley, Winchester civilian*

After nearly a week of fighting, the 6th Louisiana returned to its old winter quarters along the Rappahannock River for the remaining weeks of May, where it enjoyed the warm spring weather and light duty. All was quiet along the Rappahannock, as Hooker's army remained north of the river, licking its wounds and pondering its lost opportunities. The peaceful period gave the regiment "a much needed repose," Captain Ring noted in his diary. In his letter written on May 30 from the 6th Louisiana's camp, "Chester" told readers of a Mobile newspaper: "We are now entirely rested, and the boys are ready for another charge."[1]

General Lee was making plans for that charge, one that would again carry the war to the North. But first he had to reorganize his army in light of the losses of Jackson and thousands of others at Chancellorsville and Fredericksburg. In those battles, the Army of Northern Virginia lost about 12,821 officers and men, killed, wounded, missing, or captured—about 22 percent of Lee's effective strength. While the Union losses were higher—nearly 17,300—the total was only 13 percent of Hooker's much larger army. Still, perhaps the greatest loss to the Confederacy was the tragic death of General Jackson. Lee realized he could not replace Stonewall Jackson, and that it would be almost impossible to continue operating the army in its present two-corps arrangement, which had worked so well with Jackson and Longstreet. At the end of May, the Confederate commander divided his army into three corps composed of three divisions each. Longstreet remained in charge of the First Corps, and A. P. Hill was promoted to lieutenant general and given command of a new Third Corps. To command Jackson's old Second Corps, Lee promoted Richard S. Ewell to lieutenant general.[2]

The Louisianians had grown fond of eccentric old Dick Ewell while fighting under him as their division commander, and were happy to have him named to command the corps—even though it meant being stuck with grumpy Jubal Early as their permanent division commander. "Old Bald Head," as Ewell was affectionately known, had lost a leg at Groveton (Second Manassas Campaign), but had recuperated sufficiently to take the field—although he had to be lifted onto his horse and strapped in the saddle. After defeating Hooker's army at Chancellorsville, Lee believed the time was again right to raid into Maryland and Pennsylvania, which would compel the Federal army to vacate Virginia and provide his army with much-needed supplies and provisions. The move north also would upset any offensive plans Hooker might have for the summer campaign season, and perhaps relieve some of the growing pressure mounting against Lt. Gen. John C. Pemberton's army at Vicksburg in Mississippi.[3]

After a month of rest, the 6th Louisiana was ready for action. On June 3, the regiment received a boost in morale and strength through the return of 50 men who had been captured in the recent battles, now paroled and exchanged at Hamilton's Crossing. That brought the number present for duty to somewhat over 200 officers and men, hardly more than one-fifth of the number originally mustered. The returned ex-prisoners had barely settled into camp when orders came on the morning of June 4 to "hold ourselves in readiness to move at a moment's notice," as Captain Ring noted in his diary. The Army of Northern Virginia was stirring to execute Lee's grand strategy to take the war to the North.[4]

Leaving Hill's Third Corps in place to hold Fredericksburg against Hooker's army across the river, Lee ordered Longstreet and Ewell to begin their march toward the Blue Ridge Mountains. To mask the army's withdrawal, Jubal Early's Division waited until after dark to begin the move. Just after midnight on June 5, the 6th Louisiana began tramping its way northwest toward Culpeper Court House. Captain Ring started the all-night march with a wistful hope that this would be "a final campaign." His diary gives a detailed account of the demanding march north. The first night and day covered 23 miles, the next day 11 miles "through a drenching rain." When the march reached the Rapidan River on the third day, "we rolled up our pants and into it we went," passing within sight of Cedar Mountain, site of last August's battle, to the outskirts of Culpeper Court House, a distance of 21 miles.[5]

By June 8, the area around the town was crawling with Confederate troops. Both Ewell's and Longstreet's corps were in the vicinity, and Jeb Stuart's cavalry corps was conducting a grand, full-dress review under the eyes of General Lee on the grassy rolling plains around nearby Brandy Station. Neither Lee nor Stuart knew that Hooker had dispatched his cavalry, under Brig. Gen. Alfred Pleasonton, up the north bank of the Rappahannock to pounce upon the large force of Confederate cavalry reported to be near Culpeper. At dawn on June 9, Stuart's sleepy troopers found themselves under attack by Pleasonton's 9,500 cavalrymen, who splashed across Beverly and Kelly's Fords on the Rappahannock and came thundering down upon the unprepared Confederates. The surprise attack precipitated the largest cavalry battle of the war, a clash involving 18,000 horsemen and covering several square miles of low hills, open fields and woods around Brandy Station. The 14-hour battle raged from dawn till dusk, ending more or less in a bloody draw with the Federal cavalry withdrawing back across the Rappahannock. The 6th Louisiana, with the rest of Early's Division, was marched to the battlefield in mid-afternoon to support Stuart's hard-pressed men, who managed to drive off the Federals without infantry help. The Louisianians camped that night on a battlefield strewn with dead horses, human corpses, mangled wagons, and broken equipment.[6]

The hard march resumed at daylight on June 10, heading north through Sperryville and Little Washington, across the Blue Ridge at Chester Gap, and down the mountain into Front Royal, scene of the regiment's first battle more than a year earlier. The people of Front Royal gave the marching men, who had tramped 130 miles in eight days, an enthusiastic reception. Young Lucy Buck, who had thrilled to the liberation of the town a year earlier, heard martial music that morning and looked out to see the vanguard of Ewell's Corps, with the one-legged general riding in his carriage. Then came the column of happy foot-soldiers. "Oh how the gallant boys cheered and shouted," she recalled. "Ma and I went up on the house and when they saw us they waved and hurrahed us. Oh! it was glorious!" Arriving in Front Royal on June 12, the 6th Louisiana was only a day's march from Winchester, a place that seemed to exert a kind of magnetic pull for the men of this regiment. They had fought there once before, would fight there now, and would return to fight there yet again.[7]

Winchester, Virginia, a city of 4,400 at the northern end of the Shenandoah Valley, was one of those unfortunate few Civil War crossroads towns that lay in the heavy traffic lanes of the war. The armies of North and South repeatedly fought over control of the town because its strategic location made it crucial to control of the great agricultural valley to its south and to the river crossings over the Potomac some 25 miles to its north. Winchester changed hands no fewer than 70 times during the war as control of the area ebbed and flowed like an uncertain tide between the two contending armies.[8]

Lee had sent Ewell's Corps over the Blue Ridge to clear out the only major body of Federal troops that stood in his way on the invasion route to Pennsylvania. Headquartered at Winchester, Maj. Gen. Robert H. Milroy commanded a garrison of about 9,000 troops in and around the town and the nearby outposts of Berryville and Martinsburg. Milroy had earned the enmity of Winchester's townsfolk by his tyrannical style of rule over what he called the "rebel" populace, which included confiscating their belongings to furnish his headquarters on Main Street, and ejecting an invalid woman from her beautiful home to provide a fine house for Mrs. Milroy. Milroy's "outrages on the citizens of the Valley" were infamous enough to have raised the ire of Confederate soldiers, including one 5th Louisiana officer who branded him "that notorious old blackguard and tyrant Milroy," in a letter written just after the battle.[9]

The Union general had been urged by his superiors in Washington to abandon Winchester and retreat to a more secure position at Harpers Ferry on the Potomac, but he was reluctant to do so. He was confident he could hold out against the small Confederate force known to be operating in the area. He was also certain he would have plenty of warning of the approach of any substantial part of Lee's army, which was assumed to be still well to the south. On June 12, he had brushed aside a cavalry officer's report of sighting Confederate cavalry, infantry and artillery in large force near Cedarville, only 12 miles from Winchester, for he "deemed it impossible that Lee's army, with its immense artillery and baggage trains, could have escaped from the Army of the Potomac and crossed the Blue Ridge. . . ."[10]

That sighting was of Ewell's vanguard, then marching north from Front Royal to begin encircling Winchester to entrap Milroy. Ewell pushed two of his divisions toward Winchester—Early's, which moved north up the Valley Turnpike, so familiar from the campaign under Jackson a year earlier, and the Brig. Gen. Edward "Allegany" Johnson's

Division, which marched along the Front Royal-Winchester pike. (Ewell's third division, commanded by Brig. Gen. Robert E. Rodes, was sent northeast to Berryville to capture Milroy's 1,800-man outpost.) Toward the rear of Early's column, the Louisiana Brigade forded the Shenandoah River at Front Royal before dawn on Saturday, June 13, then marched northwest to strike the Valley pike, arriving about three miles south of Winchester before noon. Hays' skirmishers clashed with the outer perimeter of Milroy's defensive line, driving the Federals back to the fortifications around Winchester in the afternoon, before lying down for the night under a drenching downpour.[11]

Winchester was strongly fortified. General Milroy commanded 6,900 men who occupied a series of earthworks bristling with artillery, supported by rifle pits dug into the hills overlooking the town. The main fort, known as Fort Milroy but called the "Flag Fort" by the Confederates, was on a hill less than a mile northwest of town. Mounted with 22 cannon, its enclosure could hold 2,200 men. About a mile north of it lay another large fort, known as the "Star Fort" for its shape, which held eight guns and up to 400 men. Roughly three-quarters of a mile west of these two, on higher ground, the Federals had under construction a smaller earthen work, midway between two main roads into town—the Northwest turnpike from Romney, and the Pughtown road. This fort was open to the rear and was the weakest of the three. It occupied higher ground, though, and with its six guns commanded the other pair of forts, which made its capture crucial to collapsing Milroy's defenses. The fortifications were strong in one sense, yet they were vulnerable, because there was a wooded ridge to the west, called Little North Mountain, which overlooked the forts and which would provide cover for infantry and favorable ground for artillery.[12]

Conferring early on Sunday morning, June 14, Ewell and Early agreed to make the unfinished west fort the target of attack. Leaving Gordon's Brigade on Bower's Hill at the southwest edge of the town to demonstrate in front of Milroy, Early took his other three brigades on a roundabout, uphill march of some eight miles, skirting through woods and over fields with the aid of a local citizen guide to reach the slope of Little North Mountain, overlooking the Confederate's target. The day was "extremely hot," Early recalled, and the men reached the wooded ridge parched and exhausted about 4:00 p.m. "So silently was the march performed that we did not encounter on the way a picket or scout of the enemy," Captain Seymour remembered. Confident he had flanked the enemy position without being detected, Early allowed his weary men to lie down in the shade of the woods for an hour's rest.[13]

Generals Early and Hays, together with Captain Seymour, crept though the woods to get a closer look at their target. The Federals had not thrown out pickets in their direction and seemed to be totally unaware of the Confederate force hidden behind them. The oblivious Federals, Early reported, were "looking intently in the direction of Gordon's position," successfully distracted by the noisy demonstration the feisty Georgian was putting on to their south against some Union skirmishers. Conditions were ideal for a surprise attack.[14]

Early selected Hays' Louisianians for the attack as Col. Hilary Jones' gun crews quietly rolled 20 artillery pieces into position, 12 guns to the skirt of an old orchard on the right and eight guns to the edge of a cornfield on the left—"excellent positions," boasted Early, within easy range of the unsuspecting Federals. General Hays formed his brigade into line on the slope in the woods, with the 6th, 7th and 9th Louisiana regiments in the front line, and the 5th and 8th regiments in supporting position behind them. When Hays signaled that he was ready, Jones' gunners put their muscles to the cannon wheels, rolling them quietly out of the woods into firing position. At about 5:00 p.m., Early gave the signal to commence firing.[15]

The roar of 20 cannon and the eruptions of the earth about them gave the stunned Federal troops in the fort their first notice of the enemy behind them. The west fort was held by the 110th Ohio, commanded by Col. J. Warren Keifer, plus one company of the 116th Ohio and a battery of the 5th U.S. Artillery. Shells exploded over the Ohioans' heads and into their earthen dugout, showering them with dirt and metal fragments and throwing them into general confusion. The U.S. Artillery battery began to return the Confederate fire, but the concentrated shelling from Colonel Jones' 20 guns was so devastating that soon the caissons and limber carriages inside the fort were blown up or wrecked, 50 artillery horses were killed, and four of the six Union cannon were disabled, according to Keifer. "So well directed was this fire," Hays reported, "that in a few minutes the enemy were forced to seek shelter behind their works, and scarcely a head was discovered above the ramparts." The artillery exchange, a decidedly lopsided contest, continued for about 45 minutes. With the Federals hunkering down under the shelling, Hays ordered his men forward about 6:00 p.m.[16]

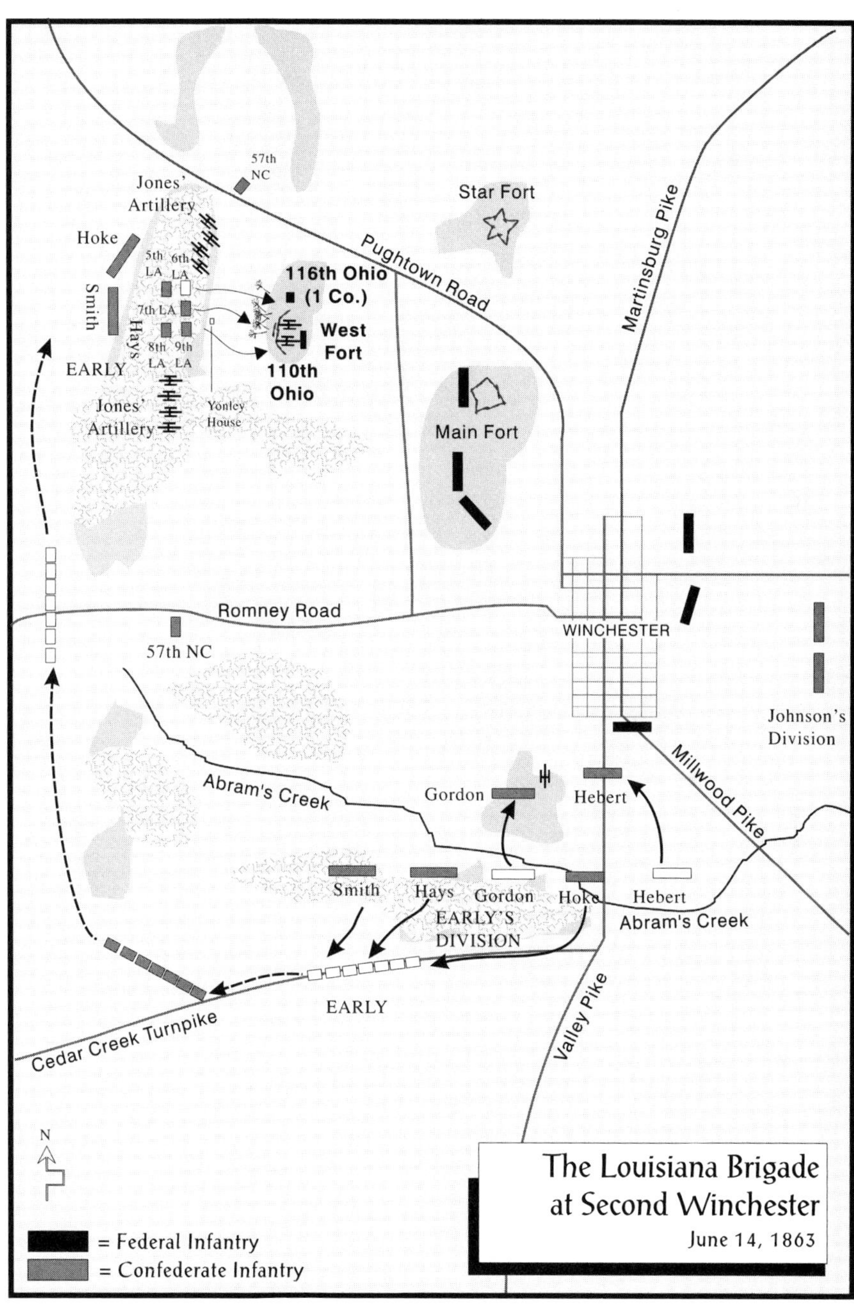

The Louisiana Brigade at Second Winchester

June 14, 1863

As the brigade moved forward, the 6th Louisiana was on the right, the 9th Louisiana in the center, and the 7th Louisiana on the left of the front line of attack, with the 5th and 8th Louisiana a short distance behind. Colonel Monaghan led his regiment out of the woods and across a cleared field to the base of the steep hill on which the west fort was built. The Confederate artillery kept the Union defenders suppressed as the Louisianians began climbing the hill toward the fort.[17]

On the slope stood a small stone farmhouse occupied by the Yonley family. As the Louisiana battle line swept by their home, Lizzie and Alma Yonley watched with rapt attention from their front door. The boys in gray "marched by our house with banners flying and our own and the enemy's shells screaming over," Lizzie Yonley, the older of the two sisters, wrote years after the war. "The storming of those breastworks was the grandest sight my eyes ever beheld."[18]

As Hays' men steadily advanced up the hill, Confederate guns kept up a heavy barrage on the fort. "So hot was the fire of our artillery that the Yankee infantry had to keep close behind the breastworks that they did not observe us until we had reached an abatis of felled timber some 150 yards from the redoubt," Captain Seymour wrote. At this point, Early's artillery had to quit firing for fear of hitting their own men. When the guns ceased firing, "the enemy immediately arose from their hiding places behind their works and discovered us. . ." Hays reported. The Louisiana brigadier shouted, "Charge!," and with their shrill rebel yell his excited Tigers surged up the hill into a hail of musket fire and canister. "The infantry and artillery opened fire on [the Confederates] with fearful effect," the Federal commander reported, "mowing down his advance regiment almost to a man." In its front-line position, the 6th Louisiana was hardly "mowed down," but many of its officers and men were falling killed and wounded as the Confederates charged the fort.[19]

Hays' Brigade came on so fast that the Union defenders had time to fire only "a few volleys of musketry and only four or five rounds of canister from their field pieces," before the surging Louisianians were upon them, Hays reported. The first man to jump over the parapet of the fort was Lt. John Orr of the 6th Louisiana, adjutant of the regiment, a 23-year-old native of Ireland. Scrambling over the top, Orr spotted a Federal color-bearer carrying off his flag, accompanied by two guards. Leaping down, Orr slashed at the three men with his sword while grabbing the flag-standard. His adversaries escaped after one of them thrust a bayonet through Orr's body, a wound from which he amazingly recovered. As Orr fell bleeding, his 6th Louisiana comrades piled into the fort along with men of the other regiments. Most of the panicked Federals ran for the safety of the Flag Fort below, leaving behind about 40 men who were killed, wounded or captured. A 5th Louisiana officer, writing to his brother two days after the battle, claimed the Union soldiers refused to stand their ground in the fort. "But few of them dared to cross bayonets with us, the balance outrunning quarter horses," Capt. Samuel Chisholm wrote. "All of those who stood their ground were soon rolling in their own blood, and many who ran away were shot in the back."[20]

General Ewell had watched the action from his headquarters on a ridge to the east of Winchester, where Johnson's Division had been demonstrating to keep the Federals' attention while Early moved into position behind them. "The firing was terrific and yet all of us crowded on the heights to see Early's charge," remembered cavalryman Harry Gilmor, who had just returned from a scouting mission to report to Ewell. "We could hear his skirmishers keeping up a continual rapid fire, and occasionally a volley and a yell as he charged some advance position; and we could tell. . .that he was getting the advantage." The grandeur of Early's battle and the Louisianians' advance captured Gilmor's attention. "Every piece seemed to be turned on him, but amid the thunders of 30 or 40 guns, there broke on our expectant ears heavy volleys of musketry, and the terrible, long, shrill yell of the two brigades of Louisiana Tigers who were charging up those heights." The Federals held their ground for but a short while, "and old Ewell was jumping about on his crutches, with the utmost difficulty keeping the perpendicular." Gilmore remembered that when the Federals began to fall back, "the Louisianians, with their battle flag, appeared on the crests charging the redoubts. The general [Ewell], through his glass, thought he recognized old Jubal Early among the foremost mounted, and he became so much excited that, with moistened eyes, he said, 'Hurrah for the Louisiana boys! There's Early. I hope the old fellow won't be hurt.'"[21]

Once inside the fort, the Louisianians made quick work of dispatching the last defenders. "The Yankee artillerymen, who were regulars," wrote Captain Seymour, "strove hard to save their guns, but by shooting the horses we prevented them from taking away a single piece or caisson." Hays' men captured all six Federal cannon in the west fort, plus two more in a smaller redoubt some 150 yards away that the Unionists abandoned when they saw their comrades overrun. Shortly after these two earthworks were taken, the Federals in the Flag Fort below tried to organize a counter-attack, forming in three columns. But some of the 6th Louisiana infantrymen helped drive them off by manning two of the captured Union guns. As Captain Seymour told it, "a party of volunteer cannoneers from the 5th and 6th Regts. turned the captured guns and by a few well directed shots drove them away."[22]

After watching the Louisiana men overrun the Federal fortifications, an elated General Early galloped up the hill to congratulate Hays and survey the situation. He ordered Colonel Jones to bring up the guns and begin shelling the larger fort below. It was too dark by then, however, to attempt an assault on that heavily-fortified position, the division commander concluded. As the 6th Louisiana and Hays' other regiments settled down to spend the night in the captured earthworks, Early sent General Ewell a message stating his view that Milroy probably would try to evacuate Winchester during the night. "It was very apparent that the enemy's position was now untenable," Early recalled later, "and that he must either submit to a surrender of his whole force or attempt to escape during the night." General Milroy came to the same conclusion, and at 1:00 the next morning began evacuating Winchester for Martinsburg, leaving his artillery, supplies, and wagons behind. Ewell, however, had anticipated his enemy's move and had dispatched Johnson's Division to cut him off. A few miles north of Winchester, most of Milroy's force was captured, though the general himself escaped with about 300 of his men.[23]

The charge of Hays' Louisianians, which was the key to the capture of Winchester, added luster to the legend of the Louisiana Tigers. The ecstatic Ewell decreed that henceforth the range of hills west of Winchester would be shown on military maps as "Louisiana Heights" or "Louisiana Ridge." Even the hard-to-please Early was enthusiastic in his official report: "The charge of Hays' brigade upon the enemy's works was a most brilliant achievement." One Confederate artillerist later said that of all the famous charges he and his colleagues had seen during the war, including George Pickett's at Gettysburg and the Irish Brigade's at Fredericksburg, "we were generally agreed that for intrepidity, steadiness, and all the other qualities which made up the veteran soldier we never saw this charge excelled, even in Lee's army."[24]

One soldier singled out for special praise after the battle was the 6th Louisiana's Lieutenant Orr. In his report, General Hays praised the "cool, steady and unflinching bravery" shown by all his men, adding, "particularly would I call attention to the conspicuous gallantry of

Lieutenant Orr, adjutant of the Sixth Regiment, who was the first to mount the parapet of the enemy's redoubt, receiving while doing so a severe bayonet wound in the side." General Ewell's report echoed Hays' praise of Orr. Though he was painfully disabled, Orr at least had these accolades from his generals to console him.[25]

The victory at the Second Winchester was as complete as any the men of the 6th Louisiana would experience during the rest of the war. The Confederate prizes, Ewell reported, included 4,000 prisoners, all of Milroy's artillery, totaling 23 guns, 300 loaded wagons, more than 300 horses, and a large amount of military stores. To the chagrin of Early, (who evidently didn't really mean that the Louisianians could steal as much as they pleased now, as he had exclaimed on May 4), much of the booty was plundered by his men. At least some of Hays' soldiers got their share of the spoils of victory. One 9th Louisiana soldier told his family that he had scooped up clothing, sugar, coffee, rice "and everything else I wanted," including "Yankee paper, pens, ink & envelopes" which he used to write his letter to home.[26]

In addition to 4,000 captives, Milroy's losses included 95 dead and 348 wounded. While the Union force was effectively destroyed, Confederate casualties at Winchester were light. Ewell's entire corps lost only 47 killed and 219 wounded, most of them from Early's Division. Hays' Brigade, which engaged in the hottest fighting, lost 14 killed and 78 wounded. For the 6th Louisiana, however, fighting at Winchester continued the string of battles in which it played the role of the hard-luck outfit of the Louisiana Brigade. Once again the 6th had endured the heaviest casualties in the brigade, with as many killed as the other four regiments combined. Early's casualty list showed seven killed and 36 wounded in Colonel Monaghan's regiment, but regimental records recorded eight killed and 55 wounded—roughly one-third of the men who went into the battle. Counting the mortally wounded who died after the battle, the death toll ran as high as 12. Monaghan's countrymen again dominated the list of the dead—seven of the killed and mortally wounded were Irish-born. Among them was 29-year-old Cpl. Robert Cahill of Company F, for whom Winchester was a most unlucky place. Wounded in the right arm in the first battle there in May 1862, Cahill received a mortal wound in the Second Battle of Winchester and died six days later.[27]

Among the wounded were several officers, including Major Manning, Captain Ring—shot in the left ankle, who would be disabled and away from the regiment for nine months—and Capt. John J. Rivera, commanding the Mercer Guards, who was shot in the side. Years after the war, Rivera recalled lying in the home of the Yonley sisters, which was used as a hospital, and holding the hand of Alma Yonley, as a surgeon probed to find the bullet in his body. The Yonley sisters, Rivera wrote, "went among the stricken soldiers and ministered to their needs in every practicable way. That entire night they were zealous in their attentions, and for several weeks they kindly nursed several, the severity of whose wounds did not permit removal."[28]

The Confederate victory cleared the Lower Valley of Federal forces and opened a route for Lee's army to move north. Morale ran high as Ewell's triumphant columns marched north to the Potomac River. On June 22, the 6th Louisiana passed through Shepherdstown and forded the river there. The men stripped before plunging into the cold water, shouting as they sank in. "The [water] was very high and it was amusing to see the long lines of naked men fording it—their clothing and accountrements slung to their guns and carried above their heads to keep them dry," Captain Seymour wrote in his diary.[29]

The long gray column crossed Maryland, marching through Sharpsburg, past the battlefield on which these Confederates had suffered nine months earlier, and on to Waynesboro in Pennsylvania. Back in enemy territory, Lee's army lived off the land, which was rich in livestock and foodstuffs. The commanding general had forbidden any plundering, destruction of private property or molestation of civilians, and the Louisianians were on their best behavior—comporting themselves in the land of the enemy better than they did in Virginia, some officers observed. Supplies taken from mills, storehouses and farmers were paid for, albeit with Confederate money that was worthless in the North. Some farm families readily offered food to the passing troops, asking only that their barns and homes be spared. General Early made an exception to Lee's rule, however, in burning down the iron furnace and mills owned by Congressman Thaddeus Stevens, a radical, anti-slavery Republican from Pennsylvania. While there, the men of the 6th Louisiana and the rest of the brigade helped themselves "most bountifully to the products of his broad and fertile acres," Captain Seymour wrote.[30]

By the night of June 26, the Louisiana Brigade reached the outskirts of Gettysburg, where Early's Division dispersed some green and easily-scared Pennsylvania militiamen. It was during this first visit to Gettysburg that some members of Hays' Brigade, most likely including a number of Colonel Monaghan's Irishmen, went on a drunken spree. Hays had consented to giving his soldiers a pint ration of whiskey. Men who didn't drink alcohol passed theirs on to those who did, and soon numerous Louisianians were stinking drunk, triggering both hilarity and fisticuffs. Some of the men stole into Gettysburg and managed to secure more liquor. It was a hung-over brigade that stumbled along the road the next morning. "Resumed the march at daylight," Captain Seymour recorded, "the men having had too much free access to liquor, of which there were large quantities in Gettysburg, many of them were drunk and caused me much trouble to make them keep up with the column." The most difficult stragglers were put into the cooks' wagons, "where they had a rough and disagreeable ride on the sharp sides and projecting legs of the pots & kettles, which sobered them speedily."[31]

Their drinking binge over, the Louisiana troops continued the march northeast with Early's Division, which had been ordered to advance to the town of York to cut the railroad there and to burn bridges over the Susquehanna River. They now were moving through the lush farmland of the Pennsylvania Dutch, dotted with sturdy barns literally bursting with oats, wheat and corn. The countryside was strangely denuded of horses and mules, which the Confederate army much needed. "The Pennsylvania farmers had sent most of their horses and mules to the other side of the Susquehannah River to prevent their falling into our hands," Captain Seymour explained. The quartermasters were ordered to scour the country for them. "Horses were found in bedrooms, parlours, lofts of barns and other out-of-the-way places." The quartermaster of the Louisiana Brigade, Maj. John G. Campbell, heard that the owner of one large, fine house had a splendid horse, but the man denied it. "The Major quietly opened the door and there in an elegant parlour, comfortably stalled in close proximity to a costly rosewood piano, stood a noble looking horse," which the major took, paying in Confederate currency.[32]

The Louisianians reached York on June 28, the same day Lee learned the Federal army had crossed the Potomac River and was marching hard to meet him. With his army strung out over many miles, Lee decided to concentrate in the vicinity of Gettysburg, and ordered his scattered corps to hasten there. "On the morning of the 30th," Lt. Michael Murray of the 6th Louisiana's Company F, wrote, "we turned back towards Gettysburg, where important business awaited us."[33]

Chapter Nine

The Turning Point: GETTYSBURG

"On every face was most legibly written the firm determination to do or die."
— *Captain William J. Seymour*

The "important business" awaiting at Gettysburg was nothing less than the pivotal battle of the war for Lee's army. As the general hurried his scattered divisions to their fateful rendezvous with the Army of the Potomac, Maj. Gen. Ulysses S. Grant was strangling the besieged garrison trapped inside Vicksburg, the key to control of the Mississippi River. While a victory in Pennsylvania might not assist General Pemberton's army in Mississippi, a defeat north of the Potomac River, coupled with another out west, would spell catastrope for the South.

On June 30, as the 6th Louisiana reversed its northeastward march and turned back toward Gettysburg along with the rest of Early's Division, the prospects for inflicting a crippling blow on the Federal army seemed promising. The Union army, demoralized after its stunning defeat at Chancellorsville almost two months earlier, was again in the throes of another upheaval in command. On June 28, President Lincoln abruptly removed "Fighting Joe" Hooker and installed Maj. Gen. George G. Meade in his place. Meade, the untested former commander of the Federal Fifth Corps, was thoroughly surprised at his sudden appointment, found himself in charge of some 100,000 men stretched out along a 25-mile front in Maryland, groping for Lee's 75,000-man army he believed was on the loose in his native Pennsylvania. He would not even enjoy the luxury of getting used to the idea of being fully responsible for the Army of the Potomac before it would collide with the confident army of the seemingly invincible Lee.[1]

Gettysburg was a town of 2,400 people in-mid-1863. More importantly as far as the armies were concerned, it was a hub where ten roads converged like the spokes on a wheel, reaching out in all directions as if to pull in everything on the move in the surrounding region. Lee recognized the strategic value of controlling this road network and thus chose the area as the place to concentrate his forces. After a copy of Lee's orders reached him late on June 29, General Early put his division on the march to Gettysburg the next morning. The Louisiana Brigade hiked 22 miles that day, camping that night in the vicinity of Heidlersburg, some 10 miles north of Gettysburg. The Louisiana men knew that the turnabout suggested a battle was imminent, "and it was inspiring to see the spirits of our men rise at the prospect of a fight," Captain Seymour recorded in his diary. "We all knew that were Meade's Army to be defeated, the roads to Washington, Baltimore and Philadelphia would be open to us."[2]

The Battle of Gettysburg opened in upside-down fashion on the morning of Wednesday, July 1, with the Army of Northern Virginia advancing from the west and north, and the Army of the Potomac marching up from the south. Hays' Louisianians were marching southwest on the Harrisburg Road early that morning when the first clash occurred on the low ridges just northwest of Gettysburg. There the advance brigade of Maj. Gen. Henry Heth's Division of Hill's Corps, marching from nearby Cashtown, ran into the dismounted troopers of Maj. Gen. John Buford's Federal cavalry division, who were gamely fighting to hold back the heavy gray columns long enough for Federal infantry to arrive. The Louisianians were still several miles from this morning collision when it began to widen and intensify, as elements of the Federal I Corps under Maj. Gen. John Reynolds arrived. Heth, meanwhile, fed more of his men into the unplanned and now escalating conflict. Lee had warned his subordinates to avoid a general engagement until he had concentrated all his troops, but the fight now took on the properties of a whirlpool, sucking in brigades and divisions as they came within its awful pull.[3]

"The heavy booming of cannon told us that the conflict had begun and we pushed on with great rapidity," Captain Seymour recalled. Marching at the rear of Early's column, The Louisiana Brigade arrived within a mile-and-a-half north of the town shortly after noon. Robert Rodes' Division, deployed on high ground to the right called Oak Hill, was already engaged. South of Rodes and on his right was A. P. Hill's Third Corps, pushing hard toward Gettysburg from the west. Early swung John Gordon's Brigade into position to the left of Rodes and joined the advance, as Hays hurried the Louisiana regiments down the road to form his line of battle.[4]

As the brigade deployed, the 6th Louisiana, with about 220 officers and men present, was commanded by Lieutenant Colonel Hanlon. The regiment's regular commander, Colonel Monaghan, had taken sick after the battle at Winchester. Hanlon, a 32-year-old former New Orleans newspaper reporter, had spent but little time with the regiment on campaign and had never led it in battle. Severely wounded at First Winchester in May 1862, Hanlon spent nearly a year recuperating, missing Jackson's Valley Campaign, the Peninsula Campaign, Second Manassas, Antietam and all the other actions of 1862. Not long after rejoining the regiment, he was captured at Fredericksburg on May 4, 1863, and missed the Second Winchester battle. He returned to the 6th Louisiana as it advanced into Pennsylvania. In neither experience nor appearance was Hanlon especially impressive. Irish-born and fair skinned, with hazel eyes and brown hair, Hanlon was slight of build, standing 5 ft. 7 in. With Hanlon at its head, the 6th Louisiana entered the action without a battle-tested commander.[5]

About 2:00 p.m., Hays put the 5th and 6th Louisiana on the right of the Harrisburg Road, next to Gordon's men, and placed the 7th and 8th Louisiana on the left, with the 9th Louisiana in the center straddling the road. From the high plateau on the extreme left of Hays' line, Lt. J. Warren Jackson of the 8th Louisiana "could see Rodes on our right driving the Yankees like sheep before him." It was, he wrote to his brother, "the prettiest sight I ever saw."[6]

The Federals opposing Early's men were from Maj. Gen. Oliver O. Howard's XI Corps, the same German-Americans who had been routed by Jackson at Chancellorsville and tagged, somewhat unfairly, as "flying Dutchmen." It would be their destiny, over the next two days, to face the "fighting Irish" of the 6th Louisiana and the rest of Hays' confident Tigers, and the outcome would do nothing to restore their tarnished reputation. Before Hays ordered the Louisianians forward, Gordon had advanced his brigade through a field of golden wheat against blue troops massed on a wooded knoll just across Rock Creek, which skirts the town on the east. Charging across the creek and up the hill, Gordon's Georgians smashed into the division of Brig. Gen. Francis Barlow, driving it back in panic and capturing many prisoners, including the severely wounded Barlow. Seeing Gordon's success, Early ordered Hays' brigade and Hoke's North Carolina Brigade (temporarily commanded by Col. Isaac Avery) across Rock Creek to join in the assault sweeping toward town.[7]

Barlow's division was shattered and the entire Union XI Corps line was unraveling as the Confederate columns stormed down from the north (Rodes) and northeast (Early). Concurrently, A. P. Hill's Third Corps was turning up the pressure from the west. With the North Carolina brigade on his left, Hays pushed his eager Louisiana Tigers across the creek toward a ragged line of Federals. These men were remnants of Barlow's beaten division (from the brigades of Brig. Gens. Adelbert Ames and Leopold von Gilsa) attempting to rally near the Almshouse. Despite what Hays called an "unusually galling" barrage of artillery fire from nearby Federal batteries, the screaming Louisiana attackers drove Ames and von Gilsa back and pushed on towards the railroad tracks that skirted the edge of the town.[8]

There, at a brickyard operated by John Kuhn, the Louisiana regiments smashed through a brigade of New Yorkers and Pennsylvanians rushed forward from the XI Corps position on Cemetery Hill south of the town. The three regiments of this brigade—commanded by Col. Charles R. Coster, of Brig. Gen. Adolph Von Steinwehr's division—fared no better than Barlow's beaten men, falling back through the streets of the town or throwing down their arms and surrendering as the Louisianians rushed upon them. "On we pushed, driving the enemy in great confusion upon the town, taking whole regiments belonging to the 11th Corps," Captain Seymour wrote. "One Dutch Colonel at the head of about 250 men came up to me and cried out that he surrendered. . . .I made him throw his sword upon the ground and sent the whole party back to our rear guard under the escort of only one Confederate soldier."[9]

With their route of escape through the town of Gettysburg nearly cut off, hundreds of men from Howard's shattered corps surrendered. The Louisiana Brigade swept through the town "clearing it of the enemy and taking prisoners at every turn," in Hays' words. "We ran them thro the town & caught hundreds of them in the houses & cellars," the 8th Louisiana's Lieutenant Jackson reported. Captain Seymour wrote that the Louisianians faced "very severe" fire of musketry and artillery in the town, where two cannon were posted to sweep the street on which they were advancing, but "on they swept, capturing the two pieces of cannon and driving the enemy pell mell through and beyond the town."

Seymour claimed that the brigade captured 3,000 prisoners—about double its own strength—though that seems exaggerated in light of official reports that the XI Corps lost 1,510 missing or captured for the entire battle. Hays reported the number of prisoners taken "exceeded in numbers the force under my command."[10]

Captain Michael O'Connor, the Irish-born commander of the 6th Louisiana's Company F, considered the action a commendable day's work by his Irish lads. His company, he wrote, "advanced under a heavy fire of artillery and infantry" in its charge upon the XI Corps regiments, to whom he generously gave credit for "showing a stubborn resistance." "We drove him back with great loss and captured the town, which we occupied during the night." O'Connor, a 37-year-old former storekeeper in New Orleans, had just returned to his duties after recuperating from a severe wound received at Chantilly nine months earlier.[11]

As Gettysburg citizens who hadn't already fled town huddled in their cellars, the 6th Louisiana and the rest of Hays' men secured the streets, rounding up the last of the surrendering Unionists, and formed a battle line along a street in the middle of the town. There they finally had a chance to rest, savoring what General Early called "a brilliant victory" in which he said 6,000 to 7,000 Federal troops and two cannon had been captured. Nevertheless, Early, Hays and some other Confederate commanders were not yet satisfied with the day's success, for they sensed a chance to turn a brilliant victory into a decisive one.[12]

The survivors of the two shattered Federal corps who managed to escape through Gettysburg were digging in along the hills and ridges southeast of town. Cemetery Hill, topped by Evergreen Cemetery and its two-story arched brick gate-house, and heavily-wooded Culp's Hill, just to its east, rose from the plain less than half-mile below Gettysburg. A long, low ridge ran south from these two heights to another pair of rocky, wooded hills two miles away called Round Top and Little Round Top. General Early, who recognized Cemetery Hill as a commanding position and superb ground for defense, saw an opportunity to capture the eminence. The hill appeared to be lightly defended by tired and demoralized troops, and most of Meade's army was still on the roads marching hard toward Gettysburg. The victorious Confederates outnumbered them now, but by morning the odds would tip in favor of the Federals. As daylight faded on the first day of the battle, there was an opportunity beckoning to be seized.[13]

This photograph depicts the crest of Cemetery Hill, which was captured by Harry Hays' Louisiana Brigade after a decisive attack and sharp hand-to-hand struggle on the evening of July 2, 1863. When promised reinforcements failed to arrive, Hays was forced to relinquish this key piece of terrain. *James P. Gannon*

And the aggressive Early ached to seize it. After he was satisfied that his men had secured the town, he rode out in search of Ewell or Hill or Rodes, "for the purpose of urging an immediate advance upon the enemy, before he could recover from his evident dismay and confusion." Rodes' men were beginning to enter the town from the west, while Hill and his troops remained out and beyond Seminary Ridge, a mile or more west of town. Early sent a courier to Hill to say that if Hill "would send a division forward we could take the hill to which the enemy had retreated." Early then found Ewell, but when he made his case for an attack, Early hesitated. Major Harry Gilmor, commanding a Maryland Cavalry unit, heard Early say to Ewell, "I can take my division and drive the enemy beyond those heights; and if this is not done, you will find a line of works there in the morning that will cost us dear." Ewell, who had been issued a discretionary order from Lee urging an attack on the hills if he "could do so to advantage," said he wanted to await the arrival of General Johnson's Division, which was still marching toward Gettysburg from Carlisle, before attempting any assault.[14]

Back in town, the Louisiana troops, their blood still up from the excitement and glory of the day, were beginning to wonder why they had not pursued the defeated Federals further. As Ewell hesitated and daylight faded, some of them began to grumble that their old corps commander, Stonewall Jackson, would not have let the beaten Federals escape to those commanding heights beyond the town. Captain Seymour recalled hearing many Louisiana officers and men lament that Jackson was not there to lead them. "Here we all felt the loss of Gen. Jackson most sensibly," Seymour wrote in his diary. "Had he been alive and in command when we charged through the town, I am sure that he would have given his usual orders under like circumstances, 'push on the infantry,' and time would not have been afforded the enemy to make their position impregnable."[15]

Ewell, though, wasn't Jackson, and no one else was either. Ewell's orders from Lee directed him to make the attack if he thought he could do so successfully, which he likely interpreted to mean that he must be certain of success—and he wasn't confident he could take those hills without Johnson's Division. Johnson, however, was delayed by a false report of Federal troops approaching from the east and arrived too late for an attack to be attempted before darkness had fallen.[16]

When it became clear that the day's fighting was over, the men of the 6th Louisiana lay down to sleep in the town, happy with the day's result but with anxiety for the morrow. Considering the fighting they had done in the last few hours, they were lucky not to have had a single man killed and only a few wounded. The whole Louisiana Brigade emerged with amazingly light casualties for the day. Hays reported his losses as seven killed, 41 wounded, and 15 missing, and guessed that the casualties of the enemy forces facing him exceeded his "by at least six to one." The 6th Louisiana emerged from the day's fighting without any killed or wounded for a change, but with five men missing.[17]

While there was reason for satisfaction as the day ended, so too was there reason for anxiety. As the Louisiana soldiers drifted into sleep, the muffled sounds from Cemetery Hill foretold something of the fear to be faced with the dawn. The noises echoing off the hillock were those of shovels and bayonets digging into rocky ground, of axes biting into tree trunks, and trees falling to provide breastworks behind which veteran infantry would await them. And thousands more were arriving on the field that night. The battle was not over; in fact, it had only just begun.

The fitful sleep of the 6th Louisiana's weary foot soldiers did not last long in those pre-dawn hours of July 2. Around midnight, General Early ordered the Louisiana Brigade commander to make a reconnaissance of the ground between the town and Cemetery Hill, to look for a position from which to attack. After surveying the situation, Hays roused his men about 2:00 a.m. and moved them forward and to the left, into an open field beyond the edge of town, near the red brick home of farmer William Culp. There they lay down behind the doubtful protection of a low hill that intervened between them and the northeast face of Cemetery Hill, about 600 yards distant, where the Union troops were digging rifle pits, taking up positions behind low stone fences, and positioning batteries of artillery.[18]

"All night long the Federals were heard chopping away and working like beavers, and when the day dawned the ridge was found to be crowned with strongly built fortifications and bristling with a most formidable array of cannon," Captain Seymour's diary reports. It was exactly as Early had predicted to Ewell the evening before. The Louisiana troops, and Avery's North Carolinians just to their left, faced an imposing, 100-foot hill now strongly fortified against an expected attack. The odds had shifted heavily in favor of the Federals.[19]

Lee's plan of attack for July 2 called for the main assault to be made by two divisions from Longstreet's Corps on the left, or southerly end, of the fishhook-shaped Federal line. Ewell's Corps would demonstrate against the right of the Union line, along the curve formed by Cemetery and Culp's hills. Ewell was ordered to hold his fire until he heard the guns announcing Longstreet's attack, and he was given freedom to convert his action into a full-scale assault if such a course seemed promising. Johnson's Division was assigned the arduous task of assaulting Culp's Hill, while Early's men were to take Cemetery Hill. However, only two of Early's four brigades—Hay's Louisianians and Avery's North Carolinians—were put in line for the assault. Gordon's Georgians remained in reserve behind the Tigers and Tar Heels, while "Extra Billy" Smith's Virginians were well in the rear, guarding the York road. Ewell's third division, commanded by General Rodes, was posted to the right of Early's and was expected to assault Cemetery Hill from the northwest after Johnson and Early engaged, thus squeezing the bend in the Federal line from three sides.[20]

When the rays of the morning sun began lighting their position, the Louisiana regiments saw that they were in a precarious place, hugging the ground below the cannons on the crest of Cemetery Hill and the infantrymen crouching in rifle pits and along stone walls on its slope. Hays' 1,200 men were strung out in a little ravine along a small stream called Winebrenner's Run. They had expected to attack early in the morning, but as the sun rose high and the day wore on, they remained prone and miserable, unable to move. General Ewell wanted to pull Early's men back when he became aware that Longstreet's attack would be delayed, but he could not do so. Ewell "expressed great anxiety to withdraw our Brigade," Captain Seymour wrote, but it was impossible to move the Louisianians without exposing them to murderous fire. "So we had to remain there—more than five hundred yards in advance of Ewell's main line of battle—hugging the ground behind a very low ridge which only partially covered us from the enemy's fire. It was almost certain death for a man to stand upright and we lost during the day forty-five men in killed and wounded from the fire of the enemy's sharpshooters, who were armed with long-ranged Whitworth rifles that would kill at a distance of twelve hundred yards." While Hays did not describe in his official report his brigade's formation as it waited for the attack, one authority on the battle has the brigade deployed in a single line with the 5th Louisiana on the right, and the 6th, 9th, 7th and 8th regiments in turn to its left.[21]

Lieutenant Colonel Hanlon and his Irishmen, their bodies pressed to the earth as they listened to bullets whiz by, must have wondered why they were spending the whole day under a deadly fire and a broiling July sun. Lee had wanted the attack to begin much earlier, but Longstreet took hours to march his divisions, by a circuitous route, into the assigned positions for launching the attack along the Emmitsburg Road, near Little Round Top. It was almost 5:00 p.m. before Ewell heard the distant booming of cannon, signaling that Longstreet finally had begun the assault on the Union left.[22]

Moments later, the roar of cannon boomed along the front that Early's men prepared to attack. Confederate batteries posted on Benner's Hill, a half-mile in the rear, opened a barrage on Cemetery Hill. For an hour Maj. Joseph W. Latimer's artillery pummeled the Unionists on that crest, but Latimer's gun crews caught hellfire from an even larger number of Federal cannon responding from Culp's and Cemetery hills. The contest, Captain Seymour recalled, was an unequal one, with "the Federals bringing at least 50 pieces to bear upon our 18 guns; their guns were protected by earth works while ours were placed on the bald top of a hill with no covering of any kind to guns or men." The Louisiana soldiers stretched out on the field below, between the dueling batteries, were awestruck by the spectacle. As Seymour remembered it, "the roar of the guns was continuous and deafening; the shot and shell could be seen

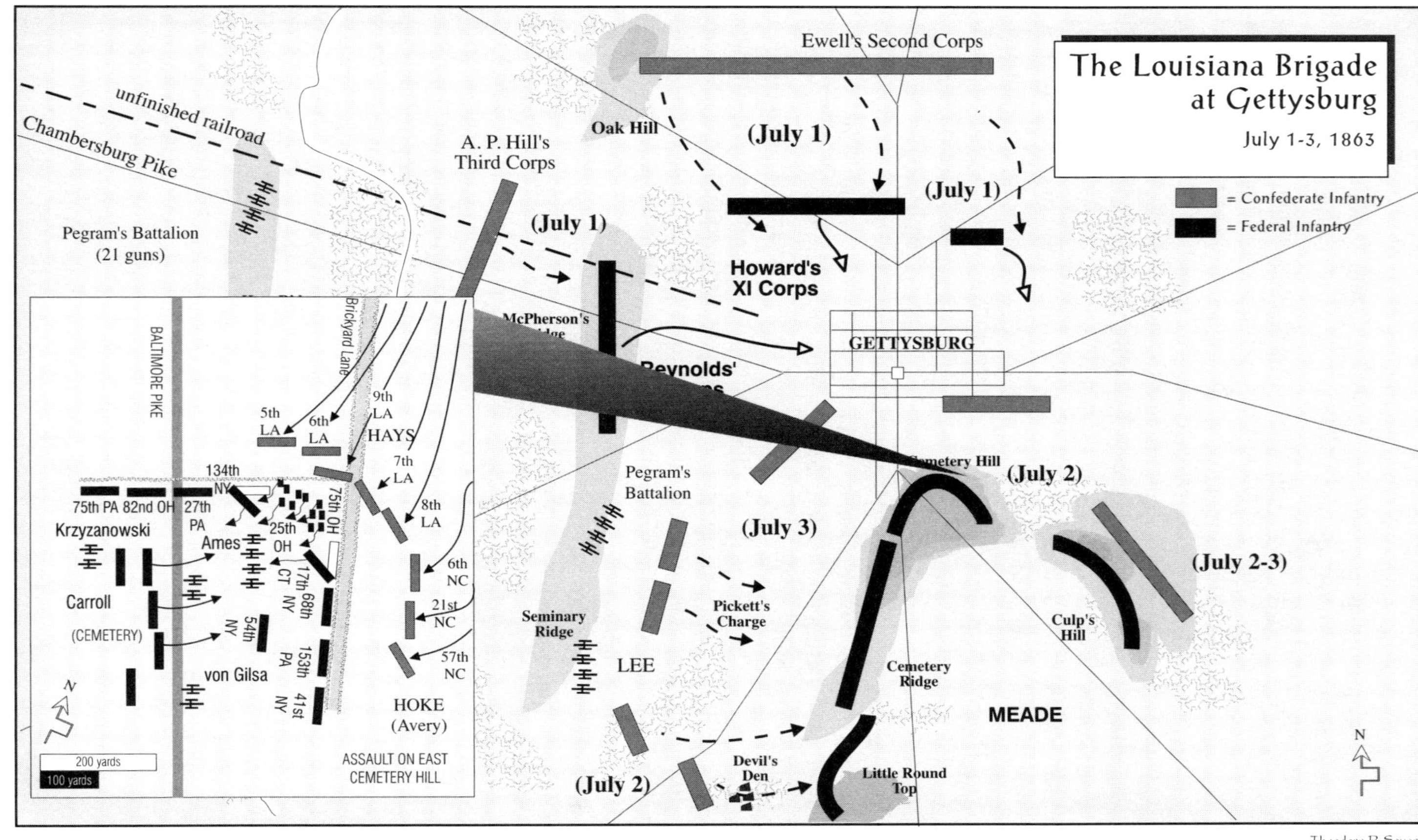

Theodore P. Savas

tearing through the hostile batteries, dismounting guns, killing and wounding men and horses, while ever and anon an ammunition chest would explode, sending a bright column of smoke far up towards the heavens."[23]

The cannonade continued for an hour until the survivors of the hard-hit Confederate batteries were forced to abandon Benner's Hill. The sun had sunk in the west, behind the two hills targeted for the Confederate assault, when the Louisianians first heard the rattle of musketry off to their left, indicating that Johnson's men were beginning their long, hard climb up steep Culp's Hill. They knew then that their time also had come to leave what little protective cover they had enjoyed and face uphill into the guns on Cemetery Hill. "The quiet, solemn mien of our men showed plainly that they fully appreciated the desperate character of the undertaking," wrote Captain Seymour, "but on every face was most legibly written the firm determination to do or die." Lieutenant Jackson of the 8th Louisiana, immediately to the right of Hanlon's men, put it in more personal terms: "I felt as if my doom was sealed, and it was with great reluctance that I started my skirmishers forward."[24]

After the artillery barrage ended, Ewell ordered Johnson to assault Culp's Hill and told Early to advance his two brigades upon Cemetery Hill. Rodes' Division, deployed in the town itself, was ordered to support Early and strike the hill from the northwest. The attack might have been suicidal, had all the Federal forces originally posted on the two hills remained there. Meade had been sufficiently alarmed by Longstreet's furious assault on his left and center, however, that he had shifted a large part of his force from Culp's Hill to blunt Longstreet's attack. The wooded and rocky slopes were now but thinly defended, and the only forces on Cemetery Hill were the ill-fated men of Howard's XI Corps, whose rout of the previous day remained fresh in their minds as they crouched behind their stone walls and in their rifle pits, awaiting the attack as dusk fell.

It was nearly 8:00 p.m. when Early gave the order to attack. Lieutenant Colonel Hanlon led his 6th Louisiana up the low rise behind which they had hidden for almost 18 hours. Exercising cramped limbs, they jogged to the crest, where Union gunners and riflemen saw them dimly outlined against the darkening horizon, silhouettes on the run. In Hays' words, his men "had gone but a short distance when my whole line became exposed to a most terrific fire from the enemy's batteries from the entire range of hills in front, and to the right and left." As

Seymour remembered it. "The Yankees have anticipated this movement and now thirty pieces of cannon vomit forth a perfect storm of grape, canister, shrapnel, etc., while their infantry pour into us a close fire from their rifles."[25]

As some of the silhouetted figures crumpled to the ground, the Louisiana line surged on. Soon the Louisianians reached the little valley at the foot of Cemetery Hill, where they encountered the first of three lines of Federal infantry who blindly discharged their weapons into the dark mass rolling toward them. Artillery also opened on the advancing Southerners. The musket fire and canister were heavy, but not particularly destructive, as the Federal missiles "are hissing, screaming & hurtling over our heads, doing but little damage," recalled Seymour. "Owing to the darkness of the evening, now verging into night, and the deep obscurity afforded by the smoke of the firing," Hays reported, "our exact locality could not be discovered by the enemy's gunners, and we thus escaped what in the full light of day could have been nothing else than horrible slaughter."[26]

Slaughter it was not, but still men were falling wounded and dead on the upslope, among them the North Carolinians' commander, Colonel Avery, who was fatally shot from his horse. One of the 6th Louisiana men who fell in the dimming twilight was Color Sergeant Phillip Bolger, who had assumed the dangerous assignment after John Heil was killed at Sharpsburg. General Hays, who joined his men on foot for the assault, urged his men forward and the Louisianians plunged through and over the first wavering line of Federal skirmishers and on toward the second line, posted behind a stone wall at the base of the hill. The men crouching behind the low L-shaped wall, firing at the shadowy figures rushing toward them, were some of the same troops that Early's men had beaten badly the day before—the brigades of Generals Ames and von Gilsa. Ames' brigade, temporarily under command of Col. Andrew L. Harris (Ames was commanding the division in place of the captured General Barlow), mustered only about 650 rifles in three Ohio regiments and one from New England. The 25th Ohio manned the angle of the wall's L, facing both north and east, with the 107th Ohio to its left, facing north, and the 75th Ohio and 17th Connecticut to its right, facing east. To their right, the 500 men of von Gilsa's thin brigade held the southern end of the wall—three New York Regiments, the 41st, 54th and 68th, composed mostly of German immigrants, and the 153rd Pennsylvania, which included many men of German descent.[27]

With the memory of yesterday's beating still vivid in their minds, these startled Federals put up some fight but hardly proved to be an immovable obstacle to the onrushing Louisiana Tigers, now in full-throated fury screaming their Rebel yell. "On we went over fences, ditches, thro marshy fields and we 'botch up' at a stone fence behind which Mr. Yank had posted himself and did not want to leave," the 8th Louisiana's Jackson wrote. "But with bayonets and clubbed guns we drove them back." A sergeant in the 25th Ohio regiment remembered that Hay's Louisianians "put their big feet on the stone wall and went over like deer, over the heads of the whole. . .regiment."[28]

The Confederates' success in overrunning the Union line posted behind the stone wall was aided by an ill-timed decision just before the attack, when General Ames moved the 17th Connecticut regiment out of its place in line to a position left of von Gilsa's brigade, creating a gap that the Louisiana attackers exploited. Col. Andrew L. Harris of the 75th Ohio regiment, commanding Ames' Second Brigade, reported that the gap left by the 17th Connecticut was left "unoccupied, excepting by a few of the 25th Ohio Volunteers." To the surprised Harris, it seemed like the charging Louisianians were all around him. "About dusk the enemy attacked the regiment in front and on the flank and rear at nearly the same time, having come through the space which had been vacated by the removal of the 17th Connecticut Volunteers," he reported. "From this attack but few escaped, and those only in the darkness and smoke; the greater portion were no doubt made prisoners."[29]

Many of the Federals overrun at the stone wall were captured. "We passed such of the enemy who had not fled, and who were still clinging for shelter to the wall, to the rear as prisoners," Hays reported. Nearing the top of the hill, his men had to climb over an abatis of felled trees before reaching the third line of Howard's men, hunched down in rifle pits. At least some of them were not in a fighting mood, for Hays reported that this line, too, was quickly breached and his men "found many of the enemy who had not fled hiding in the pits for protection." These captives also were ordered to the rear as the Louisianians raced the last few steps to the crest of the hill, where they approached the objective of their charge, two Federal batteries that were furiously belching canister at the dark mass rolling up the hill toward them. The gunners of Capt. Michael Weidrich's New York battery and Capt. R. Bruce Rickett's Pennsylvania battery bravely stood to their guns and kept firing as the attackers neared. When the Confederates rushed among them, the gunners grabbed whatever weapons they could lay their hands on and continued the fight.[30]

The right wing of Hays' line, which included the 6th Louisiana, would have been closer to Weidrich's battery than to Ricketts' guns when the Louisianians reached the top of the hill, and it is probable that whatever number of Hanlon's men actually reached the crest fell upon the New York gunners. It may have been only a handful of the regiment, for many had fallen killed or wounded. In the darkness and the frenzy of the charge all organization was lost, and men of various Louisiana regiments mingled in a swarming mass as they crashed upon the Union guns. A brief but savage hand-to-hand battle between Hays' Tigers and the XI corps cannoneers swirled around the smoke-shrouded guns. While accounts of the fighting around Weidrich's battery are sparse, the ferocity of the fighting can be imagined from the report filed by Captain Ricketts, whose crews were attacked by a mixed gang of Louisianians and North Carolinians. "A heavy column of the enemy charged on my battery and succeeded in capturing and spiking my left piece," Ricketts later reported. "The cannoneers fought them hand to hand with handspikes, rammers and pistols and succeeded in checking them for a moment. . . ."[31]

Major Harry Gilmor, the Maryland cavalryman who had watched and described the Louisiana Brigade's grand charge at Second Winchester on June 14, was also on hand at Gettysburg and volunteered to accompany Hay's men in the charge on East Cemetery Hill. Gilmor's account of the "terrible fight" around the guns at the crest of the hill captures the bravery displayed by the Louisianians and the stout defense offered by the Federals:

> While advancing on the main line of works, I saw one of our color-bearers jump on a gun and display his flag. He was instantly killed. But the flag was seized by an Irishman, who, with a wild shout, sprang upon the gun, and he too was shot down. Then a little bit of a fellow, a captain, seized the staff and mounted the same gun; but as he raised the flag, a ball broke the arm which held it. He dropped his sword, and caught the staff with his right before it fell, waved it over his head with a cheer, indifferent to the pain of his shattered limb and the whizzing balls around him. His third cheer was just heard, when he tottered and fell, pierced through the lungs.[32]

It was "a simultaneous rush from my whole line," according to Hays, that swept over the Union guns, where the screaming Louisianians "captured several pieces of artillery, four stand of colors and a number of prisoners." For now, at least, the guns were quiet. "At that time every piece of artillery which had been firing upon us was silenced," Hays wrote. "A quiet of several minutes now ensued." The Louisianians listened, hoping to hear the sound of the support they had been promised. Waiting in the quiet and the dark about the captured Federal guns, the Louisiana general and his men may have realized that they had not only penetrated Meade's line, but had captured a commanding position which could make his entire system of defenses untenable if it could be held. From this position the Confederates could turn the artillery and enfilade the spine of the Federal line, which stretched along low-lying Cemetery Ridge toward the Round Tops—a potentially devastating fire that would drive the enemy from their position with great loss. Cemetery Hill was perhaps the key to the whole battle—if it could be held.[33]

That big "if" weighed heavily on Hays. "General Hays immediately reformed his line and anxiously waited to hear Rodes' guns co-operating with us on the right," Captain Seymour recalled. The Louisiana general had understood that Rodes would advance to his support from the northwest side of Cemetery Hill when he attacked on the northeast. He waited apprehensively to hear Rodes' promised advance, or perhaps the arrival of Gordon's Brigade, which Early had held back near the town in a position to provide support if needed. Now it was needed. Before too many minutes had passed, Hays heard troops approaching, but in the blackness surrounding him it was impossible to know whether they were friend or foe. He had been "cautioned to expect friends" coming to his support from Rodes, and even when the approaching line of infantry let loose a volley of musketry, their commander ordered his Tigers to hold their fire, for these might be Confederates advancing and mistakenly firing at his men. Stabs of flame pierced the darkness a second time—another volley—but still Hays held his fire. When a third volley rang out, "the flashing musketry disclosed the still-advancing line to be one of the enemy," so finally the Louisiana general gave his men the order to fire, which checked the advance of the dimly-seen Federals briefly. Soon Hays could make out a second line of infantry behind the first, and another one behind that, signifying a counter-attack in force.[34]

After the Louisianians delivered a volley at Hays' command—a blast delivered "full in the faces of the enemy" at only 20 feet, according to

Captain Seymour—the first line of Federals seemed to have "melted away in the darkness." But soon after, "another and heavier line was discovered in our front," Seymour wrote, "while two columns were heard advancing upon our flanks, threatening to surround and capture our little Brigade and the few men of Hoke's [North Carolina] Brigade who charged with us." These troops approaching from the front and flanks were XI Corps regiments rushed to the scene by General Howard when he heard the Louisianians' yell as they fell upon the guns. Others were men from John Caldwell's division of Maj. Gen. Winfield Scott Hancock's II Corps, who were responding for a plea for help from Howard.[35]

The first Federals to reach the Tigers around Wiedrich's battery probably were two XI Corps regiments, the 58th and 119th New York, of Col. Wladimir Krzyzanowski's brigade. Along with his division commander, Maj. Gen. Carl Schurz, the Polish-born colonel double-quicked his two regiments a short distance across the Baltimore Pike to the battery's position on East Cemetery Hill. To his "great surprise," General Schurz said, "we found a general melee in the battery itself" with the Confederates holding "some of the guns" and the cannoneers "defending themselves valiantly." The 119th New York, advancing first with bayonets fixed, was only 200 strong, but with a "vigorous rush" crashed upon the Louisianians and drove them down the hill. When they reached the base, the New Yorkers dropped down as Weidrich's guns blasted canister at the retreating Confederates, who probably would have included any 6th Louisiana men who had reached the crest.[36]

A separate counterattack against the Confederates in the Union gunpits was made by Col. Samuel S. Carroll's brigade. They had come on a run from their position back of the cemetery, along the ridge where Hancock's corps was posted. Carroll double-quicked three of his four regiments to the trouble, the 14th Indiana in the lead, followed by the 7th West Virginia and the 4th Ohio. They crossed the Baltimore Pike and dashed in the direction of Ricketts' battery. "We found the enemy up to and some of them in among the front guns of the batteries," Carroll reported. In the gloom and smoke it was nearly impossible to make out just where the Confederates were until the shooting started. "It being perfectly dark, and with no guide, I had to find the enemy's line entirely by their fire," Carroll reported. For a time, some of Carroll's men found themselves in a crossfire from the Louisiana and North Carolina Confederates on the hill and behind nearby stone walls, but soon the weight of Carroll's numbers overwhelmed the Southerners.[37]

In his report, General Hays claimed his retreat to the stone wall at the base of the hill was "quietly and orderly effected." He gave the order to withdraw when he concluded he was "beyond the reach of support" and facing overwhelming force. After briefly halting behind the stone wall, the Louisiana regiments were ordered back another 75 yards to a fence to await events. Had it not been for the darkness, "the enemy would have cut us up terribly with his re-captured artillery as we fell back from the Hill," Captain Seymour wrote. Even after he had withdrawn his men from the hill, General Hays momentarily entertained hope of renewing the attack when an officer came with word that Gordon's Brigade was advancing to his support. When Gordon did not show up, and when Hays rode back to look for the Georgian and his regiments, he found him "occupying the precise position in the field occupied by me when I received the order to charge the enemy on Cemetery Hill, and not advancing." By 10:00 p.m. it was over.[38]

LT. JEFFERSON D. VAN BENTHUYSEN

The cost of Gettysburg for Lt. Jefferson Van Benthuysen was his right eye, which he lost when shot in the head during the charge on East Cemetery Hill on July 2, 1863. Captured and hospitalized after the battle, the young officer was imprisoned on Johnson's Island in Ohio after he recovered. He was promoted to captain of Company G, 6th Louisiana, in March of 1864 while still imprisoned, and was not released until February 1865. *Tulane University Library*

Deep disappointment and anger pervaded the ranks as the 6th Louisiana and Hays' other regiments moved back toward the town. They had bravely seized a crucial position within the Union line, and when they needed the support they were promised, it had not come. They had seen comrades killed and wounded to no purpose. "A madder set of men I never saw," wrote a Federal prisoner who witnessed their return. "They cursed their officers in a way and manner that showed experience in the business. . . .It was simply fearful."[39]

The men had good reason to feel resentment. Timely support from Rodes' Division on the right, coupled with Gordon's assistance, might have put enough pressure on the Union line at Cemetery Hill to collapse it entirely. Rodes, unfortunately, was not ready to attack when the crucial time came because he failed to get his men deployed in time. In his memoirs, Early wrote that when he saw that Rodes was not advancing during the attack by his two brigades, he rode out "to urge him forward." He found Rodes "getting his brigades into position" to attack, but he had not done so because he had learned that the division on his immediate right had no plans to advance. Eventually, Rodes expressed willingness to attack if Early thought it proper, but by then Early had heard that his two brigades were retreating, so he told Rodes it was "too late." Early, in turn, explained his failure in sending Gordon to support the attack by arguing that it "would have been a useless sacrifice" to send the Georgia Brigade up Cemetery Hill unless Rodes' Division advanced at the same time. Thus did one general blame the next one for this failure to exploit what was the day's most promising chance for a breakthrough that could have changed the outcome of the Battle of Gettysburg.[40]

Historians have long argued over the what-ifs of this brilliant but ultimately unsuccessful assault. What if Early had ordered Gordon to take his six splendid Georgia regiments to Hays' aid? What if Rodes had not called off his attack? Might the Confederates have overrun Cemetery Hill? Perhaps. "The whole of the three days' battle produced no more tragic might-have-been than this twilight engagement on the Confederate left," wrote Army of Northern Virginia historian Douglas Southall Freeman. To the very end of the war, the men of the 6th Louisiana remembered this night with bittersweet regrets. As he composed the brief history of the regiment in the trenches around Petersburg in the dying days of the conflict, Major Manning wrote with pride and sadness that at Gettysburg, the 6th Louisiana "took part in the charge on the Cemetary Hights on the 2 of July (1863) and if the Regiment was supported we could have held them."[41]

General Ewell's report credited the Louisiana and North Carolina brigades for their outstanding assault and agreed that "the want of coopertion on the right" prevented the attack from succeeding. If the attack had been supported by Rodes, he wrote, "I have every reason to believe, from the eminent success attending the assault of Hays and Avery, that the enemy's lines would have been carried." Early also was full of bitter regrets. Overlooking his own failure to use Gordon, he wrote that if Rodes and the other divisions to the right hadn't held back, the attack by the Louisiana and North Carolina brigades, and that of Johnson's Division, would have succeeded and "Cemetery Hill would have been carried, and the victory would have been ours."[42]

These might-have-beens were no consolation to the men of the 6th Louisiana. Five men of the regiment were killed and three others mortally wounded in the July 2 attack, including Capt. Louis A. Cormier, who fell leading his St. Landry Light Guards in their charge up East Cemetery Hill. Besides the five killed outright, 34 men of the regiment were officially reported wounded (including three who would die of wounds) and 14 captured or missing. Among those severely wounded and captured were the regiment's color bearer, Sgt. Phillip Bolger, who was shot through the arm and lung, and Lt. Jefferson D. Van Benthuysen, who took a shot to the head at the expense of his right eye. The regiment's losses represented about 25 percent of the 222 men reported present for duty on the day before the fighting at Gettysburg began. For the Louisiana Brigade as a whole, the July 2 casualty ratio was not quite as high. Hays' Brigade had 26 killed, 153 wounded and 55 missing, nearly 20 percent of those engaged.[43]

The wounded were carried to a nearby barn which served as a field hospital for Hays' Brigade, where they were tended to the next day by several women of Gettysburg. Among them was Captain Cormier, who was dying of a painful stomach wound. He was a young handsome man, less than 20 years of age, whose suffering attracted the attention of the sympathetic ladies. The young captain told them that he knew he had only hours to live and asked them to stop by later in the day "to see him die." About noon, they gathered round him again. Cormier told them of his mother and two sisters at home, whom he wished were with him, and asked the ladies to kiss him good-bye—which they did, one by one, as he took his final breaths.[44]

After their failed attack on East Cemetery Hill, the survivors of the 6th Louisiana spent a restless night on the edge of the town, close to the spot from which they launched the assault. About daybreak, Hays responded to an order of General Early to move his brigade back into town, in line of battle along Middle Street, which they had occupied two days earlier. There, the Louisianians spent an anti-climactic day even as the Battle of Gettysburg reached its dramatic climax with Lee's last desperate assault on the center of Meade's line—the disaster forever immortalized as "Pickett's Charge." The mid-afternoon attack, spearheaded by the division of Maj. Gen. George E. Pickett and two others led by Johnston Pettigrew and Isaac Trimble, briefly penetrated the center of the Union line but was broken up and driven back with horrendous losses. For General Lee, who accepted blame for the disaster, withdrawal from Gettysburg was now unavoidable.[45]

The 6th Louisiana had spent the entire day of July 3 in the town as Confederate hopes bled away in the valley fronting Cemetery Ridge. The regiment moved out of Gettysburg before the dawn on July 4. Lee, who was anticipating an attack from Meade, ordered Ewell to move his corps to Seminary Ridge, a mile west of town, to be in position to receive it, and there the Louisiana Brigade was put in line of battle as a drenching rain fell on this gloomy Independence Day. Meade, however, remained in a defensive posture and allowed Lee to slip away with his battered forces. [46]

Lee had raided into Pennsylvania with fewer than 75,000 men and he left behind 20,451 of them—a devastating blow from which the Army of Northern Virginia would never fully recover. Meade suffered grievous losses also, officially reported as 23,049, but this represented a smaller portion of his army, which could be more easily reinforced from the North's larger pool of manpower. If this was the "high water mark" of the Confederacy, as it later became known, it was like the high water of a flood, leaving the ground scattered with its debris and its dead.

Such was Gettysburg, a glorious disaster for the South, a disastrous glory for the North, a turning point in the war.[47]

Chapter Ten

Autumn of Disaster: RAPPAHANNOCK STATION

"The affair was disastrous to our Army."
— *Col. William Monaghan, 6th Louisiana*

The march back to Virginia from Gettysburg was an ordeal for the 6th Louisiana and all of Lee's army. For ten days after the battle, the soldiers slogged and the wagons sluiced along roads made soupy by heavy rains, over South Mountain and down into Maryland. Ammunition was low, food was scanty, and the troops were weary and vulnerable to a counterattack from Meade. An 18-mile long train of supply wagons and ambulances had to move first, hauling the thousands of wounded in their agony on a wrenching ride of 42 miles to the Potomac River. The wagon train left on July 4, followed by Hill's Corps and then Longstreet's. In the dark and the downpour, Ewell's divisions departed about 2:00 a.m. on July 5, bringing up the rear of the army.[1]

Colonel Monaghan's men, who could not have numbered more than 150 or so after their losses in battle, were among the last to leave, as Early's Division served as the army's rear guard on the retreat. Though they left Gettysburg in defeat, the spirit of the Louisiana men and the rest of the Confederates remained remarkably high. The Louisiana chaplain, Father Sheeran, observed these men "wading to their knees in the mud and mire," and was struck by their high morale. "They were as cheerful a body of men as I ever saw," he wrote, "and to hear them, you would think they were going to a party of pleasure instead of retreating from a hard fought battle." General Ewell was impressed by that same defiant ebullience, reporting after the retreat, "Their spirit was never better than at this time, and the wish was universal that the enemy would attack." The enemy did not attack, although Meade dispatched bodies of cavalry and infantry to watch the Confederates closely, which provoked some spirited clashes with Early's rear guard. On July 5, there was some "lively skirmishing during the afternoon with the enemy's cavalry and flying artillery," Captain Seymour recalled, before the Louisianians bivouacked for the night near Fairfield, at the foot of South Mountain. That first day's march covered only about six miles.[2]

Crossing the mountain, the 6th Louisiana marched 15 miles on July 6 to Waynesboro, followed by an 11-mile march the following day to near Hagerstown, Maryland. There, the men were ordered to begin preparing defensive positions in anticipation of an attack by the enemy. Lee's army was in a perilous position, gathered in a tight pocket with its back to a rain-swollen and unfordable Potomac River. The only pontoon bridge, at Williamsport, had been destroyed by enemy raiders. If Meade attacked in force now, the Confederates would have little room to maneuver and no way to retreat. Lee ordered a system of defenses constructed and his weary marchers began digging in. "On the 10th, [we] formed line of Battle awaiting the enemy and so remained building breastworks and doing picket duty until the night of the 13th," Captain O'Connor of the 6th Louisiana's Company F noted. "Early on the morning of the 12th," Captain Seymour wrote, "the enemy appeared in heavy force in our front and proceeded to fortify. We were all very anxious to have the Yankees attack us, for our position was a very strong one and we felt perfectly confident that we could defend it successfully."[3]

If the Louisianians, still angry and resentful about the failures at Gettysburg, were eager to fight, Lee was not. He realized the precariousness of the situation and the dire need to get his army across to Virginia, where it could rest and re-equip. An improvised pontoon bridge was being constructed at Falling Waters, a few miles below Williamsport, even as Meade's army was moving toward Lee's, probing his defenses to find a place to attack. The Union commander was under pressure from Lincoln to attack Lee before he could recross the Potomac, but his corps commanders were reluctant to hazard a battle against Lee's strong defensive lines. Meade relayed the information to Washington that he would attack soon, probably on July 14.[4]

The swollen Potomac had subsided a little by July 13, but rain began falling again that afternoon, raising the risk that the river would flood again and perhaps even wash away the makeshift pontoon bridge. Lee decided he could wait no longer and ordered the crossing to begin at dark. Longstreet and Hill marched their corps to the bridge at Falling

Waters, while Ewell's Corps moved to Williamsport to ford, armpit-deep, across the dangerous and rising river. At Williamsport, General Early found the river too deep for the artillery to cross, so he detailed Hays' Louisianians to accompany it to the bridge at Falling Waters. The men of the 6th finally marched back into Virginia about four o'clock in the morning of July 14. "The passage of the Potomac was a very hazardous undertaking," Captain Seymour wrote. "The waters were very high, and the crossing was effected in the face of a watchful and powerful enemy. But it was accomplished with no loss of material except a few disabled wagons & two pieces of cannon which the horses were unable to drag through the deep mud. . . .The rain descended in torrents during the whole night and we all were soaked through to the skin." When Meade awoke the next morning, the day of his promised attack, he found the Confederate trenches empty and Lee's army across the river, its rickety pontoon bridge cut loose to float downstream. Other than a brief cavalry thrust against a portion of Hill's Corps (Heth's Division), Lee escaped from Falling Waters unscathed.[5]

Following Lee's retreat, military operations in Virginia entered an unusual summer lull for several weeks as both armies rested and recovered from the trauma of Gettysburg. The 6th Louisiana's two-week march through the Shenandoah Valley, across the winding and steep roads over Massanutten Mountain and the Blue Ridge east to their new camp just south of the Rapidan River in Orange County, Virginia, ended on August 1. The regiment covered more than 185 miles, according to Captain Seymour's daily log. Most of them arrived exhausted, and many were barefoot; all were in dire need of a respite from fighting and marching.[6]

From August 1 to mid-September, the regiment enjoyed that welcome break as the Louisiana Brigade recuperated in camp three miles south of the Rapidan. "Here a long rest of about two months was afforded our weary men, and in the scanty pleasures of camp life we partially forgot the trials of the past and prepared ourselves for those of the future," one 9th Louisiana private wrote. Though there had been additional desertions along the march route into Pennsylvania and back, officers of the 6th Louisiana were pleased to find some men returning to the ranks. Lt. John Orr, whose bravery at Winchester had earned him a promotion to adjutant of the brigade, wrote in mid-August, "The brigade is rapidly filling with convalescents and deserters, some of whom we never expected to meet again." Three soldiers who had deserted from Company K, for instance, rejoined the company at this time—Pvts. Cain Comfort, Adolph Hale and James Torpey. On the other hand, some 6th Louisiana men wounded in battle found opportunities to desert from their hospital beds, which was one of the most common routes to desertion throughout the war. Company B's records show that Pvt. John Curry deserted from the hospital in Richmond on July 18, and Pvt. Charles Murphy absconded from a hospital in Charlottesville on August 10.[7]

With the return of sick and wounded, the regiment recouped a measure of its lost strength, reporting 214 present for duty at the end of August—almost the number that had arrived at Gettysburg two months before. The summer hiatus ended on September 14 when the regiment marched with the rest of Hays' Brigade to Raccoon Ford on the Rapidan River. The Louisianians were deployed against a threatened crossing by Meade's army, which had moved into position across the Rapidan from the Army of Northern Virginia. Raccoon Ford was one of several crossings along the Rapidan where opposing pickets faced each other at close range and often engaged in deadly skirmishing. The skirmishing on September 14, for example, killed three 6th Louisiana men: Sgt. Duncan Crawford, a Scotsman in Company H; Sgt. Amos Lacomb, a St. Landry man in Company C; and Pvt. Edward Shaw, an English immigrant from New Orleans. The men took their turns on the picket line, a dangerous duty none of them relished. "Remained at Raccoon Ford building breastworks and doing severe picket duty in the rifle pits without shelter," Captain O'Connor of Company F wrote in his muster roll report. The picketing lasted until October 8, when the regiment pulled out as part of a general movement known as the Bristoe Campaign.[8]

General Lee wanted to resume the offensive against Meade but felt he could not do so because he had temporarily lost Longstreet's Corps, transferred to the war in Georgia. When he learned, however, that Meade's army also had been weakened by a similar transfer of two corps, the Confederate commander ordered another bold flanking move against his familar enemy. Lee proposed to sweep around the Army of the Potomac in a march to the northwest and take a stand between the Federals and Washington, just as he had done 14 months earlier in the flanking movement by Jackson's Corps against John Pope that resulted in the Battle of Second Manassas. When Meade got wind of Lee's move, he immediately began marching his army back toward Washington, triggering a foot race northward. Meade wanted to get back to a defensive line behind Bull Run and Lee wanted to cut him off before he got there.[9]

It was a hard march for the 6th Louisiana. The regiment trudged along from dawn till well past dark for five days, reaching Warrenton on

October 13. The next day, the Louisianians moved out at daylight, "the enemy retreating and firing close in front," Captain O'Connor reported, with the 6th Louisiana "occasionally forming line of battle and double-quicking all day after the most severe march we have had during the war." Coming from a veteran of Jackson's forced marches in the Valley, the superlative had meaning.[10]

The clash of the two armies came on October 14 at Bristoe Station, along the Orange and Alexandria Railroad, where the Louisiana Brigade had battled Hooker's men just before Second Manassas. This time, the fight went badly for the Confederates. General Hill, arriving first at Bristoe with Heth's Division, hastily attacked with only two of Heth's brigades, unaware that three full divisions of the Federal II Corps lay in wait behind a deep railroad embankment. The Southern brigades were severely cut up and Heth lost more than 1,800 men—more than three times Federal casualties. The 6th Louisiana arrived at the battle site about 5:00 p.m., after Hill's repulse, and formed in line of battle. Luckily, the unfortunate affair was over and the Louisiana troops were not engaged. They spent the night in battle formation, listening to the wails of the wounded and dying, unable to assist them because of the nearness of the enemy's lines.[11]

The morning's light revealed that the Northern army had withdrawn up the railroad to Manassas, where Meade formed his defenses behind Bull Run. Lee had failed to cut him off, so there was little to salvage from this operation except to destroy the railroad, which he set his troops to doing before marching them back toward the Rappahannock River. While mopping up the area, a detachment of the 6th Louisiana rounded up some prisoners, stragglers from Meade's army, including one whose capture must have astounded and humiliated them. Among the captives, Captain Seymour recounted in his diary, "was a deserter from the Sixth La. Regt. of our Brigade, who was caught in a Federal uniform." This was the worst of all possible offenses—not merely deserting but turncoating—taking up arms against one's former comrades. Such Confederates who joined the Union army were known as "galvanized Yankees," having taken on an outer coating of Federal blue just as a sheet of steel takes on a zinc coating when galvanized.[12]

This newly-minted Federal soldier was recognized by his former comrades. John Conley, formerly of Company K, had fought with the 6th Louisiana through May 1862 and deserted the following month during Jackson's Shenandoah Valley Campaign. He now stood before them at

Bristoe in the enemy's uniform. There is no record of what his shocked captors said to him, nor how he may have explained his changing sides in this war. As he stood surrounded, he must certainly have known the awful fate awaiting him. The courts martial process would take time, and would lead to an occasion of bitter sadness six weeks later.[13]

For now, there was nothing more that could be done with John Conley, so the men of the 6th Louisiana pitched in to help with the railroad-wrecking that Lee had ordered before resuming the southward march to the Rappahannock. It was late October, and the chilling rains and cold nights foretold the coming of more winter suffering, for which the men in the regiment were grimly ill-prepared. Their uniforms were ragged and thin, their shoes disintegrating or gone, and blankets and coats were so few as to be considered luxuries. "More than half the company were barefooted on the march" to and from Bristoe Station, Lt. Joseph G. Davis, commanding Company D, wrote in his muster roll report. "They want at present Shoes, Blankets, pants, shirts, drawers, socks and overcoats. For the want of such, they complain much." Captain O'Connor of Company F was complaining, too. "During these two months of severe duty," he wrote, "the men were in great need of shoes, under clothing & blankets. Some of them were actually Barefooted." Lt. John Shay, commanding the Germans of Company G, put the needs simply and sweepingly: "Clothing of every description needed." So it was a ragged and somewhat grumpy regiment that crossed the Rappahannock River and went into camp in a belt of woods between Brandy Station, the scene of last June's great cavalry battle, and Culpeper Court House. The men began erecting log huts for winter quarters, unaware that events would prevent them from occupying their new quarters that winter.[14]

Harry Hays' Louisiana Brigade was part of the contingent assigned to defend Rappahannock Station, where the Orange & Alexandria Railroad crossed the Rappahannock River nine miles northeast of Culpeper Court House. The railroad bridge had been burned there, but a pontoon bridge spanned the river 800 yards upstream and had been left in place to allow the army to recross the waterway. While the rest of the Confederate army camped south of the river, one brigade was assigned to hold the bridgehead on its north bank, where a series of rifle pits and earthworks had been constructed. The duty of manning the bridgehead alternated between brigades in Early's and Johnson's divisions. On November 6, this duty fell to Hays' Louisianians, who marched over the bridge at sunrise to take up positions in the rifle pits and two small earthen forts. Colonel Monaghan's 6th Louisiana was ordered out as skirmishers about a quarter-mile in front of the earthworks. They held the extreme right of the Confederate position, which formed a crescent enclosing the pontoon bridge, its flanks anchored above and below the bridge on the riverbanks. The other regiments took up positions in and around the works. Their first day on the north bank of the river passed quietly. The second day, however, would not.[15]

As a defensive position the bridgehead left much to be desired. The rifle trenches were neither deep nor wide, and the two earthen redoubts were not protected by any obstructions in front, such as ditches or felled trees. The entire trench line was commanded by a higher ridge several hundred yards in front, behind which enemy forces could mass unseen for an attack. On the extreme right, where the 6th Louisiana was posted, the railroad approached the river on an elevated embankment, with a tunnel through it for passage of a road just in front of the works. The railroad embankment could conceal an advancing force until it charged through the roadway tunnel near the rifle pits. The river behind the Louisianians was wide and deep, and backed up by a mill dam just downstream, creating a large pond. Thus the only viable escape route was over the pontoon bridge. General Early pronounced the Confederate defensive position "very inadequate, and not judiciously laid out or constructed," or at least he said so after disaster struck. It was certainly not a position from which a brigade or two of Confederates would want to face an aggressive superior Federal force.[16]

And a superior force was exactly what General Meade intended to launch against the bridgehead. The Union commander began a general advance of his army on the morning of November 7, ordering the V and VI Corps, both under command of General Sedgwick, toward Rappahannock Station, and his three remaining corps toward Kelly's Ford, a few miles downstream. Meade planned to force a crossing of the river at both points to confront Lee in battle. The first signs of this Federal advance began to show up about noon that day.[17]

Confederate cavalry scouts reported an enemy column moving down a road toward Kelly's Ford. Captain Seymour investigated these reports with Col. Davidson B. Penn of the 7th Louisiana, who was temporarily in command of the brigade in the absence of General Hays, who was serving on a court martial. "[We] discovered that a very heavy force was marching towards our right," wrote the captain. Just before noon, Penn sent a message alerting General Early to this threat, but the division commander and his remaining brigades were five miles distant, near Brandy Station, and he did not receive the warning until nearly 2:00 p.m. Early ordered his remaining brigades—scattered and at work constructing winter huts—to form and march to the river, after which he galloped ahead to survey the situation. By 1:15 p.m., the isolated Louisianians on the north bank of the Rappahannock could see an enemy line of battle forming on the edge of a woods a mile or more away. Skirmishers were advancing in front. Soon, a second line of battle formed behind the first, and then a third was seen in the distance. "This movement revealed to us the overwhelming numbers of the force opposed to us," Seymour recorded in his diary. Still there had been no response from Early, and no sign of reinforcements.[18]

As he hurried toward the trouble, Early was overtaken by General Lee, who had not received a message sent to warn him of the Federal advance. The two Confederate generals rode to the river together, arriving a little past 3:00 p.m. Early, crossing the pontoon for a closer look, found a "heavy force" of Federals about a mile or so away, advancing slowly, and concluded that the Louisiana Brigade was "manifestly too small" to defend the thinly-manned trench line. Some 900 men occupied the earthworks, along with four rifled cannon of the Louisiana Guard Artillery—a tiny force facing the advance of two Federal Corps totaling some 30,000 men.[19]

Early rode back across the river to confer with Lee as the advancing Federals drove in the Confederate skirmishers. Colonel Monaghan's men fell back on the right, and the 8th Louisiana drew back from its advanced position on the left, so that all of Hays' regiments huddled in the rifle pits and redoubts, with the 6th Louisiana holding the extreme right of the line, nearest the railroad. The roar of Federal cannon rent the air. "The enemy soon got three heavy batteries in position on the high ground in our front and opened on us a furious fire, most of his shots being aimed at our bridge," Captain Seymour wrote. At the same time, skirmishers advanced to within a few yards of the river on the right, pouring a deadly fire on the bridge to prevent any retreat or reinforcement. Under this hail of lead, Seymour shuttled messages back and forth across the bridge—crossing eight times in all—while "the balls whistled around my head in a manner that was not musical in the least." On the south bank of the river, Confederate batteries attempted to respond to the Federal artillery, but the long range rendered their fire ineffective.

Early conferred with Lee on reinforcing the bridgehead; the Confederate commander agreed to send no more than one additional brigade across. Shortly after 4:00 p.m., when General Hays returned to resume command of his men, Early sent three regiments of Hoke's North Carolina brigade, now commanded by Col. A. C. Godwin, across the pontoon to join the Louisianians in the trenches. The force north of the river by 5:00 p.m. numbered nearly 2,000 men, hunkering down under what Hays termed a "rapid and vigorous" barrage from six Union batteries posted on the left, right, and front.[20]

While afternoon faded into dusk, Lee and Early watched from a hill on the south side of the river as the Federal batteries poured shot and shell upon their targets. A strong wind blowing from the south carried sound away from them, so the two Confederate generals could hear little from their vantage point across the river. As darkness obscured their view, the artillery firing ceased. Stabs of flame pierced the darkness—soundless flashes from the muzzles of muskets. The flashes subsided after some minutes, however, so the Southern generals concluded it must have been shooting from and at the enemy's skirmishers. Lee became convinced that the Federal advance against the bridgehead was merely a feint, designed to cover the main attack of the enemy downstream at Kelly's Ford. Early remembered Lee telling him that "it was too late for the enemy to attempt anything serious that night," just before the Confederate commander rode off into the darkness to retire for the evening.[21]

Lee had misjudged his opponent. While the Southern commanders were observing the near-silent darkness across the river (prior to Lee's departure), Union troops opposite the bridgehead fixed bayonets and waited for the order to charge. Two brigades of Brig. Gen. David A. Russell's division of the VI Corps would lead the attack. Col. Peter Ellmaker's brigade crept forward under the crest of a hill a few hundred yards from the Confederate trenches on the right, where the 6th Louisiana waited nervously. Col. Emory Upton positioned his brigade opposite the Confederate left. When all was ready, Russell ordered Ellmaker to unleash his attack on the right and center of the Confederate line.[22]

Out of the darkness they came at a run. Without firing a shot, the attackers dashed toward the rifle pits with a lusty yell. One column moved down the far side of the railroad embankment and burst upon the 6th Louisiana's position from the roadway tunnel on its right. The startled

1. In order to threaten the flank of any Federal force attempting to cross the river at Kelly's Ford, General Lee fortified a bridgehead north of the Rappahannock River west of the destroyed Orange & Alexandria Railroad bridge. The only way for the Confederates to reach this position was by a pontoon bridge. The bridgehead was manned on November 7, 1863, by Hay's Louisiana Brigade and four pieces of artillery, and was later reinforced by Hoke's Brigade, under Archibald Godwin.

2. As Federal guns pounded the position, heavy columns from the Sixth Corps stormed the works in the early evening darkness. Hand-to-hand fighting broke out and the bayonet was freely used.

3. With the line pierced in several places, the bridgehead collapsed quickly. Hays' Louisiana Brigade lost roughly three-quarters of its 900 men, with the 6th Louisiana losing nearly one-half of its strength, or 91 killed, wounded and captured.

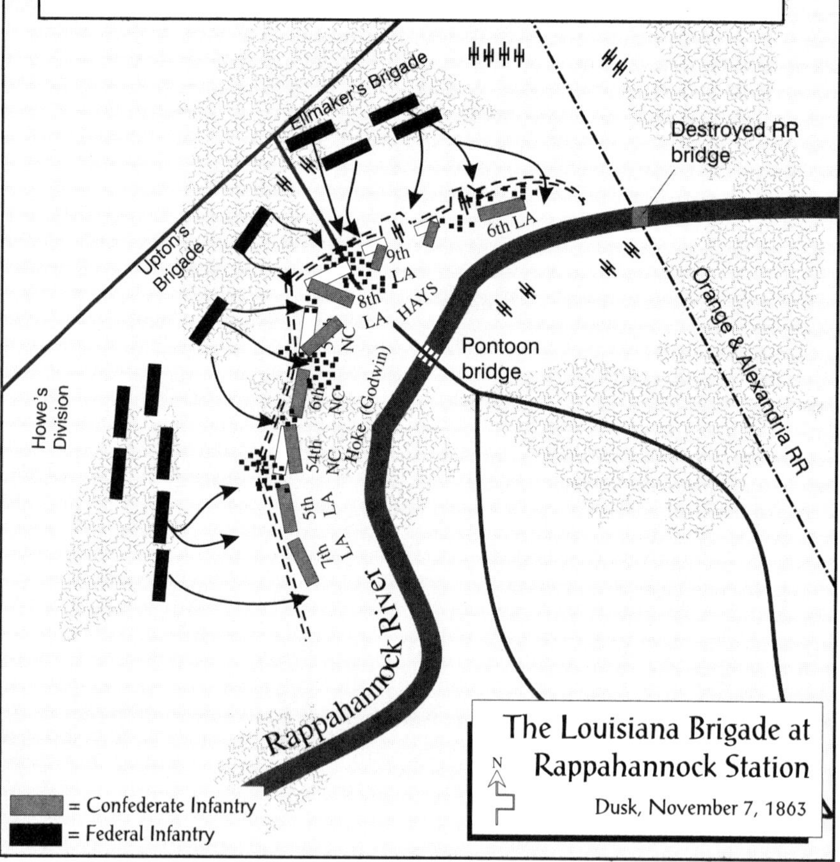

Louisiana men unleashed a volley of musketry—the muzzle flashes Lee and Early saw from across the river—that dropped scores of attackers from the 6th Maine and 5th Wisconsin regiments, which led the attack against the Confederate right. "The fire grew heavier as the line neared the works, and the men were struck down with fearful rapidity," the 6th Maine's commander, Maj. George Fuller, reported, "but unwavering, with wild cheers, the survivors reached the fortifications and springing over them engaged the enemy in hand-to-hand combat." The Confederates appeared "astonished and bewildered" by the sudden attack and gave way, many fleeing to the river, others to the line to the left, which hadn't yet been assaulted, Fuller wrote.[23]

The first Northerner to dive into the works was a Maine sergeant who found himself surrounded. He called out that he surrendered, but as his comrades leaped over the parapet, he shouted, "I take it back!" and grabbed for the colors of the 8th Louisiana. Desperate hand-to-hand fighting spread along the line. "Again and again they were hurled back from the trenches, our men fighting most stubbornly with bayonets and clubbed muskets," Captain Seymour wrote. The 5th Wisconsin poured into the melee on the heels of the 6th Maine, and was soon followed by two Pennsylvania regiments, the 49th and the 119th. The daring tactics and the sheer weight of the four charging regiments overpowered the men of the 6th, 8th, and 9th Louisiana. "The enemy poured in yelling like so many demons," the horrified Seymour recalled, claiming that they had been "stimulated by a free use of whiskey" and made the charge "in a state of beastly drunkenness." There is no evidence to support such a claim, however.[24]

Hays' line had been pierced in two places and his three regiments on the right found themselves cut off from the North Carolina regiments and the 5th and 7th Louisiana on the left. Surrounded, the Louisianians on the right had little choice but to surrender, except for those daring enough to make a dash for the river and plunge into the icy water, which some did. As Ellmaker's men overran the right and center of the Confederate position, Upton's brigade attacked on the left, ultimately surrounding the three North Carolina regiments and Hays' remaining two regiments on that end of the line. Realizing the situation was hopeless, some 6th Louisiana men managed a desperate escape in the darkness. Colonel Monaghan and Major Manning were among those who plunged into the dark, frigid waters of the river and successfully reached the opposite bank. Others trying the same method of escape either drowned or were shot in the water. General Hays was surrounded by enemy soldiers and was resigned to being captured when his frightened horse suddenly bolted and ran toward the bridge, Hays holding on for dear life. Somehow, horse and rider managed to get across "amid a shower of bullets," in the words of Captain Seymour, who similarly escaped, though his horse was wounded.[25]

One Southern officer described the final moments of the disaster:

> The Louisiana Guard battery discharged their pieces when the enemy were upon them and two of their number were bayoneted at the guns. Many of the officers threw away their swords to avoid surrendering them, and Lieutenant Charles Pierce of the Seventh Louisiana broke his sword on his knee and handed the hilt to the officer—the effect of which can easily be imagined. . . .General Harry T. Hays ran the gauntlet of the pontoon bridge under an enfilading fire of the enemy. Colonel Monaghan swam his horse across the river. Colonel Terry and a few others successfully swam across, but many lost their lives in the attempt.[26]

When General Early learned that the bridgehead had been overrun by the enemy, he rode to the river to see "if anything could be done to retrieve the disaster." He quickly concluded it would be a "useless sacrifice" to send more men across the bridge, while unleashing artillery would have endangered his surrounded men. "I had the mortification to hear the final struggle of these devoted men and to be made painfully aware of their capture, without the possibility of being able to go to their relief," he lamented. For his part, General Hays insisted that his men remained "fighting well to the last," and "there was no effort made by any one in my command to recross the river until nothing else remained but to surrender."[27]

The embarassing affair was indeed "a disaster." The mortifying event devastated the proud Louisiana Brigade, which became a mere shadow of itself after Rappahannock Station. The killed and wounded were few, due to the fact that the Federals stormed the works without firing a shot. Hays reported only two killed and 16 wounded. The disaster of Rappahannock Station, however, is measured by the long list of captives. Nearly three-fourths of his roughly 900 men were captured. The missing totaled 684, including 58 officers, among them those commanding the 5th, 7th, and 8th regiments. The 6th Louisiana had one man killed and another mortally wounded, but seven officers and 82 enlisted men were taken prisoner, a casualty total of 91—nearly half of the regiment. The unlucky soul killed there was Sgt. James J. Conway of Company F, a 42-year-old Irishman from New Orleans who had been wounded the previous year at the Battle of Chantilly. Among the 6th Louisiana officers captured were two Irish-born captains, Thomas Redmond, commanding Company B and Michael O'Connor of Company F, and Lieutenant Orr, the regiment's adjutant. All three would be held prisoner until February 1865.[28]

The affair practically eliminated the Louisiana and North Carolina brigades as fighting units. Colonel Godwin was captured along with some 900 of his North Carolinians. It was a glorious victory for the Union men, especially General Russell, who reported that his two brigades captured 103 commissioned officers and 1,200 enlisted men, four cannon, 1,225 stand of arms and eight Confederate colors—at a relatively low cost of 328 Federal casualties. Russell had used surprise and brilliant tactics, while the Confederate commanders had displayed poor judgment and overconfidence, greatly underestimating their enemy's skill and courage. They had placed too few men in too perilous a position, and then didn't take the threat seriously when overpowering numbers gathered in their front. Lee had blundered, and his men knew it. "You and every one else will wonder why those brave men were not reinforced in time to save them from destruction," one Louisianian wrote home. "Nobody knows but General Lee, who I hope will account satisfactory for it."[29]

Early was bitter about what occurred at Rappahannock Station, which he felt was the first stain on his outstanding record of command. "This was the first serious disaster that had befallen any of my immediate commands, either as a brigade or division commander, since the commencement of the war," he later remarked, "and I felt I was not responsible for it, though I bitterly regretted it." Lee offered little excuse for what he called "this unfortunate affair," and absolved the troops engaged from any blame. Their "courage and good conduct," he wrote, had been tested too often to leave room for doubt of their valor. Throughout the South, the news of the loss of the Louisiana Brigade came as a shock, for it had developed a reputation for glory and daring. In an editorial lament, the *Richmond Whig* pronounced, "We must be permitted. . .to express our sincere regret at the capture of a large portion of Hays' brigade. Decimated as it was, the nine hundred remaining Louisianians were worth their weight in gold to the army." The brigade's "imperishable record," continued the editorial, "had endeared it to the whole country and particularly to the people of Virginia. . . .If they are now lost to Lee's Army, we know not where the material will be found to replace them."[30]

For the men of the 6th Louisiana, November 7, 1863, ranked as one of the blackest days of the war. Scores of their comrades were off to Northern prison camps and the regiment was reduced in size to little more than a full company. The mood of the moment can be read in one sentence penned by Colonel Monaghan in his muster roll report: "The affair was disastrous to our Army." Disastrous, indeed; at the end of December only 103 men stood present for duty, less than half the number two months earlier. Four of the regiment's ten companies had fewer than ten men present at that time, and the largest one, Company C, reported only 19 men.[31]

On the day after the disaster, the shadow regiment fell back with the rest of Lee's army to return to its old defensive line behind the Rapidan River. Besides the successful attack at Rappahannock Station, Meade had thrust three corps over the river at Kelly's Ford, wrecking Lee's defensive posture behind the Rappahannock and forcing a retreat southward. There, the 6th Louisiana resumed picket duty on familiar ground around Raccoon Ford, and Colonel Monaghan temporarily assumed command of the much-reduced Louisiana Brigade, numbering less than 500 men. Due to General Ewell's absence on sick leave, Early moved up to command the corps and Hays took his place in command of the division, opening the way for Monaghan, as senior colonel, to manage the brigade. Monaghan's slide up the chain of command left Major Manning at the head of the 6th Louisiana. Lieutenant Colonel Hanlon, who would have replaced Monaghan, was still suffering from his severe wounds and was absent on what turned out to be a nine-month sick leave.[32]

All remained quiet along the Rapidan until November 26, when Meade moved to get around the Confederate right flank, crossing the Rapidan downstream, and forcing Lee to shift his army to the right to oppose the Federal threat. In a "bitter cold" night maneuver, the poorly dressed Louisianians, many lacking coats, blankets and shoes, "suffered severely during the march," Captain Seymour recalled. "Those of us who were on horseback were so benumbed by the cold that we were compelled to dismount whenever the column halted and dance around on the frozen ground in order to restore circulation." The suffering of the mounted officers, however, could hardly have matched that of the foot soldiers, as the armies maneuvered into opposing positions on hills overlooking a northward-flowing tributary of the Rapidan called Mine Run. On succeeding days, they marched, dug trenches, skirmished with the enemy and spent miserable nights pelted by freezing rain and chilled by bitter cold, with no shelter to protect them.[33]

Meade's Mine Run Campaign, as this indecisive face-off came to be known, accomplished little and ended December 1 when the Union commander gave up hope of overcoming the Confederates in their entrenched position and withdrew back across the Rapidan. During the face-off, the 6th Louisiana dug in along Mine Run creek. The men spent "four days under severe cannonading," according to one officer's muster-roll report, and dangerous skirmish duty cost the regiment several casualties. Company I had two men badly wounded on the skirmish line and Company D reported one man wounded and one taken prisoner on such duty. According to the official casualty report written by Monaghan for the brigade, the 6th Louisiana had three men wounded (one of which proved to be mortal) and three captured at Mine Run.[34]

It was during this frigid stand-off that the tragedy of Pvt. John Conley played out to its inevitable climax. The fate of Conley, captured in Federal uniform at Bristoe Station, was sealed by General Order No. 100, dated November 20, 1863, which published the findings of the court martial held on the charge of desertion. The charge specified that he deserted near Woodstock, Virginia, in June 1862, "and was found in the ranks of the enemy" near Bristoe Station on October 13, 1863. The court found him guilty as charged, and with two of its three members concurring, sentenced him "to be shot to death with musketry at such time and place as the general commanding may direct." The sentence was to be carried out "in the presence of his Brigade."[35]

Captain Seymour, as adjutant of the brigade, supervised the execution on November 30, "and a more unpleasant and revolting duty it had never been my misfortune to discharge," he wrote. Orders to carry out the sentence "came from Division Head Quarters in the morning, and soon after the prisoner arrived at our lines, securely manacled and guarded." Seymour reacted to the condemned man with disdain bordering on contempt, describing the prisoner as "a sullen, cross, ugly fellow, who seemed to be entirely devoid of pride or sensibility." Conley was a young man, only twenty years old, a former newsboy in New Orleans before he enlisted for the war. He had been born in Ireland, and like most of his countrymen in the 6th Louisiana, was a Roman Catholic. Seymour sent to the field hospital to secure a Catholic priest to provide "spiritual consolation" to the condemned man. The priest arrived about four o'clock that afternoon.[36]

Half an hour later, Seymour "ordered the brigade to form on the breastworks, officers & men with only their side arms." A grave was dug fifty paces from the brigade's line. Conley was marched to the edge of the grave. His shackles had been removed, but his arms were pinned behind his back. Seymour vividly recalled the scene: "The Priest was by his side, talking to him & uttering prayers, at the same time holding before the prisoner a small crucifix of our Savior, which he kissed several times." After the priest finished his final prayers, Seymour stood before the condemned man to read the charges against him, the findings of the court martial, and its sentence of death. "Connolly, apparently unmoved, listened attentively & after I had finished said that he had never pulled a trigger against his old comrades and that notwithstanding he had joined the Federal Army, he had resolved never to do so." Then the doomed soldier turned to Seymour to say "that he had no hard feelings against me for the part I was taking in his execution, for he was fully aware that I was but discharging my duty."[37]

The prisoner then addressed his final words to the firing squad, made up of 12 New Orleans men from his own company, the Violet Guards. He had marched with them and fought beside them for a year before deserting, and he had one final request. It would be "an act of mercy," the condemned man said, for them "to take sure aim and kill him immediately." Seymour then ordered the officer commanding the firing squad to proceed with the grim task. "The word of command was given, the muskets leveled, a simultaneous discharge followed and the vital spark fled forever from the body of John Connolly[sic]." Nine balls pierced his head, and one penetrated his heart, "and his death was instantaneous." It was over, but it would not be forgotten. "I hope that I may never witness a like scene again," Seymour wrote in disgust.[38]

Executions such as that of the 6th Louisiana turncoat were intended as examples to deter others from desertion, but if they had any effect it was fleeting. Desertions from Lee's army would increase in the last 18 months of the war, as hopes for the Southern cause ebbed and the hardships suffered by the Confederate soldiers increased. Those hardships intensified as this third winter of the war subjected the men to the most difficult conditions they had yet endured. Nature seemed intent on punishing them and the Confederate government seemed incapable of providing even the bare necessities to the men offering their lives to preserve and protect it.

The 6th Louisiana marched back to Raccoon Ford as December began, resuming the Rapidan line following Meade's abandonment of the Mine Run campaign. "The weather is bitter cold and our poor fellows, standing picket on the high, bleak, banks of the River, suffer terribly from want of sufficient clothing," Captain Seymour recorded. "In our Brigade there are two hundred and fifty men who have neither blankets nor overcoats. It is a great wonder that these men do not freeze to death these terribly cold nights." The coatless privates covered themselves with pine boughs as a shield against the cold wind, "while others sit up by the fires all night and, borrowing the blankets of their more fortunate comrades, sleep during the day." The men endured the suffering "with scarcely a murmur," which Seymour found remarkable, particularly because "they could so easily desert to the Yankee Army, where they would be comfortably clad and supplied with an abundance of food."[39]

There was no abundance of either food or clothing on the Confederate side, at least not for the enlisted men. "They are in great need of blankets, overcoats and shoes, some being without either blanket or overcoat & others totally barefooted," Lt. James E. Weymouth, temporarily commanding Company K of the 6th Louisiana, wrote in his December muster roll report. Echoing that complaint, Lt. Michael Murray, commanding Company F in the absence of the captured Captain O'Connor, wrote in his report: "The men are suffering for want of blankets and shoes, there being only four men now in the company who have shoes fit to leave camp with on any duty." In his report for the period, Colonel Monaghan resorted to sarcasm in mentioning the scarcity of blankets and shoes, adding, "Overcoats would be too great a luxury to mention."[40]

By Christmas time, the Louisianians made themselves a little more comfortable by erecting winter huts about three miles back from the river, rotating the picket duty every ten days or so, during which about a third of the brigade would be posted at the riverbank. "We have had plenty of wood and water, but very little meat and bread," an officer of the 6th Louisiana's Company D wrote in an unsigned muster roll report that winter. Rations were short, and the men literally foraged for things to eat.[41]

Private William Trahern, of Company D, wrote long after the war that the only time he remembered going hungry was in that winter of 1863-64 along the Rapidan. "Our supplies were cut off by high water in some stream that flowed between Clark's Mountain and our camp," Trahern recalled. "This misfortune kept us without provisions for three or four days. It was a trying time, and we lived solely on wild onions and water-cress—I mean of course the private soldier only underwent this tribulation." Trahern got a glimpse of the contrast between the subsistence grub of the foot soldiers and the diet of the field and staff officers when his captain recommended him to substitute for the regimental quartermaster when the latter was ill. "I found the charge very agreeable," wrote Trahern, "and in more senses than one":

> First, the supply of food was abundant and of the best quality; secondly, sweet rest and respite from picket duty for two or three weeks. Just to think of the private soldier almost starving, whilst his highest Commanders in his own regiment were feasting upon the best of old-time foods, such as coffee and tea, ham and eggs, bacon, flour and cornbread, and I am almost certain that there was a goodly supply of old Bourbon. Everything in this rich manner was for a time in my possession, and it pleased me to take full advantage. If it could have been possible, I would have conveyed some of it to my suffering comrades.[42]

The suffering of his comrades was alleviated somewhat that winter when various commanders from Lee's army appealed to Virginians for help. Their requests produced blankets and clothing, given either as donations or in response to demands. Records of the 6th Louisiana indicate that citizens of the city of Lynchburg supplied the brigade with coats and blankets after a "levy" was placed on the city. A February 1864 muster roll report of Company D credits Major Daniel, assistant adjutant general of Early's Division "for his benevolent appeal to the people of Va. on our behalf," which produced a coat and blanket "to every man of our Brigade by subscription from the people of Lynchburg." For five months, from December 1863 through April 1864, the 6th Louisiana held to its camp near the Rapidan as the two opposing armies waited out the long and hard winter. Beyond occasional skirmish fire along the river, there was little military action of note. The Louisianians amused themselves by building a wooden theater and staging minstrel shows, and by occasional snowball fights.

As the spring thaw arrived, one officer wrote in his end-of-April muster roll report that "nothing has transpired" in the previous two months "excepting the regular routine of camp and picket duty." Everything else, he added, "has been unusually serene."[43]

Chapter Eleven

The Overland Campaign: WILDERNESS & SPOTSYLVANIA

"There has been the most desperate struggle that I have ever seen."
— *Capt. George P. Ring*

By the time the campaign of 1864 opened, the Army of Northern Virginia numbered some 64,000 men, outnumbered nearly two-to-one by the 118,000-man Union army force encamped across the Rapidan River. The Army of the Potomac was prepared to push forward under yet another commander. Though Meade remained in command of the army, Lt. Gen. Ulysses S. Grant—the hero of Vicksburg, Chattanooga and other battles in the Western Theater—was appointed general-in-chief of all the Union armies in March. Grant took up headquarters in Culpeper and designed a spring offensive which he would personally oversee and direct, with Meade executing his wishes.[1]

The Confederate commander, who had an uncanny ability to anticipate his opponents' moves, assembled his corps and division commanders on May 2 at the signal station atop Clark's Mountain, just south of the river separating the two opposing armies. With the aid of field glasses, the officers surveyed the sprawling enemy encampments across the way in Culpeper County. The Southern generals could see signs of activity in that white-dotted landscape of tents and covered wagons, hints of an army loosening up to move. Off to the east, south of the river and beyond Mine Run, they could see the tangled green mass known as The Wilderness, a desolate thicket of vines, brambles, scrub oak, pine and cedar whose name implied its character, a place where no man would wish to live—or to die. But that was where Lee wanted to meet Grant, on ground that would tend to neutralize his opponent's advantages in numbers and artillery. Looking down the Rapidan toward its junction with the Rappahannock River to the east, General Lee pointed toward

Germanna and Ely's fords and predicted to his assembled commanders that Grant would cross the Rapidan in a move southeast toward Richmond. Within 36 hours, the Union army did precisely that.[2]

And that was just fine with the Confederate commander, for the narrow roads from the fords would guide the Federal army through the Wilderness, where his outnumbered veterans could fall upon it while it was strung out and vulnerable. The Confederates had survived a rough winter, scrimping by on short rations and in worn-out clothes and shoes. Still, by most accounts morale was remarkably good. The gaunt but hardened men "took their privations cheerfully, and complaints were seldom heard," Brig. Gen. Evander Law, one of Longstreet's brigade commanders, recalled later. "The morale of the army at this time was excellent, and it moved forward confidently to the grim death-grapple in the wilderness of Spotsylvania with its old enemy, the Army of the Potomac." Father Sheeran, who made the rounds among his Catholic constituents among the Louisiana troops, noted the same spirit. "I never saw our men more cheerful than on this occasion," he wrote on May 5. "The poor fellows had little idea of the terrible contest in which they were about to engage."[3]

Their spirits surely were lifted by the warmth of the spring sun and the greening of the countryside, as well as the arrival back in camp of old comrades. Some 500 men of Hays' Brigade captured at Rappahannock Station had been exchanged and returned to camp in March, helping fill out the regiments, which yet remained scanty. The 6th Louisiana's William Trahern, by then promoted to corporal, remembered the "sweet, balmy air and some song birds' notes" on the morning of Wednesday, May 4 as the regiment assembled, ready to march. "I was ordered to call the regiment's roll of men. This was what was left, one hundred and sixty men, with only fourteen of my original company. What a dreadful showing, compared to the day of the opening of hostilities. Then it was twelve hundred and fifty in the regiment (6th La.) and one hundred and twenty five in Co. D."[4]

The Louisianians moved out around noon that day as General Ewell put his Second Corps in motion along the old turnpike from Orange Court House to Fredericksburg, while A. P. Hill's Third Corps divisions marched on a parallel route to the south along the Orange Plank Road, followed by James Longstreet's First Corps. Lee's army was threading its way east to intercept Grant, who had crossed the Rapidan into the Wilderness.[5]

This image looks east into Saunder's Field from the Confederate trench line. Some of the battle's fiercest fighting took place here. *James P. Gannon*

Dick Ewell, who was under orders from Lee to avoid a general engagement until Longstreet's Corps came up, was advancing cautiously along the Orange Turnpike. A half-dozen Virginia regiments from Brig. Gen. John M. Jones' Brigade of Johnson's Division led Ewell's advance. Around 6:00 a.m., the van of the column reached a large clearing. Enemy soldiers could be seen lurking at the edge of the woods beyond. Ewell deployed Johnson's Division astride the turnpike, instructing Jones and other brigade commanders to fall back slowly if attacked. Johnson's brigades hastily threw up logs and dirt to form a defensive line across the turnpike at the wooded western edge of the open field, extending the line northward toward the Rapidan deep into the vine-tangled cover of the Wilderness forest. At this point the 6th Louisiana remained well back on the turnpike with the rest of Hays' Brigade, marching with Early's Division at the rear of the corps' column.[6]

The Orange Turnpike at this point bisected one of the few extensive clearings in the Wilderness, known as Saunders' Field. The open ground was an old corn patch about 400 yards deep and 800 yards wide. Halfway across the clearing ran a deep swale, cutting roughly north to south across the turnpike, which divided the field in rough halves as it ran west to east. Piney woods, tangled with vine and brushy undergrowth, bordered the field on all sides. The trees were not the majestic hardwoods of virgin forest common to much of Virginia, but the scrubby,

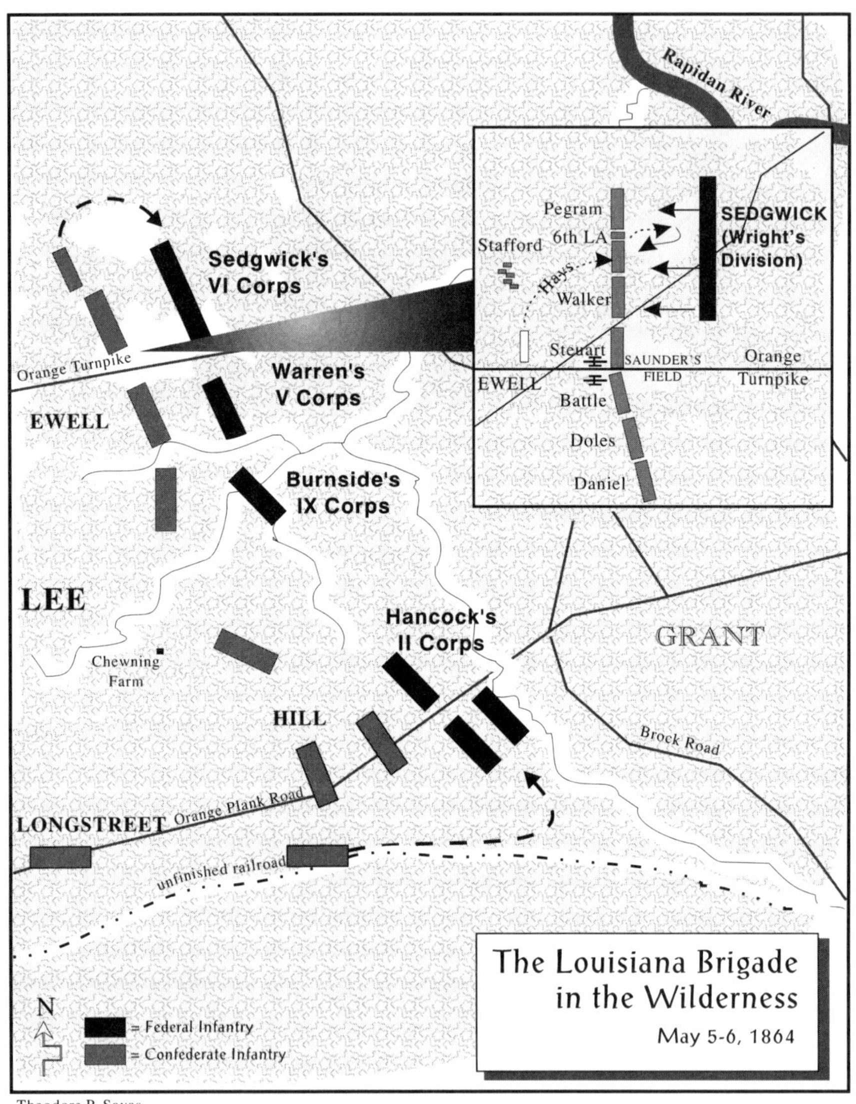

Theodore P. Savas

second-growth timber found in areas that have been logged—a denser, brush-filled cover difficult to penetrate and easy to become lost in. This characteristic of the dense, green tangle known as the Wilderness would give the impending battle a special (and hideous) character that would be remembered decades later by the soldiers fortunate enough to have survived its unique horrors.[7]

The battle opened in earnest about 1:00 p.m. when a line of Unionists swept out of the pines and across Saunders' Field. The soldiers marched down to the swale and then up the ascent toward Johnson's Confederates, who were hunched down behind their makeshift works in the brush on the western edge of the field. The attacking force was the division of Brig. Gen. Charles Griffin of Meade's V Corps, commanded by Maj. Gen. Gouveneur K. Warren. One of Griffin's brigades attacking north of the turnpike was driven back with bloody losses by Johnson's Confederates, who enjoyed a clear field of fire and took advantage of it. A second brigade under Brig. Gen. Joseph Bartlett struck with greater determination south of the road in what Captain Seymour later described as a "furious assault." Bartlett's regiments were aimed at Jones' Virginians, most of whom, Seymour claimed, "broke and ran in the greatest confusion," rupturing Johnson's line. Desperately trying to rally his panicked troops, General Jones was killed in the brief and violent struggle. A brilliant counterattack by the Georgia Brigade led by General Gordon, who would distinguish himself for higher command in this battle, drove back the Federals and plugged the gap in Ewell's line.[8]

Cpl. William E. Trahern

Corporal Trahern of the 6th Louisiana's Company D was one of the wounded survivors of the Battle of the Wilderness. More than 60 years after the battle, Trahern vividly recalled the action and his wounding on May 5, 1864, when he wrote a memoir of his life for his family. He died in Virginia at age 89, more than 66 years after enlisting in the Tensas Rifles in 1861. *Courtesy of James Trahern Micklem*

The 6th Louisiana and Hays' other regiments, which had been held in reserve during the early action, were now called upon to strengthen the line north of the turnpike. Anxious to extend his left against threatened flank attack, Ewell ordered Hays' Brigade and the Virginia brigade of Brig. Gen. John Pegram to double-quick through the woods and take up a position on the left of Johnson's Division. There was urgency to the movement, for Ewell had become aware of a strong Federal column—Brig. Gen. Horatio Wright leading four brigades—advancing toward Johnson's exposed left flank. Hays and Pegram hurried to get into position before Wright, one of General Sedgwick's VI Corps veterans, could strike. As the Louisianians moved through the choked terrain, they came upon one of the sad casualties of the day's initial Union assault—the prone figure of Brig. Gen. Leroy Stafford. Formerly of the 9th Louisiana, Stafford had been severely wounded leading the 2nd Louisiana Brigade. "We passed poor Stafford, lying under a tree on the side of the road and suffering terribly from his wound," Captain Seymour recounted. Vowing his willingness to die for the Confederate cause, Stafford urged the passing Louisianians "to fight the enemy to the last." The capable brigadier died three days later, a loss that would have important consequences for the organization of the Louisiana troops in Lee's army.[9]

It was about 2:00 p.m., according to Captain Ring, once again commanding Company K of the 6th Louisiana, when "our Brigade got into the thickest of it." The Louisianians formed on the left of the Stonewall Brigade, commanded by Brig. Gen. James Walker, with orders to attack the approaching Federals as soon as they were in position. Hays sent his adjutant, Captain Seymour, to tell General Walker of these orders "and he promised to accompany us, but for some unexplained reason, he failed to do so." Hays ordered his regiments forward. "For half a mile, we advanced through a thick woods, driving the Yankees easily before us," Seymour recalled. "We then emerged into an open field and there we could see that the Federals outflanked us by the breath of an entire brigade." Their fighting blood up, the Louisianians "were too eager and impetuous to be halted," and rushed headlong into the clearing toward a line of Unionists deployed along the edge of the woods across the field. This line of the enemy was composed of the brigades of Brig. Gens. Thomas Neill and David Russell (the latter being the officer who led the successful Federal attack at Rappahannock Station six months earlier). "The line of battle was ordered forward at a charge," Corporal Trahern of the 6th Louisiana recalled many years after the war. "Moving forward at a rapid gate, [we] encountered the enemy as we crossed the skirmish line, passing over dead and wounded. My regiment reached the bottom of a slight slope in the land, and began to ascend. The enemy opened a broad-side into our ranks."[10]

Neill's and Russell's men took deadly aim at the reckless Louisianians bulling their way across the field. The rolling volleys of musketry from the pine woods sliced through the gray line of Louisiana men, which was unsupported except for the presence of the 25th Virginia. The line staggered as scores fell dead and wounded, among them Corporal Trahern, who took a bullet just above the knee. Russell and Neill ordered their troops forward, threatening to surround the Confederate attackers. "It soon became apparent that the enemy were rapidly closing in upon both of our flanks," Captain Seymour wrote, "with the intention of enveloping our Brigade." Hays frantically ordered his men to retreat, which had to be done under a "murderous fire" that multiplied his casualties. "We had a hard fight but for want of support were forced to retire with pretty heavy loss," Captain Ring wrote to his wife on the following day. "I went into the fight with twenty-four men and came out with nine—the rest either killed, wounded or taken prisoner." As Ring's letter indicates, the regiment suffered a heavy loss: four men killed, five wounded, and 61 captured—ranking May 5 in the Wilderness along with Fredericksburg and Rappahannock Station as disasters for the number of men taken prisoner. Among the captured were Major Manning and Capt. Parnell Scott, commanding Company C. Hays' Brigade "lost heavily in this engagement," Seymour reported, its casualties totaling 254, "more than one third of its strength." The 25th Virginia, surrounded in the retreat, lost 300 men captured.[11]

The 61 men of the 6th Louisiana captured in the battle were in for a dreadful experience as prisoners. They were initially sent to the Federal prison camp at Point Lookout, Maryland, on the Chesapeake Bay, a place familiar to some of them who had spent time there after being captured at Rappahannock Station. In mid-August, they were loaded on dirty cargo ships and sent off to a new prison facility at Elmira, New York, a place which would become notorious among even these hardened men as a "hell on earth." The unsanitary, overcrowded, poorly managed Elmira camp was a nightmare of sickness, hunger, nakedness and cruelty, compounded by bitter winter weather that killed weakened men by the hundreds each week. Those who would survive Elmira to be released the next spring were the lucky ones. Of a total 12,123 Confederates imprisoned at the camp, 2,963 died of illness, exposure and associated causes.[12]

Those Louisianians lucky enough to escape capture that afternoon retreated back to the woods, where they dug in for a possible counterattack. The fighting continued sporadically throughout the afternoon as the Confederates hunkered down in shallow, log-lined trenches which faced similarly dug-in Union troops in the dense woods ahead. Much of the time, the hostile forces could not see each other through the leafy tangle of the Wilderness, aiming only at sounds and firing "by earsight." The opposing lines, according to a surgeon in Neill's brigade, ran along slight ridges on opposite sides of a wooded marsh about 300 yards wide. "The rattle of musketry," he recalled, "would swell into a continuous roar as the simultaneous discharge of 10,000 guns mingles in one grand concert, and then after a few minutes became more interrupted. . . .Then would be heard the wild yells which always told of a rebel charge, and again the volleys would become more terrible and the broken crashing tones would swell into one continuous roll of sound, which would presently be interrupted by the vigorous manly cheers of the northern soldiers, so different from the shrill yell of the rebels, and which indicated a repulse of their enemies."[13]

It had been a deadly afternoon for Colonel Monaghan's men, but their fighting on this first day in the Wilderness was not yet over. About 6:00 p.m., the Federals attempted another attack aimed at turning the Confederate left flank, held by Pegram's Virginians, who were positioned just left of Hays' Brigade. The 6th Louisiana was deployed on the left end of Hays' line, and thus connected with Pegram's men. It was a most unfortunate spot, and the regiment was soon caught up in a fierce assault against Pegram's front. Captain Seymour credited Monaghan's regiment with helping turn the tide against the Northerners. "The 6th La. Regiment, on the left of our Brigade, gave great assistance to Pegram in repelling the assault, by a left oblique fire which they poured into the thick Yankee columns as they advanced," he wrote. "The losses of the enemy were frightful and when day dawned the next morning the ground was found to be literally covered with dead bodies."[14]

The attack by Brig. Gen. Truman Seymour's Federal brigade involved some of the same unfortunate troops the 6th Louisiana had overrun at Second Winchester the previous June. General Seymour, who had taken command of Milroy's old brigade of Ohioans, Pennsylvanians and Marylanders only that morning, began his attack "under the impression that we overlapped the enemy's left, and that he was weak in our front from the detaching of troops to his right." Instead, his four regiments ran into a nasty surprise. "A vigorous advance was made and the enemy was soon found," Truman Seymour wrote, "but sheltered by log breast-works and extending so far beyond me that his fire came upon the prolongation of our line with the greatest severity." Caught in the open, the unlucky Federals took heavy casualties—especially the 110th Ohio regiment, which "suffered severely." The Ohio outfit, led by Col. J. Warren Kiefer (who was wounded in the attack), was the same regiment chased from the western fort at Winchester in the Louisianians' legendary charge eleven months earlier.[15]

As night fell on the first day's battle, the opposing lines dug into their forest trenches. From his post opposite the Louisiana Brigade's position, General Seymour listened to the Confederates preparing for the next day's fighting. "The enemy through the night was constantly strengthening his line; the cutting and felling of trees was continual, and the movement of guns to his left was distinctly heard," the Union general reported. Fires lit by the discharge of arms spread through the thick undergrowth and into the dry sedge and grasses of the open fields, bringing with it torture and a hideous death to those wounded unable to crawl away from the lapping flames. Some soldiers reported hearing the "pop-pop-pop" of exploding cartridges carried on the bodies of the dead and wounded. The discharges inflicted yet more suffering on the already luckless men. With the lines of armed men facing each other in the smoky-dark Wilderness, there was little the living could do to relieve the pain of the dying or save the remains of the dead, trapped on the smoldering battlefield.[16]

Corporal Trahern, who had the good fortune to be carried off the battlefield in a blanket by two members of his Company D, was half a mile to the rear in a field hospital tent. "At night. . .the surgeons of various commands began their rounds," he remembered. "With star candles mostly in use, they performed wonderful operations. As I lay there, stiff sore, thinking of friends far away, this Corps of able, hard-working officers halted at the tent next to mine and immediately took off the leg of an infantry soldier. My turn came next," he recalled with some trepidation, "and to my delight they pronounced my wound not at all dangerous. Although the night had long since shaded the earth, bullets were still flying through the trees, and sometimes through the tents."[17]

It had been a day of fighting unlike any seen before by the veterans of either army. They had spent it shooting at unseen enemies and being shot at from the leafy thickets in return; men and whole regiments lost their sense of direction in the brushy growth and wandered aimlessly into enemy lines and were captured. Except when the fighting was done in clearings, such as Saunders' Field, it was a case of the blind groping for the invisible, a mad game of panic and confusion, fought in an environment straight out of a bad dream. As darkness ended the nightmare for a few hours, the exhausted men within the choking blackness of the Wilderness knew that the morrow would bring another day of it, as sure as the sunrise.

While Ewell's three divisions were fighting off the Federal assaults on the left wing of Lee's army on Thursday, two divisions of A. P. Hill's Third Corps on the right fought a separate battle along the Orange Plank Road, which sliced through the green tangle some three miles south of the Saunders' Field and the Turnpike. Though badly mauled, the divisions of Maj. Gens. Henry Heth and Cadmus Wilcox managed to hold their ground, albeit just barely, against repeated ferocious assaults by Winfield Hancock's II Federal Corps. The first day's fighting on both fronts ended in a bloody draw. The Union general-in-chief planned to concentrate his attack the next morning against Lee's right, where Hill's battered brigades anxiously awaited the arrival of James Longstreet's First Corps, which was still miles back and advancing up the Plank Road. Longstreet's men had only recently returned to the army from a disappointing and trying several months in Georgia and Tennessee. Grant's plan called for five divisions of John Sedgwick's and Gouverneur Warren's corps to keep Ewell pinned down, while seven divisions from Hancock's II Corps and Ambrose Burnside's IX Corps swarmed over A. P. Hill's own pair of thinned divisions. Grant knew that Longstreet was not yet up, and he wanted to destroy Hill's Corps before "old Pete" arrived. If Hill's front could be collapsed, there was a good chance Grant could decisively defeat Lee's army.[18]

The dawn on Friday, May 6, brought with it a determined Federal assault on Hill's overmatched and weary fighters. Although they put up a determined resistance, they were unable to hold and fled rearward. Fortunately, Longstreet's veterans arrived and drove the enemy back, sealing the breach in the line. As Lee watched with obvious relief while Longstreet restored the left-front of his army, less vigorous fighting broke out in Ewell's sector, where Federal V Corps commander Warren stubbornly declined to renew the attacks across Saunders' Field that had failed so miserably the previous day. The Union VI Corps lay in the woods just to the north of Warren. Its commander, General Sedgwick, responded to Grant's prodding by sending the General Seymour and his battered brigade on yet another sortie against Ewell's northern flank. About 8:00 a.m., Seymour's men bushwhacked through the undergrowth, shooting blindly at the sound of muskets ahead, and stumbled into the sector occupied by Pegram's Brigade, adjacent to the 6th Louisiana's position. Pegram's Virginians, safely crouched behind their log and dirt dugouts, riddled the Federals with musket volleys that knocked all the momentum from their charge. In the brief but bloody exchange, Seymour's Ohio regiments again suffered high losses before being driven back, but the fight was costly for the Virginians, too, who lost their commander when Pegram was severely wounded in the leg.[19]

The 6th Louisiana's Captain Ring apparently was in the middle of writing a letter to his wife when Seymour's attack hit just to his left that morning. "We have now been engaged for forty eight hours and by the favor of God I am still uninjured but have been struck by two glancing balls," he began his May 6 letter. After summarizing the previous day's battle he promised to write again that evening, "if I get through safe." He was about to sign off when all hell broke loose. "With a firm trust in Providence for his continued favor and the hope, darling, that this will be the final fight and that I will escape safely, with all my love for"—here the flow of his words was broken, and resumed later— "I had got this far when the Enemy made a severe attack on us, which lasted half an hour, when they fled to the shades of obscurity. I am now out with my company skirmishing and the bullets are whistling all around me. I have just had another man killed but this is nothing when you get used to it." The war was hardening Captain Ring, as it hardened all the men who endured it.[20]

Fighting slackened during the rest of the day, which was characterized by what Ewell called "partial assaults on my line" and "efforts to find my flank," which were "promptly checked." Hays' adjutant also noted an easing of the fighting in front of the Louisianians. "During the remainder of the day," Captain Seymour noted, "the Yankees did not make any further attempt on our part of the line, though heavy skirmishing was kept up, without intermission, until night fall." During the comparative lull on Ewell's front, one of the war's most furious battles raged to the south along the Plank Road. After Hancock's early-morning juggernaut had been beaten back by Longstreet, the First Corps commander learned that Hancock's left flank was vulnerable to attack. Longsreet's assault fell like a giant hammer and rolled up the Federal wing "like a wet blanket." In a misfortune that eerily echoed the tragedy that struck Stonewall Jackson a year earlier and just a few miles away, Lee's "old war horse" was severely wounded by his own men when they mistook his party riding along the Plank Road for enemy cavalry. Unlike Jackson, Longstreet would survive his crippling wounds, but his loss blunted the Confederate counter-offensive just when it might have crippled Grant's army.[21]

Another opportunity for the Southerners on Dick Ewell's front was squandered the same day because of indecision on the part of the Confederate corps commander. Since early morning, the aggressive John Gordon had sought approval to launch an attack against Sedgwick's left flank, which he found on reconnaissance to be exposed and unsupported ("wholly unprotected," in Gordon's words.) Early opposed the attack as unsafe, insisting against the Georgian's first-hand evidence that Burnside's corps was in reserve behind Sedgwick's line. The issue was brought to Ewell, who displayed the same indecisiveness that had gripped him at Gettysburg. Ewell equivocated much of the day before reaching a decision late in the afternoon. Finally unleashed at 6:00 p.m., Gordon's flank attack stunned the Federals, rolled up the VI Corps line, and shattered two brigades. Gordon's assault killed and wounded 400 Federals and captured several hundred more—including brigadier generals Alexander Shaler and the luckless Truman Seymour. Stiff resistance by Neill's brigade and the gathering darkness ground the Georgian's advance to a halt. Given another hour of daylight and proper support, the attack, claimed Gordon, "would have resulted in a decided disaster to the whole right wing of General Grant's army, if not its entire disorganization."[22]

Gordon's attack was begun too late and involved too small a force to wreck Grant's right wing, but it shook the Union commander's confidence in his generals. The Army of the Potomac had barely escaped double disasters on May 6, first with Longstreet's counterattack against Hancock's flank, and then Gordon's flanking assault against Sedgwick. As it was, the two days of Wilderness fighting were disastrous enough for the Federals, whose casualties totaled 17,666 killed, wounded and captured—roughly twice those of Lee's army. Confederate losses at the Wilderness were never officially reported, but various estimates range between 7,750 and 11,000 men. The only tally of casualties in Hays' Brigade is Captain Seymour's figure of 254, which represented "more than one third of its strength." Unfortunately, Seymour did not provide a breakdown as to killed, wounded, and captured. For the two days of fighting, the 6th Louisiana suffered heavily, losing five killed, six wounded and 61 missing—more than 40 percent of the men present for duty when the fighting began.[23]

After two horrifying days the fighting in the Wilderness was over. The human suffering, however, had just begun. Thousands of bleeding and dying men covered the battlefield. "The loss of human life is shocking," Father Sheeran, chaplain to the Louisiana troops, wrote in his journal. The day after the battle, he reported, "was one of my most laborious days: it being spent from morning till late at night hearing confessions, administering Extreme Unction [the Catholic last rites for the dying], baptizing, and in washing and dressing wounds." Corporal Trahern of the 6th Louisiana, himself one of the wounded, offered a glimpse into the suffering he and others endured. On Saturday evening, Trahern and other wounded men were loaded into wagons and transported to Orange Court House to await a railroad train to Lynchburg's hospital system. The ride to the train station, over bumpy plank roads in a "common trucker's cart without springs," was a lesson in human endurance for Trahern and his badly wounded companion:

> Just think of two soldiers packed in an old box cart, one with a gaping flesh wound near the knee, the other with a leg amputated at the hip, and you will have a picture that could scarcely ever fade from human memory. My suffering was nothing to be compared to that of my comrade. We were tossed about often, and sometimes violently, and every time this occurred a solemn wail came from my companion of such sorrowful nature as to almost break my heart.

At the rail station, Trahern found "more than a thousand suffering" men lying in wait for the train. "Hundreds of box cars were on the siding, awaiting to take us to Lynchburg. Here I separated from my companion, he being placed in a special car for the desperately wounded, never to look upon his face again, or hear his once agonizing voice." Trahern would spend five months recuperating before he was able to return to the regiment that October.[24]

While the fighting in the Wilderness had not been decisive, Lee could take some satisfaction from the fact that he had inflicted heavy casualties on the Federals and fought Grant to a standoff even against two-to-one odds. In the past this had been enough to prompt the Army of the Potomac to retreat behind the nearest river, but Grant was not McClellan (or Burnside or Hooker). As President Lincoln said of him at this time, Grant "has the grit of a bulldog. Once let him get his teeth in, and nothing can shake him off." The Union's bulldog-general was eager to get out of the Wilderness, but rther than retreat, Grant chose to move southeast toward Richmond. He would find a better place to fight Lee again, this time out in the open.[25]

The morning of Saturday, May 7, was strangely quiet along the lines in the Wilderness. The solitude led to speculation on both sides that Grant was about to disengage and retreat. By late afternoon, however, it became apparent that the Federal commander harbored no such intention. The threads of his army were beginning to march, but their direction was south, not back toward the Rapidan River. His objective was the small and quiet crossroads village of Spotsylvania Court House, about a dozen miles down the Brock Road. If Grant could reach it first, his army would be between Lee and the Confederate capital, a strategic situation that would force Lee to attack him on ground of Grant's choosing. When darkness fell, Grant's infantry began a night march toward Spotsylvania, with Gouverneur Warren's V Corps in the lead.[26]

Sifting through confusing intelligence information, Lee guessed at Grant's design and dispatched Longstreet's Corps, now under command of Maj. Gen. Richard H. Anderson, to march to Spotsylvania early the next morning. Fitz Lee's Confederate cavalry reached the area first and slowed the Federal advance just long enough to allow Anderson's troops, coming on a run, to deploy moments before Warren's infantry arrived on the scene in force. While this race was on, the 6th Louisiana remained with Hays' Brigade back in the Wilderness, helping bury the dead and round up the wounded in what the visually descriptive Captain Seymour described as a ghastly environment where "the atmosphere for miles around was filled with the noisome odors that came up from the putrifying corpses."[27]

Ewell had received orders from Lee late Saturday to extend his line to the right, and if at daylight he found no large force in his front, to follow Anderson to Spotsylvania. According to Seymour, this sidewise shift was done so cautiously, in deference to the Federal troops believed to be immediately in front, that by dawn the Louisianians had marched only one-and-a-half miles. Captain Ring provides a somewhat different version of the night movement of the 6th Louisiana. In a letter home datelined "Battle Field, Spotsylvania C.H., May 9," Ring told his wife that "the enemy fell back on Saturday night, and we have been on the march ever since to get this new base. It was the most fatiguing march I have ever made. We were all Saturday night moving about 7 miles; we had to feel for the enemy all the way, and yesterday [Sunday, May 8] was exceedingly hot, not only from the sun, but part of the forest was on fire and we had to march often through a wall of fire and smoke." Ewell confirmed in his report that it was "a very distressing march through intense heat and thick dust and smoke from burning woods." For his part, Ring was clearly showing the signs of exhaustion and stress that must have been common through the ranks after the hard fighting and hellish marching: "I am nearly broke down from the want of sleep, but I am sustained by the hope that this campaign will decide the war."[28]

While on the march to Spotsylvania, the men of the 6th Louisiana learned that their brigade was to be transferred from Early's Division to Johnson's, and consolidated with the 2nd Louisiana Brigade. "I wish you to transfer Hays' Brigade to Johnson's Division, so that the two La. brigades may be together, they being so much reduced and Genl. Stafford being disabled," Lee wrote in a confidential message to Ewell that Sunday. This move was part of a broader reorganization that Lee was forced to make following his serious losses in the Wilderness. Two of his three corps commanders were not at their posts: Longstreet was severely wounded, and A. P. Hill was sick and disabled. With Anderson leading Longstreet's Corps, Lee tapped Jubal Early to command the Third Corps in Hill's absence. Early's new assignment opened a division level command, which might have gone to Harry Hays as the senior colonel but instead went to John Gordon, who had displayed such aggressive brilliance in the Wilderness. The consolidation of the two Louisiana brigades under Hays' command, and the shift of the unified brigade to Johnson's Division, conveniently moved Hays aside in favor of Gordon, while offering the Louisianian the consolation prize of commanding all the Louisiana regiments. In his special order formalizing the changes, Lee specified that although the two Louisiana brigades would be united under Hays, "each brigade will retain its present organization." The move was merely the first step toward a full consolidation of the two brigades, which would come by autumn. For the final year of the war, all the Louisiana troops in Lee's army—now dwindled to barely

1,000 men from the 12,000 that arrived in Virginia at the start—would fight together.[29]

When the Louisianians finally reached their assigned place in the Spotsylvania line—Captain Seymour puts the time at 1:00 a.m., Monday, May 9—they immediately went to work with shovels, picks, bayonets, tin cups and whatever tools they had to build their log-and-dirt fortifications. "Though our supply of entrenching tools was very limited, our men toiled with such a will that by daylight we had quite a strong line of works to fight behind," marveled Seymour. "These were further improved and strengthened during the day." When the men saw the overall plan of the defensive line and their place in it, however, there was much grumbling. The three-mile line of fortifications around Spotsylvania Court House took the shape of a ragged and inverted V, with the angle jutting out northward where the line followed the high and generally open ground of a low ridge overlooking the meandering Ny River to the east. The Confederates weren't happy with this salient, which its defenders, in deference to its shape, called the Mule Shoe. Straightening the line, however, would have surrendered the high ground to Federal artillery, so the angle was the lesser of the evils. As the Army of Northern Virginia settled into its new line, Anderson's men held the left (facing northwest), Ewell's occupied the center (facing north), and Early's divisions—Hill's Third Corps—filed into position on the army's right (facing east).[30]

To the dismay of the Louisianians, Johnson's Division, which they had joined only the day before, was placed smack at the apex of the salient, which was vulnerable to attack from both sides and front. "Our men did not like it at all," Seymour observed. "It was so liable to be enfiladed by artillery and would be a dangerous trap to be caught in should the line be broken on the right or left. . . .An unfortunate work it turned out to be."[31]

Just how unfortunate would remain unclear for three more days. For the present, as they settled into their newly dug works to await whatever might come, the 6th Louisiana veterans faced nothing more than sporadic skirmishing. This included lively exchanges between the sharpshooters of both sides, who by this time in the war were becoming a deadly factor with the widespread use of high-powered rifles, such as Enfields and English scope-equipped Whitworths. Such weapons could kill at up to 1,000 yards, and one of them in Confederate hands did just that. The Federal VI Corps commander, Maj. Gen. John Sedgwick, was fatally wounded only moments after he had brushed aside the danger of sharpshooters, remarking, "They couldn't hit an elephant at this distance."[32]

Tuesday morning, May 10, found the 6th Louisiana anxiously awaiting attack. Captain Ring stole a few moments to write again to his wife—his third letter in five days. "Another day has passed and we are still hard at it," he wrote. "We have got the enemy right before us, and trust today may decide the contest. Heavy skirmishing is now going on, and bullets are whistling about like birds on a spring morning." The weary Ring remained hopeful, however. "All accounts agree that the enemy is very much demoralized; and we have positive information that we yesterday killed Gen. Sedgwick, who is considered one of their best Generals. I am still uninjured," he added, "and will write by every chance."[33]

That afternoon brought a major effort by Grant to break the Confederate line. About 4:00 p.m., Warren's Corps launched an attack on Anderson's Corps along the western flank of the inverted "V" line well to the left and behind the position held by the Louisiana troops. The assault was repulsed with heavy loss to the Federals. Shortly after 6:00 p.m., a second attack directly against the western face of the Mule Shoe scored a stunning breakthrough into the Confederate works. Colonel Emory Upton, the same officer who had led the devastating attack against the Louisianians at Rappahannock Station the previous November, spearheaded a sudden assault on the salient at the position held by the Brig. Gen. George Doles' Georgia Brigade. Upton's 12 regiments, nearly 5,000 men, struck in a formation three regiments wide and four deep. They dashed up to the Confederate works on the run without firing a shot and tore a gap in the line, pouring over Doles' men and penetrating deep within the Mule Shoe. The Louisiana troops found Union soldiers advancing toward them from their rear. "The situation of our Division was extremely critical and we were entirely cut off from the remainder of the army, the enemy being in our rear," Captain Seymour wrote. Once again, it was General Gordon to the rescue. His division (formerly Early's) was in reserve as a kind of rapid-reaction force, ready to move wherever trouble beckoned. The counter-charge by Gordon's brigades drove the Federal troops back and restored the original Confederate line, amid great slaughter on both sides.[34]

The Louisiana troops suffered a particularly painful loss when General Hays was severely wounded by a stray bullet or a sharpshooter.

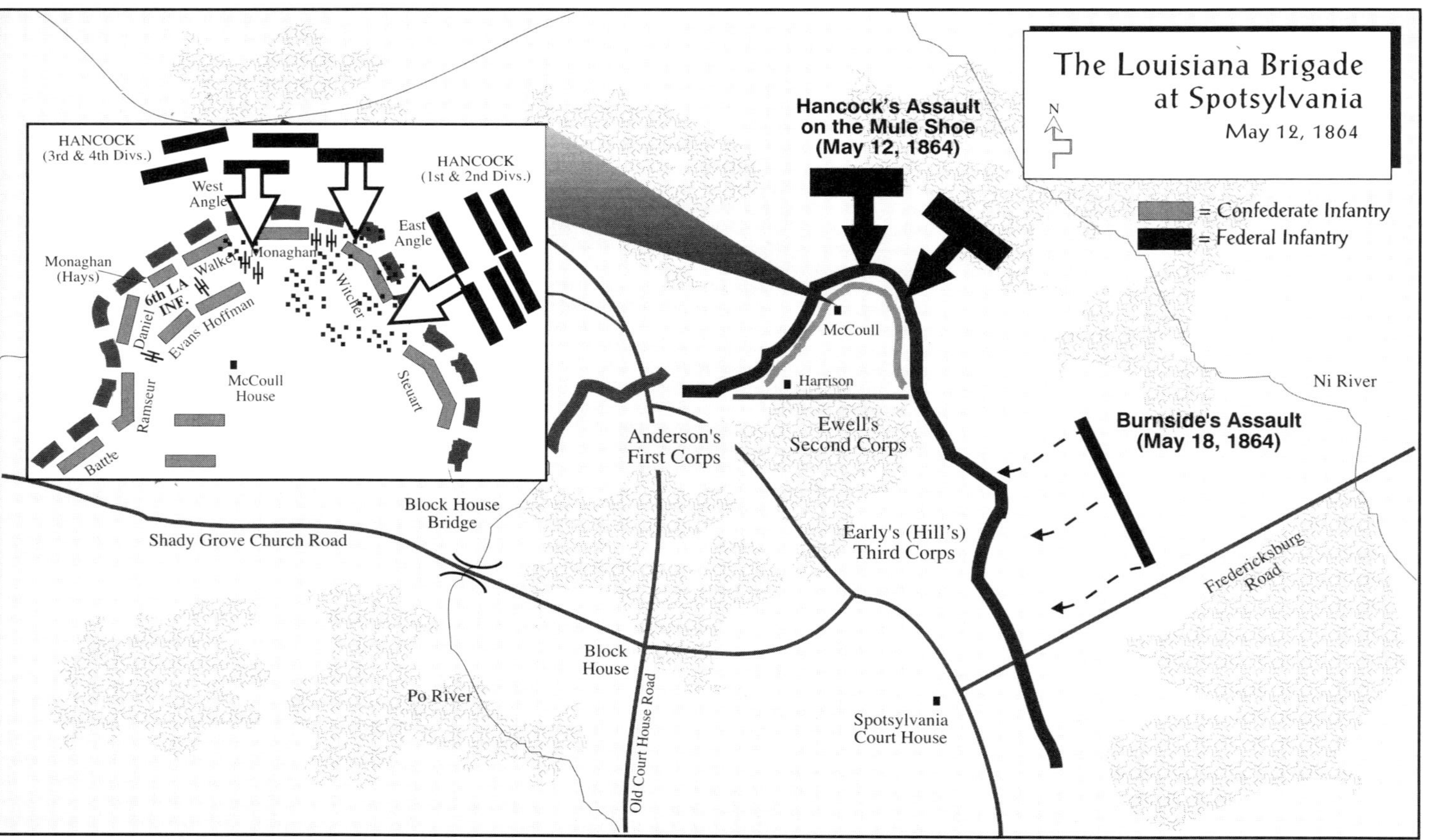

Theodore P. Savas

Although he would survive the wound, he would never again lead the Louisianians in battle. His absence opened the way for the 6th Louisiana's Colonel Monaghan to temporarily assume command of the combined Louisiana Brigade—an honor that the old Irishman probably never expected, and one which would require exacting demands in the coming days. Monaghan's elevation left the 6th Louisiana strapped for a replacement commander. Lieutenant Colonel Hanlon was absent sick at this time and Major Manning had been captured in the Wilderness. According to a letter written by Captain Ring on May 12, command of the regiment passed to its senior captain, John J. Rivera of Company E, the Mercer Guards, who was a New York-born former newspaper printer from New Orleans.[35]

Upton's attack on the western face of the salient had failed because it was not vigorously supported as planned by Grant, but its momentary success in breaking the Confederate line encouraged the Union commander to try it again on a larger scale. Wednesday, May 11, was a day of heavy rain and little fighting, as Grant busied himself planning an all-out attack for the next day, which he decided to throw at the apex of the salient, its weakest point. That afternoon, he ordered Hancock to move his command under darkness of night to mass in front of the Confederate salient for an attack to be launched at 4:00 a.m. on Thursday, May 12.[36]

On the Confederate side of the lines, troops also were being moved about in anticipation of further assaults. About 10:00 a.m., according to Seymour, the combined Louisiana Brigade was divided in two when Ewell ordered the five regiments of Hays' old brigade, including the 6th Louisiana, to the left, into the place of Doles' battered men, while leaving the five regiments Stafford's old brigade in their place in the apex of the salient. Hays' Louisianians grumbled about the change, for they did not want to occupy a position that had been overrun the day before. Considering what was about to take place, the move was a gift from Providence. Under a steady rain, Monaghan moved his five regiments to the left into Doles' muddy trenches. This was considered "the weakest portion of our works" Seymour recalled, because the Federal line ran up so close to it that there would be little warning of attack. "Our men did not like the change at all," grumbled one officer, but they were mollified and flattered when they heard that Ewell personally asked for "the best and most reliable Brigade in the Corps" to be posted at this vulnerable point.[37]

There was anxiety in those muddy trenches that damp and dreary night. Something was going on out in the blackness on the Union side, and nobody was sure just what it was. The sound of a large troop movement had been picked up late in the day. "Toward night the enemy were reported withdrawing from Anderson's front and were heard moving to our right," Ewell reported. This was the movement of Hancock's corps, getting into position for an attack at dawn, but the movement was misinterpreted by the Confederates. Anderson's front was down the western flank of the "V," which meant the Federals were moving east. Lee had received similar reports of such movements from his cavalry, which suggested either a retreat toward Fredericksburg or a move to get around the Confederate right flank, as Grant had done twice already, moving from Culpeper to the Wilderness and the Wilderness to Spotsylvania. Either way, Lee wanted to be ready to move quickly, so he ordered Ewell to withdraw the artillery from Johnson's front in the Mule Shoe to give it a head start on the muddy roads. Before sundown, the apex of the salient was stripped of the 22 defending guns it would so desperately need in just a few hours. Lee's intuition resulted in a disastrous tactical error.[38]

In the gloomy fog and drizzle inside the Mule Shoe, the departure of the artillery could only have increased the growing anxiety as midnight approached. The muffled sounds in the woods beyond their fortifications continued, convincing some officers, including Colonel Monaghan, that the Union forces were massing for an attack. Monaghan dispatched Captain Seymour to relay those fears to General Johnson. The division commander had been getting similar reports from other officers and scouts on the picket line, all pointing to a massive morning attack. Alarmed by this intelligence, Johnson urgently requested that Ewell send the artillery back. Ewell agreed and ordered the guns returned. But in the rain and blackness and mud, the movement was slow—just moments too slow, as it turned out.[39]

The veterans of the 6th Louisiana barely rested that stormy night in the rain. "Our men were on the qui vive all night and stood with muskets in hand, ready to receive hostile visitors," Seymour recalled. During the lull of this rainy day, they had collected the rifles of the dead Federals that were strewn all about the trenches where they had overrun Doles' men. They loaded the guns and stacked them at hand. "Each man had at least three guns, which would enable him to fire as many times without stopping to reload."[40]

Soon they would need them, and more. The rain-muffled sounds they had heard hours before came from the thousands of shuffling feet and clanking arms of Hancock's four divisions as they shifted eastward on a narrow road through the woods to a point fronting the apex of the salient. There, about 1,200 yards from the Confederate trenches, Hancock readied his 20,000 men for a frontal assault pointed squarely at that vulnerable bulge where the Louisiana troops stood fingering triggers, wondering when their artillery would return to the gun pits.[41]

The artillery was just moments away, but so was the massive enemy wave that was about to break on the Mule Shoe. Dawn of May 12 was held back by a heavy fog and drizzle that obscured whatever was out in the woods in front. The Louisianians' anxieties were somewhat eased in finding that Gordon's and Pegram's brigades had formed behind them to help repel the expected assault. "It was the first time that our Brigade had been supported by two lines of battle, and we all felt confident of resisting any force that could be brought against us," Seymour recorded.[42]

That confidence was misplaced. The wave that was about to break on the Confederate salient was signaled first by the scattered popping of skirmish fire that broke the silence at 4:35 a.m. The Confederate pickets got off only a few shots before the hazy figures emerging from the woods in front appeared, not as individual soldiers, but as a rolling mass of blue—regiment upon regiment, brigade upon brigade, coming at a run with the deep, full-throated roar of a Yankee cheer, so distinctively different from the high-pitched rebel yell. "Just at the dawn of day," Seymour remembered, "there suddenly burst upon our startled ears a sound like the roaring of a tempestuous sea; the woods before us fairly rang with the hoarse shouts of thousands of men." One of Monaghan's men, pointing to the right toward the apex of the angle, shouted, "Look out boys! We will have blood for supper!"[43]

"Click, click, sounded along our ranks, as each man cocked his musket and every eye was strained to discover, in the dim light of early morn, the first appearance of the Yankee line as it emerged from the woods," wrote Seymour, who penned one of the best personal accounts of the attack:

> Some moments elapsed before we could see a single Yankee, when suddenly the enemy poured out of the woods in front of our right, and marching obliquely to the left (our right), reached the broad open field in front of Jones's Brigade. Never have I seen such an exciting spectacle as then met my gaze. As far as

This photograph depicts the section of the breastworks held by the 6th Louisiana Infantry on the morning of May 12, 1864, along the west face of the "Mule Shoe." *James P. Gannon*

> the eye could reach, the field was covered with the serried ranks of the enemy, marching in close columns to attack. This was the time for our artillery to open, but not a shot was heard, our guns, unfortunately, not having gotten into position. The Yankees advanced with twelve lines of battle, and unmolested by artillery, soon reached the works behind which the remnant of Jones' Brigade, so cut up and demoralized at the Wilderness, was posted. These troops, formed in a single line and unsupported, and seeing the overwhelming force advancing against them, became panick stricken and ingloriously fled the field without firing scarcely a shot.[44]

Hancock's men had come on at a run, breaking into their deep-chested cheer about halfway to the Confederate line before rolling, as their proud corps commander later reported, "like an irresistible wave into the enemy's works." The Federals swarmed over the parapets into the salient, fanning out to the left and the right to charge the stunned brigades adjacent to Jones' panicked men, taking them in flank and rear. The Louisiana regiments of Stafford's old brigade—the 1st, 2nd, 10th, 14th and 15th—which had been left at the apex when Monaghan moved his five regiments down the line to the left, were overrun and mostly taken prisoner, as were the men of Brig. Gen. George Steuart's Brigade and Walker's Stonewall Brigade. Johnson's Division was gobbled up, and both Generals Johnson and Steuart were among the thousands of prisoners being collected and sent over to the Federal side. "They poured through our line in immense numbers," Ewell said of the Union attack, "taking possession of the right and left of the Salient."[45]

The artillery that Johnson so desperately needed suddenly arrived at a gallop—just in time to be captured by the swelling enemy mass of troops pushing deeper into the bloody chaos of the Mule Shoe. As Hancock's attackers crashed upon Jones' Brigade at the apex of the salient, General Johnson later reported, he saw the artillery just coming into sight. "I ordered the artillery to drive up at a gallop," Johnson wrote, but it was too late. The cannons did not fire a shot, he said, before they were captured. "It arrived only to have its horses shot dead in their traces, and its men mowed down in the act of unlimbering," wrote a correspondent for the *London Herald*, who was with the Confederates inside the Mule Shoe.[46]

After destroying the Confederate brigades at the toe of the Mule Shoe, the Union onslaught swept down the leg of the apex toward Monaghan and his five undermanned regiments, including the 6th Louisiana. The *London Herald* correspondent described what happened next:

> While the Stonewall brigade fought and fell back, that next on its left—Hays's—had time to swing around. Col. Monaghan, its senior colonel being in command, it confronted the rushing advance to the left. Standing behind a traverse that extended perpendicularly from the original position of the brigade, it presented a front as firm as a ledge of rock. The wave of the enemy's triumph surged up to that barrier; but having broken upon it in mere spray, left the honor of the arrest of its overflow on that side of the field to these houseless, landless warriors of Louisiana.[47]

Hancock's attackers, Seymour wrote, had captured the majority of four full brigades, plus "thirty eight men from the extreme right of our Brigade who had not heard the order to withdraw" when Monaghan withdrew the Louisianians 150 yards to the left and changed front to the right to confront the Federals. The Louisianians, thus repositioned, were in the sector defended by Brig. Gen. Junius Daniel's North Carolina brigade, on a small rise where a battery was posted, according to Seymour. "The enemy, greatly elated by this easy success, came sweeping down the line of our works, yelling like devils; arriving at the foot of the hill on the crest of which we were posted, they reformed and made repeated efforts to ascind, but were as often met by such a steady and murderous fire that they soon gave up the attempt and retired to the works they had captured." Monaghan's Louisianians joined Daniel's Carolinians in halting the Federal advance down the western side of the salient.[48]

By 5:15 a.m., the Northern troops had driven deep into the salient from the apex, overrunning about three-quarters of a mile of Ewell's front. They had achieved a stunning breakthrough, capturing nearly all of Johnson's Division, almost 4,000 men, and 20 pieces of artillery. The breakthrough threatened to split Lee's army in two, but at this point the momentum of the attack was all but spent and Hancock's forces were scattered and disorganized. The Confederate cause hovered on the brink of disaster, and only a timely and well-delivered counterblow could prevent it. Once again, the mantle of responsibility fell to General Gordon. The Georgian somehow managed to assemble his three scattered brigades and mount a screaming counterattack that drove the Federals back toward the eastern face of the works enclosing the Mule Shoe. On the western face of the salient, where the 6th Louisiana was helping hold the Union advance in check, a counterattack by Brig. Gen. Stephen Ramseur's North Carolina brigade brought some relief to the hard-pressed Louisianians. "At 7 A.M.," Captain Seymour recalled, "Ramseur's N.C. Brigade formed on our right and advanced at a charge; the steadiness with which they went forward, fighting at every step, was most admirable and elicited loud cheers from our men."[49]

Along with other Confederate counter-strikes, these moves finally pushed Hancock's troops across the original lines of the salient, where the survivors hunkered down along the outer walls of the fortifications to begin what would be more than 20 hours of close-order fighting, with Union and Confederate troops facing each other just yards away on opposite sides of the log-and-dirt walls. Grant also threw General Wright's VI Corps (formerly Sedgwick's) into the fight on the western face of the angle and Burnside's IX Corps on the eastern side, in an all-out effort that ultimately failed to overrun Lee's army. The battle, which had begun so promisingly for the Federals, evolved into a stalemate of slaughter and bloodshed on a level none of the veterans had ever witnessed.[50]

Somehow in the midst of this murderous day, Captain Ring of the 6th Louisiana found time to write again to his wife. From about 5:00 a.m. until about 3:00 p.m.—the latter being the hour Ring said he was writing—"there has been the most desperate struggle I have ever seen," this veteran of many battles wrote. "We have succeeded in driving them back and have retaken our defenses. Fighting is still going on, the enemy fighting sullenly and retiring slowly. The loss on both sides must be very great. . ." When General Hays was wounded and Monaghan moved up to replace him, Ring added, "the command of this Regiment devolved upon Captain Rivera, who is now missing, as well as two other Captains, leaving me once more in command of the gallant 6th." Ring counted himself lucky to have escaped thus far with "a slight lick to the ankle joint, which is painful, but nothing more," but his mental state bordered on desperate, as his letter shows. He prayed that Grant would react to the slaughter as other Federal commanders had—by retreating. "I trust this is the last desperate effort of the enemy, and that to-morrow's sun may find most of them over the Rappahannock. God grant it, for I am nearly dead with fatigue and want of sleep, having had nothing but short naps of a few minutes duration for the last 3 days and nights. During the fight of this morning it rained very hard, and I am now sitting in mud 6 inches deep, besides being wet and hungry."[51]

As this seemingly endless day of fighting ground on, the opposing troops on opposite sides of the Confederate works struggled amid ankle deep mud in bloody trenches filled with the dead bodies of both friend and foe, pouring point-blank fire across the few yards separating them. Upton's brigade even wheeled cannon right up to the Confederate works to pour canister at short range into the foes on the other side. The carnage on both sides was among the worst of the war. A cold, drenching rain fell during the battle, which didn't finally sputter out until about 3:00 a.m. on the 13th, after more than 20 hours of some of the most brutal slaughter any soldiers had ever seen.[52]

Captain Ring certainly had never witnessed anything like it. "I have, as you know, been through a good many hard fights, but I never saw anything like the contest of the 12th," he wrote to his wife three days later. "We lay all day and night in the Breastworks, in mud 5 inches deep with every kind of shot & shell whistling over us, among us, in us and about us, so that it was as much as your life was worth to raise your head above the works." Ring lamented that Johnson's Division "was completely broken up," and was critical of Johnson's other brigades which he claimed had been captured without putting up a fight. "All of them too, Virginia troops, among them the far famed Stonewall Brigade, one Regiment of which as the Yankees charged the works jumped over with their colors and surrendered without a shot." Ring was justifiably proud of the role the Louisianians had played in helping stop the Federal assault inside the salient. "Gen. Ewell says that our Brigade saved his Left by the determined stand we made which checked the Enemies' advance. I hope he will mention it in his report." Ewell, who did not write a report until ten months later, made no mention of Monaghan's stand, which is well-documented in both Seymour's journal and the *London Daily Herald* article written just after the battle.[53]

As the bloodletting of May 12 raged on, Lee's engineers rushed to finish a fall-back line of defense across the base of the salient they had begun on the previous day. Convinced that it was futile to try to hold the old lines encompassing the Mule Shoe, Lee ordered a pullback to the new line after dark. "At midnight, my forces were quietly withdrawn to it and artillery placed in position," Ewell reported. The new line was some 800 yards behind the peak of the salient, but the shattered remnants of Johnson's Division were moved even further back and placed in reserve. The 6th Louisiana, according to Ring's May 15 letter, pulled back two miles about daylight on May 13, to try to recruit missing members of the regiment. "Our Division had been so badly shattered that it was withdrawn from the front & placed in reserve for the purpose of reorganization," Captain Seymour wrote.[54]

The battle of May 12 was marked by a ferocity rarely matched in the history of war. It was killing on a grand scale, yet up close and personal, as the desperate men on opposite sides of the same earthworks endured hour after hour of nearly face-to-face slaughter. The muddy trenches ran red with blood, and the musketry was so intense and prolonged—soldiers reported having spent 400 or more cartridges each—that oak trees up to two feet in diameter were shredded by bullets and toppled on Confederates beneath them. The fiercest fighting was along the western face of the salient, where Monaghan's survivors hung on, and this sector acquired the name by which it is known in history: The Bloody Angle. After the war, survivors of this nearly 24-hour ordeal of meat-grinder combat scarcely expected to be believed when they attempted to describe the horrors of May 12.[55]

The battle had been disastrous for the Louisianians and shattered the newly-combined brigade that Monaghan led during the fight. The old 2nd Louisiana Brigade, which had been Stafford's, had been in the salient and had now almost disappeared. The old 1st Louisiana Brigade, Hays' regiments, lost fewer captured but had many killed and wounded. The losses of the five regiments of the brigade were never officially reported. The 6th Louisiana went into the battle with about 100 men and lost more than one-quarter of them. Incredibly, none were killed outright, although at least two of the eight wounded would die of their wounds, and another 20 men were captured.[56]

The devastated 6th Louisiana had lost nearly two-thirds of its strength during the first two weeks of May, from the opening of the Wilderness through the conclusion of Spotsylvania. It had begun the campaign with 173 men in the ranks, and on the morning of May 13, only 60 men answered roll call. When Father Sheeran went to inspect the area where his Louisiana men had fought, he was so stunned and revolted that he nearly passed out. "May God grant that I may never again experience such sensations or witness such scenes as I this night felt and beheld," the priest's wrote in his journal on May 19. "We passed over the ground enclosed in the angle where Grant broke through our lines on the morning of the 12th. The thousands of Yankees slaughtered on that memorable morning are lying there decomposed and unburied." The soggy terrain, which was "low and swampy," added to the repulsive atmosphere, which was "densely impregnated with the offensive effluvia of the dead bodies of men and horses. The sights are shocking," added Sheeran, and "the smell is still more offensive."[57]

For their part in the battle of May 12, the 6th Louisiana and the other four regiments under Monaghan's command have never received proper credit. They played an important role in containing the Federal breakthrough on the western side of the salient. Many historians overlook the fact that the newly-combined Louisiana Brigade was split up on the eve of the battle, and that Monaghan's five regiments were not swallowed, like those of Stafford's old brigade, in the initial success of Hancock's attackers. Terry Jones, an authority on the Louisiana brigades in Lee's Army, wrote of the May 12 battle: "Virtually all accounts of the battle cite Gordon as saving Lee's army by rushing in reinforcements to seal the breach and ignore the critical role Monaghan's men played. If not for Monaghan's quickness in laying out a defensive position perpendicular to the trenches, the Yankees would have continued flanking the rebel brigades all the way down the western side." Captain Ring's hope that Ewell would repeat in his official report what he apparently told these men—that "our Brigade saved his Left"—was never realized, but there is enough other evidence to support the belief that the Irishmen of the 6th and their comrades in the other four Louisiana regiments deserved some honor and recognition for their courage and tenacity on one of the worst days of the Civil War.[58]

The bloody struggle of May 12 did not end the battle of Spotsylvania. Heavy rain for several days limited the conflict to only sporadic fighting. When the weather cleared on May 17, Grant ordered Hancock to attack across the apex of the salient, which had been abandoned by the Confederates, to the new line in its rear. The morning assault of May 18 fell directly on Ewell's new defensive works across the base of the salient. The battle was a one-sided slaughter which displayed "the immense power of artillery well handled," in the words of Ewell's chief of artillery, Brig. Gen. Armistead Long. Two Federal divisions, attacking across the abandoned Mule Shoe, were cut up and scattered by 29 guns posted along Ewell's line, while the Confederate infantry mainly looked on in awe as spectators. The one-sided carnage lasted barely two hours before the bloodied Northerners withdrew, never having reached the new Confederate line.[59]

In almost two weeks of operations around Spotsylvania, the Union army suffered more than 18,000 casualties, exceeding the heavy toll extracted in the Wilderness. Confederate casualties are uncertain, and are estimated at perhaps 9,000 to 10,000, including about 4,600 captured from Ewell's Corps alone. Though Grant's stunning losses shocked the Northern public, he showed no slackening of resolve to fight it out with Lee. He had wired Washington on May 11 that he was prepared "to fight it out on this line if it takes all summer."[60]

On May 15, Captain Ring penned a final letter home to his wife from the Spotsylvania battlefield. "This is the eleventh day of this great fight," he informed her, "and still we are at it." His words reflected a mixture of awe and disgust at Grant's willingness to sustain such an appalling loss of human life:

> We have such a man this time who either does not know when he is whipped or who cares not if he loses his whole army so that he may accomplish an end. I wrote to you on the 12th during the most severe fight of this war and thought at the time that Grant would be convinced from that day's experience of the folly of his attacks, but he seems determined to die game if he has to die at all.[61]

It was beginning to dawn on the exhausted Confederates that they were facing a new kind of warrior.

Chapter Twelve

The Gates of Washington: MONOCACY

"They were met by a tempest of bullets, and many of the brave fellows fell at the first volley."
– *Maj. Gen. John B. Gordon*

The 6th Louisiana was now no larger than a company in effective strength, and it would remain so for the rest of the war. But, the dwindling few gamely soldiered. Nearly a year of campaigning and fighting lay ahead. The final campaigns would carry them into the Shenandoah Valley for a third time, back into Maryland, and then to the very gates of Washington. For the remaining few, there still were hundreds of miles to march and many battles to fight.[1]

Operations around Spotsylvania Court House ended May 19 when General Grant again began moving his army in a southeasterly direction toward Richmond. As Lee countered Grant's flanking move, the 6th Louisiana marched first to a position along the North Anna River, 23 miles north of Richmond, and then to Cold Harbor, a dozen miles east of the Confederate capital, at the end of May. In neither of these places was the 6th Louisiana seriously engaged. At Cold Harbor, the regiment was posted within a cannon shot of the place where their beloved old leader, Colonel Seymour, fell two years earlier at Gaines' Mill, sometimes called the first battle of Cold Harbor. But this time, when the heavy fighting came on June 3, the regiment was posted on the extreme left of Lee's defensive line when Grant's dawn attack by 60,000 men slammed into the Confederate center and right. Nevertheless, one 6th Louisiana soldier was killed and several men, including Lieutenant Colonel Hanlon, were wounded, one mortally. The poorly planned Federal assault turned into a disaster that cost the Union army some 7,000 men, while the dug-in

Confederates lost only 1,500. In one month of nearly continuous fighting, Grant had lost 50,000 men and Lee roughly 30,000.[2]

The heavy losses in the two Louisiana brigades prompted eight Louisiana members of the Confederate Congress to ask President Jefferson Davis to grant them a 90-day furlough and return them to service in their home state. In their June 13 letter to the president, the legislators noted that the long, proud service of these 10 regiments in the Army of Northern Virginia had devastated their ranks. "These brigades are mere skeletons, the two hardly equal to half a regiment. We are daily appealed to by them to ask for their transfer home, where they could be recruited. . . .Three years of hardships and dangers ought to entitle the few survivors of this once magnificent corps to this small boon," they wrote. Davis expressed sympathy with the plea, but Lee's need for every soldier he could find made such requests unthinkable.[3]

Brig. Gen. Zebulon York

One of the richest landowners in pre-war Louisiana, York was a native of Maine. He served with the 14th Louisiana through most of the war in the Eastern Theater. He was promoted to brigadier general at the end of May 1864, to lead the fragments of the Army of Norther Virginia's pair of Louisiana brigades. His left arm was amputated after a shell fragment shattered the limb at Winchester on September 19, 1864. The wound effectively ended his military career. *Generals in Gray*

The combined Louisiana Brigade would remain with Lee, but under a new leader. On June 3, Col. Zebulon York was promoted to brigadier general and given command. York was a 44-year old native of Maine who had moved to Louisiana to become a wealthy planter before the war. He enjoyed a reputation for rash bravery and frightful profanity, and had done well at the head of the 14th Louisiana regiment. Since Harry Hays had been shot in the Wilderness, the 6th Louisiana's Colonel Monaghan had been temporarily in command of the Louisiana Brigade.

but Monaghan took ill and went to the hospital at Richmond about June 1. The nature of his illness isn't clear, but it kept him away from the brigade until late summer. With Lieutenant Colonel Hanlon absent due to his Cold Harbor wound and Major Manning locked up in a Federal prison camp, the 6th Louisiana was temporarily under command of its senior captain, Charles Pilcher.[4]

Similar organizational changes were also taking place in the army's upper echelons of command. General Ewell, broken down and ill, was relieved of command of the Second Corps and replaced by Jubal Early, who in turn was rewarded with the rank of lieutenant general. John B. Gordon was promoted to major general and given command of the shattered remnants of Johnson's Division, which included the combined Louisiana Brigade, the survivors of several Virginia regiments commanded by Brig. Gen. William Terry, and Gordon's old brigade, now under the leadership of Brig. Gen. Clement Evans.[5]

In early June, General Lee received word of a new threat in the Shenandoah Valley, where an 18,000-man Union army under Maj. Gen. David Hunter had captured the important railroad town of Staunton and was threatening Lynchburg, a vital supply base for Lee's army. Though he was outnumbered in defending Richmond against Grant, the Confederate commander decided to detach part of his army to chase "Hunter's raiders," who were laying waste to the Valley of Virginia and threatening Lee's communications and supply lines. Lee had initially dispatched Maj. Gen. John C. Breckenridge, the former vice president of the United States and presidential candidate in 1860, together with his small division of 2,100 Virginians. This force though, was obviously not large enough to defeat Hunter's army. On June 12, Lee ordered Early to take his 8,000 infantrymen of the Second Corps, together with much of his artillery, to the Valley. Two years after it had ended its campaign under Stonewall Jackson, the Army of the Valley was being reincarnated.[6]

As if to recapture that Jacksonian legend, Early's orders from Lee included authorization for one of the most daring moves of the war, one that he hoped might "strike a decisive blow." After driving Hunter's force out of the Valley, Early was to march down (north) the Valley and cross the Potomac River into Maryland, and threaten Washington and Baltimore—if he saw the opportunity to do so. If Early could clear the Valley of Union troops and endanger the Federal capital, Lee believed Grant would be forced to detach significant forces to meet Early's threat, thus relieving the pressure on Lee's lines defending Richmond. Early and his Army of the Valley would operate as an independent command with wide latitude to strike where opportunity presented itself, possibly even at Washington itself.[7]

"Old Jube," the irascible and aggressive Virginian known for hard cussing and even harder fighting, pulled his weary men from Cold Harbor at 2:00 a.m. on the morning of June 13 to begin the long march to the Shenandoah Valley. The men of the 6th Louisiana, like the rest of Early's men, had been fighting and marching almost continuously for forty days in battles more intense than anything they had seen before. Now the 8,000 veterans had to march 80 miles in four days to reach Charlottesville, where they were put on the railroad cars to Lynchburg to meet Hunter's army. They were ragged, tattered and battle-weary, but they were the right troops to send into the Valley, for they knew every mountain pass, back road and river crossing from their campaigns with Jackson and Ewell in the two previous years. Their experience and hardness would make up for their dwindling numbers. As it turned out, Hunter had no stomach to face Early's men. By the time Early moved all his troops to Lynchburg and prepared to attack on June 19, Hunter's force had retreated in the face of danger, retiring into the mountains of western Virginia. After three days of chasing them, Early broke off the pursuit and rested his troops for a day. The march northward, down the Shenandoah Valley toward the Potomac River, resumed on June 23.[8]

MAJ. GEN. JUBAL EARLY.

The cantankerous West Point graduate (1833) presided over many of the 6th Louisiana's triumphs–and defeats. "Old Jube," whom many found personally disagreeable, was a talented combat leader at the brigade, division, and corps level. He was promoted beyond his abilities in late 1864 and his soldiers suffered as a consequence. Early, the architect of the "Lost Cause," utilized that post-war springboard to enhance his checkered war record. *Library of Congress*

General Breckinridge and his small division had joined Early at Lynchburg, and with additional cavalry battalions, the Army of the Valley grew to about 10,000 infantry and 4,000 cavalry and artillery. To give Breckinridge a command suitable to his status, Early shifted Gordon's Division to his command, forming a small corps of two divisions. The march down the valley was long and hard, past many landmarks familiar to the men of the 6th Louisiana, who remembered marching here with Stonewall in what must have seemed like another era, when they were young and hopeful. Almost half the men in Early's long gray column were barefooted, and the march left bloody traces in the dust of the road.[9]

By the second of July the Louisianians were in Winchester, where they received a joyous welcome, and three days later they forded the Potomac River at Shepherdstown with Gordon's Division. This was their third raid into Maryland, but unlike the celebratory crossings of 1862 and 1863, there were no bands playing "Maryland, my Maryland" and no crowds of excited Virginians cheering their move into enemy territory. The hardened soldiers waded across the river, some of them cutting their feet on sharp rocks and shells on the bottom, aware that the last two incursions north of the Potomac had come to grief and that this time, they marched with a force that was a mere shadow of the great armies that crossed this river in days past.[10]

Soon the alarm spread in the North that the Confederates were raiding once again. Early's cavalry extracted a $20,000 ransom from Hagerstown, Maryand, to spare that town from destruction, and Early himself demanded $200,000 from the city of Frederick, which he reached early on the morning of Saturday, July 9. Word that a Southern army was again across the Potomac and threatening Baltimore and Washington had its desired effect on Grant, who on July 6 rushed Maj. Gen. John B. Ricketts' division to Baltimore. Soon he would send the rest of Wright's VI Corps to defend the Northern capital, whose defenses had been stripped to replace the huge losses in Grant's army facing Richmond.[11]

Before the arrival of Grant's veterans, the only troops in the area were Maj. Gen. Lew Wallace's 2,500-man detachment from Baltimore. Most of these men had never seen the face of battle. Even when Ricketts' veterans arrived, the combined Federal force was outnumbered by Early's small army. Nevertheless, Wallace hoped at least to delay the Confederates long enough for reinforcements from Grant to get to

Washington. After Ricketts arrived July 8 with about two-thirds of his division, Wallace deployed his motley collection of untested recruits and old veterans, totaling about 5,800 men, along the banks of the Monocacy River three miles southeast of the city of Frederick. It was a place critical to the defense of both Baltimore and Washington, where the Baltimore Pike and the Georgetown Pike—the direct routes to the two cities—and the Baltimore and Ohio Railroad crossed the Monocacy. It also was a position of considerable defensive strength, with the river covering Wallace's entire front and the high eastern banks commanding the low, open ground that the Confederates would have to cross to reach difficult fords.[12]

The Monocacy is a small, meandering river that flows south to the Potomac through the lovely green hills and dales of Maryland, which in the flush of summer presented a panorama of wooded slopes and checkerboard fields of green corn and yellow grain. "It was a beautiful day in this beautiful country," one veteran of the battle wrote. "The air was laden with the perfume of flowers; the birds were singing in bush and tree; all the fields were green with growing crops. . . .It was a day and hour to impress all." The scene on that Saturday morning, July 9, 1864, seemed to confirm one of the odd truths of the war: the ugliest fighting often took place on the fairest of fields, where the blood flowed into the greenest of pastures, as it had at Antietam and Gettysburg and all the eye-catching battlefields of the Shenandoah Valley. The veterans of 6th Louisiana had seen them all and had left men dead on each of them. Now they were preparing to do it again.[13]

From the hills east of Frederick overlooking the river, Early and his men could see thousands of enemy soldiers across the Monocacy, defending the bridges that brought the railroad and the two main roads to Washington and Baltimore across the shimmering river. To Early's left (north), the Baltimore Pike crossed a stone bridge. To his right, some two-and-a-half miles downstream to the south, the river was spanned by the iron railroad bridge and not far below it a long, shingle-roofed covered bridge that carried the Georgetown Pike, angling off southeast toward Washington. The green fields of young corn beyond the river were dotted with dark lines of soldiers deployed by General Wallace. The Federals watched as the Confederate columns approached on the roads from Frederick.[14]

About 9:00 a.m., the Confederate commander ordered Maj. Gen. Dodson Ramseur's Division to challenge Wallace's front at the river,

This photo nicely illustrates the undulating terrain of the Monocacy field. The Worthington house is on the extreme right. The 6th Louisiana attacked across this farm. *Christopher Gannon*

around the bridges for the railroad and the Georgetown Pike. Rodes' Division moved in on Ramseur's left, fronting the bridge carrying the Baltimore Pike. As the opposing forces traded skirmish fire and exploratory cannonading across the river during the morning, Early reconnoitered the ground and concluded that a frontal assault across the stream, with its high, slippery banks, would be too perilous. He looked downstream for a ford to send in Gordon's Division on a flanking attack on the enemy's left, which would position it to gain control of the road to Washington.[15]

One of Early's cavalry brigades, led by Brig. Gen. John McCausland, had already found the route to Wallace's left flank, and crossed the river at a ford about a mile-and-a-half below the covered bridge housing the Georgetown Pike. About 11:00 a.m., some 800 of McCausland's dismounted troopers boldly attacked Ricketts' veteran infantrymen, partly concealed behind a long wooden fence that divided the farms of the Worthington and Thomas families. With banners waving, the Confederate troopers approached the waiting Union riflemen through waist-high corn. Suddenly rising from behind the fence, the Federals delivered a devastating volley that riddled McCausland's men and sent them scattering rearward. Rallied for a second assault, the outgunned horsemen were easily repulsed again. Though unsuccessful, the gallant cavalry stroke showed Early the key to the battle. He sent a courier galloping off for Gordon's Division with orders to hurry to the ford found by the troopers and cross to attack the left of the Federal line.[16]

It was after 2:30 p.m. when Gordon got his men, including the Louisiana troops, across the shallow ford. He hoped to strike with surprise and enough force to roll up the Federal line. Ricketts, however, anticipated the move and had changed front to face the assault. By the time Gordon approached, Ricketts' veterans were ready and standing firm. When Gordon rode out to survey the field, he did not like what he saw. The enemy's long blue line was posted along a fence on the crest of a ridge, in front of which lay an open field commanded by his artillery. Behind the Federal line the ground sank to a small valley, where a second line of battle waited. The field that Gordon's infantrymen would have to cross under fire was traversed by fences, which they would have to climb, and was studded by huge grain-stacks recently piled up by harvesters, which would break up their line of battle. It was hardly an encouraging prospect, but their general felt that "if any troops in the world could win victory against such adverse conditions," it was these high-spirited men from Virginia, Georgia and Louisiana.[17]

Gordon deployed his brigades by placing Clement Evans and his Georgians on the right, under cover of a dense woods about 700 yards from the enemy's left. Lining up on Evans' left were York's Louisianians, including some 50 men of the 6th regiment, again commanded by Lieutenant Colonel Hanlon, who had recovered from his Cold Harbor wound. General Terry's brigade of Virginians, remnants of the division shattered at Spotsylvania, formed behind York's men in support. The attack would begin by brigades, starting on the right with Evans. The Georgians crossed the open fields on the Worthington farm and advanced across the foot of a knoll known as Brooks' Hill, which was wooded on its western side but cleared on the east. Emerging from the woods on the eastern slope of the hill, in full view of the left of Ricketts' line, the Georgians immediately came under heavy artillery and infantry fire. Evans was one of his brigade's first casualties, falling from his horse seriously wounded. Several regimental commanders were also hit and killed, which caused some confusion in the ranks. The line slowed for a few moments and then continued on.[18]

Next the Louisianians dashed forward with "much spirit," reported Gordon, alongside the rallying Georgians. The two Confederate brigades charged toward the enemy line. "As we reached the first line of strong and high fencing, and my men began to climb over it," Gordon remembered later, "they were met by a tempest of bullets, and many of the brave fellows fell at the first volley." More men fell as the screaming Southerners dodged around the grain stacks, breaking up regimental alignments but barely slowing the onslaught. Officers were collapsing dead or maimed, leaving their men to their own initiative. "It was one of those fights where success depends largely on the prowess of the individual soldier," Gordon wrote. Men were deprived of the support given by a compact line, "where the elbow touch of comrade with comrade gives confidence to each and sends the electric thrill of enthusiasm through all. But nothing could deter them. Neither the obstructions nor the leaden blast in their front could check them." Thinking back, Gordon later wrote that he could not recall any charge of the war, "except for that of the 12th of May against Hancock, in which my brave fellows seemed so swayed by an enthusiasm which amounted almost to a martial delerium."[19]

In that delirium his men crashed upon Ricketts' forward line, manned by battle-hardened regiments from New York, New Jersey, Pennsylvania, Ohio and Vermont. The impetuous attack drove it back upon the second line in the little stream-cut valley behind the crest. There, fierce fighting at close range erupted, the battle swaying to and fro across the little brook, which ran red for 100 yards with the mingled blood of the killed and wounded from North and South. It was in this little vale, along the crimson stream, that nearly half of Gordon's men fell.[20]

After brief but ferocious fighting, the Louisianians and Georgians of Gordon's Division drove the second Federal line back, as the Northerners "ran like sheep without a Shepherd," according to General York. Even then, the battle wasn't won, for Ricketts' men had fallen back to rally with other troops strongly posted in deep cuts along the Georgetown Pike. Gordon ordered an attack by Terry's Brigade of Virginians, which had not yet been engaged. The Virginians' assault finally precipitated "the complete rout of the enemy's forces," Gordon reported. Union General Wallace, who concluded when he saw Gordon's attack formations that "it was time to get away," ordered Ricketts to withdraw to the road to Baltimore, leaving the field, littered with dead and wounded, in the hands of the victorious Confederates. By 4:30 p.m., it was over. "This battle," reported Gordon, "though short, was severe."[21]

In just two hours Gordon had lost 698 men from his division, which did by far the most fighting on the Confederate side on this day. There are no official casualty figures breaking down Gordon's loss by brigade or regiment, but it's certain that the Louisiana troops suffered severely. General York, who called Monocacy the bloodiest and fiercest encounter he had ever taken part in, claimed the Louisiana Brigade's losses ran from 25 percent to 50 percent. The intensity of the fighting along the Louisiana line is confirmed by the fact that the two Federal regiments directly opposing it—the 14th New Jersey and 151st New York of Ricketts' division—had the most killed of all the Union regiments engaged on the field. Each of those regiments reported 24 men killed; the 14th New Jersey suffered 140 total casualties, while the 151st New York recorded 101 men lost at Monocacy.[22]

Looking over the battlefield the following day, the Louisiana Brigade's chaplain, Father Sheeran, wrote: "On the crest of the hill where our men first attacked the enemy, we saw a regular line of dead Yankee bodies. A little in the rear they were seen lying in every direction and position, some on their sides, some on their faces, some on their backs with their eyes and mouths open, the burning sun beating upon them and their faces swarmed with disgusting flies."[23]

Young Glenn Worthington, only six years old at the time, watched the battle from the cellar of his father's house, which stood on the farmland crossed by the Confederates in their attack. Years afterward, he recalled gathering sheaves from the wheat field with which to make a pallet in the shade for the wounded men. One of them, he wrote, was Lt. Col. John J. Hodges of the 9th Louisiana, who "had his upper arm bone shattered by a leaden bullet and suffered great pain."[24]

For the 6th Louisiana, the Monocacy battle continued the long, slow process of bleeding the regiment into non-existence. At least five men were killed and two mortally wounded, with another dozen wounded less seriously, and a few captured. The dead included Lt. Michael Murray, commanding Company F, and the wounded again included the unlucky Lieutenant Colonel Hanlon, who nevertheless remained in the ranks for duty. Six of the seven men who were killed or mortally wounded were Irishmen from New Orleans. Among those captured was Lt. Robert Lynn, an Irishman in command of Company E who was wounded in the shoulder. After recuperating in a Federal hospital, Lynn spent the rest of the war in prison camps.[25]

Early had won the battle, inflicting 1,294 casualties on the Union force, but he had lost precious time by spending a full day fighting at the Monocacy River. Wallace, though defeated, had achieved his main objective of delaying the Confederates to buy time for Grant's reinforcements to reach Washington. After the battle, the Union general proposed that a monument to his dead be erected on the field, with the inscription: "These men died to save the National Capital, and they did save it."[26]

Events would ultimately prove Wallace correct, but the capital wasn't yet saved when the sun sank on July 9. The victory cleared the road to Washington, and Early yearned to seize the opportunity and glory that presented itself as night fell. If only he could get to Washington quickly, he might overwhelm its defenses before reinforcements arrived.

The time lost at Monocacy, however, combined with the exhaustion of his men and the beastly July weather, conspired to frustrate Early's hopes. The march resumed at daylight on Sunday as the battle-fatigued Confederates trudged 30 miles under a broiling sun on roads untouched by rain for weeks, producing dust clouds which coated their ragged uniforms and choked their parched throats. After a night of oppressive heat and little rest near Rockville, a town 10 miles from the District of Columbia line, the men resumed the march on Monday, a day even hotter than the one before. Early tried to push them but they were played out. The column shuffled along slowly, with hundreds of footsore men falling behind. Thinned by straggling, the Confederate army passed Silver Spring to approach Washington via the Seventh Street Pike, arriving by late afternoon in front of Fort Stevens.

The defensive bastion was one of 50 constructed in a circle, 37 miles around, that protected the approaches to the capital. At Fort Stevens, straight north of Washington and about a mile from the Maryland line, Early's soldiers were within four miles of the city, within sight of the Capitol dome. No Confederate forces had ever been as close to the Federal capital, and these Southern fighters were closer to Washington than Union troops had ever been to Richmond. Early wanted to attack on arrival, as he found the earthworks only feebly manned, "but the men were almost completely exhausted and not in a condition to make an attack." He would wait until morning.[27]

The delay provided just enough time for the rest of Horatio Wright's VI Corps to arrive in Washington, along with elements of the XIX Corps, newly transferred from New Orleans. Had Early reached the outskirts of Washington even a day earlier, perhaps he could have marched into the city, which was in a state of alarm. But the delaying action fought at Monocacy had prevented that. Gordon later asserted that the defenses remained so thinly manned on the afternoon of the 11th that Early's army surely could have marched into Washington, but it's not so clear what they would have done then, for the danger of being trapped in the city as Federal reinforcements arrived was great. When Early held a council of war with his generals on the night of the 11th, they joked about installing John Breckinridge in the vice president's chair in the U. S. Senate, which he formerly occupied, but there was "not a dissenting opinion" among them that it would be unwise to enter the city, according to Gordon. Early remained reluctant to abandon the idea of attacking, but became convinced of its folly at dawn the next morning when he saw the parapets lined with veteran infantry.[28]

There was no choice but retreat. Hunter's force was reported moving on Harpers Ferry, raising the risk that Early's line of withdrawal might be blocked if he delayed moving. After remaining in front of Fort Stevens and fighting off a probing move by a Union brigade during the day of July 12, Early retreated under cover of darkness to White's Ferry on the Potomac, crossing back into Virginia near Leesburg on the morning of the 14th.

Early's raid on Washington was another of the great Confederate "almosts" of the Civil War.[29]

Chapter Thirteen

Luck Runs Out: THIRD WINCHESTER

"The ladies of Winchester came into the streets and begged them, crying bitterly to make a stand for their sakes if not for their honor, but with no avail."

— *Captain George P. Ring*

The war was in its fourth summer as the few survivors of the 6th Louisiana accompanied Jubal Early's retreat back into Virginia. The young New Orleanians of 1861 probably never dreamed they would still be marching, fighting and dying as ragged-looking, barefooted men in the summer of 1864. There were less than 100 of them remaining in the regiment as the gray column snaked along dusty roads through Loudoun County, Virginia. Whatever satisfaction these weary Louisianians may have felt after throwing Washington into a summer panic was destined to dissolve in a long, frustrating fall campaign in the Shenandoah Valley. [1]

The weeks after their return to Virginia in mid-July were a blur of constant marching, skirmishing, counter-marches, cavalry raids and pitched battles—and relatively little rest in between. Early kept his forces in nearly constant motion in the lower Valley, feinting toward the Potomac and occasionally moving across it. By keeping his army in motion and showing up at points all over the compass, Early hoped to give the impression that his force was much larger than it really was. His objectives were to maintain a threatening attitude toward Washington, to prevent Federal use of the Baltimore and Ohio Railroad and the Chesapeake and Ohio Canal, both running parallel with the Potomac, and to tie down as large a force as possible from the Union army.[2]

The campaign nearly extinguished any hope the Louisianians still had for a favorable outcome of the war. On July 23, after crossing the Blue

Ridge into the Valley, the 6th was camped with the Valley Army near Strasburg, when Early learned that a Federal force under Maj. Gen. George Crook was concentrating near Winchester. The aggressive Virginian decided to attack.[3]

At dawn on Sunday, July 24, Early marched his army north toward Winchester, with Gordon's Division in the van. The weather was hot and dry as the 50-odd men of 6th Louisiana, under command of Lieutenant Colonel Hanlon, marched down the Valley Turnpike. At Kernstown, three miles south of Winchester, near the same ground where Jackson's small army battled General Shields in March 1862, the Confederates found the enemy infantry and cavalry waiting to meet them. Though Early clearly expected a battle, the 6th Louisiana's Captain Ring was surprised to find the enemy there. He wrote to his wife three days after the battle: "On last Sunday we left our camp at Strasburg and started once more toward the Potomac. When we had arrived within five miles of Winchester, to our surprise (as we had been told that the enemy had left) we saw the troops being placed into position and soon after the sharp, quick sound of the minie was heard, affording palpable evidence that there was work ahead for us."[4]

That work was on familiar ground. Ring was struck by the coincidence of fighting again near Winchester, where he had been wounded in June 1863 by a ball that knocked him out of action for eight months. "Our Division filed off at exactly the same point as last year," he wrote, "and the thought struck me rather forcibly, I wonder if we will continue the coincidence and be fortunate enough to get another nice eight-month furlough wound." (Ring had spent much of his lengthy furlough recuperating in Alabama, near his transplanted family.) Approaching the 9,500 infantrymen and cavalry of Crook's Army of West Virginia, Early deployed Breckinridge's old division, commanded by Brig. Gen. Gabriel Wharton, on the right of the Valley Pike and Gordon's Division on the left of the road, while Ramseur's Division was sent far to the left to get around the enemy's right flank. Discovering that the Federal left flank was exposed, Early ordered Wharton to attack it.[5]

Wharton's attack came about noon, striking the enemy's unprotected flank in open ground and doubling it back, throwing the entire Federal line into confusion, according to Early, who called the attack "handsomely executed." As Wharton's three brigades of Virginians rolled up the left of the Union line, Gordon's Division advanced across open fields, divided by rock walls, toward its center. Ring heard the famous Rebel yell from the right, which "spoke plainly as 'the handwriting on the wall' that we were driving them before us." The 6th Louisiana captain was impressed by his division commander's bravery. "Our gallant Gordon. . .led us at a quick step toward the foe who could be plainly seen flying through the stubble field about a mile in our front—striking them on the flank." The regiment "Pass[ed]under a heavy fire of artillery from a high hill (the same on which I was wounded)," recalled Ring, and "we came up with our double-quicking friends and our sharpshooters gave them a fire that covered the ground with killed and wounded." The Louisianians passed prisoners to the rear as they pushed forward, but the advance was slowed by the heavy and accurate Union cannon fire, which impressed the veteran Louisiana captain. "I must say," he informed his wife, "that if all other branches of their service fought and was handled as well as their artillery, we would not have so easy a time." Advancing cautiously, the Southerners slowly drove Crook's men into the town of Winchester. Up to that time, which Ring puts about 4:00 p.m., York's Louisiana Brigade "had not been able to fire a shot with the exception of that done by the sharpshooters," according to the 6th Louisiana officer, and the men feared that "we would have no chance to repay the loss that they had inflicted upon us."[76]

When they reached the edge of the city, Ring was temporarily pressed into service by General Breckinridge, who ordered him to take command of the Confederate sharpshooters as they entered the city. After leading the riflemen through Winchester's streets, Ring found the Federal infantry, artillery, and cavalry reformed in a formidable line just beyond the town's boundries. Waiting anxiously for the infantry to come up, "I saw the strong position taken by the enemy [and] I thought that at last we will have some raw work to do." Ring's concern dissipated, however, when he witnessed a charge of Confederate cavalry drive the enemy line back. Despite his long service in most of the army's battles, it was the first cavalry charge he had seen in the war, he told his wife. Watching as he sat on his horse behind his line of sharpshooters, "I could hardly contain myself and resist the strong impulse, that I under the exciting scene had to gallop over and take part in the affair."

The cavalry charge did not end the confrontation, however, for the Federal line reformed to face the approaching Confederate infantry, which was passing out of the town. Ring feared that the clash would be bloody, but it would not be so. "To my utter astonishment the moment our men emerged from the rock walls behind which they had been sheltered, then away start our Yankee friends. . .of all the tall traveling I have ever seen, they did some of the tallest from that time until night." His comrades, the captain added, "breathed a sigh of relief" and took up the pursuit "with many humorous remarks about the race we were running."[7]

The event wasn't humorous to General Crook, who was obliged to report that 3,000 to 4,000 of his dismounted cavalry and infantry "broke to the rear at the first fire, and all efforts to stop them proved to no avail." Most of the fugitives scampered all the way to Martinsburg, some 20 miles north. Some of his infantrymen were captured trying to evade Crook's provost guards, the chagrined Federal general admitted. "I lost over one-third of my cavalry in this way," he wrote. The Federals suffered 100 killed, over 600 wounded, and nearly 500 captured in the rout at Kernstown, in which Early reported only "very light" casualties. The 6th Louisiana lost two killed and four wounded, one mortally. The Louisiana Brigade lost 13 men.[8]

Captain Ring marveled at the luck the Louisianians had enjoyed in three years of fighting around "my old stomping ground" at Winchester. "It is a very singular coincidence, darling," he wrote, "that for three successive years our Army has driven the enemy out of Winchester, and each time on a Sunday, and also that the La. Brigade by the fortune of war have been the first to enter the city." Little did he know that the luck of the Louisianians at Winchester was about to run out.

For a few days, though, there was time to savor the rout of Crook's discouraged army, which retreated across the Potomac into Maryland. As the Valley Army marched north in pursuit, the signs of the panicky Federal retreat were all about them. "The road from Winchester to this point [Martinsburg] was black with the debris of the trains which they destroyed on their retreat," Ring told his wife. Early counted 72 wagons and 12 caissons abandoned along the route, most of them burned. Three days after the fight at Kernstown, the 6th Louisiana was "hard at work tearing up the Baltimore & Ohio Railroad for the fifth time," Ring wrote from Martinsburg. As July ended, the Confederates were in complete control of the Shenandoah Valley and in a strong position to threaten the North. The belligerent Early shocked and outraged Northerners with his decision to retaliate against Federal burning of homes in the Valley. "I came to the conclusion it was time to open the eyes of the people of the North to this enormity, by an example in way of retaliation," he wrote. The Southern commander sent his cavalry on a raid to Chambersburg, Pennsylvania, with a demand for $500,000 in United States currency in compensation for the Federal burnings. When town officials refused to pay, General McCausland ordered his troopers to torch the town, the center of which was reduced to ashes on July 30. The burning of Chambersburg was the astonishing if ugly exclamation point at the end of a month of Confederate triumphs. Jubal Early's Valley Campaign thus far had been a solid, if unspectacular, military success.[9]

The rout of Crook's army at Kernstown and the burning of Chambersburg convinced General U. S. Grant that a stronger army under a more combative commander was needed to sweep the Confederates from the Shenandoah Valley. In early August, Grant named Maj. Gen. Philip H. Sheridan to command all the Union forces in the region, merging the commands of Hunter, Sigel and Crook. Sheridan's newly designated Army of the Shenandoah would be the largest Federal army ever deployed in the Valley, bringing together the three infantry divisions of Wright's VI Corps, two infantry divisions of the XIX Corps and two more from Crook's Army of West Virginia, otherwise known as the VIII Corps. These 35,000 foot soldiers would be augmented with 8,000 cavalry in three divisions and a dozen batteries of field artillery. If the 5,000-man Federal garrison at Harper's Ferry was included, the new Union commander had 48,000 troops at his disposal.[10]

The man in charge of this powerful force was himself a powerful, if miniature, figure. "Little Phil" Sheridan was a five foot, three-inch, 115-pound firecracker with a short fuse—a combative, headlong fighter whose rise in the Union army had been meteoric, from captain of infantry in 1861 to major general in 1863. "He is short, thickset and common Irish-looking," one Union colonel wrote. Like many in the 6th Louisiana, Sheridan was born of Irish immigrant parents, and his approach to war displayed a fierceness that the lads of New Orleans would come to recognize as Celtic fire. Sheridan had fought under Grant as an infantry division commander in Mississippi and Tennessee, then followed his mentor to Virginia to command the cavalry of the Army of the Potomac. He was only 33 years old when Grant sent him to the Valley; some Washington officials believed he was too young for the command.[11]

Against this Irishman with attitude and his muscular army, Jubal Early at the beginning of August commanded only 13,000 to 14,000 men in all three branches of his force. His 9,000 foot soldiers and 4,000 cavalry, supported by 800 artillerists with 40 guns, would be outnumbered by three to one throughout the rest of the Valley Campaign. The crafty Southern commander's tactic for dealing with this disparity was to undertake a whirlwind of activity to make it appear that he had forces everywhere, moving in all directions. As General Gordon later put it, throughout the month of August and the first half of September, "Early's little army was marching and counter-marching toward every point of the compass in the Shenandoah Valley, with scarcely a day of rest, skirmishing, fighting, rushing hither and thither to meet and drive back cavalry raids, while General Sheridan gathered his army of more than double our numbers for his general advance up the valley."[12]

The hot days of August became a blur of motion for the weary men of the 6th Louisiana as they marched up and down the Valley with Early. Jed Hotchkiss, Stonewall Jackson's former cartographer, kept a running account in his diary of the army's itinerary that August, which clearly demonstrates the dizzying pace of activity: August 4—From its camp at Bunker Hill, north of Winchester, the Confederates sweep down the Valley to the Potomac. August 5—With Gordon's Division, the 6th Louisiana crosses the river to Sharpsburg, Md., scene of its 1862 disaster, where the Confederates skirmish with Federal cavalry. August 7—Back at Bunker Hill. August 9-12—Early, getting intelligence of a large Federal army assembling at Harper's Ferry under Sheridan, pulls his army back to Winchester, then further south to Fisher's Hill near Strasburg, awaiting attack. August 17—After watching Sheridan advance his army to Fisher's Hill and probe the Southern position, Early sees the Federals withdraw and immediately orders a pursuit. August 18-24—The Confederates press the Union rear, maneuvering first to Winchester, then to Bunker Hill, finally to Charlestown, clashing with cavalry and rear guards. "Sheridan," concluded Hotchkiss," up to this point, had not lived up to his reputation as a fighter."[13]

The Union general was still getting to know his new command and learning the terrain of the region, and was deliberately playing a cautious game. His level of caution increased in mid-August when he learned from Grant that Lee had sent reinforcements to Early: Joseph Kershaw's Division of infantry, Fitzhugh Lee's Brigade of cavalry, and additional artillery, all under command of Maj. Gen. Richard Anderson of the First Corps, were heading to the Valley. Moreover, it was an election year, and Sheridan knew that a major defeat for Union forces in the Shenandoah could spell political disaster for Lincoln. "I deemed it necessary to be cautious, and the fact that the Presidential election was impending made me doubly so," Sheridan later admitted in his memoirs. All these factors contributed to his decision to avoid a confrontation with

Early at Fisher's Hill and retreat to a defensive position at Halltown, near Harpers Ferry.[14]

Sheridan's Confederate counterpart read all this as a sign of timidity in the Union general, and pursued his aggressive campaign with increased vigor and daring. On August 25, leaving Kershaw's Division in front of Sheridan's army, Early pushed the rest of his force north toward Shepherdstown, "in order to keep up the fear of an invasion of Maryland and Pennsylvania." This feint toward the Potomac was a risky and questionable tactic that would have fatal consequences.

The 6th Louisiana at this time welcomed back a friendly face and valuable officer. The regiment's veteran colonel, the 47-year-old William Monaghan, had taken sick leave in Richmond about July 1, and had missed the fighting at Cold Harbor, Monocacy and Kernstown. He returned to duty in late July or early August and resumed command of the five regiments of Hays' old brigade. Colonel Eugene Waggaman, meanwhile, still led the remnants of Stafford's old brigade, and both organizations operated under the eye of Brig. Gen. Zebulon York, who commanded all the Louisianians. It wasn't much of a command. Only about 800 men remained in the combined Louisiana Brigade in late August. The 6th Louisiana, under the command of the once-wounded and twice-captured Lieutenant Colonel Hanlon, could barely muster 60 men.[15]

COL. WILLIAM MONAGHAN

This faded image (shown here computer enhanced) is the only known likeness of the first captain of Company F and the third colonel of 6th Louisiana. Monaghan was captured at Strasburg on June 2, 1862, and wounded at Ox Hill on September 1. He was killed in action near Shepherdstown, West Virginia, on August 25, 1864, where he was buried. *New Orleans newspaper (unidentified)*

This little band of Louisianians marched with Gordon's Division near the head of Early's long column as it moved northwest from Charlestown toward the Potomac early on Thursday, August 25. After the sun rose, the day became very warm. As the Confederates marched through Leetown toward the railroad village of Kearneysville, two divisions of Sheridan's cavalry under command of Maj. Gen. Alfred T. A. Torbert were trotting through Kearneysville toward the advancing Southern column. About a mile and a half north of Leetown, the Union mounted divisions of Brig. Gens. Wesley Merritt and James Wilson, advancing in parallel columns, spotted in a woods ahead some gray-clad horsemen that they took to be Confederate cavalry. In fact, it was the van of Early's army.[16]

Believing that "nothing but cavalry was in our front," Torbert sent out a mounted brigade on each of his flanks and ordered an attack by two brigades in front. The Confederates, seeing the Union horsemen deploy for battle, filed into line, Wharton's Division on the left of the road and Gordon's on the right. Monaghan steadied his Louisiana veterans for the anticipated cavalry charge. The thundering hoofbeats and yells of the Federal horsemen announced the Union attack. Up and down the Confederate line Southern riflemen aimed their muskets. The rippling discharge of their volley must have astonished the horse soldiers; it certainly surprised their commander. "Soon after the attack was commenced," Torbert reported, "it was found that we were fighting infantry." This was hardly what the Federals had bargained for, but once they were committed they fought gamely in what Early called "a sharp engagement with small arms and artillery." After stopping the initial charge of the cavalry, Early's foot soldiers counterattacked with spirit. "The attack was so sudden and vigorous the division was thrown in complete confusion and back three-quarters of a mile," the Union commander reported. "We soon drove the enemy off," Jed Hotchkiss noted in his diary, "with considerable loss on both sides."[17]

The loss was especially grievous for the 6th Louisiana, because one of those killed was Colonel Monaghan. Exactly when or how he fell is unknown, but it was probably during the Confederate counter-charge, which Monaghan led on his horse with his Louisiana Tigers running and yelling behind him. "Fighting became heavy" as the line advanced, one Confederate veteran of the battle wrote, and at one point the Federal horsemen made a charge and captured a few of Gordon's men, before being driven back. Union General Torbert claimed that the Confederates lost 250 killed and wounded, "together with one brigade commander." While his numerical estimate is almost certainly too high, it is plausible that his reference to the fallen "brigade commander" was Monaghan. It is also possible, however, that Monaghan was killed in a second clash which occurred a bit later, when Merritt's troopers reformed and made a stand on the Charlestown Road near Shepherdstown, which Hotchkiss reported that "Gordon repulsed with Terry's Brigade on the left, then York and Evans on the right." In this second fight, the Confederates "came near surrounding and capturing a considerable portion" of Merritt's division, Early wrote, "but it succeeded in making its escape across the Potomac." Official records simply state that Monaghan's death occurred at Shepherdstown, which could suggest he fell in the clash near the river.[18]

Regardless of where he fell, Monaghan's death was a blow not only to his men but to an army that could hardly afford to lose veteran colonels who had proven their valor through three years of war. Early remembered the colonel's death long after the event and wrote about it in his memoirs. "In this affair, a valuable officer, Colonel Monaghan of the 6th Louisiana Regiment, was killed," penned the former commander. Coming from ornery Old Jube, who was often harsh in his judgment of subordinates, this passing mention rates as a high compliment.[19]

Monaghan had led the 6th Louisiana for nearly two years and had served in the war three years and two months. He had been wounded once, captured once, and had plunged into an icy river to avoid capture a second time at Rappahannock Station; he had led his men on the battlefields from First Manassas to Spotsylvania Court House and at most of the major engagements in between. Monaghan was the third colonel of the 6th Louisiana killed in battle—a record few Southern regiments could match—and the second Irish-born colonel to die at the head of his beloved regiment. His war began at the Olive Branch Coffee House in New Orleans, where he recruited his company of Irishmen, and ended at Shepherdstown, (West) Virginia. He lies buried there in Elmwood Cemetery, along the road to Kearneysville, under a simple limestone tablet with the words: "Col. Wm. Monaghan, 6th La."[20]

Monaghan's death left Joseph Hanlon as the regiment's ranking officer. The lieutenant colonel, also a native of Ireland, had been shot through the body in the first battle of Winchester on May 25, 1862, and had never fully recovered from that near-fatal wound. The sickly Hanlon had been away from the regiment for stretches of months during the war, twice on extended sick leaves and twice as a prisoner of war after being captured near Strasburg in June 1862 and again at Fredericksburg in April 1863. The unforunate officer would be captured a third time and spend the final months of the war in prison at Fort Delaware. Hanlon's final months at the head of the regiment encompassed a time of defeat and discouragement for his dwindling band of comrades.[21]

By the end of August, the toll of Early's vigorous campaign in the Valley was clearly showing on the few survivors of the 6th Louisiana. Since leaving Lee's army around Richmond in mid-June, they had marched more than 800 miles, engaged in 17 battles and skirmishes, and had been "almost constantly in the presence of the enemy, either in the advance or in retreat," according to a report of inspection conducted August 19, 1864. Reporting on conditions in the unified Louisiana Brigade, Maj. Edwin L. Moore, assistant inspector general, found discipline in the command to be lax. "It is to be remembered that York's brigade is composed of the discordant fragments of Hays' and Stafford's brigades. . . .Both officers and men bitterly object to their consolidation into one brigade. Strange officers command strange troops, and the difficulties of fusing this incongruous mass are enhanced by the constant marching and frequent engagements," Moore wrote. This unhappy condition applied equally to the Louisiana regiments in York's command and the Virginia units in General Terry's conglomerated brigade. Endorsing this report, Moore's superior, H. E. Peyton, added, "The troops of the old organizations feel that they have lost their identity, and are without the chance of perpetuating the distinct and separate history of which they were once so proud." Though this loss of pride and prestige affected morale and discipline in Gordon's Division, Major Moore noted, "in spite of all defects, the division has fought with conspicuous gallantry and constant success."[22]

Though they continued to fight well, there were very few of them left to fight at all. The August inspection found only five officers and 47 enlisted men present for duty in the 6th Louisiana. Additionally, two officers and 15 men were away on detached duty. Another eight men were sick. That gave the regiment a nominal strength of 82 officers and men, but it could put barely 50 muskets—less than half a company—into battle. The other regiments in York's command were hardly better off, ranging from only 24 present for duty in the 10th Louisiana to 132 in the 9th. In total, the ten regiments of the combined Louisiana Brigade counted only 614 officers and men present for duty, which was less than the strength a typical regiment could field in the early days of the war.[23]

The inspection report highlighted another serious problem in 6th Louisiana, as well as the whole brigade—desertion and other unauthorized absence. In contrast to the 82 men still with the regiment, an astonishing 188 men were absent without leave. This probably included some stragglers who would eventually show up in camp and some men who may have overstayed furloughs, but the total obviously encompassed many who had deserted and would never be seen again. The 6th Louisiana was hardly alone in this problem. The 7th Louisiana had even more men absent without leave—212 according to the inspection report. The 8th Louisiana listed 182 absent without permission. York's ten regiments combined listed 764 men absent without authority. Not all were deserters, but probably the great majority were. In addition to the hundreds absent without leave, there were more Louisianians listed as prisoners in the hands of the enemy (971) than there were present for duty in the ranks of Early's Valley army.[24]

What accounts for the serious desertion problem in the Louisiana regiments? Some authorities have blamed the problem on the high percentage of foreign-born, both Irish and German, in the 6th and other Louisiana regiments, arguing that these non-citizens felt less attachment to the Confederate cause than did native-born Southerners. That seems a plausible explanation for desertions that occurred early in the war, when men seized the first chance available to get out of the army. It seems less persuasive when applied to desertions in the third or fourth year of the war, which involved soldiers who had already proven their devotion to duty through years of fighting. Moreover, there seems to be no direct correlation between the number of immigrants in a regiment and its desertion ratio. The 6th Louisiana had far more foreign-born soldiers than did the 7th Louisiana, for instance, yet the latter regiment reported more men AWOL in August 1864 than did the mostly Irish regiment. Nationality of the troops may have had something to do with the desertion rate, but it was hardly the controlling factor.[25]

The inhuman suffering that the war imposed on the Confederate soldier in its later stages had much to do with the increasing problem of desertion. The long war and desperate physical condition of the Confederate soldier simply made desertion a more rational choice than it had been to most of these men. Moreover, as the war brought devastation and Federal occupation to larger areas of the South, more Confederate soldiers received urgent appeals from desperate wives and families to come home. The fact that many left the army under these conditions is no surprise. It is perhaps more the wonder that so many Confederate soldiers, including many immigrant Irish and others, stuck it out in the worst of conditions, even when hope had virtually vanished.

The August inspection report illustrates just how poor the condition of the Louisiana regiments was at that time. They were dressed in rags and odds and ends taken from the dead. The inspection found the condition of their clothing "bad" in the entire brigade and listed specific shortages: 195 men in Monaghan's five regiments—45 percent of the total present—lacked shoes, nearly all had no stockings, 298 needed trousers, 315 lacked underclothes and shirts. "The military appearance of the command cannot be otherwise than indifferent after the arduous campaign through which it has recently passed," the inspecting officer wrote. "There is a great need of clothing in this command; pants are particularly needed." But the inspector found the Louisianians' arms "as serviceable as need be," and ammunition plentiful. In other words, as ragged as they might be, these veterans could still keep on fighting.[26]

Sheridan, however, was not much inclined to fight during most of August and early September. The Union commander remained cautiously on the defensive, wary of attacking Early while he was reinforced with Anderson's First Corps veterans. Sheridan's caution led the Confederate commander to misjudge his adversary. "The events of the last month had satisfied me that the commander opposed to me was without enterprise, and possessed an excessive caution which amounted to timidity," he wrote. Early was so confident that he could handle the "timid" Sheridan that he agreed in mid-September to return Kershaw's Division to Lee's army at Petersburg. On September 14, after a fight near Berryville, General Anderson led Kershaw and his crack fighters across the Blue Ridge marching southeast, seriously weakening the outnumbered Army of the Valley. Early's men would pay dearly for their commander's underestimation of Sheridan in the weeks ahead.[27]

The Union commander extracted the first payment on Monday, September 19 near Winchester, where he pounced on Jubal Early's tactical blunder that left the Confederates vulnerable to attack. Dividing his little army in the face of a stronger enemy, Early on September 19 had marched Gordon's and Rodes' divisions toward Martinsburg, 20 miles north of Winchester, to drive off a Union work party reported to be repairing the railroad there. It was duty better suited to cavalry, but Old Jube had little faith in his mounted men, so he dragged half his infantry up the Valley Pike toward Martinsburg, leaving Ramseur's isolated division to defend the line along Opequon Creek, three miles east of Winchester. The 6th Louisiana's Captain Ring recalled the "forced march" to Martinsburg, where his men engaged in a "brisk little skirmish" before returning south again, covering 31 miles on that busy

Sunday. Failing to find any Union work party repairing the railroad, Early turned his two divisions back toward Winchester, but they were strung out along the Valley Pike when they went into camp on that rainy Sunday night; Sheridan was preparing to attack with the dawn on Monday.[28]

The 6th Louisiana was with Early's northernmost infantry division at Gordon's camp in Bunker Hill, 14 miles north of Ramseur's position east of Winchester, when Sheridan's cavalry, followed by his infantry, began advancing westward along Berryville Pike toward Winchester. Early, camped with Rodes' Division several miles south of Gordon when the Union attack fell on Ramseur's 1,700 infantrymen, ordered his two scattered divisions to hurry to the battle. Marching south toward Winchester, the men of the 6th Louisiana heard the distant sound of cannon ahead as Ramseur's outnumbered men exchanged fire with Union cavalry at the head of Sheridan's advancing column. Luckily for Early, the Union attack was seriously delayed by a traffic jam created when Sheridan's entire force had to file through a narrow ravine that squeezed the Berryville Pike west of Opequon Creek. The resulting tangle of wagons, cannon, horses and men ruined Sheridan's great opportunity to overwhelm Ramsuer's isolated division before Early could reconcentrate his army. Ramseur's veterans held their ground for five hours as Early rushed Gordon's and Rodes' divisions to the battlefield, while the Union infantrymen untangled themselves from the mess.[29]

Gordon arrived on the field about 10:00 a.m. Led by their ramrod-straight, black-haired Georgian, his three brigades filed into a woods on a farm known as Hackwood, which was dominated by the imposing limestone mansion erected in 1777 by a local Revolutionary war hero. Evans' Georgians took position on the extreme left, close by the sparkling brook known as Red Bud Run. The 6th Louisiana with the rest of York's command formed the center of Gordon's line, while Terry's Virginians moved in on the Louisianians' right. Rodes arrived soon after and moved into position on the right of Gordon, while Ramseur's hard-pressed men slowly pulled back to align with the new Confederate front. Scarcely had Early made these dispositions before the Union infantry massed for an attack all along the line, about a mile and a half east of the city. The battlefield encompassed an undulating elevated plateau, partly wooded but broken by large open fields, between Red Bud Run on the north and Abraham's Creek on the south, with the Berryville Pike slanting southwest toward Winchester between the two streams.[30]

The five dozen or so veterans of the 6th Louisiana, commanded by Lieutenant Colonel Hanlon, "had taken up a position on the edge of a wood, when the enemy appeared in a wood opposite us," Captain Ring wrote to his wife two days after the battle. Across an open field of perhaps 600 yards, clearly visible from the Confederate woods on the Hackwood farm, the infantrymen in the Union woods were deploying for battle. The Federals that Ring saw there were infantrymen of the XIX Corps' Second Division, commanded by Brig. Gen. Cuvier Grover. Grover put Brig. Gen. Henry Birge's brigade, composed of six regiments from New England and New York, in the Union woods opposite the Louisianians' position, while Col. Jacob Sharp's brigade of five regiments, mostly from New York, extended the front line to Birge's left. Grover's two other brigades were placed in a second line behind Birge and Sharpe, while troops of Wright's VI Corps extended the Union line southward opposite Rodes and Ramseur.[31]

It was 11:45 a.m. when the whole Union line moved forward to attack. Ring saw the enemy emerge from the woods and found the sight thrilling. "They marched out into the field in beautiful order with their bright barreled guns reflecting back the rays of the sun in a way to make your eyes wink," he wrote. "Gen. Early, who happened to be just behind our command, ordered Gen. York to meet them half way. No sooner said than done and out we stepped, and I had the pleasure of seeing and participating in the prettiest stand-up, fair, open fight that I have ever seen."[32]

Captain William Seymour, the brigade adjutant who had returned to duty in late August after a lengthy sick leave, corroborates Ring's account that Early ordered York to attack when the Unionists began advancing, "and the beautiful & rare sight was presented of two opposing lines charging at the same time." Out in that sunny clearing, the blue and gray lines halted to face each other in a stand-up shoot-out, both lines blazing away with muskets despite mounting casualties. "We fought in this way about ten minutes as near as I could judge, with only a space of two hundred yards between our lines," Ring reported. From across Red Bud Run, above the northern flank of Gordon's line, six cannon of the Confederate horse artillery enfiladed the bleeding Union line with an iron rain of canister. Finally, in Ring's words, "Southern pluck was too much for our Yankee friends and they turned to seek the woods again. We of course raised a Louisiana yell and [went] after them, pouring a fire into their backs that soon made the ground black with their hateful

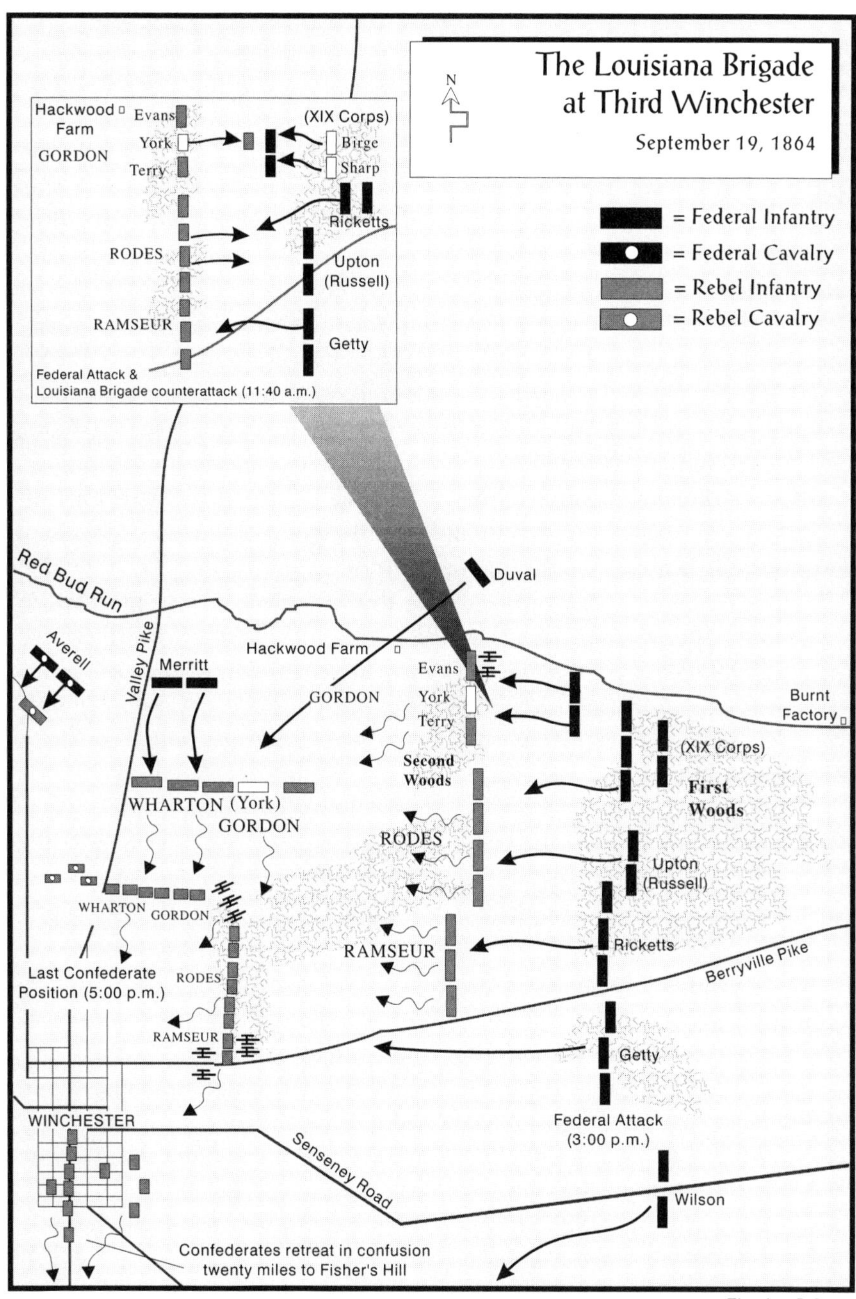

Theodore P. Savas

fire into their backs that soon made the ground black with their hateful bodies."[33]

The Louisianians were driving the Federals back to the woods, but to their left, Grover's troops had pushed back the Georgians of Evans' Brigade, threatening Early's flank. While York's yelling Tigers advanced across the clearing, the Georgians were driven deep into the Confederate woods, with Birge's rightmost regiments in pursuit. "This caused a pause in our advance and the position was most critical, for it was apparent that unless this force was driven back the day was lost," Early wrote in his memoirs. The Confederate position was saved by the steadfast gunners of Lt. Col. Carter Braxton's battalion of seven cannon, posted near Red Bud Run on the northern end of Early's line. Under Braxton's steady, well-directed fire, Early recounted, the Federals "staggered, halted and commenced falling back," pursued by a brigade of Rodes' Division, which came up in support. Meanwhile, the enthusiastic pursuit of retiring Federals by York's Brigade put the Louisianians in an exposed position, well ahead of the rest of Gordon's line, in the center of the clearing between the two woods. "We drove them in our front about a half-mile," Ring wrote, "and had the left of our line met with the same success, we would have made it a rout," but the plight of the Georgians forced Ring and his Louisiana fighters to retire to safer ground. "We had to fall back a short distance, losing about half the ground we had gained," he wrote.[34]

Over the next hour, Gordon's infantrymen and artillery delivered a devastating fire that wrecked two Union attempts to counter-charge, the first by Grover's two reserve brigades, the second by the other XIX Corps division led by Brig. Gen. William Dwight. In both cases, the Federals suffered horrific casualties, caught in the open between the two woods under a Confederate hell-fire of cannon and musketry. At some point in this mid-day slaughter, the Louisiana Confederates heard a rumor that the troops immediately opposing them were from a Federal regiment raised in Union-occupied New Orleans. The news turned the fight into a grudge match. "You ought to have seen our boys when they learned this fact," Ring wrote to his wife. "I never saw our Brigade fight better in my life, the fact of these renegades being opposed to us seemed to nerve each man's arm and make his aim more certain. I think and firmly believe that every man in Hays & Staffords Brigades killed his man that day. I for the first time took up a musket and did it too," Ring boasted, claiming that "I saw two of my marks tumble." Though there were no Federal troops from Louisiana on the Third Winchester battlefield, the mere thought of such an outrage had instilled a fighting spirit of revenge in the men from New Orleans.[35]

By 1:00 p.m., the fight along Gordon's part of the line settled down to lively skirmishing, which lasted for about four hours. The timely arrival of Gordon's and Rodes' divisions on the field that morning had saved Ramseur from certain defeat and had driven the Federals back, leading Early to think he had won a "splendid victory." While Gordon's men were wrecking the Federal XIX Corps, Rodes Division inflicted heavy losses on two divisions of the VI Corps. Early found it "a grand sight to see this immense body hurled back in utter disorder before my two divisions, numbering a very little over 5,000 muskets." Sheridan had suffered a miserable morning, but he was far from finished. The Confederates had also suffered grievous losses which included the death of the dashing and talented Robert Rodes. The commander was "killed in the very moment of triumph," lamented Early, while leading the attack of his division. The Louisianians lost their commander as well. As the battle was raging, a bullet shattered Zebulon York's wrist, a crippling wound that required the amputation of his arm.[36]

The weight of Sheridan's larger army began to tell against the weakening Confederate line. The Union commander called up his reserves, two divisions of General Crook's Army of West Virginia, which crossed Red Bud Run and massed north of the Hackwood farm. Early's line was stretched thin, and he had no reserves left from which to draw. He had already summoned Wharton's infantry division, which had spent the morning holding off Sheridan's cavalry to the north, to Winchester to shore up his tenuous position. By mid-afternoon, Crook sent his Ohioans and West Virginians storming across the boggy ground of Red Bud Run, pressing Gordon and Wharton from the northeast, while Sheridan's cavalry came thundering down the Valley Pike on the left flank and rear of Early's embattled army. By 5:00 p.m., the Confederates were pressed back into an L-shaped line on the outskirts of Winchester, facing strong pressure on all sides, as Wharton and Gordon held the north-facing line and Rodes and Ramseur defended the east-facing line, connected at a right angle defended by artillery. Late in the afternoon, two divisions of Federal cavalry broke around the Confederate left flank, getting in the rear of Early's line, which precipitated an unraveling of the Southern position.[37]

"Our situation at this time was extremely critical," wrote Captain Seymour of the Louisiana Brigade. "In front of us was the enemy's infantry four times larger than our own, while in the rear on the flank of our left wing was his cavalry which itself outnumbered our infantry. Of course, there was nothing left but to retreat and as soon as the order was given, our line broke & the men poured through Winchester in greatest confusion." Captain Ring blamed Early's overmatched cavalry for the collapse of the Confederate position. "After a feeble resistance, as usual, our worthless Cavalry gave way," he wrote with obvious disgust, "exposing the infantry flanks and causing them to give way, at first slowly, but as the Yankees pressed on with an unusual vigor, it soon became a rout on our part."[38]

Ring had been ordered by General York to stand watch from a hill 75 yards in the rear of the brigade's position, to keep track of developments on the left "so as to notify our line when to fall back." From that vantage point overlooking the battle he saw the debacle unfold. "As we came out on the open fields immediately above Winchester," Ring wrote, "I saw the jig was up with our Army unless some extraordinary dispensation of Providence. All over the plain men were to be seen flying to the rear, officers riding to and fro trying to rally and reform the men. It was a mortifying but very exciting scene." Ring saw the Confederate line fall to pieces. Just as one officer rallied his command to make a stand, the next one would give way, unraveling the position piecemeal. The scene unfolded before Ring like an exciting panorama, as Confederate artillerists stood to their guns even as their infantry supports retreated. "The Enemy advanced from the wood in splendid order, by Regiment and Brigade, halt until they could get their whole line formed when several Batteries that were in position would open upon them, causing their columns to melt away with terrible loss to them," he reported. "I never saw as fine a sight in my life as our noble Gen. Gordon presented, as he galloped down the line with a stand of colors in his hand, his hat off and long hair streaming back in the wind." Gordon galloped up to Ring, who held the colors of Stafford's Brigade in his hand, with a few men about him, and as the general passed he called out to Ring: "Form your men, Captain! I know they will stand by me." But it was too late.[39]

By this time, in Early's words, "the whole line had given away," and demoralized Confederates fled through the city. Some commands retired in good order, but there was a panicky rush by others through the streets of Winchester, now caught up in a scene of chaos as Southerners streamed to the south. "The ladies of Winchester came into the streets and begged them," Ring wrote, "crying bitterly to make a stand for their sakes if not for their honor, but with no avail. The cowards did not have the shame to make a pretense of halting, but would push by those noble women, resisting tears, entreaties and reproaches as each was used." Among the women trying to shame the troops back on to the battlefield was Mrs. Gordon, the general's wife, who, according to Ring's letter, "seized a Division HdQtrs flag, and running into the street called upon any of her husband's Division to rally around her flag and she would lead them. She rallied a party of near two hundred men and led them back to the field." But the battle was over. The beaten Confederates streamed through the town and stumbled in the darkness up the Valley Pike. They finally halted when reached Fisher's Hill twenty miles south, which Early called "the only place where a stand could be made."[40]

Regrouping at Fisher's Hill, about a mile south of Strasburg, the Confederates counted their losses. The dawn-to-dusk battle at Winchester (styled the Battle of the Opequon by the Federals) had extracted a damaging toll. The Southern general reported his loss in the infantry and artillery at 226 killed and 1,567 wounded. In addition, Early counted 1,818 missing, though he admitted that many of them were "stragglers and skulkers" rather than captured. Losses in the overmatched Southern cavalry, not officially tallied for this battle, may have added another 1,000. Overall, Early lost more than a third of his already outnumbered Valley army at Third Winchester.[41]

Sheridan's losses were numerically larger but represented a much smaller proportion of his army. The Army of the Shenandoah counted 697 killed, 3,983 wounded and 338 missing, or a total of 5,018. That represented about 12 percent of Sheridan's force. The heaviest union losses occurred in Cuvier Grover's division of the XIX Corps, which attacked Gordon's Division and was shattered by the Confederate artillery and the counter-attack of the Louisianians and Gordon's two other brigades in the fighting between the two woods on the Hackwood farm. Grover lost 1,773 officers and men, more than half of his command.[42]

While Sheridan could afford such losses, Early could not. The battle severely depleted the Confederate infantry units, including the Louisiana Brigade. The only known tally of the brigade's losses is found in Captain Ring's letter from Fisher's Hill, which states that 154 Louisianians were killed, wounded, or captured in the fight—roughly one-fourth of the brigade's effective strength. Losses in the 6th Louisiana were once again heavy. "I lost four officers out of five, wounded, and ten men wounded," Ring recorded. Company E went into the battle with only two men, and both were shot. For Pvt. John Shannon, an Irish-born barkeeper from New Orleans, it was his third wound (Manassas and Fredericksburg comprising the previous pair); Pvt. John H. Murray, also an Irish immigrant, was shot through both legs and disabled for the rest of the war. As the 6th Louisiana survivors joined the mass of Early's army stumbling toward Fisher's Hill in the darkness that night, they may have realized that their luck in the Shenandoah Valley had run out. Third Winchester was the first major defeat for a Confederate army in the Valley. It would not be the last.[43]

Chapter Fourteen

Valley of Humiliation: FISHER'S HILL & CEDAR CREEK

"Our men are shoeless, pantless, jacketless, sockless and miserable. . . If this war lasts much longer, all of my gallant company will be gone."
— *Capt. George P. Ring*

Humiliated by the debacle at Winchester, the men of the 6th Louisiana reached Fisher's Hill on the morning of the 20th and began digging in. There was much grumbling and debate about what had happened at Winchester. "Whose fault it was that this disaster occurred is the subject of much discussion in the army," Captain Ring wrote from Fisher's Hill on September 21. "All blame the Cavalry and the general impression is that if the Yankee infantry fought half as well as their Cavalry, we would not have any army here this morning."

To his wife, the Louisiana veteran poured out his frustration over the pitiful condition of his comrades. "One of the principal causes of our defeat on Monday," he penned, "was the miserable condition of the Army in the way of shoes. I have heard from reliable authority that we had over four thousand men able to bear arms but who were not armed on account of being barefooted. And if we are forced once more to make a rapid retreat up this Valley," the captain predicted, "we will lose a great number of prisoners on this account alone."[1]

The captain saved some of his bitterness for the authorities in Richmond, who failed to properly equip his men. "When will our government learn sense enough to let the fancy men about the departments go without shoes and clothing, and give all and every article that it receives or manufactures to the fighting men in the field?" he lamented. "Our men are shoeless, pantless, jacketless, sockless and miserable. . . . God grant that our leaders may soon learn that men cannot march and fight when they are half naked and with feet that leave bloody marks wherever they step." Ring was also discouraged that his company and regiment were bleeding away. Lamenting the death of three of his wounded men, the captain dolefully predicted that "if this war lasts much longer all of my gallant company will be gone."[2]

Despite his discouragement, Captain Ring nevertheless felt confident that the outnumbered Confederates could hold their strong defensive position on Fisher's Hill. With the enemy "in plain sight," he wrote, "We have just received orders to man the breastworks and we are anxious for them to come at us here as we think we can get even for the repulse of Monday. I don't think they will attack us here as they were too badly hurt on Monday last to make more than a demonstration, but that they will fall back once more to protect Washington."[3]

Like the Confederate commanding general, however, Ring underestimated General Sheridan. It was true that the Confederate position on Fisher's Hill was strong. The Shenandoah Valley narrowed at this point to about four miles across, with Fisher's Hill commanding the ground in front, and the Shenandoah River and the mountains securing Early's flanks. Fisher's Hill, which some Southerners called their "Gibraltar," rose steeply with its rocky face looking north toward Strasburg. This imposing bluff, creased by ravines, frowned over the Valley Pike and commanded the ground in its front like a natural fortress. Six weeks earlier, Sheridan had found Early's army dug in there and declined to attack. Fisher's Hill provided the Southern commander with his only fair chance to stop Sheridan's drive south up the Valley, but the odds now were much less favorable than they had been in August. The Army of the Valley was down to fewer than 10,000 effectives, and faced more than three times that number. Early was forced to stretch his line thinly over a four-mile front. With too few infantrymen to cover the ground between the river and North Mountain, the Confederate commander made a curious decision: he posted his demoralized cavalry, in which he had little confidence, on his weak left flank.[4]

The Union commander, flushed with his victory at Winchester, did not delay in moving to confront Early again. After marching his army twenty miles to Strasburg on the 20th, Sheridan pushed his forces toward Fisher's Hill the following day. "On the morning of the 21st of September, great clouds of dust appeared hanging over the [Valley] pike, indicating the advance of the enemy," Captain Seymour of the Louisiana Brigade wrote in his journal. He described the "animating spectacle" that he saw through his telescope: "First came about five thousand cavalry, their arms glistening in the sun; then long columns of infantry, followed by immense trains of ambulances & waggons; & after them came the artillery." The long blue columns filed off left and right, some two miles in front of the Confederates. Union skirmishers were thrown forward and the prelude to battle, the incessant crackle of small arms fire, erupted in the distance. Night fell, however, before any general engagement got underway.[5]

Captain Seymour and the Louisiana regiments were with Gordon's Division in the center of Early's line. Gordon's front stretched over the high bluff from the Valley Pike and across the line of the Manassas Gap Railroad, which reached the hill on a trestle that spanned a deep ravine cut by Tumbling Run, a fast-flowing stream at the base of Fisher's Hill. Gabriel Wharton's Division of Virginians was posted to the right of Gordon, between the Valley Pike and the river. On Gordon's left were the brigades that had been Ramseur's, but now were commanded by Brig. Gen. John Pegram, a 32-year-old Virginian and West Pointer who had recently joined the division as a brigade commander. Ramseur had just been transferred by Early to command the four brigades of Alabamians, North Carolinians, and Georgians that had lost their beloved General Rodes at Third Winchester. Rodes' old veterans were posted on Pegram's left. Anchoring the Confederate line on the extreme left were the dismounted troopers of Maj. Gen. Lunsford Lomax's cavalry, an undermanned, poorly armed, and demoralized bunch of horsemen. Lomax's troopers were Early's weakest fighters, yet he posted them on low ground at the end of his line that was most vulnerable to attack—a decision he never explained, but one which many Confederates later blamed for what was about to happen.[6]

On the morning of September 22, while five Union divisions of the VI Corps and the XIX Corps of Sheridan's army demonstrated in front of Fisher's Hill, probing and skirmishing, two VIII Corps divisions under General Crook made a flanking march under cover of woods and ravines to the eastern slope of Little North Mountain, for a surprise descent on the poorly defended Confederate left. Crook's march to the wooded mountain took much of the day, during which the massed Federal divisions facing Fisher's Hill banged away with artillery and made menacing moves suggesting an attack. By late afternoon, Crook had silently moved his 5,500 footsoldiers to a point where about half of them had passed to the rear of the Confederate line, which was perpendicular to Crook's column. Forming his men in two parallel lines of battle, the Union general edged them down the mountain slope to within a half-mile of Early's line.[7]

It was about 4:00 p.m. when Crook's mountain-climbers charged down behind Early's weak left flank, scattering the three brigades of dismounted Confederate horsemen in panicky flight. The Southern cavalry were "thunderstruck" when Crook's troops swept down the mountain "all yelling like madmen," in the words of future president Col. Rutherford B. Hayes, the commander of one of Crook's two divisions. As the cavalry fled, opening the flank and rear of the Confederates, Early's line came unhinged from left to right as regiment after regiment bolted. The cavalry "broke & fled & the enemy swept down our line from left to right with irresistable force," Captain Seymour wrote. The rugged, up-and-down ground crossed by Crook's men—a series of ridges and ravines covered with rocks, brush and cedar thickets—broke up his formation, "but without halting to reform, with cheer upon cheer the charge was continued for a distance of four miles, up hill and down hill, across fields and through woods, after the disordered and rapidly retreating foe," the Union general reported.

When Crook's attack fell upon Early's flank, Sheridan ordered the divisions facing Fisher's Hill to charge, pressuring the Southern line from two sides at once. The Confederate front began falling back in retreat, grudgingly at first; within minutes the retreat escalated into a rout. The Louisiana regiments and the rest of Gordon's veterans "remained in the works until nearly surrounded," Captain Seymour wrote. When the order for retreat finally was given, "It was altogether too late to retire in order, for it required the greatest fleetness of foot to enable us to keep from being captured." Along with their comrades, the 6th Louisiana men bolted from the line in an every-man-for-himself escape. At least one man of the regiment was wounded and nine captured. Among those not fleet enough to avoid being captured were an Irish-born private, Richard Nolan of Company I, who had been wounded at Winchester three days earlier, and Lt. Archibald Duncan, one of the two Scotsmen in the nearly all-Irish Company B.[8]

General Gordon later wrote that the Battle of Fisher's Hill could be summarized in one word that all experienced soldiers understand: "flanked." Early, who claimed afterwards that he knew that his position was untenable and that he planned to retreat south on the night of the 22nd, blamed his cavalry, as usual, for precipitating the rout. Yet Early refused to accept any blame himself for deploying his unreliable troopers on his most vulnerable flank. Instead, he appealed to General Lee for help. "Kershaw's division had better be sent to my aid, through Swift Run Gap, at once," Early wired to his commander on the day after the Fisher's Hill debacle.[9]

While Confederate casualties had not been excessively heavy, the Valley Army had suffered its second major defeat in three days. Early counted his losses in the infantry and artillery (cavalry, with him, didn't seem to count) as 30 killed, 210 wounded and 995 missing, a total of 1,235. Only about half the missing men were captured, he estimated, and the rest "took to the mountains." Many of the missing soon returned to his army. Confederate losses were about double the 528 casualties the Union forces sustained in the attack. In addition, Early lost 12 cannon which he unfairly charged were "not captured by the enemy but abandoned by the infantry." The Army of the Valley was eroding away, battle by battle. "My troops are very much shattered, the men very much exhausted, and many of them without shoes," Early wrote to Lee three days after his disaster at Fisher's Hill. Despite that small expression of compassion, Early's verdict on the affair was harsh. His ineffective cavalry, he complained to Lee, "has been the cause of all my disasters." When his dismounted cavalry gave way at Fisher's Hill, Early reported, his infantry was seized by panic over the fear of being flanked, "and without being defeated they broke, many of them fleeing shamefully."[10]

Luckily for the beaten Confederates, Sheridan did not pursue Early vigorously after Fisher's Hill. The Federal commander believed that the Southerners were defeated and he turned his attention to carrying out another mission—the destruction of the Valley as a Confederate supply source. Sheridan's cavalrymen sheathed their swords and hoisted the torch, laying waste what had been the breadbasket of the Confederacy. Barns and mills were burned, crops destroyed, warehouses and stores wrecked in a scorched-earth policy designed to deny food and forage to the Southern army. Unable to stop the destruction, Early's tired foot soldiers retreated up the Valley as far as Waynesboro, more than 80 miles from the scene of their latest defeat.[11]

It was about this time that Captain Ring took it upon himself to seek promotions for his superior officers in the 6th Louisiana. Four days after the debacle of the 22nd, Captain Ring wrote a letter to Adjutant and Inspector General Samuel Cooper. "Owing to the death of Col. Wm. Monaghan, 6th La. Regt. Infty., who was killed in an engagement near Shepherdstown, Va. 25th Aug. 1864, the names of the following officers are respectfully forwarded and recommended for promotions in the 6th La. Regt.: 1st, Lt. Col. Joseph Hanlon to be Colonel; 2nd, Major Wm H. Manning to be Lt. Col.; 3rd, Capt. John J. Rivera, Co. E., to be Major." This curious letter, signed "George P. Ring, Capt., Comdg. Regt.," evidently embarrassed Hanlon, who was absent sick and had not authorized it. On October 11, Hanlon wrote to the secretary of war disavowing Ring's request and asking it be withdrawn. His effort was unnecessary, for General Lee had no intention of approving the promotions. A note signed by Lee vetoing the recommendation said: "The condition of this regiment and of the company to which the enclosed recommendation appertains show the necessity for some action looking to the consolidation of these commands." That was a hint of a move to come that would end the regimental status of the 6th Louisiana. Hanlon never made the rank of colonel, and in fact would be a prisoner of war within days after he wrote to disavow Ring's unauthorized letter.[12]

In late September, in response to Early's plea after Fisher's Hill, General Lee sent Joseph Kershaw's Division back to reinforce the weakened Army of the Valley. Lee also sent a blunt admonition that Early must use this additional muscle to arrest the Federals' "present tide of success." "I have given you all I can," declared Lee, who was himself exhausted and ill. "You must use the resources you have so as to gain success. The enemy must be defeated, and I rely upon you to do it. One victory will put all things right." It is doubtful whether even the optimistic Lee believed such a thing.

The arrival of Kershaw's "dashing South Carolinians," numbering about 2,700 men, reawakened the enthusiasm of Early's army, which had been dulled by the defeats Third Winchester and Fisher's Hill. In early October, when Sheridan moved his army back down the Valley to Strasburg, Early followed, looking for a chance to repay the Federals for the two beatings he had sustained. Prodded by Lee and emboldened by Kershaw's arrival, Early "burned to have another trial of strength & valor with the Yankees at Fisher's Hill," Captain Seymour wrote.[13]

He was soon to get his chance, though not at Fisher's Hill. Writing from the 6th Louisiana's camp there on October 14, Captain Ring told his wife of a "nice little time" his men had on the previous day, when Early sent his five infantry divisions on a reconnaissance-in-force down the Valley Pike to probe the Union army's position behind Cedar Creek, north of Strasburg. When a Confederate battery opened fire that morning on the Federal camp beyond the creek, the surprised Unionists "skedaddled worse than we did at this place" on September 22, Ring boasted. Two Federal brigades, expecting to meet only dismounted cavalry, crossed Cedar Creek to confront the Southern troops but were bloodied badly and sent scrambling back across the stream. "Our attack seemed to take them completely by surprise and I think if we had pressed right on that we could have routed their whole army," Ring declared. After all they had been through, Early's ragged few still had plenty of spirit. "Our men never acted better and seemed more eager for a fight than on yesterday," Ring wrote. "The general feeling is this army is to have one more good chance, and if they do not amply retrieve the disgrace of Winchester and Fisher's Hill, it is not for the want of hard fighting."[14]

The chance came five days later on Wednesday, October 19, and for a few shining hours it appeared that the Confederate retribution would be as glorious as any Southerner could have prayed for. On the previous Monday, Generals John Gordon and Clement Evans, together with cartographer Jed Hotchkiss, climbed to the signal station on the northernmost peak of Massanutten Mountain. The imposing hill overlooked the Federal camps, and the officers were seeking the most promising route of attack. What Gordon saw through his field glasses from that lofty position excited his soldier's blood. Below him lay Sheridan's army, stretched out as if in miniature, with every division camp, every line of breastworks, every gun emplacement, in clear view. The approaches to the Union camps were only lightly guarded at the base of the steep mountain, because the Federals assumed that the terrain and the North Fork of the Shenandoah River, which flowed alongside Massanutten, would prohibit any Confederate attack upon that flank. Sheridan had left that end of his line "with no protection save the natural barriers and a very small detchment of cavalry on the left bank of the river," Gordon wrote. Hotchkiss drew a rough map of the Union camps as a plan of attack leaped to Gordon's mind, "the turning of Sheridan's flank where he least expected it, a sudden eruption upon his left and rear, and the complete surprise of his entire army." The route the Confederates would have to take to Sheridan's exposed flank looked nearly impassable for an army, but Hotchkiss found a "dim and narrow pathway" along the foot of the mountain paralleling the Shenandoah River. Gordon's infantrymen would have to walk in single file over this steep, narrow woods trail, and would take many hours to move a division or more into position for the attack.[15]

Early, who had decided he must either attack or retreat far up the Valley because the burned-out region around him could no longer sustain his army, seized upon the plan presented by Hotchkiss and Gordon. At a council of war on October 18, Early outlined the plan of attack for the following morning. Gordon was ordered to take the three Confederate Second Corps divisions—Ramseur's, Pegram's and his own, to be led by General Evans—after nightfall and move them by the path along the foot of the mountain and cross the North Fork of the Shenandoah at Bowman's Ford, just below the mouth of Cedar Creek. His column would then move silently to a white farmhouse, which Gordon had seen from the mountain top, about a mile and a quarter north of the ford and directly opposite the Union camp east of the Valley Pike. Meanwhile Generals Kershaw and Wharton were to move their divisions up the Valley Pike, with Kershaw filing off to the right at Strasburg to cross Cedar Creek at Bowman's Mill Ford, where he could strike the front of the force that Gordon would strike from the flank. Wharton would advance to the bridge carrying the pike over the creek and cross after the attack began. Most of the Confederate cavalry, under Maj. Gen. Thomas L. Rosser, would protect Early's left flank from the heavy Union cavalry concentrated there. The attack by Gordon, Kershaw and Rosser's cavalry was to begin at 5:00 a.m.[16]

In the camp of the Louisiana Brigade, the four dozen men of the 6th Louisiana were given orders by Major Manning, who had taken command of the regiment only days before. The 26-year-old major returned to duty in mid-October after spending more than five months in prison after his capture at the Wilderness. A Northerner by birth and a Confederate by choice, Manning would lead the remnants of the 6th Louisiana for the rest of the war. He was in charge of the regiment because his superior, Lieutenant Colonel Hanlon, had been given command of the Louisiana Brigade. That, at least, is the testimony of Captain Ring, who wrote in his October 14 letter from Fisher's Hill that Manning returned to duty and that "Col. Hanlon is now in command of Hays' & Staffords" brigade. If Hanlon was in command of the unified brigade, as indicated by Ring, it was a measure of the scarcity of field officers. The army was preparing for another battle, and there was not a single full colonel to lead the Louisianians.[17]

Preparing for the night's march, the 6th Louisiana men and all of Gordon's troops were stripped of their canteens, tin cups and anything else that might clank and alert the Union pickets, for it was essential to maintain surprise. Corporal William Trahern, who had just returned to the 6th Louisiana at Fisher's Hill after recuperating from his serious wound received at the Battle of the Wilderness, recalled the suspense generated by the daring operation. "After much mysterious preparation during the day," he wrote long after the war, "it was ordered in camp that no officer should allow his sword to beat against anything, nor the private soldier to carry his tin cup. It was to make the march as silent as possible." As darkness fell, Gordon's three divisions set out on the long trek. "It was a fearful, winding tramp, consuming nearly the whole night," Trahern remembered. The Louisiana men groped along the narrow trail in single file, aided by the tree-filtered light of a moon just past full. As Gordon remembered it, the men spoke only in whispers if at all, striving to suppress every sound as "the long gray line like a great serpent glided noiselessly along the dim pathway above the precipice."

After an exhausting march of seven hours, Gordon's men settled down along the river at the ford, one hour before the appointed time of attack. A heavy fog blanketed the low ground. It was a time of contemplation and prayer, for every soldier knew that the day might be his last. They were about to attack an army much larger than their own. The 6th Louisiana's Trahern had gotten a glimpse of Sheridan's sprawling camp from some high point before the battle. "It was the largest encampment of soldiers I ever looked upon," he wrote some years later. "They were stretched across the pike for a distance of five miles on each side, consisting of the Nineteenth, Eighth and Eleventh Corps, with a large body of cavalry on their extreme right."[18]

That huge Union army, however, was mostly asleep in its tents when Gordon ordered his infantry across the river about 4:30 a.m. to get into position for attack. Shrouded by the fog, the men waded through the cold, waist-deep waters of the Shenandoah, chilled by frosty October nights, and double-quicked a mile and a quarter along a dark farm road to the white house that Gordon had spied from the top of Massanutten. The house was immediately opposite the northern end of the camp of the Second Division of Crook's VIII Corps, commanded by Col. Rutherford B. Hayes. Crook's First Division, under Col. Joseph Thoburn, was about a mile to the south, in trenches on the ridge overlooking Bowman's Mill, where Kershaw's South Carolinians were preparing to attack. Gordon's corps had reached the chosen point of attack undetected, having scattered the few Union mounted videttes at the river without raising any general alarm. Evans' Division, including the 6th Louisiana, had double-

Surprised Federal troops jump to the other side of their works as John B. Gordon's Confederates rush through the XIX Corps camps in their rear. *Alfred R. Waud.*

quicked about a mile toward the designated jumping-off point for the attack when an outbreak of musketry was heard in the distance, signaling the beginning of Kershaw's assault. General Evans hurriedly lined up his three brigades on the Confederate left, with the Louisiana Brigade in the middle of his line. Ramseur's Division extended Evans' line to the right, northward, while Pegram's Division fell in behind Evans in support. Shortly after 5:00 a.m., all was ready.[19]

"Forming immediately with sharpshooters in front we dashed in, in good style encountering the enemy after advancing a half mile," General Evans wrote to his wife three days after the battle. Evans' Confederates rushed forward across rough ground, over hills and through ravines heavily wooded to reach Colonel Hayes' Federals, who had just been rudely awakened and were trying to scramble into line, some only half-dressed. According to Corporal Trahern, the startled Federals put up little resistance. "Just as our army had orders to move forward rapidly, one lone shot was heard fired by the Yankees' picket," Trahern recalled. "We were then inside the Federal lines, and moving with an almost hurricane speed, swept everything before us. Many Federal soldiers hastily drawn up in line to meet our advance met sudden death. Some were in the death ranks without pants or shoes. . . .It seems to me they were ushered into eternity with only a moment's warning." Trahern saw dead Union soldiers with "feet to the wood fire" who had been cooking their breakfast at their tents when death swept down upon them. A Virginian in Pegram's Division wrote that "Gordon's men struck the extreme left of the enemy's line so suddenly that men were captured in their beds, not knowing or even suspecting that we were nearer than Fisher's Hill."[20]

General Evans, writing just after the battle, said Hayes' men managed to put up "a pretty heavy but badly directed fire," at the charging Confederates. Many of Hayes' 1,445 foot soldiers tumbled from their tents half-dressed and half-awake, trying to focus on the ghostly gray figures springing toward them through the thick fog, screaming like demons. Was it a nightmare or was it really happening? "They sprang from their beds to find Confederate bayonets at their breasts," as Gordon rather melodramatically described it. "Large numbers were captured. Many hundreds were shot down as they attempted to escape." Hayes tried to get as many men as possible into line, but their stand lasted only a few moments. Evans, in an unpublished battle report only recently discovered in his personal papers, called Hayes' effort "a brief but somewhat stubborn resistance," with some Federals holding on to engage in hand-to-hand fighting before they fled. General Wright of the VI Corps, in command of the army that morning because Sheridan had taken a trip to Washington, was in Hayes' camp when the attack hit. "The surprise was complete, for the pickets did not fire a shot," Wright reported, "and the first indication of the enemy's presence was a volley into the main line where the men of a part of the regiments were at reveille roll-call without arms."[21]

While Evans and Ramseur were shattering Hayes' division, Kershaw's attack across Cedar Creek was producing the same result in Thoburn's ranks, sending the whole of Crook's corps streaming down the Valley Pike toward Middletown, about 2 miles to the north. The Louisianans swept through Hayes' camp eastward toward the pike, where the camp of the Union XIX Corps stretched out on the plateau just across the highway, below the mansion known as Belle Grove, Sheridan's headquarters. The vast and well-equipped Federal camps impressed the 6th Louisiana's Trahern, who looked with envy upon the comforts, equipment, and accommodations of the Union army. "Stretched as they were across the Winchester Pike, they looked as you approached like a beautiful city, and engineering ability was wonderfully displayed. Milk cows were here and there staked, for the accommodation of Generals and minor officers. Large stable-tents for the accommodation of head and staff, artillery and cavalry." The scene was a stark contrast to the threadbare camps Southern soldiers were accustomed to.[22]

In the camp of the XIX Corps, Maj. Gen. William H. Emory had his men up and under arms before daylight, but when the Confederate attacks hit, the fog was so heavy he could not see the enemy or tell the direction of the Confederate advance. Emory, the XIX Corps commander, tried to make a stand with his two divisions near the turnpike, but the forces of Kershaw and Gordon, which converged at that point, pushed back his men, who joined in the flight with Crook's fugitives seeking safety north of Middletown. Wright was appalled at the rout of the XIX Corps. "Influenced by a panic which often seized the best troops. . .the line broke before the enemy fairly came in sight, and under a slight scattering fire retreated in disorder down the pike," he reported.[23]

By 8:00 a.m., the Confederates had scattered most of Sheridan's army in disarray from the battlefield. "Two entire corps, the Eighth and Nineteenth, constituting two thirds of Sheridan's army, broke and fled, leaving the ground covered with arms, accoutrements, knapsacks, and the dead bodies of their comrades," Gordon wrote. General Evans claimed his division was joined with Kershaw's on the left and Ramseur's on the right in pursuing the fleeing Unionists beyond Belle Grove, Sheridan's headquarters, where the pursuit halted about 8:00 a.m. The jubilant Confederates had smashed five divisions of Sheridan's army and captured 18 cannons and 1,300 prisoners—at virtually no cost in Southern casualties. At that hour, Evans reported, he resumed command of his brigade and Gordon resumed command of the division, because General Early had taken command on the battlefield. It was here that Gordon's successful attack ended, and Early's hesitant management of the battle began.[24]

Unfortunately, it is impossible to trace the precise movements and action of the Louisiana Brigade, much less the few dozen men of the 6th Louisiana. This is particularly the case after the initial morning attack. Trahern's sketchy memoir, written five decades after the battle in the twilight of the old soldier's life, is the only known account by a member of the regiment. Confederate accounts of Cedar Creek are few, and even the official records are unusually thin. No report for the Louisiana Brigade has ever been located. General Gordon claimed in his memoirs that he compiled one, but it has never was published.[25]

The early morning action left Sheridan's army on the edge of defeat, but not all of the Union men had given up the fight as the ascending sun burned the fog off the field. The veterans of Horatio Wright's VI Corps, who had saved Washington from Early in July, had been camped farthest from the point of attack, on high ground north of Belle Grove and west of Middletown. After the collapse of Crook's and Emory's two corps, Wright's hardened soldiers stiffly resisted the Confederate advance west of the turnpike along Meadow Brook ravine around 7:30 a.m., and held that position against repeated Southern charges until Early massed his artillery along the turnpike and drove the VI Corps from its position. Wright's Second Division, commanded by Brig. Gen. George W. Getty, held out under the iron and lead rain for over an hour, until it retired in orderly fashion to join a new line of defense formed by Wright, perpendicular to the Valley Pike about two miles north of Middletown. This would become the final Union line from which the afternoon battle would be fought.[26]

A long pause in the fighting consumed the rest of the morning and the early hours of the afternoon—"the fatal halt," Gordon labeled it—that would cause bitter controversy after the battle. In his memoirs, Gordon claimed that he urged a full-scale attack on the VI corps during its "sullen, slow and orderly retreat," but that Early vetoed it, saying "this is glory enough for one day." Early contended that the Confederate troops were too weary, too disorganized, and too distracted by looting the Union camps to attempt a further offensive. Whatever the reasons, a delay of four to five hours ensued during which many of the Confederates wandered off from their commands to gather up Union plunder, including desperately needed rations and equipment, shoes, and clothing. "It was stated that during the lull in the battle that day," wrote Corporal Trahern, "more than five thousand Confederate soldiers deliberately left their commands and went to plundering." Trahern defended the looting in light of "the desperate condition of our army" and the overwhelming temptation presented by the rich store of goods in the Union camp. "We were ending this great battle by 'fighting on our stomachs,'" he remembered. "Thousands of pounds of sugar, hams, bacon, lard, etc., figured in this great haul and quieted the hostile feeling of the inner man. We killed much valuable time during our voluntary digression. . . .The lost hours and opportunities lasted from about 11:30 to nearly four o'clock."[27]

While Early hesitated and Gordon supposedly fumed over the lost opportunity, the commanding general of the Army of the Shenandoah was galloping to the battlefield. Alerted by the sound of cannon to the south, Sheridan raced from Winchester, where he had spent the night after returning from a conference in Washington. By the time he reached Newtown, six miles north of the battlefield in mid-morning, he found thousands of scared, disorganized Union soldiers milling about in disarray behind Wright's line. Early's delay, however, gave Sheridan time to reorganize his forces along the line established by Wright north of Middletown. The Confederates, meanwhile, formed an opposing line stretching for three miles, perpendicular to and straddling the turnpike, about a mile south of Sheridan's new line. The 6th Louisiana men were close to the far left flank of this line, where Evans' Division anchored the western end of the Southern army's position. It would prove to be an unfortunate position for them.[28]

Except for a half-hearted Confederate advance that Early ordered about 1:00 p.m., which did little more than probe the Union line in the woods north of town, the fighting subsided for the rest of the afternoon until about 4:00 p.m. As the hours ticked away, Early worried about Union cavalry probes on his right. Gordon sensed a massing of Union forces on his western end of the Confederate line that portended a counterattack by Sheridan. Gordon knew that his position was vulnerable, for his left flank was exposed and there was a dangerous gap between his two westernmost brigades. The Louisianans were posted at that vulnerable position. A quarter-mile gap yawned between the left of the Louisiana Brigade and the right of the next and last Confederate brigade, Evans' Georgians. Gordon, without explaining why this "long gap" was left open "with scarcely a vedette to guard it," worried about his position and sent repeated messages to Early for reinforcements, without result.[29]

At 4:00 p.m., Sheridan struck with vengeance. The Union commander ordered his whole line forward, and a phalanx of men poured out of the woods to confront the Southerners, some of whom enjoyed the protection of stone walls and rail breastworks. The attack stalled initially against what the Union commander called "very determined" resistance. On Gordon's end of the line, one of the Union's XIX Corps divisions finally overwhelmed Evans' Georgia Brigade on the extreme left and poured into the gap next to the Louisianians. At that moment, about 4:30 p.m., as the Union infantrymen who had overrun the Georgians prepared to fall upon the open flank of the Louisianans, the Federal cavalry division led by Brig. Gen. George A. Custer appeared across the open ground to their left-front. With a charge, Custer's aroused troopers came thundering into the gap. "Just as the last rays of the setting sun glowed upon our heads," Corporal Trahern remembered, "Sheridan's Cavalry came down like an avalanche. . . .Completely routed, we were scattered like sheep." Trahern and his Louisiana comrades ran for their lives, reliving the awful moments of cavalry-induced terror of exactly one month earlier at Winchester. As the Louisianans broke away, Early's line began to unravel. "Regiment after regiment, brigade after brigade, in rapid succession was crushed," Gordon wrote, "and like hard clods of clay under a pelting rain, the superb commands crumbled to pieces." As he saw the flight of the soldiers on his left, Dodson Ramseur ordered his brigades to fall back to a stone wall, where the Confederacy's youngest major general received a mortal wound from which he died the following day.[30]

As Ramseur lay bleeding, the sun was setting on both the battlefield and Confederate hopes in the Shenandoah Valley. Sweet victory had curdled into sour defeat at Cedar Creek. "We lost before nightfall one of the most important and glorious victories of the war," lamented Trahern in his old age. "This was one of the most brilliant victories of the war turned into one of the most disgraceful defeats, and all owing to the delay in pressing the enemy after we got to Middletown," complained Jed Hotchkiss in his journal. Hotchkiss quoted Early with a damning summary of the day that makes the lieutenant general's subsequent reports and reconstructions of the battle ring hollow. "The Yankees got whipped and we got scared," Old Jube had confessed to his mapmaker.[31]

Early's timidity turned to fury as he watched his army dissolve into the twilight, with Sheridan's horsemen galloping and slashing through the running gray mass of humanity as it flowed southward toward Strasburg. Nothing could be done to rally his men, a mortified Early reported to his commanding general. The rout "was as thorough and disgraceful as ever happened to our army." As Confederate wagons and artillery streamed through Strasburg, a bridge on the Valley Pike at Spangler's Mill broke, preventing any of the vehicles or cannon from crossing, which compounded Confederate losses. Early lost all the Union artillery pieces captured in the morning plus 23 cannon of his own, in addition to many wagons, ambulances and badly needed supplies. Southern casualties were never officially reported, but Early later calculated his losses as about 1,860 killed and wounded, plus about 1,000 captured, or nearly 2,900. The fact that Early's fighters had caused even greater losses in the Union army—officially reported as 5,665— was little consolation, for the Confederate army's military power in the Shenandoah Valley was forever broken.[32]

Early was bitter and vengeful toward his own officers and men in defeat. In an intemperate tirade filed as his official report, the Confederate commander blamed the loss on Gordon's Division giving way, causing other divisions in the line to fall back, "not because there was any pressure on them, but from an insane idea of being flanked." He fumed, "We had within our grasp a glorious victory and lost it by the uncontrollable propensity of our men for plunder, in the first place, and the subsequent panic among those who had kept their places, which was without sufficient cause. . . ." Early blamed everyone but himself for the loss, claiming he had very few officers "worth anything" and condemning the troops for "bad conduct." Mortified, he offered to resign, an offer Lee did not take up at this time. General Evans, in compelling letter to his wife shortly after the battle, claimed Early's effort to blame the defeat on plundering was a cover-up. "There was plundering done on this as on every other battle field," he insisted, "but it was Early's miserable

Generalship which lost the battle. If history does not say so it will not speak the truth."[33]

Cedar Creek was a disaster for the 6th Louisiana as well. Its leadership was shattered. Lieutenant Colonel Hanlon, the regiment's commanding officer, was captured for a third time at Strasburg during the retreat and was imprisoned for the rest of the war. The remaining ranking officer was Major Manning, who had returned to the regiment shortly before the battle. The 6th's faithful and valuable diarist, Capt George Ring, was seriously wounded at Cedar Creek and would never return to serve with his regiment. With his departure, there wasn't a single captain left commanding any of the regiment's ten companies. Six of them were prisoners of war, two were absent wounded, and two were detailed to other duties. Only a few lieutenants remained to lead the dwindling number of men, reduced again by casualties.[34]

While there is no official return of casualties for the regiment at Cedar Creek, a study of the 6th Louisiana's compiled service records shows that at least two men were killed, at least three others were wounded, and three were captured.[35] The Louisiana Brigade was so devastated by the four-month campaign in the Valley that it had to be reorganized again, as Lee had hinted it would be in rejecting Hanlon's promotion. Its ten regiments were combined into a single battalion made up of six companies. The 5th, 6th and 7th Louisiana regiments were combined into Company A, commanded by Major Manning. At the end of October, this company consisted of three officers and 120 men. The entire brigade—or battalion—numbered only 563. The fabled Louisiana Brigade had passed into history and was now only a memory; the 6th Louisiana no longer existed, except in the hearts and minds of its approximately 50 surviving members.[36]

Cedar Creek was the last major battle in the Valley of Virginia, which had been a cradle of war for over three years. By the end of 1864 it was a scene of devastation and ruin. For the next six weeks, the survivors of the 6th Louisiana grimly endured more marching up and down the Valley and some light skirmishing. In mid-November, mapmaker Jed Hotchkiss wrote in his journal that "to this date we had marched, since the opening of the campaign, sixteen hundred and seventy miles, and had seventy-five battles and skirmishes." The few men of the 6th Louisiana who had survived this ordeal were thoroughly worn down. On December 8, they boarded trains at Staunton for Richmond and bid farewell to the Shenandoah Valley for the final time.[37]

Chapter Fifteen

The Bitter End: PETERSBURG & APPOMATTOX

"Tell Louisiana, when you reach her shores, that her sons in the Army of Northern Virginia have made her illustrious on every battle-field."
— *Brig. Gen. Clement A. Evans*

When they arrived at Petersburg during that last, bitter winter of the war, the survivors of the 6th Louisiana numbered about five dozen. They took up their position with the Louisiana Brigade near Hatcher's Run, on the extreme right of Lee's lines. By this time, they were almost without officers. Major Manning was in command of the remnants of the three regiments collectively known now as Company A. In mid-December, Lt. Joseph B. Bresnan, one of the original officers of Joseph Hanlon's Irish Brigade company, was promoted to captain. Lt. John S. Gilbert was also there from the regiment's old A Company. Other than those men, there were just a few non-commissioned officers left to lead the privates. The Louisiana Brigade was under the command of the 9th Louisiana's Col. William R. Peck, who replaced the wounded General York. Known as "Big Peck," the six-foot, six-inch, 300-pound colonel was a popular commander who had risen from the rank of private.[1]

When Peck's Louisianians looked around at each other, they saw a grim company of gaunt men clad in threadbare clothes, slouched in muddy trenches and huddled near fires or under tent flaps to ward off biting wind and bone-chilling rain, sleet, and snow. Petersburg, a city of 18,000 at the start of the war, was a crucial transportation hub where five railroads converged, a gateway to Richmond, 23 miles to the north. The city had been under siege by Gen. U. S. Grant since June. The Union commander had failed in his efforts to either destroy the Army of Northern Virginia or take Richmond, and so he shifted his considerable force south across the James River and assaulted Petersburg. Somehow, a thin line of reservists and a handful of veterans had fought Grant's advance to a standstill just outside the logistical center, buying the time Lee's infantry needed to arrive in force. Out of options, Grant settled for a siege of both Richmond and Petersburg.

As 1865 began, Lee's ragged and hungry army of about 55,000 men was strung out along a 34-mile line of trenches, earthworks, and forts in an arc around the cities. Grant's richly-equipped and well-fed armies (Army of the Potomac, and Army of the James) numbered more than 120,000 and were dug in facing the Confederate works, which so far had proved too formidable for the Union army to overwhelm. But time was running out for the depleted Confederacy, and Lee's army—unable to maneuver and barely able to subsist—was dying.[2]

The condition of the 6th Louisiana's survivors reflected this desperate plight. "The appearance of the troops is good considering the state of their clothing, which is much worn," wrote an officer who conducted an inspection of the Louisiana troops at the end of December, 1864. "The arms are in fair condition. Accoutrements are greatly needed." Discipline was found to be good, which is something of a surprise considering the lack of officers and the miserable circumstances of the army. In Company A, the unit embracing the survivors of the 5th, 6th and 7th Louisiana, three officers and 133 men were present for duty. That number was far outweighed by the 355 absent *with* leave, of whom most were prisoners in Federal hands. Another 310 men were absent *without* leave, a figure which reflected the continuing desertion problem that would worsen substantially during these last, hopeless months of the war. Many Confederates who had endured more than three years of fighting finally gave up hope and left. One of these was Pvt. Edward Fitzgerald, a New Orleans Irishman in Company I. Fitzgerald had been badly wounded at the first battle of Winchester, captured in the Wilderness, and survived four months of imprisonment at Point Lookout in Maryland. The final winter in Petersburg proved too much for him, and on January 29, 1865, he went over to the Union lines, took the Oath of Allegiance to the United States at City Point, and was sent north to New York City as an ex-soldier. He was soon followed by thousands more.[3]

Writing home to his sister from Petersburg, Pvt. Theodore H. Woodard of the 6th Louisiana's Tensas Rifles lamented the sad condition in which he found the Louisiana regiments when he returned to his command from seven months in the Federal prison camp at Point Lookout. "I came out to our command on Friday last," Woodard wrote in mid-January 1865, "and found only four men in the company. The 5th, 6th & 7th Regiments are temporarily consolidated into one Company, numbering only 60 men out of over 3,000. Now you can imagine the loss we have sustained."[4]

The Confederates battled hunger and bad weather at Petersburg as well as Grant's troops. Private Woodard complained to his sister that conditions for the Southern soldiers were no better than those of the Confederate captives in Northern prisons. While he was in Richmond on the way back to his command, Woodard said, he sought the help of an influential friend there to try to get him a transfer to some other unit, preferably Col. John S. Mosby's Rangers. "He is trying to get me with Mosby, but I don't know whether he will succeed or not," Woodard wrote. "I sincerely hope he does, for this place is enough to kill the dead. We do not positively get any more to eat here than we did at Point Lookout."[5]

Major General John B. Gordon, who had been given command of the three divisions of the Second Corps, was as distressed as his troops over the lack of food. Gordon was informed soon after he arrived at Petersburg "that it was impossible for the Government to supply us with more than half-rations, and even these were by no means certain." The general scavenged for food and forage in the back country nearby, scraping up what paltry supplies he could find for his men and animals. "Starvation, literal starvation, was doing its deadly work," he wrote years later. "It was a harrowing but not uncommon sight to see those hungry men gather the wasted corn from under the feet of half-fed horses, and wash and parch and eat it to satisfy in some measure their craving for food." The Federal troops were aware of the plight of the hungry rebels and occasionally acted with admirable compassion. One starving soldier of the 9th Louisiana crawled out between the lines one day after a sympathetic Yankee held up a large chunk of meat and offered it to him. Shrugging off warnings from his Southern comrades that it might be a trick, he shouted, "Yank, don't shoot! I came after that piece of meat." He was rewarded with meat, hardtack, bread and coffee which he brought back to his appreciative, if astonished, comrades.[6]

The weather was so bad it prevented much serious fighting that winter. The only significant battle involving the 6th Louisiana's veterans came in early February. Grant made an effort to get around the Confederate right flank, which was held by Gordon's troops, to cut the logistically important Boydton Plank Road. The result was a two-day clash on February 5 and 6, 1865, known as the Battle of Hatcher's Run. The action began on the morning of February 5 when a division of Union cavalry, followed by two infantry corps of five divisions, swung south and west of Petersburg in an attempt to capture or destroy Confederate wagon trains on the plank road. That afternoon, an indecisive clash occurred between elements of Henry Heth's Confederate division and the Federal II Corps, now commanded by Maj. Gen. Andrew A. Humpheys. The Louisianians moved forward with Clement Evans' Division to support Heth, but were not heavily engaged in the fighting north of Hatcher's Run. Exposed to the frigid weather, both sides suffered through a bitterly cold night.[7]

The heaviest fighting for Peck's Louisiana Tigers occurred on the following day. After a quiet morning, both sides sent out reconnaissance parties to probe the enemy. General Gouverneur Warren, commanding the Federal V Corps, ordered Maj. Gen. Samuel Crawford's division to move south of Hatcher's Run along a road leading to Dabney's saw mill to find the Confederate position. On the Confederate side, Gordon sent Pegram's Division on a similar scouting mission. One of Pegram's brigades ran into Crawford's advancing men in the vicinity of the old steam saw mill, and the resulting clash about 2:00 p.m. began pulling in reinforcements from both sides. The severest fighting occurred about a half-mile south of Hatcher's Run around an immense heap of saw dust from the mill, which some Union soldiers initially mistook as a Confederate fort.[8]

When Pegram's men were attacked and pushed back from Dabney's Mill by Crawford's Federal division, Evans' Division rushed to Pegram's support. Peck moved his small brigade of Louisianians "as rapidly as possible to our picket line south of Hatcher's Run," he reported. Peck arrived with only 250 or so in his command, having left 150 men on picket back at the Petersburg lines. Peck reported that his "mere handful" of Louisianians went into line in a woods near the sawmill between Terry's Virginia Brigade on his left and Walker's Brigade of Pegram's Division on his right[9]

With such a tiny fighting force, the Louisiana colonel was forced to conform his movements entirely to the movements of the larger brigades on each side. "Advancing twice to the edge of the woods, and driving the enemy from the sawdust pile in the field, we were each time forced to retire by the wavering and falling back of the line on our left," Peck reported. According to one contemporary account, Gordon ordered a third charge, and the Louisianians surged toward the sawdust pile. "With a yell, Peck's Louisianians struck the heap of saw dust and carried it," according to the Atlanta newspaper account, which said the fight became "very fierce" at this stage. During what he called the "constant and severe" fighting, Union corps commander Warren called up the division of Maj. Gen. Romeyn B. Ayres to bolster Crawford. On the Confederate side, Maj. Gen. William Mahone's Division of A. P. Hill's Corps arrived to fill a gap between Evans and Pegram. With Mahone's help, a final Confederate charge drove the Federals east of Dabney's Mill as the Union battle line "gave way and fell back rapidly," an unhappy Warren reported. When Mahone's fresh division arrived to spearhead the final Confederate charge, Peck reported, "many of my men had by this time been killed and wounded and the command was short of ammunition." After having "fired away the last round we had," Peck pulled his troops back and apparently played no role in the final charge.[10]

A freezing rain fell during the last hours of the battle, causing terrible suffering for the untended wounded of both sides. The Confederates lost about 1,000 casualties, the most significant of whom was Brig. Gen. John Pegram. The capable and recently-married brigadier was shot through the body near the heart and died almost as soon as he hit the ground. Among the Louisianians, Colonel Peck reported six killed and 17 wounded. The number of 6th Louisiana casualties is uncertain, but at least one man, Pvt. Gabriel Porter, was severely wounded.[11]

The casualties among the Louisianians further reduced a fighting force that was already pitifully small. The day after the fighting, a Confederate artillery officer who had known the Louisiana Brigade in its glory days was shocked and saddened to see what had become of this proud group of regiments. On February 7, Maj. William Owen Miller, adjutant of the Washington Artillery of New Orleans, was told by General Gordon that the Louisiana Brigade would come to serve as infantry support for his gunners. Owen could barely believe his eyes when he saw them:

> Soon after, a small body of troops, not over 250, came marching towards me through the ice-covered pines, and I recognized at the head of the column the giant form of Col. Peck. And this was all that was left of the 'Louisiana brigade' that had numbered over 3,000 muskets before Richmond in the Seven Days' battles!. . . .This extraordinary diminution of numbers showed plainly what it had gone through, and the truly gallant, unconquerable Louisiana brigade, now of 250 brave hearts, tempered like fine steel in the fiery blasts of battle, was all that was left for me to depend upon to support my guns.[12]

Like the steady erosion of the Louisiana regiments, Confederate hopes also were dying. Even General Lee, who rarely betrayed any sign of despair, warned Richmond of the impending catastrophe. He knew his troops could not endure much more suffering. Two days after the Battle of Hatcher's Run, which he said occurred during the worst weather of that brutal winter, Lee wrote to Secretary of War James A. Seddon, complaining that his hungry men went into the fight without having any meat for three days, "and all were suffering from reduced rations and scant clothing, exposed to battle, cold, hail and sleet." He ordered his chief commissary, "who had not a pound of meat at his disposal," to go to Richmond to see if nothing could be done about the food supply. "The physical strength of the men, if their courage survives, must fail under this treatment," he wrote. His cavalry had been dispersed because of lack of forage for the horses. Under such conditions, he warned, "you must not be surprised if calamity befalls us."[13]

Faced with nearly intolerable conditions, more of Lee's troops melted away in desertion, either to their homes or to enemy lines. "Hundreds of men are deserting nightly," Lee had complained in January, warning Richmond that he could "not keep the army together unless examples are made" of convicted deserters. Official records show that 2,934 soldiers deserted from the Confederate lines in the month following the fight at Hatcher's Run. By the end of February, the Louisiana Brigade, wracked by sickness and desertion, was down to only 401 men available for duty. The Louisianians were moved from their position near Hatcher's Run, on the right of Lee's lines, to the trenches on the left, near the scene of the "Crater." The giant cavity was created by the infamous exploding mine of the previous July, when the Federals tried to blow up Lee's lines by tunneling below them. Their last brigade commander, Col. Eugene Waggaman of the 10th Louisiana, took charge at this time and replaced Colonel Peck, who was promoted to brigadier general and transferred west. The popular and deeply religious Waggaman, a Louisiana sugar planter before the war, had distinguished himself with his bravery at Malvern Hill in July 1862, where he had been taken prisoner.[14]

By March, it was clear to the men in the trenches that the end was near. One sign came when Major Manning received orders to compile a brief history of the 6th Louisiana and each of its companies, recording for posterity the details of their formation, their record in the war, and memorable campaigns and battles. Manning penned the history on March 13, compressing four incredible years into about 500 inadequate words, noting apologetically that no records remained to guide him. His only resources were his memories and those of the few men remaining with him.

He and Captain Bresnan shared the duty of writing brief company histories, hampered by the fact that some companies numbered only two or three men. In a memo "done in the trenches near Petersburg, Va.," on March 20, Bresnan briefly summarized the record of his Irishmen in Company I, noting with some sadness that only one officer and three men remained of its original 90-plus members. Bresnan was a 34-year-old Irish immigrant from New Orleans who had worked as a clerk before the war. He was completely unaware when he produced his historical notes that one more battle loomed at Petersburg, a vicious affair that would prove almost fatal for him.[15]

General Lee, convinced that he must break out of Grant's encirclement or ultimately face surrender, asked his trusted Second Corps commander to study the Federal lines and recommend a plan to allow the Army of Northern Virginia to escape the Union stranglehold. General Gordon spent a week studying the Federal entrenchments and forts and finally recommended a daring assault upon an earthen redoubt known as Fort Stedman. The target, one of a series of enclosed fortifications along the Union line, stood directly east of Petersburg about a mile south of the Appomattox River. Steadman was just opposite a bulge in the Confederate works known as Colquitt's Salient, which narrowed the distance between the opposing lines. A boy with a strong arm, Maj. Henry Kyd Douglas later observed, could have thrown a stone from the Confederate fortifications into the Union lines.[16]

Gordon's plan was a bold and desperate last-chance gamble. Success would require surprise, stealth, deception, and daring—in addition to good luck. The plan called for a sudden, pre-dawn assault from the Confederate salient upon Fort Steadman, where the opposing trenches were no more than 150 yards apart. Stedman was armed with four guns and was supported by batteries on the north (Battery X) and the south (Batteries XI and XII). About a half-mile south of the fort stood another Union redoubt, Fort Haskell. Gordon's plan called for the three divisions of his corps, supported by four brigades borrowed from other commands, to dash across the open ground between the lines in darkness, capture Fort Stedman and then fan out left and right, up and down the Union trenches. The Union batteries, once captured, would be turned to enfilade the enemy, while supporting troops and cavalry poured through the gap torn open by the initial assault.[17]

The ground in front of Fort Stedman was criss-crossed with picket trenches and bristled with abatis, a tangle of felled trees piled together.

The fort was also protected by breast-high sharpened logs, angled toward the enemy. Its obstacles were daunting, but Gordon conceived plans to deal with them. The assault would be preceded by fifty strong men with sharp axes who would hack at the obstructions to clear a path for the attacking infantry. Three hand-picked groups of 100 men, each led by one officer, would rush past Fort Stedman into the Union rear, pretending to be Federals driven back by the Confederate assault, using the names of Union officers known to be in that sector in order to gain passage beyond Fort Stedman. These three columns of 100 masqueraders were to rush to three small forts thought to be in rear of Stedman, capture them and turn their guns on the Federal lines. Once all this was done, massed Confederate infantry and cavalry would pour through the gap and collapse Grant's left wing, cutting his army in two.[18]

Gordon's scheme was so elaborate as to be fanciful, but Lee was desperate enough to approve it. The assault was scheduled to begin at 4:00 a.m. on March 25. Colonel Waggaman was summoned to a council of war to discuss the plan with Gordon and his division commanders. Suddenly General Evans turned to the Louisiana colonel and said: "On account of the valor of your troops, you will be allowed the honor of leading off the attack. This you will make with unloaded arms." It was a dubious honor, but one the proud Louisianian could hardly decline. His men were to capture or silence the Federal pickets in the no-man's-land between the lines without firing a shot, so as not to alert the Union defenders in the forts; they would also assist in clearing away obstructions for the infantry to follow.[19]

An hour before the assault was set to begin, the Louisianians assembled at their jumping-off point. Gordon was there, ready to personally supervise the attack. When 4:00 a.m. arrived, the corps commander mounted the Confederate breastworks opposite Fort Stedman with a single rifleman at his side, who was to fire one shot to signal the attack. In the darkness, some of Gordon's men pushed aside the Confederate obstructions in front of their own trench-line, making a noise that alerted a Federal picket who called out, "What are you doing over there Johnny? What is that noise? Answer quick or I'll shoot." Gordon was paralyzed with concern. Any shots from the pickets would alert the gunners in Fort Stedman. The quick-witted private at his side cried out: "Never mind, Yank. Lie down and go to sleep. We are just gathering a little corn. You know our rations are short over here." The Union picket responded, "All right, Johnny—go ahead and get your corn. I'll not shoot at you while you are drawing your rations." When Gordon ordered his clever private to fire the signal shot for the assault, pangs of conscience nagged at the soldier, who felt obliged to return the Yank's courtesy. As Gordon repeated the order to fire the shot, the rifleman called out, "Hello, Yank! Wake up. We are going to shell the woods. Look out, we are coming!"[20]

A lone rifle shot rang out. Confederates who had crawled within yards of their Union counterparts sprang upon them, silencing them without a shot. Some of the Confederates, according to Union officers, fooled the Union pickets by posing as deserters coming across the no-mans land to surrender with their rifles, a common practice that had been encouraged by the Federals. Gordon's axemen dashed across no-man's land and quickly opened a gap in the obstructions in front of the Union stronghold. The three squads of 100 men picked to impersonate retreating Federals came next, followed on their heels by packed columns of infantry.[21]

The Louisianians were in the forefront as the first Southern troops sprang upon the Federal trenches and into the fort. According to one account published in a Richmond newspaper a week after the attack, Gordon's sharpshooters led the assault, followed by the consolidated Louisiana Brigade. The first Confederates to enter the fort were Lt. R. B. Smith of the 2nd Louisiana and eight of his men. "Their situation was a critical and perilous one, but with remarkable coolness and bravery, they held it until reinforcements arrived, when the Fort was assaulted and its garrison captured or killed." According to the newspaper account:

> While this was going on, and almost simultaneously, the Louisiana brigade, being the head of the supporting column, was a short distance to the left, attacking works surrounding another battery of several guns, defended by a garrison of two hundred men. With their accustomed intrepidity and gallantry, the task assigned them was soon accomplished. In a moment they were at the base of the fortifications; they escaladed and stormed the breastworks, penetrated the Fort by forcing their way through the embrasures, while a shower of grape, canister and musketry was poured upon them from within, and captured every thing within the redoubt save the few who escaped under cover of darkness or those who were slain. The guns were left in charge of Captain Bressman of the 6th Louisiana, who a few moments afterwards relinquished them to a company of artillery, who turned them and opened fire on the enemy. These feats of valor were not performed without serious losses. Lieutenant Ryan of the 10th Louisiana was mortally wounded and died the next day, while

> Captain Bressman and Lieutenant Kendall lie seriously wounded. Many gallant men shared the fate of these officers.[22]

The 6th Louisiana captain seriously wounded in the wild and hand-to-hand brawl inside the fort was Captain Bresnan, the same officer who had recently penned the regiment's history. Bresnan took a bayonet in the abdomen and miraculously lived to tell about it. The New Orleans Irishman was stabbed during the "rough and tumble fighting" that in one account had the opposing soldiers "locked together like serpents" and fighting "as if they had drunk two quarts of brandy."[23]

The attacking Confederates overpowered Fort Stedman's gunners, men of the 14th New York Heavy Artillery, and fanned out up and down the Federal trenches, capturing a long stretch of the Union line including Batteries X, XI and XII. Brig. Gen. Napoleon McLaughlen, commanding a Federal brigade in this sector, was awakened by the noise of the attack and rode his horse to Fort Stedman, where he began issuing orders to the soldiers inside the dark enclosure. Unaware that they were Confederates, he was quickly surrounded and sent packing across no-man's-land to surrender to General Gordon. It was still well before dawn and the attack had succeeded almost better than Gordon could have hoped. Before sunrise, his men had captured the fort, nine heavy cannon, eight mortars and more than 500 prisoners, at only a small loss in casualties. A hole nearly 1,000 yards wide had been opened in the Union line. Gordon, reaching Fort Stedman himself, sent word to Lee that he had taken the fort and that his 300 masqueraders were on their way to the Federal rear.[24]

The meticulously planned attack quickly went awry. Gordon received a message from the officer leading one of his three groups of 100 men that he had successfully cleared the Federal infantry lines by passing himself off as a colonel of a Pennsylvania regiment. His guide, however, was lost and could not find the fort in the rear of the lines he was to capture. The same thing happened to the other two columns. The Confederate attack stalled as Maj. Gen. John F. Hartranft, commanding a Federal IX Corps division in charge of this part of the Union lines, organized six regiments for a counterattack. Federal artillery batteries and forts along the line, plus field pieces advanced to the hills behind it, began pounding the Southerners. With Hartranft's Pennsylvania regiments arrayed in a deadly semi-circle around Gordon's men, the Confederates could not go forward and could not long hold the position they had captured. Reporting this to Lee, General Gordon received orders to withdraw.[25]

Retreat, however, was a difficult and deadly proposition. Falling back between the lines meant a death-defying dash across no-man's-land under the concentrated fire of Federal guns. "A consuming fire on both flanks and front during this withdrawal caused a heavy loss to my command," Gordon wrote years later. The brave took their chances and fled through the storm of lead and iron back to their starting point. According to one account, Colonel Waggaman lost half the Louisianians who made the attack. General Evans' unpublished list of casualties, however, claims the Louisiana Brigade suffered three killed, 26 wounded and 25 missing in the attack. In addition to the bayonetted Captain Bresnan—who somehow made it back to the Confederate lines and was rushed to a Petersburg hospital—the 6th Louisiana's wounded included Sgt. Samuel Jenkins of Company B, who was mortally struck in the thigh and died two weeks later, and Pvt. Joseph Husselby of Company B, who took a shot that fractured his right arm, which was amputated after the battle. Among the captured were Lt. James E. Weymouth and Pvt. James P. McGough of Company A and Pvt. John Coleman, an Irishman in Company K. Hundreds of discouraged Southerners simply surrendered rather than face the risk of retreat across that deadly zone of fire. By 8:15 a.m., it was all over. The Federals claimed 1,949 prisoners, including 71 commissioned officers. The attack and retreat had cost Lee's shrinking army at least 4,000 killed, wounded, and captured. Gordon's desperate gamble had ended in a spectacular and bloody failure. It was, he recalled, "the last supreme effort" to break Grant's grip, "the expiring struggle of the Confederate giant."[26]

It all unraveled quickly after the failure at Fort Stedman. Like the old gray Confederate uniforms, worn thin by years of war, the fabric of Lee's defenses around Petersburg simply came apart, piece by piece. General Grant skillfully used the powerful cavalry divisions of "Little Phil" Sheridan, who arrived on the Petersburg front in late March after wrecking Early's skeletal army in the Valley, together with a column of infantry to smash through the Confederate forces commanded by General Pickett at Five Forks on April 1. Pickett's defeat collapsed the Confederate right flank. Lee warned President Davis that he could no longer defend Richmond and made plans to abandon the Petersburg-Richmond defenses and escape in southwest Virginia. His only hope was to link the Army of Northern Virginia, which had shrunk to less than 40,000 men, with the Confederate army led by Gen. Joseph Johnston in North Carolina.[27]

The days in the muddy trenches on Gordon's front after the failure at Fort Stedman were a blur of skirmishes, mortar attacks, and sharpshooters' duels. These were the dying hours of a lost cause. The small band of survivors from the 6th Louisiana must have known the war was lost, veteran soldiers as they were. Certainly they were able to read the signs of defeat as well as the faces of their commanders. At dawn on Sunday, April 2, the day after Pickett's disaster at Five Forks, fighting erupted all along the Petersburg lines as Grant launched his long-awaited final assault. Lee's thinly manned lines were broken in several places, including Gordon's sector, where the defenders stood as much as 15 feet apart. Union troops of the IX Corps broke through one part of the line near the Crater but were hemmed in when Waggaman threw the Louisiana Brigade into the breach and recaptured 200 yards of the works. Gordon was frantically organizing such counterattacks when a messenger from Lee came with the grim news that overwhelming Union forces were approaching from the right where A. P. Hill's lines had collapsed. The Third Corps commander himself had been killed during the initial breakthrough. There was no point in Gordon sacrificing more men to restore his lines. Instead, he was asked to hold off the advancing Federals until nightfall, while Lee withdrew his other commands to begin the retreat. When the rest of the army had evacuated the fortifications, Gordon was to fall back over the Appomattox River and move west, serving as rear guard of the army. In a battle that stretched 22 hours from start to finish, the Louisiana Brigade held on grimly with Gordon's men, as one by one Lee's divisions pulled out from Petersburg and Richmond. At about 10:00 p.m., Colonel Waggaman ordered his weary men from their trenches and marched them over the bridge spanning the rain-swollen Appomattox River, which was burned not long after they crossed.[28]

The retreat aimed for Amelia Court House, 36 miles west of Petersburg, where Lee had ordered supplies to be sent by railroad. Fighting by day and marching by night, the Louisianians dragged themselves along, exhausted, hungry and dispirited. The retreat was slow, the columns of infantry halting, waiting, then starting again as the wagons and guns creaked on ahead. Half-starved, surviving on a daily ration of one biscuit and one ounce of bacon, the Louisiana men may have been sustained by the thought of trainloads of food awaiting them at Amelia. But when Lee's troops arrived there, they learned that the trains had not shown up, and no one knew why. This was the final straw for some of the exhausted soldiers, unable to continue the retreat and unwilling to fight for a government that could not even feed them. Some fell out along the road merely to find food or rest, while others decided at last that desertion was the only course left. Many threw down their arms and simply walked away. As it struggled west in the rain and mud, Lee's army shed men and muskets like a dying animal might shed hair, skin, and flesh, reducing itself to its bony core. Decades later, the march stood out vividly in Gordon's memory: "Fighting all day, marching all night, with exhaustion and hunger claiming their victims at every mile of the march, with charges of infantry in the rear and cavalry on the flanks, it seemed the war god had turned loose all his furies to revel in havoc." In this seemingly endless moving battle, the last 55 survivors of the 6th Louisiana endured the final week of the war.[29]

They arrived at a little village called Appomattox Court House on the evening of Saturday, April 8, as part of an army that bore little resemblance to the magnificent fighting machine of earlier years. Two days before, nearly 8,000 men (one-quarter of Lee's army) had been captured and hundreds more killed and wounded at Sayler's Creek, on the road to Appomattox. Watching the fighting, Lee had exclaimed, "My God! Has the army dissolved?" The prisoners included several generals, among them Dick Ewell and Joseph Kershaw. Lee's army was reduced to two corps—Gordon's and Longstreet's, about 30,000 infantry—and was surrounded on all sides but the north by an adversary that had nearly 100,000 men. Lee's men were numbed by lack of sleep and weakened by lack of food, but those who remained in the ranks were not yet ready to quit.[30]

On Saturday night, April 8, the last Confederate council of war was held as Generals Lee, Gordon, Longstreet and a few others gathered around a fire, sitting on blankets and saddles in a stand of timber. The discussion ranged from the exchange of letters over the past two days between Grant and Lee, feeling out the possible terms of surrender, to the future of the Southern people following the Confederacy's defeat. The talk turned to the army's last remaining options other than immediate surrender, including one final attempt to break though the cordon of Union troops blocking the path west, toward the mountains and a possible linkup with Johnston's army. Lee believed that only Union cavalry was in his front (to the west), in which case the attack might succeed. But, he added, if the attack found Grant's infantry supporting the cavalry, he would seek terms. After some discussion, it was decided that Gordon's infantry divisions and Maj. Gen. Fitzhugh Lee's cavalry corps would try a breakout in the morning.[31]

Before dawn on Palm Sunday, April 9, 1865, the last survivors of the 6th Louisiana fell into line of battle with Gordon's divisions. Due to heavy desertions and straggling, Gordon probably fielded less than 2,000 armed men ready to fight that morning. They filed off a half-mile west of the court house, on the edge of a freshly plowed field, with Fitzhugh Lee's 2,400 mounted troopers extending the line to the west beyond Gordon's right. The Confederate line obliquely cut across the Richmond-Lynchburg Stage Road. Evans' Division, on the far left of Gordon's line, was south of the Stage Road, but about half of the infantry and all the Southern cavalry were north of it. To seize and protect the Stage Road for the contemplated escape to Lynchburg, the plan of attack called for the battle line to swing like a gate, hinged on the left where Evans' three brigades stood, so that the right swept down south of the road. Colonel Waggman had only 150 soldiers deployed for battle that morning, less than half the number of Louisianians who would subsequently surrender. Such absenteeism was typical of most Confederate brigades on this final morning of the war in Virginia.[32]

Lining up for what would be the last attack of the war, the thinly-clad Confederates shivered in the pre-dawn chill. A fog had settled over the field before them, limiting vision. In the dim light of dawn, Major Manning and his handful of 6th Louisiana men may not even have seen the enemy soldiers, who were waiting across the field crouched behind light breastworks thrown up during the night. Between 5:00 a.m. and 7:00 a.m., Confederate skirmishers began to feel out the Federal position. It was probably after the latter hour when the Confederate line began moving forward. Lee's cavalrymen spurred their horses into a charge around the Union left flank, capturing two Union guns posted on the Stage Road west of the village. The Confederate infantry line began its gate-like swing, advancing en echelon by brigades, the far right brigade moving first, followed at 100-yard intervals by the next, and so on down the line. Artillery boomed on both sides as the attack developed. Stumbling across the soft, furrowed field, the Louisiana Tigers raised the Rebel yell for the last time, perhaps remembering similar moments of past glory, perhaps believing that once more they could do the impossible. Certainly, they did not act like defeated men. Gordon, knowing the odds were stacked against them, was thrilled at their spirit. "I take especial pride," he wrote in his memoirs, "in recording the fact that this last charge of the war was made by the footsore and starving men of my command with a spirit worthy of the best days of Lee's Army."[33]

Gordon's troops swept over the dismounted blue cavalry behind the fence line, driving them into the woods. The happy Louisianians, who captured an enemy battle flag, joyfully waved their own banners and cheered. The Confederates had captured two cannon and driven the Union troops back, but Gordon soon saw a heavy column of infantry advancing on his right and rear. More Federal cavalry appeared on the left. Longstreet's Corps, serving as Lee's rear guard some four miles east near New Hope Church, was under attack and could not come to Gordon's aid. The hope of a breakthrough was gone. When Lee sent a message asking Gordon's situation, he responded: "Tell General Lee that I have fought my corps to a frazzle, and I fear I can do nothing unless I am heavily supported by Longstreet's corps."[34]

Colonel Waggaman was still leading his Louisianians forward toward a Federal battery in a woods beyond the plowed field when orders arrived for them to fall back to their original line. The men could not understand why they would break off a successful attack. A white flag of truce appeared on the field soon after, and rumors began swirling through the ranks, raising the most dreaded word of all. Many sank to the ground and looked at each other, bewildered and unbelieving, as the whispers spread up and down the line. Finally, it had come to this—surrender![35]

So few of them had endured it all, right down to this bitter end. The 6th Louisiana regiment was gone, but its heroes were here, huddled near the village of Appomattox Court House. They were a fair cross-section of the regiment—nearly half Irish born, nearly half Louisianians, with a sprinkling of men from Prussia, France, Virginia, North Carolina, New York. They were young and old. There was young Tommy Cavanaugh, a mere Irish lad of 15 when he enlisted in New Orleans as drummer, now an aged and war-weary 19. There was old James Donovan, an Irish-born former sailor, who was 44 years old and wracked by rheumatism. As befits such an Irish regiment, there were two Patrick Murphys among them, both born in Ireland—a 31-year-old former butcher, one of Henry Strong's original recruits in Company B, and a 37-year-old former laborer, one of Joseph Hanlon's original men. Amazingly, at least 30 of the 52 who surrendered at Appomattox were the original volunteers of June 1861. They had traveled every step of the war's long road to its very end. Most of the others were recruits of 1862.[36]

Many bore wounds from the 6th Louisiana's long list of battles. Prussian-born John Welk, a private in the mostly-German Company G, had been wounded and disabled at the First Battle of Winchester in 1862, but had served thereafter as a teamster and ambulance driver. Irish-born Pvt. Malachi Davis of Company I carried a wound from Port Republic, while Daniel Keegan, the fifer from Company F, bore a similar injury from the Second Battle of Winchester in June 1863. There were wounds from Sharpsburg (Cpl. J. T. Bolton, Company A), from Manassas (Sgt. Pierce P. Hickey, Company K), from Fredericksburg (Pvts. Thomas Quinalty, Company B, and William Lucas, Company K) and from Spotsylvania Court House (Cpl. J. H. Reynolds, Company A.)

Nearly half of those surrendering—23 in all—had been captured in battle and imprisoned in the North, some more than once. Private Daniel Riordan, an Irishman in Company F, had the distinction of being a three-time loser: first at Fredericksburg in April of 1863, a second time at the disaster of Rappahannock Station in November of that same year, and a third time in the Wilderness in May of 1864. He had spent a total of 14 months in three Federal prisons—Old Capitol in Washington, Point Lookout in Maryland, and Elmira in New York. Eight of the surrendering men had been captured at Fredericksburg, seven at Rappahannock Station, six at the Wilderness.[37]

The names of the 52 men surrendering—Lynch and Moran, Kennedy and Donovan, Lejeune and Fontenot, Steinmutz and Pfister, Briggs and Smith—reflected both the dominant Irish character of the regiment as well as its ethnic diversity. Any differences between them had paled and lost their meaning when measured against the overpowering common experience of sacrifice, pain, death, grief, and glory they had shared in the past four years. They had something in common now that other men who had not marched this long, incredible journey would never know or feel. What they had endured together had created a bond that would outweigh all the divisive tendencies of ethnicity, religion, birth, and station. They had survived this war to its humiliating end. Now, for the last time, they huddled together as brothers.

On the afternoon of Sunday, April 9, General Lee surrendered the Army of Northern Virginia to General Grant in a simple and dignified meeting in the home of Wilmer McLean in the village of Appomattox Court House. After two days of arranging details and preparing lists of all those to be surrendered and paroled, Lee's army assembled for the last time on the morning of Wednesday, April 12. Behind their General

Gordon, who rode erect but with eyes downcast, the last of the 6th Louisiana veterans marched in column into the village and halted. On the left and the right of the road, two Federal brigades stood silently at attention. The Confederate line turned to face south. At an order from officers, bayonets were fixed. Then, on command, the men in ragged gray and brown uniforms stepped forward four paces across the road and stacked their arms. Cartridge boxes were hung from the stacked muskets. Color sergeants folded regimental flags and laid them on the stack. The soldiers turned and marched past the court house. Their war was over.[38]

Four officers and 48 enlisted men of the 6th Louisiana took part in the Appomattox surrender ceremony. Enduring to the end, they comprise a special honor roll. These are the final 52, the last fighters of this brave regiment:

Officers: Maj. William H. Manning; 2nd Lt. John S. Gilbert, Company A; Ensign Godfrey Gaiser; Assistant Surgeon William B. Watford, Sgt.-Maj. John Tobin.

Company A: Sgt. T. J. Gilbert; Cpls. J. T. Bolton, J. H. Reynolds; Pvts. J. R. Traylor, James S. Davis, William T. Jordan, Richard Ussery, Phillip Ussery, S. B. Wininger, James H. Briggs, B. J. Smith.

Company B: Pvts. John G. Ricker, Andrew Kennedy, Louis Shidell, Thomas Quinalty, James Donovan, Timothy Britt, Patrick Lynch, Thomas P. Cavanaugh, Patrick Murphy.

Company C: Sgt. James M. Hull; Cpl. John Cox, Pvts. Alcee Bertrand, Edmund Lejeune, Benjamin Fontenot, Thomas Smith.

Company D: Sgt. William F. Wells.

Company E: Sgt. Charles Moran, Pvts. Henry C. Hall, William A. Beard, G. Paul Burce.

Company F: Drum-Major Daniel Keegan, Pvt. Daniel Riordan.

Company G: Pvts. J. Augustus Steinmutz, Leonard Pfister, Pierre Lievre, John Welk.

Company H: Pvt. Louis Bertrand.

Company I: Pvts. Patrick Murphy, Malachi Davis, William Hart.

Company K: Sgt. Pierce P. Hickey, Pvts. Cain Comfort, Michael Eagan, William Lucas, Michael McCue, James Russell.[39]

On the day before the formal surrender ceremonies, their commanding generals issued their farewells. More than 130 years later, their words cannot be improved upon as a tribute to the 6th Louisiana and to the regiments that fought with it in the two Louisiana brigades of the Army of Northern Virginia.

Their division commander, General Clement Evans, addressed his farewell speech to Colonel Waggaman:

> The sad hour has arrived when we who have served in the Confederate Army so long together must part at least for a while, but the saddest circumstance connected with the separation is that it occurs under a heavy disaster to our cause. To you, Colonel, and to our brother soldiers of Hays' and Stafford's Brigades, I claim to say, that you can carry with you the proud consciousness that, in the estimation of your commander, you have done your duty. Tell Louisiana, when you reach her shores, that her sons in the Army of Northern Virginia have made her illustrious on every battle-field, from the first Manassas to the last desperate blow struck by your command on the hill at Appomattox Court House, and tell her, too, that as in the first, so in the last, the enemy fled before the valor of your charging lines. To the sad decree of an inscrutable Providence let us bow in humble resignation, awaiting for the pillar of cloud to be lifted. To you, your officers and devoted men I shall always cherish the most pleasant memories, and when I say farewell it will be with a full heart, which beats an earnest prayer for your future happiness.[40]

With equal eloquence, General Gordon, commanding Lee's Second Corps, paid his final tribute to his fighting Louisianians on the same day:

> In parting with the Louisiana Brigade of this Army, I cannot omit to offer this tribute, which is due to as heroic a devotion as ever illustrated in the armies of any people; coming with glorious ardor to the support of a cause sacred in itself, doubly consecrated today by its dead. You have carried your enthusiasm into a hundred battles, filling your comrades and countrymen with pride and your enemy with fear. Steady and unshaken have you passed through the struggle with unstained record. Your name is without the shadow of a stain. Your conduct in the closing hour is as lofty as when with full ranks, you struck and exulted in victory. Take with you, soldiers, in parting, the unfeigned admiration of my heart.[41]

Conclusion

Reflections on the Irish Rebels

"Strange people, these Irish! Fighting everyone's battles, and cheerfully taking the hot end of the poker."
— *Maj. Gen. Richard Taylor*

Looking back on it now, from a distance of thirteen decades, it is a marvel that any men could have traveled that incredible odyssey of the 6th Louisiana from Camp Moore in Louisiana to Appomattox Court House in Virginia. None of them could have known, in that hopeful Confederate springtime of 1861, what they would have to endure to reach the end of that road, in the hopeless spring of 1865. Many of them signed up for a summertime lark, only to find they were harnessed to the war-horses of hell. And yet they struggled on, duty-bound and honor-bound, when only duty and honor remained, when victory was a fading memory and defeat was the inevitable future.

Many of them fell with honor on the battlefields, but many others lost heart and fell out along the road of war. The record of the 6th Louisiana is a bittersweet story of glory and honor, of despair and disgrace. The Civil War was a struggle of heroic proportions which drew out and enlarged the human qualities of the men who fought it, magnifying both their strengths and their weaknesses. The 6th Louisiana produced heroic leaders in men such as Isaac Seymour and William Monaghan, just as it produced a coward in Nathaniel Offutt and a turncoat in John Conley. In the ranks, it boasted hundreds of men willing to charge headlong into the guns at Port Republic or Malvern Hill or Gettysburg, even as it harbored scores of others who would desert rather than face the danger or endure the suffering.

For suffering and sacrifice, consider the case of young Allan S. Nethery. A 21-year-old blacksmith in the Mississippi River town of

Waterproof, Louisiana, Nethery joined the Tensas Rifles in the spring of 1861. Private Nethery went to Virginia with the 6th Louisiana and was wounded in the hip at the First Battle of Winchester on May 25, 1862. After he recovered, the private returned to duty in time for the Battle of Chantilly on September 1, 1862, where he was wounded seriously a second time. Returning to the regiment in May 1863, he fought through the Gettysburg Campaign only to be wounded a third time at Mine Run on November 30. By the spring of 1864, Nethery was well enough to fight at the Battle of the Wilderness, where he was captured. As a prisoner, he spent three months at Point Lookout, Maryland, before being transferred in August to the notorious Federal prison camp at Elmira, New York, where he passed a brutal winter. Released as a sick man in February 1865, he was sent to a Richmond hospital with smallpox in March. On March 31, ten days before Robert E. Lee surrendered at Appomattox Court House, Allan Nethery died at the age of 25.[1]

Like Private Nethery, scores of men in the regiment suffered through months of captivity in Federal prisons. Some men were imprisoned two or three times during the war. The compiled service records of the 6th Louisiana reveal at least 17 men who died in Federal prisons, and numerous others who died not long after being released, victims of the deprivations they had suffered. Pvt. John W. Murphy of the Mercer Guards was captured three times—at Fredericksburg, Rappahannock Station, and finally at the Wilderness—and survived two stretches in prisons before dying as a POW at Point Lookout, Md., in July 1864. Pvt. James Kelly, an Irishman in the Tensas Rifles, drowned in 1862 while attempting to escape from Fort Delaware, a man-made island in the Delaware River south of Wilmington, Deleware. Private Henry P. Tracy, a Northern-born Irishman captured at Gettysburg, received a serious stab wound to the abdomen attempting to escape Fort Delaware in 1864, and retired to the Invalid Corps.[2]

It would ill-serve the memory of these men either to gild the glory that they earned or to whitewash the disgrace that some brought on the regiment by cowardice and desertion. The statistics summarizing what happened to the 6th Louisiana over the course of those four horrendous years suggest the dimensions of both. A total of 1,146 men were enrolled in the 6th Louisiana during the war, according to an official state tally published in 1890. Of that total, the report listed 219, or 19%, killed in battle—just under one in five. Another 104 men died of disease or other non-combat causes, five were killed accidentally, one drowned and one—

the infamous John Conley—was executed for desertion. Thus, 330 men died while serving in the regiment, a 29 percent fatality rate.[3]

To compile a full roster of the 6th Louisiana, I reviewed the service records of every man in the regiment on the microfilmed files at the National Archives. More than 1,250 soldier's files were carefully examined. Some names were discarded when it appeared that they never actually served with the 6th Louisiana, as was the case with many 1862 bounty jumpers, who signed a recruiting muster roll (and thus are in the archived files) but never showed up for service. Discarding such cases, I found 1,215 men whose service, however brief or lengthy, could be verified.

Based on these 1,215 records—considerably more than the adjutant general's count of 1890—I was able to verify that 180 men were killed or mortally wounded in battle. The higher official count of 219 may be accurate but the records no longer exist to confirm it. The rate of battle deaths among the 10 companies of the regiment shows some interesting variations. The two companies with the highest fatality rates in battle were Company K, with 23 out of 125 men killed (18.4%), and Company G with 20 out of 109 (18.3%). These companies were dominated by immigrants—Germans in G, Irish in K. The lowest rates of battle deaths were found in two companies dominated by American-born men—only 7 of 90 men (7.7%) in Company E and 10 of 104 men in Company D (9.6%) were killed. Perhaps not too much should be made of this, but it does suggest that the Irish and German immigrants of the regiment more than equally shared in the bloody sacrifice of war.

As for desertions, there were many, though it is difficult to pin down an exact number. For his study of the two Louisiana brigades in the Army of Northern Virginia, Historian Terry Jones counted the number of desertions for each regiment, as recorded in the regimental record rolls housed at Tulane University. Jones tallied 232 desertions in the 6th Louisiana, a number far higher than he found for any of the other seven regiments for which desertions are recorded. The others ranged from a low of 53 desertions in the 7th Louisiana, to 130 in the 15th Louisiana.[4]

My own tally of desertions in the regiment, based on the service records of 1,215 men, found 269 who were recorded as deserters, or 22 percent of the total. By company, desertion rates ranged from a low of about 13 percent in Company A, the country soldiers from Union and Sabine parishes, to a high of 41 percent in Company E, the Mercer Guards from New Orleans. Although about one-third of Company E's men were foreign born (considerably less than five other companies), it had the highest percentage of men born in the North—about one-fourth of the company—and this mix of transplanted Northerners and foreigners produced the regiment's highest desertion rate.

In general, desertion rates were highest in the companies with large numbers of foreign-born members, who may have felt less attachment to the Southern cause than men born in the Confederacy. Some disaffected 6th Louisiana men deserted, while others apparently allowed themselves to be captured by the enemy and then took the oath of allegiance to the United States to escape the war. For this reason, the best measure of the desertion problem involves combining the statistics for outright desertions with those for men who took the oath after capture. For the regiment as a whole, the combined desertion/oath tally is 368, or just over 30% of the total. The companies that stand out with higher-than-average rates by this combined tally had high proportions of immigrants and transplanted Northerners. Nearly 45% of Company E's members abandoned the war by desertion or oath, closely followed by 43% of the mostly-German Pemberton Rangers, Company G. As for the predominantly Irish companies, Company I led with a rate of nearly 38%, Company F followed at 35%, and Company B recorded a 32% combined desertion/oath rate. On the other end of the scale, only 15% of Company A's men and 18% of Company C's soldiers abandoned their comrades.

Whatever the exact numbers, desertion was a problem in the regiment. Major Manning took note of the issue in writing his brief historical memos of various companies which he composed at Petersburg near the end of the war. In his memo about Company E, he wrote: "This roll contains a black list of Deserters but still it only shows to more advantage the few (though not many) that did stand by the cause they vollenteered to support through all misfortunes and all disasters."[5]

The numerous desertions, however, do not subtract an ounce of glory from the great majority in the regiment who marched, fought, bled and died in more than 25 major battles and dozens of other actions and skirmishes during four years of war. In terms of impact on significant events, the 6th Louisiana can fairly be credited with an important role in Jackson's Valley Campaign of 1862—particularly at its climactic battle at Port Republic. In 1863, at the Second Battle of Winchester, the charge of the 6th Louisiana and her sister regiments in Harry Hays' Brigade was the key to victory for Generals Early and Ewell. In 1864, the regiment stood firm under Col. William Monaghan at Spotsylvania to help stem the tide of the massive Federal breakthrough of May 12 at the

Bloody Angle. From First Manassas to Antietam, from Gettysburg to the Wilderness, from Cedar Creek to Petersburg, the 6th Louisiana was in the thick of the fight. Their itinerary is a road map to the entire war in the East Theater, step-by-step from the first clash to the last.

That so many of these men were foreign-born makes their story of endurance and sacrifice all the more remarkable. It is hard enough to understand how those born in the South, rooted in her soil and culture and traditions, could have toughed it out from the beginning to the end of this war. It is even more impressive that so many Irishmen, and not a few Germans and others who were immigrants, trod that same road in lockstep with men born in the South.

The Irish of the 6th Louisiana were mostly common men, rough men, not well educated and not much inclined toward debating the great moral and political questions that the Civil War presented to the country. They held no love for the black man, with whom they competed for jobs in the pre-war years, but on the other hand they had no stake in slavery. A great many of them were not even citizens and had no right to vote when the war began, and thus could have declared alien status and avoided service—as indeed some immigrants did. But these Irishmen volunteered to fight, and earned a reputation as cheerful, willing fighters who would, as General Taylor testified, "follow their officers to the death."

One of the many paradoxes of the Civil War is the fact that so many Irish fought with such conviction and passion for both sides, North and South. Their courage in battle and their endurance under hardship were well-noted on both sides of the line, and stood out after the war in the memories of Union and Confederate generals. Shortly after the war, John Francis Maguire, a member of the British Parliament from Ireland, traveled North and South gathering material for his study on the Irish in America, including their role in the Civil War. His observations, based on talking with many veterans of the blue and gray, including several generals who led them, help explain the paradox of Irish attachment to both the Union and the Confederacy.

North and South, the Irish attached themselves and gave their loyalty to the community which took them in and gave them a new start as Americans. As Maguire observed, "they acted, as they felt, with the community amid whom they lived, and with whom their fortunes were identified. The feeling was the same on both sides of the line. The Irish in the South stood with the state to which, as they believed, they owed their first allegiance, and, as was the case in the North, they caught the spirit of the community of whom they formed part."[6]

The Irish took to heart the sentiments of the majority of the people with whom they lived. "The Northern Irishman went into the war for the preservation of the Union—the Southern Irishman for the independence of his State," according to Maguire. The northern Irishman, he wrote, "could not comprehend how it was that the Southern Irishman. . .could possibly take up arms against the Union—against the Stars and Stripes—that 'terror of tyrants and hope of the oppressed.'" But in the same way, "the Southern Irishman could not reconcile it to his notions of consistency, that the very men who sought to liberate their native land from British thralldom should join with those who were doing their utmost to subjugate and trample under foot the liberties of a people fighting for their independence."[7]

Indeed, this perceived similarity between England's oppression of an Ireland yearning to be free, and the North's determination to keep the Southern states tied to a Union from which they sought to break, was a powerful parallel for the Irish of the South. It was easy for them to think of the Southern states' desire for independence as comparable to Ireland's centuries-old quest for freedom, and the North's policy of military suppression of their rebellion as no different from England's armed oppression of the Irish.

In fact, that was a common view of the American situation from Ireland at the time. An example of that viewpoint appeared in the *Daily True Delta*, a newspaper in New Orleans identified with the city's Irish community, in the early weeks of the war. The newspaper reprinted an article from the *Dublin Nation* of July 20, 1861, which argued in outraged tones that Lincoln's national government was acting just as Europe's monarchs and despots had always acted in suppressing the "rebellion" of the Southern states. "Well may we despair of popular liberty in the presence of the sight the world sees today" in America, the Dublin journal commented. "A republican people, whose liberties were won by a rebellion, whose independence was snatched by a secession, parrot as glibly as any minions of Old World tyranny 'the rebels' and 'the rebellion' as phrases of reproach! Those who profess to hold sacred the popular will, to reverence the desire for self-government, proceeding to drown the popular will in blood, and to answer the desire for self-government by butchery and slaughter!" The South had a stronger case justifying secession than the American colonies had in rebelling from Britain, the

Dublin journal argued, because the states of the Confederacy were sovereign and independent, not mere colonies of a distant empire. "We say that. . .this bloody war to force union on the southern people at the point of the sword—to saber them into brotherhood, and dragoon them into 'liberty!' is a blot upon humanity."[8]

Such sentiment appealed strongly to the Irish in the Confederacy, who also fought to prove themselves worthy citizens. "Foreigners and aliens they would have proved themselves to be, had they stood coldly aloof, or shown themselves insensible to the cause which stirred the heart of the nation to its depths," Maguire wrote. "They vindicated their citizenship not alone by their services, but by their sympathies, and in their terrible sacrifices." The Irish preferred to fight alongside their own countrymen, and thus tended to join regiments composed of their own kind, Maguire noted. They reveled in their identification as Irishmen, whether it was with the 69th New York of the Union army or the 6th Louisiana of the Confederate. The Irishman fought, Maguire contended, not only "to maintain the honor of his regiment, but also to maintain the honor of his country; for if he fought as an American citizen, he also fought as an Irish exile." Besides the "natural love of a fight that seems inherent in the Irish blood," this sense of upholding the honor of Irishmen as soldiers helps explain "the desperate courage displayed on every occasion where they were engaged." Whether it was the Federal Irish Brigade storming Marye's Heights at Fredericksburg, or the Irish of the 6th Louisiana charging the guns at Port Republic or East Cemetery Hill at Gettysburg, the Irish soldier was driven to courage and sacrifice by a desire to bring honor and respect to his race.[9]

The Irish fought with abandon and won plaudits from their generals for their courage, their cheerfulness, their endurance and their loyalty. During his post-war travels, Maguire spoke with a Confederate general who, he said, "commanded a Southern brigade, in which half. . .were Irish." On the quality of the Irish as soldiers, he quotes the general as follows:

> If tomorrow I wanted to win a reputation, I would have Irish soldiers in preference to any others, and I tell you why. First, they have more dash, more elan than any other troops that I know of; then they are more cheerful and enduring—nothing can depress them. Next, they are more cleanly. The Irishman never failed to wash himself and his clothes. Not only were they cheerful, but they were submissive to discipline when broken in—and where they had good officers that was easily done; but once they had

> confidence in their officers, their attachment to them was unbounded. And confidence was established the moment they saw their general in the fight with them. . . .They required strict discipline; but they always admitted the justice of their punishment when they believed their commander was impartial. . .There was one great element of strength in these men—they were volunteers, every man of them. Many could have been excused on the ground of their not being American citizens, as not more than one-third of them had a right to vote at the time; but they joined of their own free will—no Irishman was conscripted. I repeat, if I had to take from one to 10,000 men to make a reputation with, I'd take the same men as I had in the war—Irishmen from the city, the levees, the river, the railroads, the canals, or from ditching and fencing on the plantations. They make the finest soldiers that ever shouldered a musket."[10]

It is unfortunate that Maguire did not identify the Southern general by name. If the quote and the description of the general's troops are accurate, such a statement hardly could have been made by anyone but a general commanding the Louisiana Irish, such as Harry Hays or Richard Taylor. His description of the men who fought for him—"the Irish from the city, the levees, the river, the railroads, the canals, or from ditching and fencing on the plantations"—perfectly describes the Irish immigrants of Louisiana. It fits the 6th Louisiana like a glove, and as a tribute to the quality of the regiment's Irish fighters, it is unmatched.

I realized during the course of researching and writing this work, that there is something quintessentially Irish about the Confederate cause. The Irish are intimately familiar with hopeless fights for independence. Theirs was a Lost Cause for four centuries—a history of failed attempts to achieve independence from an oppressive English government. Fighting for glory, even for martyrdom, when there was little or no hope of winning was a long-standing tradition of the Irish, who would fight simply because not to fight meant to submit, and that was worse than death.

Two Civil War scholars have tried to make the case that the essential cultural difference between the North and the South was one of ethnicity. "Yankee culture was in large part transplanted English culture; southern culture was Celtic—Scottish, Scotch-Irish, Welsh, Cornish, and Irish," Grady McWhiney and Perry D. Jamieson write *Attack and Die*, their provocative study of Civil War military tactics and the Southern heritage. They cite the Anglo-Saxon and Teutonic qualities that charactertized the Northern approach to war—an emphasis on organization, order, discipline and commercial superiority, in contrast with the Celtic qualities that characterized the Southern side—an aggressive penchant for attack, a romantic attachment to the land and to a sacred cause, a boldness bordering on reckless abandon.[11]

Such was the Celtic way of waging war for 2,000 years against the Romans, Anglo-Saxons and others, according to McWhiney and Jamieson. Rebellion was a way of life for the Irish and the Scots; they fought fiercely if not wisely, usually against overwhelming odds. So too did the Celtic Southerners of 1861-65. "From the war's outset the Confederates fought in the traditionally Celtic way: they attacked." Attacking strongly defended positions, such as at Gettysburg, reflected Celtic recklessness, the two authors argued. They concluded:

> Southerners lost the Civil War because they were too Celtic and their opponents were too English. The distinguished historian of the war's common soldiers, Bell I. Wiley, concluded that in many ways Johnny Reb and Billy Yank were quite different. Rebels fought 'with more dash, elan and enthusiasm'; they were more emotional, more religious, more humorous and poetical, says Wiley. They also had a more 'acute sense of the ludicrous, the dramatic or the fanciful.' Yanks, on the other hand, were more practical, more materialistic, more literate, and they displayed 'more of tenacity, stubbornness en masse and machinelike efficiency'. . . .All of the differences that Wiley recognized are cultural characteristics that separated not merely the Rebels and Yankees but Celts and their historic enemies from antiquity to the American Civil War."[12]

All of this suggests that the Irishmen of the 6th Louisiana must have felt at home fighting for the Confederacy. They were rebels at heart, romantics by tradition, fighters by heritage. They were Irish by blood, but Americans by bloodshed—exultant in victory, unbroken in defeat, enduring to the end.

Illustration by Thomas Tepper

Storming the Breastworks

Appendix A: Roster

Field & Staff

The 6th Louisiana Volunteers were commanded by three colonels during the war, and all three were killed in battle—a distinction few Civil War regiments could match. The field and staff officers of the regiment were a diverse lot. Seven were foreign-born: four from Ireland, one each from France, Germany and Scotland. Five were native Louisianians, but they were outnumbered by five from other Confederate states and four born in states in the North. Birthplaces of four others are not known. During the war, four of the officers listed below were killed in battle, six resigned their commissions, five were transferred out of the regiment, two were discharged, one retired to the Invalid Corps and three—Major Manning, Assistant Surgeon Watford and Ensign Geiger—surrendered with General Lee's army at Appomattox Court House on April 9, 1965. The regiment's Field and Staff Officers are listed below in order of rank and seniority.

This roster of the 6th Louisiana Volunteers was assembled through a careful review of the microfilmed Compiled Service Records of the regiment held at the National Archives in Washington, D.C. The great majority of the information presented herein is derived from the individual soldiers' files on the eleven rolls of microfilm for the 6th Louisiana Infantry, in Record Group 109, File M320, Compiled Service Records of Confederate Soldiers Who Served in Organizations from the State of Louisiana, Rolls 163 through 173.

These records are far from complete, and certainly are not without many errors and omissions, but they are the best records available. Many other sources of information were used to supplement the microfilmed service records. The author examined all the original muster rolls of the regiment that are preserved at the National Archives, as well as the record rolls of the 6th Louisiana kept at the Howard-Tilton Library at Tulane University. Additional information was derived from various sources, including cemetery records, private collections of documents held by descendants of 6th Louisiana officers and soldiers, and state of Louisiana records, including widow's proofs and soldier's proofs of service under state legislation granting land warrants to Civil War veterans.

The aim of this roster is to present a capsule look at the service record of each member of the regiment. Some of the individual soldier's files are quite detailed and complete, others sketchy and incomplete. Where such information was available, the individual entries include name, rank, date of enlistment, promotions and significant details of the man's war experience—any record of being killed, wounded, captured, imprisoned, discharged, or of transfer, retirement, resignation or death. Biographical information—place of birth, occupation, residence, age, marital status, is given when recorded. The age listed is usually the soldier's age at enlistment. Physical descriptions—height, hair and eye color, complexion, etc.—were found for some but not all of the men. For most men, the records cite date of enlistment as June 4 or 5, 1861, when the 6th Louisiana was formed at Camp Moore, La., though most men actually enrolled in an individual company a few days or weeks earlier.

In format, each entry gives name, rank and enlistment first, then significant details of service. The soldier's presence or absence with the regiment is indicated in muster rolls within the file. These are summarized in the entries. "Present to 6/62," for example, means the soldier was present on all available muster rolls up to June, 1862. Absent wounded, 9-12/62, means the soldier was away from the regiment due to wounds (usually hospitalized) from some time in September 1862 to some time in December of that year. Hospital records are cited where they give significant details of a wounding or illness, or date and cause of death, or length of hospitalization.

Abbreviations are used throughout the roster. Dates are abbreviated, so that 6/4/61 means June 4, 1861. Standard abbreviations for ranks (Pvt. for Private, Sgt. for Sergeant, etc.) are used. The rank cited with the name of each soldier is normally the highest rank attained during his service. Spelling of names is a problem. The files of any individual soldier may contain several spellings of his name. The spelling used in this roster is the one under which his service records are filed, except where there is evidence (such as a written signature) that makes it clear another spelling is the correct one. Records of soldiers with common names — in this regiment, the Murphys, Ryans, and Sullivans as well as the Smiths — are often misfiled under the name of another. The author has sorted these out to the extent possible, but some confusion and conflict remains in a few cases.

Key to Abbreviations:

En.: Enlistment date.
CM: Camp Moore, La.
Occ.: Occupation at enlistment.
Res.: Residence at enlistment
N.O.: New Orleans
La.: Louisiana
POW: Prisoner of war.
Hosp.: Hospital.
Cem.: Cemetery

Seymour, Isaac Gurdon, Col. Commissioned by Gov. T.O. Moore, 5/21/61. En. 6/4/61, CM, as col. Present to 6/62. Killed at Gaines' Mill, Va., while commanding 1st La. Brigade, 6/27/62. Born: Savannah, Ga. (1804). Occ.: Newspaper editor. Res.: N.O. Age 56, married. Buried at Rose Hill Cem., Macon, Ga.

Strong, Henry B., Capt./Col. En. 6/5/61, CM, as capt. of Co. B. Elected lt. col., 5/8/62. Appointed col., 8/16/62, to take rank from 6/27/62. Present to 2/62. Detailed to recruiting in N.O., 2-3/62. Present, 4-9/62. Killed at Sharpsburg, Md., 9/17/62. Born: Ireland. Occ.: Clerk. Res.: N.O. Age 40, married. Buried in Washington Confederate Cem., Hagerstown, Md.

Monaghan, William, Col. Commissioned by Gov. T.O. Moore as captain of Irish Brigade Company B, 5/8/61. Enrolled as captain of Company F, 6th Louisiana, 6/4/61, CM. Present to 6/62. Captured at Strasburg, Va., 6/2/62. POW, Old Capitol Prison, Washington, exchanged 8/5/62. Promoted to major, 6/27/62. Wounded at Chantilly, Va., 9/1/62. Absent wounded, 9-10/62. Promoted to colonel, 11/7/62. Present 11/62 to 6/64. Absent sick, 6-7/64. Present, 8/64. Killed near Shepherdstown, Va. [W.Va.], 8/25/64. Born: Ireland. Occ.: Notary Public. Res.: N.O. Age 44, married. Buried in Elmwood Cem., Shepherdstown, W.Va.

Lay, Louis, Lt. Col. En. 6/4/61, CM. Present to 2/62. Resigned 2/21/62, at Camp Carondolet, (Manassas) Va. Born: France. Occ: Cotton classer. Res.: N.O. Age 40, married.

Offutt, Nathaniel G., Lt. Col. Commissioned by Gov. T.O. Moore as captain of St. Landry Light Guards, 4/23/61. Enrolled in 6th Louisiana, 6/4/61, CM. Wounded at Winchester, Va., 5/25/62. Promoted to major, 5/27/62, following death of Maj. Arthur McArthur Jr. Promoted to lt. col., upon promotion of Henry Strong to col., 6/27/62. Present to 8/62. Admitted to Genl. Hosp. No 2., Lynchburg, Va., 8/11/62. On list of officers AWOL from Ewell's Div., 9/22/62. Submitted letter of resignation from Lynchburg, 10/5/62. Resignation effective 11/7/62. Record dated 3/13/65 at Petersburg states: "Resigned under charges of cowardice." Born: La. Occ.: Planter. Res.: Washington, La. Age 30, single.

Hanlon, Joseph, Lt. Col. En. 5/3/61, N.O., as 1st lt. of Irish Brigade Company A. Enrolled in 6th Louisiana and promoted to captain of Company I, 6/5/61, CM. Present to 5/62. Severely wounded and captured at Winchester, Va., 5/25/62. POW, Baltimore, Md., exchanged 8/5/62. Promoted to major, 9/17/62. Promoted to lt. col., 11/7/62. Captured at Fredericksburg, Va., 4/29/63. POW, Old Capitol Prison, Washington, paroled 5/18/63. Present, 7-8/63. Absent sick, 9/63 to 5/64. Wounded at Cold Harbor, Va., 6/2/64. Present, 7-10/64. Captured at Strasburg, Va., [Battle of Cedar Creek] 10/19/64. POW, Fort Delaware, Del., released 7/20/65. Born: Ireland. Occ.: Reporter. Res.: N.O. Age 28, married, 5'7", hazel eyes, brown hair, fair complexion. Died 7/3/90. N.O.

James, Samuel L., Maj. En. 6/4/61, CM., as captain of Company I. Appointed major, 6/5/61. Resigned 12/1/61. Born: Tennessee. Occ.: Engineer. Res.: N.O. Age 35, married.

Christy, George W., Maj. Commissioned by Gov. T.O. Moore as 1st Lt., Pemberton Rangers, 5/9/61. En. 6/4/61, CM, as 1st lt., Company G. Elected major, 11/22/61. Record dated 3/15/65 at Petersburg states: "Did not present his name for re-election at reorg. in May 1862 and now retains his rank as Maj. of Artillery." Born: La. Occ.: Lawyer. Res.: N.O. Age 40, married.

McArthur, Arthur Jr., Maj. En. 6/4/61, CM, as captain of Company A, Union and Sabine Rifles. Elected major, 5/9/62. Killed at Winchester, Va., 5/25/62. Born: Connecticut. Occ.: Planter. Res.: Union Parish. Age 35, single.

Manning, William H., Maj. Enrolled as captain of Company K, 6/4/61, CM. Promoted to major, 11/7/62. Present to 6/63. Wounded at Winchester, Va., 6/14/63. Absent wounded, 6-10/63. Admitted to CSA Hosp., Charlottesville, Va., 7/4/63, returned to duty 10/14/63. Present, 10-12/63. Admitted CSA Hosp., Charlottesville, 12/26/63, returned to duty, 1/27/64, chronic rheumatism. Present, 1-5/64. Captured at Wilderness, Va., 5/5/64. POW, Fort Delaware, Del., transferred to Hilton Head, S.C., 6/21/64. Present, commanding regiment, 10/64 to 4/65. Surrendered at Appomattox C.H., 4/9/65. Born: New York. Occ.: Cooper. Res.: N.O. Age 23, married. Died 8/3/80, N.O.

Graham, Lewis, Lt., Adjutent. En. 6/4/61, CM, in Company H. Appointed adjutent, 6/4/61, CM. Promoted from 2nd lt. to 1st lt., 7/17/62. Resigned, 11/7/62. Residence: N.O.

Orr, John, Lt., Adjutent En. 6/4/61, CM, as jr. lt., Company F. Promoted to 2nd lt., 6/27/62. Promoted to 1st lt. and adjutent, 11/26/62. Wounded at Sharpsburg, Md., 9/17/62. Absent wounded, 9-10/62. Present 11/62 to 6/63. Wounded at Winchester, Va., 6/14/63. Absent wounded, 7-8/63. Present, 9-11/63. Captured at Rappahannock Station, Va., 11/7/63. POW, Johnson's Island, Sandusky, Ohio, transferred to Point Lookout, Md., 3/14/65. Born: Ireland. Occ.: Clerk. Res.: N.O. Age 21, single.

McKelvey, P. Beckman, Surgeon. En. 6/4/61, CM. Present to 1/62. Resigned, 1/20/62. Occ.: M.D. Res.: N.O.

Robertson, William A., Surgeon. En. 6/4/61, CM, as pvt. in Company C. Promoted to asst. surgeon, 7/61.Promoted to surgeon, 1/20/62. Present to 10/63. Absent sick, 10/63 to 4/64. Roll for 3-4/64 states: "Assigned to duty in Georgia and dropped April 29, 1864." Assigned to Lee Hosp., Columbus, Ga. Born: La. Occ.: M.D. Res.: St. Landry Parish. Married.

Todd, Charles H., Surgeon. Appointed asst. surg., 12/4/62. Present on rolls, 3/63 to 1/64. Absent on furlough, 1-2/64. Promoted to surgeon, 2/25/64. Present to 7/64. Captured at Frederick, Md., after Battle of Monocacy, 7/10/64. Admitted to USA Gen. Hosp., Frederick, Md., 7/10/64, transferred to Baltimore, 7/30/64, transferred to Fort Delaware, Del., released 8/8/64. Record dated 3/13/65 at Petersburg states: "Transferred to Pegram's Brigade." Born: Kentucky. Occ.: M.D.

Hunter, Andrew, Asst. Surgeon. Date of commission: 9/11/61. Wounded at Winchester, Va., 5/25/62. Present to 11/62. AWOL, 11-12/62. Dropped from rolls by order of Sec. of War, 1/63. Born: Virginia. Occ.: M.D. Res.: Virginia.

Traylor, F.M., Asst. Surgeon. En. 6/4/61, CM, as cpl. in Co. A. Present to 12/62. Present as hospital steward, 1-2/63. Promoted to asst. surgeon, 3/3/63. Killed at Fredericksburg, Va., 5/4/63. Occ.: M.D. Res.: Union Parish, La.

Watford, William B., Asst. Surgeon. Assigned to 6th La., 5/15/63. Present to 7/63. Roll for 7-8/63 states: "Left in charge of wounded at Hagerstown, Md., July 1863." Captured at Williamsport, Md., 7/14/63. POW at Harrisburg, Pa., transferred to Fort Delaware, Del., 8/16/63, exchanged 11/23/63. Absent on furlough, 11-12/63. Present, 1/64 to 4/65. Surrendered at Appomattox C.H., 4/9/65. Born: North Carolina. Occ.: M.D. Res.: North Carolina.

Heard, T.R. Quarter Master. No enlistment data recorded. Present on 1861 rolls. Transferred to Trans-Mississippi Department, date unknown. Occ.: Merchant. Res.: N.O.

Shaw, Franklin, Capt./Asst. Quarter Master. No enlistment record. Roster of commissioned officers, undated, states: "Dropped Feb. 24, 1862." Record dated 3/13/65 at Petersburg states: "Resigned in 1861."

Reed, Isaac, Capt./Asst. Q.M. En. 6/4/61, CM, as jr. 2nd lt., in Company D. Elected 1st lt., 10/9/61. Promoted to asst. quarter master, 11/18/62. Present to 7/62. Absent sick, 7-11/62. Present, 12/62 to 7/63. Captured at Gettysburg, 7/4/63. POW, Fort Delaware, Del., 7/10/63, transferred to Johnson's Island, Sandusky, Ohio, 7/18/63, exchanged 3/14/65. Born: La. Occ.: Clerk. Res.: St. Joseph, La.

Gruber, John F., Capt./Asst. Q. M. Promoted from 7th La. Regt., to Asst. Q.M., 6th La., 12/19/63 at Orange C.H., Va. Present to 9/64. Absent on detached service in La., after 9/64. Born: Germany. Occ.: Clerk. Res.: N.O.

Jackson, N. Hart, Sgt. Major. En. 6/4/61, CM, in Co. E. Appointed Sgt. Major, 6/61. Present to 6/62. Discharged on medical certificate of disability, 6/23/62, disease of eyes. Born: Charleston, S.C. Occ.: Clerk. Res.: N.O. Age 25, 5'7", dark eyes, black hair, dark complexion.

Butler, Benjamin R., Sgt. Maj. En. 6/4/61, CM, in Co. C. as pvt. Appointed sgt. maj., 7/15/62. Present to 9/62. Discharged on surgeon's certificate due to gunshot wound in thigh, 9/26/62. Born: La. Occ.: Engineer. Res.: Washington, La. Single.

Tobin, John, Sgt. Maj. En. 6/4/61, CM, as 1st sgt., Co. E. Promoted to sgt. maj., 11/7/62. Present to 9/64. Wounded and captured at Winchester, Va., 9/19/64. Admitted USA Field Depot Hosp., Winchester, 9/19/64, wound in left side perforating intestines and splintering lumbar vertebra. Transferred to Baltimore, Md., POW, Fort McHenry, Md., transferred to Point Lookout, Md., 2/20/65. Retired to Invalid Corps at Osyka, Miss., 3/9/65. Born: Pennsylvania. Occ.: Clerk. Res.: N.O. Age 22, single.

Campbell, John G., Commissary Sgt. En. 6/4/61, CM, as 2nd sgt. Promoted to regimental commissary sgt., 7/27/61. Present to brigade commissary sgt., 12/61. Wounded at Wilderness, Va., 5/5/64. Record dated 3/13/65 at Petersburg states: "This officer is not expected to go into action, being Brigade C.S., was promoted from the ranks." Born: Scotland. Res.: N.O. Age 28, single.

Gaisser, Godfrey, Ensign. (aka Gaizer) En. 2/21/62, N.O. Present to 11/63. Captured at Rappahannock Station, Va. 11/7/63. POW, Point Lookout, Md., exchanged 3/10/64. Present, 5/64 to 4/65. Promoted from pvt. to cpl., 2/1/63. Promoted to ensign, 11/26/64. Surrendered at Appomattox C.H., 4/9/65. Born: N.O. Occ.: Clerk. Res.: N.O. Age 19, single.

Company A: Union and Sabine Rifles

One of the three companies of the 6th Louisiana recruited from outside of New Orleans, Company A was composed of men from Union and Sabine Parishes. Of the 120 men who served in the company, 16 were killed or mortally wounded in battle, 30 died of disease, 13 were discharged, 16 deserted, two were captured and took the oath of allegiance to the U.S., two retired to the Invalid Corps, and 11 surrendered at Appomattox Court House. The record roll for the company does not give place of birth, residence, occupation or age of enlistment. Birthplaces are unknown for 112 men of the company, though it is likely that the majority were native Louisianians. Among those whose birthplaces are recorded, one was a native of Louisiana, five were from other Confederate states, and two from Union states.

Captains:

McArthur, Arthur Jr., Capt., Major. En. 6/4/61, CM. Elected major, 5/9/62. Present to 5/62. Killed at Winchester, Va., 5/25/62. Born: Connecticut. Occ.: Planter. Res.: Union Parish. Age 35, single.
Callaway, Allen M., Lt./Capt. En. 6/4/61, CM, as 1st lt. Present to 5/62. Elected captain 5/8/62, upon election of Arthur McArthur to major. Killed at Sharpsburg, 9/17/62. Born: Alabama. Occ.: Sheriff of Union County. Res.: Farmerville, La. Age 32, married.
Phillips, Joseph F., Lt./Capt. En. 6/4/61, CM, as 2nd lt. Present to 12/62. Promoted to 1st lt., 5/8/62. Promoted to capt., 9/17/62, upon death of Allen M. Callaway. Absent sick, 1-2/63. Absent furloughed, 3-4/63. Present, 5-10/63. Absent furloughed, 11-12/63. AWOL, 1-2/64. Present, 3-4/64. Roll for 5-8/64 states: "Retired from duty." Inspection report dated 10/31/64 states: "Appeared before Med. Board for retirement." Admitted Genl. Hosp. No. 4, Richmond, 11/18/64, furloughed to residence in Forestville, N.C., 12/2/64, chronic rheumatism. Retired to Invalid Corps., 12/7/64.

* * *

Archer, Henry, Pvt. En. 6/4/61, CM. Absent sick at Louisiana Hosp., Richmond, 10/61. On roll of sick and wounded, Camp Carondolet, Va., 2/62, chronic rheumatism. Discharged on surgeon's certificate, 2/1/62.
Ardry, R.D., Pvt. En. 6/4/61, CM. Present to 6/62. Recorded as deserted, 6/62.
Bath, Hyman, Pvt. En. 6/4/61, CM. Captured at Fredericksburg, Va., 4/29/63. POW, Old Capitol Prison, Washington, exchanged 6/3/63. Captured at Wilderness, Va., 5/5/64. POW, Elmira, N.Y., 8/15/64 to 2/20/65.
Beard, William, Sgt. En. 6/4/61, CM, as pvt. Present to 11/63. Captured at Rappahannock Station, Va., 11/7/63. POW, Point Lookout, Md., exchanged 3/9/64. Promoted to sgt., 4/1/64. Captured at Fisher's Hill, Va, 9/22/64. POW, Point Lookout, exchanged 2/10/65.
Bentley, Joseph, Pvt. En. 3/18/62, Union Parish. Present to 11/62. Absent sick in hospital, 11/62 to 2/63. Remarks: "Left at White Post, Va., sick. When last heard from about Nov. 15, 1862, he was in a dying condition." Age, 28.
Boatright, John, Pvt. En. 3/12/62, Union Parish. Died in hospital, Richmond, Va., 4/24/62.
Bolton, James H., Cpl. En. 6/4/61, CM. Discharged on certificate of disability, 8/10/62. Born: Sabine Parish. Occ.: Overseer. Age 34, 5' 8", fair complexion, blue eyes, dark hair.
Bolton, J.T., Cpl. En. 6/4/61, CM. Wounded at Sharpsburg, Md., 9/17/62. Absent wounded until 4/21/63. Captured at Wilderness, Va., 5/4/64. POW, Point Lookout, Md., transferred to Elmira, N.Y., 8/15/64. exchanged 10/24/64. Surrendered at Appomattox C.H., Va., 4/9/65. Age 29, 5' 9", dark complexion, blue eyes, dark hair. Res.: Union Parish.
Bradley, J., Pvt. En. 6/4/61, CM. Present on 1861 rolls. Absent on furlough, 3-4/62. No record thereafter.
Brantley, J.L., Pvt. En. 7/26/61, Union Mills, Va. Present to 11/61. Admitted to Chimborazo Hosp., Richmond, 11/11/61, typhoid fever. No record thereafter.
Brantley, G. W., Pvt. En. 6/4/61, CM. Present to 10/61. Died at regimental hospital near Centreville, Va., 10/1/61.
Briggs, James H., Pvt. En. 6/4/61, CM. Promoted to 5th sgt., 8/1/61. Present to 7/62. Detatched as regimental blacksmith, 7/17/62. Served as 6th La. blacksmith, 1863 and 1864. Captured at High Bridge, near Farmville, Va., 4/6/65. Surrendered at Appomattox C.H., 4/10/65. Res.: N. O. 5'8", blue eyes, fair complexion, dark hair.
Butt, Ed W., Pvt. En. 6/4/61, CM. Killed at Winchester, Va, 5/25/62.
Butt, James, Pvt. En. 3/18/62, Union Parish, La. Admitted to Chimborazo Hosp., Richmond, 4/21/62, cardiac disease. Discharged on certificate of medical disability, 6/24/62.
Cadell, W. B., Sgt. En. 6/4/61, CM. Present to 7/63. Captured at Gettysburg, 7/3/63. POW, Fort Delaware, Del. Died at Fort Delaware, 9/21/63, chronic diarrhea.

Caldwell, Robert, Pvt. En. 64/61,CM. Present to 10/61. Died at General Hosp., Culpeper, Va., 10/19/61, typhoid fever. Buried in Fairview Cem., Culpeper, Va.

Carson, G.W., Pvt. En. 3/7/62, Union Parish. Absent sick, 5-6/62. Present 9/62 to 4/63. Captured at Fredericksburg, Va., 4/29/63. POW, Point Lookout, Md., exchanged 6/3/63. Captured at Rappahannock Station, Va., 11/7/63. POW, Point Lookout, exchanged 3/10/64. Captured at Wilderness, Va., 5/5/64, POW, Point Lookout, transferred to Elmira, N.Y., 8/15/64, exchanged 2/25/65.

Carson, R. D., Pvt. En. 6/4/61, CM. Present to 4/63. Captured at Fredericksburg, Va., 4/29/63. POW, Old Capitol Prison, Washington, exchanged 6/3/63. Present to 2/64. Deserted from camp near Raccoon Ford, (Rapidan River), Va., 2/20/64.

Carter, Harry, Pvt. En. 6/4/61, CM. Present to 9/62. Captured at Frederick, Md., 9/12/62. Admitted to USA General Hosp., Frederick, Md., 9/18/62. POW, Fort Delaware, Del., exchanged 11/10/62. Present 1-4/63. Captured at Fredericksburg, Va., 4/29/63. POW, Old Capitol Prison, Washington, exchanged 6/3/63. Wounded at Winchester, Va., 6/14/63. Captured at Wilderness, Va, 5/4/64. POW at Point Lookout, Md. Died at POW camp hospital, Point Lookout, 7/23/64, acute dysentery.

Coley, J.F. Pvt. En. 6/4/61, CM. Died in hospital at Fairfax Station, Va., 7/6/61.

Cook, Thomas J., Pvt. En. 6/4/61, CM. Present to 9/62. Wounded at Sharpsburg, Md., 9/17/62. Admitted to CSA Hosp., Charlottesville, Va., 12/4/62, foot wound, furloughed 5/13/63. No record thereafter.

Cook, T.M., Pvt. En. 6/4/61, CM. Died at Camp Bienville, Centreville, Va., 8/3/61. Cause: "Unknown (suddenly.)"

Cook, Shaderick, Pvt.. En. 6/4/61, CM. Discharged on surgeon's certificate, 9/20/61, general debility from chronic diarrhea.

Corley, B.J., Pvt. En. 6/4/61, CM. Absent in hospital, 7-8/61. Present, 9-10/61. Admitted to CSA Hosp., Charlottesville, Va., 4/23/62, died 5/2/62, typhoid fever.

Corley, Joseph, Pvt. En. 3/7/62, Union Parish, La. Absent in hospital, 4-5/62. Died at Charlottesville, Va., 5/27/62, cause unstated.

Curtis, Isaiah, Cpl. En. 6/4/61, CM. Present to 9/62. Killed at Chantilly, Va., 9/1/62.

Curtis, John. J., Pvt. En. 6/4/61, CM. Present to 5/64. Absent on furlough, wounded (place unstated), 8/64. On roll of POWs of the 6th Louisiana Field Battery, Light Artillery, surrendered at New Orleans 5/26/65, paroled at Natchitoches, La., 6/6/65. Residence: Sabine Parish, La.

Davis, James, Pvt. En. 6/4/61, CM. Present, 7-8/61. Absent sick, Louisiana Hosp., Richmond, 8/61. Absent sick in hospital, 11/62 to 3/63. Present, 3/63 to 5/64. Captured at Wilderness, 5/4/64. POW, Point Lookout, Md., transferred to Elmira, N.Y., 8/15/64, paroled 3/10/65. Surrendered at Appomattox C.H., 4/9/65. Res.: Sabine Parish, La. Age 26. 5'11", blue eyes, dark hair, dark complexion.

Davis, T.L., Pvt. En. 3/7/62, Union Parish, La. Absent in hospital, 3-11/62. Present, 11-12/62. Absent in hospital, 1-2/63. Captured at Fredericksburg, 4/29/63. POW, Fort Delaware, Del., exchanged 6/3/63. Wounded at Winchester, 6/14/63. Present, 7-11/63. Captured at Rappahannock Station, Va., 11/7/63. POW, Point Lookout, Md., exchanged 3/10/64. Roll for 5-8/64 states: "Deserted 3/10/64."

Dean, J.A., Pvt. En. 6/4/61, CM. Present to 6/62. Wounded at Port Republic, Va., 6/9/62. Absent, wounded at home on extended furlough, 9/62 to 3/64. Deserted from furlough, 3/24/64.

Dickerson, S. T., Pvt. En. 3/7/62, Union Parish, La. Absent in hospital, 5/62 to 1/63. Present, 1-2/63. Absent in hospital, 3-4/63. Died at Lynchburg Gen. Hosp., 4/10/63, debility.

Demaign, Francis X., Sgt. En. 6/4/61, CM. Transferred from Company H by order of Col. Seymour, 7/1/61. Killed accidentally near Manassas, Va., 7/18/61. Roll for 7-8/61 states: "Killed by Miss. piquets on the morning of July 18 while making his way to his co., having been cut off 17 July while on piquet at Fairfax Station, Va."

Eichelberger, E. H., Sgt. En. 6/4/61, CM. Present to 9/62. Wounded at Chantilly, 9/1/62. Admitted to General Hosp. No. 21, Richmond, 10/5/62, gun shot wound, right shoulder blade. Absent, wounded, 9-12/62. Captured at Fredericksburg, Va., 4/29/63. POW, Old Capitol Prison, Washington, exchanged 6/3/63. Wounded at Winchester, 6/14/63. Captured at Rappahannock Station, Va., 11/7/63. POW, Point Lookout, Md., released on taking oath of allegiance, 3/30/64. Residence: Union Parish, La. Age 33, 5'8", blue eyes, black hair, dark complexion.

Feason, A.M., Pvt. En. 6/4/61, CM. Present to 10/62. Absent sick, 11/62 to 12/63. Roll for 1-2/64 states: "Deserted. Sent to hosp. in fall of 1862, has not returned since."

Fitz, H.S., Pvt. En. 3/20/62, Union Parish. Admitted to General Hosp., Orange C.H., Va., 4/3/62, fever. Absent in hospital 4/62 to 4/64. Roll for 3-4/64 states: "Supposed to be dead. At hospital since spring 1862."

Freeman, O.P., Pvt. En. 4/2/62, Union Parish. Captured at Fredericksburg, Va., 4/29/63. POW, Fort Delaware, Del., exchanged 6/3/63. Absent sick in hospital at Lynchburg, Va., 6-12/63. Present, 1-5/64. Captured at Wilderness, Va., 5/5/64. POW, Point Lookout, died 6/25/64.

Gaynus, J.G., Pvt. En. 6/4/61, CM. Present to 10/62. Recorded as deserted, 10/62.

Gilbert, A.H., Pvt. Transferred to 6th La. from the 3rd Arkanasas Battalion at Fredericksburg, 10/11/62. Present to 4/63. Captured at Fredericksburg, 4/29/63. POW, Old Capitol Prison, Washington, exchanged 6/3/63. Present to 5/64. Admitted to CSA Hosp., Richmond, 5/17/64, wound in lungs, died 5/26/64.

Gilbert, C.J., Pvt. En. 6/4/61, CM. Present to 2/62. Absent on sick furlough, 2/62. Roll for 6/63 states: "Absent at home on extended sick furlough. Left. Co. in Feby. 1862." Recorded as "deserted from furlough," 3/24/64.

Gilbert, J.R., Pvt. En. 6/4/61, CM. Present to 9/62. Wounded at Chantilly, Va., 9/1/62. Absent wounded, 9/62 to 2/63. Admitted to Howard's Grove Hosp., Richmond, 1/30/63, died 2/4/63, smallpox.

Gilbert, John S., Lt. En. 6/4/61, CM. Present to 3/62. Absent in hospital, 3-9/62. Present, 9/62 to 4/63. Captured at Fredericksburg, Va., 4/29/63. POW, Old Capitol Prison, Washington, exchanged 6/3/63. Present 6/63 to 1/64. AWOL, 1-2/64. Present, 3/64 to 4/65. Surrendered at Appomattox C.H., 4/9/65. Res: Union Parish. Age 30, 5'10", gray eyes, dark hair, dark complexion.

Gilbert, R.M., Pvt. En. 3/13/62, Union Parish. Present to 6/62. Wounded at Port Republic, Va., 6/9/62. Absent wounded, on furlough, 9/62 to 3/64. Recorded as "deserted from furlough," 3/24/64.

Gilbert, T.F., Cpl. En. 7/26/61, Union Mills, Va. Present to 4/63. Promoted to cpl., 12/1/62. Wounded at Fredericksburg, Va., 12/13/62. Captured at Fredericksburg, 4/29/63. POW, Old Capitol Prison, Washington, exchanged 6/3/63. Present 6/63 to 5/64. Captured at Spotsylvania C.H., 5/20/64. POW, Point Lookout, Md., transferred to Elmira, N.Y., 7/6/64, exchanged 2/25/65.

Gilbert, T.J., Sgt. En. 6/4/61, CM. Present to 9/62. Wounded at Sharpsburg, Md., 9/17/62. Absent in hospital, 9-12/62. Absent, detached as hospital ward master at Lynchburg, Va., 1/63 to 4/64. Present, 4/64 to 4/65. Surrendered at Appomattox C.H., 4/9/65. Age 30, 6'3", hazel eyes, dark hair, dark complexion.

Godwin, J.D.S., Pvt. En. 6/4/61, CM. Present to 4/63. Killed at Fredericksburg, Va., 4/29/63.

Goings, A.M., Pvt. En. 6/4/61, CM. Present to 9/62. Wounded and captured at Sharpsburg, Md., 9/18/62. POW, Fort McHenry, Md., exchanged 10/25/62. Discharged, 12/14/62.

Goldsby, H.K., Pvt. En. 6/26/61, Union Mills, Va. Present to 3/62. Absent in hospital, 3-4/62. Mortally wounded at Port Republic, Va., 6/9/62. Died in hospital at Lynchburg, Va., 6/22/62.

Goldsby, M.W., Pvt. En. 8/5/61, Centreville, Va. Present to 11/61. Discharged 11/25/61.

Gully, J.M., Pvt. En. 6/4/61, CM. Present to 9/62. Wounded at Chantilly, Va., 9/1/62. Absent wounded, on furlough, 9-10/62. Discharged due to disability caused by minie ball wound blinding right eye, 10/29/62.

Hays, W.A., Pvt. En. 3/7/62, Union Parish. Absent in hospital, 5/62 to 7/63. Present, 7/63 to 4/64. Absent on sick furlough, 5-9/64. No record thereafter.

Hayslip, C.C., Pvt. En. 6/4/61, CM. Present to 3/62. Absent in hospital 3-12/62. Absent on sick furlough, 1-2/63. Absent sick, 3-9/63. Present, 9-10/63. Absent sick, 11/63 to 6/64. Absent detailed to hospital as nurse, 6/27/64.

Heard, Charles A., Sgt. En. 6/4/61, CM, as sgt. Reduced to pvt., 8/3/61. Present, 9-10/61. Absent in hospital, 3-4/62. Discharged on surgeon's certificate of disability, 6/18/62, shortening of left leg. Born: Alabama. Occ.: Lawyer. Age 27.

Heath, George, Pvt. En. 3/15/62, Union Parish. Absent in hospital, 3-7/62. Present, 9/62 to 5/64. Captured at Wilderness, Va., 5/5/64. POW, Point Lookout, Md., transferred to Elmira, N.Y., 8/15/64, released on oath of allegiance, 6/27/64. Res.: Alabama Landing, La. 5'8", blue eyes, red hair, dark complexion.

Hodges, A.B., Pvt. Present to 8/61. Died at Camp Bienville, Centreville, Va., 8/20/61, gastric enteritis.

Hodges, Samuel B., Pvt. En. 6/4/61, CM. Present to 9/62. Absent sick in hospital, 9/62 to 6/63. Captured at Gettysburg, 7/4/63. POW at Baltimore, exchanged 8/23/63. Admitted to Gen. Hosp., Petersburg, 12/4/63, syphlis. On furlough, 1-2/64. Sick in Louisiana Hosp., Richmond, 2/64 to 4/65. Captured in hospital, 4/3/65. POW, Newport News, Va., released 6/16/65. Residence: Sabine Parish.

Honeycutt, Christopher, Pvt. En. 3/15/62, Union Parish. Absent sick, 4/62. Died in Banner Hosp., Richmond, 4/13/62, cause unstated.

Howard, John, Pvt. En. 6/4/61, CM. Present to 5/64. Captured at Wilderness, 5/5/64. POW, Point Lookout, transferred to Elmira, N.Y., 8/15/64, transferred to West Bldg. Hosp., Baltimore, Md., 2/15/65. POW, Fort McHenry, Md., 5/9/65 to 6/10/65.

Johnson, W. J., Pvt. No enlistment data. Remustered for the war at Camp Carondolet, Va., 2/11/62. Appears on an undated list of Confederates wounded at the Battle of Antietam, 9/17/62, who died at nearby hospitals. Remarks: "Buried on the battlefield of Antietam."

Johnson, Wyatt R., Pvt. En. 6/4/61, CM. Present to 4/63. Captured at Fredericksburg, Va., 4/29/63. POW, Old Capitol Prison, Washington, exchanged 6/3/63. Wounded and captured at Gettysburg, 7/5/63. POW, Fort McHenry, Md., transferred to Point Lookout, Md., 8/22/63. Released on joining U.S. Army, 2/27/64.

Joiner, G. W., Sgt. En. 6/4/61, CM. Present to 9/62. Killed at Sharpsburg, Md., 9/17/62.

Jordan, William T., Pvt. En. 3/15/62, Union Parish. Present to 4/63. Captured at Fredericksburg, Va., 4/29/63. POW, Fort Delaware, Del., exchanged 6/3/63. Present 7/63 to 4/65. Surrendered at Appomattox C.H., 4/9/65.

Kalker, Christian, Pvt. En. 6/4/61, CM. Present to 9/62. Roll for 9-10/62 states: "Absent. Left sick on the road before army crossed into Md." Roll for 3-4/64 states: "Supposed to be dead. Not heard from since summer 1862."

Keener, James B., Pvt. En. 3/15/62, Union Parish. Admitted to General Hosp., Orange C.H., Va., 4/3/62, fever. Present, 9-10/62. Absent in hospital, 11/62 to 1/63. Discharged on surgeon's certificate of disability, 1/13/63, extreme disability. Born: Barbor County, Alabama. Res.: Farmerville, La.

Lassiter, W. R., Pvt. En. 10/17/61 at Camp Reserve (Centreville) Va. Died at General Hosp., Manassas, Va., 11/10/61, typhoid fever.

Lawhorn, D.H., Pvt. En. 6/4/61, CM. Present to 3/62. Absent sick in hospital, 3-6/62. Died at CSA Hosp., Danville, Va., 6/21/62, chronic diarrhea.

Lee, George M., Cpl. En. 6/4/61, CM. Present to 2/62. Died at Camp Carondolet, Va., (Manassas) 2/19/62, pneumonia.
Lee, R.L., Pvt. En. 4/2/62, Union Parish. Present to 5/62. Died at General Receiving Hosp., Gordonsville, Va., 5/18/62, enteritis.
Lee, William C., Pvt. En. 7/26/61 at Union Mills, Va. Absent detached as sutler, 8/61. Present, 9/61 to 3/62. Admitted to Chimborazo Hosp., Richmond, 4/21/62, gonorrhea. Absent sick in hospital, 4-12/62. Discharged at Danville Gen. Hosp., on certificate of disability, 12/16/62. Born: Wilcox County, Alabama. Age 25, 6'0", blue eyes, dark hair, fair complexion.
Little, Micajah, Lt. En. 6/4/61, CM, as 1st sgt. Elected 2nd Lt., 5/9/62. Present to 9/62. Killed at Sharpsburg, Md., 9/17/62.
Lowe, William H., Pvt. En. 6/4/61, CM. Present to 4/63. Captured at Fredericksburg, Va., 4/29/63. POW, Old Capitol Prison, Washington, exchanged 6/3/63. Wounded at Winchester, Va., 6/14/63. Absent wounded, 6-11/63. Present 11/63 to 9/64. Admitted to CSA Genl. Hosp., Charlottesville, Va., 9/25/64, gunshot wound in left knee. Appears on a register of deceased soldiers, undated.
Maines, R.A., Sgt. (aka Manes) En. 6/4/61, CM. Present to 9/62. Wounded at Sharpsburg, Md., 9/17/62. Present to 5/64. Captured at Spotsylvania C.H., Va., 5/20/64. POW, Point Lookout, Md., transferred to Elmira, N.Y., 7/3/64, exchanged 2/25/65. On roll of POWs surrendered at New Orleans, 5/26/65, paroled at Natchitoches, La., 6/15/65.
Martin, John, Pvt. En. 6/4/61, CM. Present to 4/63. Captured at Fredericksburg, Va., 4/29/63. POW, Old Capitol Prison, Washington, exchanged 6/3/63. Present, 6/63 to 1/64. Admitted to Genl. Hosp. No. 9, Richmond, 1/30/64, furloughed for 30 days. Roll for 3-4/64 states: "Deserted from furlough, Mar. 24, 1864."
McCabe, J.H., Pvt. En. 6/4/61, CM. Present to 9/61. Absent, detached as brigade teamster, 9/61 to 2/64. Roll for 1-2/64 states: "Deserted. Left waggon yard in Feb. on a bought furlough."
McGough, James P., Pvt. En. 3/13/62, Union Parish. Present to 10/62. Absent, detailed as hospital steward, 10/62 to 8/63. Present, 9/63 to 3/65. Captured near Petersburg, Va., 3/25/65. POW, Point Lookout, Md., released 6/29/65. Hazel eyes, red hair, fair complexion, 5'11".
McLanahan, V., Pvt. En. 6/4/61, CM. Present to 4/62. Died at Genl. Hosp., Orange C.H., Va., 4/7/62, cause unknown.
McLemore, J.G., Pvt. En. 3/15/62, Union Parish. Absent in hospital, 6-7/62. Died at Genl. Hosp. No. 1, Lynchburg, Va., 7/4/62, chronic diarrhea.
Montgomery, George, Cpl. (aka T. Montgomery) En. 6/4/61, CM. Present to 6/62. Mortally wounded at Port Republic, Va., 6/8/62. Died at CSA Genl. Hosp., Charlottesville, Va., 6/17/62. Hospital record states: "Died 15 minutes after entering this hospital."
Morris, S.W., Pvt. En. 6/4/61, CM. Present to 9/62. Wounded at Sharpsburg, Md., 9/17/62. Admitted Chimbozaro Hosp., Richmond, 11/21/62, gunshot wound in foot, furloughed 60 days from 12/5/62. Absent wounded to 8/63. Present, detailed as ambulance driver, 8/63 to 5/64. Roll for 5-8/64, dated 11/2/64 states: "Dead."
Murphy, James, Pvt. En. 6/4/61, CM. Present on 1861 rolls. No record thereafter.
Nash, Christopher C., Lt. En. 6/4/61, CM, as 3rd sgt. Elected 2nd jr. lt., 4/28/62. Promoted to 1st lt., 9/23/62. Present to 4/63. Captured at Fredericksburg, Va., 4/29/63. POW, Old Capitol Prison, Washington, exchanged 6/3/63. Present, 6-11/63. Captured at Rappahannock Station, Va., 11/7/63. POW, Johnson's Island, Sandusky, Ohio, released 6/13/65. Res.: Many, La. Age 28, 5'8", dark eyes, dark hair, dark complexion.
Orbison, W.C., Pvt. En. 6/4/61, CM. Present to 10/62. Roll for 9-10/62 states: "Discharged Oct. 1, being over 45 years of age." Admitted to Confederate Soldiers Home, Richmond, Va., 7/18/89.
Patterson, William, Pvt. En. 6/4/61, CM. Present to 3/63. Absent, detailed as clerk in Adjutent's office, 4-12/63. Absent on furlough, 1-2/64. Roll for 3-4/64 states: "Deserted from furlough March 24, 1864."
Pearson, Benjamin F., Pvt. En. 6/4/61, CM. Present to 4/63. Wounded at Bristoe Station, Va., 8/27/62. Captured at Fredericksburg, Va., 4/29/63. POW, Old Capitol Prison, exchanged 6/3/63. Present, 6/63 through 8/64. Surrendered at New Orleans, 5/25/65, paroled at Monroe, La., 6/15/65. Born: Alabama. Occ.: Farrier. Age 28, 5'8", blue eyes, light hair, fair complexion.
Pendry, John, Pv. En. 6/4/61, CM, in Co. H. Transferred to Co. A, 10/31/61. Present on 1861 rolls. Remustered for the war, 2/7/62 at Camp Carondolet, (Manassas) Va. Roll for 3-4/62 states: "Absent, furlough expired." Born: Missouri. Occ.: Engineer. Res.: N.O.
Poston, R. H., Pvt. En. 3/20/62 at Union Parish. Died at South Carolina Hosp., Charlottesville, Va., 5/4/62, pneumonia.
Province, Thomas, Pvt. En. 6/4/61, CM. Present to 4/63. Captured at Fredericksburg, Va., 4/29/63. POW, Old Capitol Prison, Washington, exchanged 6/3/63. Present to 5/64. Captured at Wilderness, Va., 5/5/64. POW, Point Lookout, Md., transferred to Elmira, N.Y., 8/15/64, exchanged 2/13/65. Admitted to Genl. Hosp. No. 9, Richmond, 2/20/65. Surrendered at Lynchburg, Va., 4/14/65.
Pugh, William J., Pvt. En. 3/15/62, Union Parish. Present to 4/63. Absent, detailed to hospital duty, 4/63 to 4/64. Present, 4-6/64. Mortally wounded at Cold Harbor, Va., 6/3/64, admitted to Chimborazo Hosp., Richmond, 6/4/64, wounded in thigh, fractured by shell. Died in hospital, 6/12/64.
Ratcliffe, T.G. (aka Radcliffe) En. 6/4/61, CM. Present to 10/31. Died at Camp Reserve (Centreville), Va., 10/31/61, typhoid fever.

Reynolds, J.H., Cpl. En. 3/15/62, Union Parish. Present to 5/63. Captured at Fredericksburg, Va., 5/3/63. POW, Fort Delaware, Del., exchanged 5/23/63. Present 6/63 to 5/64. Wounded in side and arm at Spotsylvania C.H., Va., 5/10/64. Furloughed for 60 days from Louisiana Hosp., Richmond, to Mount Mugs, Ala., 5/31/64. Present, 10/64 to 4/65. Surrendered at Appomattox C.H., Va., 4/9/65. Age 17, 5'7", gray eyes, dark hair, light complexion.

Reynolds, Robert N. En. 3/7/62, Union Parish. Present to 4/63. Captured at Fredericksburg, Va., 4/29/63. POW, Fort Delaware, Del., exchanged 6/3/63. Absent sick in hospital, 6-11/63. Present, 11/63 to 9/64. Wounded at Spotsylvania C.H., Va., 5/12/64. Admitted to Genl. Hosp. No. 9, Richmond, 5/16/64, wounded in thigh, furloughed 60 days to Thomaston, Ga. Died at Genl. Hosp. No. 9, Salisbury, N.C., 3/13/65, tuberculosis.

Roach, P.P., Pvt. En. 3/15/62, Union Parish. Present to 8/62. Wounded at Manassas, 8/29/62. Absent wounded, 8/62 to 4/64. Roll for 5-6/63 states: "Absent at home on extended furlough. Wounded, one arm amputated." Roll for 3-4/64 states: "Deserted from hospital, Apr. 4, 1864."

Scarborough, B.O., Pvt. En. 6/4/61, CM. Present to 4/63. Captured at Fredericksburg, Va., 4/29/63. POW, Old Capitol Prison, Washington, exchanged 6/3/63. Wounded at Winchester, 6/14/63. Roll for 5-6/63 states: "Died at Jordan Springs Hosp., 18 June 1863 of a wound rec'd at Winchester 14 June 1863 in the celebrated charge of Hays' La. Brigade."

Shepherd, James, Pvt. (aka Shepard) En. 3/20/62, Union Parish. Present to 4/63. Captured at Fredericksburg, Va., 4/29/63, exchanged 6/3/63. Present, 6-11/63. Captured at Rappahannock Station, Va., 11/7/63. POW, Point Lookout, Md., exchanged 3/10/64. Roll for 5-8/64 states: "Deserted March 20, 1864." Age 36.

Sibley, Reddick W., Pvt. En. 6/4/61, CM. Present to 4/63. Captured at Fredericksburg, 4/29/63. POW, Old Capitol Prison, Washington, exchanged 6/3/63. Wounded at Winchester, Va., 6/14/63. Roll for 5-6/63 states: "Left wounded at New Town, leg amputated." Absent wounded, 6/63 to 1/64. Retired to Invalid Corps, 4/1/64. Res: Sabine Parish, La.

Smart, R.J., Pvt. En. 6/4/61, CM. Absent in hospital, 7-8/61. Discharged at Charlottesville, Va., on surgeon's certificate of disability, 9/10/61.

Smith, B.J., Pvt. En. 6/4/61, CM. Present to 9/62. Captured at Sharpsburg, Md., 9/19/62. POW, Fort McHenry, Md., exchanged 10/27/62. Absent sick, 11-12/62. Present 1-2/63. Present, detailed as ambulance driver, 3/63 through 1864. Surrendered at Appomattox C.H., 4/9/65.

Smith, J.F., Lt. En. 6/4/61, CM, as jr. 2nd lt. Present to 11/61. Admitted Moore Hosp., Danville, Va., 12/29/61, diarrhea. Roster of Commissioned Officers, undated, states: "Dropped April 28, 1862."

Speight, M.K., Jr. En. 6/4/61, CM. Present on 1861 rolls. Absent in hospital, 5-6/62. No record thereafter.

Stringer, T.J., Pvt. En. 6/4/61, CM. Present to 10/62. Roll for 9-10/62 states: "Discharged Oct. 1, being under 18 years of age."

Taylor, John F., Pvt. En. 3/20/62, Union Parish. Admitted to Chimborazo Hosp., Richmond, 4/17/62, died 5/19/62, typhoid fever.

Taylor, M.L., Pvt. En. 3/14/62, Union Parish. Absent sick in hospital, 4/62 to 4/63. Captured at Fredericksburg, 4/29/63. POW, Old Capitol Prison, Washington, exchanged 6/3/63. Absent sick in hospital, 7/63 to 4/65. Surrendered at Lynchburg, Va., 4/15/65. Age 22.

Thomas, John, Pvt. En. 4/2/62, Union Parish. Present to 4/63. Captured at Fredericksburg, 4/29/63. POW, Old Capitol Prison, Washington, exchanged 6/3/63. Present, 6-11/63. Captured at Rappahannock Station, Va., 11/7/63. POW, Point Lookout, Md., exchanged 3/10/64. Absent sick in hospital, 5-10/64. Present, 11-64. Surrendered at Lynchburg, Va., 4/15/65.

Thompson, D.R., Pvt. En. 3/7/62, Union Parish. Present to 6/62. Captured at Cross Keys, Va., 6/9/62. POW, Steamer Coatzacoalas,exchanged 8/5/62. Wounded at Chantilly, Va., 9/1/62. Absent wounded, 9/62 to 1/64. Roll for 1-2/64 states: "Deserted. Sent to Hosp. slightly wounded Sept. 1, 1862, not heard from since."

Traylor, A.J., Cpl. En. 6/4/61, CM. Present to 4/63. Captured at Fredericksburg, Va., 4/29/63. POW, Old Capitol Prison, Washington, exchanged 6/3/63. Rolls for 5-8/63 state: "Absent, detailed to nurse R.W. Sibley at New Town." Recorded as deserted, 9/1/63.

Traylor, F.M., Cpl./Asst. Surgeon. En. 6/4/61, CM, as cpl. Present to 12/62. Present, detached as hospital steward, 1-2/63. Promoted to Asst. Surgeon of 6th La., 4/3/63. Killed at Fredericksburg, Va., 5/4/64. Occ.: M.D. Res.: Union Parish.

Traylor, J.R., Pvt. En. 6/4/61, CM. Present to 4/63. Captured at Fredericksburg, Va., 4/29/63. POW, Old Capitol Prison, Washington, exchanged 6/3/63. Present to 4/65. Surrendered at Appomattox C.H., 4/9/65. Res.: DeSoto Parish, La. Age 40.

Tubb, Joseph, Pvt. En. 3/15/62, Union Parish. Absent in hospital, 3-4/62. Died at Banner Hosp., Richmond, 4/17/62, cause unstated.

Tubb, Lewis, Pvt. En. 6/4/61, CM. Present on 1861 rolls. Roll for 3-4/62 states: "Died at Culpeper C.H., Apr. 16, 1862."

Ursery, Phillip, Pvt. (aka Ussery, Ursing) En. 3/23/62, Union Parish. Present to 4/63. Captured at Fredericksburg, Va., 4/29/63. POW, Old Capitol Prision, Washington, exchanged 6/3/63. Present, 6/63 to 6/64. Wounded in thigh at Cold Harbor, Va., 6/4/64. Admitted Chimborazo Hosp., Richmond, 6/4/64, furloughed 30 days from 6/30/64. Present, 8/64 to 4/65. Surrendered at Appomattox C.H., 4/9/65.

Ursery, Richard, Pvt. En. 3/23/62, Union Parish. Present to 4/63. Wounded at Manassas, Va., 8/29/62. Captured at Fredericksburg, Va., 4/29/63. POW, Old Capitol Prison, Washington, exchanged 6/3/63. Present, 6-10/63. Absent sick, 11-12/63. Present 1-5/64. Captured at Wilderness, Va., 5/5/64. POW, Point Lookout, Md., transferred to Elmira, N.Y., 8/15/64, exchanged 2/10/65. Present to 4/65. Surrendered at Appomattox C.H., 4/9/65.
Vincent, Charles, Pvt. En. 6/4/61, CM. Present to 9/62. Killed at Chantilly, Va., 9/1/62.
Weymouth, James E., Lt. En. 7/9/61 at Fairfax Station, Va., as pvt. Present to 7/63. Wounded in left hip at Gettysburg, 7/2/63. Admitted to Gen. Hosp. No. 4, Richmond, 7/29/63, returned to duty 8/7/63. Present to 9/64. Wounded in right leg at Winchester, Va., 9/19/64. Admitted USA Depot Field Hosp, transferred 10/11/64, place unstated. Captured at Petersburg, Va., 3/25/65 [attack on Fort Stedman]. POW, Fort Delaware, Del., released 6/17/65. Res.: N.O. Grey eyes, dark hair, ruddy complexion, 6'3".
White, J.C., Sgt. En. 6/4/61, CM, as pvt. Promoted to sgt., 8/1/61. Present to 4/63. Captured at Fredericksburg, Va., 4/29/63. POW, Old Capitol Prison, Washington, exchanged 6/3/63. Left sick and captured at Gettysburg, 7/5/63. POW, DeCamp Gen. Hosp., David's Island, N.Y., exchanged 9/18/63. Present, 1-5/64. Captured at Wilderness, Va., 5/5/64. POW, Point Lookout, Md., exchanged 2/10/65.
Paroled 4/10/65, place unstated. Res.: Danville, Texas. Age 36, hazel eyes, light hair, fair complexion.
White, T.P., Pvt. En. 7/22/61 at Camp Walker, Va. Wounded at Manassas, Va., 8/29/62. Wounded at Sharpsburg, Md., 9/17/62. Present to 4/63. Captured at Fredericksburg, Va., 4/29/63. POW, Old Capitol Prison, Washington, exchanged 6/3/63. Absent in hospital, 6-8/63. Recorded as deserted about 8/1/63.
Williams, W. B., Sgt. En. 6/4/61, CM. Present to 4/63. Captured at Fredericksburg, Va., 4/29/63. POW, Old Capitol Prison, Washington, exchanged 6/3/63. Wounded at Winchester, Va., 6/14/63. Absent wounded to 11/63. Present, 11/63 to 4/64. Absent detailed as hospital guard at Lynchburg, Va., 4/64 to 4/65. Surrendered and paroled at Lynchburg, 4/13/65.
Wineberg, Simon, Pvt. (aka Weinburg, Wyndburg) En. 6/4/61, CM. Present to 9/62. Roll for 9-10/62 states: "Absent, left with Dr. Robertson, M.D." POW, place of capture unstated, paroled 9/27/62. Present, 11/62 to 5/64 Wounded at Wilderness, Va., 5/5/64. Admitted La. Hosp., Richmond, amputated middle finger of left hand, furloughed to Columbus, Ga., 5/20/64. Surrendered at N.O., 5/26/65.
Wininger, S.B., Pvt. En. 3/15/62, Union Parish. Present to 9/62. Wounded at Chantilly, Va., 9/1/62. Absent wounded 9-12/62. Present, 1-4/63. Captured at Fredericksburg, Va., 4/29/63. POW, Old Capitol Prison, Washington, exchanged 6/3/63. Present to 11/63. Captured at Rappahannock Station, Va., 11/7/63. POW, Point Lookout, Md., exchanged 3/10/64. Present, 4/64 to 4/65. Surrendered at Appomattox C.H., 4/9/65.

Company B: Calhoun Guards

Recuited by Henry Strong in New Orleans, Company B was one of the predominantly Irish companies of the regiment. Of the 162 men who served with the company, 128 were born in Ireland. Another 20 were immigrants of other countries—Germany, England, Scotland, Wales and Holland—so that 91 percent of the company was foreign-born. Only two men were native Louisianians. Of the total, 23 men were killed in battle or mortally wounded, another 11 died of disease, 21 were discharged (including 10 who were discharged as aliens), 30 deserted, 22 were captured and took the oath of allegiance, five were retired to the Invalid Corps, two transferred to other services, and two joined the U.S. Army to gain their release as prisoners of war. Nine men of the company surrendered at Appomattox Court House.

Captains:

Strong, Henry B., Capt./Col. En. 6/5/61, CM, as capt. Elected lt. col., 5/8/62. Appointed col. of 6th La., 8/16/62, to take rank from 6/27/62. Present to 2/62. Detailed to recruiting in N.O., 2-3/62. Present, 4-9/62. Killed at Sharpsburg, Md., 9/17/62. Born: Ireland. Occ.: Clerk. Res.: N.O. Age 40, married.
Redmond, Thomas, Sgt./Capt. En. 6/5/61, CM, as 2nd sgt. Elected 1st Lt., 1/25/62. Promoted to captain, 5/8/62, upon Henry Strong's election to lt. col. Present to 11/63. Captured at Rappahannock Station, Va., 11/7/63. POW, Old Capitol Prison, Washington, transferred to Johnson's Island, Sandusky, Ohio, 11/11/63, released 6/13/65. Born: Ireland. Occ.: Clerk. Res.: N.O. Age 25, single.

* * *

Adams, Charles, Pvt. En. 6/5/61, CM. Absent, detailed at brigade HQ, 7/62 to 12/62. Absent sick in hospital, Charlottesville, Va., 11/16/63 to 1/23/64. Absent, detailed as courier at brigade HQ., 1/64 to 4/64. Absent, wounded in left forearm, in hospital, 5-9/64. Born: Kentucky. Occ.: Paperhanger. Res.: N. O. Age 21, single.

Avenholtz, Christopher, Pvt. En. 6/5/61, CM. Present to 7/62. Roll for 8/62: "Deserted since last report. Taken the oath." Born: Amsterdam. Occ.: Paperhanger. Res.: N. O. Age 25, married.
Avenholtz, Mrs. Christopher. Laundress. On roll of recruits dated 3/21/62, N. O.
Bartels, John, Pvt. En. 3/31/62, N. O. Captured at Strasburg, Va., 6/2/62. POW, Fort Delaware, Del., exchanged 8/5/62. Took oath of allegiance to U.S. at Fort Delaware, 8/10/62. Born: Hanover, Germany. Age 18.
Boyne, Richard, Pvt. En. 6/5/61, CM. Present thru 1/63. Absent sick in hospital, Charlottesville, 3-10/63, ulcer of leg. Present, 11-12/63. Absent sick in hospital, 1-8/64. Retired to Invalid Corps, 12/5/64. Born: Ireland. Occ.: Laborer. Res.: N. O. Age 36, married.
Britt, Timothy, Pvt. En. 6/5/61, CM. Present, all rolls through 1864. Surrendered at Appomattox C.H., 4/9/65. Born: Ireland. Occ.: Laborer. Res.: N. O. Age 28, single.
Brown, Carl, (aka Charles) Pvt. En. 6/5/61, CM. Present through 2/64. Absent, detached to the Naval Dept., Richmond, 3/64. Born: Prussia. Occ.: Sailor. Res.: N. O. Age 22, single.
Brown, James, Pvt. En. 6/5/61, CM. Present to 12/62. Discharged as alien, 12/2/62. Affidavit states Brown was born in County Donegal, Ireland and arrived in New Orleans three years earlier, not intending to remain permanently in U.S., a non-citizen and subject of Great Britain. Born: Ireland. Occ.: Laborer. Res: N. O. Age 22, single.
Byrnes, Thomas, (aka Burns, Thomas) Sgt. En. 6/5/61, CM. Present to 7/64. Wounded at Gettysburg, 7/2/63. Promoted to sgt., 1863. Killed at Kernstown, Va., 7/24/64. Born: Ireland. Occ: Laborer. Res.: N.O. Age 26, single.
Campbell, Mathew A., Pvt. En. 5/29/61, N.O. Present to 7/62. Killed at Malvern Hill, Va., 7/1/62. Born: Ireland. Occ.: Laborer. Res.: New Orleans. Age 22, single.
Carbery, Patrick S., Pvt. En. 6/5/61, CM. Present to 9/62. Captured at South Mountain, Md., 9/13/62. POW at Fort Delaware, Del., exchanged 10/2/62. Affidavit signed at Richmond, Va., dated 10/9/62 states he came to U.S. at age 16 but never intended to remain or become a citizen. Discharged as alien, 11/7/62. Born: County Westmeath, Ireland. Occ.: Laborer. Res.: N.O. Age 23, single.
Carlos, Michael, Pvt. En. 6/5/61. Present to 5/63. Captured at Fredericksburg, Va., 5/4/63, took oath of allegiance to U.S. Born: Ireland. Occ.: Laborer. Res.: N.O. Age 22, single.
Carson, John, Pvt. En. 6/5/61, CM. Admitted to Chimborozo Hosp., Richmond, 3/14/62, died 4/4/62, pulmonary consumption. Born: County Carlow, Ireland. Occ.: Laborer. Res.: N.O. Age 28. 5'8", blue eyes, dark brown hair, fair complexion.
Casey, Thomas, (aka Cassey), Sgt. En. 6/5/61, CM. Promoted to 1st sgt., 7/20/62. Present to 7/63. Killed at Gettysburg, Pa., 7/2/63. Born: Ireland. Occ.: Laborer. Res.: N.O. Age 23, single.
Cavanaugh, John, Pvt. En. 3/2/62, N.O. Admitted to CSA General hosp., Charlottesville, Va., 4/5/62, acute diarrhea, transferred to Lynchburg., Va. Died in General Hosp. No 2, Lynchburg, Va., 7/1/62, tuberculosis. Born: County Longford, Ireland. Occ.: Laborer. Res., N.O. Age 46, married.
Cavanaugh, Thomas P., Pvt.. En. 3/4/62 as drummer. Present as pvt., 7/62 to 11/63. Detailed as orderly at regimental HQ., 11/63. Surrendered at Appomattox C.H., 4/9/65. Born: Ireland. Occ.: Laborer. Age 15, single.
Cavanaugh, William C.,Pvt. En. 3/6/62, N.O. AWOL, 7-8/62. Present to 7/63. Wounded at Gettysburg, Pa. 7/2/62. Captured in hospital at Gettysburg, transferred to General Hosp., Gettysburg, 7/22/63, slight leg wound. Roll for 4/64 states: "Dropped as deserter. Taken prisoner at Gettysburg July 1863 and took the oath of allegiance." Born: Ireland. Occ.: Laborer. Res.: N.O. Age 34, married.
Clayton, Thomas, Pvt. En. 6/4/61. Present to 1/63. Present, detailed at regimental wagon yard. 1-8/63. On extra duty as ordnance wagon driver for brigade, 11/63-4/64. Wounded in left elbow and forearm at Monocacy, Md., 7/9/64. Admitted to CSA Hosp., Charlottesville, Va., 7/26/64, furloughed 7/29/64. Severely wounded in chest at Cedar Creek, Va., 10/19/64. Admitted to CSA Hosp., Charlottesville, 11/3/64, furloughed 11/15/64. Born: England. Occ.: Laborer. Res.: N.O. Age 21, single.
Coffey, William, Pvt. En. 5/29/61, N.O. Present to 10/64. Captured at Strasburg after Battle of Cedar Creek, Va., 10-19-64. POW, Point Lookout, Md., paroled 1/17/65. Admitted to Way Hosp., Meridian, Miss., 2/10/65 as "furloughed paroled prisoner, wounded." Born: Ireland. Occ.: Cab driver. Res.: N.O. Age 19, single.
Collins, John, Cpl. Transferred in from Wheat's Special Battalion. On muster roll of Jackson Hosp., Richmond, employed as guard, 9/7/63. Retired to Invalid Corps, assigned to Jackson Hosp., Richmond, 9/16/64. On roll of POWs captured at Richmond hospitals, 4/3/65. Record dated 2/10/65 at Petersburg, states: "Was transferred to this company. He lost his arm. He belonged to Wheat's Btn., he is on guard at Camp Jackson."
Collins, Patrick, Pvt. En. 3/25/62, N.O. Captured at Woodstock, Va., 6/3/62. POW, Fort Delaware, Del., took oath of allegiance, 8/10/62. Born: County Tipperary, Ireland. Occ.: Laborer. Age 19. 5'4", gray eyes, red hair, fair complexion. (Appears to be the same man as Patrick Collins who enlisted in Company F, 3/11/62 in New Orleans, collecting $50 bounty on both enlistments.)
Conlon, John, Pvt. (aka Conlin) En. 3/31/62, N. O. Captured at Harrisonburg, Va., 6/15/62. POW, Fort Delaware, Del., took oath of allegiance to U.S., 8/10/62. Born: Ireland. Occ.: Laborer. Res.: N.O. Age 23, single.
Cooney, William, Pvt. En. 3/18/62, N.O. Present to 5/63. Wounded at Fredericksburg, Va., 5/4/63. Absent wounded, 5-8/63. Present to 1/65. Deserted at Petersburg 1/28/65. Took oath of allegiance to U.S. at City Point, Va., 1/29/65. Record dated 2/10/65 at Petersburg states: "Deserted on Jan. 28 to the Yanks. He was a good soldier." Born: Ireland. Occ.: Laborer. Res.: N.O. Age 27, single, 5'8", blue eyes, dark hair, dark complexion.

Cullen, Bernard, Pvt. (aka Cullum) En. 3/31/62, N.O. Present to 6/63. Killed at Winchester, Va., 6/14/63. Born: County Cavan, Ireland. Occ.: Laborer. Res.: N.O. Age 28, single, 5'1", blue eyes, brown hair, dark complexion.
Cullen, James, Pvt. (aka Culomn) En. 6/5/61, CM. Present to 7/62. Killed at Malvern Hill, Va., 7/1/62. Born: Ireland. Occ.: Laborer. Res.: N.O. Age 22, single.
Cunningham, Patrick, Pvt. En. 3/8/62, N.O. Present, 7-8/62. Captured near Poolesville, Md. by 8th Illinois Cavalry Regt., 9/9/62, sent to Washington, D.C., 9/10/62. Recorded on rolls for 9-10/62 as deserted. Born: Ireland. Occ.: Laborer. Res.: N.O. Age 28, single, 5'8", gray eyes, fair hair, ruddy complexion.
Curry, John, Pvt. En. 6/5/61,CM. Present to 9/62. Captured at Frederick, Md., 9/12/62. POW, Fort Delaware, Del., exchanged 11/10/62. Present, 11/62 to 5/63. Wounded at Fredericksburg, Va., 5/4/63. Admitted to Howards' Grove Hosp., Richmond, 5/9/63, left shoulder wound, returned to duty 7/18/63. Deserted from hospital, 7/18/63. Record dated 2/10/65 at Petersburg states: "Joined cavalry and since killed." Born: Ireland. Occ.: Laborer. Res.: N.O. Age 24, single.
Devan, Charles, Pvt. (aka Dever, Divers) En. 6/5/61, CM. Present to 5/63. Wounded and captured at Fredericksburg, Va., 5/4/63. POW, Old Capitol Prison, Washington, paroled 6/25/63. Present, 9/63 to 9/64. Wounded severely in right breast at Winchester, 9/19/64. Admitted to CSA Hosp., Charlottesville, 9/25/64, transferred to Lynchburg Hosp., 10/25/64. Captured at High Bridge, near Farmville, Va., 4/6/65. POW, Newport News, Va., released 6/25/65. Born: Ireland. Occ.: Sailor. Res.: N.O. Age 24, single, 5'6", blue eyes, dark hair, dark complexion.
Devine, James, Pvt. En. 3/6/62, N.O. Present to 11/63. Captured at Rappahannock Station, Va., 11/7/63. POW, Point Lookout, Md., took oath of allegiance to U.S., 3/14/64, released and sent to Baltimore, Md. Born: Ireland. Occ. Laborer. Res.: N.O. Age 29, married.
Dillon, Edward, Pvt. En. 6/5/61, CM. Present to 8/62. Killed at Manassas, 8/29/62. Born: Ireland. Occ.: sailor. Res.: N.O. Age 28, single.
Donovan, James, Pvt. En. 6/5/61, CM. Present to 9/62. AWOL, 9-12/62. Absent sick at Lynchburg, 1-4/63. Present, 5/63 to 4/64. Absent in hospital, 5-8/64. Surrendered at Appomattox C.H., 4/10/65. Record dated 2/10/65 at Petersburg states: "Old age is on him and rheumatick pains is on him." Born: County Westmeath, Ireland. Occ.: Sailor. Res.: N.O. Age 40, married, 5'8", gray eyes, dark hair, florid complexion.
Downey, Peter, Pvt. En. 3/4/62, N.O. Present, 7-8/62. Deserted, 8/26/62. Born: Erie County, N.Y. Occ.: Clerk. Res.: N.O. Age 21, 5'6", blue eyes, fair hair, fair complexion.
Doyle, John, Pvt. En. 3/24/62, N.O. Present to 4/63. Captured at Fredericksburg, Va., 4/29/63. POW, Old Capitol Prison, Washington, took oath of allegiance to U.S., 4/29/63. Born: County Roscommon, Ireland. Occ.: Laborer. Age 32, married, 5'4", brown eyes, black hair, fair complexion.
Duncan, Archibald, Lt. En. 6/5/61, CM, as pvt. Present 7-10/61 as cpl. Elected 1st Lt., 5/10/62. Present to 7/63. Wounded at Gettysburg, Pa., 7/2/63. Present 9/63 to 9/64. Captured at Fisher's Hill, Va., 9/22/64. POW, Fort Delaware, Del., released 6/17/65. Born: Scotland. Occ.: Cook. Res.: N.O. Age 24, single.
Dunn, Bernard, Pvt. En. 6/5/61, CM. Present to 7/62. Detatched as regimental wagon driver, 7/62 to 8/64. Wounded at Sharpsburg, Md., 9/17/62. Record dated 2/10/65 at Petersburg states: "Joined cavalry on 8 Sept. 64." Born: Ireland. Occ.: Laborer. Res.: N.O. Age 36, married.
Edwards, John, Pvt. En. 3/25/62, N.O. Roll for 7-8/62 states: "Deserted since last report." Born: London, England. Occ.: Bookkeeper. Age 25.
Eichoff, Lewis, Pvt. En. 6/5/61, CM. Present to 6/62. Captured at Woodstock, Va., 6/2/62. POW, Fort Delaware, Del., took oath of allegiance, 8/10/62.
Ennis, Patrick, Pvt. En. 6/5/61, CM. Present to 7/63. Captured at Williamsport, Md., on retreat from Gettysburg, 7/14/63. POW, Fort Delaware, Del., paroled 9/14/64. Admitted to Genl. Hosp. No. 9, Richmond, 9/22/64, transferred to Louisiana Hospital, Richmond. Affidavit signed by him at New Orleans 3/9/65, states he deserted while on furlough from hospital in September 1864, went to N.O. and took oath of allegiance. Born: Ireland. Occ.: Painter. Res.: N.O., age 23, single.
Enright, Timothy, Pvt. En. 6/5/61, CM. Present to 12/62. Discharged as an alien, 12/2/62. Born: County Limerick, Ireland. Occ.: Painter. Res.: N.O. Age 29, single.
Fay, John, Pvt. En. 6/5/61, CM. Present to 9/63. Wounded at Raccoon Ford, Va., 9/14/63. Admitted to Jackson Hosp., Richmond, 9/21/63, minie ball in breast, returned to duty 11/17/63. Present to 9/64. Captured at Fisher's Hill, Va., 9/22/64. POW, Point Lookout, Md., exchanged 11/1/64. Record dated 2/10/65 at Petersburg states: "Got crippled with a ball in his lungs, returned to serve his country, he is a good man." Born: Ireland. Occ.: Waterman. Res.: N.O. Age 24, single.
Fitzpatrick, Daniel, Pvt. En. 6/10/61. Present to 6/62. Killed at Port Republic, Va., 6/9/62. Born: Ireland. Occ.: Cook. Res.: N.O. Age 24, single.
Flanagan, Patrick, Sgt. En. 6/5/61, CM. Present to 11/62. Absent sick, 11-12/62. Present, 1/63 through 4/64. Resigned as 1st sgt., 5/10/63. Severely wounded at Kernstown, Va., 7/24/64. Admitted to Genl. Hosp., Winchester, Va., 7/64, gunshot wound in left thigh. Admitted to CSA Genl. Hosp., Charlottesville, 10/18/64, transferred to Lynchburg hospital, 10/25. Paroled at Montgomery, Ala., 5/9/65. Born: Ireland. Occ.: Carpenter. Res.: N.O. Age 22, single.

Flanagan, Thomas, Pvt. En. 6/5/61. Present to 11/62. Detailed to regimental wagon yard, 11/62 to 5/63. Present to 7/63. Captured at Gettysburg, 7/3/63. POW, Fort Delaware, Del., paroled and forwarded for exchange, 3/7/65. Born: Ireland. Occ.: Carpenter. Res.: N.O. Age 21, single, 5'9", blue eyes, dark hair, dark complexion.

Flannery, John, Pvt. En. 6/5/61, CM. Present to 9/62. AWOL, 9-10/62. Discharged as alien, 11/22/62. Born: County Tipperary, Ireland. Occ.: sailor. Res.: N.O. Age 23, single.

Foley, Patrick, Pvt. En. 3/31/62, N.O. Present to 8/62. Wounded at Manassas, Va., 8/29/62. Absent wounded, crippled in foot, detailed for guard duty, Gordonsville, Va., 11/63. Detailed as nurse at Lynchburg, Va. 9/64. Surrendered at Lynchburg, 4/15/65. Born: Ireland. Occ.: Laborer. Res.: N.O. Age 28, single.

Fox, John, Pvt. En. 6/4/61, CM. Present to 6/62. Wounded at Port Republic, Va., 6/9/62. Admitted to CSA Hosp., Charlottesville, Va., 11/19/62. Died at Lynchburg hospital, 12/62, secondary hemorrhage. Record dated 2/10/65 at Petersburg states: "Got discharged for being overage and went into the fight, got killed."Born: Ireland. Occ.: Waterman. Res.: N.O. Age 40, married.

Freelander, Herman, Pvt. (aka Frielander) En. 3/18/62, N.O. Recorded as deserted, 8/62. Born: Prussia. Occ.: Laborer. Res.: N.O. Age 18, single.

Freret, Miles, Pvt. (aka Frerrett, Ferrett) En. 6/10/61. Present to 4/63. Wounded and captured at Fredericksburg, 4/29/63. POW, Fort Delaware, Del., exchanged 6/3/63. Wounded at Winchester, 6/14/63. Absent wounded, 6-12/63. Absent on furlough, 1-2/64. Present 5-8/64. Retired to Invalid Corps, Mobile, Ala., 11/27/64. Record dated 2/10/65 at Petersburg states: "Crippled in left leg and both hands, he was a noble honest man also a good soldier." Born: Ireland. Occ.: Waterman. Res.: N.O. Age 27, married.

Gaffney, Thomas, Pvt. En. 6/5/61, CM. Present to 7/63. Wounded and captured at Gettysburg, 7/2/63. Roll dated 3-4/64 states: "Taken prisoner at Gettysburg July 1863 and took the oath of allegiance." Born: Ireland. Occ.: Bricklayer. Res.: N.O. Age 27, married.

Gahon, Michael, Pvt. En. 6/5/61, CM. Present to 7/62. Absent sick, 9-10/62. Admitted to CSA Hosp., Charlottesville, 12/2/62, died 4/7/63, consumption. Born: Ireland. Occ.: Laborer. Res.: N.O. Age 26, single.

Gallagher, James, Pvt. En. 3/8/62, N.O. Present to 12/62. Wounded in right leg at Fredericksburg, Va., 12/13/62. Absent wounded, 12/62 to 3/64. Present, 3-9/64. Wounded at Kernstown, Va., 7/24/64. Captured at Fisher's Hill, Va., 9/22/64. POW, Point Lookout, Md., exchanged 2/15/65. On roll of POWs at New Orleans, La., captured at Gentilly Road, La., 5/1/65, released on taking oath of allegiance, 5/8/65. Born: Ireland. Occ.: Laborer. Res.: N.O. Age 28, single, 5'5", blue eyes, brown hair, light complexion.

Gannon, James, Pvt. En. 6/5/61, CM. Present to 2/62. Absent on furlough in N.O., 2/14/62 to 4/5/62. Recorted as deserted, 7/62. Record dated 2/10/65 at Petersburg states: "Went to New Orleans, took the oath." Born: Ireland. Occ.: Striker. Res.: N.O. Age 23, single.

Gleason, Henry, Pvt. En. 3/17/62, N.O. Present to 8/62. Killed at Manassas, Va., 8/29/62. Born: Ireland. Occ.: Laborer. Res.: N.O. Age 29, married.

Good, John, Pvt. (aka Goode) En. 6/4/61, CM. Present to 3/63. Absent on furlough in N.O., 2/63 to 4/63. Present to 7/63. Killed at Gettysburg, 7/2/63. Born: Ireland. Occ.: Laborer. Res.: N.O. Age 28, single.

Gray, Daniel, Pvt. En. 3/6/62, N.O. Present to 8/62. AWOL, 9-12/62. Record dated 2/10/65 at Petersburg, states: "Deserted, took the oath." Born: Northhampton, England. Occ.: Carpenter. Res.: N.O. Age 19, single.

Green, Bernard, Pvt. En. 6/5/61, CM. Present to 6/62. Captured at Woodstock, Va., 6/2/62. POW, Fort Delaware, Del., took oath of allegiance, 8/10/62. Born: Ireland. Occ.: Striker. Res.: N.O. Age 24, single.

Grinstead, Robert W., Pvt. (aka Grimstead) En. 8/1/61, Manassas, Va. Roll for 9-10/61 states: "Present, substitute for Wm. E. Murphy, Oct. 1, 1861." Present to 5/63. Wounded at Fredericksburg, Va., 5/4/63. Absent wounded 5-6/63. Present 7/63 to 9/64. Wounded at Fisher's Hill., Va., 9/22/64. On wounded furlough, 11/64 to 2/65. Retired to Invalid Corps at Mobile, Ala., 2/16/65. Record dated 2/10/65 at Petersburg, states: "Crippled in the left hand at Fisher's Hill." Born: Missouri. Occ.: Painter. Res.: N.O. Age 29, single.

Hall, Edward, Pvt. En. 6/4/61, CM. Present to 11/62. Discharged as alien, 11/7/62. Born: Ireland. Occ.: Seafarer. Res.: N.O. Age 31, single.

Hanley, Matthew, Pvt. En. 6/4/61, CM. Present to 11/63. Captured at Rappahannock Station, Va., 11/7/63. POW, Point Lookout, Md., exchanged 3/10/64. Captured at Fisher's Hill, Va., 9/22/64. POW, Point Lookout, exchanged 2/10/65. Paroled and signed oath of allegiance at Montgomery, Ala., 6/2/65. Born: Ireland. Occ.: Mailboy. Res.: N.O. Age 26, single.

Heart, John, Pvt. En. 3/7/62, N.O. Present to 5/64. Captured at Wilderness, Va., 5/5/64. POW, Point Lookout, Md., transferred to Elmira, N.Y., 8/15/64, released 5/17/65. Born: County Roscommon, Ireland. Occ.: Slater. Res.: N.O. Age 36, married, 5'4", blue eyes, sandy hair, fair complexion.

Henderson, John, Pvt. En. 6/5/61, CM. Present to 7/62. Recorded as deserted, 11/62. Record dated 2/10/65 at Petersburg states, "Joined the artillery, got killed at Port Hudson." Born: Ireland. Occ.: Laborer. Res.: N.O. Age 23, single.

Henderson, Peter, Pvt. En. 6/5/61, CM. Present to 7/62. Recorded as deserted, 11/62. Record dated 2/1/65 at Petersburg states: "Joined the artillery, died with disease." Born: Ireland. Occ.: Tinsmith. Res.: N.O. Age 21, single.

Hennessy, John, Pvt. En. 6/4/61, CM. Present to 7/62. Recorded as deserted, 10/62. Record dated 2/10/65 at Petersburg states: "Joined the cavalry." Born: Ireland. Occ.: Hatter. Res.: N.O. Age 24, single.

Henry, William, Cpl. En. 3/31/62, N.O. Present to 5/63. Wounded at Fredericksburg, Va., 5/3/63. Promoted to cpl., 7/2/63. Present 7-11/63. Captured at Rappahannock Station, Va., 11/7/63. POW, Point Lookout, Md., exchanged 3/10/64. Present to 7/64. Severely wounded and captured at Battle of Monocacy, Md., 7/9/64. Admitted to USA Genl. Hosp., Frederick, Md., 7/9/64, gunshot wound in left thigh, transferred to Baltimore, Md., 9/20/64. POW, Point Lookout, Md., exchanged 10/29/64. Retired to Invalid Corps at Richmond, 2/14/65. Born: County Down, Ireland. Occ.: Laborer. Age 30, blue eyes, brown hair, fair complexion, 5'6".

Herron, Michael, Pvt. En. 3/29/62, N.O. Present to 9/62. Recorded as deserted, 10/62. Born: County Wexford, Ireland. Occ.: Drayman. Age 27, 5'10", gray eyes, black hair, fair complexion.

Herron, Nicholas, Pvt. En. 6/5/61, CM. Present to 10/62. Discharged as alien, 10/7/62. Born: County Wexford, Ireland. Occ.: Bricklayer. Res.: N.O. Age 20, single, 5'6", blue eyes, black hair, dark complexion.

Hines, Robert, Pvt. En. 3/11/62, N.O. Present to 1/64. Absent sick, 1-2/64. Present, 3-11/64. Record dated 2/10/65 at Petersburg states: "Went to N. Carolina recruiting, he is a good soldier." Born: Ireland. Occ.: Waterman. Res.: N.O. Age 26, single.

Hodgins, Thomas, Pvt. En. 3/3/62, N.O. Absent sick 3-12/62. On furlough, 60 days from 12/3/62. Admitted to CSA Gen. Hosp., Charlottesville, Va., 5/30/62, returned to duty 9/10/62, chronic dysentery. Recorded as deserted from Charlottesville, 1-2/63. Born: County Tipperary, Ireland. Occ.: Baker. Res.: N.O. Age 29, married, 5'8", blue eyes, brown hair, fair complexion.

Hogan, Jeremiah, Lt. En. 6/5/61, CM, as 2nd Lt. Dropped from rolls, 4/28/62. Record dated 2/10/65 at Petersburg, Va., states: "Threw out of office May 1862." Born: Ireland. Occ.: Clerk. Res.: N.O. Married.

Houlohan, John, Pvt. En. 7/21/63 at Mobile, Ala. Present 7/63 to 4/65. Surrendered at Lynchburg, Va., 4/13/65. Record dated 2/10/65 at Petersburg, Va., states: "He is a old man, got transferred to this company August 1863."

Houlohan, Michael, Pvt. En. 7/25/63 at Mobile, Ala. Present to 11/63. Captured at Rappahannock Station, Va., 11/7/63. POW, Point Lookout, Md., released on taking oath of allegiance, 3/30/64. Born: Ireland. Occ.: Carpenter. Res.: N.O. Age 36, married, 5'9", gray eyes, black hair, dark complexion.

Hughes, George, Pvt. (aka George Hewes) En. 3/3/62, N.O. Present to 4/63. Captured at Fredericksburg, Va., 4/29/63. POW, Old Capitol Prison, Washington. Took oath of allegiance in Washington, undated. Born: County Fermanagh, Ireland. Occ.: Bricklayer. Age 30, 5'5", blue eyes, brown hair, fair complexion.

Hughes, Michael, Pvt. En. 6/5/61, CM. Present to 7/62. Wounded at Malvern Hill, Va., 7/1/62. Absent wounded, 7-8/62. Present, 9-10/62. AWOL, 11/62 to 3/63. Present, 3-11/63. Captured at Rappahannock Station, Va., 11/7/63. POW, Point Lookout, Md., released on taking oath of allegiance, 3/10/64. Born: Ireland. Occ.: Laborer. Res.: N.O. Age 28, single.

Hughes, Peter, Pvt. (aka Peter Hewes) En. 6/5/61, CM. Present to 11/63. Captured at Rappahannock Station, Va., 11/7/63. POW, Point Lookout, Md., took oath of allegiance, 3/15/64. Born: Ireland. Occ.: Bricklayer. Res.: N.O. Age 29, single.

Husselby, Joseph, Pvt. (aka Husselbee) En. 3/10/62, N.O. Present to 7/63. Wounded at Gettysburg, 7/2/63. Absent in hospital at Staunton, Va., 11/63. Wounded 3/25/65 (attack on Fort Stedman, Petersburg), admitted to CSA Hosp., Petersburg, compound fracture of right arm, amputated. Captured in hospital at Petersburg, 4/3/65, transferred to Point of Rocks, Va., hospital, 5/11/65. Record dated 2/10/65 at Petersburg states: "He was wounded 3 times severely, never missed a fight." Born: England. Occ.: Bricklayer. Res.: N.O. Age 36, married.

Jenkins, Samuel, Sgt. En. 6/5/61 as pvt. Promoted to 3rd sgt., 7/62. Present on every muster roll taken during the war. Wounded at Gettysburg, 7/2/63. Wounded at Petersburg, 3/25/65 (attack on Fort Stedman), minie ball causing compound fracture of right thigh. Died at Washington Street Hosp., Petersburg, 4/11/65. Born: Ireland. Occ.: Engineer. Res.: N.O. Age 20, single.

Jones, Stephen, Pvt. En. 3/18/62, N.O. Present to 9/62. Killed at Chantilly, Va., 9/1/62. Born: Wales. Occ.: Slater. Res.: N.O. Age 27, married, 5'8", hazel eyes, black hair, dark complexion.

Kavanagh, Peter, Pvt. (aka Kavanaugh, Cavanaugh) En. 3/1/62, N.O. Present to 8/62. Deserted 8/27/62. Born: County Longford, Ireland. Occ.: Marble cutter. Res.: N.O. Age 32, single.

Keane, James, Pvt. (aka Kain, Kane) En. 3/18/62. Present to 12/62. Wounded at Fredericksburg, Va., 12/13/62. Absent wounded, 12/62 to 3/63. Present, 3/63 to 3/64. Absent detached to Navy Yard at Richmond, 3/63. Transferred to Navy, 4/4/64. Born: County Roscommon, Ireland. Occ.: Sailor. Res.: N.O. Age 23, single.

Keegan, James, Pvt. En. 3/26/62, N.O. Present to 12/62. Wounded at Fredericksburg, Va. 12/13/62. Present 1-6/63. Killed at Winchester, Va., 6/14/63. Born: County Meath, Ireland. Occ.: Laborer. Res.: N.O. Age 39, single, 5'8", blue eyes, brown hair, fair complexion.

Kennedy, Andrew, Sgt. En. 3/7/62, N.O, as pvt. Present on all rolls through 1864. Promoted to cpl., 5/63. Promoted to sgt., 9/63. Wounded at Winchester, Va., 6/14/63. Wounded at Spotsylvania C.H., Va., 5/12/64. Admitted to Chimborazo Hosp., Richmond, 6/4/64, gunshot wound in left thigh, furloughed 40 days from 7/7/64. On list of Confederate POWs not present with their commands for parole and afterwards taken up by U.S. Cavalry and paroled according to the terms of surrender at Appomattox C.H., 4/9/65. Born: County Tipperary, Ireland. Occ.: Soda manufacturer. Res.: N.O. Age 27, 5'6", gray eyes, brown hair, fair complexion.

Kennedy, Robert G., Pvt. En. 3/3/62, N.O. Present to 9/62. Captured near Poolesville, Md., 9/9/62. Roll for 9-10/62 states: "Deserted since last report." Record dated 2/10/65 at Petersburg states: "Deserted and took the oath." Born: County Monaghan, Ireland. Occ.: Waiter. Res.: N.O. Age 23, single, 5'5", blue eyes, sandy hair, fair complexion.

Kennedy, William E., Pvt. En. 6/5/61, CM. Present to 6/63. Promoted to sgt., 5/4/63. Wounded in left leg at Winchester, Va., 6/14/63. Resigned as sgt., 7/4/63. Absent wounded, 6/63 to 9/64. Present 9/64 to 4/65. Captured at Petersburg, Va., 4/3/65. POW, Hart's Island, New York, released 6/14/65. Born: Ireland. Occ.: Laborer. Res.: N.O. Age 21, single.

Kesler, Joseph, Pvt. En. 3/14/62, N.O. Present to 9/63. Wounded at Manassas, Va., 8/28/62. Wounded at Gettysburg, 7/2/63. Wounded at Raccoon Ford, Va., 9/17/63. Absent wounded, 9-10/63. Present 11/63 though 1864. Captured at Waynesboro, Va., 3/2/65. POW, Fort Delaware, released 5/10/65. Record dated 2/10/65 at Petersburg states: "He is crippled with three wounds, he is a good soldier." Born: Prussia. Occ.: Laborer. Res.: N.O. Age 37, single.

Keyes, Thomas, Pvt. (aka Keys, Keese) En. 6/5/61, CM. Present to 12/62. Discharged as alien, 12/2/62. Born: County Donegal, Ireland. Occ.: Laborer. Res.: N.O. Age 24, single.

Kilane, John, Pvt. En. 2/2/62, N.O. Present to 6/62. Died 6/11/62. Record dated 2/10/65 at Petersburg states: "Died coming over the Mountain to Richmond, 11 June, 1862." Born: Ireland. Occ.: Laborer. Res.: N.O. Age 26, single.

Killacky, John, Pvt. En. 6/5/61, CM. Present to 5/63. Captured at Fredericksburg, Va., 5/3/63. POW, Fort Delaware, exchanged 6/3/63. Admitted to CSA Genl. Hosp., Charlottesville, Va., 6/9/62, wound in knee. Wounded at Gettysburg, 7/2/63. Absent wounded, 7-8/63. Captured at Rappahannock Station, Va., 11/7/63. POW, Point Lookout, Md., released on taking oath of allegiance, 3/30/64.

Killane, Patrick, Pvt. (aka Killale) En. 3/6/62, N.O. Absent sick, 7-8/62. Roll for 9-10/62 states: "Deserted since last report." Born: County Longford, Ireland. Res.: N.O. Age 46.

Krieger, Herman, Pvt. (aka Kreeger, Kruger) En. 6/5/61, CM. Present to 3/63. Absent sick, 3-4/63. Present 5-7/63. Wounded at Gettysburg, 7/2/63. Absent wounded 7-10/63. Captured at Rappahannock Station, Va., 11/7/63. POW, Old Capitol Prison, Washington, took oath of allegiance, 3/15/64. Born: Germany. Occ.: Laborer. Res.: N.O. Age 21, single, 5'8", blue eyes, light hair, dark complexion.

Lahey, William, Pvt. En. 3/31/62, N.O. Absent sick, 7-8/62. Present, 9-10/62. Absent sick, 11-12/62. Roll for 1-2/63 states: "Deserted at Richmond Jan. 11, 1863 and has gone to New Orleans." Born: County Cavan, Ireland. Occ.: Laborer. Res.: N.O. Age 18, single.

Laird, John, Pvt. En. 6/5/61, CM. Present to 8/62. Captured at Bucketstown, Va., date unstated. POW, Fort Delaware, exchanged 10/2/62. Discharged as alien, 10/12/62. Born: Scotland. Occ.: Laborer. Res.: N.O., 36, single.

Larramore, John, Pvt. En. 7/31/63 at Mobile, Ala. Present to 11/63. Captured at Rappahannock Station, Va., 11/7/63. POW, Point Lookout, Md., took oath of allegiance, 3/30/64. Born: Ireland. Occ.: Carpenter. Res.: N.O. Age 26, single, 5'7", blue eyes, brown hair, sandy complexion.

Lavelle, Edward, Sgt. En. 6/5/61, CM, as 4th sgt. Present to 5/62. Discharged 5/10/62. Born: Ireland. Occ.: Clerk. Res.: N.O. Age 40, married.

Lavelle, James, Pvt. En. 7/1/61 at Fairfax, Va. Present to 7/62. Roll for 7-8/62 states: "Discharged since last report at Lynchburg." Born: N.O. Occ.: Laborer. Res.: N.O. Age 17, single.

Lawler, Patrick, Pvt. En. 6/5/61, CM. Present to 8/62. Wounded at Manassas, 8/29/62. Present to 11/63. Absent sick at Lynchburg, Va., 11/63 to 11/64. Record dated 2/10/65 at Petersburg states: "He is a old man, he is not fit for duty." Born: Ireland. Occ.: Laborer. Res.: N.O. Age 36, married.

Long, Henry, Lt. En. 6/5/61, CM, as 3rd sgt. Promoted to 1st sgt., 1/25/62. Elected 2nd Lt., 5/9/62. Present to 1/63. Absent furlough, 1-2/63. Present 3/63 to 9/63. Absent furlough, 9/63 to 3/64. Present 3-9/64. Severely wounded in right arm at Winchester, Va., 9/19/64. Absent wounded to 2/65. Retired to Invalid Corps at Charlottesville, Va., 2/27/65. Born: Ireland. Occ.: Clerk. Res.: N.O. Age 23, single.

Long, Thomas, Sgt. En. 6/5/61, CM. Present to 2/62. Discharged on surgeon's certificate of disability, 2/19/62, hernia and vericose veins. Born: County Tipperary, Ireland. Occ.: Clerk. Res.: N.O. Age 30, single.

Long, Thomas, Pvt. En. 3/5/62, N.O. Absent sick, 7/62 to 12/63. Recorded as deserted, 2/64. Record dated 2/10/65 at Petersburg states: "Went to the hospital, never heard from him since." Born: County Tipperary, Ireland. Occ.: Carpenter. Res.: N.O. Age 25, single.

Lynch, Patrick, Pvt. En. 6/5/61, CM. Present to 7/62. Absent detached as brigade butcher, 7/62 to 5/64. Present, 5/64 to 4/65. Surrendered at Appomattox C.H., 4/9/65. Born: Ireland. Occ.: Butcher. Res.: N.O. Age 24, single.

Mack, John, Pvt. En. 6/5/61, CM. Present to 9/62. Absent detached as teamster in division wagon yard, 9/62 to 5/64. Present after 5/64. Born: Ireland. Occ.: Laborer. Res.: N.O. Age 27, single.

Mahon, James, Pvt. (aka James Maher) En. 3/17/62, N.O. Regimental record roll at Tulane University records him as killed at Winchester, 6/14/63, though his name is not on official casualty lists for that battle. Mahon's compiled service record in National Archives contains only one entry, a record dated 2/10/65 at Petersburg, Va., which states: "He fell nobly defending his flag of his adoption." Born: Ireland. Occ.: Laborer. Res.: N.O. Age 27, single.

Mahoney, John, Pvt. En. 6/5/61, CM. Present to 9/62. Absent captured, 10/62. Roll for 1-2/63 states: "Deserted at Richmond after being exchanged by the enemy." Born: Ireland. Occ.: Laborer. Res.: N.O. Age 27, single.

Maloney, John, Pvt. En. 6/5/61, CM. Present to 5/62. Severely wounded at Winchester, Va., 5/25/62. Absent wounded, 5/62 to 3/63. Present 3/63 to 11/63. Captured at Rappahannock Station, Va., 11/7/63. POW, Point Lookout, Md., exchanged 3/9/64. Roll for 5-8/64 states: "Absent in Richmond, detailed as courier." Surrendered at Lynchburg, Va., 4/14/65. Born: Ireland. Occ.: Laborer. Res.: N.O. Age 32, married.
Mann, Henry, Cpl. En. 6/5/61, CM. Present to 1/62. Died at hospital, place unstated, 1/25/62. Born: Ireland. Occ.: Carpenter. Res.: N.O. Age 19, single.
Marron, Peter, Pvt. En. 6/5/61, CM. Present to 2/62. Died at Camp Carondolet (Manassas), Va., 2/22/62, pneumonia. Born: Ireland. Occ.: Laborer. Res.: N.O. Age 32, single.
Martin, James, Pvt. En. 6/18/61 at Lynchburg, Va. Present to 2/62. Absent on furlough, 2-4/62. No record thereafter.
Masterson, John, Pvt. En. 6/10/61, CM. Present to 8/62. Recorded as deserted, 10/62. Record dated 2/10/65 at Petersburg states: "Took the oath to the Yanks." Born: Ireland. Occ.: Butcher. Res.: N.O. Age 29, single.
McCarthy, James, Pvt. En. 6/5/61, CM. Present to 10/62. Discharged as alien, 11/7/62. Record dated 2/10/65 at Petersburg states: "Joined artillery, got killed at Port Hudson." Born: County Dublin, Ireland. Occ.: Baker. Res.: N.O. Age 24, single.
McCauly, Bernard, Pvt. (aka McCalia) En. 6/5/61, CM. Present to 7/62. Roll for 7-8/62 states: "Died July 16, 1862." Record dated 2/10/65 at Petersburg states: "Died in camp at Richmond." Born: Ireland. Occ.: Finisher. Res.: N.O. Age 23, single.
McClune, Bernard, Pvt. En. 2/62, N.O. Present to 6/62. Record dated 2/10/62 states: "Died with sun struck on the mountain." Born: Ireland. Occ.: Laborer. Res.: N.O. Age 32, single.
McClune, Robert, Pvt. En. 3/5/62, N.O. Present to 8/62. No record thereafter. Born: County Down, Ireland. Occ.: Shoemaker. Age 39.
McClung, James, Pvt. En. 6/5/61, CM. Present to 6/62. Captured at Woodstock, Va., 6/2/62. POW, Fort Delaware, took oath of allegiance, 8/10/62. Born: Ireland. Occ.: Laborer. Res.: N.O. Age 28, single.
McClung, John, Pvt. En. 6/5/61, CM. Present to 11/62. Absent sick in hospital, 11/62 to 3/63. Present, 3-6/63. Killed at Winchester, Va., 6/14/63. Born: Ireland. Occ.: Laborer. Res.: N.O. Age 24, single.
McDonald, Michael, Pvt. En. 3/4/62, N.O. Present to 7/62. Mortally wounded at Malvern Hill, 7/1/62. Died at St. Charles Hosp., Richmond, 7/14/62. Record dated 2/10/62 at Petersburg states: "He fell nobly defending his country." Born: County Tipperary, Ireland. Occ.: Drayman Res.: N.O. Age 28, married.
McDonough, James, Pvt. En. 6/5/61, CM. Present to 7/62. Absent detached at regimental wagon yard, 7-11/62. Present 11/62 to 8/63. Roll for 7-8/63 states: "Deserted July, joined Jenkins Cavalry." Record dated 2/10/65 at Petersburg states: "Joined cavalry, got killed on the 16 Nov., 1863." Born: Ireland. Occ.: Butcher. Res.: N.O. Age 27, single.
McEvoy, Patrick, Sgt. En. 6/5/61, CM, as pvt. Promoted to 3rd sgt., 6/1/63. Present to 9/64. Wounded at Battle of Monocacy, Md., 7/9/64, captured 7/10/64. POW, West Bldg. Hosp., Baltimore, Md., flesh wound of left knee. Transferred to Fort McHenry, Md., 8/30/64, tranferred to Point Lookout, Md., 10/25/64, exchanged 10/30/64. Born: Ireland. Res.: N.O. Age 29, single.
McFaull, George, Sgt. (aka McFall, McFaul) En. 6/5/61, CM. Present to 7/62. Recorded as deserted, 7/20/62. Record dated 2/10/65 states: "Took the oath, joined the Yankee army." Born: Ireland. Occ.: Laborer. Res.: N.O. Age 27, married.
McGillick, Patrick, Pvt. En. 6/5/61, CM. Present to 7/62. Absent, detached at brigade HQ., 7-8/62. Absent, detached at Richmond with the Quartermaster, 9-12/62. Roll for 1-2/63 states: "Deserted from Richmond and reported at Mobile, Alabama." Born: Ireland. Occ.: Laborer. Res.: N.O. Age 21, single.
McGovern, James, Pvt. En. 6/5/61, CM. Present to 8/62. Killed at Manassas, Va., 8/29/62. Born: Ireland. Occ.: Laborer. Res.: N.O. Age 25, single.
McGuinn, Patrick, Sgt. En. 6/5/61, CM. Present to 7/62. Absent, detached at regimental wagon yard, 7/62 to 3/63. Promoted to sgt., 6/1/63. Reported missing at Gettysburg, 7/2/63. Roll for 11-12/63 states: "Taken prisoner at Gettysburg, July 2, 1863." Record dated 2/10/65 at Petersburg states: "Killed 2 July, '63." Born: Ireland. Occ.: Baker. Res.: N.O. Age 23, single.
McGuinness, James K., Cpl. En. 6/45/61, CM. Present to 6/62. Wounded at Gaines' Mill, Va., 6/27/62. Absent wounded after 6/62. Roll for 1-2/64 states: "Died from wounds received at Gaines' Mill, June 27, 1862." Roster of non-commissioned officers, undated, states: "Killed at Gain's Mills." Born: Ireland. Occ.: Carpenter. Res.: N.O. Age 22, single.
Meahan, John, Pvt. En. 3/24/62, N.O. Present to 5/63. Reported as missing at Battle of Fredericksburg, Va., 5/3/63. Roll for 5-6/63 states: "Deserted." Born: County Limerick, Ireland. Occ.: Blacksmith. Res.: N.O. Age 26.
Meyers, John H., Pvt. En. 6/5/61, CM. Present to 9/62. AWOL, 9-12/62. Record dated 2/10/65 at Petersburg states: "Joined cavalry under the gallant Morgan." Born: N.O. Occ.: Laborer. Res.: N.O. Age 17, single.
Meyers, Zelestine, Pvt. En. 3/4/62, N.O. Present to 7/62. Killed at Malvern Hill, Va. 7/1/62. Born: Baden (Germany). Occ: Steamboatman. Res.: N.O. Age 46, married.
Miller, Louis, Pvt. En. 6/5/61, CM. Present to 11/63. Captured at Rappahannock Station, Va., 11/7/63. POW, Point Lookout, Md., released on joining U.S. Army, 2/1/64. Born: Prussia. Occ.: Baker. Res.: N.O. Age 19, single.

Muldowney, Hugh, Lt. En. 6/5/61, CM, as cpl. Elected 2nd jr. lt., 5/9/62. Present to 11/63. Absent sick, 11/63-1/64. Present to 8/64. Detailed to recruiting service at Alexandria, La., 8/64 to 6/65. Surrendered and paroled at Alexandria, La., 6/11/65.

Murdock, Edward, Pvt. En. 6/5/61, CM. Present to 5/62. Admitted to CSA Hosp., Charlottesville, Va., 5/30/62, syphlis, transferred to Lynchburg Hosp., 6/16/62. Discharged on surgeon's certificate of disability, 10/26/62. Born: County Longford, Ireland. Occ.: Weaver. Res.: N.O. Age 35, single.

Murphy, Charles, Pvt. En. 6/5/61, CM. Present to 7/63. Wounded at Gettysburg, 7/2/63. Admitted to CSA Hosp., Charlottesville, Va., 7/12/63, deserted from hospital, 8/10/63. Record dated 2/10/65 at Petersburg states: "He joined cavalry, since not heard from." Born: Ireland. Occ.: Laborer. Res.: N.O. Age 22, single.

Murphy, John, Pvt. En. 6/5/61, CM. Present to 7/63. Wounded at Fredericksburg, Va., 5/3/63. Wounded at Gettysburg, 7/2/63, and captured 7/5/63. POW, DeCamp Genl. Hosp., David's Island, N.Y., leg wound. Admitted to Episcopal Church Hosp., Petersburg, Va., 9/15/63, right foot amputated, returned to duty, 2/8/64. Detailed to Provost Guard duty at Staunton, Va., 3/5/64. Record dated 2/10/65 at Petersburg states: "Crippled, taken prisoner, he was a good man." Born: Ireland. Occ.: Laborer. Res.: N.O. Age 25, single.

Murphy, Patrick, Pvt./Musician. En. 6/10/61, CM, as musician. Present to 11/63. Wounded at Gettysburg, 7/2/63. Absent sick in hospital, 11/63 to 2/64. Present, 2/64 to 4/65. Record dated 2/10/65 states: "Drummer, present in camp." Surrendered at Appomattox C.H., Va., 4/9/65. Born: Ireland. Occ.: Butcher. Res.: N.O. Age 27, single.

Murphy, Thomas, Pvt. En. 6/5/61, CM. Present to 5/62. Killed at Winchester, Va., 5/25/62. Born: Ireland. Occ.: Slater. Res.: N.O. Age 20, single.

Murphy, Thomas A., Pvt. En. 6/5/61, CM. Present to 9/62. Roll for 9-10/62 states: "Discharged since last report." Born: Ireland. Occ.: Laborer. Res.: N.O. Age 17, single.

Murphy, William E., Pvt. En. 6/5/61, CM. Present to 10/61. Discharged, 10/61. Roll for 9-10/61 states: "Discharged—Substituted by Robt. Grimstead by order Oct. 1, 1861." Born: Ireland. Occ.: Laborer. Res.: N.O. Age 22, single.

Neary, Thomas, Pvt. En. 6/5/61, CM. Present to 6/62. Captured at Woodstock, Va., 6/2/62. POW, Fort Delaware, took oath of allegiance, 8/10/62. Born: Ireland. Occ.: Laborer. Res.: N.O. Age 27, single.

O'Brien, James, Pvt. En. 3/8/62, N.O. Absent sick in hospital, 7/62 to 4/63. Absent, detailed as nurse in hospital, 4-8/63. Discharged on surgeon's certificate of disability, Charlottesville, Va., 8/21/63, chronic rheumatism. Born: County Fermanagh, Ireland. Occ.: Policeman. Res.: N.O. Age 44, single.

O'Brien, Michael, Pvt. En. 6/5/61, CM. Present to 6/62. Captured at Woodstock, Va., 6/2/62. POW, Fort Delaware, took oath of allegiance, 8/10/62. Born: Ireland. Occ.: Laborer. Res.: N.O. Age 29, single.

O'Connell, Jeremiah, Pvt. En. 6/5/61, CM. Present to 8/62. Roll for 9-10/62 states: "Discharged since last report." Born: Ireland. Occ.: Laborer. Res.: N.O. Age 42, married.

O'Neil, John, Pvt. En. 3/25/63. Roll for 3-4/63 states: "Present, substitute for C.H. Ragen on the 25th of March, 1863." Present to 11/63. Captured at Rappahannock Station, Va., 11/7/63. POW, Point Lookout, Md., exchanged 3/10/64. Absent, detailed at Richmond, 5-8/64. Absent sick in hospital, 8/64 to 4/65. Surrendered and paroled at Winchester, Va., 4/24/65. Age 50, 5'8", brown eyes, black hair, dark complexion.

O'Neil, John, Cpl. (aka O'Neal) En. 6/5/61, CM, as 3rd cpl. Present on 1861 rolls. On register of payments to discharged soldiers, discharge dated 2/10/62. Born: Ireland. Occ.: Carpenter. Res.: N.O. Age 40, married.

O'Neil, Patrick, Pvt. En. 3/6/62, N.O. Present to 6/62. Captured at Harrisonburg, Va., 6/15/62. POW, Fort Delaware, took oath of allegiance, 8/10/62. Born: County Longford, Ireland. Occ.: Carriage driver. Age 27.

O'Neil, Peter, Cpl. En. 6/5/61, CM. Present on 1861 rolls. Discharged on surgeon's certificate of disability, 4/21/62, hernia. Born: County Carlow, Ireland. Occ.: Carpenter. Res.: N.O. Age 36, married.

O'Neil, Thomas, Lt. En. 6/5/61, CM. Present to 1/62. Resigned 1/3/62. Voucher for pay dated 1/3/62 states: "Lieut. O'Neil entered the service again and is now captain of Co. K in 20th Regt. La. Vols." Born: Ireland. Occ.: Clerk. Res.: N.O. Married.

Quinalty, Thomas, Pvt. En. 6/5/61, CM. Present to 12/62. Wounded in right ankle at Fredericksburg, Va., 12/13/62. Absent wounded to 7/62. Present 7/63 to 4/65. Surrendered at Appomattox C.H., 4/9/65. Born: Ireland. Occ.: Laborer. Res.: N.O. Age 24, single.

Raftery, John, Pvt. (aka Rafferty) En. 3/18/62. Present to 9/62. Wounded at Chantilly, Va., 9/1/62. Absent sick, 10/62 to 3/63. Wounded at Fredericksburg, Va., 4/29/63. Present 4-6/63. Captured at Gettysburg, 7/4/63. POW, Fort McHenry, Md., transferred to Fort Delaware, released on joining U.S. 3rd Maryland Cavalry, 9/22/63. Born: County Roscommon, Ireland. Occ.: Cab driver. Res.: N.O. Age 31, single.

Ready, John H., Pvt. (aka Reedy) En. 6/5/61, CM. Present to 9/62. Severely wounded in leg at Chantilly, Va., 9/1/62. Absent wounded, 9/62 to 3/64. Roll for 3-4/64 states: "Absent detailed as nurse at Gen. Hosp., Charlottesville, Va." Absent detailed, 4/64 to 5/65. Paroled at Charlottesville, 5/16/65. Born: Ireland. Occ.: Laborer. Res.: N.O. Age 26, single.

Regensburger, David (aka Ragenburger) En. 3/18/62. Present to 10/62. Discharged on surgeon's certificate from Louisiana Hosp., Richmond, 10/20/62, due to "youth and deblility." Born: Germany. Occ.: Clerk. Res.: N.O. Age 17, single.

Ricker, John G., Sgt. En. 6/5/61, CM, as pvt. Present to 11/63. Captured at Rappahannock Station, Va., 11/7/63. POW, Point Lookout, Md., exchanged 3/10/64. Present, 2/64 to 4/65. Promoted to 4th sgt., 10/19/64. Surrendered at Appomattox C.H., 4/9/65. Born: Ireland. Occ.: Laborer. Res.: N.O. Age 19, single.
Rosenberg, Henry, Pvt. (aka Rosenburgh, Rusenberger, Rougenburgh) En. 3/14/62. Present to 12/62. Killed at Fredericksburg, Va., 12/13/62. Born: Germany. Occ.: Laborer. Res.: N.O. Age 38, single.
Ryan, James, Cpl. En. 3/17/62, N.O. Present to 12/62. Wounded at Fredericksburg, Va., 12/13/62. Present, 1-11/63. Captured at Rappahannock Station, Va., 11/7/63. POW, Point Lookout, Md., took oath of allegiance, 3/14/64. Born: County Tipperary, Ireland. Occ.: Carpenter. Res.: N.O. Age 40 married.
Shanahan, Michael, Pvt. En. 6/5/61, CM. Present to 10/62. Recorded as absent sick, 11/62 to 12/63. Roll for 1-2/64 states: "Reported to have deserted to the enemy from Liberty, Va." Born: Ireland. Occ.: Laborer. Res.: N.O. Age 29, single.
Shaw, Edward, Pvt. En. 6/5/61, CM, as pvt. Promoted to sgt., 4/5/62. Resigned as sgt., 6/1/63. Present to 9/63. Killed at Raccoon Ford, Va., 9/14/63. Born: England. Occ.: Sailor. Res.: N.O. Age 24, single.
Shaw, R.J., Pvt. En. 6/5/61, CM. Present on 1861 rolls. Absent on furlough to N.O., 2-4/62. Record dated 2/10/65 at Petersburg states: "He deserted in 1861, took the oath." Born: Ireland. Occ.: Sailor. Res.: N.O. Age 24, single.
Shidell, Louis, Pvt. (aka Slidell) En. 6/5/61, CM. Present, all rolls to 4/65. Surrendered at Appomattox C.H., 4/9/65. Born: Baden (Germany). Occ.: Sailor. Res.: N.O. Age 21, single.
Sullivan, John, Pvt. En. 6/5/61, CM. Present, all rolls to 3/65. Admitted CSA Hosp., Farmville, Va., 3/16/65, returned to duty 3/21/65, chronic rhreumatism. On roll of POWs at USA Hosp., Farmville, 4/7/65 to 6/15/65. Paroled at Farmville, 4/20/65. Born: Ireland. Occ.: Laborer. Res.: N.O. Age 23, single.
Summers, George J., Lt. En. 6/5/61 as jr. 2nd lt. Present to 4/62. Roster of commissioned officers, undated, states "dropped, April 28, 1862." Record dated 2/10/65 at Petersburg states: "Threw out of office. Joined cavalry, since K[illed]." Born: Virginia. Occ.: Plumber. Res.: N.O.
Tiner, Michael, Pvt. En. 3/17/62, N.O. Absent sick, 7-10/62. Died at Gen. Hosp., Lynchburg, Va., 9/30/62. Born: County Cork, Ireland. Occ.: Blacksmith. Res.: N.O. Age 27, married.
Usedon, Theodore, Pvt. (aka Usedorn, Uesdon) En. 6/4/61, CM. Present to 7/62. Discharged as alien, 7/31/62. Born: Prussia. Occ.: Clerk. Age 31.
Walker, John, Pvt. En. 6/5/61, CM. Present to 9/62. Absent, detailed as nurse, 9/62 to 7/63. Present, 7/63 to 10/64. Severely wounded and captured at Cedar Creek, Va., 10/19/64. POW, USA Gen. Hosp., Baltimore, Md., gunshot wound in left chest, passing through left lung. Transferred to Point Lookout, Md., 10/28/64, exchanged 11/15/64. Admitted La. Hosp., Richmond, 12/3/64, transferred to Lynchburg, 4/8/65. Born: Ireland. Occ.: Sailor. Res.: N.O. Age 32, single.
Ward, Patrick H., Pvt. En. 6/5/61, CM. Present to 6/62. Severely wounded at Gaines' Mill, Va., 6/27/62, right leg amputated, 10/6/62. Absent wounded to 9/64. Retired to Invalid Corps at Columbia, S.C., 9/23/64. Born: Ireland. Occ.: Baker. Res.: N.O. Age 19, single.
Wilkinson, James D., Pvt. En. 6/5/61, CM. Present to 9/62. Absent, detached as baker at Lynchburg, Va., 9/62 to 10/64. Died at Gen. Hosp. No. 2, Lynchburg, 10/23/64, pneumonia. Born: Ireland. Occ.: Baker. Res.: N.O. Age 23, single.
Williams, John, Pvt. En. 3/19/62, N.O. Captured at Gettysburg, 7/3/63. POW, Fort Delaware, exchanged 3/7/65. Born: County Cork, Ireland. Occ.: Laborer. Age 34.

Company C: St. Landry Light Guards

Recruited from St. Landry Parish, the men of this company were mostly natives of Louisiana. Of the 147 men who served in the company, at least 84 were born in Louisiana, eight were Irish immigrants, eight were born in Germany, one in France and one in Italy. Another 15 men were from other states of the Confederacy, and seven were from Northern states. Birthplaces of 23 are unknown. Company A had 20 men killed or mortally wounded in battle, while another 13 died of disease. Eighteen men deserted, nine more were captured and took the oath of allegiance, and seven were captured and joined the U.S. service to win release from Federal prisons. Seven men retired to the Invalid Corps, and six from the company surrendered at Appomattox Court House.

Captains:

Offutt, Nathaniel G., Capt./Lt. Col. Commissioned by Gov. T.O. Moore, 4/23/61. En. 6/4/61, CM, as Capt. See Field and Staff Roster.
Ritchie, H. Bain, Capt. En. 6/4/61, CM, as 2nd lt. Promoted to capt. from 1st lt., 5/26/62. Present to 9/62. Killed at Sharpsburg, Md., 9/17/62. Born: La. Occ.: Farmer. Res.: Big Cane, La. Single.

Cormier, Louis A., Capt. En. 6/4/61, CM, as orderly sgt. Promoted to 2nd jr. lt., 10/31/61. Promoted to 2nd lt., 5/26/62. Promoted to 1st lt., 7/1/62. Promoted to capt., 9/17/62. Absent sick in hospital, 9-10/62. Present, 11/62 to 7/63. Mortally wounded at Gettysburg, Pa., 7/2/63, died 7/3/63. Born: La. Occ.: Farmer. Res.: Washington, La. Single.

Scott, Pannill, Sgt./Capt. En. 6/4/61, CM., as 2nd sgt. Promoted to 2nd jr. lt., 6/11/62, to 2nd lt., 7/1/62, to 1st lt., 9/17/62, to capt., 7/2/63. Present to 6/63. Wounded at Sharpsburg, Md., 9/17/62. Wounded at Fredericksburg, Va., 5/4/63. Wounded at Winchester, Va., 6/14/63. Absent wounded, 6-10/63. Present to 5/64. Captured at Wilderness, Va., 5/5/64. POW, Fort Delaware, Del., released 5/5/65. Born: La. Occ.: Farmer. Res.: Washington, La. Single, 5'10", gray eyes, sandy hair, fair complexion.

* * *

Andrus, Abraham, Pvt. En. 6/4/61, CM. Detached as hospital ward, 8/1/61. Present 1/62 through 2/63. Absent sick in hospital, 3-6/63. Absent on furlough, 1-2/64. Deserted while on furlough, 4/64. Born: La. Res.: Big Cane, La. Married.

Arden, William, Pvt. En. 6/4/61, CM. Present to 1/63. Wounded at Fredericksburg, Va.,12/13/62. Absent sick in hospital, 1/63 to 8/63. Captured at Fisher's Hill, Va., 9/23/64. POW, Point Lookout, Md., 10/3/64 to 2/10/65. Born: La. Occ.: Carpenter. Res.: Washington, La. Single.

Ashford, Christopher C., Pvt. En. 6/4/61, CM. Present to 2/62. Discharged on surgeon's certificate of disability ,2/9/62, chronic rheumatism. Born: St. Landry, La. Occ.: Farmer. Res.: Washington, La. Age 28, married, 5' 9", light complexion, light eyes, dark hair.

Baddeaux, Arvillien, Pvt. En. 6/4/61, CM. Present to 8/61. No record thereafter.

Badeaux, Charles, Pvt. Absent sick in hospital, 5-10/62. Present 11/62 to 4/63. Absent sick in hospital, 5/63 through 8/64. On roll of POWs, captured in hospital, Richmond, 4/3/65. Born: La. Occ.: Farmer. Res.: Washington, La. Married, 5' 7", gray eyes, dark complexion, dark hair.

Barton, Alexander, Pvt. En. 6/4/61, CM. Present to 5/63. Wounded at Fredericksburg, Va., 5/3/63. Absent, detailed as nurse to attend wounded, 5-6/63. Present 7/63 to 11/63. Captured at Rappahannock Station, Va.,11/7/63. POW, Point Lookout, Md., exchanged 3/9/64. Captured at Wilderness, Va., 5/5/64. POW, Point Lookout, transferred to Elmira, N.Y., 8/16/64, exchanged 7/25/65. Born: La. Occ.: Mechanic. Res.: Washington, La. Married.

Bellow, Charles S., Pvt. En. 6/4/61, CM. Present to 6/62. Detailed as teamster, 6/15/62. Absent sick in hospital, 9-10/62. Deserted, 3/8/63.

Benileau, J., NR. No enlistment record. Roll for 5-6/62 states: "Wounded June 9. Discharged on the 14th of June."

Bertrand, Alcee, Pvt. En. 3/3/62, St. Landry Parish. Absent sick in hospital 5-8/62. Present 9/62 to 5/64. Captured at Wilderness, Va., 5/5/64. POW, Point Lookout, Md., transferred to Elmira, N.Y., 8/15/64. Paroled 2/25/65, Elmira. Surrendered 4/9/65 at Appomattox C.H. Res.: St. Landry, La. Age 21, 5' 3", black eyes, dark hair, dark complexion.

Bihm, Milton, Pvt. En. 6/4/61, CM. Present through 8/61. Absent sick, 9-10/61. Absent sick in Louisiana, 5/62 to 2/63. Born: La. Occ.: farmer. Res.: St. Landry. Single.

Bihm, R.L. (Lewis), Pvt. En. 6/4/61, CM. Discharged on surgeon's certificate of disability, 7/27/62, diabetis. Born: St. Landry, La. Occ.: planter. Age 30, 5' 10", dark hair, gray eyes, dark complexion.

Blair, Alex W., Pvt. En. 3/3/62, St. Landry. Present to 11/62. Absent sick in hospital, 11/62 through 8/63. Recorded as deserted 9-10/63. Born: Kentucky. Occ.: Mechanic. Res.: Washington, La. Single.

Bollendorf, Nicholas, Pvt. En. 6/4/61, CM. Present to 6/62. Captured at Front Royal, Va., 6/2/62. On roll of POWs aboard steamer Coatzacoalas, undated. Detailed as a tailor at Confederate clothing bureau, Richmond, Va., 9-11/63. Captured at Wilderness, Va., 5/5/64. POW, Point Lookout, Md. Admitted to Point Lookout hospital, 5/22/64, died 5/30/64, pneumonia. Born: Germany. Occ.: Laborer. Res.: Washington, La. Single.

Bolton, Alex, Pvt. En. 6/4/61. Born: Tennessee. Occupation: clerk. Residence: Washington, La. Single.

Bolton, Moses, Pvt. En. 6/4/61, CM. Present to 9/61. Absent sick in hospital, 9-10/61. Discharged 12/2/61.

Bonham, E., Pvt. No enlistment record. Signed voucher for bounty, $50, 10/25/62. On list of paroled prisoners, undated.

Bowen, William, Pvt. En. 3/3/62, St. Landry. Absent sick in hospital, 5-8/62. Present 9/62 through 4/63. Absent, detailed as brigade teamster, 5-6/63. Present, 7-11/63. Captured at Rappahannock Station, Va., 11/7/63, POW, Point Lookout, Md., took oath of allegiance, 3/30/64. 5'6", gray eyes, black hair, dark complexion.

Bundick, George W., Pvt. En. 5/26/61, Washington, La. Absent sick in hospital, 7-9/61. Discharged on certificate of disability, 9/2/61. Born: La. Occ.: Farmer. Res.: Big Cane, La. Single.

Bushnell, Nathaniel, Pvt. En. 6/4/61, CM. Present to 11/62. Absent sick in hospital, 11-12/62. Present, 1-4/63. Absent sick, 4-5/63. Present, 7-10/63. Captured at Rappahannock Station, Va., 11/7/63. POW, Point Lookout, Md., exchanged 3/10/64. Listed as killed at Wilderness, Va., 5/5/64, on 6th Louisiana casualty list in Museum of Confederacy, Richmond, Va. Born: La. Occ.: Mechanic. Res.: Washington, La. Single.

Butler, Benjamin R., Sgt. Maj. See Field & Staff roster.

Cassidy, A.D., Pvt. En. 8/24/61, N.O. Mortally wounded at Gaines' Mill, Va., 6/27/62, died 7/15/62.

Charles, Cyprian, Pvt. En. 3/2/62, Washington, La. Admitted to CSA Hosp., Charlottesville, Va., 4/16/62. Discharged on surgeon's certificate, 7/4/62, due to "epilepsy and feeble constitution." Born: St. Landry Parish. Occ.: Farmer. Res.: Washington, La. Age 37, married. 5'8", dark eyes, dark hair, dark complexion.

Chenier, Tesson M., Pvt. (aka T.N. Chenier) En. 3/3/62, St. Landry, La. Absent sick in hospital, 5-6/62. Present, 7-8/62. Captured at Frederick, Md., 9/12/62. POW, Fort Delaware, exchanged 11/10/62. Recorded as deserted, 12/63. Born: La. Occ.: Mechanic. Res.: Washington, La. Married.

Clow, Albert B., Cpl. En. 6/4/61, CM. Discharged on surgeon's certificate, 1/3/62, due to injury to vertebra, paryalysis. Born: La. Occ.: Clerk. Res.: Washington, La. Age 23, married, 6'0", light eyes, light hair, light complexion.

Cole, Jonathan H., Pvt. En. 6/4/61, CM. Present to 4/62. Admitted to CSA Hosp., Charlottesville, Va., 4/23/62, typhoid fever, returned to duty 5/27/62. Discharged on surgeon's certificate, 7/25/62, chronic diarrhea and general debility. Born: St. Landry Parish, La. Occ: Overseer. Age 36, married, 5'4", dark eyes, dark hair, light complexion.

Cormier, Emile T., Lt. En. 6/4/61, CM, as pvt. Promoted to sgt., 6/15/62. Elected 2nd jr. lt., 9/26/62. Present to 12/63. Absent on furlough, 1-2/64. Wounded at Battle of Monocacy, 7/9/64, and captured at Frederick, Md., 7/10/64. Admitted to U.S. Genl. Hosp., Baltimore, Md., 7/27/64, left leg wound. POW, Fort McHenry, Md., transferred to Point Lookout, Md., 9/27/64, exchanged 9/30/64. Admitted to Gen. Hosp. No. 4, Richmond, 10/7/64, left leg wound, furloughed 10/12/64. Record dated 3/13/65 at Petersburg, states: "Dropped from rolls." Born: La. Occ.: Druggist. Res.: Washington, La., married.

Cox, John, Cpl. En. 3/3/62, St. Landry. Absent, detached as ambulance driver, 5-8/62. Present, 9/62 to 4/65. Promoted to from pvt. to cpl., 1/1/64. Surrendered at Appomattox C.H., Va., 4/9/65. Born.: Virginia. Occ.: Teamster. Res.: Washington, La. Age 27, single, 6'1", gray eyes, dark hair, dark complexion.

Craig, Thomas, Sgt. En. 6/4/61, CM. Present to 11/63. Promoted from pvt. to cpl., 5/63. Promoted to sgt., 9/14/63. Captured at Rappahannock Station, Va., 11/7/63. POW, Point Lookout, Md., exchanged 3/17/64. Present, 5-8/64. On roll of POWs surrendered at New Orleans, 5/26/65, paroled at Washington, La., 6/16/65. Born: Ireland. Occ.: Cooper. Res.: Washington, La. Age 23, 5'9", hazel eyes, dark hair, fair complexion.

Cunningham, Daniel, Pvt. En. 6/4/61, CM. Present to 9/62. Captured at Hagerstown, Md., 9/11/62. POW, Fort Delaware, Del., exchanged 11/10/62. Present, 11/62 to 5/63. Wounded at Fredericksburg, Va., 5/4/63. Absent wounded, 7-8/63. Present, 9-11/63. Captured at Rappahannock Station, Va., 11/7/63. POW, Point Lookout, Md. Released on joining U.S. Army, 2/1/64. Born: County Clare, Ireland. Occ.: Mechanic. Res.: Washington, La. Age 24, married, 5'10", blue eyes, dark hair, fair complexion.

Curtis, Reuben, Pvt. En. 6/4/61, CM. Present to 11/62. Absent sick in hospital, 11-12/62. Absent on furlough, 1-2/63. Transferred to 1st Field Battery, Louisiana Artillery (St. Mary's Cannoneers), by special order dated 4/29/63. Surrendered as cpl., 1st. Field Battery, at Tyler, Texas, 5/26/65, paroled at Franklin, La., 6/19/65. Born: Texas. Occ.: Clerk. Res.: Washington, La. Single.

Darby, L.J., Pvt. En. 6/4/61, CM. Present to 5/62. Absent sick, 5-8/62. Present 9/62 to 7/63. Captured at South Mountain, Md., 7/5/63. POW, Fort Delaware, exchanged 3/7/65. Born: La. Occ.: Merchant. Res.: Big Cane, La. Single.

Derosier, P., Pvt. En. 3/3/62, St. Landry. Absent sick in hospital, 5/62 to 7/63. Roll for 9-10/63 states "supposed to have died at Winchester, Oct. 1862."

Desbrest, Antoine, Pvt. En. 6/4/61, CM. Present to 7/62. Absent sick in hospital, 7-8/62. Present, 9/62 to 5/63. Killed at Fredericksburg, Va. 5/3/63.

Douglas, William, Pvt. En. 6/4/61, CM. Present to 7/61. Absent detached as teamster, 7/61 to 7/63. Captured in Washington County, Md., 7/7/63. POW, Camp Chase, Ohio, transferred to Fort Delaware, 7/14/63. Took oath of allegiance, 12/64. Born: Ohio. Occ.: Merchant. Res.: Washington, La. Age 31, single, 6'0", blue eyes, black hair.

Drinkard, Frank M., Pvt. En. 6/4/61, CM. Present to 11/63. Captured at Rappahannock Station, Va., 11/7/63. POW, Point Lookout, Md., took oath of allegiance, 5/6/64. Occ.: Clerk. Res.: Washington, La. Single.

Dykes, James C., Pvt. En. 6/4/61, CM. Present to 10/61. Admitted to Chimborozo Hosp., Richmond, 10/18/61, chonic diarrhea, died 4/12/62. Born: La. Occ.: Farmer. Res.: Washington, La. Single.

Fisher, Ulysses W., Cpl. En. 6/4/61, CM, as pvt. Present to 9/62. Wounded at Sharpsburg, Md., 9/17/62. Admitted to Chimborazo Hosp., Richmond, 10/24/62, foot wound, returned to duty 12/15/62. Promoted to cpl., 1/1/63. Severely wounded and captured at Gettysburg, 7/2/63, gunshot wound in thigh. POW, DeCamp Genl. Hosp., David's Island, N.Y., died 9/6/63.

Fitch, Daniel A.., Sgt. En. 6/4/61, CM, as pvt. Present to 6/62. Killed at Port Republic, Va., 6/9/62. Born: La. Occ.: Engineer. Res.: Washington, La. Single.

Fitch, John M., Pvt. En. 7/23/61, Union Mills, Va. Present to 11/62. Detached as ambulance driver, 11/62 to 3/63. Present, 3-11/63. Captured at Rappahannock Station, Va., 11/7/63. POW, Point Lookout, Md., took oath of allegiance, 3/20/64. Born: St. Landry, La. Occ.: Mechanic. Res: Washington, La. Single.

Fitzgerald, Thomas, Pvt. En. 6/4/61, CM. Present to 3/62. Died at Moore Hosp., Manassas Junction, Va., 3/5/62, typhoid fever. Born: Ireland. Occ.: Farmer. Res.: Washington, La. Single.

Fontenot, Benjamin, Pvt. En. 6/4/61, CM. Present to 4/62. Absent sick, 4-5/62. Present to 5/64. Captured at Mine Run, Va., 5/12/64. POW, Point Lookout, Md., transferred to Elmira, N.Y., 8/15/64. Paroled at Elmira and sent to

James River for exchange, 2/25/65. Surrendered at Appomattox C.H., 4/9/65. Born: La. Occ.: Farmer. Res.: Washington, La. Single.

Fontenot, Emile, Pvt. En. 6/4/61, CM. Present to 6/62. Wounded at Port Republic, Va., 6/9/62. Absent wounded 6-11/62. Present to 5/63. Wounded at Fredericksburg, Va., 5/5/63. Absent wounded to 1/64. Retired to Invalid Corps, 4/64. Born: La. Occ.: Farmer. Res.: Washington, La. Single.

Fontenot, Oreal S., Pvt. En. 6/4/61, CM. Present to 9/62. Wounded at Chantilly, Va., 9/1/62. Absent wounded to 11/63. Discharged on surgeon's certificate of disability, 5/64. Born: La. Occ.: Farmer. Res.: Washington, La. Single.

Fontenot, Paul, Sgt. En. 3/2/62, St. Landry, La. Wounded at Bristoe Station, Va., 8/27/62. Promoted to sgt., 4/7/64. Captured at Wilderness, Va., 5/5/64. POW, Point Lookout, Md., transferred to Elmira, N.Y., 8/15/64, exchanged 2/25/65. Born: La. Occ.: Farmer. Res.: Washington, La. Single.

Fontenot, U., Pvt. En. 3/3/62, St. Landry, La. Absent sick, 5-11/62. Discharged on surgeon's certificate, 11/62. Born: La. Occ.: Farmer. Res.: Washington, La. Single.

Fontenot, Viale, Pvt. En. 3/3/62. Present to 5/64. Captured at Wilderness, Va., 5/5/64. POW, Point Lookout, Md. Died at Point Lookout, 6/20/64. Born: La. Occ.: Farmer. Res.: Washington, La. Married.

Foote, A.. S., Pvt. En. 6/2/61, CM. Present to 6/62. Discharged on surgeon's certificate, 6/16/62, necrosis of the nasal bones. Born: La. Occ.: Overseer. Res.: Big Cane, La. Single.

Ford, Alex M., Pvt. En. 6/4/61, CM. Present to 9/62. Absent sick in hospital, 9/62 to 4/63. Wounded at Winchester, Va., 6/14/63. Retired to Invalid Corps, 10/28/64.

Ford, Lewis S., Pvt. En. 8/4/61, Camp Bienville (Centreville) Va. Present to 11/61. Discharged on surgeon's certificate, 11/11/61. Born: La. Occ.: Mechanic. Res.: Big Cane, La. Single.

Frith, Charles H., Pvt. En. 6/4/61, CM. Transferred to Company C from Company H., 7/1/61. Present to 2/62. Discharged on surgeon's certificate of disability, 2/12/62, chronic rheumatism and injury to left arm. Born: Mississippi. Occ.: farmer. Age 24.

Fusilier, John, Pvt. En. 3/3/62, St. Landry, La. Present through 12/64. On roll of POWs of diverse companies and regiments, detached, surrendered at Citronelle, Ala., 5/4/65. Paroled at Meridian, Miss., 5/12/65. Born: La. Occ.: Farmer. Res.: Washington, La. Married.

Gale, J. Scott, Pvt. En. 6/4/61, CM. Present to 8/62. Captured at Manassas, Va., 8/62. POW, place unstated, exchanged at Aikin's Landing, Va., 11/10/62. Present to 4/63. Captured at Fredericksburg, Va., 4/29/63. POW, Old Capitol Prison, Washington, exchanged 6/3/63. Present, 7-1/63. Captured at Rappahannock Station, Va., 11/7/63. POW, Point Lookout, Md., released 2/1/64 on joining the U.S. Army.

Gleavy, John, Pvt. En. 6/4/61, CM. Present to 5/63. Wounded at Fredericksburg, Va., 5/4/63. Present to 7/63. Captured at Gettysburg, 7/3/63. POW, Fort Delaware, Del. Released 5/65. Born: Ireland. Occ.: Farmer. Res.: St. Landry Parish, La. Single, 5'9", hazel eyes, dark hair, ruddy complexion.

Going, Edward J., Cpl. En. 6/4/61, CM. Present to 7/62. Detailed as ambulance driver, 7/62 to 1/64. Absent on furlough, 1-2/64. Deserted while on furlough, 3/64. On roll of POWs surrendered at New Orleans, 5/26/65, paroled Alexandria, La., 6/3/65. Born: Mississippi. Occ.: Clerk. Res.: Washington, La. Single.

Gordon, Charles P., Pvt. En. 6/4/61, CM. Present to 5/62. Absent sick in hospital, 5-8/62. Detailed as clerk in hospital, 9/62 to 1/63. Present, 1-2/63. Detailed as clerk for Brigade surgeon, 3-8/63. Present, 8/63 to 5/64. Captured at Wilderness, Va., 5/5/64. POW, Point Lookout, Md., transferred to Elmira, N.Y., 8/15/64, exchanged 10/29/64. On roll of POWs of Co. C., commanded by Lt. E.T. Cormier, surrendered at N.O., 5/26/65, paroled at Washington, La., 6/16/65. Born: St. Landry Parish, La. Occ.: Clerk. Res.: St. Landry Parish. Single.

Graham, Holmes, Sgt. En. 6/4/61, CM, as pvt. Promoted to cpl., 6/15/62, to sgt., 6/28/62, to 1st sgt., 9/14/63. Present to 11/63. Captured at Rappahannock Station, Va., 11/7/63. POW, Point Lookout, Md., took oath of allegiance, 3/30/64. Born: Ireland. Res.: St. Landry Parish, La. Single.

Guillory, Achille, Pvt. En. 3/3/62, St. Landry Parish, La. Present to 5/62. Died in Genl. Hosp. No. 1, Lynchburg, Va., 5/17/62, typhoid fever. Born: La. Occ.: Cooper. Res.: St. Landry Parish. Single.

Guillory, Augustave, Pvt. En. 3/3/62, St. Landry Parish, La. Present to 5/63. Absent sick in hospital, 5-6/63. Present, 7-8/63. Absent sick in hospital, 9-10/63. Present, 11/63 to 3/64. Absent sick, 3-4/64. Present, 4/64 to 4/65. On list of Confederate soldiers who surrendered giving individual paroles, Greensboro, N.C., 5/5/65. Born: La. Occ.: Farmer. Res.: St. Landry. Single.

Guillory, Zenon, Pvt. En. 3/3/62, St. Landry, Parish, La. Present to 5/63. Absent sick, 5-6/63. Present, 7-11/63. Absent on furlough, 11-12/63. Present, 1-5/64. Captured at Wilderness, Va., 5/5/64. POW, Point Lookout, Md. Died at POW Hospital, Point Lookout, 7/3/64, fever.

Haines, James D., Pvt. En. 6/4/61, CM. Detached as wagon driver, 8/61 to 11/62. Present to 7/63. Killed at Gettysburg, Pa., 7/2/63. Born: New York. Occ.: Farmer. Res.: St. Landry, La. Single.

Hall, Benjamin, Pvt. En. 6/4/61, Mobile, Ala. Transferred from 3rd Alabama Regiment, 4/1/64. Captured at Woodstock, Va., 10/21/64. POW, Point Lookout, Md., exchanged 1/17/65. Born: La. Occ.: Farmer. Res.: St. Landry, La. Married.

Hanna, Gordon W., Sgt. En. 6/4/61, CM. Present to 9/62. Promoted to sgt., 6/15/62. Wounded in finger at Sharpsburg, Md., 9/17/62. Absent wounded, 9-10/62. Present 11/62 to 11/63. Wounded and captured at Rappahannock Station, Va., 11/7/63, gunshot wound in left ankle. POW, Old Capitol Prison, Washington, took oath of allegiance, 3/22/64. Born: Ohio. Occ.: Clerk. Res.: St. Landry Parish. Single, 5'8", blue eyes, brown hair, dark complexion.

Hardy, Constantine, Pvt. En. 6/4/61, CM. Present to 6/62. Recorded as missing since Battle of Port Republic, 7-11/62. Recorded as deserted, 12/62. Born: La. Occ.: Farmer. Res.: St. Landry Parish. Single.

Hardy, Flavius, Pvt. En. 3/3/62, St. Landry Parish. Present to 5/63. Wounded at Fredericksburg, Va., 5/4/63. Absent wounded 5-12/63. Absent, detailed as guard at Bellona Arsenal, Chesterfield County, Va., 1-11/64. Captured at Salisbury, N.C., 4/12/65. POW, Camp Chase, Sandusky, Ohio, released 6/13/65. Born: La. Occ.: Clerk. Res.: St. Landry Parish. Age 42, married, blue eyes, dark hair, florid complexion, 5'6".

Hebert, William, Pvt. En. 6/4/61, CM. Present to 9/62. Absent, detailed as provost guard at Winchester, Va., 9-10/62. Present 1-12/63. Absent sick in hospital, 1/64 to 1/65. Retired to Invalid Corps, 1/65, impaired eyesight. Born: La. Occ.: Merchant. Res.: St. Landry Parish. Age 24, single.

Hickman, John C., Lt. En. 6/4/61, CM, as 1st Lt. Present to 9/61. Resigned, 10/25/61. Born: La. Occ.: Engineer. Res.: Washington, La. Single.

Higgenbotham, Perry, Pvt. En. 6/4/61, CM. Present to 7/62. Mortally wounded at Malvern Hill, Va., 7/1/62, died 7/8/62. Born: Texas. Occ.: Farmer. Res.: St. Landry Parish. Single.

Hull, James M., Sgt. En. 6/4/61, CM, as drummer. Present to 10/61. Detailed as teamster, 10/61 to 2/62. Detailed as superintendent of brigade ambulance train, 3/63 to 4/65. Surrendered at Appomattox C.H., 4/9/65. Record dated 3/13/65 at Petersburg, Va., states: "In charge of ambulance corps and present at all fights." Born: La. Occ.: Farmer. Res.: St. Landry Parish. Single.

Humble, Oliver, Pvt. En. 6/20/62 in Charlottesville, Va. Present, 6-9/62. Absent detailed as hospital nurse, 9/62 to 3/63. Present, 3-7/63. Wounded at Gettysburg, 7/2/63. Absent wounded, 7-8/63. Present 9/63 to 5/64. Captured at Wilderness, 5/5/64. POW, Point Lookout, Md., transferred to Elmira, N.Y., 8/15/64, exchanged 2/13/65. Paroled at Genl. Hosp., Greensboro, N.C., 4/26/65.

Jackson, Preston, Pvt. En. 3/6/62, St. Landry. Present to 6/62. Captured at Woodstock, Va., 6/2/62. POW, Fort Delaware, Del., exchanged 8/5/62. Absent sick in hospital, 8/62 to 3/63. Present, 3-4/63. Absent sick, 5-6/63. Captured at South Mountain, Md., 7/5/63. POW, Fort Delaware. Died at Fort Delaware, 10/24/63, smallpox.

Jacobs, Philip, Pvt. En. 6/4/61, CM. Present to 8/62. Detached as clerk in Quartermaster's office, 8/62 to 3/63. On detached service in Louisiana with General Richard Taylor from 7/1/63 on. Born: Prussia. Occ.: Clerk. Res: St. Landry Parish. Single.

Johnson, Barrien, Pvt. En. 6/4/61, CM. Present to 9/62. Captured at Antietam, Md., 9/27/62. POW, Fort McHenry, Md., exchanged 10/20/62. Present, 10/62 to 5/64. Captured at Wilderness, Va., 5/5/64. POW, Point Lookout, Md., transferred to Elmira, N.Y., 8/15/64, exchanged 2/25/65. Surrendered and paroled at Tallahassee, Fla., 5/12/65. Born: Florida. Occ.: Farmer. Res.: St. Landry. Single.

Kerol, Felix, Sgt. (aka Carroll) En. 6/4/61, CM. Promoted to cpl., 7/11/62. Present to 7/63. Wounded at Gettysburg, 7/2/63. Absent wounded 7-9/63. Present 10/63 to 7/64. Captured near Harper's Ferry, Va., 7/8/64. POW, Old Capitol Prison, Washington, transferred to Elmira, N.Y., 7/23/64, exchanged 3/2/65. Captured at Petersburg, Va., 4/3/65. POW, Hart's Island, N.Y., released 6/14/65. Born: La. Occ.: Barber. Res.: St. Landry. Single.

Labarge, William, Pvt. En. 3/3/62, St. Landry Parish. Present to 7/63. Detailed as regimental butcher, 7/63 to 1/64. Present 1-5/64. Captured at Wilderness, Va., 5/5/64. POW, Point Lookout, Md., transferred to Elmira, N.Y., 8/16/64. Exchanged 10/29/64. Born: La. Occ.: Farmer. Res.: St. Landry. Married.

Lacomb, Amos, Sgt. En. 6/4/61, CM, as pvt. Promoted to sgt., 6/15/62. Present to 9/63. Killed at Raccoon Ford, 9/14/63. Born: La. Occ.: Engineer. Res.: St. Landry. Single.

Lacomb, Austin, Pvt. En. 6/4/61, CM. Present to 5/64. Captured at Wilderness, Va., 5/5/64. POW, Point Lookout, Md., transferred to Elmira, N.Y., 8/15/64, exchanged 2/25/65. Admitted to Louisiana Hosp., Richmond, 3/13/65. Paroled at Charleston, W.Va., 5/1/65. Born: La. Occ.: Farmer. Res.: St. Landry. Age 22, single, 5'6", blue eyes, light hair, fair complexion.

Lafleur, Ernest, Cpl. En. 6/4/61, CM. Promoted to cpl., 6/28/62. Present to 9/62. Captured at Sharpsburg, Md., 9/19/62. POW, Fort McHenry, Md., exchanged 11/10/62. Present 11/62 to 5/63. Captured at Fredericksburg, Va., 5/3/63. POW, Fort Delaware, Del., exchanged 6/3/63. Captured at Rappahannock Station, Va., 11/7/63. POW, Point Lookout, Md., exchanged 2/10/65. Born: La. Occ.: Farmer. Res.: St. Landry. Single.

Lambert, Fritz, Pvt. En. 6/4/61, CM. Present to 8/62. Wounded at Bristoe Station, Va., 8/27/62. Absent wounded, 8/62 to 4/64. Roll for 3-4/64 states: "Deserted, dropped as deserter." On list of prisoners taken and paroled at Warrenton, Va., 9/29/62. Last paid at Richmond, 10/16/62, on furlough. Born: Germany. Occ.: Merchant. Res.: St. Landry Parish. Single.

Launey, Arthur, Pvt. En. 6/4/61, CM. Present to 6/62. Detailed as hospital nurse, 6-12/62. Present, 1-4/63. Captured at Fredericksburg, Va., 4/29/63. POW, Fort Delaware, Del., exchanged 6/3/63. Wounded at Winchester, 6/14/63. Absent wounded, 6-11/63. Present 12/63 to 5/64. Captured at Wilderness, Va., 5/5/64. POW, Point Lookout, Md., transferred to Elmira, N.Y., 8/15/64, exchanged 3/10/65. Paroled at Charleston, W.Va., 5/1/65. Born: La. Occ.: Mechanic. Res.: St. Landry Parish. Age 21, single, 5'5", black eyes, dark hair, dark complexion.

Lejeune, Edmond, Pvt. En. 3/3/62, St. Landry Parish. Absent sick, 5-11/62. Present 11/62 to 4/65. Surrendered at Appomattox C.H., Va., 4/9/65. Born: La. Occ.: Farmer. Res.: St. Landry Parish. Age 19, single, 5'6", hazel eyes, brown hair, light complexion.

Lejeune, John, Pvt. En. 3/3/62, St. Landry. Present to 11/63. Captured at Rappahannock Station, Va., 11/7/63. POW, Point Lookout, Md., exchanged 3/10/63. Captured at Wilderness, Va., 5/5/64. POW, Point Lookout, transferred to Elmira, N.Y., 8/15/64, paroled 2/13/65. Transferred to Point Lookout Hospital, 2/17/65, smallpox. Deserted from hospital, 3/28/65. Born: La. Occ.: Farmer. Res.: St. Landry Parish. Single.

Lewis, Edward D., Pvt. En. 6/4/61, CM. Present to 5/62. Absent sick in hospital, 5-7/62. Discharged on surgeon's certificate of disability, 7/5/62, asthma. Born: Henrico County, Va. Age 32.

Manuel, Azelien, Pvt. En. 3/3/62, St. Landry. Present to 7/63. Captured at South Mountain, Md., 7/5/63. POW, Fort Delaware, Del, released 5/5/65. Born: La. Occ.: Farmer. Res.: St. Landry Parish. Single, 5'7", black eyes, dark hair, dark complexion.

McCaulay, Stephen D., Lt. En. 6/4/61, CM, as 2nd jr. lt. Promoted to 1st lt., 5/26/62. Present to 7/62. Killed at Malvern Hill, Va., 7/1/62. Born: La. Occ.: Farmer. Res.: Washington, La. Single.

McCauley, Jesse M., Pvt. En. 6/4/61, CM. Present on 1861 rolls. No record thereafter. Born: La. Occ.: Farmer. Res.: St. Landry Parish. Single.

McCrory, Robert R., Pvt. En. 6/4/61, CM. Present to 9/61. Discharged on surgeon's certificate of disability, Camp Bienville (Centreville) Va., 9/4/61, general debility and bronchitis.

McGee, John, Pvt. En. 3/3/62, St. Landry. Admitted CSA Hosp., Charlottesville, Va., 4/29/62. Died 5/19/62, pneumonia. Born: La. Occ.: Farmer. Res.: St. Landry. Married.

McGee, Lucien, Pvt. (aka Magee) En. 3/3/62, St. Landry. Present to 7/62. Absent sick in hospital, 7-12/62. Absent on furlough, 12/61-1/63. Roll for 3-4/63 states: "Deserted on 1st March." Born: La. Occ.: Farmer. Res.: St. Landry. Single.

McKinney, Archibald, Pvt. (aka McKenny) En. 6/4/61, CM. Present to 6/62. Wounded at Port Republic, Va., 6/9/62. Absent wounded, 6-9/62. Present, 9/62 to 5/63. Wounded at Fredericksburg, Va., 5/4/63. Absent wounded, 5-6/63. Present 7-11/63. Captured at Rappahannock Station, Va., 11/7/63. POW, Point Lookout, Md., released on joining U.S. service, 1/24/64. Born: Ireland. Occ.: Farmer. Res.: St. Landry. Single.

McPherson, John, Pvt. En. 12/20/61 at Camp Carondolet, Va. Present to 6/62. Captured at Woodstock, Va., 6/2/62. Roll for 7-8/62 states: "Exchanged prisoner, absent without leave." Recorded as deserted, 10/62. Born: La. Occ.: Farmer. Res.: St. Landry. Single.

Metivier, Leon, Pvt. En. 6/4/61, CM. Present to 6/62. Wounded at Port Republic, Va., 6/9/62. Absent wounded to 3/64. Retired to Invalid Corps at Staunton, Va., 4/1/64.

Morgan, James, Cpl. En. 6/4/61, CM, as pvt. Promoted to cpl., 10/1/62. Present to 5/62. Absent sick in hospital, 5-6/62. Absent detached as nurse, 7-8/62. Present, 9-11/62. Admitted to Louisiana Hosp., Richmond, 12/13/62, died 12/26/62, double pneumonia. Born: La. Occ.: Farmer. Res.: St Landry. Single.

Morris, Jack, Pvt. En. 6/4/61, CM. Present to 8/62. Wounded at Manassas, Va., 8/29/62. Present, 9/62 to 11/63. Captured at Rappahannock Station, Va., 11/7/63. POW, Point Lookout, Md. Released 2/1/64 on joining U.S. Army. Born: Mississippi. Occ.: Farmer. Res.: St. Landry. Single.

Mullholland, James, Pvt./Musician. (aka Mullhollin, Mulhollan, Jake) En. 6/4/61, CM, as drummer. Present to 11/62. Absent sick, 11-12/62. Present, 1-7/63. Reported missing at Gettysburg, 7/3/63. Roll for 7-8/63 states: "Absent, supposed to have been taken prisoner on the retreat from Gettysburg." Roll for 3-4/64 states: "Taken the oath of allegiance to the U.S., dropped as deserter." Born: Pennsylvania. Occ.: Farmer. Res.: St. Landry. Single.

Mullen, Joseph, Pvt. En. 6/4/61, CM. Present to 4/63. Captured at Fredericksburg, Va., 4/29/63. POW, Old Capitol Prison, Washington, exchanged 6/3/63. Present, 6-11/63. Captured at Rappahannock Station, Va., 11/7/63. POW, Point Lookout, Md., released on oath of allegiance, 3/30/64.

O'Connor, Thomas, Pvt. En. 3/3/62, St. Landry. Present to 4/63. Captured at Fredericksburg, Va., 4/3/63. POW, Old Capitol Prison, Washington, transferred to Fort Delaware, exchanged 6/3/63. Severely wounded in leg at Gettysburg, 7/2/63, and captured 7/5/63. POW, USA Genl. Hosp., West Bldg., Baltimore, Md., paroled 9/25/63 and transferred to City Point, Va., for exchange. Absent on furlough, 10-12/63. Absent wounded thereafter. Born: La. Occ.: Mechanic. Res.: St. Landry. Married.

Oger, Pierre, Pvt. En. 3/3/62, St. Landry. Absent sick in hospital, 5-6/62. Present, 6-9/62. Mortally wounded at Sharpsburg, Md., 9/17/62. Roll for 11-12/62 states: "Died from wound rec'd at Sharpsburg." On list of Confederate wounded at the Battle of Antietam who died at hospitals near Antietam, place of death, Grove's Warehouse. Born: Tennessee. Occ.: Mechanic. Res.: St. Landry. Married.

Olds, Walton R., Pvt. En. 6/4/61, CM. Present to 9/62. Wounded in leg at Chantilly, Va., 9/1/62. Absent wounded, 9/62 to 9/63. Roll for 9-10/63 states: "Absent, detailed as guard at hospital, Richmond." Absent, detailed after 9/63. Certificate of disability dated 11/12/64 at Richmond states: "Fracture of right fibula and loss of bone." Occ.: Mechanic. Res.: St. Landry. Married.

O'Riley, Edward, Lt. En. 6/4/61, CM, as cpl. Present to 6/62. Promoted to 1st sgt., 6/11/62. Wounded at Gaines' Mill, Va., 6/27/62. Elected 2nd jr. lt., 7/9/62. Absent wounded, 6/62 to 20/63. Promoted to 1st Lt., 7/2/63. Absent,

The tattered remains of the flag of Company D, Tensas Rifles, 6th Louisiana Volunteers, awaits restoration at Confederate Memorial Hall in New Orleans. The Flag featured a blue quarter with a cotton bale bearing the name Tensas Rifles," surrounded by eight golden stars, with bars of red, white, and blue.

detached in Louisiana by order of Gen. E.K. Smith, 11/63 to 2/64. Ordered to rejoin command, 3/11/64. Present to 9/64. Killed near Winchester, Va., 9/19/64. Born: La. Occ.: Cooper. Res.: Washington, La. Single.

Overall, Thomas N., Pvt. En. 6/4/61, CM. Present to 7/62. Absent sick in hospital, 7-12/62. Present, 1/63 to 5/64. Roll for 5-8/64, dated 11/2/64, states: "Dead." Born: North Carolina. Occ.: Farmer. Res.: St. Landry. Single.

Pfiel, Auguste, Sgt. En. 6/4/61, CM, as cpl. Promoted to 1st sgt., 7/9/62. Present to 9/62. Wounded at Chantilly, Va., 9/1/62. Absent wounded to 4/63. Roll for 5-6/63 states: "Discharged on surgeon's certificate." Born: Germany. Occ.: Mechanic. Single.

Pitre, Leon, Pvt. En. 3/3/62, St. Landry Parish. Present to 5/62. Captured at Front Royal, Va., 5/30/62. POW, Steamer Coatzacoalas, exchanged 8/5/62. Absent sick in hospital, 9-12/62. Present, 1-5/63. Killed at Fredericksburg, Va., 5/4/63. Born: Mississippi. Occ.: Overseer. Res.: St. Landry. Married.

Porter, Gabriel, Pvt. En. 6/4/61, CM. Present to 10/61. Absent detached as teamster, 10/61 to 5/64. Present 5/64 to 2/65. Wounded at Hatcher's Run, Va., 2/13/65. Admitted to Jackson hospital, Richmond, gunshot wound in right leg, fracturing tibia. Captured in hospital, 4/3/65. POW, USA Genl. Hosp., Point Lookout, Md., released 7/7/65. Born: La. Occ.: Farmer. Res.: St. Landry. Single.

Quinlan, Jerry, Pvt. En. 6/4/61, CM. Present to 11/62. Captured at Berryville, Va., 11/29/62. POW, Old Capitol Prison, Washington, exchanged 3/17/63. Present, 4-5/63. Roll for 5-6/63 states: "Absent, wounded accidentally, shot himself through the arm on picket." Absent wounded, 5/63 to 2/65. Retired to Invalid Corps, 2/13/65, gunshot wound of left arm resulting in paralysis. Born: Limerick, Ireland. Occ.: Farmer. Res.: St. Landry. Age 34, 5'5", black eyes, dark hair, dark complexion.

Reina, Frank, Pvt. En. 6/4/61, CM. Present on rolls through 10/61. No record thereafter. Born: Germany. Occ.: Shoemaker. Res.: St. Landry. Single.

Renaud, Alfred, Pvt. En. 6/4/61, CM. Present to 7/63. Captured at Gettysburg, 7/5/63. POW, Fort McHenry, Md., transferred to Fort Delaware, Del., 7/12/63. Released on joining U.S. 3rd Maryland Cavalry Regt., 8/30/63. Roll of POWs states: "Born in France; gave up Gettysburg." Born: France. Occ.: Painter. Res.: St. Landry. Married.

Richard, L., Pvt. En. 3/3/62, St. Landry. Wounded at Port Republic, 6/9/62. Absent wounded, 6/62 to 2/64. Roll for 3-4/64 states: "Deserted."

Richmond, Charles N., Pvt. En. 6/4/61, CM. Present to 7/62. Absent detailed as teamster, 7/62 to 7/63. Present, 7-11/63. Captured at Rappahannock Station, Va., 11/7/63. POW, Point Lookout, Md., exchanged 3/10/64. Admitted Genl. Hosp. No. 9, Richmond, 3/23/64, furloughed 30 days. No record thereafter. Born: La. Occ.: Cooper. Res.: St. Landry. Single.

Rose, Washington, Pvt. En. 6/4/61, CM. Present to 7/62. Roll for 9-10/62 states: "Present. Deserted about the 10 Aug., 1862 and returned to his company on 19 Sept., 1863." Present to 5/64. Captured at Wilderness, Va., 5/5/64. POW, Point Lookout, transferred to Elmira, N.Y., 8/15/64, exchanged 2/25/65. Born: Georgia. Occ.: Cooper. Res.: St. Landry. Single.

Samuels, Abraham, Pvt. En. 6/4/61, CM. Present on 1861 rolls, no record thereafter. Born: Prussia. Occ.: Merchant. Res.: St. Landry. Single.

Sarvant, Benjamin, Pvt. (aka Savant, Sarvaunt) En. 6/4/61, CM. Present to 11/63. Captured at Rappahannock Station, Va., 11/7/63. POW, Point Lookout, Md., released on joining U.S. Army, 2/6/64. Born: La. Occ.: Farmer. Res.: St. Landry. Single.

Sarvant, Frank, Pvt. (aka Savant) En. 6/4/61, CM. Present to 9/61. Absent sick, 9/61 to 2/62. Discharged on surgeon's certificate of disability, 2/4/62, chronic rheumatism. Born: La. Occ.: Laborer. Res.: St. Landry. Age 25, single.

Schenk, A. Pvt. En. 12/18/61 at Centreville, Va. Present to 6/62. Wounded at Gaines' Mill, Va., 6/27/62. Absent wounded, 6/62 to 3/63. Admitted to Genl. Hosp. No. 18, Richmond, 10/30/62, gunshot wound in back. Recorded as deserted, 3/1/63. Born: La. Occ.: Farmer. Res.: St. Landry. Single.

Scott, Isaac R., Pvt. En. 6/4/61, CM. Present to 6/62. Captured at Harrisonburg, Va., 6/15/62. POW, Steamer Coatzacoalas, exchanged 8/5/62. Present, 9/62 to 6/63. Wounded at Winchester, Va., 6/14/63. Captured at Jordan Springs (Va.) Hosp., 7/26/63. Roll for 9-10/63 states: "Died of wounds while in the enemy's hands at Winchester in Aug. 1863." Born: Virginia. Occ.: Clerk. Res.: St. Landry. Single.

Senn, John, Cpl. (aka Sands, Sane) En. 6/4/61, CM. Promoted to cpl., 9/1/63. Present to 1/64. Absent on furlough, 1-2/64. Roll for 3-4/64 states: "Deserted while on furlough of indulgence." Surrendered at New Orleans, 5/26/65, paroled at Alexandria, La., 6/3/65. Born: Germany. Occ.: Farmer. Res.: Washington, La. Single.

Simpson, P.P., Pvt. En. 3/3/62, St. Landry. Present to 6/62. Captured at Woodstock, Va., 6/2/62. POW, Steamer Coatzacoalas, exchanged 8/5/62. Absent sick, 8/62 to 4/63. Roll for 3-4/63 states: "Deserted on 1st March." Surrendered at New Orleans, 5/26/65, paroled at Washington, La., 6/16/65. Born: Germany. Occ.: Farmer. Res.: St. Landry. Married.

Slone, E., Pvt. (aka Sloane) En. 3/3/62, St. Landry. Present to 9/62. Killed at Sharpsburg, Md., 9/17/62. Born: La. Occ.: Farmer. Res.: St. Landry. Married.

Smith, Frank, Pvt. No enlistment record. Captured 11/2/62 in Gilmore County, Va., after deserting. POW, Wheeling, Va., released on taking oath of allegiance, 12/25/62. Born: Cincinnati, O. Occ.: Boatman. Res.: Louisville, Ky. Age 21.

Smith, John A.B., Pvt. En. 6/4/61, CM. Present on 1861 rolls. Absent sick, 5-10/62. Recorded as deserted, 11/62. Born: Georgia. Occ.: Farmer. Res.: St. Landry. Single.

Smith, Ozemus, Pvt. En. 3/3/62, St. Landry. Present to 6/63. Wounded at Winchester, Va., 6/14/63. Roll for 5-6.63 states: "Died from wound received at Battle of Winchester, June 14, 1863." Born: La. Occ.: Farmer. Res.: St. Landry. Married.

Smith, Thomas, Pvt. En. 3/3/62, St. Landry. Present to 11/63. Captured at Rappahannock Station, Va., 11/7/63. POW, Point Lookout, Md., exchanged 3/10/64. Present, 4/64 to 4/65. Surrendered at Appomattox C.H., 4/9/65. Res.: St. Landry. Age 22, 5'4", dark eyes, black hair, dark complexion.

Soileau, Faustin, Pvt. En. 6/4/61, CM. Present on 1861 rolls, no record thereafter.

Soileau, Trassimo, Pvt. En. 6/4/61, CM. Present to 11/61. Admitted to Genl. Hosp. No. 18, Richmond, 11/15/61. Discharged, 1/6/62. Born: La. Occ.: Farmer. Res.: St. Landry. Married.

Stagg, Benjamin, Sgt. En. 6/4/61, CM, as pvt. Detailed on recruiting service, 2/62. Killed at Gaines' Mill, Va., 6/27/62. Born: La. Occ.: Clerk. Res.: St. Landry. Single.

Stephens, Jackson, Pvt. En. 3/3/62, St. Landry. Absent sick, 5-6/62. Present, 7/62 to 5/63. Absent, detailed as nurse in Richmond, 5-8/63. Absent on sick furlough, 11/63 to 3/64. Roll for 3-4/64 states: "Absent sick in La., rec'd certificate of disability in March 1864." Surrendered at New Orleans, 5/22/65, paroled at Washington, La., 6/16/65. Born: La. Occ.: Farmer. Res.: St. Landry. Married.

Stout, F.N., Pv. En. 3/3/62, St. Landry. Absent sick, 5-8/62. Absent detailed as cook in hospital, 8-12/62. Present 1-6/63. Wounded at Fredericksburg, Va., 5/4/63. Severely wounded at Winchester, Va., 6/14/63. Furloughed from Genl. Hosp. No. 21, Richmond, to Jackson, Miss., 9/9/63, amputated leg at thigh. Absent wounded after 6/63. Surrendered at New Orleans, 5/26/65, paroled at Washington, La., 6/16/65. Born: La. Occ.: Wheelwright. Res.: St. Landry. Single.

Strother, Alphonse, Pvt. En. 6/4/61, CM. Present to 2/62. Discharged on medical certificate of disability, 2/5/62, chronic diarrhea. Born: Kentucky. Occ.: Well digger. Age 50.

Swan, Appleton G., Pvt. En. 6/4/61, CM. Present to 9/62. Wounded at Chantilly, Va., 9/1/62. Admitted CSA Hosp., Danville, Va., 9/24/62, gunshot wound. Discharged at Danville on surgeon's certificate of disability, 10/25/62. Born: La. Occ.: Carpenter. Res.: St. Landry. Age 25, single.

Teer, John, Pvt. En. 3/3/62, St. Landry. Present to 7/62. Admitted to CSA Hosp., Charlottesville, Va., 6/22/62. Discharged on surgeon's certificate of disability, 8/29/62, cataracts. Born: La. Occ.: Wheelwright. Res.: St. Landry. Single.

Tessendore, Louis, Pvt. En. 6/4/61, CM. Present to 4/63. Captured at Fredericksburg, Va., 4/29/63. POW, Old Capitol Prison, Washington, exchanged 6/3/63. Present, 7-11/63. Captured at Rappahannock Station, Va., 11/7/63. POW, Point Lookout, Md., released on joining U.S. Army, 2/1/64. Born: Italy. Occ.: Artist. Res.: St. Landry. Single.

Trainor, John O., Sgt. En. 6/4/61, CM, as 3rd sgt. Rolls after 1861 list rank as pvt. Present to 6/62. Captured at Woodstock, Va., 6/2/62. POW, exchanged 8/5/62. Roll for 7-8/62 states: "Absent, wounded on the 27th August." Absent to 3/63. Present, 3-4/63. Discharged on surgeon's certificate of disability, 6/63. Born: La. Occ.: Clerk. Res.: Washington, La. Married.

Tubre, Henry O., Sgt. En. 6/4/61, CM, as pvt. Promoted to cpl., 6/28/62. Promoted to sgt., 10/1/62. Present to 11/63. Captured at Rappahannock Station, Va., 11/7/63. POW, Point Lookout, Md., exchanged 3/10/64. Roll for 3-4/64 states: "Absent, paroled prisoner since March 17, 1864." No record thereafter. Born: La. Occ.: Farmer. Res.: St. Landry. Single.

Vable, Alfred, Pvt. (aka Wible, Wable) En. 3/3/62, St. Landry. Present to 4/63. Captured at Fredericksburg, Va., 4/29/63. POW, Old Capitol Prison, Washington, exchanged 6/3/63. Absent sick, 6-9/63. Present, 9-11/63. Captured at Rappahannock Station, Va., 11/7/63. POW, Point Lookout, Md., exchanged 3/10/64. No record thereafter. Born: La. Occ.: Farmer. Res.: St. Landry. Single.

Vable, Honore, Pvt. En. 3/3/62, St. Landry. Absent sick, 5-9/62. Present 9/62 to 6/63. Roll for 7-8/63 states: "Absent, was left with the wounded at Jordan Springs, Winchester." Reported missing at Gettysburg, 7/2/63. Absent captured on rolls to 8/64, no record thereafter. Born: La. Occ.: Farmer. Res.: St. Landry. Single.

Vanney, Asa M., Pvt. (aka Vannoy) En. 6/4/61, CM. Present to 6/62. Discharged on surgeon's certificate of disability, 6/17/62, pneumonia and general debility. Born: La. Occ.: Farmer. Res.: St. Landry. Age 20, married.

Vannoy, Jesse L., Pvt. (aka Venoy) En. 6/4/61, CM. Present to 9/62. Killed at Chantilly, Va., 9/1/62. Born: La. Occ.: Farmer. Res.: St. Landry. Single.

Vidrine, J.B., Pvt. (aka Vidre) En. 3/3/62, St. Landry. Present to 4/63. Captured at Fredericksburg, Va., 4/29/63. POW, Old Capitol Prison, Washington, exchanged 6/3/63. Present to 11/63. Captured at Rapphannock Station, Va., 11/7/63. POW, Point Lookout, Md., exchanged 3/10/64. Surrendered at N.O., 5/26/65, paroled at Washington, La., 6/16/65. Born: La. Occ.: Farmer. Res.: St. Landry. Married.

Wade, John, Pvt. En. 6/4/61, CM. Present to 6/62. Wounded at Port Republic, Va., 6/9/62. Roll for 5-6/62, dated 10/25/62, states: "Wounded June 9. Died." Born: La. Occ.: Farmer. Res.: St. Landry. Single.

Wilsy, Jacob, Pvt. En. 6/4/61, CM. Present to 12/61. ADmitted to Moore Hosp., Danville, Va., 12/26/61, transferred to Richmond. Died at Louisiana Hosp., Richmond, 1/6/62, cause unstated. Born: La. Occ.: Farmer. Res.: St. Landry. Single.

Winkler, Anthony W., Pvt. En. 3/3/62, St. Landry. Present to 7/63. Wounded and captured at Gettysburg, 7/5/63. POW, DeCamp Hosp., David's Island, N.Y., exchanged 9/16/63. Absent wounded, 9-12/63. Present, 1-5/64. Captured

at Wilderness, Va., 5/5/64. POW, Point Lookout, Md., transferred to Elmira, N.Y., 8/15/64. Died at Elmira, 2/15/65, smallpox. Born: La. Occ.: Farmer. Res.: St. Landry. Single.
Winkler, Frank E., Pvt. En. 6/4/61, CM. Present to 7/63. Wounded (7/2/63) and captured at Gettysburg, 7/5/63. Right foot amputated at field hospital, sent to Gen. Hosp., 7/22/63, transferred as POW to DeCamp Gen. Hosp., David's Island, N.Y., exchanged 9/16/63. Absent wounded in hospital, 9/63 to 2/64. Retired as invalid, 4/1/64. Surrendered at N.O., 5/26/65, paroled at Washington, La., 6/16/65. Born: La. Occ.: Farmer. Res.: St. Landry. Single.
Young, Alfred B., Cpl. En. 3/3/62, St. Landry. Promoted to cpl., 1/1/63. Present to 4/63. Captured at Fredericksburg, Va., 4/29/63. POW, Old Capitol Prison, Washington, exchanged 6/3/63. Wounded at Winchester, Va., 6/14/63. Absent wounded, 6-9/63. Present, 9-11/63. Captured at Rappahannock Station, Va., 11/7/63. POW, Point Lookout, Md., exchanged 3/10/64. Captured at Wilderness, Va., 5/5/64. POW, Point Lookout, transferred to Elmira, N.Y., 8/15/64, exchanged 3/10/65. Born: La. Occ.: Farmer. Res.: St. Landry. Age 23, single.
Young, Henry, Pvt. En. 3/13/62, St. Landry. Present to 1/64. Absent on furlough, 1-2/64. Roll for 3-4/64 states: "Deserted while on furlough of indulgence." Surrendered at N.O., 5/28/65, paroled at Washington, La., 6/16/65. Born: La. Occ.: Farmer. Res.: St. Landry. Single.

Company D: Tensas Rifles

Raised in Tensas Parish in northeast Louisiana, this was another of the three non-New Orleans companies in the 6th Louisiana. Less than one-fifth of its members were native Louisianians, however. Of the 104 men who served in Company D, only 18 were born in Louisiana, while 27 came from other Confederate states, including 20 from nearby Mississippi. Thirty men were foreign-born: 20 from Ireland, six from Germany, two from France, one each from England and Scotland. Eleven men were born in Northern states. Birthplaces for another 18 are unrecorded. Of the 104 men, 10 were killed or mortally wounded in battle, 15 died of disease and three were killed in accidents, including the company's first captain. Twenty-one men deserted and five more were captured and took the oath of allegiance. Twenty-one were discharged, three retired to the Invalid Corps, and two surrendered at Appomattox Court House.

Captains:

Tenney, Charles B., Capt. En. 6/4/61, as capt. Roll for 9-10/61 states: "Died from pistol shot wound, Oct. 3, 1861." Died at Camp Reserve (Fairfax) Va., 10/3/61, of accidental wounding. Born: Mississippi.
Buckner, David, Capt. En. 6/4/61. Present as 1st lt., 7-8/61. Elected to captain, 10/9/61, replacing Charles Tenney, deceased. Present 5-6/62. Wounded Malvern Hill, Va., 7/1/62. Admitted to Chimborazo Hosp., Richmond, 7/4/62, wound in side. Present, 9-10/62. Wounded at Fredericksburg, Va., 12/13/62. Returned to duty from hospital, 1/2/63. Present 1-4/63. Wounded at Fredericksburg, 5/4/63. Admitted to General Hosp., Richmond, gun shot wound, 5/6/63, transferred to Jackson, Miss., 6/6/63. Absent wounded, on recruiting service in La., 7/63 to 4/64. Captured 4/28/64 on Mississippi River while attempting to return to his command. POW, Camp Chase, Ohio, transferred to Fort Delaware, Del. Paroled at Fort Delaware and forwarded for exchange, 2/27/65. On roll of POWs paroled 5/20/65, place unspecified. Born: Mississippi. Res.: St. Joseph, La. Age 31. 5'10", gray eyes, light hair, dark complexion.

* * *

Allen, Ethan, Pvt. En.6/4/61, CM. Wounded severely in chest at Winchester, Va., 5/25/62. Absent wounded, 7/62 to 12/63. Discharged, date unknown. On roll of POWs in Taylor Gen. Hosp., surrendered at New Orleans, 5/26/65. Paroled at Nachitoches, Miss., 6/6/65. Born: La. Occ.: Farmer. Res.: N. O. Age 21, single.
Allen, John C., Cpl. En. 6/4/61, CM. Present, 7-10/61.Absent sick, 5-12/62. AWOL, 1-2/63. Present, 3-4/63. Absent sick, 5-6/63. Discharged due to pulmonary consumption, 6/18/63. Born: Tennessee. Occ.: Farmer. Res.: Kirksferry, La. Age 23, single.
Brady, James, Pvt. En. 6/4/61, CM. Deserted 6/11/61. Born: Ireland. Occ: Laborer. Residence: N. O. Age 25, single.
Brumley, John A., Pvt. En. 6/4/61, CM. Present, 1861. Absent sick, 5-6/62. Absent under arrest in jail at Charlottesville, 7/62 to 12/62. Present under arrest on charge of AWOL, 1-2/63. Confined by sentence of general court martial, 3-6/63. Present, 7-11/63. AWOL, 1-2/64. Under arrest for desertion, 3-4/64. Deserted from provo guard house, 5/64. Born: Alabama. Occ.: Farmer. Res.: Winsboro, La. Age 26, married.
Burgoyne, Marshall K., Pvt. En. 6/4/61, CM. Present under arrest on charge of desertion, 9-10/61. Captured at Fredericksburg, Va., 5/3/63. POW, Fort Delaware, exchanged 6/3/63. Present, 7-8/63. Captured at Mine Run, Va., 11/27/63. POW, Old Capitol Prison, Washington, released on oath of allegiance, 3/18/64. Born: Virginia. Occ.: Painter. Residence: Waterproof, La. Age 24, single. 5'7", gray eyes, brown hair, dark complexion.

Cassidy, John, Pvt. En. 6/4/61, CM. Present to 6/62. Killed at Gaines' Mill, Va., 6/27/62. Born: Ireland. Occ.: Brick mason. Res.: St. Joseph, La. Age 20, single.
Chew, T. Holland, Pvt. En. 6/4/61. Present to 7/62. Absent sick, 7/62 to 12/62. Absent on sick furlough to 4/64. Deserted on sick furlough in La., 4/64. Born: La. Occ.: Farmer. Res.: St. Joseph, La. Age 26, single.
Clarke, William M., Pvt. En. 6/4/61, CM. Present 7-8/61. Absent sick, 9/61 to 5/62. Discharged on surgeon's certificate, 5/31/62, cardiac disease. Born: La. Occ.: Farmer. Res.: Kirksferry, La. Age 21, single.
Clifton, D.C., Pvt. En. 3/4/62, St. Joseph, La. 5-6/62. Absent sick. Discharged on surgeon's certificate, 7/26/62, hernia. Born: Tennessee. Occ.: Blacksmith. Age 40, 5'8", gray eyes, light hair, light complexion.
Cobb, Richard, Pvt. En. 3/4/62, St. Joseph, La. Admitted to General Hosp., Orange C.H., Va., 4/7/62, died 4/17/62, cause unstated.
Cobb, William, Pvt. En. 3/20/62, St. Joseph, La. Admitted to CSA Hosp., Charlottesville, Va., 4/16/62, died 4/25/62, typhoid fever. Born: La. Occ.: Farmer. Res.: Winsboro, La.
Cochran, Edward, Pvt. En. 3/4/62, St. Joseph, La. Absent sick, 5-6/62. Admitted to Camp Winder Hosp., Richmond, 5/10/62, returned to duty 6/2/62, diarrhea. Admitted to CSA Hosp., Charlottesville, Va., 6/24/62, returned to duty 8/11/62, debility. Discharged due to sickness, 8/18/62. Born: Mississippi. Occ.: Farmer. Res.: St. Joseph, La. Age 25, married.
Cochran, William E., Pvt. En. 6/4/61. Present to 6/62. Wounded at Port Republic, 6/9/62. Admitted to CSA Hosp., Charlottesville, Va., 6/21/62. Discharged on surgeon's certificate, 8/6/62 due to "gun shot fracture of the skull at Port Republic June 9th." Born: Mississippi. Occ.: Farmer. Res.: St. Joseph. Age 20, single.
Coffey, Isaac N., Sgt. En. 6/4/61, CM. Present as pvt., 7-10/61. Present as 4th sgt., 5/62 to 4/63. Wounded at Sharpsburg, Md., 9/17/62. Captured at Fredericksburg, Va., 4/29/63. POW, Old Capitol Prison, Washington, 5/10/63. Absent on furlough 7-8/63. Absent sick, 9-10/63. Present, 11-12/63. AWOL, 1-2/64. POW, Harper's Ferry, Va., 3/9/64, "surrendered himself to cavalry pickets March 7, 1864 at Bunker Hill, Va." Took oath of allegiance, 3/9/64. Born: Kentucky. Occ.: Farmer. Res.: St. Joseph, La. Age 22, single, 5'11", gray eyes, dark hair, florid complexion.
Coleman, James W., Sgt. En. 6/4/61,CM. Appointed 3rd sgt., 10/23/61. Died in hospital at Lynchburg, Va., 5/8/62, cause unstated. Born: Kentucky. Occ.: Merchant. Res: St. Joseph, La. Age 40, single.
Coleman, James, Sgt. En. 6/4/61, CM. Present to 6/63. Wounded at Sharpsburg, Md., 9/17/62. Wounded severely at Fredericksburg, Va., 5/4/63. Retired to Invalid Corps at Raleigh, N.C., 3/6/65. On list of Confederate soldiers in Libbey Prison, Richmond, 4/10/65, listed as "deserter." Born: Ireland. Occ.: Clerk. Age 19, single.
Coulliard, John C., Pvt. En. 3/4/62, St. Joseph, La. Present to 5/63. Wounded in right foot at Fredericksburg, 5/4/63. Admitted to Howard's Grove Hosp., Richmond, 5/9/63, returned to duty 7/18/63. Absent sick, 9-10/63. Received furlough of indulgence to Mississippi, 1/22/64. Record dated 3/13/65 states, "Furloughed, crossed Miss., not returned, since expired." Born: Maine. Occ.: Clerk. Res.: St. Joseph. Age 21, single.
Craig, George, Pvt. En. 6/4/61, CM. Absent sick at Culpeper, Va., 7-10/61. Absent sick, 5-9/62. Admitted to Chimborazo Hosp., Richmond, 8/22/62, discharged on surgeon's certificate 9/8/62, consumption. Born: Scotland. Occ.: Brickmason. Age 28, 5'5", blue eyes, light hair, light complexion.
Cushing, Timothy, Pvt. (aka Cushin) En. 6/4/61, CM. Present to 6/62. Captured at Strasburg, Va., 6/6/62. POW, Fort Delaware, took oath of allegiance, 8/10/62. Born: Ireland. Occ.: Laborer. Res.: St. Joseph, La. Age 24, single.
Davis, Joseph G., Lt. En. 6/4/61 as sgt. Present to 7/62. Absent sick, 7-8/62. Present 9-12/62. Promoted to lt., 12/27/62. Present 1/63 to 5/64. Captured at Wilderness, Va., 5/5/64. POW, Fort Delaware, 5/17/64, paroled 9/28/64. Admitted to Genl. Hosp. No. 4, Richmond, 10/7/64, chronic diarrhea, furloughed 10/12/64. Inspection report dated 2/27/65 states, "Paroled prisoner and furloughed in Oct. 1864, whereabouts not known." Born: Mississippi. Occ.: Farmer. Res.: St. Joseph, La. Age 26, single.
Donohue, John, Pvt. En. 6/4/61, CM. Present to 6/62. Wounded at Port Republic, Va., 6/9/62. Absent wounded, 6-12/62. Roll for 1-2/63 states, "Absent, discharged from hospital at Lynchburg 1/10/63, has not reported." Record dated 3/13/65 states, "deserted." Born: Ireland. Occ.: Laborer. Age 21, single.
Doyle, Edward, Pvt. En. 6/4/61, CM. Present to 5/62. Killed at Winchester, 5/25/62. Born: Ireland. Occ.: Laborer. Age 22, single.
Dreyfus, Herman, Cpl. En. 6/4/61, CM. Present to 12/61. Discharged 12/21/61, no reason stated. Born: Germany. Occ.: Clerk. Res.: Waterproof, La. Age 20, single.
Facundus, McKie, Pvt. En. 6/4/61, CM. Present to 10/61. Admitted to Chimborazo Hosp., Richmond, 10/18/61, jaundice, returned to duty 12/17/61. Present to 3/62. Admitted to Chimborazo Hosp., 3/21/62. Deserted from hospital, 5/19/62. Born: La. Occ.: Laborer. Age 28, single.
Farnham, Volney L., Pvt. (aka Farnum) En. 6/4/61, CM. Present to 7/62. Absent sick, 7-8/62. Wounded at Sharpsburg, Md. 9/17/62. Absent on furlough, 11/62 to 11/63. Roll for 3-4/64 states: "Deserted. Wounded at Battle of Sharpsburg, supposed to have been accidentally killed going on furlough." Record dated 3/13/65 at Petersburg, states: "Supposed dead." Born: La. Occ.: Farmer. Age 18, single.
Farnum, James, Pvt. En. 6/4/61, CM. (aka Farnham) Died at Camp Moore, La., 6/6/61. Born: La. Occ.: Farmer. Res.: Kirk's Ferry, La. Age 21, single.
Farrar, Thomas P., Jr., Lt. En. 6/4/61, CM. Present to 6/62. Wounded at Port Republic, Va., 6/9/62. Absent wounded to 12/62. Died of wounds received at Port Republic, 12/3/62. Born: La. Res.: St. Joseph, La.

Fisher, N.R., Pvt. En. 6/4/61, CM. Absent in hospital at Warrenton, Va., 8/61. Record dated 3/13/65 at Petersburg, Va., states: "Died at Camp Bienville, Va." Age 21, single.

Flinn, W.G., Pvt. En. 6/4/61, CM. (aka Flynn) Died at General Hosp., Culpeper C.H., Va., 8/25/61, typhoid fever. Born: Mississippi. Occ.: Carpenter. Age 48, single.

Ford, Percival F., Pvt. En. 6/4/61, CM. Present to 5/62. Absent sick, 5/62 to 10/62. Present, 11/62 to 7/63. Wounded at Gettysburg, 7/2/62. Absent on furlough, 8/63 to 1/64. Roll for 3-4/63 states: "Deserted. Away on a wounded furlough in La. Supposed to have been taken prisoner while coming back." Born: Mississippi. Occ.: Farmer. Res.: St. Joseph, La. Age 27, single.

Frank, Christian, Pvt. En. 6/4/61, CM. Present to 5/62. Absent sick, 5/62 to 12/62. Captured at Fredericksburg, Va., 4/29/63. POW, Fort Delaware, took oath of allegiance. Born: Germany. Occ.: Laborer. Res.: St. Joseph, La. Age 22, single.

Gibson, William H., Lt. En. 6/4/61, CM, as sgt. Promoted to jr. lt., 10/9/61. Present to 5/62. AWOL, 5/62 to 3/63. Admitted to CSA Genl. Hosp., Charlottesville, Va., 6/9/62, gonorrhea. Deserted from hospital, 6/17/62. Letter from Gibson to Col. I.G. Seymour, dated Camp Bragg, Va., 5/12/62, submits his resignation as 2nd jr. lt. Roll for 3-4/63 states: "Deserted. AWOL since 24th of May 1862. Dropped from the rolls by Genl. Order." Born: Maryland. Res.: New Carthage. Age 23, single.

Gilbert, Jacob M., Pvt. En. 6/4/61, CM. Present to 3/62. Absent sick, 3-4/62. Present, 5-8/62. Absent sick, 9/62 to 3/63. Present, 3/63 to 8/63. Absent sick, 8/63 to 3/64. Roll for 3-4/63 states: "Deserted. Absent sick since Aug. 1863." Born: La. Occ.: Farmer. Res.: Kirks Ferry, La. Age 21, single.

Gilbert, John K., Pvt. En. 6/4/61, CM. Present to 9/62. Wounded at Chantilly, Va., 9/1/62. Absent on furlough, 9-10/62. Present 11/62 to 5/63. Absent detached to Division Signal Corps, 5/63. Surrendered and paroled at Staunton, Va., 5/1/65. Born: La. Occ.: Farmer. Res.: Kirksferry, La. Age 26, single, 5'4", gray eyes, black hair, fair complexion.

Gleason, James, Musician. En. 2/20/63 at Fredericksburg, Va. Present to 5/63. Admitted to Genl. Hosp. No. 9, Richmond, 5/21/63. Absent sick in hospital, 5/63 to 3/64. Recorded as "deserted, never paid," 3/64.

Green, O.B., Pvt. En. 6/4/61, CM. Present to 8/62. Wounded at Bristoe Station, Va., 8/27/62. Absent wounded to 11/62. Present, 11/62 to 5/63. Wounded at Fredericksburg, Va., 5/4/63. Admitted to Chimborazo Hosp., Richmond, 5/6/63, gunshot wound in shoulder. Transferred to Tredegar Works, Richmond, 1/30/64. On Detached service as machinist in Richmond after 1/64. Born: Vermont. Occ.: Machinist. Res.: St. Joseph, La. Age 28, single.

Gray, Edward, Pvt. En. 6/4/61, CM. Present to 9/62. Roll for 1-2/63 states: "Left in Md. with sprained ankle, believed to be a deserter." Admitted to USA Genl. Hosp., Frederick, Md., 9/62, transferred to place unspecified, 10/22/62. Record dated 2/13/65 at Petersburg, Va., states: "Deserter." Born: Ireland. Occ.: Laborer. Res.: N.O. Age 23, single.

Griffing, Joseph F., Sgt. En. 6/4/61, CM. Discharged, 12/23/61. Record dated 3/13/65 at Petersburg, states: "Furnished a substitute." Born: Mississippi. Occ.: Farmer. Res.: St. Joseph, La. Age 19, single.

Guice, Benjamin D., Pvt. En. 6/4/61, CM. Present to 9/61. Absent sick in hospital, 9-10/61. Present, 5/62 to 9/62. Absent sick, 9/62 to 4/63. Roll for 3-4/63 states: "Deserted. Absent since Sept. 1, 1862, believed to have joined Page County [Va.] Cavalry in the Valley." Born: Mississippi. Occ.: Farmer. Res.: St. Joseph, La. Age 18, single.

Harris, William H., Pvt. En. 4/4/63, Camp Buchanan, Va. Absent sick, 5-8/62. Present, 9/62 to 11/63. Absent detailed after 5/64. Record dated 3/13/65 at Petersburg states: "Transferred—exchanged with Miss. Regt." Born: Mississippi. Occ.: Farmer. Res.: Waterproof, La. Age 21, single.

Hayes, Benjamin F., Pvt. En. 6/4/61, CM. Absent in hospital at Warrenton, Va., 7-8/61. Discharged on surgeon's certificate of disability, 10/7/61. Born: La. Occ.: Farmer. Res.: Waterproof, La. Age 21, single.

Hayes, Thomas T., Pvt. En. 6/4/61, CM. Present to 8/62. Wounded at Bristoe Station, Va., 8/27/62, gunshot wound in arm. Absent on furlough, 9-12/62. AWOL, 3/63 to 3/64. Recorded as deserted, 4/64. Born: La. Occ.: Farmer. Res.: Waterproof, La. Age 20, single.

Higgins, William, Pvt. En. 6/4/61, CM. Present to 6/62. Captured at Port Republic, Va., 6/9/62. Took oath of allegiance, place and date unstated. Born: Ireland. Occ.: Laborer. Age 30, single.

Hilliard, John C., Pvt. En. 6/4/61, CM. Present to 3/63. Wounded at Chantilly, Va., 9/1/62. Absent on detached duty as nurse in Richmond, 3-11/63. Present 11/63 to 5/64. Captured at Wilderness, Va., 5/5/64. POW, Point Lookout, Md., transferred to Elmira, N.Y., 8/15/64, exchanged 2/20/65. Died at Genl. Hosp. No. 9, Richmond, 3/5/65.

Isenhood, James, Sgt. En. 6/4/61, CM, as pvt. Promoted to 5th sgt., 8/1/63. Present to 10/61. Absent sick, 10-11/61. Present to 7/62. Absent sick, 7-8/62. Present to 5/64. Captured at Wilderness, Va., 5/5/64. POW, Point Lookout, Md., exchanged 2/10/65. Admitted to Genl. Hosp. No. 9, Richmond, 2/14/65. Surrendered at Jackson, Miss., 5/20/65. Born: Mississippi. Occ.: Carpenter. Res.: St. Joseph, La. Age 22, single.

Kelly, James, Pvt. (aka Kilby) En. 6/4/61, CM. Present to 6/62. Captured at Woodstock, Va., 6/2/62. POW, Fort Delaware. Record dated 3/13/65 at Petersburg states: "Drowned while attempting to escape from prison at Fort Delaware." Born: Ireland. Occ.: Laborer. Age 23, single.

Kelly, Martin, Pvt. En. 6/4/61, CM. Present to 9/64. Captured at Winchester, Va., 9/19/64. POW, Point Lookout, Md., exchanged 2/18/65. Surrendered at Charleston, W.Va., 3/9/65, listed as "rebel deserter." Born: Ireland. Occ.: Laborer. Res.: N.O. Age 24, single.

Kelly, Peter, Pvt. (aka Patrick Kelly) En. 6/4/61, CM. Present to 6/62. Captured at Woodstock, Va., 6/2/62. POW, Fort Delaware, exchanged 8/5/62. Recorded as deserted, 10/62. Record dated 3/13/65 at Petersburg states: "Escaped from Fort Delaware, afterwards deserted, joined cavalry since." Born: Ireland. Occ.: Laborer. Age 22, single.

King, Justus C., Pvt. En. 6/4/61, CM. Present to 1/63. Detached as clerk in Quartermaster Dept., 1-8/63. Present, 8/63 through 2/65. Born: Mississippi. Occ.: Farmer. Res.: Waterproof, La. Age 26, single.

Kraft, Samuel, Pvt. En. 6/4/61 as musician. Present to 8/61. Discharged on surgeon's certificate of disability, 8/19/61.

Kruse, George J., Sgt. (aka Cruse) En. 6/4/61, CM. Present to 8/62. Wounded at Bristoe Station, 8/27/62. Absent wounded after 8/62. Roll for 3-4/64 states: "Deserted. In consequence of a bad wound, he was furloughed in 1862 to La., not heard of him since." Born: Germany. Occ.: Butcher. Res.: Waterproof, La. Age 24, single.

Lee, Israel S., Cpl. En. 6/4/61, CM. Wounded at Sharpsburg, Md., 9/17/62. Present to 4/63. Captured at Fredericksburg, Va., 4/29/63. POW, Old Capitol Prison, Washington, exchanged 6/3/63. Present 6-11/63. Captured at Rappahannock Station, Va., 11/7/63. POW, Point Lookout, Md., exchanged 3/10/64. Captured at Wilderness, Va., 5/5/64. POW, Point Lookout, transferred to Elmira, N.Y., 8/15/64, exchanged 2/25/65. Admitted to Way Hosp., Meridian, Miss., 3/21/65. Born: Mississippi. Occ.: Brickmason. Res.: St. Joseph, La. Age 16, single.

Lewis, Thomas, Pvt. En. 6/4/61, CM. Present to 3/62. Deserted 3/10/62. Born: Indiana. Occ.: Carpenter. Age 22, single.

Lilly, Henry, Pvt. En. 6/4/61, CM. Present to 9/62. Wounded at Chantilly, Va., 9/1/62. Absent wounded, 9/62 to 12/63. Detailed as hospital attendant at Lynchburg, Va., 12/63 to 11/64. Present, 11/64 to 4/65. Surrendered at Appomattox C.H., 4/9/65.

Mann, Thomas A., Pvt. En. 6/4/61, CM. Present to 8/61. Record dated 3/13/65 at Petersburg states: "Died (at) Camp Bienville, Va., Aug., 1861." Born: Germany. Occ.: Carpenter. Res.: St. Joseph, La., Age 28, married.

Mansel, William F., Pvt. En. 6/4/61, CM. Present to 9/62. Killed at Sharpsburg, Md., 9/17/62.

McCormick, Philip, Pvt. En. 6/4/61, CM. Present to 9/62. Killed at Chantilly, Va., 9/1/62. Born: Ireland. Occ.: Laborer. Age 28, single.

McNamara, Edward, Pvt. Transferred from 19th Mississippi Inf. Regt. at Raccoon Ford, Va., 1/64. Present to 9/64. Wounded at Winchester, Va., 9/19/64. Admitted to CSA Hosp., Charlottesville, Va., 9/25/64, wound in right hip, transferred to Wayside Hosp., Richmond, 10/27, furloughed 60 days from 10/27/64. Born: Ireland. Occ.: Laborer. Res.: Vicksburg, Miss. Age 30, single.

Meinhart, Philip, Pvt. En. 6/4/61, CM. Present to 7/62. Wounded at Malvern Hill, Va., 7/1/62. Absent wounded, 7-11/62. Present 11/62 to 5/63. Severely wounded at Fredericksburg, Va., 5/14/63. Absent wounded at Louisiana Hosp., Richmond, 5/63, amputated right leg at thigh. Retired to Invalid Corps, 3/27/65. Born: Germany. Occ.: Blacksmith. Res.: Waterproof, La. Age 22, single.

Mildoon, James M., Pvt. En. 6/4/61, CM. Present to 11/63. Captured at Rappahannock Station, Va., 11/7/63. POW, Point Lookout, Md., exchanged 3/10/64. Admitted to Wayside Hosp., Richmond, 3/19/64, furloughed 30 days. Absent sick, 5/64 through 2/65. Record dated 3/13/65 at Petersburg states: "Detailed on light duty at Lynchburg, Va." Surrendered at Lynchburg, Va., 4/13/65. Born: Ireland. Occ.: Laborer. Res.: St. Joseph, La. Age 42, single.

Mortimer, James, Pvt. (aka Mortimore) En. 6/4/61, CM. Present on 1861 rolls. No record thereafter.

Murdock, Andrew, Pvt. En. 6/4/61, CM. Present to 7/62. Admitted CSA Hosp., Charlottesville, Va., 7/22/62, wounded, transferred to Genl. Hosp., Lynchburg, Va., 8/11/62. Roll for 9-10/62 states: "Deserted. Sent to Richmond on account of accidental wound. Afterwards deserted to White's cavalry."

Neathery, Allan S., Pvt. En. 6/4/61, CM. Present to 6/62. Wounded at Winchester, Va., 5/25/62. Admitted to CSA Hosp., Winchester, 5/27/62, hip wound. Absent wounded to 9/62. Wounded at Chantilly, Va., 9/1/62. Absent wounded to 5/63. Present, 5-11/63. Wounded at Mine Run, Va., 11/30/63. Present, 1-5/64. Captured at Wilderness, Va., 5/5/64. POW, Point Lookout, Md., transferred to Elmira, N.Y., 8/15/64, exchanged 2/25/65. Admitted Wayside Hosp., Richmond, 3/3/65. Died at Howard's Grove Hosp., Richmond, 3/31/65, smallpox. Born: La. Occ.: Blacksmith. Res.: Waterproof, La. Age 21, single.

Nevers, John L., Pvt. En. 6/9/61, CM. Present to 7/62. Absent sick, 7-10/62. Present, 11/62 to 4/63. Captured at Fredericksburg, Va., 4/29/63. POW, Old Capitol Prison, Washington, exchanged 6/3/63. Present, 7/63 to 5/64. Captured at Wilderness, Va., 5/5/64. POW, Point Lookout, Md., exchanged 2/10/65. Paroled at Columbus, Miss., 5/23/65. Born: France. Occ.: Cook. Age 20, single.

Offin, Thomas, Pvt. En. 6/4/61, CM. Present to 9/62. Absent sick, 9-12/62. Admitted Chimborazo Hosp., Richmond, 11/6/62, died 12/25/62, typhoid/pneumonia. Born: England. Age 20, single.

Oglethorpe, James, Pvt. En. 6/4/61, CM. Present to 9/61. Absent sick, 9-10/61. Record dated 3/13/65 at Petersburg states: "Died in hospital in the summer of 1861." Occ.: Farmer. Age 28, married.

Paxton, John H., Pvt. En. 6/4/61, CM. Present to 3/62. Absent sick in hospital, 3-8/62. Present, 9/62 to 4/63. Killed at Fredericksburg, Va., 4/29/63. Born: Virginia. Occ.: Farmer. Res.: St. Joseph, La. Age 24, single.

Phillips, John, Pvt. En. 6/23/61 at Camp Pickens, Va. Present on 1861 rolls. Record dated 3/13/65 at Petersburg states: "Deserted Jan. 1, 1862." Age 23, single.

Phillips, Isaac, Pvt. En. 6/4/61, CM. Present to 11/63. Captured at Rappahannock Station, Va., 11/7/63. POW, Point Lookout, Md., exchanged 3/10/64. Record dated 3/13/65 at Petersburg states: "Received furlough, never returned." Born: La. Occ.: Painter. Res.: N.O. Age 25, single.
Pitman, David S., Sr. En. 6/4/61, CM. Absent sick in hospital, 7-8/61. Absent detailed as nurse at Warrenton, Va., 9-10/61. Discharged on surgeon's certificate of disability ("incomplete paralysis of left side. . .he is 50 years of age"), Chimborazo Hosp., Richmond, 10/7/62. Born: Adams County, Mississippi. Occ.: Farmer. Res.: New Carthage, La. Age 50.
Pitman, David S., Jr., En. 6/4/61, CM. Absent sick in hospital, 7-8/61. Roll for 9-10/61 states: "Discharged for sickness by certificate of disability, Oct. 5, 1861." Occ.: Farmer. Res.: New Carthage, La. Age 15, single.
Reed, Alexander, Pvt. En. 6/4/61, CM. Present to 5/62. Absent sick in hospital, 5/62 to 7/63. Present, 7-11/63. Captured at Rappahannock Station, Va., 11/7/63. POW, Point Lookout, Md., exchanged 3/10/64. Present 4-9/64. Captured at Fisher's Hill, Va., 9/22/64. POW, Point Lookout, exchanged 2/10/65. Born: Kentucky. Occ.: Carpenter. Res.: Kirksferry, La. Age 25, single.
Reed, Isaac, Lt. En. 6/4/61, CM, as jr. 2nd lt. Elected 1st lt., 10/9/61. Promoted to Assistant Quarter Master with rank of captain, 11/18/62. See Field and Staff Roster.
Reinfrank, Adolph, Pvt. En. 6/4/61, CM. Present to 5/62. Absent on leave, 6-12/62. Present, 1-4/63. Killed at Fredericksburg, Va., 4/29/63. Born: La. Occ.: Shoemaker. Res.: St. Joseph, La. Age 18, single.
Reinhart, Charles, Pvt. En. 6/4/61, CM. Present to 5/63. Killed at Fredericksburg, Va., 5/4/63. Born: France. Occ.: Silversmith. Res.: N.O. Age 28, single.
Richardson, Henry B., Pvt. En. 6/4/61, CM. Present to 5/62. Absent on detached service, 5-8/62. Commended by Gen. Richard Taylor, commanding brigade, for "valuable services" in scouting enemy position at Battle of First Winchester, 5/25/62, recommended for promotion. Promoted to 1st lt. and transferred to the Corps of Engineers on Gen. R.S. Ewell's staff, 8/11/62. Wounded at Sharpsburg, Md., 9/17/62. Promoted to capt. and chief engineer for Ewell's Division, 10/4/62. Wounded captured at Gettysburg, 7/5/63. POW, DeCamp Genl. Hosp., David's Island, N.Y., 7-9/63, transferred to Johnson's Island, Sandusky, Ohio, 9/18/63, transferred to Point Lookout, Md., 3/14/65. Paroled at Chattanooga, Tenn., 5/26/65. Res.: Tensas Parish, La. Blue eyes, black hair, light complexion, 5'9".
Riley, S.J., Pvt. En. 6/23/61 at Camp Pickens, Va. Present to 8/62. Wounded in right arm at Bristoe Station, Va., 8/27/62. Absent wounded, 8/62 to 4/63. Absent detailed as nurse in Richmond, 4-9/63. Present, 9/63 to 3/64. Absent detailed, 4/64 to 3/65. Discharged by special order, 3/7/65. Born: New York. Occ.: Carpenter. Res.: St. Joseph, La. Age 24, married.
Riley, Thomas, Pvt. En. 6/4/61, CM. Present to 9/62. Roll for 9-10/62 states: "Killed at the blowing up of a bridge at Frederick City, Md." Record dated 3/13/65 at Petersburg states: "Accidentally killed at Monocacy Bridge, Sept. 8, 1862." Born: Mississippi. Age 26, single.
Rosson, James M., Pvt. En. 6/4/61, CM. Present to 11/63. Captured at Rappahannock Station, Va., 11/7/63. POW, Point Lookout, Md., exchanged 3/10/64. Present to 7/64. Wounded at Monocacy, Md., 7/9/64. Admitted Chimborazo Hosp., Richmond, 7/22/64, gunshot wound in breast. Absent wounded, 7-64 to 4/65. Surrendered and paroled at Lynchburg, Va., 4/15/65. Occ.: Farmer. Res.: St. Joseph, La. Age 24, single.
Schrick, Charles, Pvt. En. 6/4/61, CM. Present to 9/61. Absent sick, 9-10/61. AWOL, 5-6/62. Recorded as deserted, 8/62.
Shillings, William W., Pvt. En. 6/4/61, CM. Present to 3/62. Discharged on medical certificate of disability, 4/15/62, "old age." Born: Mississippi. Occ.: Overseer. Res.: St. Joseph, La. Age 55, married.
Sloan, Ferdinand M., Pvt. En. 6/4/61, CM. Present to 7/62. Wounded at Malvern Hill, Va., 7/1/62. Admitted to Chimborazo Hosp., Richmond, 7/4/62, gunshot wound in back. Discharged on surgeon's certificate of disablity, 11/20/62, gunshot wound fracturing spinal column. Born: La. Occ.: Farmer. Res.: St. Joseph, La. Age 30, single.
Smith, Alfred, Pvt. En. 6/4/61, CM. Present to 9/61. Roll for 9-10/61 states: "Absent at the Insane Asylum, Charlottesville, Va." Discharged, date unknown. Born: Missouri. Occ.: Carpenter. Age 23, single.
Smith, Green R., Pvt. En. 6/4/61, CM. Absent sick, 6-7/61. Died at Genl. Hosp., Culpeper C.H., Va., 7/25/61, cause unstated. Occ.: Brick Mason. Res.: St. Joseph, La. Age 22, single.
Smith, John J., Pvt. En. 6/4/61, CM. Present to 6/62. Captured at Woodstock, Va., 6/2/62. Exchanged 8/5/62. Roll for 7-8/62 states: "Deserted." Born: Pennsylvania. Occ.: Laborer. Res.: St. Joseph, La. Age 21, single.
Smye, Joseph H., Pvt. En. 6/4/61, CM. Present to 9/62. Absent on detached service with Pioneer Corps, 9/62 to 3/65. Occ.: Carpenter. Age 22, single.
Starks, James S., Pvt. En. 6/4/61, CM. Present to 5/62. Roll for 5-6/62 states: "Died May 12 in hospital." Born: Kentucky. Occ.: Shoemaker. Age 19, single.
Stewart, Charles, Pvt. En. 6/4/61, CM. Present to 12/61. Absent sick, 12/61 to 7/62. Discharged at Richmond on surgeon's certificate of disability, 7/30/62, anemia. Born: Dublin, Ireland. Occ.: Tailor. Res.: St. Joseph, La. Age 33.
Sugrue, John, Pvt. En. 6/4/61, CM. Present to 7/62. Killed at Malvern Hill, Va., 7/1/62. Born: Ireland. Occ.: Laborer. Res.: N.O. Age 28, married.
Sullivan, Timothy, Pvt. En 6/4/61, CM. Present to 9/62. Wounded at Chantilly, Va., 9/17/62. Absent wounded to 4/63. Absent detailed as nurse at Richmond, 4/63 to 4/64. Roll for 3-4/64 states: "Deserted. Disabled on account of

wound received in battle." Record dated 3/13/65 at Petersburg states: "Disabled in leg. Serving in cavalry." Born: Ireland. Occ.: Laborer. Age 24, single.

Tenney, John B., Cpl. En. 6/4/61, CM. Present to 9/61. Absent in Mississippi with leave, 9-10/61. Absent on furlough, 5-6/62. AWOL, 7-8/62. Roll for 9-10/62 states: "Forged a furlough on 4 Oct. 1861 and went to Fayette, Miss., where he still remains. Deserted." Born: Mississippi. Res.: Winsboro, La. Age 22, single.

Trahern, William E., Cpl. (aka Traham) En. 6/4/61, CM, as cpl. Present to 11/61. Absent sick, 11/61 to 9/62. Detached as clerk at Chimborazo Hosp., Richmond, 10/62 to 3/64. Present, 4-5/64. Wounded in left leg at Wilderness, Va., 5/5/64. Absent wounded, 5-10/64. Present, 10/64 to 2/65. Absent sick in Richmond, 3-4/65. Captured in Richmond, 4/3/65, paroled 4/15/65. Born: Jackson, Miss. Occ.: Clerk. Res.: St. Joseph. Age 21.

Walker, W.W., Pvt. En. 6/4/61, CM. Present to 8/61. Discharged on surgeon's certificate of disability, 8/26/61. Born: La. Occ.: Farmer. Res.: St. Joseph. Age 15, single.

Weeks, Frederick, Pvt. En. 6/4/61, CM. Present to 5/62. Absent sick, 5-11/62. Discharged by order of medical director, 8th Brigade, 11/26/62. Born: North Carolina. Occ.: Carpenter. Age 50, married.

Wells, William F., Sgt. En. 6/4/61, CM. Present to 9/62. Wounded in chest and captured at Sharpsburg, Md., 9/17/62. POW, Fort McHenry, Md., exchanged 10/18/62. Admitted Chimborazo Hosp., Richmond, 10/23/62, furloughed 30 days. Present, 11/62 to 9/64. Wounded at Gettysburg, 7/2/62. Wounded in right leg at Winchester, 9/19/64. Surrendered at Appomattox C.H., 4/9/65. Born: Mississippi. Occ.: Farmer. Res.: Fayette, Miss. Age 29, single.

Welsh, Michael, Pvt. En. 6/4/61, CM. Present to 8/62. Wounded in chest at Bristoe Station, Va., 8/27/62.
Absent wounded, 8/62 to 6/63. Absent, detailed as nurse at Richmond, 7/63 to 9/64. Retired to Invalid Corps at Columbia, S.C., 9/26/64, permanently disabled with wound in left lung. Born: Prussia. Occ: Baker. Res.: Waterproof, La. Age 26, single.

Wheelan, William, Pvt. (aka Whelan) En. 6/4/62, CM. Present to 5/62. Wounded at Winchester, Va., 5/25/62. Absent wounded to 1/63. Discharged on surgeon's certificate of disability, 8/29/62, gunshot wound through right foot. Appears on report of men in Hays' Brgd. on extra duty, as "Surgeon Robertson's orderly," 8/5/63. Born: Ireland. Occ.: Laborer. Res.: N.O. Age 24, single.

White, Richard, Pvt. En. 6/4/61, CM. Present to 6/62. Wounded at Port Republic, Va., 6/9/62. Absent wounded, 6-11/62. Present, 11/62 to 5/63. Killed at Fredericksburg, Va., 5/4/63. Born: Ireland. Occ.: Laborer. Res.: St. Joseph. Age 24, single.

Williams, Weldon, Pvt. En. 6/4/61, CM. Present on 1861 rolls. Absent sick, 5-9/62. Present, 9-10/62. Absent sick, 11/62 to 4/63. Detailed as nurse in hospital, 4/63 to 1/64. Present, 1-5/64. Captured at Wilderness, Va., 5/5/64. POW, Point Lookout, Md., transferred to Elmira, N.Y., 8/15/64. Died at Elmira, 2/4/65, pneumonia. Born: Ireland. Occ.: Carpenter. Res.: St. Joseph Age 50, married.

Wise, Lewis, Pvt. En. 6/4/61, CM. Present to 7/62. Absent sick, 7-11/62. Discharged on surgeon's certificate of disability, 11/15/62, chronic sciatica. Born: Tennessee. Occ.: Farrier. Age 39, 5'11", blue eyes, light hair, light complexion.

Word, William R., Sgt. En. 6/4/61, CM, as pvt. Promoted to 4th sgt., 10/23/61. Present to 12/62. Wounded at Fredericksburg, Va., 12/13/62. Absent, detached as clerk to regimental quartermaster, 1-6/63. Present, 7/63 to 5/64. Captured at Wilderness, Va., 5/5/64. POW, Point Lookout, Md., transferred to Elmira, N.Y., 8/15/64, exchanged 2/25/65.

Woodard, Theodore H., Pvt. En. 6/4/61, CM. Present to 7/62. Absent sick, 7-12/62. Absent detached as nurse in hospital, 1/63 to 4/64. Captured at Wilderness, Va., 5/5/64. POW, Point Lookout, Md., exchanged 11/5/64. Present to 3/65. Transferred to Latcher Artillery, 3/7/65. Born: Mississippi. Occ.: Farmer. Res.: St. Joseph. Age 27, single.

Company E: Mercer Guards

Raised in New Orleans, this company was an amalgam of Irish and German immigrants, transplanted Northerners, city natives and others. The smallest company of the regiment, with 90 men total, Company E had the highest rate of desertions (41 percent) and fewest men killed in the regiment. Of the 90 men, 15 were natives of Ireland, 13 were from Germany and 22 were born in the North. Sixteen were born in Louisiana, six in other Confederate States, three from England, two from Canada and one from Scotland. Birthplaces are unknown for 12 men. Seven men were killed or mortally wounded in battle and only three died of disease. However, 37 deserted and three more were captured and took the oath of allegiance. Fourteen were discharged, five retired to the Invalid Corps, four transferred to other units, and five surrendered at Appomattox Court House.

Captains:

Walker, Thomas F. Commissioned by Gov. T.O. Moore as captain, 5/1/61. En. 6/4/61, CM. Present to 8/61. Resigned at Camp Bienville, Va., 8/61. Appointed capt. and aide de camp to Brig. Gen. E.L. Tracy, 1st Brgd., 1st Div., Louisiana Militia, New Orleans, 10/17/61.

Rivera, John J. Commissioned as 2nd lt. by Gov. T.O. Moore, 5/1/61. En. 6/4/61, CM. Elected captain 10/7/61, replacing Thomas F. Walker. Present to 9/62. Wounded at Chantilly, Va., 9/1/62. Absent wounded, 9-10/62. Present, 11/62 to 6/63. Wounded at Winchester, Va., 6/14/62. Absent wounded, 6-9/63. Present 10/63 to 5/64. Captured at Spotsylvania C.H., Va., 5/10/64. POW, Fort Delaware, released 6/14/65, listing residence as Galveston, Tex. Born: New York. Occ.: Printer. Res.: N.O. Age 25, married, 5'11", blue eyes, light hair, dark complexion.

* * *

Aborn, Charles, Pvt. En. 6/4/61, CM. Present to 5/62. Deserted 5/14/62. Born: England. Occ.: Painter. Res.: N. O. Age 25, single.

Aitkins, John F., Pvt. En. 6/4/61. Present to 9/62. Captured at North Mountain Station, Va., 9/12/62. POW, Camp Chase, Ohio, 9/17/62, transferred to Cairo, Ill, 9/29/62, exchanged at Vicksburg, Miss., 11/1/62. Returned to duty, 12/8/62. Present to 6/63. Mortally wounded in thigh at Fredericksburg, Va., 5/4/63, died in Louisiana Hosp., Richmond, 6/3/63. Born: N. O. Occ.: Clerk. Age 18, single, 5'7", gray eyes, sandy hair, fair complexion.

Alexander, Robert, Pvt. En. 7/3/61, Fairfax, Va. Present to 8/62. Deserted 8/20/62. Born: Canada. Occ.: Carpenter. Age 23, single.

Beard, William A., Sgt. En. 6/4/61 in Co. H, as pvt. Transferred to Co. E, 7/1/61. Promoted to sgt., 8/7/61. Detached as clerk for adjutent general, brigade HQ, 9/1/61 through 12/64. Surrendered at Appomattox C.H., 4/9/65. Born: Va. Occ.: Clerk. Res.: N. O. Age 30, single. Listed residence on parole as Rockbridge County, Va.

Bell, C.R., Pvt. En. 6/4/61, CM. Present to 10/61. Deserted 10/24/61. On undated roll of POWs who took oath of allegiance, Washington, D.C. Letter dated Headquarters, Third Brigade, Porter's Division, Army of Potomac, 10/30/61, states Bell was captured at Hunter's Mill, Va., and stated that the 6th Louisiana then had 920 men stationed at Centreville, Va. Born: Mississippi. Occ.: Painter. Res., N. O. Age 36, single.

Benoas, Charles M., Pvt. (aka C.M. DeBenoas) En. 6/4/61, CM. Present to 3/62. Discharged on certificate of disability, 3/24/62. Certificate signed by Capt. John J. Rivera states Benoas had been sick in hospital and "is dirty in appearance and dress (habitually) and is unfit to be a soldier on many other grounds." Born: Frankfurt, Germany. Occ.: Clerk. Res.: N. O. Age 21, single.

Black, Robert, Sgt. En. 6/4/61, CM. Promoted from cpl. to sgt., 6/1/62. Wounded at Chantilly, 9/1/62. Absent wounded, 11-12/62. Present, 1-6/63. Wounded at Winchester, 6/14/63. Absent wounded, 7/63 to 8/64. Retired from service, 8/64. Born: N. O. Occ.: Clerk. Res.: N. O. Age 18, single.

Brady, James W., Pvt. En. 6/4/61. Present to 8/62. Wounded in left knee at Manassas, Va., 8/29/62. Absent wounded, 9/62 to 9/63. Absent wounded in Mobile and Greenville, Ala., hospitals, 9/63 to 4/64. Retired to Invalid Corps, 10/21/64. On roll of sick and wounded, Army of Tennessee: died 2/1/65, tuberculosis. Born: Ireland. Occ.: Laborer. Res.: N. O. Age 35, married.

Brensel, Henry, Pvt. (aka Brensel, M. and Brentzel, Henry) En. 6/4/61, CM. Present to 10/62. Recorded as deserted, 10/31/62. List of engagements shows him captured at Chantilly, Va., 9/1/62. Born: Pennsylvania. Occ.: Tailor. Res.: N. O. Age 20, single.

Brisbin, George M., Lt. En. 6/4/61. Captured at Union Mills, Va.,7/17/61, took oath of allegiance.

Brugniens, Louis, Pvt. En. 6/4/61. Present to 7/62. Deserted 7/7/62. Born: N. O. Occ.: Painter. Res.: N. O. Age 20, single. Record dated 2/10/65 at Petersburg states: "Deserted but doing duty in the Cavalry service."

Buckholtz, Nicholas, Pvt. En. 6/4/61, CM. Present to 8/62. Wounded at Bristoe Station, Va., 8/27/62. Present on duty at commissary dept., 9/62 to 8/63. Present to 2/64. Deserted 2/8/64. Born: Germany. Occ.: Butcher. Res.: N. O. Age 24, single. Record dated 2/10/65 states: "Deserted but at present in the Cavalry."

Burce, G. Paul, Pvt. (aka G.P. Burci or Barci) En. 6/4/61, CM. Present to 9/62. Wounded in Achilles tendon at Sharpsburg, Md., 9/17/62. Absent wounded, 9/62 to 4/63. Transferred to Atlanta, Ga., 4/63. Furloughed to Augusta, Ga., 1/5/64. Present, 2-4/65. Surrendered at Appomattox, Va., 4/9/65. Occ.: Clerk. Residence: N. O. Age 19, single.

Burce, Joseph, Pvt. En. 6/4/61. Present to 9/62. Absent sick, 9/62 to 10/63. Deserted, 10/63. Occ.: Clerk. Age 22, single. Record dated 2/10/65 at Petersburg states: "Deserted but at present in the cavalry."

Burgess, Henry, Pvt. En. 6/4/61, CM. Present to 7/62. Absent sick, 7/62 to 3/63. Present 4-7/63. Captured in Maryland, 7/13/63. POW, Camp Chase, Ohio, 7/22/63 to 2/29/64. Transferred to Fort Delaware, Del., 2/29/64. Paroled and forwarded for exchange, 3/7/65. Oath of allegiance sworn at Knoxville, Tenn., 4/21/65. Born: Nova Scotia. Occ.: Carpenter. Res.: N. O. Age 30, married, 5'11", dark eyes, dark hair, dark complexion.

Byrne, T.T., Sgt. En. 6/4/61. Present to 8/62. Promoted to sgt., 8/62. Absent sick, 9-12/62. Died at Louisiana Hosp., Richmond, Va., 5/21/63, consumption. Born: New York. Occ.: Painter. Res.: N. O. Age 26, single.

Campbell, John G., Sgt. En. 6/4/61, CM, as 2nd sgt. Promoted to regimental commissary sgt., 7/61. See Field & Staff roster.

Carney, John F., Pvt. (aka John Kearney) En. 3/1/62, N.O. Absent sick, 7/62 to 4/63. Recorded as deserted, 4/63, with remarks: "Deserted. Recruit sent to hospital at Richmond, July 20/63. On gun boat in James River." Record dated 2/10/65 at Petersburg states: "Transferred to the Navy." Born: La. Occ.: Painter. Res.: N.O. Age 22, married.
Cenas, Augustus, Pvt. En. 6/4/61, CM. Present to 9/62. Mortally wounded at Sharpsburg, Md., 9/17/62, died at Grove's Warehouse, Sharpsburg, 11/6/62. Born: N.O. Occ.: Clerk. Res.: N.O. Age 20, single.
Cooper, Edward B., Pvt. En. 6/4/61, CM. Present to 6/62. Deserted 6/21/62. Born: Ohio. Occ.: Painter. Res.: N.O. Age 25, single.
Cullen, Michael, Pvt. (aka Colomn) Present to 6/63. Wounded at Winchester, 6/14/63. Present 11/63 to 5/64. Captured at Wilderness, 5/5/64. POW, Point Lookout, Md., exchanged 2/10/65. Born: Ireland. Occ.: Printer. Res.: N.O. Age 20, single.
Deisler, Constance A., Sgt. En. 6/5/61, CM. Promoted from 3rd sgt. to 2nd sgt., 8/61. Reduced to cpl., 11/15/61. Discharged on surgeon's certificate of disability, 12/31/61, mercurial paralysis of right leg. Born: La. Age 25, 5'7", gray eyes, sandy hair, light complexion.
Delaney, A.H., Pvt. En. 6/4/61, CM. Present to 5/62. Deserted 5/14/62. Born: New York. Occ.: Barber. Res.: N.O. Age 24, single.
Donelon, Martin, Pvt. En. 6/4/61, CM. Present to 8/62. Deserted 8/25/62. Record dated 2/10/65 at Petersburg, Va. states: "Deserted, at present in Cavalry." Born: N.O. Occ.: Cab driver. Res.: N.O. Age 18, single.
Dreyfus, H.J., Pvt. En. 6/4/61, CM. Roll for 7-8/61 states: "Transferred to 8th La. Vols. in exchange for Wm. Wells." Born: La. Occ.: Painter. Res.: N.O. Age 22, married. Record dated 2/10/65 at Petersburg states: "Trans. to 8th La. and killed at Battle of Sharpsburg."
Driscoll, John, Pvt. En. 6/4/61, CM. Present to 8/62. Deserted 8/62. Born: Ireland. Occ.: Steward. Res.: N.O. Age 20, single.
Elmore, William, Pvt. En. 6/4/61, CM. Present to 11/62. Absent sick, 11/62 to 5/63, rheumatism. Employed as guard, General Hosp., Staunton, Va., 11/62, returned to duty 4/29/63. Present, 5-6/63. Recorded as deserted, 7/2/63, Gettysburg, Pa. Record dated 2/10/65 at Petersburg states: "Deserted and joined the cavalry service, at present in prison." Born: N.O. Occ.: Brick mason. Res.: N.O. Age 19, single.
Etriss, E.J., Pvt. En. 6/4/61, CM. Present to 8/62. Deserted, 8/20/62. Born: Missouri. Occ.: Painter. Res.: N.O. Age 22, single.
Evans, Michael, Pvt. En. 6/4/61, CM. Present to 1/62. Admitted to Moore Hosp., Danville, Va., 12/26/61, catarrh fever. Discharged on certificate of disability, 1/28/62. Born: Ireland. Occ.: Seaman. Res.: N.O. Age 30, married, 5'7", blue eyes, dark hair, dark complexion.
Faber, John, Pvt. En. 6/4/61, CM. Present to 7/62. Deserted, 7/7/62. Born: Germany. Occ.: Laborer. Res.: N.O. Age 20, single.
Gleason, Michael, Pvt. En. 6/4/61, CM. Present to 6/63. Killed at Winchester, Va., 6/14/63. Born: Ireland. Occ.: Carpenter. Res.: N.O. Age 23, single.
Gorman, Eugene F., Pvt. En. 6/4/61, CM, as drummer. Discharged on surgeon's certificate, 2/3/62, hernia. Born: Germany. Occ.: Musician. Res.: N.O. Age 20, married.
Hagan, P., Pvt. En. 6/4/61, CM. Wounded at Chantilly, 9/1/62. No record thereafter.
Hall, Henry C., Pvt. En. 6/4/61, CM. Present to 8/62. Wounded at Bristoe Station, Va., 8/27/62. Captured at Wilderness, Va., 5/5/64. POW, Point Lookout, Md., exchanged 8/31/64. Admitted to Gen. Hosp., Richmond, 11/29/63, returned to duty 12/3/64. Surrendered at Appomattox, Va., 4/9/65. Born: N.O. Occ.: Blacksmith. Res.: N.O. Age 17, single.
Harney, Edward T., Pvt. En. 6/4/61, CM. Present to 8/62. Killed at Manassas, Va., 8/29/62. Born: Ireland. Occ.: Laborer. Res.: N.O. Age 22, single.
Hayes, John, Pvt. En. 6/4/61, CM. Present to 7/62. Recorded as deserted, 7/7/62. Born: Ireland. Occ.: Baker. Res.: N.O. Age 23, single.
Hubert, Benjamin, Pvt. En. 6/4/61, CM. Detailed as clerk at brigade headquarters, 7/61 to 9/62. Discharged by order of Sec. of War, 9/3/62, medical disability, chronic diahrrea. Born: N.O. Occ.: Clerk. Res.: N.O. Age 18, single.
Hutchins, David M., Pvt. En. 6/4/61, CM. Present to 8/62. Reported as deserted, 8/20/62. Born: Pennsylvania. Res.: N.O. Age 16, single.
Hutchings, William H., Cpl. En. 6/4/61, CM. Present to 7/72. Recorded as deserted, 7/7/62. Born: Pennsylvania. Occ.: Clerk. Res.: N.O. Age 18, single.
Jackson, N. Hart, Pvt/Sgt. Major. See Field & Staff roster.
Kane, Frank, Pvt. En. 6/4/61, CM. Present to 8/62. Wounded at Bristoe Station, Va., 8/27/62. Absent wounded 8/62 to 3/63. Wounded at Fredericksburg, Va., 5/4/63. Absent wounded 5/63 to 4/64. Disabled and detailed after 4/64 as courier at Stuart Hosp., Richmond. Retired to Invalid Corps at Augusta, Ga., 1/6/65. Paroled at Augusta, 5/9/65. Born: New Jersey. Occ.: Engineer. Res.: N.O. Age 21, single.
Kelly, James, Pvt. En. 6/4/61, CM. Present to 2/62. Detailed on recruiting service, 2/62. Roll for 5-6/62 states: "Was sent on recruiting service with Lt. Lynne and procured a substitute who failed to report for duty." Record dated 2/10/65 at Petersburg records him as "deserted". Born: Ireland. Occ.: Cooper. Res.: N.O. Age 24, single.

Kelly, Henry R., Pvt. En. 6/4/61, CM. Present to 8/62. Wounded at Cedar Mountain, Va., 8/9/62. Roll for 7-8/62 states: "Deserted Aug. 25." Born: England. Occ.: Painter. Res.: N.O. Age 30, married.
Kelly, William P., Pvt. En. 6/4/61, CM. Present to 4/62. Transferred by special order dated 4/14/62 to Dea's Artillery, Maryland Line. Born: New York. Occ.: Grocer. Res.: N.O. Age 22, single.
Lacklen, William, Sgt. En. 6/4/61, CM. Promoted to sgt., 11/1/61. Present to 6/62. Captured at Port Republic, Va., 6/9/62. POW, Fort Delaware, exchanged 8/5/62. Present, 9/62 to 5/63. Wounded at Fredericksburg, Va., 5/4/63. Wounded at Wilderness, Va., 5/4/64. Absent wounded after 5/64. Retired to Invalid Corps, 3/6/65. Born: Pennsylvania. Occ.: Carpenter. Res.: N.O. Age 36, single.
Lambert, Nick, Pvt. En. 6/4/61, CM. Present to 5/62. Roll for 5-6/62 states: "Deserted May 14, 1862." Born: England. Occ.: Painter. Res.: N.O. Age 23, single.
Leslie, Samuel J., Sgt. En. 6/4/61 as cpl. Promoted to 1st sgt., 6/15/62. Present to 8/62. Killed at Manassas, Va., 8/29/62. Born: Arkansas. Occ.: Clerk. Res.: N.O. Age 24, single.
Lewis, William J., Pvt. En. 6/4/61, CM. Present to 11/61. Roll for 12/61 states: "Deserted 11/15/61." Born: Alabama. Occ.: Carpenter. Res.: N.O. Age 20, single.
Lynne, George, Lt. En. 6/4/61, CM, as 2nd sgt. Elected 2nd jr. lt., 8/7/61. Present to 9/62. Killed at Sharpsburg, Md., 9/17/62. Born: Ireland. Occ.: Painter. Res.: N.O. Age 22, single.
Lynne, Robert E., Lt. En. 6/4/61 as 1st Lt. Present to 7/62. Absent sick, 7-9/62. Present 9/62 to 2/63. Absent on recruiting service, ordered to raise a company of sharpshooters, 2/63 to 3/64. Present, 3-7/64. Wounded and captured at Battle of Monocacy, Md., 7/9/64. POW, West Bldg. Hosp., Baltimore, Md., wound in right shoulder. Transferred to Fort McHenry, Md., 8/30/64, transferred to Fort Delaware, 10/25/64, released 6/12/65. Born: Ireland. Res.: N.O. Age 24, single.
Madden, James, Pvt. En. 6/4/61, CM. Present to 8/62. Absent sick, 8/62 to 4/63. Roll for 3-4/63 states: "Deserted. Absent sick from Aug. 26, 1862, since deserted." Born: New York. Occ.: Hatter. Res.: N.O. Age 22, married.
Maroney, Patrick, Pvt. (aka Marooney) En. 6/4/61, CM. Present to 5/62. Wounded at Winchester, Va., 5/25/62. Record dated 2/10/65 at Petersburg states: "Deserted." Born: Illinois. Occ.: Printer. Res.: N.O. Age 24, single.
McCormack, John T., Pvt. En. 6/4/61, CM. Present to 8/62. Roll for 7-8/62 states: "Deserted Aug. 20." Born: Ireland. Occ.: Plumber. Res.: N.O. Age 22, single.
McMahon, George, Pvt. En. 2/24/62, N.O. Present to 6/62. Captured at New Market, Va., 6/6/62. POW, Fort Deleware, took oath of allegiance, 8/10/62. Born: New Orleans. Occ.: Schoolboy. Res.: N.O. Age 18, single.
Meissner, Charles, Pvt. En. 6/4/61, CM. Present to 8/62. Roll for 7-8/62 states: "Deserted Aug. 24, took oath to U.S." Born: Germany. Occ.: Clerk. Res.: N.O. Age 24, single.
Moore, Thomas, Sgt. En. 6/4/6, CM. Promoted to sgt., 11/1/61. Present to 8/62. Roll for 7-8/62 states: "Deserted Aug. 20." Born: Ireland. Occ.: Carpenter. Res.: N.O. Age 24, single.
Moran, Charles E., Sgt. En. 6/4/61, CM, as 3rd sgt. Detailed as Regimental Commissary Sergeant, 8/6/61. Present, detailed to Commissary Dept., 8/61 to 4/63. Absent sick in hospital, 5-6/63. Present, detailed, 7-8/63. Absent sick, 10-12/63. Absent, detached as clerk in Provost Marshall's office, Lake Shore District., La., 1-10/64. Captured at Osyka, Miss., 10/7/64. POW, Ship Island, Miss., transferred to Elmira, N.Y., 11/19/64, exchanged 2/13/65. Admitted to Wayside Hosp., Richmond, 2/20/65. Surrendered at Appomattox C.H., 4/9/65.
Moran, James, Pvt. En. 6/4/61, CM. Present to 8/62. Discharged 8/24/62. Born: Shreveport, La. Age 25, 5'5", blue eyes, dark hair, dark complexion.
Moran, James A., Pvt. En. 2/24/62, N.O. Present to 5/63. Captured at Fredericksburg, Va., 5/3/63. POW, Fort Delaware, exchanged 6/3/63. Present 6/63 to 5/64. Captured at Wilderness, Va., 5/5/64. POW, Point Lookout, Md., exchanged 2/10/65. Surrendered at Citronelle, Ala., 5/4/65, paroled at Meridian, Miss., 5/10/65. Born: N.O. Occ.: Clerk. Res.: N.O. Age 18, single.
Moynan, Alex F., Pvt. En. 6/4/61, CM. Present to 11/62. Absent sick, 11/62 to 2/63. Present, 2-5/63. Captured at Fredericksburg, Va., 5/4/63. POW, Fort Delaware, exchanged 5/23/63. Present 7/63 to 5/64. Roll for 5-8/64, dated 11/2/64, states: "Dead."
Moynan, Jefferson, Pvt. En. 3/62, N.O. Present to 9/62. Discharged on surgeon's certificate at Richmond, 9/18/62, due to "youth, 15 years old."
Murdock, Edward, Pvt. (aka Ned Murtha) En. 9/10/62, Mobile, Ala. Captured at Wilderness, Va., 5/5/64. POW, Point Lookout, Md., transferred to Elmira, N.Y., 8/15/64, released 5/13/65. Record of POWs at Elimira states he was an Irishman, immigrated to America 12 or 13 years before, was in N.O. at outbreak of war, desires to go to New York, where relatives reside.
Murdock, William, Pvt. En. 6/4/61, CM. Present to 7/63. Wounded at Bristoe Station, Va., 8/27/62. Absent sick after 7/63. Roll for 3-4/64 states: "Deserted July 12, 1863." Record dated 2/10/65 at Petersburg states: "Deserted, has done active service in cavalry, is now in Y.P. [Yankee Prison?]." Surrendered and paroled at Winchester, Va., 5/17/65. Age 20, 5' 7"gray eyes, dark hair, dark complexion.
Murphy, Edward, Pvt. En. 6/4/61, CM. Present on 1861 rolls. Admitted to Chimborazo Hosp., Richmond, 3/14/62. Record dated 2/10/65 at Petersburg states: "Deserted to the enemy."
Murphy, John W., Pvt. En. 6/4/61, CM. Present to 8/62. Roll for 7-8/62 states: "Deserted Aug. 20." Roll for 3-4/63 states: "Present, rejoined from desertion, Apr. 8, '62." Captured at Fredericksburg, Va., 5/3/63. POW, Fort Delaware,

exchanged 6/3/63. Present to 11/63. Captured at Rappahannock Station, Va., 11/7/63, POW, Point Lookout, Md., exchanged 3/10/64. Present to 5/64. Captured at Wilderness, Va., 5/5/64, died as POW at Point Lookout, 7/1/64. Born: New York. Occ.: Gas fitter. Res.: N.O. Age 23, single.

Murray, John H., Pvt. En. 3/3/62, N.O. Present to 7/62. Absent sick, 7-12/62. Absent detailed in Quartermaster's Dept., Staunton, Va., 1-10/63. Captured at Rappahannock Station, Va., 11/7/63. POW, Point Lookout, Md., exchanged 3/15/64. Present, 3-9/64. Severely wounded at Winchester, Va., 9/19/64. Declared unfit for field duty by Medical Examining Board at Augusta, Ga., 12/19/64, unhealed wounds in both thighs. Detailed to Quartermaster's office, Augusta, 2/26/65. Record dated 2/10/65 at Petersburg states: "Wounded at Winchester, still suffering from wounds." Surrendered at Augusta, 5/5/65. Born: N.O. Occ.: Clerk. Res.: N.O. Age 19, single.

Obermeyer, Morris, Pvt. En. 6/4/61, CM. Present on 1861 rolls. Record dated 2/10/65 at Petersburg states: "Discharged." Born: Germany. Occ.: Storekeeper. Res.: N.O. Age 20, single.

Palmer, Archibald, Pvt. En. 6/4/61, CM. Present to 6/62. Recorded as deserted, 6/21/62. Born: Kentucky. Occ.: Painter. Res.: N.O. age 23, single.

Park, John P., Sgt. En. 6/4/61, CM, as 5th sgt. Present to 6/62. Recorded as deserted, 6/21/62. Record dated 2/10/65 at Petersburg states: "Deserted and joined, at present in the cavalry." Born: N.O. Occ.: Printer. Res.: N.O. Age 21, single.

Regan, James, Pvt. En. 6/4/61, CM. Present to 8/62. Roll for 7-8/62 states: "Deserted Aug. 27, took oath to U.S. Govt." Born: New York. Occ.: Blacksmith. Res.: N.O. Age 25, single.

Robinson, John W., Pvt. En. 6/4/61, CM. Present to 8/62. Discharged at Gordonsville, Va., on certificate of disability, 8/17/62. Born: N.O. Occ.: Clerk. Res.: N.O. Age 24, married.

Robinson, Robert, Pvt. En. 6/4/61, CM. Present to 6/62. Roll for 5-6/62 states: "Deserted June 19, 1862." Born: Ireland. Occ.: Laborer. Res.: N.O. Age 23, single.

Romer, Daniel, Pvt. (aka Roma, Roemer) En. 6/4/61, CM. Absent detached as nurse in hospital, 7-9/61. Present, 5-6/62. Absent detached on hospital duty, 7/62 to 10/63. Roll for 9-10/63 states: "Deserted to the enemy Oct. 20, 1863." Captured at Catlett's Station, Va., 10/23/63. POW, Old Capitol Prison, Washington, released on taking oath of allegiance, 12/17/63. Born: Germany. Occ.: Clerk. Res.: N.O. Age 25, single.

Rosch, Frederick, Pvt. (aka Rosh, Ross) En. 6/4/61, CM. Present to 8/62. Wounded at Bristoe Station, Va., 8/27/62. Absent wounded, 8/62 to 6/63. Roll for 3-4/63 states: "Absent wounded from Aug. 27, right arm amputated." Discharged on surgeon's certificate of disability, 6/1/63. Born: Germany. Occ.: Shoemaker. Res.: N.O. Age 24, single.

Rusha, Edward M., Pvt. En. 6/4/61, CM. Present to 9/61. Discharged at Camp Bienville, Va., on surgeon's certificate of disability, 9/23/61, angina pectoris. Born: N.O. Occ.: Clerk. Res.: N.O. Age 20, single.

Sattele, Emile, Pvt. (aka Settle) En. 6/4/61, CM. Present to 7/64. Captured at Battle of Monocacy, Md., 7/9/64. Admitted to USA Gen. Hosp., Frederick, Md., 7/10/64, transferred to Baltimore 8/23/64. Record dated 2/10/65 at Petersburg states: "Captured at the Monocacy, at present paroled." Admitted to CSA Hosp., Richmond, 3/1/65, "debilitas." Born: Germany. Occ.: Barkeeper. Res.: N.O. Age 16, single.

Shannon, John M., Pvt En. 6/4/61, CM. Present to 9/62. Wounded at Chantilly, 9/1/62. Absent wounded, to 4/63. Wounded at Fredericksburg, Va., 5/4/63. Admitted to Louisiana Hosp., Richmond, gunshot wound in shoulder, furloughed 30 days to Mobile, Ala., 6/10/63. Absent wounded to 7/64. Present, 7-10/64. Wounded at Cedar Creek, Va., 10/9/64. Record dated 2/1-/65 at Petersburg states: "Wounded four times, at present in hospital." Paroled at Augusta, Ga., 5/11/65. Born: Ireland. Occ.: Barkeeper. Res.: N.O. Age 19, single.

Shaw, Augustus, Pvt. En. 6/4/61, CM. Present to 8/62. Recorded as deserted, 8/20/62. Record dated 2/10/65 at Petersburg states: "Deserted but said to be Engineer on one of our boats." Born: Germany. Occ.: Blacksmith. Res.: N.O. Age 24, single.

Sherwood, Charles J., Cpl. En. 6/4/61, CM. Present to 1/62. Discharged at Manassas Jct., Va., on surgeon's certificate of disability, 1/25/62, typhoid fever. Born: Mississippi. Occ.: Clerk. Res.: N.O. Age 17, single.

Skallon, James P. (aka Scallon) En. 6/4/61, CM. Present to 6/63. Wounded in left shoulder at Winchester, 6/14/63. Furloughed from Louisiana Hosp., Richmond, for 60 days to Selma, Ala., 11/3/63. Roll for 3-4/64 states: "Absent on furlough from Feb. 10, disabled from wound." Born: Ireland. Occ.: Gas fitter. Res.: N.O. Age 25, married.

Smith, James H., Pvt. En. 6/4/61, CM. Present to 9/62. Wounded at Sharpsburg, Md., 9/17/62. Present to 6/63. Wounded at Winchester, Va., 6/14/63. Wounded at Gettysburg, 7/2/63, and captured there. POW, admitted to US Gen. Hosp., Baltimore, Md., 9/27/63, wound to left elbow, disabling hand. Exchanged 9/27/63. Absent wounded, 9/63 to 5/64. Present, 5-8/64. Retired to Invalid Corps at Mobile, Ala., 12/9/64, discharged 2/11/65. Born: New York City. Occ.: Blacksmith. Res.: N.O. Age 21, single.

Strohfeldt, William, Sgt. En. 6/4/61, CM, as pvt. Promoted to sgt., 11/1/61. Present to 9/62. Wounded in arm at Chantilly, Va., 9/1/62. Absent wounded, 9/62 to 3/63. Roll for 5-6/63 states: "Deserted from hosp. in Lynchburg in March 1863." Surrendered at Fayette County, Va., 4/27/63. POW, Camp Chase, Ohio, transferred to Johnson's Island, 6/14/63, released on taking oath of allegiance, 10/9/63. Born: Prussia. Occ.: Carpenter. Res.: N.O. Age 30, married.

Tobin, John, Sgt. Major. See Field & Staff roster.

Williams, David M., Sgt. En. 6/4/61, CM, as cpl. Promoted to 3rd sgt., 8/7/61. Present to 6/62. Recorded as deserted, 6/21/62. Born: Kentucky. Occ.: Stone cutter. Res.: N.O. Age 20, single.

Williams, James B., Pvt. En. 6/4/61, CM. Present to 9/62. Killed at Chantilly, Va., 9/1/62. Born: Kentucky. Occ.: Stone cutter. Res.: N.O. Age 22, single.
Wills, John B., Sgt. En. 6/4/61, CM. Promoted to 3rd sgt., 11/61. Present to 6/62. Recorded as deserted, 6/21/62. Born: Germany. Occ.: Painter. Res.: N.O. Age 22, single.
Wills, William, Pvt. En. 6/4/61, CM. Roll for 7-8/61states: "Received in exchange [from 8th La. Regt.] for H.J. Dreyfus." (See above.) Present to 8/62. Recorded as deserted 8/20/62. Born: Germany. Res.: N.O. Age 20, single.
Wilson, Samuel, Pvt. En. 6/4/61, CM. Present to 9/61. Discharged at Camp Bienville, Va., on surgeon's certificate of disability, 9/24/61, due to "injury." Born: New York. Occ.: Clerk. Res.: N.O. Age 20, single.

Company F: Irish Brigade Company B

This predominantly Irish company was recruited in New Orleans by its first captain, Irish-born William Monaghan, later colonel of the regiment. Originally named Irish Brigade Company B, it became Company F of the 6th Louisiana when it joined the regiment at Camp Moore in June 1861. Of the 115 men who served in the company, at least 100 were born in Ireland. Most of the four men whose birth places are unrecorded and the four men in the company born in Northern states also had common Irish names. The company also included three native Canadians, two men from England, one Scot and just one Louisiana native. During the war, 20 men of Company F were killed or mortally wounded, four died of disease and one was murdered in camp (they were, after all, a rough bunch). Thirty two men deserted and eight more were captured and took the oath of allegiance. Eight were discharged, six retired to the Invalid Corps, four gained release from Federal prisons by joining the U.S. Army, two transferred out, and two surrendered at Appomattox Court House.

Captains:

Monaghan, William, Capt., Col. Commissioned 5/8/61 by Gov. T.O. Moore. En. 6/4/61, CM. Promoted to Major of 6th La., 6/27/62. See Field and Staff Roster.
O'Connor, Michael, Capt. Commissioned 5/8/61 by Gov. T.O. Moore. En. 6/4/61, CM, as 1st Lt. Promoted to captain, 6/27/62. Present to 9/62. Wounded at Sharpsburg, Md., 9/17/62. Absent wounded, 9-12/62. Present, 1-/4, 63. Wounded at Fredericksburg, Va., 4/29/63. Admitted to CSA Hosp., Charlottesville, Va., 5/1/63, wound in forearm, returned to duty 8/12/63. Present 9-11/63. Captured at Rappahannock Station, Va., 11/7/63. POW, Old Capitol Prison, transferred to Johnson's Island, Sandusky, Ohio, 11/11/63, forwarded to City Point, Va., for exchange, 2/24/65. Born: Ireland. Occ.: Storekeeper. Res.: N.O. Age 35, married.

* * *

Adams, John. Pvt. En. 6/4/61, CM. Present to 7/62. Mortally wounded in chest and arm Malvern Hill, Va. 7/1/62. Died at Chimborazo Hosp., Richmond, Va., 7/15/62. Letter of Col. William Monaghan dated 4/63 stated that before Adams died he asked that the pay due him be given to his messmate John Carroll for debts owed. Monaghan wrote that Carroll "is an excellent man and gallant soldier. I would like to see the wishes of his late comrade gratified." Born: Ireland. Occ.: Laborer. Res: N. O. Age 30, single.
Austin, Frank. Pvt. En. 6/4/61, CM. Present to 9/62. Wounded at Sharpsburg, Md., 9/17/62. Absent in hospital, 10/62. Present 11/62 to 6/63. Wounded at Winchester, Va., 6/14/63. Absent wounded, 7-10/63. Present, 11-12/63. Absent, detailed in shoemakers' shop, Lynchburg, Va., 1-9/64. Wounded 2/6/65 at Hatchers' Run, Va. Captured 4/2/65 at Petersburg, Va. POW, Hart's Island, N.Y., released 6/14/65. Born: Ireland. Occ.: Laborer. Res.: N. O. Age 27, single. 5'9", gray eyes, brown hair, light complexion.
Bennett, Anthony, Sgt. En. 6/4/61, CM. Promoted from pvt. to sgt., 7/31/61. Present to 7/62. Absent sick in hospital, 7/62 to 11/62. Deserted from Louisiana Hosp., Richmond, 11/62. Born: Ireland. Occ.: Laborer. Res.: N. O. Age 34, married.
Bowe, Thomas. Sgt. En. 6/8/61, CM. Present to 9/62. Wounded in right elbow at Chantilly, Va., 9/1/62. Absent in hospital, 9/62 to 11/63. Detailed as courier at Jackson Hosp., Richmond, 11/62-8/64. On register of Invalid Corps dated 2/17/65 at Woodville, Miss. Born: Ireland, County Carlow. Occ.: Laborer. Res.: N. O. Age 28, single. 5'8", blue eyes, fair hair, fair complexion.
Brennan, John. Pvt. En. 6/4/61, CM. Present to 9/62. Wounded at Chantilly, Va., 9/1/62. Absent wounded to 3/64. Detailed to provost marshall guard, Lynchburg, Va., 4/20/64. Surrendered at Lynchburg, 4/13/65. Born: Ireland. Occ.: Laborer. Res.: N. O. Age 40, single.

Bruslan, William. Pvt. En. 6/4/61. Present through 10/61. Admitted to hospital in Richmond, 3/9/62, remittant fever. On register of hospital in Danville, Va., 6/29/62, returned to duty 7/2/62. Listed as AWOL, 5-8/62, recorded as deserted, 10/62. Born: Ireland. Occ.: Blacksmith. Res.: N. O. Age 20, single. 5'5", gray eyes, dark hair, dark complexion.

Burns, James. Pvt. En. 6/8/61, CM. Present to 5/62. AWOL, 5/62-8/62. Recorded as deserted, 10/62. Rejoined from desertion, 11/62. Wounded at Fredericksburg, Va., 12/13/62. Deserted 3/18/63 at Rappahannock River. POW, Old Capitol Prison, Washington, 3/20/62, listed as deserter. Born: Ireland. Occ.: Laborer. Res.: N. O. Age 25, single.

Cahill, Martin, Pvt. En. 6/4/61, CM. Present to 5/62. Sick in hospital, 5-12/62. Present 1-4/63. Captured at Fredericksburg, Va., 4/29/63. POW, Old Capitol Prison, Washington, took oath of allegiance 5/25/63. Born: Ireland. Occ.: Laborer. Res.: N.O. Age 30, single.

Cahill, Robert, Cpl. En. 6/4/61, CM. Present to 5/62. Wounded at Winchester, 5/25/62. Admitted to CSA Hosp., Charlottesville, Va., 6/9/62, wounded in right arm. Present 7/62 to 6/63. Mortally wounded at Winchester, 6/14/63, died 6/20/63. Born: Ireland. Occ.: Laborer. Res.: N.O. Age 27, single.

Carroll, John, Pvt. En. 6/4/61, CM. Present through 12/62. Absent on furlough, 1-2/63. Present 3-7/63. Killed at Gettysburg, 7/2/63. Born: Ireland. Occ.: Laborer. Res.: N.O. Age 40, single.

Casey, Michael, Pvt. En. 6/4/61, CM. Present to 6/62. Wounded at Port Republic, Va., 6/9/62. Absent wounded, 7-8/62. Present 9/62 to 4/63. Killed at Fredericksburg, Va., 5/4/63. Born: Ireland. Occ.: Laborer. Res.: N.O. Age 40, married.

Caughlin, Patrick, Pvt. En. 6/4/61, CM. Present to 5/62. Wounded at Winchester, 5/25/62. Admitted to CSA Hosp., Charlottesville, Va., 6/9/62, compound fracture of arm. Absent wounded, 7/62 to 12/63. Roll for 1-2/64 states absent, "disabled from wound received at Winchester, May 25, 1862." Born: Ireland. Occ. Laborer. Res.: N.O. Age 40, married.

Cleary, Dennis, Pvt. En. 6/4/61, CM. Present to 8/62. Absent sick in hospital, 9/62 to 12/62. Reported deserted from hospital, 12/62. Returned from desertion, 5/6/63. Deserted near Fredericksburg, Va., 5/19/63. On register of POWs, Army of Potomac, received 5/21/63, took oath of allegiance, 6/63. Born.: Ireland. Occ.: Laborer. Res.: N.O. Age 29, single.

Collins, Patrick, Pvt. En. 3/11/62, N.O. See Patrick Collins of Company B.

Connolly, John, Pvt. En. 6/4/61, CM. Present to 11/63. Captured at Rappahannock Station, Va., 11/7/63. POW, Point Lookout, Md., paroled 3/9/64, exchanged 3/14/64. Captured at Wilderness 5/5/64. POW, Point Lookout, transferred to Elmira, N.Y., 8/15/64, released 5/29/65. Listed residence upon release as Rock Island, Ill. Born: Ireland. Occ.: Laborer. Res.: N.O. Age 39, single, 5'5", blue eyes, dark hair, dark complexion.

Conroy, D.W., Pvt. En. 6/4/61, CM. Absent sick in hospital, 7-8/61. Died in General Hosp., Culpeper, Va., 8/8/61, apoplexy. Born: Ireland. Res.: N.O. Age 50, single.

Conway, James J., Sgt. En. 6/4/61 as ensign. Appointed sgt., 7/7/61. Present to 9/62. Wounded at Chantilly, Va., 9/1/62. Absent wounded 9-10/62. Present 11/62 to 11/63. Killed at Rappahannock Station, Va., 11/7/63. Born: Ireland. Occ.: Laborer. Res.: N.O. Age 40, single.

Copeland, George, Pvt. Enlisted at unspecified date in 1864 in Virginia. Killed at Cold Harbor, Va., 6/3/64. Born: England. Res.: N.O. Age 25, single.

Copeland, G.F., Pvt. No enlistment recorded. POW, received at Point Lookout, Md., from White House, VA., captured at "Old Church," Va., 5/29/64. Released on joining U.S. Army, 6/11/64.

Crimmins, Daniel, Pvt. En. 6/4/61, CM. Present to 7/62. Wounded at Malvern Hill, Va., 7/1/62. Admitted to Chimborazo Hosp., Richmond, 7/4/62, gunshot wound in left leg, returned to duty 9/23/62. Present 10/62 to 4/63. Absent detached as hospital nurse at Winchester, 5-8/63. Captured at Rappahannock Station, Va., 11/7/63. POW, Point Lookout, Md., exchanged 3/10/64. Reported as deserted, 6/64. Born: Ireland. Occ.: Laborer. Res.: N.O. Age 26, single.

Croake, John, Pvt. En. 6/4/61, CM. Present to 6/62. Killed at Port Republic, Va., 6/9/62. Born: Ireland. Occ.: Laborer. Res.: N.O. Age 26, single.

Crossan, John, Pvt. (aka Crossland) En. 6/4/61, CM. Present 7-8/61. Detailed as teamster 10/61 to 3/63. Deserted 3/63. Born: Ireland. Occ.: Laborer. Res.: N.O. Age 29, married.

Cummings, Thomas, Pvt. En. 6/4/61, CM. Present to 7/63. Captured at Gettysburg, 7/3/63. POW, Fort Delaware, exchanged 9/30/64. Took oath of allegiance at New Orleans, 1/14/65. "Deserter came into the lines at Pass Manchac (La.) Jan. 6, 1865." Born: Ireland. Occ.: Laborer. Res.: N.O. Age 40, single, 5'3", blue eyes, dark hair, light complexion.

Drady, John C., Cpl. En. 6/4/61, CM. Present to 5/62. Wounded at Winchester, 5/25/62. Admitted to CSA Hosp., Charlottesville, Va., 6/9/62, wound in right elbow, discharged on surgeon's certificate of disability, 8/29/62. Born: Ireland. Occ.: Laborer. Res.: N.O., Age 30, single.

Duggan, Phillip, Pvt. En. 6/4/61, CM. Record dated 3/20/65, Petersburg, Va., states: "Deserted at Camp Moore, La." Born: Ireland. Occ.: Laborer. Res.: N.O.

Dunn, Patrick J., Cpl. En. 6/4/61, CM. Present to 5/62. AWOL, 5-6/62. Reported as deserted, 9-10/62. Born: Ireland. Occ.: Laborer. Res.: N.O. Age 26, single.

Edmonds, Michael J., Cpl. En. 6/4/61, CM. Present to 6/62. Wounded in left thigh at Gaines' Mill, Va., 6/27/62. Absent wounded, 6/62 to 7/63. Present 7-10/63. Absent, detailed at Jackson Hosp., Richmond, 11/63 to 1/65. Retired to Invalid Corps at Woodville, Miss., 1/30/65. Born: Ireland. Occ: Laborer. Res.: N.O. Age 28, single.
Fahey, James, Pvt. En. 3/8/62, N.O. Present to 11/62. Absent in hospital, 11/62 to 3/63. Present, 3/63 to 8/64. Admitted to Gen. Hosp. No. 9, Richmond, 6/64, transferred to Louisiana Hosp., Richmond. Deserted 12/15/64. Born: County Galway, Ireland. Occ.: Laborer. Res.: N.O.
Farrell, Thomas F., Pvt. En. 6/4/61, CM. Present to 7/62. Captured at Pughtown, Va., 7/6/62. POW, Old Capitol Prison, Washington, transferred to Fort Monroe, 8/1/62. Recorded as deserted, 10/62. Born: Ireland. Occ.: Teacher. Res.: N.O. Age 30, single.
Fitzgerald, Joseph, Pvt. En. 6/4/61, CM. Present to 6/62. Wounded at Port Republic, Va., 6/9/62. Detached as orderly to Col. Monaghan, 9/15/62. Admitted to CSA Hosp., Charlottesville, Va., 7/7/63, furloughed. Admitted to CSA Hosp., Charlottesville, 8/17/63, transferred to Lynchburg, Va., 9/21/63, wounds with gangrene. Detailed to provost guard, Gordonsville, Va., 11/21/63. Born: Ireland. Occ.: Laborer. Res.: N.O. Age 35, single.
Fitzhenry, James, Pvt. En. 6/4/61, CM. Present to 5/62. Detached to regimental wagon yard, 5/62 to 11/62. Present, 11-12/62. Absent sick in hospital, 1-4/63. Detailed as ship's carpenter to Navy Yard, Richmond, by special order dated 5/15/63. Born: Ireland. Occ.: Mechanic. Res.: N.O. Age 30, single.
Flannegan, Lawrence, Pvt. (aka Flanigan) En. 6/4/61, CM. Present to 4/63. Captured at Fredericksburg, Va., 4/29/63. POW, Old Capitol Prison, Washington, took oath of allegiance, 6/8/63, forwarded to Philadelphia, Pa. Born: Ireland. Occ.: Laborer. Res.: N.O. Age 45, single.
Flannegan, Michael, Pvt. En. 6/4/61, CM. Present to 8/62. Absent sick in hospital, 11/63 through 1864. Admitted to Ross Hosp., Mobile, Ala., 10/6/63, asthma. On list of permanently disabled soldiers transferred to Eufala, Ala., 4/26/64, emphysema. Born: Ireland. Occ.: Laborer. Res.: N.O. Age 45, single.
Fleury, Daniel, Cpl. En. 6/4/61, CM. Present to 4/63. Captured at Fredericksburg, Va., 4/29/63. POW, Old Capitol Prison, Washington, exchanged 6/3/63. Present 6-11/63. Captured at Rappahannock Station, Va., 11/7/63. POW, Point Lookout, Md., exchanged 3/10/64. Wounded at Winchester, 9/19/64, gunshot wound in hip. Admitted to USA Field Hospital, Winchester, 9/19/64. POW, Point Lookout, Md., exchanged 10/30/64. Captured in hospital, Richmond, 4/3/65, transferred to Libbey Prison. Released at Newport News, Va., 6/15/65. Born: Ireland. Occ.: Laborer. Res.: N.O. Age 40, single, 5'10", blue eyes, gray hair, fair complexion.
Fox, Bernard, Pvt. En. 6/4/61, CM. Present to 5/62. AWOL, 5-6/62. Present, 7-8/62. Recorded as deserted, 9/62. Born: La. Occ.: Laborer. Res.: N.O. Age 30, single.
Fox, William, Pvt. En. 6/4/61, CM. Present to 5/62. Wounded at Winchester, Va., 5/25/62. Admitted to CSA Hosp., Charlottesville, Va., 6/8/62, wound in arm, transferred to Lynchburg Hosp., 6/16/62. Admitted to CSA Hosp., Danville, Va., 9/7/62, diarrhea, returned to duty 1/17/63. Present to 4/63. Captured at Fredericksburg, Va., 4/29/63. Recorded as absent, captured thereafter. Born: Ireland. Occ.: Teacher. Res.: N.O. Age 30, single.
Gallagher, Thomas, Pvt. En.6/4/61, CM. (aka Gallaher) Present to 6/62. Killed at Port Republic, Va., 6/9/62. Born: Ireland. Occ.: Laborer. Res.: N.O. Age 22, single.
Gannon, Patrick, Pvt. En. 6/4/61, CM. Present to 5/62. AWOL, 5-8/62. Recorded as deserted, 9-10/62. Born: Ireland. Occ.: Laborer. Res.: N.O. Age 23, single.
Gillen, Samuel, Pvt. En. 6/4/61, CM. Present to 2/62. Discharged on surgeon's certificate of disability at Manassas, Va., 2/15/62, tuberculosis. Born: County Galway, Ireland. Occ.: Cook. Res.: N.O. Age 21, single, 5'6", brown eyes, auburn hair, fair complexion.
Grady, Edward, Cpl. En. 6/4/61, CM. Present to 9/62. Wounded at Chantilly, Va., 9/1/62. Absent wounded in hospital, 9-12/62. Present 1-7/63. Captured at Gettysburg, 7/3/63. POW, Fort Delaware. Record dated 3/20/65 at Petersburg states: "Captured July 3, 1863, taken the oath to U.S." Born: Ireland. Occ.: Laborer. Res.: N.O. Age 24, single.
Hall, Martin, Pvt. En. 6/4/61. Present to 5/62. AWOL, 5-8/62. Recorded as deserted 9/62. Born: Ireland. Occ.: Laborer. Res.: N.O. Age 30, married.
Hanley, James, Pvt. En. 6/4/61, CM. Present to 5/62. Absent sick in hospital, 5/62 to 2/63. Captured at Fredericksburg, Va., 4/29/63. POW, Old Capitol Prison, Washington, exchanged 6/3/63. Present to 5/64. Captured at Wilderness, Va., 5/5/64. POW, Point Lookout, Md., transferred to Elmira, N.Y., 8/17/64. Released 5/16/65. Born: Ireland. Occ.: Laborer. Res.: N.O. Age 45, single.
Hanlon, Patrick, Pvt. En. 6/4/61, CM. Present to 4/63. Roll for 5-6/63 states: "Killed in action April 29, 1863 at Fredericksburg, Va." Hays' Brigade list of casualties at Fredericksburg lists him as missing, 4/29/63. Record dated 3/20/65 at Petersburg states: "Killed May 1, 1863." Born: Ireland. Occ.: Laborer. Res.: N.O. Age 28, single.
Harmon, H., Pvt. No enlistment record. Captured at Rappahannock Station, Va., 11/7/63. POW, Point Lookout, Md., released on joining U.S. service, 1/28/64.
Hayes, Michael, Pvt. En. 6/4/61, CM. Present to 4/63. Captured at Fredericksburg, Va., 4/29/63. POW, Old Capitol Prison, Washington, exchanged 6/3/63. Wounded and captured at Gettysburg, 7/2/63. POW, DeCamp Genl. Hosp., David's Island, N.Y. Absent wounded, 7/63 to 1/64. Present to 5/64. Captured at Wilderness, Va., 5/5/64. POW, Point Lookout, Md., released 5/14/65. Born: Ireland. Occ.: Baker. Res.: N.O. Age 28, single.

Healy, Dennis, Pvt. En. 6/4/61, CM. Present to 4/63. Captured at Fredericksburg, Va., 4/29/63. POW, Old Capitol Prison, exchanged 5/13/63. Present to 7/63. Captured at Gettysburg, 7/5/63, after being left to attend wounded. POW, Fort McHenry, Md., released 2/25/64 on joining U.S. Army. Born: Ireland. Occ.: Teamster. Res.: N.O. Age 25, married.

Healy, Thomas, Pvt. En. 6/4/61, CM. Present to 10/61. Discharged on surgeon's certificate, date unstated. Born: Ireland. Occ.: Laborer. Res.: N.O. Age 37, single.

Hickey, John, Pvt. En. 6/4/61, CM. Present to 6/62. Captured at Strasburg, Va., 6/2/62. POW, Fort Delaware, took oath of allegiance to U.S., 8/10/62. Born: Ireland. Occ.: Laborer. Res.: N.O. age 29, single.

Hill, Samuel William, Pvt. En. 6/4/61, CM. Present to 9/62. Wounded at Chantilly, Va., 9/1/62. Absent wounded, 9/62 through 12/63. Absent, detailed to Engineer's Dept., Mobile, Ala., 1/64. Appointed 2nd Lt., Engineer's Corps, Heth's Division, 10/28/64. Surrendered and paroled with Heth's Division, 4/9/65. Born: Ireland. Occ.: Engineer. Res.: N.O. Age 40, single.

Hogan, Michael, Pvt. En. 6/4/61, CM. Present to 7/62. Wounded at Malvern Hill, Va., 7/1/62. Absent wounded, 7/62 to 2/63. Roll for 3-4/63 states: "Died in hospital of wounds received in action." Record dated 3/20/65 states: "Killed May 1st, 1863." [Battle of Fredericksburg] Born: Ireland. Occ.: Laborer. Res.: N.O. Age 25, married.

Holland, Peter, Pvt. En. 6/4/61, CM. Present to 7/62. Absent detached to Brigade wagon yard, 7-12/62. Absent sick in hospital at Mobile, Ala., 1-7/63. Recorded as deserted, 7/63 in Mobile. Born: Ireland. Occ.: Laborer. Res.: N.O. Age 28, married.

Johnson, John, Pvt. En. 6/4/61, CM. Present to 5/64. Captured at Wilderness, Va., 5/5/64. POW, Point Lookout, Md., transferred to Elmira, N.Y., 8/15/64, released 5/17/65. Born: England. Occ.: Laborer. Res.: N.O. Age 22, single.

Joyce, Martin, Sgt. En. 5/62, N.O. Detached on Pioneer Corps, 7-10/62. Present 11/62 to 4/64. Wounded at Gettysburg, 7/2/63. Promoted to cpl., 9/63. Promoted to sgt., 1/1/64. Killed at Wilderness, Va., 5/5/64. Born: Ireland. Occ.: Carpenter. Res.: N.O. Age 28, single.

Kane, Thomas, Pvt. En. 6/4/61, CM. Present to 6/62. Wounded at Port Republic, Va., 6/9/62. Absent wounded, 6-12/62. Roll for 11-12/62 states: "Died from wounds rec'd at Port Republic, June 9, 1862." Born: Ireland. Occ.: Laborer. Res.: N.O. Age 38, single.

Keating, James, Pvt. (aka Kayton) En. 6/4/61, CM. Present to 4/63. Severely wounded and captured at Fredericksburg, 4/29/63. Admitted St. Aloysius Hosp., Washington, 5/28/63, gunshot wound fracturing right leg. POW, Fort Delaware, 6/17/64, paroled 9/14/64. Detailed as guard, Jackson Hosp., Richmond, 1/65. On register of Confederate POWs sent from City Point, Va., 4/13/65, transportation furnished to Cincinnati, Ohio. Born: Ireland. Occ.: Laborer. Res.: N.O. Age 30, single.

Keating, Peter, Pvt. En. 6/4/61, CM. Present on 1861 rolls. AWOL, 5-8/62. Recorded as deserted, 10/62. Born: Ireland. Occ.: Laborer. Res.: N.O. Age 30, single.

Keegan, Daniel, Pvt., Chief Musician. En. 6/4/61, CM, as fifer. Present to 7/62. Absent sick in hospital, 7-11/62. Present 11/62 to 5/63. Transferred to non-commissioned staff, 5/18/63, as chief musician. Wounded in left foot at Winchester, Va., 6/14/63. Absent wounded, 7-10/63. Present 10/63 to 4/65. Surrendered at Appomattox C.H., Va., 4/9/65. Born: Ireland. Occ.: Musician. Res.: N.O. Age 28, single.

Kenny, Philip, Pvt. En. 6/4/61, CM. Present to 9/61. Discharged on surgeon's certificate of disability at Camp Bienville, Va., 9/16/61, chronic rheumatism. Born: County Wexford, Ireland. Occ.: Laborer. Res.: N.O. Age 32, single.

Larkin, Michael, Pvt. En. 6/4/61, CM. Present to 5/62. Absent sick, 5-9/62. Wounded at Sharpsburg, Md., 9/17/62. Absent wounded, 9/62 to 3/64. Captured at Harrisonburg, Va., 9/25/64, POW, Point Lookout, Md., released on joining U.S. Army, 10/17/64. Born: Ireland. Occ.: Laborer. Res.: N.O. Age 35, single.

Long, Mark, Sgt. En. 6/4/61, CM. Present to 5/62. Detached as regimental ordnance sgt., 5/62 to 4/65. Wounded at Manassas, Va., 8/29/62. Absent sick, 11-12/63. Present after 1/64. Born: Ireland. Occ.: Clerk. Res.: N.O. Age 21, single.

Magee, Robert, Pvt. (aka McGee) En. 6/4/61, CM. Present to 5/62. Absent sick in hospital, 5/62 to 6/63. Roll for 7-8/63 states: "Detailed to and deserted from Navy Yard, Richmond, Sept. 1863." Record dated 3/20/65 at Petersburg states: "Discharged by surgeon of regiment." Born: Ireland. Occ.: Laborer. Res.: N.O. Age 28, married.

Maloney, William, Pvt. En. 6/4/61, CM. Present to 6/62. Captured at Woodstock, Va., 6/2/62. POW, Fort Delaware, took oath of allegiance 8/10/62. Born: Ireland. Occ.: Laborer. Res.: N.O. Age 22, single.

Martin, James Owen, Lt. En. 6/4/61, CM, as 2nd Lt. Promoted to 1st Lt., 6/27/62. Wounded at Port Republic, Va., 6/9/62. Absent wounded 6-8/62. Wounded at Sharpsburg, Md., 9/17/62. Present to 12/62. Absent sick, 12/62 to 10/63. Resigned commission, 10/2/63. Letter of resignation dated 9/1/63 at Gainesville, Fla., states he is unfit for infantry field duty due to wounds and wishes to resign to join the 1st Louisiana Cavalry Regt., then operating in Tennessee. Born: Ireland. Occ.: Lawyer. Res.: N.O. Age 22, single.

McCann, Patrick, Pvt. En. 6/4/61, CM. Present to 7/62. Severely wounded at Malvern Hill, Va., 7/1/62. Admitted to Genl. Hosp. No. 7, Richmond, 7/22/62, right arm amputated, transferred to Louisiana Hosp., Richmond, 11/25/62. Absent wounded to 3/64. Detailed as watchman to Selma, Ala., 4/64. Born: Ireland. Occ.: Laborer. Res.: N.O. Age 23, single.

McCoole, Dennis, Pvt. En. 6/4/61, CM. Present to 5/64. Captured at Wilderness, Va., 5/5/64. Record dated 3/20/65 at Petersburg states: "Prisoner of war." Paroled at Stauton, Va., 5/1/65. Born: Ireland. Occ.: Gunsmith. Res.: N.O. Age 24, single, 5'10", blue eyes, light hair, fair complexion.
McCormack, Patrick, Pvt. En. 6/4/61, CM. Present to 6/62. Captured at Woodstock, Va., 6/2/62. POW, Steamer Katskill, exchanged 8/5/62. Present 8/62 to 6/63. Wounded at Winchester, Va., 6/4/63, left forearm. Present to 11/63. Captured at Rappahannock Station, Va., 11/7/63. POW, Point Lookout, transferred wounded, to Genl. Hosp., Point Lookout, 12/19/63, gunshot wound in left forearm. Exchanged 3/16/64. Absent detailed, 5/64 through 2/65. Record dated 3/20/65 at Petersburg states: "Was wounded while prisoner and now detailed." Born: Ireland. Occ.: Laborer. Res.: N.O. Age 24, single.
McCormick, James, Pvt. En. 6/4/61, CM. Present to 10/61. Roll for 9-10/61 states: "Killed by a member of the Tiger Rifles, Wheat's Battalion, Oct. 21, 1861." Report of sick and wounded for October 1861, at Camp Reserve, Va., lists date of death 10/23/61, puncture wound. Born: Ireland. Occ.: Laborer. Res.: N.O. Age 42, single.
McCormick, John, Pvt. En. 6/4/61, CM. Present to 6/62. Mortally wounded at Port Republic, Va., 6/9/62. Roll for 11-12/62 states: "Died from wound rec'd Port Republic, June 9, 1962." Born: New York. Occ.: Laborer. Res.: N.O. Age 21, single.
McCormick, Michael, Pvt. En. 6/4/61, CM. Present to 1/63 Absent sick, 1-2/63. Present 3-11/63. Captured at Rappahannock Station, Va., 11/7/63. POW, Point Lookout, Md., exchanged 3/10/64. Present to 5/64. Captured at Wilderness, Va., 5/5/64. POW, Point Lookout, transferred to Elmira, N.Y., 8/15/64, released 5/29/65. Born: Ireland. Occ.: Laborer. Res.: N.O. Age 40, single, 5'5", blue eyes, auburn hair, fair complexion.
McKenna, John, Pvt. En. 6/4/61, CM. Present to 2/62. Discharged at Camp Carondolet, Va., on surgeon's certificate of disability, 2/10/62, chronic ulcer. Born: Ireland. Occ.: Soldier. Res.: N.O. Age 28, single.
McKune, Edward, Pvt. En. 6/8/61, CM. Present through 10/61. Record dated 3/20/65 at Petersburg states: "Deserted." Born: Ireland. Occ.: Laborer. Res.: N.O. Age 29, single.
McLaughlin, James, Pvt. En. 6/4/61, CM. Present to 4/63. Captured at Fredericksburg, Va., 4/29/63.
POW, Old Capitol Prison, Washington, took oath of allegiance 5/25/63, forwarded to Philadelphia, Pa. Born: Ireland. Occ.: Laborer. Res.: N.O. Age 25, single.
Mooney, William, Cpl. En. 6/4/61, CM. Present to 7/62. Wounded at Malvern Hill, Va. 7/1/62. Admitted Chimborazo Hosp., Richmond, 7/5/62, gunshot wound in left leg, furloughed 30 days from 10/14/62. Absent wounded, 7/62 to 8/63. Present, disabled, 1/64. Record dated 3/20/65 at Petersburg states: "Detailed in Richmond and now on duty." Born: Ireland. Occ.: Laborer. Res.: N.O. Age 26, single.
Moran, Michael, Pvt. En. 6/4/61, CM. Present to 5/62. Absent sick in hospital, 5-8/62. Recorded as deserted, 10/62. Born: Ireland. Occ.: Teamster. Age 29, married.
Morgan, John, Pvt. En. 7/15/63 at Mobile, Ala. Absent sick in hospital, 7/63 to 3/64. Roll for 4-5/64 states: "Deserted Sept. 1863, Lynchburg, Va." Born: Ireland. Res.: N.O. Age 30, married.
Morrison, John, Pvt. En. 6/4/61, CM. Present to 12/62. Wounded at Fredericksburg, Va., 12/13/62. Admitted to Louisiana Hosp., Richmond, 12/16/62, transferred to Winder Hosp., Richmond, 1/14/63. Present, 3-4/63. Wounded at Fredericksburg, 4/29/63. Admitted to CSA Hosp., Charlottesville, Va., 5/2/63, returned to duty, 5/13/63. Wounded in shoulder at Winchester, Va., 6/14/63. Absent wounded and disabled, 6/63 to 5/64. Detailed as guard at Winder Hosp., Richmond, 5/26/64. Captured in Richmond hospital, 4/3/65. Born: Scotland. Occ.: Laborer. Res.: N.O. Age 30, single.
Murray, James, Sgt. En. 3/12/62, N.O. as pvt. Present to 9/62. Wounded at Chantilly, Va., 9/1/62. Present to 5/63. Wounded and captured at Fredericksburg, Va., 5/3/63. POW, Fort Delaware, exchanged 5/23/63. Present, 6-11/63. Captured at Rappahannock Station, Va., 11/7/63. POW, Point Lookout, Md., released on oath of allegiance, 3/3/64. Born: Ireland. Occ.: Laborer. Res.: N.O. Age 28, single.
Murray, Michael, Lt. En. 6/4/61, CM, as 1st sgt. Promoted to jr. 2nd lt., 9/26/62. Present to 7/64. Killed at Battle of Monocacy, Md., 7/9/64. Born: Ireland. Occ.: Laborer. Res.: N.O. Age 34, single.
Murray, Michael, Pvt. En. 6/4/61, CM. Present to 6/62. Killed at Port Republic, Va., 6/9/62. Born: Ireland. Occ.: Laborer. Res.: N.O. Age 22, single.
Murray, Richard, Pvt. En. 6/4/61, CM. Present to 5/62. Wounded at Winchester, Va., 5/25/62. Recorded as deserted, 10/62. Record dated 3/20/65 at Petersburg states: "Wounded and then deserted." Born: Ireland. Occ.: Soldier. Res.: N.O. Age 30, single.
Murray, William, Pvt. En. 6/4/61, CM. Present to 7/62. Absent detached as hospital nurse, 8/62 to 1/63. Present, 1-4/63. Captured at Fredericksburg, Va., 4/29/63. POW, Old Capitol Prison, Washington, exchanged 6/3/63. Present to 7/63. Severely wounded and captured at Gettysburg, 7/1/63. On register of sick and wounded Confederates in hospitals around Gettysburg, severe wound in knee joint, died 7/29/63. Born: Ireland. Occ.: Laborer. Res.: N.O. Age 25, married.
Nolan, Michael, Pvt. En. 6/4/61, CM. Present to 10/61. AWOL, 11/61 to 9/62. Recorded as deserted, 10/62. Born: Ireland. Occ.: Laborer. Res.: N.O. Age 30, single.
Nugent, James, Pvt. (aka Newgent) En. 7/15/63 at Mobile, Ala. Present to 7/64. Captured near Harper's Ferry, Va., 7/8/64. POW, Old Capitol Prison, Washington, transferred to Elmira, N.Y., 7/23/64, exchanged 3/10/65. Admitted CSA Genl. Hosp., Shreveport, La., 4/17/65, died 5/17/65, dysentery.

O'Brien, Terence B., Pvt. En. 6/4/61, CM. Present to 5/62. Discharged on surgeon's certificate at Camp Bragg, Rockingham County, Va., 5/5/65, chronic rheumatism. Born: Philadelpia, Pa. Occ.: Druggist. Res.: N.O. Age 20, single, 5'4", blue eyes, brown hair, fair complexion.

O'Brien, Thomas, Pvt. En. 6/4/61, CM. Absent sick, 6-7/61. Present 7-10/61. AWOL, 5-8/62. Recorded as deserted, 10/62. Born: Ireland. Occ.: Laborer. Res.: N.O. Age 25, single.

O'Brien, William, Pvt. En. 6/4/61, CM. Present to 7/62. Present, detailed as orderly to Col. William Monaghan, 8/62 to 5/64. Captured at Wilderness, Va., 5/5/64. POW, Point Lookout, Md., transferred to Elmira, N.Y., 8/15/64, released 5/15/65. Born: Ireland. Occ.: Laborer. Res.: N.O. Age 50, single, 5'10", hazel eyes, black hair, dark complexion.

O'Connor, Michael, Pvt. En. 11/18/63 at Raccoon Ford, Va. Roll for 11-12/63 states: "Present, substitute for a Mr. Ball of Miss." Present 1-4/64. Absent sick, 5-8/64. Admitted to CSA Hosp., Charlottesville, Va., 5/13/64, furloughed 60 days from 6/8/64. Record dated 3/20/65 at Petersburg states: "Substitute, deserted." Born: Ireland. Occ.: Merchant. Res.: N.O. Age 45, married.

O'Connor, Michael J., Sgt. En. 6/4/61, CM. Present to 8/62. Killed at Bristoe Station, Va., 8/27/62. Born: Ireland. Occ.: Laborer. Res.: N.O. Age 28, single.

O'Connor, Thomas, Pvt. En. 6/4/61, CM. Present to 5/62. Detached as teamster in regimental wagon yard, 5-11/62. Absent sick in hospital, 12/62 to 2/63. Died at Eastern District Hosp., Richmond, 2/6/63, chronic bronchitis. Born: Ireland. Occ.: Laborer. Res.: N.O. Age 26, single.

O'Meara, Patrick, Pvt. (aka O'Mara) En. 6/4/61, CM. Present to 8/62. Absent sick in hospital, 5/62 to 5/64. Retired to Invalid Corps, 8/16/64. Paroled at Beaver Dam, Va., 5/10/65. Born: Ireland. Occ.: Laborer. Res.: N.O. Age 25, single.

O'Neill, James, Pvt. (aka O'Neal) En. 6/4/61, CM. Present on 1861 rolls. AWOL, 5-8/62. Recorded as deserted, 10/62. Born: Ireland. Occ.: Laborer. Res.: N.O. Age 25, single.

O'Neill, Joseph, Pvt. (aka O'Neal) En. 6/4/61, CM. Present to 2/62. Absent on furlough2-4/62. Record dated 3/20/65 at Petersburg states: "Died in New Orleans in winter of 1862." Born: Ireland. Occ.: Merchant. Res.: N.O. Age 45, single.

Orr, John, Lt. En. 6/4/61, CM, as jr. lt. Promoted to 2nd lt., 6/27/62. Promoted to 1st lt. and adjutent of regiment, 11/26/62. Wounded at Sharpsburg, Md., 9/17/62. Absent wounded, 9-10/62. Present 11/62 to 6/63. Wounded at Winchester, Va., 6/14/63. Absent wounded, 7-8/63. Present, 9-11/63. Captured at Rappahannock Station, Va., 11/7/63. POW, Johnson's Island, Sandusky, Ohio, transferred to Point Lookout, Md., 3/14/65. Born: Ireland. Occ.: Clerk. Res.: N.O. Age 21, single.

Phair, William, Sgt. En. 6/4/61, CM, as pvt. Promoted to sgt., 6/6/64. Present to 8/62. Wounded at Bristoe Station, Va., 8/27/62. Absent wounded, 11/62 to 3/63. Captured at Fredericksburg, Va., 4/29/63. POW, Old Capitol Prison, exchanged 6/3/63. Present 6/63 to 7/64. Killed at Battle of Monocacy, Md., 7/9/64. Born: Ireland. Occ.: Clerk. Res.: N.O. Age 28, single.

Power, John D., Pvt. En. 6/4/61, CM. Present on 1861 rolls. Absent sick in hospital, 5/62 to 1/64. Absent detailed in hospital at Montgomery Springs, Va., 1-4/64. Record dated 3/30/65 at Petersburg states: "Deserted." Took oath of allegiance at City Point, Va., 1/29/65. Born: Ireland. Occ.: Laborer. Res.: N.O. Age 45, single.

Riley, Michael, Pvt. En. 6/4/61, CM. Present to 7/62. Wounded at Gaines' Mill, Va., 6/27/62. Absent wounded, 6/62 to 2/64. Roll for 3-4/64 states: "Deserted June 1862, Richmond, Va." Record dated 3/20/65 at Petersburg states: "Missing since July 1862." Born: Ireland. Occ.: Laborer. Res.: N.O. Age 26, single.

Riordan, Daniel, Pvt., No. 1. (aka Reardon) En. 6/4/61, CM. Present to 6/62. Captured at Port Republic, 6/9/62. POW, exchanged 8/8/62. Present 8-11/62. Absent sick in hospital, 12/62 to 7/63. Present 7-12/63. Captured at Mine Run, Va., 11/30/63. POW, Old Capitol Prison, Washington, transferred to Point Lookout, Md., 2/3/64, exchanged 2/10/65. Surrendered and paroled at Appomattox C.H., Va., 4/9/65. Born: Ireland. Occ.: Laborer. Res.: N.O. Age 28, single.

Riordon, Daniel, Pvt., No. 2. En. 2/28/62. Present to 4/63. Captured at Fredericksburg, Va., 4/29/63. POW, Old Capitol Prison, Washington, exchanged 6/3/63. Present to 11/63. Captured at Rappahannock Station, Va., 11/7/63. POW, Point Lookout, Md., exchanged 3/10/64. Captured at Wilderness, Va., 5/5/64. POW, Point Lookout, transferred to Elmira, N.Y. 8/15/64, released 5/15/65. Born: County Cork, Ireland. Occ.: Clerk. Res.: N.O. Age 25, single.

Roe, Patrick, Pvt. (aka Rowe) En. 6/4/61, CM. Present to 8/62. Wounded at Bristoe Station, Va., 8/27/62. Absent wounded, 8/62 to 5/63. Present 6-12/63. Absent on sick furlough, 1-2/64. Retired to Invalid Corps, 5/4/64. Record dated 3/20/65 at Petersburg states: "Arm amputated Aug. 1862." Paroled at Mobile, Ala., 4/25/65. Born: Ireland. Occ.: Laborer. Res.: N.O. Age 22, single.

Ryan, John, Pvt. En. 2/27/62, N.O. AWOL, 5-8/62. Recorded as deserted, 9-10/62. Born: Baltimore, Md. Occ.: Soldier. Age 24.

Ryan, John C., Pvt. En. 6/4/61, CM. Record dated 2/10/65 at Petersburg states: "Accidentally wounded and arm amputated 1861." Retired to Invalid Corps at Mobile, Ala., 10/21/64. Born: Ireland. Occ.: Laborer. Res.: N.O. Age 25, single.

Sinnott, Michael, Pvt. En. 2/21/62, N.O. Present to 9/62. Wounded at Sharpsburg, Md., 9/17/62. Absent wounded, 9-10/62. Present, 11/62 to 3/63. Roll for 3-4/63 states: "Deserted Mar. 18, 1863, Rappahannock River." Born: County Wexford, Ireland. Occ.: Soldier. Res.: N.O. Age 30, single.

Smith, John, Pvt. En. 6/4/61, CM. Present to 6/62. Killed at Port Republic, Va., 6/9/62. Born: Ireland. Occ.: Butcher. Res.: N.O. Age 39, married.
Smith, William St. Clair, Pvt. En. 6/4/61, CM. Present on 1861 rolls. Absent sick, 5-6/62. AWOL, 7-8/62. Recorded as deserted, 9-10/62. Born: Canada. Occ.: Laborer. Res.: N.O. Age 29, single.
Sweeney, Patrick, Pvt. En. 3/3/62, N.O. Present to 4/63. Captured at Fredericksburg, Va., 4/29/63. POW, Fort Delaware, Del., exchanged 6/3/63. Present to 5/64. Captured at Wilderness, Va., 5/5/64. POW, Point Lookout, Md., transferred to Elmira, N.Y., 8/15/64, released 5/19/65. Born: New York. Occ.: Laborer. Res.: N.O. Age 25, married.
Tolan, John, Pvt. En. 6/8/61, CM. Present to 6/62. AWOL, 6-9/62. Recorded as deserted, 10/62. Born: Canada. Occ.: Laborer. Res.: N.O. Age 21, single.
Tracy, Henry P., Pvt. En. 6/4/61, CM, as drummer. Present to 7/63. Captured at Gettysburg, 7/2/63. POW, Fort Delaware, exchanged 9/28/64. Admitted to Louisiana Hosp., Richmond, 1/3/65. Retired to Invalid Corps., 3/28/65, due to "incised wound of abdomen received in attempting to escape from prison." Paroled at Salisbury, N.C., 5/3/65. Born: Buffalo, N.Y. Occ.: Sailor. Res.: N.O. Age 29, single.
Twohey, Patrick, Cpl. (aka Toohey) En. 3/8/62, N.O. as pvt. Promoted to cpl., 9/63. Present to 4/63. Captured at Fredericksburg, Va., 4/29/63. POW, Old Capitol Prison, Washington, exchanged 6/3/63. Present to 12/64. Deserted at Petersburg, Va., 12/11/64, took oath of allegiance at City Point, Va., sent to New York City, 12/13/64. Born: Cork City, Ireland. Occ.: Teamster. Res.: N.O. Age 27.
Ward, Joseph, Sgt. En. 6/4/61, CM, as pvt. Promoted to cpl., 8/24/61. Promoted to 1st sgt., 1/1/64. Present to 6/62. Wounded at Port Republic, Va., 6/9/62. Absent wounded, 6-9/62. Present, 9/62 to 5/64. Captured at Wilderness, Va., 5/5/64. POW, Point Lookout, Md., transferred to Elmira, N.Y., 8/15/64, exchanged 10/11/64. Admitted to Louisiana Hosp., Richmond, 12/3/64. Retired to Invalid Corps, 2/22/65. Surrendered at Lynchburg, Va., 4/13/65. Born: County Down, Ireland. Occ.: Laborer. Res.: N.O. Age 24, single.
Welsh, Matthew, Pvt. (aka Walsh) En. 6/4/61, CM. Present to 7/62. Absent sick, 7-9/62. Present to 5/64. Captured at Wilderness, Va., 5/5/64. POW, Point Lookout, Md., exchanged 9/18/64. Present 9/64 to 3/65. Captured in Fair Grounds Hosp., Petersburg, Va., 4/3/65. Released from USA Gen. Hosp., Fort Monroe, Va., 6/17/65. Born: Ireland. Occ.: Teamster. Res.: N.O. Age 40, single.
Welsh, Michael F., Pvt. En. 6/4/61, CM. Present to 10/61. Detailed as teamster, 10/61 to 1/63. Roll for 1-2/63 states: "Deserted from camp when division teamster." Rejoined from desertion, 3/6/63. Present, 3-11/63. Captured at Mine Run, Va., 11/30/63. POW, Old Capitol Prison, Washington, released on taking oath of allegiance, 3/19/64, sent to Philadelphia. Born: Ireland. Occ: Laborer. Res.: N.O. Age 26, single.
Whelan, John, Pvt. En. 6/4/61, CM. Present to 7/62. AWOL, 7/62 to 3/63. Rejoined from desertion, 3/2/63. Roll for 5-6/63 states: "Undergoing sentence of court martial at Staunton, Va." Present, 7-11/63. Roll for 11-12/63 states: "Captured at Rappahannock Station, Nov. 7, 1863." Record dated 3/20/65 at Petersburg states: "Wounded Nov. 7, 1863 and died of his wounds." Born: Ireland. Occ.: Laborer. Res.: N.O. Age 23, single.
White, Charles, Pvt. En. 6/4/61, CM. Present to 12/61. Admitted to Moore Hosp., Danville, Va., 12/26/61, broken arm. Absent sick to 11/62. Roll for 11-12/62 states: "Discharged on surgeon's certificate of disability." Record dated 3/20/65 at Petersburg states: "Broke his arm accidentally and discharged." Born: Ireland. Occ.: Mason. Res.: N.O. Age 35, single.
White, Peter, Pvt. En. 6/4/61, CM. Present to 1861 rolls. Roll 11-12/63 states: "Joined from desertion Nov. 18, 1863, Raccoon Ford. Absent in arrest." Prisoner at Division Guard House, 1-4/64. Record dated 3/20/65 at Petersburg states: "Deserted." Born: Canada. Occ.: Blacksmith. Res.: N.O. Age 35, married.

Company G: Pemberton Rangers

Raised in New Orleans primarily among the city's large German population, Company G's ranks were more than 80 percent foreign-born. Of the 109 men enrolled, at least 61 were natives of Prussia, Bavaria or other Germanic states. Many of the 15 men whose birthplaces are unknown had common German surnames. Another 13 were Irish immigrants, seven were from France, two each from England and Italy, one from Switzerland and one from Malta. Only two men were natives of Louisiana, and four were born in Northern states. During the war, 20 men of this company were killed or mortally wounded in battle, six died of disease, two were discharged and two transferred out. Twenty-six men deserted and another 21 were captured and took the oath of allegiance. Three men joined the U.S. service to gain release from prison. Four of the company surrendered at Appomattox Court House.

Captains:

Smith, Isaac A., Capt. Commissioned by Gov. T.O. Moore as capt. of Pemberton Rangers, 5/11/61. En. 6/4/61, CM, as capt., Company G, 6th La. Present to 2/62. Detailed on recruiting service in Louisiana, 2/62. Present to 6/62. Killed at Port Republic, Va., 6/9/62.

Clarke, Frank, Capt. En. 6/4/61 as 2nd lt. Elected 1st lt. at Centreville, Va., 11/22/61. Wounded at Winchester, 5/25/62. Promoted from 1st lt. to capt., 6/9/62. Wounded at Sharpsburg, Md., 9/17/62. Absent wounded to 4/24/63. Wounded at Fredericksburg, Va., 4/29/63. Absent on detached service at conscription camp at Mobile, Ala., 5-10/63. Absent, detached at Montgomery, Ala., 11-12/63. Declared permanently disabled from field service by Medical Examining Board, Montgomery, due to fracture of left leg from gunshot wound at Fredericksburg, 12/5/63. Promoted to major, Commandant of Conscription for East Louisiana, 3/11/64.

Van Benthuysen, Jefferson D., Capt. En. 4/15/61, N.O. Elected 2nd jr. lt. 8/16/61 from ranks of Co. B, 1st La. Special Batln. Promoted to 1st lt., 6/9/62. Promoted to capt., 3/11/64. Present to 7/63. wounded in head 7/2/63 and captured 7/5/63 at Gettysburg. POW, DeCamp Gen. Hosp., David's Island, N.Y., transferred to Johnson's Island, Ohio, 9/18/63, released Fort Monroe, 2/2/65. Adm. to Stuart Hosp., Richmond, 3/22/65, catarrh. Granted leave, 3/28/65.

* * *

Abel, Joseph, Pvt. Transferred in from Wheat's 1st La. Special Battalion, 9/26/62. Present to 5/64. Captured at Wilderness, 5/6/64. POW, Point Lookout, Md., to 5/15/64, transferred to Elmira, N.Y., exchanged 3/10/65. Born: France. Occ.: Laborer. Res.: N. O.

Aboth, James, Pvt. (aka Abbott) En. 6/4/61, CM. Deserted at Knoxville en route to Va. in 1861. Born: Baden, Germany. Occ.: Saddler. Res.: N. O.

Arcenaux, J., Pvt. No enlistment record. Appears on register of sick and wounded POWs at USA Depot Field Hosp., Winchester, Va. Admitted 9/19/64, wounded in abdomen. Died 9/30/64.

Beach, Abner, Cpl. En. 2/22/62, N. O. Promoted from pvt. to cpl. 7/62. Wounded at Malvern Hill, Va., 7/1/62. Captured at Bristoe Station, Va. 8/27/62. Absent sick, 11/62 to 4/63. Record dated 3/21/65 at Petersburg states: "Deserted, took oath to U.S." Born: Auburn, N.Y. Occ.: Painter. Age 43, single.

Blef, Peter, Pvt. En. 6/4/61, CM. Captured at Wilderness, 5/5/64. POW, Point Lookout, Md., paroled and exchanged, 1/17/65.

Bock, Adolph, Cpl. En. 6/4/61, CM, as pvt. Promoted to cpl., 6/12/62. Wounded in right leg at Gaines' Mill, Va., 6/27/62. Absent wounded through 12/63. Detailed as nurse at Jackson Hosp., Richmond, 1/20/64. Surrendered at Citronelle, Ala., 5/4/65. Born: Prussia. Occ.: Laborer. Res.: N. O. Age 33, single. 5'9", hazel eyes, brown hair, dark complexion.

Bolger, Phillip, Color Sgt. Present through 6/62. Absent sick, 7-8/62. Promoted from pvt. to Color Sgt., 10/1/62. Wounded at Fredericksburg, 5/3/63. Wounded severely in lung and arm at Gettysburg, 7/2/63. Captured at Gettysburg, 7/5/63, paroled at Baltimore, Md., 8/23/63. Absent wounded, 7/63 to 5/64. Absent, disabled in Engineer Corps, 8/64. Born: N. O. Occ.: Laborer. Res.: N. O. Single.

Bolte, Emile, Pvt. En. 6/4/61, CM. Present to 11/63. Captured at Rappahannock Station, Va., 11/7/63. POW, Point Lookout, Md, released on joining U.S. Army, 1/28/64. Born: Prussia. Occ.: Cooper. Res.: N. O. Single.

Borge, Louis, Pvt. En. 2/20/62, N. O. Captured in Shenandoah Valley, Va., 6/1/62. POW, Fort Delaware, Del., took oath of allegiance 8/10/62. Born: Malta. Occ.: Laborer. Res.: N. O. Age 25, single.

Bosen, Edmond, Pvt. En. 6/4/61, CM. Present to 8/61. Detached as teamster, 8/21/61. Deserted, 2/62. Born: Prussia. Occ.: Laborer. Res.: N. O. Single.

Braun, Charles, Pvt. En. 6/4/61, CM. Captured at Woodstock, Va., 6/2/62. POW, Fort Delaware, Del., took oath of allegiance 8/10/62. Born: Berlin, Prussia. Occ.: Laborer. Res.: N. O. Age 20, single.

Braun, John, Pvt. En. 2/21/62, N. O. Captured in Shenandoah Valley, Va., about 6/1/62. POW, Fort Delaware, Del., took oath of allegiance, 8/10/62. Born: Hesse-Darmstadt, Germany. Occ.: Laborer. Age 25.

Brennan, John, Pvt. En. 6/4/61, CM. Captured in Shenandoah Valley, Va., about 6/1/62. Record dated 3/21/65 at Petersburg states: "Took oath to U.S." Born: Ireland. Occ.: Laborer. Res.: N. O. Single.

Brenning, John, Sgt. En. 6-4-61. Promoted from cpl. to sgt., 6/13/62. Wounded at Malvern Hill, Va., 7/1/62. Absent wounded, 7/62 through 8/63. Died in hospital at Richmond, 12/1/63. Record dated 3/21/65 at Petersburg states: "Deserted from hospital and afterwards died in Castle Thunder," [a political prison in Richmond, Va.]. Born: Wirtemburg, Germany. Occ.: Laborer. Res.: N. O. Single.

Brewer, William B., 2nd Lt. En. 6-4-61, CM. Commissioned as junior 2nd Lt., 5/9/61 by Gov. T.O. Moore. Resigned at Manassas, Va., 7/8/61.

Christy, George W. See Field & Staff roster.

Collins, John, Pvt. (no enlistment data) Captured at Woodstock, Va., 6/2/62. POW, Fort Delaware, Del., took oath of allegiance to U.S., 8/10/62.

Daegner, Thomas, Pvt. (aka Degnan, Dagnon) En. 6/4/61, CM. Present to 5/62. Absent sick in hospital, 5/62 to 8/63. Present, 9-10/63. Captured at Rappahannock Station, Va., 11/7/63. POW, Point Lookout, Md., exchanged 3/10/64. Present 5/64 to 9/64. Wounded in shoulder and captured at Winchester, Va., 9/19/64. POW, Point Lookout, exchanged 10/10/64. Absent in Louisiana Hosp., Richmond, 12/64. Born: Ireland. Occ.: Laborer. Res.: N.O. Age 25, single.

Dolan, John, Cpl. En. 6/4/61, CM. Promoted to cpl., 9/25/61. Present to 5/62. Deserted, 5/27/62. Born: Ireland. Occ.: Laborer. Res.: N.O. Single.

Dorsing, Theodore, Pvt. En. 6/4/61, CM. Present to 7/63. Captured at Gettysburg, 7/4/63. POW, Fort McHenry, Md., transferred to Fort Delaware, Del., released upon joining 3rd Maryland Cavalry (U.S.), 9/22/63. Born: France. Occ.: Laborer. Res.: N.O. Single.

Elkers, August, Pvt. (aka Elgas, Eldres) En. 6/4/61, CM. Present to 5/63. Absent sick, 5-6/63. Present 7-11/63. Captured at Rappahannock Station, Va., 11/7/63. POW, Point Lookout, Md., transferred to Elmira, N.Y., 7/23/64. Took oath of allegiance, 8/64. Born: Alsace, France. Occ.: Laborer. Res.: N.O. Single, 5'9", hazel eyes, dark hair, dark complexion.

Engelhart, Henry, Pvt. (aka Inglehart) En. 6/4/61, CM. Present to 5/62. Wounded at Winchester, 5/25/62. Absent wounded to 3/63. Roll for 3-4/63 states: "Died June 1862 from wounds received at Winchester May 25, 1862" Unresolved conflicting record: Name appears on register of furloughs approved, Medical Director's Office, Richmond, dated 11/27/62. Born: Bavaria. Occ.: Shoemaker. Res.: N.O. Single.

Euth, Christian, Pvt. En. 6/4/61, CM. Present to 6/62. Killed at Port Republic, Va., 6/9/62. Born: Wirtemburg, Germany. Occ.: Carpenter. Res.: N.O. Single.

Fick, George, Cpl. En. 6/4/61, CM. Present to 12/63. Promoted from pvt. to cpl., 9/62. Absent on furlough, 12/63. Present to 5/64. Captured at Wilderness, Va., 5/5/64. POW, Point Lookout, Md., transferred to Elmira, N.Y., 7/25/64, released 5/15/65. Born: Frankfort, Germany. Occ.: Moulder. Res.: N.O. Single, 5'8", blue eyes, dark hair, dark complexion.

Fitzpatrick, Patrick, Pvt. En. 6/4/61, CM. Absent in hospital, 7/61 to 12/62. Detached as baker in hospital at Lynchburg, Va., 1/63 to 11/64. Present 11-12/64. Deserted at Petersburg, Va., 12/11/64. Took oath of allegiance at City Point, Va., 12/13/64. Born: Ireland. Occ.: Baker. Res.: N.O. Single, 5'8", blue eyes, dark hair, dark complexion.

Fogle, Louis, Cpl. No enlistment recorded. Appointed cpl., 9/10/61. Died of disease, 3/2/62.

Ford, Patrick, Pvt. En. 6/4/61, CM. Present to 6/62. Detached as hospital nurse, disabled, 6/62. Captured in hospital at Winchester, Va., 6/2/62. POW, Fort Delaware, Del. Captured at Gettysburg, 7/63. POW, Fort Delaware, paroled 9/14/64. Born: Ireland. Occ.: Laborer. Res.: N.O. Single.

Fraid, Jacob, Pvt. En. 6/4/61, CM. Present to 8/62. Captured at Manassas, Va., 8/28/62. Paroled at Fort Monroe, Va., date unrecorded. Recorded as deserted, 4/63. Record dated 3/21/65 at Petersburg states: "Never returned to command after being exchanged." Born: Baden, Germany. Occ.: Laborer. Res.: N.O. Single.

Franke, Charles, Pvt. En. 6/4/61, CM. Present to 5/62. Recorded as deserted 5/15/62. Born: Prussia. Occ.: Laborer. Res.: N.O.

Gaber, C., Pvt. No enlistment recorded. Captured at Strasburg, Va., Oct. 19, 1864. POW, Point Lookout, Md., arrived 10/25/64, exchanged 2/10/65.

Geyer, George, Pvt. En. 6/4/61, CM. Record dated 3/21/65 at Petersburg states: "Deserted at Knoxville when enroute to Virginia." Born: Bavaria. Occ.: Laborer. Res.: N.O. Single.

Gold, John, Pvt. En. 6/4/61, CM. Died at Camp Bienville, Centreville, Va., 8/7/61, paralysis. Born: Prussia. Occ.: Laborer. Res.: N.O. Single.

Heil, John, Color Sgt. En. 6/4/61, CM. Present to 9/62. Promoted from pvt. to Color Sgt., 11/61. Killed at Sharpsburg, Md., 9/17/62. Born: Baden, Germany. Occ.: Laborer. Res.: N.O. Single.

Heintz, Louis, Cpl. (aka L. Hines) En. 3/10/62, N.O. Present to 9/62. Mortally wounded in thigh at Sharpsburg, Md., 9/17/62, died at Groves' Warehouse near Sharpsburg battlefield, 10/16/62. Born: France. Occ.: Barkeeper. Res.: N.O. Age 31, single.

Heyden, William F., Pvt. En. 6/4/61, CM. Present to 9/62. Present on extra duty as orderly in regimental commissary, 9/62 to 6/63. Absent sick, 9-10/63. Recorded as deserted from camp near Raccoon Ford, Rapidan River, Va., 1/26/64. Born: Prussia. Occ.: Confectioner. Res.: N.O. Married.

Hill, Andrew, Sgt. En. 6/8/61, N.O. Present to 9/62. Severely wounded at Sharpsburg, Md., 9/17/62. Absent wounded 9/62 to 3/65. Record dated 3/21/65 at Petersburg states: "When last heard from was in the Trans-Mississippi Dept." Born: Bavaria. Occ.: Laborer. Res.: N.O. Single.

Hummel, Rudolph, Pvt. En. 6/4/61, CM. Present to 6/62. Captured at Strasburg, Va., 6/2/62. POW, Fort Delaware, Del., took oath of allegiance, 8/10/62. Born: Baden (Germany). Occ.: Laborer. Res.: N.O. Single.

Husselman, Herman, Pvt. En. 6/4/61, CM. Present to 11/63. Captured at Rappahannock Station, 11/7/63. POW, Point Lookout, Md., took oath of allegiance, 1/28/64. Born: Prussia. Occ.: Laborer. Res.: N.O. Single.

Izen, Frank, Pvt. En. 6/4/61, CM. Present to 6/62. Captured at Woodstock, Va., 6/3/62. POW, Fort Delaware, Del., took oath of allegiance, 8/10/62. Born: Prussia. Occ.: Laborer. Res.: N.O. Single.

Jaeger, Ernest, Pvt. En. 6/4/61, CM. Present to 12/61. Record dated 3/21/65 at Petersburg states: "Deserted in Dec., 1861." Born: Switzerland. Occ.: Laborer. Res.: N.O. Single.

Keris, Martin, Pvt. En. 6/4/61, CM. Present to 6/62. Captured at Strasburg, Va., 6/2/62. POW, Fort Delaware, Del, took oath of allegiance, 8/10/62. Born: Prussia. Occ.: Carpenter. Res.: N.O. Single.

The flag of Company H, Orleans Rifles, 6th Louisiana, is currently housed in the Confederate Memorial Hall in New Orleans.

Kempf, Charles, Pvt. En. 6/4/61, CM. Present to 5/62. Recorded as deserted, 5/22/62. Born: Hesse-Darmstadt (Germany). Occ.: Laborer. Res.: N.O. Single.
Kleppe, Charles, Pvt. En. 6/4/61, CM. Record dated 3/21/65 at Petersburg states: "Deserted at Knoxville en route to Va. in 1861."
Klopfer, John, Sgt. En. 6/4/61, CM, as pvt. Promoted to cpl., 2/62. Promoted to sgt., 9/1/62. Present to 5/64. Wounded at Fredericksburg, Va., 5/4/63. Captured at Wilderness, Va., 5/5/64. POW, Point Lookout, Md., transferred to Elmira, N.Y., 7/25/64, took oath of allegiance, 11/4/64. Born: Wirtemburg, Germany. Occ.: Laborer. Res.: N.O. Single.
Knapp, Philip, Pvt. En. 6/4/61, CM. Present to 7/63. Captured at South Mountain, Md., 7/5/63. POW, Fort Delaware, Del., released 5/65. Born: Baden (Germany) Occ.: Moulder. Res.: N.O. Single.
Kuschke, Herman, Pvt. En. 6/4/61, CM. Held rank as Musician, 9/61 to 9/63. Present to 7/62. Absent sick, 7/62 to 5/63. Present, 5/63 to 5/64. Captured at Wilderness, Va., 5/5/64. POW, Point Lookout, Md., transferred to Elmira, N.Y., 7/26/64, released 5/15/65. Born: Prussia. Occ.: Carpenter. Res.: N.O. Age 50, married.
Lehnen, John, Pvt. (aka Leiden) En. 6/4/61, CM. Present to 6/62. Captured at Woodstock, Va., 6/2/62. Recorded as deserted, 10/62. Record dated 3/21/65 at Petersburg states: "Deserted to cavalry." Born: Prussia. Occ.: Laborer. Res.: N.O. Single.
Lievre, Pierre, Pvt. En. 6/4/61, CM. Present to 11/62. Detached as orderly to brigade quartermaster, 11/62 to 3/63. Present, 3-4/63. Detached as hospital nurse, 4/63. Detached as orderly to brigade quartermaster, 11/63. Surrendered at Appomattox C.H., Va., 4/9/65.
Linton, Joseph, Pvt. En. 3/10/62, N.O. Present to 6/62. Captured at Woodstock, Va., 6/2/62. POW, Fort Delaware, Del., took oath of allegiance, 8/10/62. Born: Prussia. Occ.: Laborer. Age 28.
Lorentz, Florence, Pvt. (aka Laurens, Lorantz) En. 6/4/61, CM. Present to 7/62. Wounded at Malvern Hill, Va., 7/1/62. Admitted to Chimborazo Hosp., Richmond, gunshot wound in head, 7/4/62. Absent wounded to 12/62. Present to 7/63. Captured at Gettysburg, 7/4/63. Roll for 7/63 states he was left behind as a nurse to attend wounded. POW, DeCamp Gen. Hosp., Davids Island, N.Y. Record dated 3/15/65 at Petersburg states: "Deserted Oct. 1, 1863, being exchanged at that time and never having reported to command." Born: France. Occ.: Laborer. Res.: N.O., Single.
Lorentz, Joseph, Pvt. (aka Lawrence) En. 6/4/61, CM. Present to 6/62. Wounded at Gaines' Mill, Va., 6/27/62. Absent wounded, 6/62 to 7/63. Absent on detached service in hospital at Lynchburg after 7/63. Born: France. Occ.: Laborer. Res.: N.O. Single.
Lucas, Edmond M., Pvt. En. 6/4/61, CM. Present to 8/62. Captured at Cedar Mountain, Va., 8/15/62. POW on board steamer Frolic, near Baton Rouge, La., 2/23/63. Present, 5/63 to 5/64. Wounded at Fredericksburg, Va., 5/4/63. Captured at Wilderness, Va., 5/5/64. POW, Point Lookout, Md., transferred to Elmira, N.Y., 8/15/64, released 5/13/65. Born: England. Occ.: Confectioner. Res: St. Louis, Mo. Married.
Ludorf, Otto, Pvt. En. 6/4/61, CM. Present to 6/62. Killed at Gaines' Mill, Va., 6/27/62.
Lush, Michael, Pvt. En. 6/4/61, CM. Present to 8/62. Wounded at Bristoe Station, 8/27/62. Absent wounded to 3/63. Present, disabled, 3-4/63. Detached as nurse at hospital in Richmond, 5/63. Roll for 1-2/64 states: "Deserted from hospital, Richmond, 1/12/64." Returned from desertion, 4/29/64. Captured at Wilderness, Va., 5/5/64. POW, Point Lookout, Md., transferred to Elmira, N.Y., 7/28/64, released 5/19/65. Born: Germany. Occ.: Laborer. Res.: N.O. Single.
Mandle, James, Pvt. (aka Mantle) En. 3/12/62, N.O. Present to 6/62. Captured at Strasburg, Va., 6/2/62. POW, Fort Delaware, Del., took oath of allegiance, 8/10/62. Born: Hamburg, Wirtemburg (Germany). Occ.: Laborer. Age 21.
Matthews, John, Pvt. En. 6/4/61, CM. Present to 5/62. Roll for 5-6/62 states: "Deserted May '62." Born: England. Occ.: Laborer. Res.: N.O. Single.
Mayer, August, Pvt. En. 6/4/61, CM. Present to 8/62. Killed at Bristoe Station, Va., 8/27/62. Born: Prussia. Occ.: Laborer. Res.: N.O. Single.
Martin, Michael, Pvt. En. 3/17/62, N.O. Present to 6/62. Killed at Port Republic, Va., 6/9/62. Record dated 3/21/65 at Petersburg states: "Killed by shot in back of head." Born: Baden (Germany). Occ.: Laborer. Res.: N.O. Age 29, single.
McDonnough, John, Pvt. En. 6/4/61, CM. Present to 9/62. Wounded at Chantilly, Va., 9/1/62. Absent wounded, 9-10/62. Present 11/62 to 4/63. Wounded at Fredericksburg, Va., 4/29/63. Absent wounded, 5-6/63. Present, 7-11/63. Captured at Rappahannock Station, Va., 11/7/63. POW, Point Lookout, Md., took oath of allegiance, 3/30/64. Born: Ireland. Occ.: Laborer. Res.: N.O. Single.
Mertlin, Bernard, Pvt. En. 3/12/62, N.O. Present to 8/62. Killed at Bristoe Station, Va., 8/27/62. Record dated 3/21/65 at Petersburg states: "Killed by shot in head." Born: Baden (Germany). Occ.: Laborer. Res.:N.O. Age 25, single.
Miller, John, Cpl. En. 6/4/61, CM, as pvt. Promoted to cpl., 9/15/61. Admitted to CSA Hosp., Charlottesville, Va., 7/23/61, returned to duty 9/10/61, diarrhea. Present 9/61 to 3/62. Admitted to Chimborazo Hosp., Richmond, 3/18/62, died 5/3/62, dropsey. Born: Wirtemburg (Germany). Occ.: Laborer. Res.: N.O. Single.
Miranda, Henry G., Pvt. En. 6/4/61, CM. Present to 10/62. Admitted to Winder Hosp., Richmond, 10/16/62, returned to duty, 3/11/63. Present 3/63 to 1/64. Roll for 1-2/64 states: "Deserted from camp near Raccoon Ford, Jan. 26, 1864."

Morse, Daniel, Pvt. En. 2/26/62, N.O. Present to 6/62. Captured at Strasburg, Va., 6/2/62. POW, Fort Delaware, Del., took oath of allegiance, 8/10/62. Born: County Tyrone, Ireland. Occ.: Laborer. Res.: N.O. Age 33, single.
Mullen, Daniel, Pvt. En. 6/7/61, N.O. Present to 6/62. Killed at Port Republic, 6/9/62. Record dated 3/21/65 at Petersburg states: "Killed instantly by shot though head." Born: Ireland. Occ.: Laborer. Res.: N.O., single.
Muller, Alexander, Pvt. (aka Miller) En. 2/20/62, N.O. Present to 5/64. Wounded at Fredericksburg, Va., 5/3/63. Died at Hospital No. 3, Lynchburg, Va., 5/2/64, chronic diarrhea. Born: Prussia. Occ.: Laborer. Res.: N.O. Age 23, single, 5'8", gray eyes, light hair, light complexion.
O'Riley, John, Pvt. (aka O'Reiley) En. 6/4/61, CM. Present to 5/62. Severely wounded in leg at Winchester, Va., 5/25/62. Discharged at Staunton, Va., on surgeon's certificate of disability, 12/20/62, amputated left leg below the knee. Born: County Mayo, Ireland. Occ.: Laborer. Res.: N.O.
O'Rourke, Patrick, Pvt. En. 6/4/61, CM. Present to 6/62. Wounded at Port Republic, Va., 6/9/62. Admitted to CSA Hospital, Charlottesville, Va., 6/15/62, amputated finger. Absent wounded to 9/62. Present, 9/62 to 11/63. Captured at Rappahannock Station, Va., 11/7/63. POW, Point Lookout, Md., took oath of allegiance, 3/30/64. Born: Ireland. Occ.:Laborer. Res.: N.O. Single.
Peters, Philip, Pvt. En. 6/4/61, CM. Present to 9/61. Absent sick in hospital, 9/61 to 4/63. Roll for 3-4/63 states: "Missing since 1st Jan., 1862, deserted." Record dated 3/21/65 at Petersburg states: "Being disabled and about sixty years old, was sent to the rear Nov. 1861 and never heard of since." Born: Prussia. Occ.: Laborer. Res.: N.O. Single.
Pfister, Leonard, Pvt. En. 6/4/61, CM. Present to 5/62. Wounded at Winchester, Va., 5/25/62. Admitted to CSA Hosp., Winchester, 5/27/62, wound in hand, finger amputated. Absent wounded, 5-11/62. Present disabled, 11/62 to 6/63. Present on duty as company commissary, 7-12/63. Present, 1-10/64. Captured at Strasburg, Va., 10/19/64 [Battle of Cedar Creek]. POW, Point Lookout, Md., exchanged 2/25/65. Surrendered at Appomattox C.H., 4/9/65. Born: Michigan. Occ.: Laborer. Res.: N.O. Age 28, single, 5'10".
Plala, John, Pvt. En. 2/20/62, N.O. Absent sick, 3-5/62. Captured at Harrisonburg, Va., 6/15/62. POW, Fort Delaware, Del., took oath of allegiance, 8/10/62. Record dated 3/21/65 at Petersburg states: "Deserted during Valley Campaign of 1862." Born: Italy. Occ.: Merchant. Res.: N.O. Age 26, single.
Reinecke, August, Pvt. En. 6/4/61, CM. Present on 1861 rolls. Absent sick, 5-11/62. Present 11/62 to 5/63. Captured at Fredericksburg, Va., 5/3/63. POW, Fort Delaware, Del. Roll for 1-2/64 states: "Deserted from Camp Lee about June 1, 1863." Born: Prussia. Occ.: Paperhanger. Res.: N.O. Single.
Renz, L., Cpl. En. 6/4/61, CM. Record dated 3/21/65 at Petersburg states: "Deserted at Knoxville en route to Va. in 1861." Born: Bavaria. Occ.: Laborer. Res.: N.O. Single.
Rodin, Vincent, Pvt. En. 3/18/62, N.O. Present to 6/62. Roll for 7-8/62 states: "Deserted near Richmond on or about the 25th of June, 1862." Born: Lambeck, Prussia. Occ.: Blacksmith. Res.: N.O. Age 29, single.
Rogers, James P., Pvt. En. 6/4/61, CM. Present to 9/62. Roll for 9-10/62 states: "Absent, left at Sharpsburg Hospital as nurse for wounded." Captured at Antietam, Md., 9/28/62. POW, Fort McHenry, Md., paroled 12/14/62. Present, 1-7/63. Roll for 5-6/63 states: "Captured by the enemy about 27 June in Pa." Absent captured, 7/63 to 3/65. Born: Ireland. Occ.: Laborer. Res.: N.O. Single.
Ryan, Anthony, Pvt. En. 6/4/61, CM. Present to 6/62. Wounded at Gaines' Mill, Va., 6/27/62. Absent wounded, 6/62 to 10/62. Roll for 9-10/62 states: "Deserted from hospital in Richmond on recovery from wound rec'd during Battle of Gaines' Mill." Born: Ireland. Occ.: Laborer. Res.: N.O. Single.
Schembri, Joseph, Pvt. En. 2/20/62, N.O. Present to 6/62. Captured at Mt. Jackson, Va., 6/13/62. POW, Camp Chase, Ohio, transferred to Vicksburg, Miss., for exchange, 8/25/62. Present, 9/62 to 3/54. Absent on detached service, fireman on gun boat, 3-4/64. Transferred to CS Navy, 4/16/64. Born: Italy. Occ.: Laborer. Res.: N.O. Age 26, single.
Schmidt, Cornelius, Pvt. En. 6/4/61, CM. Present to 6/62. Killed at Cross Keys, Va., 6/8/62. Born: Bavaria. Occ.: Laborer. Res.: N.O. Single.
Schmidt, John, Pvt. En. 6/4/65, CM. Record dated 3/21/65 at Petersburg states: "Deserted at Knoxville en route to Va. in 1861." Born: Germany. Occ.: Laborer. Res.: N.O. Single.
Schwenterman, Frank, Pvt. En. 3/11/62, N.O. Present to 8/62. Wounded in right leg at Bristoe Station, Va., 8/27/62. Absent wounded, 8-12/62. Present, 1-4/63. Captured at Fredericksburg, Va., 4/29/63. POW, Old Capitol Prison, Washington, took oath of allegiance, 6/24/64. Born: Germany. Occ.: Laborer. Age 39.
Shaw, Louis, Sgt. En. 6/4/61, CM, as cpl. Promoted to sgt., 7/1/61. Resigned as sgt., 11/10/61. Present to 4/63. Captured at Fredericksburg, Va. POW, Old Capitol Prison, Washington, took oath of allegiance, 6/24/63. Born: Baden (Germany). Occ.: Carpenter. Res.: N.O. Age 26, single.
Shay, John, Lt. En. 6/4/61, CM, as pvt. Promoted to sgt., 6/10/61. Promoted to Regimental Color Sgt., 7/4/61. Promoted to jr. 2nd lt., 11/21/61. Promoted to 2nd lt., 6/9/62. Wounded at Fredericksburg, Va., 5/4/63. Present to 11/63. Captured at Rappahannock Station, Va., 11/7/63. POW, Johnson's Island, Ohio, released 5/12/65. Born: Vermont. Occ.: Laborer. Res.: N.O. Age 26, single. Oath gives residence as New Bedford, Mass.
Shiller, Henry, Pvt. En. 6/4/61, CM. Present to 6/62. Mortally wounded at Gaines' Mill, Va. Roll for 7-8/62 states: "Died at Charlottesville, Va., Hospl., from wounds rec'd at Gaines' Mill." Born: Prussia. Occ.: Laborer. Res.: N.O. Single.

Shriver, John A., Sgt. En. 6/11/61, CM, as cpl. Promoted to 2nd sgt., 8/27/62. Present to 9/62. Wounded and captured at Sharpsburg, Md., 9/17/62. POW, Fort McHenry, Md., transferred to Fort Monroe, Va., for exchange, 10/13/62. Admitted to Chimborazo Hosp., Richmond, 10/24/62, wounded in thigh, returned to duty 11/14/62. Present to 5/64. Captured at Wilderness, Va., 5/5/64. POW, Point Lookout, Md., transferred to Elmira, N.Y., 8/15/64, exchanged 2/25/65. Present, Wayside Hosp., Farmville, Va., 2-6/65.

Smith, Charles H., Lt. En. 6/4/61, CM. Promoted to sgt., 7/61. Elected 2nd jr. lt., 6/13/62. Present to 9/62. Mortally wounded at Sharpsburg, Md., 9/17/62. Roll for 9-10/62 states: "Died at Winchester, Oct. 17, 1862 of wound received during Battle of Sharpsburg." Born: Pennsylvania. Occ.: Laborer. Res.: N.O. Single.

Smith, Edward, Pvt. En. 6/4/61, CM. Present to 5/62. Recorded as deserted, 5/62. Born: Germany. Occ.: Laborer. Res.: N.O. Single.

Smith, Henry, Pvt. (aka Schmidt) En. 6/4/61, CM. Present to 8/62. Wounded at Bristoe Station, Va., 8/27/62. Absent wounded, 8-11/62. Present to 6/64. Wounded at Cold Harbor, Va., 6/2/64. Absent wounded, 6-8/64. Present, 9-10/64. Captured at Battle of Cedar Creek, Va., 10/19/64. Born: Prussia. Occ.: Laborer. Res. N.O. Single.

Smith, James, Pvt. En. 6/4/61, CM. Present to 9/62. Captured at Hagerstown, Md., 9/14/62. POW, Fort Delaware, Del., exchanged 11/10/62. Roll for 1-2/63 states: "Present, joined from desertion Feb. 24, 1862." Present to 5/63. Severely wounded in right leg at Fredericksburg, Va., 5/4/63, absent wounded thereafter. Roll for 3-4/64 states: "Absent in hospital in Georgia." Surrendered at Savannah, Ga., 4/26/65. Born: Ireland. Occ.: Laborer. Res.: N.O. Single.

Smith, John, Pvt. Transferred from Wheat's 1st La. Special Battalion, 9/7/62. Present to 4/63. Killed at Fredericksburg, Va., 4/29/63. Born: Baden (Germany). Occ.: Laborer. Res.: N.O. Single.

Speis, Frank, Pvt. En. 3/18/62, N.O. Present to 6/62. Absent sick, 7-12/62. Admitted Louisiana Hosp., Richmond, 9/21/62, deserted from hospital, 1/10/63. Born: Bavaria. Occ.: Barkeeper. Res.: N.O. Age 31, single.

Spoonhamer, Conrad, Pvt. En. 6/4/61, CM. Present to 6/62. Mortally wounded at Port Republic, Va., 6/9/62. Roll for 7-8/62 states: "Died at White Hall Hospital from wounds received at Port Republic."

Steinmutz, J. Augustus, Sgt. (aka Steinmetz) En. 6/4/61, CM, as pvt. Promoted to sgt., 7/62. Present to 11/63. Captured at Rappahannock Station, Va., 11/7/63. POW, Point Lookout, Md., exchanged 3/10/64. Captured at Spotsylvania C.H., Va., 5/12/64. POW, Point Lookout, transferred to Elmira, N.Y., 8/15/64, exchanged 2/25/65. Present, 3-4/64. Surrendered at Appomattox C.H., 4/9/65. Born: France. Occ.: Laborer. Res.: Washington, La. Age 21, single.

Teiss, Jacob William, Pvt. (aka Tice, Theis) En. 6/4/61, CM. Present to 5/63. Wounded at Fredericksburg, Va., 5/4/63. Absent wounded to 12/63. Present, 1-6/64. Absent sick, 7/64 to 2/65. Surrendered and paroled at Lynchburg, Va., 4/15/65. Born: Prussia. Occ.: Laborer. Res.: N.O. Single.

Theobald, A., Sgt. En. 6/4/61, CM. Record dated 3/21/65 at Petersburg states: "Deserted at Knoxville en route to Va. in 1861." Born: Prussia. Occ.: Laborer. Res.: N.O. Single.

Vogel, William, Cpl. En. 6/4/61, CM. Present on 1861 rolls. Detailed on recruiting service, 2/62. Record dated 3/21/65 at Petersburg states: "Died in March 1862." Born: Baden, Germany. Occ.: Carpenter. Res.: N.O. Single.

Vogler, Joseph, Pvt. En. 2/22/62, N.O. Present to 8/62. Wounded at Bristoe Station, Va., 8/27/62. Absent wounded to 6/63. Record dated 3/21/65 at Petersburg states: "Last seen when the Army were on the Pennsylvania campaign." Born: Bavaria. Occ.: Laborer. Res.: N.O. Age 31, single.

Wagner, Christian, Sgt. En. 6/4/61, CM, as 3rd sgt. Reduced to pvt., 7/27/61. Present to 4/63. Captured at Fredericksburg, Va., 4/29/63. POW, Old Capitol Prison, Washington, took oath of allegiance 5/25/63. Born: Wirtemburg, Germany. Occ.: Cook. Res.: N.O. Age 25, single.

Waldman, Carl, Pvt. En. 6/4/61, CM. Present all rolls through 8/64. Absent on furlough, 2/65. No record thereafter. Born: Prussia. Occ.: Dyer. Res.: N.O. Single.

Weigert, Ernest, Pvt. En. 6/4/61, CM. Present to 8/62. Wounded at Manassas, Va., 8/29/62. Absent wounded, 9-10/62. Present, 11/62 to 4/63. Captured at Fredericksburg, Va., 4/29/63. POW, Old Capitol Prison, Washington, took oath of allegiance 6/24/63 at Philadelphia. Born: Hanover, Germany. Occ: Laborer. Res.: N.O. Age 28, single.

Weiner, Joseph, Pvt. (aka Wagner) No enlistment record. Captured at Gettysburg, 7/5/63. POW, Fort Delaware, Del., released on joining U.S. 3rd Md. Cavalry, 8/30/63. Born: Germany.

Weiss, John, Sgt. En. 6/4/61, CM, as 2nd sgt. Present to 8/62. Killed at Bristoe Station, Va., 8/27/62. Born: Bavaria. Occ.: Laborer. Res.: N.O. Single.

Weiss, John, Pvt. En. 6/4/61, CM. Present to 9/62. Wounded and captured at Sharpsburg, Md., 9/17/62. POW, Ft. McHenry, Md., exchanged 11/10/62. Roll for 3-4/64 states: "Deserted. Was wounded at battle of Sharpsburg, was exchanged, got well of wounds and deserted from hospital, Richmond, about Dec. 1, 1862." Born: Prussia. Occ.: Laborer. Res.: N.O. Single.

Welk, John, Pvt. (aka Wilks) En. 6/4/61, CM. Present to 5/62. Wounded in leg at Winchester, Va., 5/25/62. Captured in hospital at Winchester, 6/2/62. POW, place unstated, exchanged 8/5/62. Absent wounded to 3/63. Present, disabled, on duty at Brgd. wagon yard, 3-10/63. Detailed as ambulance driver to 10/64. Present, 2/65. Surrendered at Appomattox C.H., 4/9/65. Born: Prussia. Occ.: Brewer. Res.: Washington, La. Age 23.

Wickle, Nicholas, Pvt. En. 6/4/61, CM. Present to 7/62. Discharged at Gordonsville, Va., on surgeon's certificate of disability, due to "amputation of left arm from a gun shot wound." Born: Baden, Germany. Occ.: Laborer. Res.: N.O. Age 27, single.

Wolff, Frederick, Pvt. En. 3/15/62, N.O. Present to 5/63. Mortally wounded at Fredericksburg, Va., 5/4/63, died 5/8/63. Record dated 3/21/65 states: "Killed by shot in head." Born: Prussia. Occ.: Laborer. Res.: N.O. Single.
Young, Alois, Pvt. En. 6/4/61, CM. Present to 5/63. Mortally wounded at Fredericksburg, 5/4/63, died at Gen. Hosp. No. 1, Richmond, 5/14/63. Born: Prussia. Occ.: Laborer. Res.: N.O. Single.
Zang, Albert, Pvt. En. 6/4/61, CM. Present to 8/62. Killed at Bristoe Station, Va., 8/27/62. Born: Baden, Germany. Occ.: Laborer. Res.: N.O. Single.

Company H: Orleans Rifles

Recruited in New Orleans, this company was about 60 percent foreign-born. Of its 109 men, at least 31 were born in Ireland, 17 in Germany, 10 in England, three in Scotland, two in Canada and one in Sweden. Company H had 13 native Louisianians, 14 men born in the North, 15 whose birthplace is unrecorded, and one listed as born "at sea." During the war, 19 men were killed or mortally wounded in battle and 13 died of disease. At least 24 deserted, another 13 took the oath of allegiance after being captured, and one joined the U.S. Army to gain his release from prison. Eleven men were discharged, two retired to the Invalid Corps, and one transferred out. Three men were "drummed out" of the service after conviction on charges by a General Court Martial. Only one man of this company surrendered at Appomattox Court House.

Captains:

Buttrick, William H., Capt. En. 6/4/61 as 1st Lt. Elected captain, 8/24/61, replacing Thomas F. Fisher. Absent in hospital, 5-6/62. Resigned 7/17/62. Res.: Algiers, La.
Fisher, Thomas F., Capt. En. 6/4/61, CM. Resigned 8/20/61 at Centreville, Va. Appointed major of Quartermaster's Dept., Louisiana, 7/19/61, resigned 4/6/63.
Pilcher, Charles M., Capt. En. 6/4/61, CM, as 2nd lt. Elected 1st lt., 8/24/61. Present to 6/62. Wounded at Gaines' Mill, Va., 6/27/62. Promoted to captain, 7/17/62, replacing Willam H. Buttrick. Absent wounded, 6-10/62. Present, 10/62 to 11/63. Admitted to Gen. Hosp. No. 9, Richmond, 11/1/63, furloughed 11/11/63, pneumonia. Absent on furlough, 1-4/64. Present, 5-8/64. Absent, detached on recruiting service in Alexandria, La., 8/64 to 3/65. Paroled at Natchitoches, La., 6/6/65.

* * *

Ackerman, W.C., Pvt. En. 6-4-61, CM. Died at Lynchburg, Va., June 1861. Born: La. Occ.: Clerk. Res.: N. O.
Bertrand, Louis, Pvt. En. 6/4/61, CM. Present to 5/63. Wounded in right hip at Fredericksburg, Va., 4/3/63. Absent in hospital, 5-11/63. Present, wounded and disabled, 11-12/63. On list of permanently disabled soldiers, 4/15/64. Employed as guard at hospital, Camp Winder, Richmond, 9-12/64. Surrendered at Appomattox C.H., 4/9/65. Born: La. Occ.: Clerk. Res.: Algiers, La.
Black, Henry, Pvt. En. 6/4/61, CM. Present to 6/62. Captured at Strasburg, Va., 6/2/62. POW, Fort Delaware, Del.,took oath of allegiance 8/10/62. Born: Germany. Res.: N.O.
Bremer, Charles, Pvt. No enlistment recorded. On list of POWs at Military Prison, Wheeling, Va., 6/30/62, arrested at Cumberland, Md., 6/26/62. Transferred to Camp Chase, Ohio, 7/31/62. Transferred to Vicksburg, Miss., for exchange, 8/25/62, released on taking oath of allegiance. Occ.: Painter. Res.: N.O. Age 41. 5'6", gray eyes, dark hair, dark complexion.
Bruhns, Henry, Pvt. En. 6/4/61, CM. Present to 7/62. Absent sick in hospital, 7/62 to 4/63. Absent, assigned to commissary depot, Buchanan, Va., 10/30/63, on medical certificate of disability. Born: Germany. Res.: N.O.
Burke, William, Sgt. En. 6/4/61, CM, as pvt. Promoted to cpl., 6/1/62. Absent sick in hospital, Lynchburg, Va., 10/61. Present, 5-12/62. Promoted to 1st Sgt., 6/1/63. Killed at Winchester, Va., 6/14/63. Born: Ireland. Occ.: Plasterer. Res.: N.O.
Burns, Michael, Pvt. En. 6/4/61, CM. Present to 7/62. AWOL, 7-8/62. Present, 9-12/62. Died at Guinea Station, Va., 2/18/63. Born: Ireland. Occ.: Laborer. Res.: N.O.
Burton, Robert, Pvt. En. 6/4/61, CM. Present 7-10/61. Deserted, 2/62. Born: England. Occ.: Hatter. Res.: N.O.
Carr, Richard, Sgt. En. 6/4/61, CM. Absent detached to quartermaster dept., 7-10/61. Promoted to 3rd sgt., 1/1/62. Present, 5-9/62. Wounded at Sharpsburg, Md., 9/17/62. Absent wounded to 4/63. Present 4-7/63. Detached as regimental commissary sgt., 8/63 to 4/64. Killed at Battle of Cedar Creek, Va., 10/19/64. Born: New York. Occ.: Seaman. Res.: N.O.
Carty, Thomas, Pvt. En. 6/4/61, CM. Present to 4/62. Discharged on surgeon's certificate of disability, 4/17/62. Born: Ireland. Occ.: Cooper. Res.: N.O.

Cary, Michael, Pvt. En. 6/4/61, CM. Present to 5/62. Absent sick, 5-10/62. Admitted to Gen. Hosp. No. 7, Richmond, 7/22/62, dislocation of right shoulder. Discharged, 10/62. Born: Ireland. Occ.: Bricklayer. Res.: N.O.
Clarke, Patrick, Pvt. En. 6/4/61, CM. Present to 11/63. Captured at Rappahannock Station, 11/7/63. POW, Point Lookout, Md., transferred to Hammond Gen. Hosp., chronic diarrhea. Exchanged 3/16/64. Record dated 3/20/65 at Petersburg, Va., states, "Discharged from over age, on or about 20 Dec. 1864."
Clarke, Peter, Pvt. En. 6/4/61. Record dated 3/20/65 at Petersburg, Va., states: "Died while en route to Va., June 1861." Born: Ireland. Occ.: Seaman. Res.: N.O.
Collins, Edwin, Pvt. En. 6/4/61, CM. Present to 6/62. Captured at Woodstock, Va., 6/3/62. POW, Fort Delaware, Del, took oath of allegiance, 8/10/62. Born: England. Occ.: Seaman. Res.: N.O.
Conley, John, Pvt. En. 6/4/61, CM. Present to 8/62. Killed at Manassas, Va., 8/29/62. Born: Ireland. Occ.: Blacksmith. Res.: N.O.
Connell, Timothy, Pvt. En. 6/4/61, CM. Present to 6/62. Wounded at Gaines' Mill, Va., 6/27/62. Present, 7-8/62. Absent sick in hospital, 10/62 to 2/63. Present, 3-4/63. Captured at Fredericksburg, Va., 5/3/63. POW forwarded to Washington, D.C., took oath of allegiance, 5/4/63. Born: Ireland. Occ.: Laborer. Res.: N.O.
Crawford, Duncan, Sgt. En. 6/4/61, CM. Present to 5/63. Wounded and captured at Fredericksburg, Va., 4/4/63. POW, Fort Delaware, Del., forwarded to Old Capitol Prison, Washington. Present, 7-8/63. Killed on picket along Rappahannock River, 9/14/63. Born: Scotland. Occ.: Carpenter. Res.: N.O.
Dohrman, Henry, Pvt. En. 2/28/62, N.O. Present to 8/62. Captured at Bristoe Station, Va., 8/27/62, took oath of allegiance. Born: Hamburg, Germany. Occ: Bookkeeper. Res.: N.O. Age 28.
Drudy, Patrick, Pvt. En. 3/12/62, N.O. Captured at Strasburg, Va., 6/2/62. POW, Fort Delaware, Del., took oath of allegiance, 8/10/62. Born: County Roscommon, Ireland. Occ.: Carpenter. Res.: N.O. Age 22, 5'5", gray eyes, sandy hair, fair complexion.
Duffee, Philip, Pvt. (aka Duffy, Duffey) En. 6/4/61, CM. Present to 10/62. Absent sick in hospital, 10-12/62. Detailed for hospital duty, 4/3/63. Listed as "wounded disabled," 12/63. Detailed as nurse for Army of the Valley, Second Corps, A.N.V., 3/15/64. Surrendered at Lynchburg, Va., 4/65. Born: Ireland. Occ.: Laborer. Res.: N.O.
Farrell, Edward,Pvt. En. 3/10/62, N.O. Captured at Woodstock, Va., 6/2/62. POW, Fort Delaware, Del., exchanged 8/5/62. Present to 4/63. Captured at Fredericksburg, Va., 4/29/63. POW, Fort Delaware. Present 6/63 to 5/64. Captured at Wilderness, Va., 5/5/64. POW, Point Lookout, Md., transferred to Elmira, N.Y., 8/18/64. Paroled and sent to James River for exchange, 2/2/65. Captured at Petersburg, Va., 4/3/65. POW, Hart's Island, N.Y., released 6/14/65. Born: Ireland. Occ.: Drayman. Res.: N.O. Age 18, 5'7", gray eyes, light hair, fair complexion.
Figenschue, Venderlin, Sgt. En. 2/26/62, N.O. Present to 8/62. Absent sick in hospital, 9-10/62. Present, 11/62 to 4/63. Promoted from pvt. to cpl., 12/1/62. Captured at Fredericksburg, Va., 4/29/63. POW, Old Capitol Prison, Washington, exchanged 6/3/63. Promoted to sgt., 4/30/63. Wounded at Winchester, Va., 6/14/63. Present 7/63 to 5/64. Captured at Wilderness, Va., 5/5/64. POW, Point Lookout, Md., exchanged 2/10/65. On register of POWs captured at New Orleans, 4/1/65, released 5/8/65.
Flohr, Charles G., Pvt. En. 6/4/61, CM. Present to 1/63. Absent sick in hospital, 2/63 to 1/64. Admittted to hospital in Buchanan, Va., 4/12/63, heart disease, transferred to Gen. Hosp., Lynchburg, Va., 10/17/63. Died at Lynchburg, 1/18/64. Born: La. Occ.: Cook. Res.: N.O.
Flynne, John, Pvt. Rn. 6/4/61, CM. Present to 7/62. AWOL, 7-8/62. Present, 9/62 to 5/63. Wounded at Fredericksburg, Va., 5/3/63, gunshot wound in face. On furlough, 6-7/63. Present 7/63 to 4/64. Captured at Fisher's Hill, Va., 9/22/64. POW, Point Lookout, Md., exchanged 1/17/65. Surrendered at New Orleans, 5/26/65, paroled at Alexandria, La., 6/4/65. Born: Ireland. Res.: N.O.
Forkell, William F., Cpl. (aka F.W. Forkell) En. 6/4/61, CM. Promoted from pvt. to cpl., 10/31/61. Killed at Gaines' Mill, Va., 6/27/61. Born: Germany. Occ.: Carpenter. Res.: N.O.
Francis, George. W., Lt. En. 6/4/61, CM. Promoted from sgt. to 2nd lt., 8/26/61. Killed at Malvern Hill, Va., 7/1/62. Born: England. Occ.: Baker. Res.: N.O.
Friedlander, Aron, Pvt. En. 6/4/61, CM. Present to 10/61. Discharged on surgeon's certificate of disability, 10/8/61, rheumatism. Born: Germany. Occ.: Merchant. Res.: N.O. Age 41.
Fuge, Henry, Pvt. En. 2/22/62, N.O. Present to 6/62. Captured at Strasburg, Va., 6/2/62. POW, Fort Delaware, Del., took oath of allegiance, 8/10/62. Born: County Waterford, Ireland. Occ.: Laborer. Res.: N.O. Age 28.
Gorman, William, Pvt. No record of enlistment. Captured at Gettysburg, 7/1/63. On roll of POWs discharged by order of Sec. of War from Fort Delaware, Del., 7/63. Remarks: "Rebel deserter."
Graham, Lewis, Lt. Enlisted 6/4/61, CM. Appointed adjutent, 6/4/61. See Field & Staff roster.
Gribble, Henry, Pvt. En. 6/4/61, CM. Present to 11/63. Captured at Rappahannock Station, Va., 11/7/63. POW, Point Lookout, Md., exchanged 3/10/64. Absent on furlough, 3-5/64. Present, 5-7/64. Absent sick, 7/64 to 1/65. Present, 2-3/65. Captured near Petersburg, Va., 3/28/65. POW, Point Lookout, released 6/13/65. Born: England. Occ.: Carpenter. Res.: N.O.
Grubbs, William S., Pvt. En. 6/12/61, Morristown, Tenn. Present to 4/62. Deserted, 4/62. Born: Kentucky. Occ.: Laborer. Res.: Morristown, Tenn.
Guell, C., Pvt. (aka Henry Guell) En. 6/4/61, CM. Present to 3/62. Died at Moore Hosp., Manassas, Va., 3/6/62, typhoid fever. Born: Germany. Occ.: Clerk. Res.: N.O.

Harper, James, Musician. En. 9/1/63 at Culpeper, Va. Present to 2/65. Born: La. Res.: N.O.
Harrigan, Dennis, Pvt. En. 6/4/61, CM. Present to 9/62. Mortally wounded at Chantilly, Va., 9/1/62, date of death unstated. Born: Ireland. Occ.: Seaman. Res.: N.O.
Healey, Henry, Lt. En. 6/4/61, CM. Promoted from pvt. to Lt., 7/22/62. Present to 8/62. Mortally wounded at Manassas, Va., 8/29/62, died at Middleburg, Va., 11/8/62. Born: Ireland. Occ.: Plasterer. Res.: N.O.
Heidelberg, Henry Clay, Sgt. En. 6/4/61, CM. Present to 7/62. Promoted from pvt. to cpl., 3/1/62. Promoted to sgt., 8/31/62. AWOL, 7-10/62. Present 11/62 to 11/63. Reduced to pvt., 6/1/63. Captured at Rappahannock Station, Va., 11/7/63. POW, Old Capitol Prison. Record dated 3/20/65 at Petersburg, Va., states: "Deserted May 1864." Born: Mississippi. Occ.: Dentist.
Henderson, William, Pvt. En. 6/4/61, CM. Present to 8/62. Captured at Cedar Mountain, Va.,, 8/9/62. Paid as paroled prisoner, 9/17/62. Record dated 3/20/65 at Petersburg, Va., states: "Deserted Nov. 1862." Born: Scotland. Occ.: Laborer. Res.: N.O.
Henry, William D., Sgt. En. 6/4/61, CM. Promoted from pvt. to cpl., 7/1/61. Promoted to sgt., 9/30/61. Present to 6/62. Absent sick in hospital, 6-9/62. Recorded as deserted from hospital at Lynchburg, Va., about 8/6/62. Born: Ohio. Occ.: Painter. Res.: N.O.
Houston, Lemuel, Pvt. En. 6/4/61, CM. Present to 4/63. Killed at Fredericksburg, Va., 4/29/63. Born: Kentucky. Occ.: Painter. Res.: N.O.
Hurley, Henry V., Pvt. En. 6/4/61, CM. Detached as hospital steward, 7/61 to 7/62. Discharged on surgeon's certificate of disability, 7/27/62, chronic rheumatism. Born: New York. Occ.: Physician. Res.: N.O.
Huth, Ferd, Pvt. En. 6/4/61, CM. Present to 5/62. AWOL, 5-9/62. Recorded as deserted, 10/62, "Deserted from the Valley on or about 27 May 1862."
Iley, James A., Pvt. En. 6/4/61,CM. Present to 8/62. Roll for 9-10/62 states: "Deserted from the Rapidan River about the 8th August, 1862." On roll of POWs, undated, at Fort Monroe, Va., paroled on steamer Juniata, 9/1/62. Born: New York. Occ.: Clerk. Res.: Brownsville, Texas.
Jackson, William, Pvt. En. 6/4/61, CM. Present to 5/63. Roll for 5-6/63 states: "Deserted from camp, 14 May, 1863." Born: La. Occ.: Laborer. Res.: N.O.
Joy, John, Pvt. En. 6/4/61, CM. Present to 4/63. Wounded at Fredericksburg, 4/29/63. Admitted to Louisiana Hosp., Richmond, 5/1/63, gunshot wound of left clavicle, furloughed 40 days from 6/7/63. Absent wounded after 8/63. Record dated 3/20/65 at Petersburg states: "Permanently disabled by wound in left shoulder." Paroled 5/23/65 at Montgomery, Ala.
Kelly, Patrick, Pvt. En. 6/4/61, CM. Present to 9/62. Captured at Frederick, Md., 9/12/62. POW, Fort Delaware, Del., exchanged 11/10/62. Present 11/62 to 11/63. Wounded and captured at Rappahannock Station, Va., 11/7/63. Admitted to Lincoln General Hosp., Washington, 12/19/63, gunshot wound in right forearm (amputated.) POW, Point Lookout, Md., received 5/30/64, transferred to Elmira, N.Y., 7/9/64, exchanged 10/29/64. Retired to Invalid Corps, Richmond, 2/20/65. Captured in hospital at Richmond, 4/3/65. POW, Point Lookout, released 7/7/65. Born: Ireland. Occ.: Clerk. Res.: N.O.
Kennedy, Michael J., Sgt. En. 6/4/61, CM, as pvt. Present to 8/62. Wounded at Manassas, Va., 8/29/62, gunshot wound in right arm. Absent wounded to 12/63. Killed at Battle of Monocacy, Md., 7/9/64. Born: Ireland. Occ.: Laborer. Res.: N.O.
Koesner, Frederick, Sgt. En. 6/4/61, CM, as pvt. Promoted to cpl., 5/15/63. Promoted to sgt., 6/15/63. Wounded at Fredericksburg, Va., 5/3/63. Wounded at Gettysburg, 7/2/63. Present to 7/64. Killed at Battle of Monocacy, Md., 7/9/64. Born: La. Occ.: Bartender. Res.: N.O.
Laggerton, John, Pvt. En. 6/4/61, CM. Present to 7/62. Killed at Malvern Hill, Va., 7/1/62. Born: Sweden. Occ.: Laborer. Res.: N.O.
Langridge, John E., Pvt. (aka Henry Langridge) En. 3/18/62, N.O. Absent, left sick at Front Royal, Va., 5/62. Captured at Front Royal, 5/30/62. POW aboard steamer Coatzacoalas, exchanged 8/5/62. Absent sick in hospital, 8/62. Record dated 3/20/65 at Petersburg states: "Died in Genl. Hosp., Richmond, date unknown." Born: N.O. Occ.: Painter. Res.: N.O. Age 26, 5'6", gray eyes, dark hair, dark complexion.
Leblanc, John, Pvt. En. 3/7/62, N.O. Present to 6/62. Captured at Woodstock, Va., 6/2/62. POW, Fort Delaware, Del., took oath of allegiance, 8/10/62. Born: Canada. Occ.: Laborer. Res.: N.O. Age 26.
Little, Joseph, Pvt. En. 6/4/61, CM. Present to 8/61. Discharged on surgeon's certificate of disability, Camp Bienville, Va., 8/27/61, chronic bronchitis. Record dated 3/20/65 states: "Died in N.O., Dec. 18, 1861, disease of the heart." Born: New York. Occ.: Seaman.
Loughery, F.J., Pvt. En. 6/4/61, CM. Present to 2/62. Discharged on surgeon's certificate of disability, 2/7/62, general disability. Born: Maysville, Ky. Age 47.
Lucas, Thomas M., Lt. En. 6/4/61, CM, as pvt. Promoted to cpl., 8/24/61. Promoted to sgt., 10/1/61. Reduced to pvt., 6/1/62. Elected 1st Lt., 12/21/62. Present to 7/63. Wounded slightly at Malvern Hill, Va., 7/1/62. Wounded and captured at Gettysburg, 7/2/63. POW, Fort McHenry, Md., transferred to Johnson's Island, Sandusky, Ohio, 7/20/63, transferred to Point Lookout, Md., 2/16/65. Paroled at Greensboro, N.C., 5/4/65. Born: New York. Occ.: Map finisher. Res.: St. Louis, Mo.

Lyle, William, Pvt. En. 6/4/61, CM. Present to 10/62. Admitted to Winder Hosp., Richmond, 11/16/62, fever., recorded as deserted from hospital, 4/23/63. Roll for 1-2/64 states: "Sent to hosp., and not heard from, supposed to be dead." Record dated 3/20/65 at Petersburg states: "Discharged in Oct., 1862." Born: Scotland. Occ.: Seaman. Res.: N.O.

Mayer, Charles, Sgt. En. 6/4/61, CM, as 2nd Sgt. Present to 7/62. Severely wounded at Malvern Hill, Va., 7/1/62. Admitted Chimborazo Hosp., Richmond, 7/14/62, right leg amputated. Absent wounded after 7/62. Retired to Invalid Corps at Richmond, 2/13/65. Paroled at Richmond, 4/17/65. Born: La. Occ.: Coppersmith. Res.: N.O.

Mayer, Joseph F., Pvt. (aka F.J. Mayer) En. 6/4/61, CM. Present to 7/62. Absent detailed as nurse in hospital at Richmond, 7/62 to 9/63. Present, 9/63 to 5/64. Captured at Wilderness, Va., 5/5/64. POW, Point Lookout, Md., exchanged 2/10/65. Born: La. Res.: N.O.

McAleese, Archibald, Pvt. En. 6/4/61, CM. Present to 9/62. Absent sick in hospital, 9/62 to 1/64. Detailed to hospital duty by special order dated 8/18/63. Born: Ireland. Occ.: Plumber. Res.: N.O.

McCance, Holmes, Pvt. En. 6/4/61, CM. Present to 7/62. Wounded at Malvern Hill, Va., 7/1/62, gunshot wound in arm. Absent wounded, 7-9/62. Present 9-10/62. Absent sick, 11-12/62. Present, 1-5/63. Wounded at Fredericksburg, Va., 5/4/63, gunshot wound in forearm. Absent wounded 5/63 to 2/64. Present 2-5/64. Wounded at Spotsylvania C.H., 5/10/64. Admitted to Jackson Hosp., Richmond, 5/17/64, wound in left thigh. Retired to Invalid Corps, Charlottesville, Va., 2/27/65. Born: County Antrim, Ireland. Occ.: Shoemaker. Res.: N.O. Age 26.

McDonald, William, Pvt. En. 6/4/61, CM. Present to 11/61. Recorded as deserted, 11/20/61. Born: England. Occ.: Seaman. Res.: N.O.

Meckler, Joseph, Pvt. En. 6/4/61, CM. Present to 9/62. Mortally wounded at Sharpsburg, Md., 9/17/62. Roll for 7-8/63 states: "Died." Record dated 3/20/65 at Petersburg states: "Died of wounds at Frederick City, Md., date unknown." Born: Germany. Occ.: Laborer. Res.: N.O.

Mitchell, James G., Pvt. En. 6/4/61, CM. Present to 12/62. Absent sick in hospital, 12/62 to 3/63. Roll for 9-10/63 states: "Deserted from hosp. Lynchburg, May 1863." Born: Tennessee. Occ.: Laborer. Res.: N.O.

Morris, John F., Pvt. En. 6/4/61, CM. Present to 7/62. Absent sick in hospital, 7/62 to 5/63. Roll for 5-6/63 states: "Deserted from hosp. some time in May." Roll for 7-8/63 states: "Joined from desertion, Aug. 1863." Roll for 9-10/63 states: "Deserted from hosp., Charlottesville, Aug. '62." Born: Ireland. Occ.: Laborer. Res.: N.O.

Morrissey, John, Pvt. En. 6/4/61, CM. Present to 2/62. Record dated 3/20/65 at Petersburg states: "Deserted Feb. '62, joined from desertion Feb. 18, 1865." On register of POWs received 3/30/65 by Provost Marshall, Army of Potomac, transferred to Washington, took oath of allegiance, 4/4/65. Born: Ireland. Occ.: Laborer. Res.: N.O.

Murray, Samuel, Pvt. En. 6/4/61, CM. Present to 8/62. Captured at Cedar Mountain, Va., 8/9/62. POW, Steamer Juniata, exchanged 9/21/62. Roll for 9-10/62 states: "Deserted from the Rapidan River about the 6th of Aug., 1862." Record dated 3/20/65 at Petersburg states: "Deserted from Paroled Camp, Richmond, Va., Oct. 1862." Born: Ireland. Occ.: Painter. Res.: N.O.

Niffing, W. G., Pvt. (aka Niffirg) En. 6/4/61, CM. Present to 11/61. Tried and found guilty by General Court Martial of refusing to obey orders, drawing a weapon and charging with bayonet upon superior officers, after straggling on march; sentenced to 12 months confinement and then being drummed out of service without pay, 11/20/61. Born: La. Res.: N.O.

O'Donnell, William, Pvt. En. 6/4/61, CM. Present to 11/61. Tried and found guilty by General Court Martial of refusing to obey orders, drawing a weapon and charging with bayonet upon superior officers, after straggling on march; sentenced to 12 months confinement and then being drummed out of service without pay, 11/20/61. Born: England. Occ.: Seaman. Res.: N.O.

Ohlendorf, Frederick, Pvt. En. 6/4/61, CM. Present to 1/63. Admitted to Louisiana Hosp., Richmond, 1/17/63, died 2/11/63, typhoid fever. Record dated 3/20/65 at Petersburg states: "Detailed as Col.'s orderly June 1861. Died in hosp., Richmond, '63." Born: La. Occ.: Clerk. Res.: N.O.

Olding, Christian, Cpl. En. 3/19/62, N.O. Promoted to cpl., 11/1/63. Present to 5/64. Captured at Wilderness, Va., 5/5/64. POW, Point Lookout, Md., exchanged 2/15/65. Born: Germany. Occ.: Tailor. Res.: N.O.

Pendry, John, Pvt. En. 6/4/61, CM. Transferred to Company A, 10/31/61. See Company A roster.

Poole, William, Pvt. En. 6/4/61, CM. Present to 6/62. Discharged at Richmond on certificate of disability, 6/11/62, rheumatism. Born: England. Occ.: Seaman. Res.: N.O. Age 29.

Porter, James, Pvt. En. 6/4/61, CM. Present on 1861 rolls. Absent sick in hospital, 5-8/62. Record 3/20/65 at Petersburg states: "Deserted from Genl. Hosp., Richmond, May 1862." Born: Ireland. Occ.: Engineer. Res.: N.O.

Prest, Albert, Pvt. En. 3/10/62, N.O. Present to 6/62. Captured at New Market, Va., 6/6/62. POW, Fort Delaware, Del., took oath of allegiance, 8/10/62.

Pryor, Patrick, Pvt. En. 6/4/61, CM. Present to 10/61. Admitted to Chimborazo Hosp., Richmond, 10/22/61. Discharged on surgeon's certificate of disability, 11/1/61, chronic rheumatism. Born: Ireland. Occ.: Laborer. Res.: N.O.

Quinn, John, Pvt. En. 6/4/61, CM. Present to 3/62. Absent sick in hospital, 3/62 to 3/63. Record dated 3/20/65 at Petersburg states: "Died in Hospl., Charlottesville, date unknown." Born: Ireland. Occ.: Laborer. Res.: N.O.

Richardson, Henry V., Cpl. En. 6/4/61, CM, as pvt. Promoted to cpl., 7/61. Detailed as musician, 2/1/62. Absent sick,

5-8/62. Roll for 9-10/62 states: "Deserted from Louisa C.H. on or about 23 June 1862." Born: New York. Occ.: Seaman. Res.: N.O.

Richardson, James, Pvt. En. 6/8/61, CM. Present to 7/62. Absent sick in hospital, 7-8/62. Reported deserted from hospital, 10/62. Roll for 1-2/63 states: "Present, joined from desertion Feb. 23, 1863." Captured at Fredericksburg, Va., 4/29/63. POW, Fort Delaware, Del., exchanged 6/3/63. Present, 6/63 to 7/64. Killed at Battle of Monocacy, Md., 7/9/64. Born: Ireland. Occ.: Seaman. Res.: N.O.

Rohmick, Max, Pvt. (aka Rhomick) En. 2/24/62, N.O. Absent sick in hospital, 6-8/62. Present, 8/62 to 5/63. Killed at Fredericksburg, Va., 5/3/63. Born: Saxony (Germany). Occ.: Clerk. Res.: N.O. Age 23.

Roose, Frederick, Cpl. En. 3/6/62, N. O. Present to 9/62. Killed at Chantilly, Va., 9/1/62. Born: Germany. Occ.: Butcher. Res.: N.O.

Ryan, William, Pvt. En. 6/4/61, CM. Present to 11/64. Absent sick in hospital, 11-12/64. Died at Pratt Hosp., Lynchburg, Va., 1/5/64, enteritis. Born: Ireland. Occ.: Laborer. Res.: N.O.

Safford, Henry S., Pvt. En. 6/4/61, CM. Present to 9/62. Wounded at Sharpsburg, Md., 9/17/62. Absent wounded to 5/63. Present, 5-6/63. Absent sick, 7-10/63. Roll for 11-12/63 states: "Deserted from hosp."
Born: "At Sea." Occ.: Teamster. Res.: N.O.

Scherf, Henry, Pvt. En. 6/4/61, CM. Record dated 3/10/65 at Petersburg states: "Deserted June 1862." Born: Germany. Occ.: Painter. Res.: N.O.

Scherff, Fred, Pvt. En. 6/4/61, CM. Present on 1861 rolls. No record thereafter.

Schreiber, John H., Pvt. En. 3/3/62, N.O. Absent sick in hospital, 5/62 to 2/63. AWOL, 3-9/63. Roll for 9-10/63 states: "Deserted in the Valley, May 1862." Born: Prussia. Occ.: Merchant. Res.: N.O. Age 38.

Schultz, Henry, Pvt. En. 6/4/61, CM. Absent sick in hospital, 7-11/61. Died at Gen. Hosp., Culpeper C.H., Va., 11/1/61, dropsy. Born: South Carolina. Occ.: Laborer. Res.: N.O.

Schwartz, Charles, Pvt. En. 3/1/62, N.O. Absent sick in hospital, 5-12/62. AWOL, 1-2/63. Recorded as deserted, 3-4/63. Born: Hamburg, Germany. Occ.: Engineer. Age 23.

Scofield, James, Pvt. En. 6/4/61, CM. Captured at Strasburg, Va., 6/2/62. POW, exchanged 8/5/62. Record dated 3/20/62 at Petersburg states: "Deserted May 1862." Born: England. Occ.: Machinist. Res.: N.O.

Scofield, Lawrence, Pvt. (aka Schofield) En. 6/4/61, CM. Present to 5/63. Killed at Fredericksburg, Va., 5/3/63. Roll for 5-6/63 states: "Killed May 3, 1863, in the retreat from Lee's Hill near Fredericksburg." Born: England. Occ.: Machinist. Res.: N.O.

Scott, Patrick, Pvt. En. 6/4/61, CM. Present to 6/62. Captured at Woodstock, Va., 6/3/63. POW, Fort Delaware, Del., took oath of allegiance, 8/10/62. Born: Ireland. Occ.: Laborer. Res.: N.O.

Shannon, James F., Cpl. En. 6/4/61, CM, as cpl. Reduced to pvt., 2/28/62. Present to 6/62. Wounded at Port Republic, Va., 6/9/62. Absent wounded, 6-10/62. Present to 7/63. Captured at South Mountain, Md., 7/5/63. POW, Fort Delaware, Del., exchanged 3/7/65. Born: Ireland. Occ.: Clerk. Res.: N.O.

Singleton, George F., Pvt. En. 6/4/61, CM. Present to 6/62. Severely wounded at Gaines' Mill, Va., 6/27/62, gunshot wound in both legs. Absent wounded 6-9/62. Present, 9/62 to 6/63. Absent sick, 5-7/63. Appointed regimental hospital steward, 8/18/63. Absent detached as hosp. steward, 8/63 to 9/64. Captured at Winchester, Va., 9/19/64. POW, Harper's Ferry, Va., transferred to Elmira, N.Y., 12/16/64. Died at Elmira prison camp, 3/30/65, pneumonia. Born: Canada. Occ.: Druggist. Res.: N.O. Single.

Singery, John, Pvt. (aka Singrey) En. 6/4/61, CM. Present to 11/63. Severely wounded and captured at Rappahannock Station, Va., 11/7/63. POW, admitted to Army Square Hosp., Washington, 11/9/63, gunshot wound in right thigh, fractured. Transferred to Fort Delaware, Del., 6/15/64, exchanged 9/30/64. Born: Ohio. Occ.: Artist. Res.: Peoria, Ill.

Smith, Conrad, Pvt. En. 6/4/61, CM. Absent sick, 6/61 to 9/62. Died at Genl. Hosp. No. 1, Lynchburg, Va., 9/16/62, tuberculosis.

Snow, John, Pvt. En. 6/4/61, CM. Present to 8/61. Discharged on surgeon's certificate of disability, 10/8/61, cause unstated. Born: Ireland. Occ.: Laborer. Res.: N.O.

Sonhill, Fred, Pvt. En. 6/4/61, CM. Present to 5/62. Roll for 9-10/62 states: "Deserted from the Valley on or about 25 May 1862." Present on roll of Gen. Hosp. No. 17, Richmond, 9/18/62. No record thereafter. Born: Germany. Occ.: Carpenter. Res.: N.O.

Southorn, Francis, Pvt. En. 6/4/61, CM. Present on 1861 rolls. Absent sick, 5-9/62. Roll for 9-10/62 states: "Deserted from hospl." On roll of POWs captured 5/3/63, Army of Potomac, [near Fredericksburg, Va.], POW, Old Capitol Prison, Washington, transferred to Fort Delaware, Del, 5/7/63. No record thereafter.

Stern, Theodore, Pvt. En. 2/27/62, N.O. Present to 4/63. Wounded at Fredericksburg, Va., 4/29/63. Absent wounded, 5-6/63. Present, 7-11/63. Captured at Rappahannock Station, Va., 11/7/63. POW, Point Lookout, Md., released on joining U.S. Army, 2/1/64. Born: Bavaria. Occ.: waiter. Res.: N.O. Age 33.

Stewart, Henry, Pvt. (aka Stuart) En. 6/4/63, CM. Present to 4/63. Killed by shot to head at Fredericksburg, Va., 4/29/63. Born: Germany. Occ.: Laborer. Res.: N.O.

Templeton, Webster, Sgt. En. 6/4/61, CM, as 4th sgt. Promoted to 1st sgt., 8/24/61. Present to 7/62. AWOL, 7-10/62. Reduced to pvt., 8/31/62. Absent sick, 11-12/62. AWOL, 1-2/63. Recorded as deserted, 3/63. Born: La. Occ.: Coppersmith. Res.: N.O.

Turner, Charles H., Sgt. En. 6/4/61, CM, as cpl. Promoted to sgt., 10/31/61, resigned 12/31/62. Present to 6/62. Wounded at Gaines' Mill, Va., 6/27/62. Absent wounded, 7-8/62. Present, 9/62 to 12/64. Wounded at Sharpsburg, Md., 9/17/62. Surrendered as deserter at Buckhannon, W.Va., 12/10/64, released on taking oath of allegiance, 12/12/64. Born: N.O. Occ.: Gas fitter. Res.: N.O. Age 23.
Wachter, Frederick, Pvt. En. 6/4/61, CM. Present to 1/62. Discharged after furnishing a substitute, 1/1/62. Born: Germany. Occ.: Clerk. Res.: N.O. Age 31.
Walsh, John, Pvt. En. 6/4/61, CM. Present to 6/62. Captured, 6/62, place unstated. POW, Fort Delaware, Del., took oath of allegiance, 8/10/62. Born: Ireland. Occ.: Bartender. Res.: N.O.
Warsdell, John, Pvt. En. 6/4/61, CM. Present to 11/61. Tried and found guilty by General Court Martial of refusing to obey orders, drawing a weapon and charging with bayonet upon superior officers, after straggling on march; sentenced to 12 months confinement and then being drummed out of service without pay, 11/20/61. Born: England. Occ.: Seaman. Res.: N.O.
Williams, John, Musician. (aka William Williams) En. 6/5/61, CM. Appointed drum major, 7/1/61. Present to 1861 rolls. Record dated 3/20/65 at Petersburg states: "Deserted Feb. 1862." Born: N.Y. Occ.: Seaman. Res.: N.O.
Wilson, John, Pvt. (aka N.C. Wilson) En. 6/4/61, CM. Record dated 3/20/65 at Petersburg states: "Deserted to the enemy while on picket, July 1861." Born: Indiana. Occ.: Printer. Res.: N.O.
Windsor, Thomas, Pvt. En. 6/4/61, CM. Present to 6/62. Mortally wounded at Port Republic, Va., 6/9/62, died 6/10/62. Born: Ohio. Occ.: Boatman. Res.: N.O.
Woods, Alexander, Pvt. En. 6/4/61, CM. Present to 5/62. Took oath of allegiance at Fort Delaware, Del., 8/10/62. Record dated 3/20/65 at Petersburg states: "Captured May 1862, taken oath of allegiance to U.S." Born: Ireland. Occ.: Painter. Res.: N.O.

Company I: Irish Brigade Company A

This overwhelmingly Irish company was raised in New Orleans by its first captain, Joseph Hanlon, who later became lieutenant colonel of the regiment. Like William Monaghan's company, this unit also carried the "Irish Brigade" title before becoming Company I of the 6th Louisiana. Of the 106 men who served in the company, at least 89 were born in Ireland, and common Irish surnames dominate the eight men whose birthplace is unrecorded and the four born in Northern states. Besides the Irish, there were two men from Norway, one from Belgium, one from Tennessee (its first captain) and only one from Louisiana. During the war, 18 men of the company were killed or mortally wounded. Eleven died of disease and one was killed accidentally. Twenty-seven men deserted and 13 others were captured and took the oath of allegiance. One joined the U.S. service to gain release from prison. Three were discharged and two transferred. Two were dismissed from the service as result of regimental court martial. Three men from Company I surrendered at Appomattox Court House.

Captains:

James, Samuel L., Capt./Maj. En. 6/4/61, CM., as captain of Company I. Appointed major, 6/5/61. Resigned 12/1/61. Born: Tennessee. Occ.: Engineer. Res.: N.O. Age 35, married.
Hanlon, Joseph, Capt./Lt. Col. En. 6/4/61, CM. as 1st Lt. Promoted to Capt., 6/15/61. Promoted to major, 9/17/62. See Field and Staff roster.
Walshe, Blayney T., Capt. Commissioned as 2nd jr. lt. by Gov. T.O. Moore, 5/24/61. Elected 1st lt., 6/5/61, CM. Present to 6/62. Wounded in left foot at Gaines' Mill, Va., 6/27/62. Promoted to capt., 9/23/62. Absent wounded, 6/62 to 9/63. Absent on detached duty at Passport Office, Richmond, 9-11/63. Assigned to duty as Provost Marshall of Parishes of Livingston, St. Tammany and Washington, La., 11/63. Retired to Invalid Corps, 3/4/65. Born: County Wexford, Ireland. Occ.: Clerk. Res.: N.O. Age 22, single.
Bresnan, Joseph B., Capt. En. as 2nd lt., 6/4/61, CM. Present to 7/62. Absent sick at Winchester, Va., 7-10/62. Present 11/62-10/64. Promoted to 1st lt., 9/17/62. Absent sick in hospital, Charlottesville, Va., 8/17/64 to 9/28/64, acute diarrhea. Wounded in right shoulder, Battle of Cedar Creek, 10/19/64. Admitted to CSA Hosp., Charlottesville, Va., 10/22/64, returned to duty 1/19/65. Promoted to capt., 12/16/64. Wounded in abdomen in attack on Fort Stedman, Petersburg, Va., 3/25/65. Captured in hospital at Petersburg, 4/3/65. Born: Ireland. Occ.: Clerk. Res.: N.O. Age 30, single.

* * *

Bardon, Patrick, Pvt. En. 6/4/61, CM. Present to 8/62. Deserted at Cedar Mountain, Va., 8/9/62. Born: Ireland. Occ.: Laborer. Res.: N.O. Age 23, single.
Barrett, Timothy, Pvt. En. 6/4/61, CM. Present to 7/62. AWOL, 7-8/62. Arrested as deserter in Mobile, Ala., 12/62. Returned to duty and present, 1863-1864. Born: Ireland. Occ.: Laborer. Res.: N.O. Age 38, married.
Boland, James, Lt. En. 6/4/61, CM. Present to 10/61. Promoted to 3rd sgt., 10/24/61. Admitted as 2nd lt. to South Carolina Hosp., Charlottesville, Va., 7/22/62, died 7/24/62, laryngitis. Born: Ireland. Occ.: Clerk. Res.: N.O. Age 26, single.
Brassel, John, Pvt. En. 6/4/61. Present to 9/62. Killed at Chantilly, Va., 9/1/62. Born: Ireland. Occ.: Laborer. Res.: N.O. Age 28, single.
Broderick, Denis, Pvt. En. 6/4/61, CM. Present to 8/61. Dismissed from service by order of regimental court martial, 8/29/61.
Brown, William, Sgt. En. 6/4/61, CM. Promoted to cpl., 9/20/61. Promoted to 5th sgt., date unknown. Deserted, 6/30/62. Born: Ireland. Occ.: Sailor. Res.: N.O. Age 25, single.
Buckley, John, Sgt. En. 6/4/61, CM. Present to 6/62. Captured at Port Republic, Va., 6/9/62. POW aboard steamer Coatzacoalas, exchanged 8/5/62. Wounded at Fredericksburg, Va., 4/29/63. Present to 4/64. Captured at Wilderness, 5/5/64. POW, Point Lookout, Md., transferred to Elmira, N.Y., 8/15/64, paroled 2/25/65. On roll of refugees and deserters, surrendered at Washington, D.C., 4/17/65. Born: Ireland. Occ.: Laborer. Res.: N.O. Age 22, single.
Byrnes, Patrick, Pvt. En. 6/4/61, CM. Present to 7/62. Admitted to hospital at Charlottesville, Va., 7/25/62, died 8/2/62, chronic diarrhea. Born: Ireland. Occ.: Laborer. Res.: N.O. Age 32, married.
Byrnes, Peter, Sgt. En. 6/4/61, CM. Present to 9/62. Wounded and captured at Sharpsburg, Md., 9/17/62. POW, Fort McHenry, Baltimore, Md., sent to Fortress Monroe, Va., for exchange 10/20/62. Absent wounded, 9/62 to 8/63. Absent, detailed as watchman at medical depot, Charlotte, N.C., 8/63. Amputated left arm at shoulder joint, 2/9/64 at Louisiana Hosp., Richmond, Va. On roll of POWs of detailed men, post of Grenada, Miss., surrendered at Citronelle, Ala., 5/4/65. Born: Ireland. Occ.: Baker. Res.: N.O. Age 27, married.
Cahill, John, Pvt. En. 6/4/61, CM. Present to 8/62. Severely wounded at Manassas, Va., 8/29/62. Absent wounded through 12/63. Retired to Invalid Corps, 5/25/64. Born: Ireland. Occ.: Laborer. Res.: N.O. Age 35, single.
Cleary, Thomas, Pvt. En. 3/17/62, N.O. On roll at General Hosp., Liberty, Va., 10/62 to 2/63. Died at General Hosp. No. 3, Mobile, Ala., 4/6/63, consumption. Born: County Kildare, Ireland. Occ.: Farmer. Res.: N.O. Age 35, 5'7", gray eyes, dark hair, fair complexion.
Clark, James, Pvt. (aka Clarke) En. 6/4/61, CM. Present to 8/62. Captured at Cedar Run, Va., 8/9/62. POW, Fort Monroe, Va. Record dated 3/20/65 at Petersburg states: "Deserted Aug. 8, 1862." Born: La. Occ.: Laborer. Res.: N.O. Age 21, single.
Clark, Edward, Cpl. En. 6/4/61, CM, as pvt. Present to 5/62. Severely wounded in leg at Winchester, 5/25/62. Absent wounded, 6-11/62. Present, 11/62 to 11/63. Promoted to cpl., 5/63. Wounded at Fredericksburg, 5/4/63. Captured at Rappahannock Station, 11/7/63. POW, Point Lookout, Md., exchanged 3/10/64. Admitted to CSA Hosp., Charlottesville, Va., 9/26/64. Surrendered and paroled at Charlottesville, 5/17/65. Born: Ireland. Occ.: Laborer. Res.: N.O. Age 32, single.
Clancy, John, Pvt. En. 6/4/61, CM. Present to 7/62. Absent sick in Lynchburg, Va., 7-12/62. Present, 1-6/63. Captured in Pennsylvania (Gettysburg campaign), 7/63. Absent captured, 7-11/63. Present 11-12/63. Detailed to hospital duty in Charlottesville, 2/64 to 3/65. On register of Confederate refugees and deserters who took oath of allegiance in Washington, 3/25/65. Born: Ireland. Occ.: Sailor. Res.: N.O. Age 46, single.
Clancy, James, Pvt. En. 6/4/61 as musician. Present to 7/62. Accidentally killed in hospital, place unstated, 7/30/62. Record dated 3/20/65 at Petersburg states, "Killed by accident July 5, 1862." Born: Ireland. Occ.: Laborer. Res.: N.O. Age 44, single.
Condon, John, Pvt. En. 6/4/61, CM. Present to 5/64. Wounded at Chantilly, Va., 9/1/62. Captured at Wilderness, 5/5/64. POW, Point Lookout, Md., transferred to Elmira, N.Y., 8/15/64, exchanged 2/16/65. Captured at Petersburg, Va., 3/3/65. POW, Hart's Island, N.Y., received 4/7/65, released 6/14/65. Born: Ireland. Occ.: Laborer. Res.: N.O. Age 26, single, 5'8", dark eyes, dark hair, light complexion.
Connor, James, Pvt. En. 6/4/61, CM. Present to 8/62. Absent sick in hospital, 10-11/62. On register of CSA Hosp., Danville, Va., 8/25/62, furloughed for 60 days, 11/11/62. Record dated 3/20/65 at Petersburg, states: "Deserted July 29, 1862." Born: Ireland. Occ.: Laborer. Res.: N.O. Age 36, married.
Connor, John, Pvt. En. 6/4/61, CM. Present 7-10/61. Record dated 3/20/65 at Petersburg, Va., states: "Deserted May 30, 1862." Born: Ireland. Occ.: Plasterer. Res.: N.O. Age 23, single.
Conroy, Martin, Sgt. En. 6/4/61, CM. Promoted from cpl to 5th sgt., 9/20/61. Wounded at Gaines' Mill, Va., 6/27/62. Record dated 3/20/65 at Petersburg states: "Deserted June 28, 1862." Born: Ireland. Occ.: Laborer. Res.: N.O. Age 23, single.
Corbett, Daniel, Pvt. En. 6/4/61, CM. Present to 7/62. Wounded at Malvern Hill, Va., 7/1/62. Absent wounded, 7-8/62. Present 5-11/63. Severely wounded at Mine Run, Va., 11/29/63. Absent wounded to 3/64. Died in hospital at Gordonsville, Va. from gunshot wounds received at Mine Run and pneumonia, 3/9/64. Born: Ireland. Occ.: Laborer. Res.: N.O. Age 25, single.

Cunningham, Robert, Pvt. En. 6/4/61, CM. Present to 6/62. Captured at Woodstock, Va., 6/4/62. POW, Fort Delaware, Del., took oath of allegiance, 8/10/62. Born: Ireland. Occ.: Shoemaker. Res.: N.O. Age 23, single.
Davis, Malachi, Pvt. En. 6/4/61, CM. Present to 6/62. Wounded in shoulder at Port Republic, Va., 6/9/62. Absent wounded to 8/63. Detached for duty as nurse at hospital in Farmville, Va., 8/5/63 to 5/64. Present, 5/64 to 4/65. Surrendered at Appomattox C.H., 4/9/65. Born: Ireland. Occ.: Bricklayer. Res.: N.O. Age 28, married.
Daw, Thomas, Pvt. En. 6/4/61, CM. Present to 4/64. Transferred to CS Navy, 4/16/64. Born: Ireland. Occ.: Sailor. Res.: N.O. Age 37, married.
Delaney, Jeremiah, Pvt. En. 6/4/61, CM. Present to 7/62. Wounded at Malvern Hill, Va., 7/1/62. Captured at Fredericksburg, Va., 4/29/63. Took oath of allegiance at Philadelphia, Pa., 5/30/63. Born: County Wexford, Ireland. Occ.: Laborer. Res.: N.O. Age 24, single, 5'9", black eyes, dark hair, fair complexion.
Donk, Joseph, Pvt. En. 3/21/62, N.O. Present to 9/62. Deserted at Sharpsburg, Md., 9/16/62. Born: Belgium. Occ.: Laborer. Res.: N.O. Age 31, single, 5'10", hazel eyes, dark hair, dark complexion.
Donohue, John, Pvt. En. 6/4/61, CM. Present to 6/62. Wounded in leg at Port Republic, Va., 6/9/62. Absent wounded in hospital, 7/62 to 3/63. Killed at Fredericksburg, Va., 4/29/63. Born: Ireland. Occ.: Laborer. Res.: N.O. Age 20, single.
Donovan, Dennis, Pvt. (aka Dunivan) En. 6/4/61, CM. Present to 3/62. Deserted 3/62. Born: New York. Occ.: Laborer. Res.: N.O. Age 26, single.
Donovan, John, Pvt. (aka Dunivan) En. 6/4/61, CM. Present to 6/62. Deserted 6/8/62. Born: Ireland. Occ.: Laborer. Res.: N.O. Age 27, single.
Donovan, Patrick, Pvt. (aka Dunivan) En. 6/4/61, CM. Present to 5/63. Mortally wounded at Fredericksburg, Va., 5/4/63. Admitted to General Hosp. No. 18, Richmond, 5/10/63, died 5/29/63. Born: Ireland. Occ.: Laborer. Res.: N.O. Age 28, single.
Farrell, James, Pvt. En. 3/21/62, N.O. Admitted to CSA Genl. Hosp., Charlottesville, Va., 4/16/62, died of pneumonia 4//26/62. Born: County Kildare, Ireland. Occ.: Steamboatman. Age 30.
Finley, Andrew, Pvt. En. 6/4/61, CM. Present to 7/62. Mortally wounded at Malvern Hill, Va., 7/1/62. Died at Chimborazo Hospital, Richmond, 7/6/62, shoulder wound. Born: Ireland. Occ.: Laborer. Res.: N.O. Age 20, single.
Fitzgerald, Daniel, Sgt. En. 6/4/61, CM. Promoted from pvt. to cpl., 9/20/61. Wounded at Port Republic, Va., 6/9/62. Absent wounded, 7/62 to 6/63. Present, 7-11/63. Captured at Rappahannock Station, Va., 11/7/63. POW, Point Lookout, Md., released upon joining U.S. service, 1/24/64. Born: Ireland. Occ.: Laborer. Res.: N.O. Age 26, single.
Fitzgerald, Edward, Pvt. En. 6/4/61, CM. Present to 5/62. Wounded at Winchester, 5/25/62. Absent wounded, 7-8/62. Present, 9-12/62. Absent in hospital, 1-9/63. Present, 9/63 to 5/64. Captured at Wilderness, Va., 5/5/64. POW, Point Lookout, Md., exchanged 9/18/64. On roll of Confederate refugees and deserters, Provost Marshall General, Army of the Potomac, 1/29/65. Took oath of allegiance at City Point, Va., 1/29/65. Born: Ireland. Occ.: Laborer. Res.: N.O. Age 25, single, 6'0", blue eyes, light hair, light complexion.
Flanagan, Thomas, Sgt. En. 6/4/61, CM. Wounded, captured in hospital at Winchester, Va., 6/2/62. POW, place unspecified, exchanged 8/8/62. Captured at Fredericksburg, Va., 5/3/63. POW, Fort Delaware, Del. Wounded seriously in left leg at Mine Run, Va., 11/27/63. Absent wounded, 12/63 to 7/64. Captured at Winchester, Va., 7/21/64. POW, Wheeling, W.Va., transferred to Camp Chase, Ohio, 10/6/64, released 5/13/65. Born: Ireland. Occ.: Laborer. Res.: N.O. Age 38, single.
Flood, William, Pvt. En. 3/22/62, N.O. Mortally wounded at Port Republic, Va., 6/9/62. Record dated 3/20/65 at Petersburg, Va., states: "Killed in battle June 9, 1962." Born: Ireland. Occ.: Laborer. Age: 35.
Flynn, Thomas, Pvt. En. 6/4/61, CM. Present to 8/62. Wounded in shoulder at Manassas, Va., 8/29/62. Absent wounded to 11/1/62. Captured at Fredericksburg, Va., 4/29/63. POW, Old Capitol Prison, Washington, exchanged 6/3/63. Present to 1/64. AWOL, 1-2/64. Present under arrest, 3-4/64. Captured at Wilderness, Va., 5/5/64. POW, Point Lookout, Md., transferred to Elmira, N.Y., 8/15/64, exchanged 3/10/65. Surrendered at Burkeville, Va., 4/27/65. Born: Maine. Occ.: Laborer. Res.: N.O. Age 20, single.
Foley, Declon, Cpl. En. 6/4/61, CM. Present to 6/62. Killed at Port Republic, Va., 6/9/62. Born: Ireland. Occ.: Laborer. Res.: N.O. Age 26, single.
Frazier, Peter, Pvt. En. 3/21/62, N.O. Wounded at Winchester, 5/25/62. Killed at Bristoe Station, Va., 8/27/62. Born: Maine. Occ.: Farmer. Res.: N.O. Age 28, single, 5'8", brown eyes, dark hair, dark complexion.
Gleavy, Michael, Pvt. (aka Glavy) En. 6/4/61, CM. Present to 8/62. Discharged on surgeon's certificate of disability, 8/62, verisose veins of right leg. Born: Ireland. Occ.: Laborer. Age 29, 5'7", blue eyes, black hair, dark complexion.
Gleason, George, Cpl. En. 6/4/61, CM. Present to 3/6. Deserted, 3/62. Born: New York. Occ.: Laborer. Res.: N.O. Age 22, single.

Gleason, Patrick, Pvt. En. 6/4/61, CM. Present to 5/62. Severely wounded at Winchester, Va., 5/25/62. Admitted to CSA Hosp., Winchester, 5/27/62, shoulder wound. Record dated 3/20/65 at Petersburg, Va., states: "Died in hosp. of wound received May 25, 1862." Born: Ireland. Occ.: Laborer. Res.: N.O. Age 21, single.

Gunderson, Edward, Pvt. En. 3/21/62, N. O. Present to 5/63. Captured at Fredericksburg, Va., 5/3/63. POW, Fort Delaware, Del., exchanged 6/3/63. Wounded at Gettysburg, 7/2/63. Present to 5/64. Captured at Wilderness, Va., 5/5/64. POW, Point Lookout, transferred to Elmira, N.Y., 8/15/64, released 6/19/65. Born: Christiana, Norway. Occ.: Laborer. Res.: New Orleans. Age 25, single, 5'9", blue eyes, auburn hair, florid complexion.

Hart, William, Pvt., (No. 1) En. 6/4/61, CM. Present to 3/63. Absent sick in hospital, 3-4/63. Present 5-11/63. Captured at Rappahannock Station, Va., 11/7/63. POW, Point Lookout, Md., exchanged 3/10/64. Captured at Wilderness, Va., 5/5/64. POW, Point Lookout, transferred to Elmira, N.Y., 8/15/64, exchanged 2/13/65. Surrendered at Appomattox C.H., 4/9/65. Born: Ireland. Occ.: Laborer. Res.: N.O. Age 23, single

Hart, William, Pvt., (No. 2) En. 6/4/61, CM. Present to 9/62. Absent sick in hospital in Lynchburg, Va., 9/62 to 2/63. Captured at Fredericksburg, Va., 4/29/63. POW, Old Capitol Prison, Washington, exchanged 6/3/63. Discharged on surgeon's certificate of disability, 6/15/63, rheumatism. Born: Ireland. Occ.: Baker. Res.: N.O. Age 36, single.

Higgins, Joseph, Pvt. En. 6/4/61, CM. Present to 6/62. Wounded at Gaines' Mill, Va., 6/27/62. Absent wounded 7-12/62. Present, 5/65 to 7/64. Mortally wounded at Battle of Monocacy, Md., 7/9/64, died at USA Genl. Hosp., Fredericksburg, Md., 7/28/64, after amputation of leg from gunshot wound, knee joint. Born: Ireland. Occ.: Tinsmith. Res.: N.O. Age 24, single.

Horrogan, Daniel, Pvt. En. 6/4/61, CM. Present to 5/62. Wounded at Winchester, Va., 5/25/62. Captured in Winchester hospital, 6/2/62, transferred to Baltimore, Md., 8/1/62. POW on steamer Katskill, 8/62. Present 3/63 to 5/64. Captured at Wilderness, Va., 5/5/64. POW, Point Lookout, Md., transferred to Elmira, N.Y., 8/15/64, exchanged 2/25/65. On register of Confederate refugees and deserters surrendered at Washington, D.C., 4/17/65. Born: Ireland. Occ.: Laborer. Res.: N.O. Age 26, single.

Hughes, Thomas, Pvt. En. 6/4/61, CM. Present to 6/63. Wounded at Winchester, Va., 6/14/63. Absent wounded, 6-9/63. Present, 9-12/63. Absent furlough, 1-2/64. Present 3-5/64. Killed at Wilderness, Va., 5/5/64. Born: Ireland. Occ.: Laborer. Res.: N.O. Age 30, married.

Ivory, Thomas, Pvt. En. 6/4/61, CM. Present to 6/62. Recorded as deserted 6/29/62. Born: Ireland. Occ.: Laborer. Res.: N.O. Age 28, single.

Jordan, Mark, Pvt. Transferred to 6th La. from Wheat's 1st La. Special Battalion, 12/63. Right arm amputated after Battle of Gaines' Mill, Va., 6/27/62. Absent sick in hospital, 1-10/64. Discharged as disabled, 10/22/64. Retired to Invalid Corps, Montgomery, Ala., 10/64.

Judge, Patrick, Pvt. En. 6/4/61, CM. Present on 1861 rolls. Absent sick, 5-6/62. Record dated 3/20/65 at Petersburg states: "Died in hospital of disease," no date given. Born: Ireland. Occ.: Laboer. Res.: N.O. Age 33, single.

Keefe, John, Pvt. En. 6/4/61, CM. Present to 5/63. Wounded at Fredericksburg, Va., 5/4/63. Absent wounded, 5-9/63. Present 9/63 to 5/64. Captured at Wilderness, Va., 5/5/64. POW, Point Lookout, Md., exchanged 9/18/64. Paroled at Charlottesville, Va., 5/17/65. Born: Ireland. Occ.: Laborer. Res.: N.O. Age 35, single.

Kelleher, John, Pvt. En. 3/4/62, N.O. Present to 4/63. Captured at Fredericksburg, Va., 4/29/63. POW, Old Capitol Prison, Washington, exchanged 6/3/63. Captured at Gettysburg, 7/5/63. POW, Point Lookout, Md., released on taking oath of allegiance, 3/30/64. Born: County Cork, Ireland. Occ.: Drayman. Res.: N.O. Age 23, single.

Kelly, Daniel, Pvt. En. 6/4/61, CM. Present to 6/62. Recorded as deserted, 6/62. Born: Ireland. Occ.: Blacksmith. Res.: N.O. Age 25, single.

Kelly, Richard, Pvt. En. 6/4/61, CM. Present to 7/63. Died at Seminary Hosp., Hagerstown, Md., 7/14/63, gunshot wound to base of skull. Roll for 3-4/64 states: "Died at the hosp. at Williamsport, Md., on or about 12 July from gunshot wound received on the 8th." Record dated 3/20/65 at Petersburg states: "Killed in the discharge of his duty by an assassin." Born: Ireland. Occ.: Butcher. Res.: N.O. Age 24, married.

Kenniffe, John, Pvt. En. 6/4/61, CM. Present to 3/62. Admitted to CSA Hosp., Charlottesville, Va., 3/31/62, died 4/29/62, conjunctivitis. Born: Ireland. Occ.: Laborer. Res.: N.O. Age 25, single.

Keogh, James, Pvt. En. 6/4/61, CM. Present to 6/62. Captured at Woodstock, Va., 6/2/62. POW, Fort Delaware, Del., took oath of allegiance, 8/10/62. Born: Ireland. Occ.: Laborer. Res.: N.O. Age 26, single.

Knox, William, Pvt. En. 6/4/61, CM. Present to 5/63. Wounded at Bristoe Station, Va., 8/27/62. Absent wounded, 8-9/62. Wounded at Fredericksburg, Va., 5/4/63, gunshot wound in chest, fracturing ribs. Absent wounded 5-8/63. Present to 6/64. Wounded at Cold Harbor, Va., 6/3/64. Admitted CSA Hosp., Charlottesville, Va., 6/9/64, shell wound in neck, transferred to Lynchburg Hosp., 9/27/64. Born: Ireland. Occ.: Laborer. Res.: N.O. Age 28, single.

Lewis, James, Pvt. En. 6/4/61, CM. Present to 5/63. Killed at Fredericksburg, Va., 5/4/63. Born: Ireland. Occ.: Laborer. Res.: N.O. Age 35, single.

Lillas, Michael, Pvt. (aka Lillis) En. 3/13/62, N.O. Record dated 3/20/65 at Petersburg states: "Deserted June 9, 1862." Born: Ireland. Occ.: Laborer. Res.: N.O. Age 25, single.

Maguire, Joseph, Pvt. (aka McGuire) En. 6/4/61, CM. Present to 7/63. Wounded at Sharpsburg, Md., 9/17/63. Severely wounded in thigh and captured at Gettysburg, 7/2/63. POW, U.S. Genl. Hosp., Baltimore, Md., admitted 7/26/63, exchanged 8/24/63. Present, disabled, 9/63 to 2/64. Absent sick, 3-8/64. Record dated 3/20/65 at

Petersburg states: "Deserted Feb. 1, 1865." On register of Confederate deserters received in Washington, 2/1/65; took oath of allegiance at City Point, Va., 1/29/65. Born: Ireland. Occ.: Laborer. Res. N.O. Age 21.

Maguire, Nicholas, Pvt. (aka Magner) En. 6/4/61, CM. Present to 9/62. Killed at Sharpsburg, Md., 9/17/62. Born: Ireland. Occ. Laborer. Res.: N.O. Age 27, single.

Mahegan, David, Pvt. En. 6/4/61, CM. Present to 5/62. Record dated 3/20/65 at Petersburg states: "Deserted May 28, 1862." Born: Ireland. Occ.: Laborer. Res.: N.O. Age 28, single.

Mauder, John, Pvt. En. 3/21/62. Present to 5/62. Roll for 7-8/62 states: "Died at Winchester, May 28, 1862."

McAuliffe, Cornelius, Pvt. En. 6/4/61, CM. Present to 5/62. Wounded at Winchester, Va., 5/25/62. Captured at Winchester hospital, 6/2/62. POW on Steamer Katskill, exchanged 8/10/62. Present 9/62 to 4/63. Captured at Fredericksburg, Va., 4/29/63. POW, Old Capitol Prison, Washington, took oath of allegiance, 5/25/63. Born: Ireland. Occ.: Steamboat hand. Res.: N.O. Age 28, single.

McCarthy, Charles, Pvt. En. 6/4/61, CM. Present to 4/64. Absent sick in hospital at Charlottesville, Va., 5-8/64. Paroled at Winchester, Va., 4/24/65. Born: Ireland. Occ.: Laborer. Res.: N.O. Age 25, single.

McCarthy, James, Pvt. En. 6/4/61, CM. Present to 5/63. Wounded at Fredericksburg, Va., 5/4/63. Present to 7/63. Wounded at Gettysburg, 7/2/63. Admitted to CSA Hosp., Charlottesville, Va., 7/20/63, returned to duty, 8/5/63. Present to 4/64. Transferred to CS Navy, 4/16/64. Born: Ireland. Occ.: Laborer. Res.: N.O. Age 25, single.

McGrath, John, Pvt. En. 6/4/61, CM. Present to 2/62. Discharged on surgeon's certificate of disability, 2/21/62, paryalysis of ankle joint. Born: Ireland. Occ.: Laborer. Res.: N.O. Age 31, single.

Mehegan, Charles, Pvt. En. 6/4/61, CM. Present to 11/63. Captured at Rappahannock Station, Va., 11/7/63. POW, Point Lookout, Md., took oath of allegiance, 3/19/64. Born: Ireland. Occ.: Laborer. Res.: N.O. Age 39, married.

Modien, John, Pvt. En. 3/21/62, N.O. Present to 6/62. Record dated 3/20/65 at Petersburg states: "Killed in battle June 9, 1862." [Battle of Port Republic, Va.] Born: Christiana, Norway. Occ.: Laborer. Res.: N.O. Age 29, single.

Moffitt, Michael, Pvt. (aka Moffat) En. 6/4/61, CM. Present to 8/62. Wounded at Bristoe Station, Va., 8/27/62. Admitted to CSA Hosp., Charlottesville, Va., 9/28/62, wound in chest, returned to duty 11/11/62. Absent in hospital, 1-6/63. Captured at South Mountain, Md., 7/4/63. POW, Fort Delaware, Del., exchanged 7/31/63. Present, 9/63 to 5/64. Captured at Wilderness, Va., 5/5/64. POW, Point Lookout, Md., transferred to Elmira, N.Y., 8/15/64, exchanged 2/15/65. Surrendered at Washington, D.C., 4/17/65. Born: Ireland. Occ.: Laborer. Res.: N.O. Age 35, married.

Mullins, Jeremiah, Pvt. (aka Mullen) En. 3/17/62, N.O. Present to 4/63. Captured at Fredericksburg, Va., 4/29/63. POW, Old Capitol Prison, Washington, forwarded to Fort Delaware, Del., exchanged 5/23/63. Absent sick, 6-7/63. Present, 8/63 to 5/64. Captured at Wilderness, Va., 5/5/64. POW, Point Lookout, Md., transferred to Elmira, N.Y., 8/15/64, released 6/29/65. Born: Ireland. Occ.: Laborer. Res.: N.O. Age 35, single, 5'4", blue eyes, gray hair, florid complexion.

Mulrooney, John, Sgt. En. 6/4/61, CM. Promoted to cpl, 9/20/61. Promoted to 5th sgt., 7/1/62. Present to 11/63. Captured at Rappahannock Station, Va., 11/7/63. POW, Point Lookout, Md., exchanged 3/10/64. Present 3-5/64. Mortally wounded at Spotsylvania C.H., Va., 5/12/64. Roll for 5-8/64 states: "Dead, killed in action." Record dated 3/20/65 at Petersburg states: "Died of wounds rec'd May 12, 1864." Born: Ireland. Occ.: Laborer. Res.: N.O. Age 18, single.

Murphy, Dennis, Pvt. En. 6/4/61, CM. Present to 8/62. Wounded at Bristoe Station, Va., 8/27/62. Absent wounded to 2/63. Absent detached as hospital nurse, 2/63 to 4/64. Captured at Wilderness, Va., 5/5/64. POW, Point Lookout, Md., transferred to Elmira, N.Y., 8/15/64, exchanged 2/20/65. On roll of Confederate refugees and deserters at Washington, D.C., dated 3/28/65, took oath of allegiance. Born: Ireland. Occ.: Laborer. Res.: N.O. Age 46, single.

Murphy, Edward F., Pvt. En. 6/4/61, CM. Present to 10/61. Admitted to Chimborazo Hosp., Richmond, 10/22/61, died 12/30/61, fracture of leg and chronic rheumatism.

Murphy, Edward J., Pvt. En. 6/4/61, CM. Present to 6/62. Record dated 3/20/65 at Petersburg states: "Deserted June 9, 1862." Born: Ireland. Occ.: Laborer. Res.: N.O. Age 24, single.

Murphy, Michael, Pvt. En. 6/4/61, CM as Musician. Present to 6/62. Record dated 3/20/65 at Petersburg states: "Deserted June 28, 1862." Born: Ireland. Occ.: Laborer. Res.: N.O. Age 26, single.

Murphy, Patrick, Pvt., En. 6/4/61, CM. Present to 6/62. Captured at Winchester, Va., 6/2/62. POW, Baltimore, Md., exchanged 8/8/62. Present 8/62 to 5/65. Surrendered at Appomattox C.H., Va., 4/9/65. Born: Ireland. Occ.: Laborer. Res.: N.O. Age 41, single, 5'3", gray eyes, dark hair, dark complexion. Parole dated 4/10/65 lists residence as Washington, La.

Murray, John, Pvt. En. 6/4/61, CM. Present to 6/62. Captured at Woodstock, Va., 6/2/62. POW, Fort Delaware, Del., took oath of allegiance, 8/10/62. Born: Ireland. Occ.: Shoemaker. Res.: N.O. Age 30, single.

Newport, Stephen, Pvt. En. 3/13/62, N.O. Present on roll dated 4/15/62. No record thereafter. (Note: Bartlett's *Military Record of Louisiana* lists an S. Newport of the 6th Louisiana as killed at the First Battle of Winchester, Va., 5/25/62, but Newport's compiled service records contain only one muster roll, and say nothing of his being killed.) Born: New Ross, Ireland. Occ.: Laborer. Age 41.

Nichols, John, Sgt. En. 6/4/61, CM, as 3rd sgt. Promoted to 1st Sgt., 10/26/61. Present to 7/62. Record dated 3/20/65 at Petersburg states: "Deserted July 2, 1862." Born: Ireland. Occ.: Laborer. Res.: N.O. Age 23, single.

Nolan, John, Pvt. En. 6/4/61, CM. Present to 5/62. Absent, left in care of wounded at Winchester, Va., 6-8/62. Killed at Bristoe Station, Va., 8/26/62. Born: Ireland. Occ.: Laborer. Res.: N.O. Age 26, single.

Nolan, Richard, Pvt. En. 6/4/61, CM. Present to 8/62. Wounded at Manassas, Va., 8/29/62. Absent wounded, 9-10/62. Present, 11/62 to 5/63. Captured at Fredericksburg, Va., 5/3/63. POW, Fort Delaware, Del., exchanged 6/3/63. Wounded at Winchester, Va., 9/19/64. Captured at Fisher's Hill, Va., 9/22/64. POW, Point Lookout, Md., exchanged 2/10/65. Surrendered at Charleston, W.Va., listed as "rebel deserter," took oath of allegiance, 3/9/65. Born: Ireland. Occ.: Laborer. Res.: N.O. Age 27, married, 5'7", blue eyes, dark hair, fair complexion.

Noonan, William, Pvt. En. 6/4/61, CM. Present to 8/61. Roll for 7-8/61 states: "Dismissed the service 29th of Aug., 1861, by sentence of regimental court martial."

Normile, James, Pvt. En. 6/4/61, CM. Present to 8/62. AWOL, 8/62 to 3/63. Present, 3/63 to 5/64. Captured at Wilderness, Va., 5/5/64. POW, Point Lookout, Md., exchanged 11/15/64. Present 11/64 to 2/65. Surrendered as deserter to Provost Marshall, V Corps, Army of Potomac, [at Petersburg, Va.], 2/19/65, took oath of allegiance at Washington, 2/21/65. Record dated 3/20/65 at Petersburg states: "Deserted Feb. 18, 1865." Born: Ireland. Occ.: Laborer. Res.: N.O. Age 27, single.

Phillips, John, Pvt. En. 6/4/61, CM. Present to 8/62. Killed at Bristoe Station, Va., 8/27/62. Born: Ireland. Occ.: Painter. Res.: N.O. Age 28, married.

Quirk, William, Lt. En. 6/4/61, CM, as jr. 2nd lt. Roll for 7-8/61 states: "Resigned 15 Aug., 1861."

Rielly, James, Pvt. (aka Riley) En. 6/4/61, CM. Present to 7/62. Admitted CSA Hosp., Farmville, Va., 7/22/62, wounded hand. Absent sick in hospital, 7/62 to 4/63. Absent detailed as nurse in hospital, 4-12/63. Declared disabled by Medical Examining Board, Farmville, 8/23/64, "permanent injury of right arm from railroad accident." Retired to Invalid Corps, 12/5/64. Born: Ireland. Occ.: Laborer. Res.: N.O. Age 30, single.

Rooney, Michael, Pvt. En. 6/4/61, CM, as color bearer. Present to 9/62. Wounded in shoulder at Chantilly, Va., 9/1/62. Absent wounded, 9-10/62. Present to 4/63. Captured at Fredericksburg, Va., 4/29/63. POW, Old Capitol Prison, Washington, took oath of allegiance, 6/24/63. Born: Ireland. Occ.: Laborer. Res.: N.O. Age 22, single.

Ryan, Denis, Pvt. En. 6/4/61, CM. Present to 3/62. Absent sick in hospital, 3-5/62. Wounded at Gaines' Mill, Va., 6/27/62. Absent wounded, 6-11/62. Present to 5/63. Captured at Fredericksburg, Va., 5/3/63. POW, Old Capitol Prison, exchanged 6/3/63. Present to 11/63. Captured at Rappahannock Station, Va., 6/11/63. POW, Point Lookout, Md., took oath of allegiance 3/30/64. Born: Ireland. Occ.: Laborer. Res.: N.O. Age 27, single.

Sanderson, Henry, Pvt. En. 4/1/63 at Fredericksburg, Va. Wounded in thigh at Fredericksburg, 5/4/63. Absent wounded, 5-6/63. Present, 7-10/63. Roll for 9-10/63 states: "Deserted." Captured at Raccoon Ford, Va., 10/5/63 as "rebel deserter." POW, Old Capitol Prison, Washington, took oath of allegiance 12/17/63.

Scott, Thomas, Cpl. En. 6/4/61, CM, as cpl. Present on 1861 rolls. Resigned as cpl., 9/20/61. Record dated 3/20/65 at Petersburg states: "Deserted Jany. 1862." Born: Ireland. Occ.: Laborer. Res.: N.O. Age 23, single.

Shannon, Cornelius, Pvt. En. 3/21/62, N.O. Captured at Winchester, Va., 5/9/63, with notation: "Captured within our lines attempting to escape, is no doubt a spy." POW, Wheeling, Va., transferred to Camp Chase, Ohio, took oath of allegiance 5/28/63. Born: County Tipperary, Ireland. Occ.: Laborer. Res.: St. Charles Parish. Age 26.

Sullivan, Cornelius, Pvt. En. 6/4/61, CM. Present to 8/61. Died at Camp Bienville (Centreville) Va., 8/3/61, typhoid fever. Born: Ireland. Occ.: Laborer. Res.: N.O. Age 26, single.

Sullivan, James, Pvt. En. 6/4/61, CM. Present to 7/62. Admitted to Louisiana Hosp., Richmond, 6/30/62, deserted from hospital, 1/10/63. Born: Ireland. Occ.: Laborer. Res.: N.O. Age 25, single.

Tobin, Richard, Pvt. En. 6/4/61, CM. Present to 5/62. Wounded at Winchester, Va., 5/25/62. Absent wounded to 3/63. Detailed as nurse at hospital, 4-9/63. Present, 9/63 to 5/64. Captured at Wilderness, Va., 5/5/64. POW, Point Lookout, Md., transferred to Elmira, N.Y., 8/15/64, released 5/17/65. Born: Ireland. Occ.: Laborer. Res.: N.O. Age 28, single, 5'10", blue eyes, dark hair, florid complexion.

Valentine, James, Pvt. En. 3/13/62, N.O. Present to 6/62. Captured at Strasburg, Va., 6/5/62. POW, Fort Delaware, Del., took oath of allegiance, 8/10/62. Born: County Kildare, Ireland. Occ.: Baker. Age 33.

Walsh, Michael, Pvt. En. 6/4/61, CM. Present to 4/63. Wounded at Fredericksburg, Va., 4/29/63. Absent wounded, 5-8/63. Present, 9-11/63. Wounded and captured at Rappahannock Station, Va., 11/7/63. POW, Old Capitol Prison, Washington, transferred to Point Lookout, Md., 2/3/64, exchanged 3/10/64. Roll for 3-4/64 states: "Deserted. Took the Yankee oath at Point Lookout." Born: Ireland. Occ.: Laborer. Res.: N.O. Age 32, single.

Walshe, Edward, Lt. En. 6/4/61, CM, as commissary sgt. Present to 8/61. Roll for 7-8/61 states: "Discharged 8/22/61 due to ill health." Elected 2nd jr. lt., 12/62. Present on rolls 3-11/63. Captured at Rappahannock Station, Va., 11/7/63. POW, Johnson's Island, Ohio, forwarded to Point Lookout, Md., for exchange, 2/16/65. On roll of POWs paroled 5/15/65, place unstated. Age 21, 5'6", blue eyes, light hair, light complexion; parole lists residence as Okyka, Miss.

Waters, John, Pvt. En. 3/1/62, N.O. Present to 5/62. Record dated 3/20/65 at Petersburg states: "Deserted May 27, 1862." Born: Ireland. Occ.: Laborer. Res.: N.O. Age 28, single.

White, John, Lt. En. 6/4/61, CM, as 1st sgt. Elected 2nd jr. lt, 9/20/61. Present to 1/62. Admitted to Moore Hosp., Danville, Va., 1/2/62, died at Manassas, Va., hosp., 1/8/62, gastritis. Born: Ireland. Occ.: Laborer. Res.: N.O. Age 28 single.

Wilson, Thomas, Pvt. En. 6/4/61, CM. Present to 6/62. AWOL, 7-8/62. Record dated 3/20/65 at Petersburg states: "Deserted June 1862." Born: Ireland. Occ.: Laborer. Res.: N.O. Age 25, single.

Winn, John, Pvt. En. 6/4/61, CM. Present to 6/62. Record dated 3/20/65 at Petersburg states: "Deserted June 1862." Born: Ireland. Occ.: Laborer. Res.: N.O. Age 31, single.

Company K: The Violet Guards

This company was raised in New Orleans by its first captain, William H. Manning, who later became major and commanded the remnants of the 6th Louisiana in the last months of the war. It also was dominated by Irishmen, with at least 60 of its 125 members born in Ireland and another 19 with common Irish surnames. Two thirds of this company was foreign-born, with seven from Germany, seven from England, three from France, two from Canada and one each from Mexico, Cuba and Switzerland. Twenty-one men were native Louisianians, 13 were from Northern states, two from Confederate states, and seven whose birthplace is unrecorded. During the war, at least 23 men were killed or mortally wounded, three were accidentally killed, nine died of disease and one was executed. Thirty-eight men deserted and three were captured and took the oath of allegiance. Eight were discharged, four retired to the Invalid Corps, three transferred out and seven surrendered at Appomattox Court House.

Captains:

Manning, William H., Capt., Major. En. 6/4/61, CM as Capt. Acting Major of 6th La. after 9/17/62. Appointed Major of 6th La., 12/20/62 to take rank 11/7/62. See Field and Staff Roster.
Ring, George P., Capt. En. 6/4/61, CM. Commissioned as 1st lt. by Gov. T.O. Moore, 4/3/61. Present to 9/62. Wounded at Sharpsburg, Md., 9/17/62. Promoted to captain, 11/7/62. Present to 6/63. Wounded at Winchester, Va., 6/14/63. Admitted CSA Hosp., Charlottesville, Va., 7/4/63, wound in left ankle. Absent on detached service at Nolasuga, Ala., 7/63 to 4/64. Present, 4-10/64. Wounded at Battle of Cedar Creek, Va., 10/19/64. Admitted to Louisiana Hosp., Richmond, 11/5/64, returned to duty, 12/12/64. Inspection report dated 11/29/64 states: "Assigned to light duty at Montgomery, Ala." Paroled at Montgomery, 5/4/65. Born: Tennessee. Res.: N.O. Blue eyes, gray hair, light complexion, 5'11". Died 6/9/67, N.O.

* * *

Agaisse, J.H., Sgt. En. 6/4/61, CM. Present to 11/63. Promoted from pvt. to cpl., 8/17/61, to 3rd sgt., 6/62, to 2nd sgt., 9/17/62, to 1st sgt., 12/62. Captured at Rappahannock Station, Va., 11/7/63. POW at Point Lookout, Md, 11/11/63, took oath of allegiance, 3/30/64. Born: N.O. Occ.: Clerk. Age 28, married.
Berara, Jose, Pvt. En. 3/8/62, N.O. Deserted 6/1/62. Born: Vera Cruz, Mexico. Occ.: Laborer. Age 16.
Barrett, William, Pvt. En. 3/11/62, N.O. Deserted 10/1/62. Born: N.O. Occ: Laborer. Res.: N.O. Age 20, single.
Bartley, James, Pvt. En. 6/4/61,CM. Present through 4/64. Captured at Wilderness, Va., 5/5/64. POW, Pt. Lookout, Md., transferred to Elmira, N.Y., 8/15/64, paroled 2/25/65. Born: Ireland. Occ.: Laborer. Res.: N.O. Age 19, single.
Brogan, Charles, Pvt. En. 6/4/61, CM. Present to 3/62. Died at Moore Hosp., Manassas, Va., 3/8/62. Disease: Epilepsy.
Brogan, William, Pvt. En. 4/3/61, N.O. Record dated 2/21/65, Petersburg, Va. states: "Deserted 1861." Born: Ireland. Occ.: Laborer. Res.: N.O. Age 34, married.
Burke, David, Pvt. En. 6/4/61, CM. Discharged on certificate of disability, Camp Carondolet (Manassas), Va., hernia, 2/13/62. Born: New Brunswick, Canada. Occ.: Sailor. Res.: N.O. Age 36, single.
Burns, Edward, Sgt. En. 6/4/61, CM. Present to 9/62. Wounded in left thigh at Sharpsburg, Md., 9/17/62. Promoted from pvt. to cpl., 9/17/62. Absent wounded 11/62 to 10/63. Captured at Rappahannock Station, Va., 11/7/63. POW at Point Lookout, Md., 11/11/63, exchanged 3/10/64. Captured at Spottsylvania C.H., 5/12/64. POW at Point Lookout, transferred to Elmira, N.Y., 8/15/64. Paroled at Elmira, 2/25/65. On roll of POWs of various regiments (detached) surrendered at Citronelle, Ala., 5/4/65. Born: Ireland. Occ.: Laborer. Res.: N.O. Age 24, single.
Cahill, John, Sgt. En. 6/4/61, CM. Present, 7-10/61. Promoted from 4th sgt. to 2nd sgt, 8/1/61. Reduced to pvt., 9/17/62. Absent with leave, 1-2/63. Present, 1-7/63. Wounded at Gettysburg, 7/2/63. Absent wounded, 7-10/63. Present, 11/63 to 5/64. Captured at Wilderness, 5/5/64. POW, Point Lookout, Md, transferred to Elmira, N.Y., 8/17/64. Born: Ireland. Occ.: Clerk. Res.: N.O. Age 18, single.
Campbell, Joseph, Pvt. En. 6/4/61, CM. Present to 9/62. Killed accidentally at Bristol, Va., 9/12/62. Born: England. Occ.: Sailor. Res.: N.O. Age 37, married.
Carlin, Barney, Pvt. En. 6/4/61, CM. Present to 5/62. AWOL, 5-6/62. Present, 6/62. Discharged 8/1/62. Born: Ireland. Occ.: Laborer. Res.: N.O. Age 20, single.

Carroll, James H., Pvt. En. 6/4/61, CM. Present to 7/62. Admitted to Chimborozo Hosp., Richmond, 7/11/62, typhoid fever, returned to duty 8/24/62. Record dated 2/10/65 at Petersburg states: "Deserted Aug. 1862." Born: New York. Occ.: Laborer. Res.: N.O. Age 20, single.

Charles, John, Sgt. En. 6/4/61, CM. Promoted from pvt to 4th sgt., 8/1/61. Died 2/1/63, cause and place unstated. Born: Ireland. Occ.: Laborer. Res.: N.O. Age 24, single.

Clark, John W., Pvt. En. 6/4/61, CM. Present to 1/62. Discharged to enter CS Navy, assigned to Merrimac crew, 1/10/62.

Clark, Michael, Pvt. En. 6/4/61, CM. Present to 5/64. Wounded at Wilderness, Va., 5/5/64. Roll for 5-8/64 states: "Absent, disabled and detailed." Retired to Invalid Corps at Danville, Va., 3/6/65. Born: New Jersey. Occ.: Laborer. Res.: N.O. Age 19, single.

Cluskey, John, Pvt. En. 6/4/61, CM. Present to 6/62. Captured at Strasburg, Va., 6/2/62. POW, Fort Delaware, Del., exchanged 8/5/62. Record dated 2/10/65 at Petersburg states: "Died Nov. 10, 1863." Born: Ireland. Occ.: Laborer. Res.: N.O. Age 24, single.

Cole, James, Pvt. En. 6/4/61, CM. Present to 8/62. Deserted 8/1/62. Born: N.O. Occ.: Laborer. Res.: N.O. Age 19, single.

Coleman, John, Pvt. (aka Coalman) En. 6/4/61, CM. Present to 6/62. Severely wounded at Gaines' Mill, Va., 6/27/62. Absent wounded to 10/63. Present, 9-12/63. Absent detailed, 5-7/64. Severely wounded at Winchester, Va., 9/17/64. Present, 2-3/65. Captured at Petersburg, Va. (attack on Fort Stedman), 3/25/65. POW, Point Lookout, Md., released 6/24/65. Born: Ireland. Occ.: Laborer. Res.: N.O. Age 24, single, 5'5", blue eyes, brown hair, light complexion.

Coleman, John W., pvt. En. 6/4/61 as musician. Present to 10/64. Mortally wounded at Cedar Creek, Va., 10/19/64, died 11/7/64. Occ.: Painter. Res.: N.O. Age 27, married.

Comfort, Cain, Pvt. En. 6/4/61, CM. Present to 1/63. Wounded at Sharpsburg, Md., 9/17/62. AWOL, 1-8/63. Rejoined from desertion, 8/27/63. Absent sick, 9/63 to 2/64. Severely wounded at Spotsylvania C.H., Va., 5/12/64. Absent wounded to 2/65. Surrendered at Appomattox C.H., 4/9/65. Born: Ireland. Occ.: Laborer. Res.: N.O. Age 19, single.

Connolly, James A., Pvt. (aka Conley) En. 2/25/62, N.O. Captured at Strasburg, Va., 6/2/62. POW, Fort Delaware, Del., exchanged 8/5/62. Present 11/62 to 7/63. Captured at Gettysburg, 7/3/63. POW, Fort Delaware. Died at Fort Delaware 4/1/65, hemorrhage of lungs. Born: N.O. Occ.: Carpenter. Res.: N.O. Age 27, 5'4", gray eyes, brown hair, light complexion.

Connolly, John, Pvt. (aka Conley) En. 6/4/61. Present to 6/62. Captured at Strasburg, Va., 6/2/62. POW, Fort Delaware, Del. Joined U.S. Army, was recaptured by Confederate forces at Bristoe Station, Va., 10/13/63. Found guilty by court martial of desertion and joining the enemy, 11/20/63. Executed by firing squad at Mine Run, Va., 11/30/63. Born: N.O. Occ.: Carpenter. Res.: N.O. Age 20, single.

Conner, Thomas O., Pvt. En. 2/27/62. Killed at Gaines' Mill, Va., 6/27/62. Born: Ireland. Occ.: Sailor. Res.: N.O. Age 32, married.

Cunningham, James, Pvt. En. 6/4/61, CM. Present to 2/62. Deserted 2/1/62. Born: Ireland. Occ.: Laborer. Res.: N.O. Age 26, single.

Curry, Daniel, Pvt. (aka Currie) En. 6/4/61, CM. Present to 4/63. Absent detailed as guard in hospital in Richmond, 4/63 to 1/64. Present, 1/64 to 7/64. Mortally wounded at Battle of Monocacy and captured at Frederick, Md., 7/10/64, died at USA Genl. Hosp., Frederick, 7/16, gun-shot fracture of right leg, amputated. Buried in grave no. 250, Mount Olivet Cemetery, Frederick, Md. Born: Ireland. Occ.: Laborer. Res.: N.O. Age 30, single.

Deavitt, Owen, Sgt. En. 6/4/61, CM. Promoted from pvt. to 5th sgt., 1/1/62. Present to 10/62. Discharged on surgeon's certificate of disability, South Carolina Hosp., Charlottesville, Va., 10/7/62, due to vericose veins of leg. Born: Ireland. Occ.: Screwman. Res.: N.O. Age 26, single, 5'9", blue eyes, light hair, fair complexion.

Delmore, Chares, Pvt. En. 6/4/61, CM. Present to 7/62. Wounded at Malvern Hill, Va., 7/1/62. Admitted to Gen. Hosp. No. 7, Richmond, 7/22/62, wounded in left hip, furloughed 30 days on 9/10/62. Recorded as deserted, 12/1/62. Born: Germany. Occ.: Tailor. Res.: N.O. Age 22, married.

Dirr, Leon, Pvt. (aka Derr, Deir) En. 2/24/62, N.O. Present to 5/63. Wounded at Fredericksburg, Va., 5/4/63. Present, 7/63 to 9/64. Captured at Fisher's Hill, Va., 9/22/62. POW, Point Lookout, Md., exchanged 2/10/65. Born: Germany. Occ.: Laborer. Res.: N.O. Age 25, single.

Driscoll, Daniel, Pvt. En. 3/12/62, N.O. Present to 2/64. Record dated 2/10/65 at Petersburg, states: "Deserted Feb. 22, 1864." Born: N.O. Occ.: Laborer. Res.: N.O. Age 19, single, 5'6", gray eyes, dark hair, dark complexion.

Duffy, Michael, Pvt. En. 6/4/61, CM. Present to 8/62. Recorded as deserted, 8/62. Admitted to Louisiana Hosp., Richmond, 1/30/63, returned to duty 3/14/63. Wounded at Fredericksburg, Va., 4/29/63. Admitted to Louisiana Hosp., Richmond, 5/1/63, died 5/22/63 of wounds received at Fredericksburg. Born: Ireland. Occ.: Laborer. Res.: N.O. Age 21, single.

Dunn, P. G., Pvt. En. 6/4/61, CM. Present to 9/62. Wounded and captured at Sharpsburg, Md., 9/17/62. POW, Fort McHenry, Md., exchanged 10/13/62. Admitted to CSA Hosp., Farmville, Va., wounded in forearm, 2/2/63. Absent, detailed to drill conscripts at Camp Moore, La., 5/63 to 3/64. Recorded as deserted, 4/64. Born: Ireland. Occ.: Laborer. Res.: N.O. Age 22, single.

Eagan, Michael, Quartermaster Sgt. En. 6/4/61, CM, as cpl. Promoted to 4th sgt., 7/1/61. Promoted to QM sgt., 11/1/61. Absent detached as wagonmaster, 5-10/62. Transferred by appointment to QM sgt., 10/62. Severely wounded at Monocacy, Md., 7/9/64. Record dated 2/10/65 at Petersburg, Va., states: "Present as QMS up to 8th Oct. 1864." Surrendered at Appomattox C.H., 4/9/65, with rank of pvt., listed as "Courier at Brigade Hd. Qrtrs."
Estlow, Godfrey, Pvt. En. 6/4/61, CM. Present to 9/62. Absent sick, 9-10/62. Present, 11/62 to 3/63. Absent sick, 3-4/63. Present 5/63 to 9/64. Severely wounded at Kernstown, Va., 7/24/64. Died at Gen. Hosp., Mt. Jackson, Va., 9/7/64, gunshot wound in chest. Born: England. Occ.: Sailor. Res.: N.O. Age 30, married.
Farrell, Thomas, Pvt. En. 6/4/61, CM. Present to 7/62. Absent sick, 7-8/62. Recorded as deserted, 10/62. Born: N.O. Occ.: Laborer. Res.: N.O. Age 23, single.
Finnegan, James, Pvt. En. 6/4/61, CM. Present to 5/62. Wounded at Winchester, 5/25/62. Captured at Winchester hospital, 6/2/62, transferred to Baltimore, Md. POW, Steamer Katskill, exchanged 8/5/62. Present to 5/63. Captured at Fredericksburg, Va., 5/4/63. POW, Old Capitol Prison, Washington, took oath of allegiance, 5/12/63. Born: Ireland. Occ.: Laborer. Res.: N.O. Age 26, single.
Finnegan, John, Pvt. En. 6/4/61, CM. Present to 6/62. Wounded at Port Republic, Va., 6/9/62. Captured at Middletown, Va., 9/12/62. POW, Fort Delaware, Del., exchanged 11/10/62. Wounded at Fredericksburg, Va., 5/4/63. AWOL, 7-8/63. Absent under arrest, 9/63 to 2/64. Present, 3-4/64. Absent on furlough, 5-8/64. Born: Ireland. Occ.: Laborer. Res.: N.O. Age 27, single.
Finnegan, Patrick, Pvt. En. 6/4/61, CM. Present to 1/63. Absent, detached to Pioneer Corps, Early's Division, 1-5/63. Present 5-10/63. Absent detached, Pioneer Corps, 11/63 to 4/65. Born: Ireland. Occ.: Laborer. Res.: N.O. Age 27, single.
Fitzgerald, Edward, Pvt. En. 2/25/62, N.O. Present to 8/62. Discharged 8/1/62. Born: Ireland. Occ.: Carpenter. Res.: N.O. Age 38, married.
Fitzgerald, Thomas, Pvt. En. 6/4/61, CM. Present to 6/62. Captured at Woodstock, Va., 6/2/62. POW, Steamer Coatzacoalcos, exchanged 8/5/62. Present, 9/62 to 9/64. Severely wounded and captured at Winchester, 9/19/64. POW, Point Lookout, Md., exchanged 10/28/64. Captured in hospital, Richmond, 4/3/65, transferred to Point Lookout, 5/2/65. Admitted to USA Genl. Hosp., Point Lookout, gunshot wound in left leg, fractured tibia. Released on taking oath of allegiance at USA Genl. Hosp., Staunton, Va., 8/25/65. Born: Ireland. Occ.: Carpenter. Res.: N.O. Age 19, single.
Flatman, Nicolas, Pvt. En. 3/1/62, N.O. Absent sick in hospital, 5-6/62. Deserted, 7/62. Born: N.O. Occ.: Tinsmith. Res.: N.O. Age 18, single, 5'5", dark eyes, light hair, light complexion.
Flemming, John, Pvt. En. 6/4/61, CM. Present to 7/62. Killed at Malvern Hill, Va., 7/1/62. Born: Ireland. Occ.: Laborer. Res.: N.O. Age 21, single.
Flood, Edward, Lt. En. 6/4/61, CM. Present to 9/62. Promoted from 2nd jr. lt. to 2nd lt., 11/7/62. Absent, detatched to Division Pioneer Corps., 9/62 through 4/65.
Francisco, Joseph, Pvt. En. 3/10/62, N.O. Present to 8/62. Captured at Manassas, Va., 8/29/62, took oath of allegiance. Born: Havana, Cuba. Occ.: Tailor. Age 18, single.
Gaisser, Godfrey, Ensign. (aka Gaizer) En. 2/21/62, N.O. Present to 11/63. Captured at Rappahannock Station, Va. 11/7/63. POW, Point Lookout, Md., exchanged 3/10/64. Present, 5/64 to 4/65. Promoted from pvt. to cpl., 2/1/63. Promoted to ensign, 11/26/64. Surrendered at Appomattox C.H., Va., April 9, 1865. Born: N.O. Occ.: Clerk. Res.: N.O. Age 19, single.
Gallagher, James, Pvt. En. 6/4/61, CM. Present to 6/62. Killed at Port Republic, Va., 6/9/62. Born: Ireland. Occ.: Laborer. Res.: N.O. Age 32, single.
Graham, James, Pvt. En. 6/4/61. Present to 9/62. Wounded at Chantilly, Va., 9/1/62. Absent sick, 11-12/62. Present, 1-5/63. Captured at Fredericksburg, Va., 5/3/63. POW, Old Capitol Prison, Washington, transferred to Fort Delaware, Del. Severely wounded at Spotsylvania C.H., 5/12/64. Admitted to Jackson Hosp., Richmond, 5/18/64, died 6/6/64. Record dated 2/10/65 at Petersburg, Va., states: "Died at Lynchburg from wound received May 12 at Spotsylvania." Born: New York. Occ.: Sailor. Res.: N.O. Age 20, single.
Grasser, G. Pvt. En. 6/4/61, CM. Present to 6/63. Mortally wounded at Winchester, Va., 6/14/63, died 7/25/63. Born: France. Occ.: Laborer. Res.: N.O. Age 22, single.
Green, James, Pvt. En. 6/4/61, CM. Present to 9/62. Deserted 9/1/62. Born: England. Occ.: Sailor. Res.: N.O. Age 30, married.
Hale, Adolph, Pvt. En. 6/4/61, CM. Present to 8/63. Deserted, 8/27/63. Born: N.O. Occ.: Laborer. Res.: N.O. Age 22, married.
Hale, Joseph, Pvt. En. 3/19/62, N.O. Present to 6/62. Killed at Gaines' Mill, Va., 6/27/62. Born: Switzerland. Occ.: Laborer. Res.: N.O. Age 22, single, 5'6", gray eyes, dark hair, dark complexion.
Halper, William, Sgt. En. 6/4/61,CM. Present to 6/63. Wounded at Winchester, 6/14/63. Absent wounded 6-9/63. Promoted from pvt. to sgt., 4/64. Born: Ireland. Occ.: Slater. Res.: N.O. Age 22, single.
Harding, William H., Sgt. En. 6/4/61, CM. Present to 6/62. Promoted to sgt., 5/62. Wounded at Gaines' Mill, Va., 6/27/62. Wounded and captured at Sharpsburg, Md., 9/17/62. POW, Fort McHenry, Md. Absent detailed at Richmond as cooper, 5/63 to 3/64. Captured at Wilderness, Va., 5/5/64, transferred to Elmira, N.Y., 8/15/64, exchanged 2/25/65. Born: England. Occ.: Sailor. Res.: N.O. Age 21, single.

Hare, Peter, Lt. En. 6/4/61, CM. Promoted from pvt. to sgt., 7/61. Promoted to 2nd Lt., 11/25/62. Present to 11/63. Captured at Rappahannock Station, Va., 11/7/63. POW, Old Capitol Prison, Washington, transferred to Johnson's Island, Sandusky, Ohio, 11/14/63, released 6/13/65. Born: Ireland. Occ.: Clerk. Res.: N.O. Age 20, single, 5'7", blue eyes, dark hair, light complexion.

Healey, Patrick, Cpl. En. 6/4/61, CM. Present to 6/62. Wounded at Gaines' Mill, Va., 6/27/62. Roll for 3-4/63 states: "Deserted hospital at Lynchburg, Va. in Dec. 1862, supposed to have enlisted in Capt. White's P. Rangers." Born: Ireland. Occ.: Laborer. Res.: N.O. Age 20, single.

Hearty, O., Pvt. (aka O. Hardy) En. 6/4/61, CM. Present to 10/61. Detached as teamster in regimental wagon yard, 10/61 to 11/62. Present, 11/62 to 3/63. Detached as teamster, 3-9/64. Admitted to USA Depot Field Hospital, Winchster, Va., 9/19/64, neck wound. Record dated 2/10/65 at Petersburg, Va., states: "Killed at the Battle of Winchester, Sept. 19, 1864." Born: Ireland. Occ.: Laborer. Res.: N.O. Age 23, single.

Heine, Gustave, Pvt. En. 2/21/62, N.O. Present to 6/62. Captured at Strasburg, Va., 6/2/62. Roll for 7-8/62 states: "Deserted." Born: Germany. Occ.: Clerk. Res.: N.O. Age 21, single.

Henry, William, Pvt. En. 6/4/61, CM. Present to 6/62. Wounded at Port Republic, Va., 6/9/62. Absent wounded, 6-12/62. Roll for 3-4/63 states: "Deserted hosp. at Lynchburg, Va. in Dec. 1862, supposed to have enlisted in Capt. White's P. Rangers." Born: England. Occ.: Laborer. Res.: N.O. Age 25, single.

Hickey, Pierce P., Sgt. En. 3/4/62, N.O. Present to 8/62. Wounded at Manassas, Va., 8/29/62. Absent wounded, 9-10/62. Promoted to sgt., 11/1/62. Wounded at Fredericksburg, Va., 5/4/63. Absent wounded, 6-11/63. Present 11/64 to 6/64. Absent sick, 7-11/64. Present 2-4/65. Surrendered at Appomattox C.H., 4/9/65. Born: Ireland. Occ.: Slater. Age 19, blue eyes, fair hair, light complexion, 5'9".

Higgins, William, Pvt. En. 6/4/61, CM. Present to 6/62. Wounded at Port Republic, Va. 6/9/62. Wounded at Chantilly, Va., 9/1/62. Absent wounded 9/62 to 2/64. Recorded as deserted, 4/64. Born: N.O. Occ.: Laborer. Res.: N.O. Age 23, single.

Houlahan, Edward, Pvt. En. 6/4/61,CM. Present to 8/62. Wounded at Bristoe Station, Va., 8/27/62. Absent wounded to 3/63. Roll for 3-4/63 states: "Deserted hospital at Lynchburg, Va. in Dec. 1862, supposed to have enlisted in Capt. White's P. Rangers." Record dated 2/10/65 at Petersburg, Va., states: "Killed at Bristoe Station, August 27, 1862." Born: Ireland. Occ.: Carpenter. Res.: N.O. Age 28, single.

Howard, William, Sgt. En. 6/4/61, CM as 2nd Sgt. Promoted to Quarter Master Sgt., 8/1/61. (Later rolls give rank as pvt.) Roll for 5-6/63 states: "Joined June 9 from desertion." Wounded at Winchester, 6/14/63. Absent wounded, 7-8/63. Present 9/63 to 4/64. Transferred to CS Navy 4/4/64. Born: Maine. Occ.: Sailor. Res.: N.O. Age 28, single.

Hughes, Michael, Pvt. En. 3/11/62, N.O. Present to 5/63. Wounded at Fredericksburg, Va., 5/4/63. Present 5/63 to 11/63. Captured at Rappahannock Station, Va., 11/7/63. POW, Point Lookout, Md., paroled 3/9/64. Captured at Wilderness, 5/5/64. POW, Point Lookout, exchanged 2/13/65. Born: Ireland. Occ.: Shoemaker. Res.: N.O. Age 19, single, 5'3", gray eyes, light hair, light complexion.

Hughes, Thomas, Pvt. En. 6/4/61, CM. Present to 6/62. Wounded at Port Republic, Va., 6/9/62. Absent wounded, 6-12/62. Present, 1-4/63. Absent detailed as hospital steward at Winchester, 5/63. Captured at Winchester, 7/26/63, paroled at Jordan Springs, Va., 8/2/63. Born: England. Occ.: Laborer. Res.: N.O. Age 20, single.

Hurley, John, Pvt. En. 2/27/62, N.O. Present to 6/62. Severely wounded at Gaines' Mill, Va., 6/27/62. Absent wounded, 6/62 to 3/63. Present 3/63 to 1/64. Roll for 3-4/64 states: "Absent sick, permanently disabled." Retired to Invalid Corps, at Montgomery, Ala., 12/7/64. Record dated 2/10/65 at Petersburg, states: "Lost right arm at the Battle of Gaines' Mill, June 27, 1862." Born: Lyons, France. Occ: Hatter. Res.: N.O. Age 18, single, 5'9", gray eyes, light hair, light complexion.

Hutchings, Andrew J., Pvt. En. 6/4/61, CM. Present to 9/62. Wounded at Sharpsburg, Md., 9/17/62. Captured near Sharpsburg, 9/30/62. POW, Fort McHenry, Md., paroled 11/12/62. Present 11/62 to 7/63. Captured at Williamsport, Md., 7/14/63. POW, Seminary Hosp., Hagerstown, Md., forwarded to Fort Delaware, Del., 8/15/63, exchanged 3/7/65. Paroled at Montgomery, Ala., 5/9/65. Born: Alabama. Occ.: Carpenter. Res.: N.O. Age 24, single.

Kiehbordt, Charles, Pvt. (aka Kehbort) En. 2/26/62, N.O. Present to 6/62. Captured at Strasburg, Va., 6/2/62. Record dated 2/10/65 at Petersburg states: "Deserted June 1, 1862." Born: Bavaria. Occ.: Tobacconist. Res.: N.O. Age 24, single.

Kingston, John, Pvt. En. 6/4/61, CM. Present to 12/61. Discharged on certificate of disability, 12/14/61. Letter in file signed by Capt. William Manning dated 12/11/61 states Kingston had false right eye, which was inflamed. Born: England. Occ.: Laborer. Age 22, 5'10", gray eyes, dark hair, dark complexion. (Note: This John Kingston appears to have re-enlisted in 2/62, as his description is identical to the John Kingston listed below. The two are listed separately in Compiled Service Records, but appear to be the same man.)

Kingston, John, Pvt. En. 2/24/62, N.O. Present to 9/62. Absent sick, 9-10/62. Present 11/62 to 5/63. Wounded in left wrist at Fredericksburg, Va., 5/4/63. Absent wounded 5-9/63. Absent furlough, 11-12/63. AWOL, 1-2/64. Present, 3-5/64. Mortally wounded at Wilderness, Va., 5/5/64, died 5/9/64. Record dated 2/10/65 at Petersburg states: "Died 9th May from wound rec'd at Battle of Wilderness." Born: England. Occ.: Barkeeper. Res.: N.O. Age 22, single, 5'10", gray eyes, black hair, dark complexion.

Kirk, Samuel O., Lt. En. 6/4/61, CM, as 2nd Lt. Promoted to 1st Lt., 11/7/62. Present to 6/62. Absent sick, 6/62 to 3/63. Detached to duty at Passport Office, Richmond, 3/63 to 1/64. Honorably retired by special order, 1/19/64. Born: New York. Res.: N.O.

Kirwin, Michael, Pvt. En. 6/4/61, CM. Present to 6/63. Captured at Fredericksburg, Va., 5/3/63. POW, Fort Delaware, Del., exchanged 6/3/63. Killed at Winchester, Va., 6/14/63. Born: Ireland. Occ.: Laborer. Res.: N.O. Age 20, single.

Little, William, Pvt. En. 6/4/61, CM. Present to 8/62. Killed at Bristoe Station, Va., 8/27/62. Born: Ireland. Occ.: Laborer. Res.: N.O. Age 28, married.

Lucas, William, Pvt. En. 6/4/61, CM. Present to 5/62. Absent, detached as teamster, 5-10/62. Present, 11/62 to 5/63. Wounded at Fredericksburg, Va., 5/4/63. Absent wounded 5-9/63. Present 9/63 to 3/64. Absent sick, 3/64 to 3/65. Surrendered at Appomattox C.H., 4/9/65. Born: Ireland. Occ.: Laborer. Res.: N.O. Age 27, single.

Lyons, Michael, Pvt. En. 6/4/61, CM. Present to 6/62. Wounded at Gaines' Mill, Va., 6/27/62. Bartlett's *Military Record of Louisiana* lists a Pvt. M. Lyons as killed at Cold Harbor (Gaines' Mill) Va., 6/27/62. Lyon's Compiled Service Records do not confirm this, however. The last muster roll in his file, for 5-6/62, states: "Absent wounded at Gaines' Mill, June 27, 1862." Record dated 2/10/65 at Petersburg states: "Deserted Aug. 30, 1862." Born: Ireland. Occ.: Laborer. Res.: N.O. Age 20, single.

Madden, Patrick, Pvt. En. 6/4/61, CM. Present to 11/62. Absent sick, 11/62 to 3/63. Roll for 3-4/63 states: "Deserted hospital at Lynchburg, Va., in Dec., 1862. Supposed to have enlisted in Capt. White's P. Rangers." Born: Ireland. Occ.: Laborer. Res.: N.O. Age 26, single.

Maher, John, Pvt. En. 6/4/61, CM. Present to 5/62. Wounded at Winchester, Va., 5/25/62. Absent wounded, 5/62 to 5/63. Present, 5-11/63. Absent, detailed to regimental wagon yard, 11/63 to 3/64. Absent, detailed on guard duty, Staunton, Va., 3/64 to 2/65. Record dated 2/10/65 states: "Deserted to the enemy Feb. 1, 1865." Born: New Jersey. Occ.: Laborer. Res.: N.O. Age 21, single.

Manning, Edward, Pvt. En. 6/4/61,CM. Present to 9/62. Wounded at Chantilly, Va., 9/1/62. Present to 5/63. Captured at Fredericksburg, Va., 5/4/63. POW, Old Capitol Prison, Washington, exchanged 6/3/63. Present 6/63 to 4/64. Transferred to CS Navy, 4/25/64. Born: Ireland. Occ.: Laborer. Res.: N.O. Age 20, single.

Mathews, Pat, Pvt. En. 6/4/61, CM. Present to 10/62. Absent sick, 11-12/62. Present 1-4/63. Wounded at Fredericksburg, Va., 4/29/63. Roll for 5-6/63 states: "Died May 26, 1863 from wounds received at Fredericksburg, April 29, 1863."

Mathews, Peter T., Pvt. En. 6/4/61, CM. Present to 7/62. Roll for 7-8/62 states: "Deserted." Record dated 2/10/65 at Petersburg states: "Deserted July 30, 1862." Born: Ireland. Occ.: Laborer. Res.: N.O. Age 20, single.

McAdams, James, Pvt. En. 6/4/61, CM. Present to 8/62. Captured at Manassas, Va., 8/29/62. POW, exchanged at Fort Monroe, 9/21/62. Present to 5/63. Wounded at Fredericksburg, Va., 5/3/63. Admitted to Genl. Hosp. No. 9, Richmond, 11/8/63, transferred to Jackson Hosp., Richmond, 11/20/63, wound in right hip, Minie ball. Present to 5/64. Killed at Wilderness, Va., 5/6/64. Born: Ireland. Occ.: Laborer. Res.: N.O. Age 22, single.

McCluskey, William, Pvt. En. 3/14/62, N.O. Present to 7/62. Wounded at Malvern Hill, Va., 7/1/62. Admitted to Chimborazo Hosp., Richmond, 7/4/62, gunshot wound in right shoulder, transferred to Charlottesville hosp., 9/10/62, transferred to Lynchburg hosp., 11/11/62. Died at Ladies Hosp., Columbia, S.C., 3/13/63. Born: N.O. Occ.: Shoemaker. Res.: N.O. Age 19, single.

McCue, Michael, Pvt. En. 6/4/61, CM. Present to 9/62. Absent sick, 9-10/62. Present, 11/62 to 5/63. Absent sick, 5-6/63. Present, 7/63 to 3/64. Absent detailed at commissary department, 3-8/64. Surrendered at Appomattox C. H., Va., 4/9/65. Born: Ireland. Occ.: Laborer. Res.: N.O. Age 22, single.

McGurty, Hugh, Pvt. En. 6/4/61, CM. Present to 6/62. Severely wounded at Gaines' Mill, Va., 6/27/62, compound fracture of right femur (thigh). Absent wounded to 4/64. Absent on furlough, disabled, 5-8/64. Retired on certificate of disability, 7/64. Paroled at Montgomery, Ala., 5/17/65.

McMahon, Con., Cpl. En. 6/4/61, CM, as pvt. Promoted to cpl., 3/1/64. Present to 6/63. Absent sick, 6-7/63. Present 11/63 to 6/64. Admitted Genl. Hosp. No. 9, Richmond, 6/8/64. Absent sick thereafter. Born: New York. Occ.: Barkeeper. Res.: N.O. Age 19, single.

McNamara, Thomas, Pvt. En. 6/4/61, CM. Present to 7/62. Recorded as deserted, 7/62. Record dated 2/10/65 at Petersburg states: "Deserted July 21, 1862." Born: New York. Occ.: Corker. Res.: N.O. Age 25, single.

Mealey, Patrick, Pvt. En. 6/4/61, CM. Present to 6/62. AWOL, 5-6/62. Recorded as deserted, 8/62. Roll for 3-4/63 states: "Deserted June 11, 1862. Joined Mar. 8, 1863 from desertion." Present, 3/63 to 1/64. Record dated 2/10/65 at Petersburg states: "Deserted Jan. 22, 1864." Surrendered at Winchester, Va., 5/6/65, paroled at Staunton, Va., 5/14/65. Born: Ireland. Occ.: Laborer. Res.: N.O. Age 18, single.

Mohan, Edward, Pvt. En. 3/10/62, N.O. Present to 8/62. Recorded as deserted, 8/62. Record dated 2/10/65 at Petersburg states: "Deserted Aug. 28, 1862." Born: Canada. Occ.: Shoemaker. Res.: N.O. Age 18, single.

Monahan, Daniel, Pvt. En. 2/22/62, N.O. Present to 7/62. Captured at Malvern Hill, Va., 7/1/62. POW, Fort Columbus, New York Harbor, 7/3/62, transferred to Fort Delaware, Del., 7/9/62. Record dated 2/10/65 at Petersburg states: "Deserted Aug. 28, 1862." Born: Ireland. Occ.: Laborer. Res.: N.O. Age 25, single.

Murphy, George, Pvt. En. 2/26/62, N.O. Present to 5/63. Wounded at Fredericksburg, Va., 5/4/63. Wounded at Gettysburg, 7/2/62. Absent wounded, 7-10/63. Present 10/63 to 5/64. Captured at Wilderness, Va., 5/5/64. POW,

Point Lookout, Md., transferred to Elmira, N.Y., 8/15/64, exchanged 2/25/65. Surrendered at Staunton, Va., 5/1/65. Born: Ireland. Occ.: Laborer. Res.: N.O. Age 18, single.

Murphy, Thomas, Musician. En. 2/26/62, N.O. Present all rolls , 2/62 to 2/65. Born: Ireland. Occ.: Laborer. Res.: N.O. Age 17, single.

Murray, Patrick, Pvt. En. 6/4/61, CM. Present to 2/63. Roll for 1-2/63 states: "Killed accidentally at Camp near Liberty Church, Feb. 13, 1863." Born: Ireland. Occ.: Laborer. Res.: N.O. Age 22, single.

Myers, John, Pvt. En. 6/4/61, CM. Present to 8/62. Recorded as deserted, 8/62. Record dated 2/10/65 at Petersburg states: "Deserted Nov. 7, 1863." Born: Ireland. Occ.: Sailor. Res.: N.O. Age 27, married.

Nuss, Michael, Pvt. (aka Ness) En. 2/24/62, N.O. Present to 7/62. Absent sick, 7-10/62. Admitted CSA Hosp., Charlottesville, Va., 7/21/62, returned to duty 10/3/62, fever. Present, detailed as teamster to regimental wagon train, 8/62 to 2/65. Born: Germany. Occ.: Laborer. Res.: N.O. Age 28, single.

Noonan, James, Pvt. En. 6/4/61, CM. Present to 6/62. Killed at Port Republic, Va., 6/9/62. Born: Ireland. Occ.: Laborer. Res.: N.O. Age 22, single.

O'Hay, Christie, Pvt. (aka Ohay, Oha) En. 6/4/61, CM. Present to 3/62. Absent sick, 3-4/62. Present to 6/62. Roll for 5-6/62 states: "Absent, taken prisoner at Strasburg, June 2, 1862." Recorded as deserted, 8/62. Born: Ireland. Occ.: Laborer. Res.: N.O. Age 22, single.

Ohm, Alfred, Pvt. En. 3/4/62, N.O. Present to 6/62. Roll for 5-6/62 states: "Absent, taken prisoner at Strasburg, June 2, 1862." Record dated 2/10/65 at Petersburg states: "Deserted June 1st, 1862." Born: Hamburg, Germany. Occ.: Sailor. Res.: N.O. Age 22, single.

Pierce, Thomas, Pvt. En. 6/4/61, CM. Present to 8/62. Killed at Bristoe Station, Va., 8/27/62. Born: Ireland. Occ.: Laborer. Res.: N.O. Age 28, married.

Plunkett, Mathew, Pvt. En. 2/23/62, N.O. Present to 9/62. Wounded at Chantilly, Va., 9/1/62. Absent wounded, 9-12/62. Present, 1-2/63. Absent sick, 3-8/63. Present, 9-10/63. Absent detailed as guard at Gordonsville, Va., 11/63 to 3/64. Present, 3/64 to 3/65. Discharged at Petersburg, Va., on surgeon's certificate of disability, 3/17/65, chronic rheumatism. Born: Ireland. Occ.: Laborer. Res.: N.O. Age 49, married, 5'6", hazel eyes, gray hair, light complexion.

Russell, George C. En. 6/4/61, CM.Present to 4/63. Wounded at Fredericksburg, Va., 4/29/63. Present to 4/65. Surrendered to Provost Marshall, Army of Potomac, at Petersburg, Va., 3/31/65, transferred to Washington, took oath of allegiance, 4/4/65. Born: Albany, N.Y. Occ.: Printer. Res.: N.O. Age 28, single.

Russell, James, Pvt. En. 8/17/62 at Cedar Mountain, Va., as musician. Present all rolls, 8/62 to 4/65. Record dated 2/10/65 at Petersburg, states: "Re-enlisted Aug. 1, 1862, from Wheat's Battalion." Surrendered at Appomattox C.H., Va., 4/9/65. Born: N.O. Occ.: Laborer. Res.: N.O. Age 18, single.

Ryan, Daniel, Sgt. En. 11/19/62 at Front Royal, Va., as pvt. Promoted to sgt., 5/1/64. Present to 5/64. Wounded at Gettysburg, 7/2/63. Captured at Wilderness, Va., 5/5/64. POW, Point Lookout, Md., exchanged 2/10/65. Record dated 2/10/65 at Petersburg states: "Re-enlisted Aug. 1, 1862, from Wheat's Battalion." Born: Ireland. Occ.: Laborer. Res.: N.O. Age 20, single.

Seales, B.W., Sgt. En. 6/4/61, CM, as pvt. Promoted to cpl., 7/62, to 4th sgt., 9/17/62. Present to 6/63. Wounded at Winchester, Va., 6/14/63. Absent wounded, 6-7/63. Present to 5/64. Captured at Wilderness, Va., 5/5/64. POW, Point Lookout, Md., died at Point Lookout, 7/23/64. Born: Baton Rouge, La. Occ.: Cooper. Res.: N.O. Age 32, married.

Shay, Daniel, Pvt. (aka Shea) En. 2/21/62. Present to 6/62. Wounded at Gaines' Mill, Va., 6/27/62. Absent wounded, 6/62 to 2/64. Recorded as deserted, 3-4/64. Record dated 2/10/65 at Petersburg states: "Deserted May 12, 1863. Lost left arm at Battle of Gaines Mills." Born: Ireland. Occ.: Laborer. Res.: N.O. Age 18, single.

Shay, Michael, Pvt. En. 6/10/61, CM. Present to 8/62. Wounded at Bristoe Station, Va., 8/27/62. Present to 6/63. Severely wounded at Winchester, Va., 6/14/63, gunshot wound in jaw. Absent wounded to 4/64. Wounded at Spotsylvania C.H., Va., 5/12/64. Admitted CSA Hosp., Richmond, 5/17/64, furloughed 60 days from 6/7/64. Record dated 2/10/65 at Petersburg states: "Died Aug. 25, 1864 from wound received at Battle of Spotsylvania." Born: Ireland. Occ.: Laborer. Res.: N.O. Age 22, single.

Shelby, T.G., Pvt. En. 6/4/61, CM. Present to 9/62. Recorded as deserted, 9/14/62. Born: N.O. Occ.: Bar keeper. Res.: N.O. Age 20, single.

Slighting, Frederick, Pvt. En. 2/21/62, N.O. Present to 11/62. Absent sick, 11/62 to 3/63. Present, 3-4/63. Absent sick, 5/63 to 2/64. Recorded as deserted, 3-4/64. Record dated 2/10/65 at Petersburg states: "Deserted Sept. 20, 1862." Born: N.O. Occ.: Carpenter. Res.: N.O. Age 20, single.

Smith, Alexander, Pvt. En. 6/4/61, CM. Present to 9/62. Captured at Frederick, Md., 9/12/62. POW, Fort Delaware, Del., exchanged 11/10/62. Record dated 2/10/65 at Petersburg states: "Deserted Aug. 30, 1862." Born: New York. Occ.: Clerk. Res.: N.O. Age 22, single.

Smith, Horne, Musician. En. 6/19/61 at Lynchburg, Va., as musician. Present to 8/62. Record dated 2/10/65 at Petersburg states: "Deserted Aug. 1, 1862." Born: Ireland. Occ.: Laborer. Res.: N.O. Age 23 single.
Smith, Michael, Cpl. En. 6/4/61, CM, as cpl. Present to 8/62. Severely wounded in thigh at Bristoe Station, Va., 8/27/62. Absent wounded, 8/62 to 10/63. Discharged at Orange C.H., Va., 10/30/63, disabled. Born: Ireland. Occ.: Laborer. Res.: N.O. Age 34, married.
Sullivan, John, Pvt. (No. 1) En. 6/4/61, CM. Present to 6/62. Roll for 5-6/62 states: "Killed accidentally at Beaver Dam, Va., June 23, 1862." Born: Ireland. Occ.: Laborer. Res.: N.O. Age 27, single.
Sullivan, John, Pvt. (No. 2) En. 6/4/61, CM. Present to 6/62. Captured at Woodstock, Va., 6/6/63. POW, steamer Coatzacoalas, exchanged 8/5/62. Roll for 7-8/62 states: "Deserted." Born: Ireland. Occ.: Laborer. Res.: N.O. Age 20, single.
Sullivan, Michael, Pvt. En. 6/4/61, CM. Present to 9/62. Severely wounded and captured at Sharpsburg, Md., 9/17/62. Admitted USA Genl. Hosp., Frederick, Md., 10/3/62, transferred to Gen. Hosp. No. 1, Frederick, 1/15/63, died 4/22/63, compound fractures of both thighs. Born: Ireland. Occ.: Laborer. Res.: N.O. Age 28, single. Born: Ireland. Occ.: Laborer. Res.: N.O. Age 28, single.
Sylvester, Richard, Sgt. En. 6/4/61, CM, as ordnance sgt. Absent sick, 7-10/61. Roster of Non-commissioned officers, undated, states "died" as reason for office expiring. Record dated 2/10/65 at Petersburg states: "Honorably discharged 1861." Occ.: Finisher. Res.: N.O. Age 24, single.
Thompson, Mathew, Pvt. En. 6/4/61, CM. Present to 9/62. Recorded as deserted 9/1/62. Born: New York. Occ.: Laborer. Res.: N.O. Age 23, single.
Torpey, James, Pvt. En. 6/4/61, CM. Present to 6/62. Wounded at Gaines' Mill, Va., 6/27/62. Recorded as deserted, 7-8/62. Rejoined from desertion, 7/30/63. Present to 1/64. Recorded as deserted, 1/29/64. Born: N.O. Occ.: Tinsmith. Res.: N.O. AGe 19, single.
Wagner, Peter, Pvt. En. 3/4/62, N.O. Present to 5/64. Wounded at Gettysburg, 7/2/63. Captured at Wilderness, 5/5/64. POW, Point Lookout, Md., exchanged 2/18/65. Born: France. Occ.: Barber. Res.: N.O. Age 19, single.
Waldron, James, Pvt. En. 6/4/61, CM. Present to 6/62. Captured at Woodstock, Va., 6/2/62. POW, place unstated, exchanged 8/2/62. Present to 6/63. Wounded at Winchester, Va., 6/14/63. Absent wounded, 6-8/63. Present to 5/64. Captured at Spotsylvania C.H., Va., 5/18/64. POW, Point Lookout, Md., transferred to Elmira, N.Y., 7/3/64, exchanged 2/25/65. Born: N.O. Occ.: Laborer. Res.: N.O. Age 19, single.
Waldron, John, Pvt. En. 8/12/62 at Cedar Run, Va. Present to 11/62. Absent sick, 11/62 to 3/64. Captured at Fredericksburg, Va., 4/29/63. POW, Fort Delaware, Del. Admitted USA Post Hosp., Fort Delaware, 5/14/63, died 5/18/63, pneumonia. Born: N.O. Occ.: Laborer. Res.: N.O. Age 22, married.
Wallace, Thomas, Pvt. En. 6/4/61, CM. Present to 8/62. Severely wounded in shoulder at Manassas, Va., 8/29/62. Absent wounded, 8/62 to 1/63. Roll for 1-2/63 states: "Assigned to duty at camp of instruction at Richmond." Record dated 2/10/65 at Petersburg states: "Died at Mobile, Apr. 20, 1864." Born: Ireland. Occ.: Laborer. Res.: N.O. Age 20, single.
Walsh, John, Sgt. En. 6/4/61, CM. Present to 11/61. Discharged 11/1/61. Born: Ireland. Occ.: Laborer. Res.: N.O. Age 22, single.
Walsh, James W., Pvt. En. 6/19/61 at Lynchburg, Va. Present to 11/63. Captured at Rappahannock Station, Va., 11/7/63. POW, Point Lookout, Md., exchanged 3/10/64. Absent on furlough, 3-4/64. Absent sick, 5-9/64. No record thereafter. Born: N.O. Occ.: Laborer. Res.: N.O. Age 24, single.
Walsch, Lawrence, Pvt. (aka Welch) En. 6/4/61, CM. Present to 6/62. Wounded at Gaines' Mill, Va., 6/27/62. Absent wounded to 8/63. Absent, detailed as nurse in Richmond, 8/63 to 2/65. Retired to Invalid Corps at Ashville, N.C., 2/20/65. Born: Germany. Occ.: Shoemaker. Res.: N.O. Age 18, single.
Weibell, William, Pvt. Present to 6/62. Captured at Woodstock, Va., 6/2/62. POW, place unstated, exchanged 8/5/62. Present to 12/62. Wounded at Fredericksburg, Va., 12/13/62. Absent wounded, 1-2/62. Captured at Fredericksburg, 4/29/63. POW, Fort Delaware, exchanged 6/3/63. Present, 6/63 to 5/64. Captured at Wilderness, Va., 5/5/64. POW, Point Lookout, Md., exchanged 2/15/65. Born: N.O. Occ.: Bar keeper. Res.: N.O. Age 19, single.
Wilson, M. Pvt. En. 6/4/61, CM. Present to 6/62. Wounded at Port Republic, Va., 6/9/62. Absent wounded, 6-12/62. Roll for 3-4/63 states: "Deserted hospital at Lynchburg in Dec. 1862. Supposed to have enlisted in Capt. White's P. Rangers."
Wilson, William, Pvt. En. 6/4/61, CM. Present to 6/62. Wounded at Gaines' Mill, Va., 6/27/62. Absent wounded 6-9/62. Record dated 2/10/65 at Petersburg states: "Deserted Sept. 1, 1862." Born: Ireland. Occ.: Laborer. Res.: N.O. Age 20, single.
Young, Michael, Pvt. En. 6/4/61, CM. Present to 6/62. Wounded at Port Republic, Va., 6/9/62. Absent wounded, 6-12/62. Present 1-5/63. Absent sick, 5-6/63. Absent detailed as nurse in hospital, 7/63 to 6/64. Record dated 2/10/65 at Petersburg states: "Died at Staunton, Va., June 1, 1864, from sickness." Born: Ireland. Occ.: Laborer. Res.: N.O. Age 25, single.
Zeller, George, Pvt. En. 6/4/61, CM. Present to 9/62. Mortally wounded in abdomen at Sharpsburg, Md., 9/17/62, died 9/18/62 at Grove's Warehouse. Buried in Rose Hill Cem., Hagerstown, Md. Born: N.O. Occ.: Butcher. Res.: N.O. Age 24, single.

Appendix B

Birthplaces of 6th Louisiana men

Company	Louisiana	Ireland	Germany	Other Foreign	CSA	USA	NR
A: 120	1	—	—	—	5	2	112
B: 162	2	128	11	9	1	3	8
C: 148	84	8	8	2	15	7	24
D: 104	18	20	6	4	27	11	18
E: 90	16	15	13	5	6	22	13
F: 115	1	100	—	6	—	4	4
G: 109	2	13	61	13	—	4	16
H: 109	13	31	17	16	3	14	15
I: 106	1	89	—	3	1	4	8
K: 125	21	60	7	15	2	13	7
F&S: 27	4	4	—	—	5	4	10
Totals:							
1,215	163	468	123	73	65	88	235

Keys: The numbers following the company letters indicate the total number of men who served. CSA—Confederate states other than Louisiana. USA—States of the Union. NR—not recorded. Other foreign includes England (30), France (13), Scotland (9), Canada (9), Norway (2), Switzerland (2) and Belgium, Cuba, Mexico, Sweden, Malta, Holland, Italy and Wales (one each).

Appendix C

Statistical Summary:
Casualties, Deaths, Desertions, Discharges, etc.

	Killed	Died	Deserted	Oaths	Discharged	Inv.	ACH
Company A (120)	16	30	16	21	3	2	11
Company B (162)	23	11	30	22	21	5	9
Company C (147)	20	13	18	9	25	7	6
Company D (104)	10	15	21	5	21	3	2
Company E (90)	7	3	37	3	14	5	5
Company F (115)	20	4	32	8	8	6	2
Company G (109)	20	6	26	21	2	0	4
Company H (109)	19	13	24	13	11	2	1
Company I (106)	18	12	27	13	3	3	3
Company K (125)	23	13	38	3	8	4	7
Field & Staff	4	0	0	0	2	1	2

The table is based on the author's search of compiled service records of the 6th Louisiana at the National Archives. Killed includes those mortally wounded in battle. The "Died" column counts deaths from disease, accidents and one execution. The "Oaths" column tallies those who were captured and took the oath of allegiance as prisoners of war. "Discharged" counts discharges of all kinds, including those for sickness and disability as well as discharges of those who claimed alien (non-citizen) status. The "Inv" column records those who were disabled by wounds and retired to the Invalid Corps. "ACH" shows the number of men of each company who surrendered at Appomattox Court House, Va., on April 9, 1865. Totals are not given because the tally from the service records is necessarily incomplete, as not every death, desertion, discharge, etc. is recorded. Though incomplete, the table permits comparative looks at the various categories of one company against another.

Appendix D

List of Engagements of the 6th Louisiana Volunteer Regiment

1861	Date	Killed	Wounded	Missing
First Battle of Manassas	July 21	0	0	0
1862				
Front Royal	May 23	0	0	
Middletown	May 24	0	0	
First Battle of Winchester	May 25	5	27	
Cross Keys	June 8	1	0	
Port Republic	June 9	23	55	
Gaines's Mill	June 27	8	39	
Malvern Hill	July 1	12	27	
Cedar Mountain	Aug. 9	0	1	
Bristoe Station	Aug. 2	10	25	
Second Manassas	Aug. 28-29	7	13	
Chantilly	Sept. 1	9	32	
Harper's Ferry	Sept. 15	0	0	
Sharpsburg	Sept. 17	17	41	
Fredericksburg	Dec. 13	1	1	2
1863				
Fredericksburg	Apr. 29-May 4	20	68	99
Second Winchester	June 14	12	55	
Gettysburg	July 1-2	8	34	14
Raccoon Ford	Sept. 14	3	—	
Rappahannock Station	Nov. 7	2	—	89
Mine Run	Nov. 27	0	3	3
1864				
Battle of the Wilderness	May 5-6	5	6	61
Spotsylvania	May 10-18	4	8	20
Cold Harbor	June 3	2	5	—
Monocacy	July 9	7	12	—

Kernstown	July 24	3	3	
Third Winchester	Sept. 19	3	4	—
Cedar Creek	Oct. 19	2	3	3
1865				
Hatcher's Run	Feb. 5-6	—	1	
Fort Stedman	March 25	1	2	3
Appomattox Court House	April 9		—	—

This list of casualties is by no means a complete tally of all the men killed in battle in the 6th Louisiana. It omits many minor engagements and skirmishes in which men were killed, wounded and captured. It is presented in this form merely to provide a comparative look at the level of casualties in various major engagements. It clearly shows, for instance, that the bloodiest fights for the 6th Louisiana were Port Republic, Second Fredericksburg, Sharpsburg, and Second Winchester, in that order. The numbers in the Killed column include the mortally wounded who died after the battle. The figures are based on the author's examination of compiled service records of the regiment at the National Archives, official returns of casualties, contemporary published casualty lists, diaries and memoirs, and other sources. The numbers here presented will frequently differ from officially reported casualties, as they incorporate information available after such official returns were prepared.

Endnotes

Irish Rebels, Confederate Tigers

Preface

1. Historical Memoranda in *Record Roll, 6th Louisiana Volunteer Regiment, 1861-65,* in Louisiana Historical Association Collection (LHAC), Howard-Tilton Memorial Library, Tulane University, New Orleans, La. Major Manning's brief history of the regiment is dated "Station near Petersburg, Date March 13th, 1865." It was written in response to orders from Col. Henry M. Favrot, who was sent to Virginia in February 1865 by Louisiana's Confederate governor, Henry W. Allen, to compile the records of all Lousisiana troops fighting in Virginia. In addition to his overview of the regiment, Manning and other remaining officers wrote similar historical memos on each company of the 6th Louisiana.

2. Richard N. Current, (ed.) *Encyclopedia of the Confederacy*, vol. 2, pp. 822-823.

3. Unidentified newspaper clipping in Seymour family scrapbook, Seymour Papers, Schoff Civil War Collection (SCWC), William L. Clements Library, University of Michigan, Ann Arbor.

Introduction

1. *Daily Picayune*, New Orleans, April 28, 1861, typescript copy in the Military Library, Office of the Adjutant General, Jackson Barracks, New Orleans, vol. 103, p. 123. Hereinafter footnoted as "Jackson Barracks."

2. John D. Winters, *The Civil War in Louisiana* (Baton Rouge, 1963), p. 3-21.

3. Ella Lonn, *Foreigners in the Confederacy* (Chapel Hill, N.C. 1940), p. 481. The 1860 census figures cited by Lonn show New Orleans with 24,398 Irish-born residents and 19,752 Germans. These figures represented 14.5% and 11.7%, respectively, of the city's population of 168,000. Richmond, by contrast, had only 2,244 Irish-born residents, out of its 1860 population of 37,910. More than 38 % of New Orleans' population in 1860 was foreign-born.

4. Earl F. Niehaus, *The Irish in New Orleans, 1800-1860* (Baton Rouge, 1965), pp.25-26.

5. Ibid, p. 34. Randall M. Miller, "The Enemy Within: Some Effects of Foreign Immigrants on Antebellum Southern Cities," *Southern Studies*, vol. 24, no.1, pp. 30-53.

6. Niehaus, *The Irish in New Orleans*, pp. 44-51. Miller, "The Enemy Within," pp. 33-35. Irish and free blacks, Niehaus writes, "constituted two hostile labor forces" struggling for jobs. "In the long run the Irishman forced the Negro out of his job. . . .the lasting result was a deep hostility." According to Miller, "it was the immigrants' initial willingness to underbid local labor for any and all work that drove free blacks into despair and poverty. Immigrants ignored local taboos about 'nigger work' and crashed into free black monopolies everywhere, from drayage to barbering."

7. Niehaus, *The Irish in New Orleans,* pp. 32-36.

8. Ibid, p.158.

9. *Daily Picayune*, May 24, 1861, in Louisiana Militia archives, Jackson Barracks, vol. 105, p. 88.

10. Louisiana militia archives, Jackson Barracks, vol. 103, p. 131; vol. 105, p. 15.

11. Ella Lonn, *Foreigners in the Confederacy,* pp. 105-112; Thomas W. Brooks and Michael D. Jones, *Lee's Foreign Legion*, (Gravenhurst, Ontario, 1995) pp. 2-7.

12. Terry L. Jones, *Lee's Tigers* (Baton Rouge, La., 1987) pp. 233-254; Record roll, 6th Louisiana Volunteer Regiment, Louisiana Historical Association Collection, Tulane University. Compiled Service Records, 6th Louisiana Volunteers, record group 109, File M320, rolls 163-173, National Archives. Though the other cited sources were consulted, the statistics on birthplaces of men in the regiment were derived primarily though the author's own examination of the microfilmed service records of each and every recorded member of the regiment. Of 1,215 officers and men who served in the regiment during the war, birthplaces are known of 980, as follows: Ireland, 468; Louisiana, 163;

Germanic states, 123; other foreign, 73; northern (Union) states, 88; other Confederate states, 65. The 235 men whose birthplaces are unrecorded probably included some Irish, a few other foreign borns, and a mix of Louisianians, Northerners and other Southerners.

13. Winter, *The Civil War in Louisiana*, pp. 21-23. Louisiana Militia archives, Jackson Barracks, "Encyclopedia of Forts, Posts, Named Camps and Other Military Installations in Louisiana," pp. 122-123.

14. Compiled service records, 6th Louisiana Volunteers, record group 109, File M320, rolls 163-173. Lonn, *Foreigners in the Confederacy*, pp. 108-109. Eight of the 6th Louisiana's ten companies enlisted for the duration of the war while two—the Calhoun Guards (B) and Tensas Rifles (D)—were composed of 12-months volunteers, most of whom re-enlisted for the war in 1862.

15. "The Death of Col. Seymour," *The Commercial Bulletin*, July 30, 1862.

16. Unidentified newspaper clipping in Seymour family Civil War scrapbook, in Seymour Papers, Schoff Civil War Collection, William L. Clements Library, University of Michigan, Ann Arbor.

17. Ibid.

18. George Zeller to family, May 25, 1861, in 6th Louisiana regiment file, Antietam National Battlefield Park library, Sharpsburg, Md.

19. *Sunday Delta*, May 19, 1961, in Louisiana Militia archives, Jackson Barracks, vol. 104, p. 119

20. Diary of George P. Ring, Louisiana Historical Association Collection, Howard-Tilton Memorial Library, Tulane University. Hereinafter, documents from this collection will be footnoted as LHAC, Tulane.

Chapter One – To the Front: Virginia

1. Freeman, *Lee's Lieutenants*, vol. 1, p. 41. OR 2, p. 440, pp. 943-944. The other regiments in the brigade were the 5th and 6th Alabama.

2. Seymour to Secretary of War, June 29, 1961, in Letters Received by Secretary of War, file M437, roll 5, National Archives.

3. "Reminiscences of the War," unidentified newspaper clipping in Seymour family scrapbook, Seymour Papers, Schoff Civil War Collection, William L. Clements Library, University of Michigan, Ann Arbor. Hereinafter footnoted as SCWC, Michigan.

4. Nicholas Herron to Anne McCarthy, July 9, 1861, in Herron Family correspondence, LHAC, Tulane.

5. *The Daily True Delta*, New Orleans, July 2, 1861.

6. Freeman, *Lee's Lieutenants*, vol. 1, pp. 45-48.

7. Nicholas Herron to Anne McCarthy, Aug. 18, 1861, LHAC, Tulane. Record of events, 6th Louisiana, record group 109, file M861, roll 23, National Archives.

8. Compiled service records, 6th Louisiana, file M320, roll 165, National Archives. Demaign's service record states that he enlisted at Camp Moore in the Orleans Rifles, Company H, but was transferred to Company A on the order of Colonel Seymour on July 1, 1861. He was a transplanted Northerner, born in Maine, and lived in New Orleans before the war.

9. Herron to McCarthy, Aug. 18, 1861.

10. Freeman, *Lee's Lieutenants*, vol. 1, pp. 51-57.

11. OR, vol. 2, 536-537. Freeman, *Lee's Lieutenants,* vol. 1, pp. 53-58.

12. Ring Diary, LHAC, Tulane.

13. Herron to McCarthy, Aug. 18, 1861, LHAC, Tulane.

14. Record of Events, 6th Louisiana, record group 109, file M861, roll 23, National Archives

15. Herron to McCarthy, Aug. 18, 1861, LHAC, Tulane.

16. J. Hogan to "Friend Corbett," Aug. 12, 1861, in 6th Louisiana Regiment file, Manassas National Battlefield Park library.

17. Confederates lost 387 dead and 1,582 wounded vs. 481 killed and 1,124 wounded for the Federals. Another 1,500 Federals were captured.

18. Jones, *Lee's Tigers*, 21. Walker was a 44-year-old graduate of West Point who served in the U.S. Army in the war with Mexico, where he was seriously wounded. He joined the Confederate service in May and was named brigade commander late in August 1861.

19. Isaac G. Seymour to "Sir," September 2, 1861, Isaac Gurdon Seymour papers, SCWC, Michigan.

20. Ibid.

21. Record of events, 6th Louisiana, record group 109, file M861, roll 23, National Archives.

22. Nicholas Herron to Ann McCarthy, Aug. 31, 1861, LHAC, Tulane.

23. William E. Trahern, biographical memoir dated Sept. 21, 1926, Virginia Historical Society collection, p. 20. Hereinafter footnoted as Trahern memoir, VHS.

24. Trahern memoir, VHS, p. 22. Upon his accidental death, Tenney was succeeded as captain by 1st Lt. David Bucker, a 31-year-old, Mississippi-born resident of St. Joseph, La., who would be wounded three times in battle and captured to spend the final months of the war in Northern prisons.

25. Record of events, 6th Louisiana, record group 109, File M861, Roll 23, National Archives.

26. Report of Sick and Wounded, 6th Louisiana, muster roll files (originals), National Archives.

27. Ibid.

28. Henry E. Handerson, *Yankee in Gray*: The Civil War Memoirs of Henry E. Handerson (Cleveland, 1962), p. 90. Handerson's letter to his father is dated Septemer 11, 1861.

29. Letters of George M. Lee in "A Collection of Louisiana Confederate Letters," The Louisiana Historical Quarterly, vol. 26, October 1943, pp. 937-974.

30. Ibid. Disease took a much higher toll among the men from the more isolated rural areas, who probably had not been exposed much to contagious illness, than it did from the volunteers from New Orleans, who perhaps built up some immunity to such scourges. In Company A, from Union and Sabine Parishes, fully 25% of the men died of disease during the war (30 out of 120), while among the Irishmen of Company F, less than 4% died of disease (4 of 115 men.) These figures, derived from the author's study of compiled service records of the regiment, suggest the country men were much more vulnerable to fatal bugs than the city men, who had lived through waves of epidemics in New Orleans.

31. George Zeller letter to family dated September 4, 1961, in 6th Louisiana regimental file, Antietam National Battlefield Park, Sharpsburg, Md.

32. Record of events, Company I, 6th Louisiana, record group 109, file M 861, roll 23, National Archives. Jones, *Lee's Tigers*, p. 56.

33. George Zeller to family, October 2, 1861, in 6th Louisiana regimental file, Antietam National Battlefield Park.

34. Theodore H. Woodard to John Prichard, November 14, 1861, Louisiana Room Papers Collection, Eleanor S. Brockenbrough Library, Museum of the Confederacy, Richmond, Va. Woodard was among the first to enlist in Tensas Parish, tearing down a recruiting poster and rushing home to tell his parents of his plans to enlist, according to an undated letter from his daughter, Annie Woodard Fox, in the Confederate Museum file. The only son in a family of ten, Woodard was "petted, spoiled, humored" and loved adventure, going off to war with his body-servant, Champ, who "at the sound of the first gun. . .melted away into the night," according to Mrs. Fox. He survived the war and returned to live and raise a family in Tensas Parish.

35. Alison Moore, *The Louisiana Tigers*, (Baton Rouge, La., 1961) pp. 49-51. The quote refers to Senator John Slidell, the powerful secessionist whose political influence dominated Louisiana at the time.

36. Richard Taylor, *Destruction and Reconstruction: Personal Experiences of the Late War* (New York, 1879), p. 18. The page numbers cited herein are from the Bantam Books edition of 1992.

37. T. Michael Parrish, *Richard Taylor: Soldier Prince of Dixie* (Chapel Hill, 1992) p. 135. Walker returned to the army in March 1863, rising to major general and serving with distinction until he was killed July 22 in the opening phase of the battle of Atlanta.

38. Parrish, *Richard Taylor*, pp. 37-39. David French Boyd, *Reminiscences of the War in Virginia* (Baton Rouge: Louisiana State University) p.13.

39. Handerson, *Yankee in Gray,* p. 91. Parrish, *Richard Taylor*, pp. 72, 140.

40. Zeller to family, letter dated "the 12th, 1861", in 6th Louisiana regimental file, Antietam National Battlefield Park. Parrish, *Richard Taylor;* p, 141. Jones, *Lee's Tigers*, pp. 40-41.

41. Taylor, *Destruction and Reconstruction*, p. 20.

42. Nicholas Herron to Anne McCarthy, Dec. 20, 1961, LHAC, Tulane.

43. Herron to McCarthy, Feb. 13, 1862, LHAC, Tulane.

44. Zeller to family, January 9, 1862, Antietam file.

45. Zeller to family, February 8, 1862, Antietam file.

46. Freeman, *Lee's Lieutenants,* vol. 1, pp. 130-136.

47. Freeman, *Lee's Lieutenants*, vol. 1, p. 140. Jones, *Lee's Tigers*, p. 65. Handerson, *Yankee in Gray*, p. 39.

48. Ben Hubert to Letitia Bailey, March 13, 1862, in Ben Hubert Papers, Special Collections Library, Duke University, Durham, N.C. Hereinafter cited as Hubert Papers, SCL-DU.

49. Herron to McCarthy, March 6, 1862, LHAC, Tulane.

50. Hubert to Bailey, March 17, 1862, from Rappahannock Station, Va., Hubert Papers, SCL-DU.

Chapter Two – Service With Stonewall Jackson: The Shenandoah Valley

1. Ring diary, LHAC, Tulane. Besides the Louisianians, Ewell's Division consisted of the brigades of Brig. Gens. Arnold Elzey, Isaac Trimble and George H. Steuart.

2. Robert G. Tanner, *Stonewall in the Valley*. (Mechanicsburg, Pa., 1996 edition) p. 3, pp. 33-38.

3. Freeman, *Lee's Lieutenants*, vol. 1, p. 347. Taylor, *Destruction and Reconstruction*, p. 34. Ring diary, LHAC, Tulane.

4. Isaac G. Seymour to William J. Seymour, May 2, 1862, in Seymour papers, SCWC, Michigan

5. Tanner, *Stonewall in the Valley*, pp. 122, 141.

6. Ring diary, LHAC, Tulane. Taylor, *Destruction and Reconstruction*, pp. 43-46.

7. Isaac G. Seymour to William J. Seymour, May 2, 1862, in Seymour papers, SCWC, Michigan.

8. Ibid.

9. Unidentified New Orleans newspaper clipping in Seymour scrapbook, Seymour Papers, SCWC, Michigan.

10. Ibid.

11. Letter to Ewell dated Camp Bragg, Va., May 7, 1862 in 6th Louisiana muster roll files, National Archives. The letter was almost certainly written by Capt. William Monaghan, later colonel of the regiment, as its elegant script exactly matches the distinctive handwriting found on other letters and documents signed by Monaghan, who surely must have had the reputation of being as gifted with the pen as he was with the sword.

12. 6th Louisiana record roll, LHAC, Tulane. Arthur W. Bergeron Jr., *Guide to Louisiana Confederate Military Units, 1861-1865* (Baton Rouge, 1989) pp. 84-85. Thomas Redmond, another Irishman, succeeded Strong as captain of Company B, and Louisiana-born Allen M. Callaway succeeded McArthur in command of Company A. According to General Ewell's aide, Capt. Campbell Brown, Maj. George Christy of the 6th Louisiana "failed of a re-election" at the reorganization of May 9. Christy then "was appointed Chief of Ordinance to the division with the rank of Captain of Engineers," Brown wrote in a memo composed in 1862 and published in SHSP 10, pp. 255-261.

13. Tanner, *Stonewall in the Valley*, pp. 179-210.

14. Ibid, p.233.

15. Ring diary, LHAC, Tulane. Taylor, *Destruction and Reconstruction*, p.48.

James Cooper Nisbet, *Four Years on the Firing Line* (Jackson, TN.) 1963. p. 41.

16. William Allen, *History of the Campaign of Gen. T.J. (Stonewall) Jackson in the Shenandoah Valley of Virginia*, SHSP, vol. 43, pp. 205-207.

17. OR 12, pt. 1, p. 701. Tanner, *Stonewall in the Valley*, pp. 249-250.

18. OR 12, pt. 1, p. 555, p. 559.

19. OR 12, pt. 1, 702. Laura Virginia Hale, *Battle of Front Royal*, Warren County Civil War Centennial Commission, Front Royal, Va. 1962. p. 10.

20. OR 12, pt. 1, p. 555, p.702. Hale, *Battle of Front Royal,* pp. 10-11. Ring diary, LHAC, Tulane.

21. Hale, *Battle of Front Royal*, p. 14. Lucy Rebecca Buck, *Sad Earth, Sweet Heaven: The Diary of Lucy Rebecca Buck* (Birmingham, Ala., 1992) pp. 78-79. Hereinafter cited as Buck diary.

22. OR 12, pt. 1, p. 702. *Tanner, Stonewall in the Valley*, p. 261. Ring diary, LHAC, Tulane. Allan, *SHSP* 43, p. 209.

23. OR 12, pt. 1, pp. 556-557.

24. Taylor, *Destruction and Reconstruction,* pp. 54-55. OR 12, pt. 1, p. 557.

25. OR 12, pt. 1, p. 562, p. 702.
26. OR 12, pt. 1, p. 702, p. 800. Ring diary, LHAC, Tulane.
27. OR 12, pt. 1, p. 559, p. 703. Allan, *SHSP* 43, p. 211.
28. OR 12, pt. 1, p. 546. Tanner, *Stonewall in the Valley*, pp. 267-270.
29. Tanner, *Stonewall in the Valley*, p. 270.
30. Ibid, p. 271.
31. OR 12, pt. 1, p. 703. Taylor, *Destruction and Reconstruction*, page 56.
32. Tanner, *Stonewall in the Valley*, p. 272. Taylor, *Destruction and Reconstruction*, p. 57.
33. OR12, pt. 1, p. 800. Ring diary, LHAC, Tulane.
34. OR 12, pt. 1, p. 596.
35. OR 12, pt. 1, 705. Tanner, *Stonewall in the Valley*, pp. 279-282.
36. Tanner, *Stonewall in the Valley*, pp. 282-284. Taylor, *Destruction and Reconstruction*, p. 59.
37. Taylor, *Destruction and Reconstruction*, p. 59. Tanner, *Stonewall in the Valley*, p. 284.
38. OR 12, pt. 1, pp. 616-617, p. 619.
39. Taylor, *Destruction and Reconstruction*, pp. 59-60.
40. Taylor, *Destruction and Reconstruction*, p. 60. Worsham, *One of Jackson's Foot Cavalry*, p. 46.
41. Jones, *Lee's Tigers*, p. 79. Tanner, *Stonewall in the Valley*, p. 285. Taylor, *Destruction and Reconstruction*, pp. 60-61, 91-92. OR 12, pt. 1, pp. 616-617, p. 619-620.
42. Freeman, *Lee's Lieutenants*, vol. 1, p. 402, quoting the diary of Mrs. Hunter McDonald, wife of a Confederate colonel.
43. Nisbet, *Four Years on the Firing Line*, p. 46. Douglas, *I Rode with Stonewall*, p. 58. OR 12, pt. 1, p. 705.
44. Douglas, *I Rode with Stonewall*, p. 59.
45. Ring to wife, June 14, 1862, LHAC, Tulane.
46. OR 12, pt. 1, p. 780. Ring to wife, June 7, 1862, LHAC, Tulane University. In addition to McArthur, the 6th Louisiana's killed at Winchester included two Irish-born privates, Edward Doyle of Company D and Thomas A. Murphy of Company A, plus Pvt. Edward Butt of Company A and probably Pvt. Stephen Newport of Company I, also Irish. Newport is listed as killed in action at Winchester in Bartlett's *Military Record of Louisiana;* his compiled service records at the National Archives contain only a record of his presence on a muster roll in April 1862 and no record thereafter. Pvt. Patrick Gleason, an Irishman in Company I, sustained a severe shoulder wound and died weeks later. The wounded also included three officers: Captains Joseph Hanlon of Company I, Nathaniel G. Offutt of Company C, and Lieutenant Frank Clarke of Company G.
47. Ring to wife, June 7, 1862, LHAC, Tulane. *Confederate Veteran*, Vol. 6 (1898), p. 177 reports a postwar speech by former Capt. Blaney T. Walshe of Company I who described Hanlon's wound and said that the Irish-born New Orleanian "died shortly after the close of the war."
48. OR 12, pt. 1, p.801. Richardson received his promotion within weeks and was transferred out of the regiment.
49. Ring to wife, June 14, 1862, LHAC, Tulane.
50. Ring to wife, June 7, 1862 and June 14, 1862, LHAC, Tulane.
51. Ring to wife, June 14, 1862, LHAC, Tulane.
52. OR 12, pt. 3, p. 219-221. Tanner, *Stonewall in the Valley*, pp. 296-297.
53. Tanner, *Stonewall in the Valley*, p. 297.
54. OR 12, pt. 1, pp. 707-708. Tanner, *Stonewall in the Valley*, 329-336.
55. Taylor, *Destruction and Reconstruction*, p. 63. Tanner, *Stonewall in the Valley*, p. 331.
56. Taylor, *Destruction and Reconstruction*, p. 64. Jones, *Lee's Tigers*, pp. 81-82.
57. Tanner, *Stonewall in the Valley*, pp. 339-340. Taylor, *Destruction and Reconstruction*, pp. 64-69.
58. OR 12, pt. 1, pp. 649-650. G.F.R. Henderson, *Stonewall Jackson and the American Civil War*, 2 vols. (Secaucus, N.J., 1989 reprint) vol. 1, pp. 351-352. Tanner, *Stonewall in the Valley*, pp. 339-340. Taylor, *Destruction and Reconstruction*, pp. 68-70. In his report, Fremont did not identify the units routed by Taylor's flanking maneuver, referring only to "two small regiments" supported by eight guns. He claimed his loss in the two-hour skirmish was only seven wounded. Taylor, in his official re-

port, did not even mention the June 1 action west of Strasburg, though he recounted it in some detail in his memoirs. Henry Kyd Douglas referred to the affair as "a small skirmish and artillery duel" in his memoirs.

59. Taylor, *Destruction and Reconstruction*, pp.71-72.

60. Ibid, p. 72.

61. Ibid, p. 73.

62. Ibid, p. 73. Parrish, *Richard Taylor,* p. 194, p. 213. Taylor belittled the German-born Federal soldiers he encountered in the June 1 skirmish, arguing that Fremont had other troops—presumably American born—who could have stiffly resisted his flank attack.

63. George Ring to wife, June 7, 1862, LHAC, Tulane University. Compiled Service Records, file M320, rolls 163-173, National Archives. The estimate of at least 52 captured at Strasburg and Woodstock is based on the author's study of individual soldiers' war records. The predominance of the Irish and Germans in this large group of captured 6th Louisiana men raises the question of whether these foreign-born soldiers may have defected willingly, or offered themselves up for easy capture to get out of the fighting. The company that had the highest number captured at this time was Company G, composed mostly of German-born men. Companies B, H, and K, heavy with Irishmen, also lost large numbers. Some of these men returned to the regiment and served bravely later, but most took the oath and thus ended their participation in the war.

64. Taylor, *Destruction and Reconstruction*, pp. 73-75.

65. Ring to wife, June 7, 1862, LHAC, Tulane.

66. Ibid.

67. Freeman, *Lee's Lieutenants*, vol. 1, pp. 424-425.

68. Ring to wife, June 7, 1862, LHAC, Tulane.

Chapter Three – The 'Hell Spot': Port Republic

1. Henry Kyd Douglas, *I Rode with Stonewall*, p. 85.

2. Ring to wife, June 7, 1862, LHAC, Tulane.

3. Robert K. Krick, *Conquering the Valley: Stonewall Jackson at Port Republic*, (New York, 1996), pp. 40-53.

4. Douglas, *I Rode with Stonewall*, p. 85. Krick, *Conquering the Valley*, pp.67-70.

5. OR 12, pt. 1, p.713, p. 781. Henderson, *Stonewall Jackson,* p. 372-373. Krick, *Conquering the Valley*, pp. 139-140.

6. OR 12, pt. 1, pp. 795-596. Krick, *Conquering the Valley*, pp. 165-181. Krick devotes an entire chapter to the slaughter of the 8th New York, which he states "drained all of Fremont's initiative" for the remainder of the battle, which lasted until dark.

7. Krick, *Conquering the Valley*, p. 133, p. 149. Taylor, *Destruction and Reconstruction*, p. 78.

8. OR 12, pt. 1, pp. 801-802. Taylor, *Destruction and Reconstruction,* pp. 78-79.

9. OR 12, pt. 1, p. 802. James Cooper Nisbet, *Four Years on the Firing Line* (Jackson, TN., 1963) pp. 53-54.

10. Nisbet, *Four Years on the Firing Line,* p. 54.

11. OR 12, pt. 1, p. 802. Krick, *Conquering the Valley*, p. 252. Bartlett, *Military Record of Louisiana,* p. 61. Compiled service records, 6th Louisiana Volunteers, file M320, roll 172, National Archives.

12. OR 12, pt. 1, p. 797. Krick, *Conquering the Valley*, pp. 267-271.

13. "Taylor's Louisiana Brigade," *The Daily Picayune,* New Orleans, Sunday, June 10, 1866. This lengthy article, which describes in detail the role of the Louisianians at Port Republic, is unsigned and the author is unknown. Its vivid account suggests it could have been written only by a brigade member who participated in the battle. Hereinafter cited as "Taylor's Louisiana Brigade."

14. Krick, *Conquering the Valley*, p. 289. "Taylor's Louisiana Brigade."

15. Krick, *Conquering the Valley*, pp. 291-293.

16. Henry B. Kelly, *Port Republic*, (Philadelphia, 1886), pp. 15-16.

17. Kelly, *Port Republic*, p. 16. Taylor, *Destruction and Reconstruction*, p. 79. Krick, *Conquering the Valley*, p. 306, pp. 314-315. Though Taylor's official report, written two days after the battle, and

his memoirs, written many years later, seem to imply that he led the brigade throughout the advance, Kelly persuasively reports otherwise in his account. The 8th Louisiana commander advanced his regiment, followed by the 9th Louisiana and Wheat's battalion, to the front on the order of Jackson's aide without seeing or consulting Taylor, who came up later in company of the 6th Louisiana to take command just before the brigade made its attack.

18. Kelly, *Port Republic*, pp. 4-6. Krick, *Conquering the Valley*, p. 232-324.

19. OR 12, part 1, p. 691. Taylor, *Destruction and Reconstruction*, p. 79-80. Henderson, *Stonewall Jackson*, p. 379. Krick, *Conquering the Valley*, p. 309. The Port Republic battlefield, unspoiled by modern development, looked much the same in 1996 as it did in 1862. It is one of the prettiest places in the valley and remains largely unmarked, except for a sign along the Port Republic-to-Luray road (Route 340) and a well-marked path leading up the hill to the site of the Coaling, courtesy of the Association for the Preservation of Civil War Sites. For more detail, see Krick's *Conquering the Valley*

20. OR 12, pt. 1, pp. 695-696. Krick, *Conquering the Valley*, p. 323. Henderson, *Stonewall Jackson*, pp. 379-380.

21. OR 12, pt. 1, p. 714. Krick, *Conquering the Valley*, p. 318, p. 327.

22. Taylor, *Destruction and Reconstruction*, p. 80.

23. Ibid. Krick, *Conquering the Valley*, p. 335-337.

24. OR 12, pt. 1, p. 802. Taylor, *Destruction and Reconstruction*, p. 80. Taylor's post-war memoirs suggest that he was unaware that the 7th Louisiana had been detached by Jackson to reinforce Winder, but his official report, written two days after the battle, clearly states that the commanding general ordered him to "leave one regiment behind" for that purpose.

25. Kelly, *Port Republic*, p. 16-17. Krick, *Conquering the Valley*, pp. 348-349.

26. Kelly, *Port Republic*, p. 17. Krick, *Conquering the Valley*, pp. 350-352.

27. Kelly, *Port Republic*, pp. 17-18. Krick, *Conquering the Valley*, pp. 352-353. Taylor, *Destruction and Reconstruction*, p. 80. The jealous taste of post-war rivalry is evident in both Kelly's and Taylor's accounts. Kelly clearly seeks to show in his account that he, not Taylor, led most of the regiment up to the attack's jumping-off point, and appeared miffed that he never got credit for his part. Both Taylor's official report and his memoirs make no mention of Kelly's separate advance with most of the brigade and imply that Taylor led his men up the mountain as a body.

28. Krick, *Conquering the Valley*, p. 311, p. 405.

29. Kelly, *Port Republic*, p. 18. Krick, *Conquering the Valley*, pp. 356-362. "Taylor's Louisiana Brigade." Taylor, *Destruction and Reconstruction*, p. 80.

30. Taylor, *Destruction and Reconstruction*, pp. 80-81. Krick, *Conquering the Valley*, p. 405. "Taylor's Louisiana Brigade." Though other sources give the strength of the Louisiana Brigade as high as 2,500 men, Krick's painstakingly documented estimate of 1,700 involved in the attack on the Coaling is accepted here as the most accurate. Based on morning reports of June 11, 1862, just after the battle, and counting in the casualties of June 8-9, Krick's figures imply that the 6th Louisiana took about 480 men into the attack on the Coaling.

31. OR 12, part 1, p. 693, p. 697. "Taylor's Louisiana Brigade."

32. OR 12, pt. 1, p. 693. Krick, *Conquering the Valley*, pp. 407-498, p. 414.

33. "Taylor's Louisiana Brigade." Kelly, *Port Republic*, p. 19. Compiled service records, 6th Louisiana Volunteers, record group 109, file M320, roll 164.

34. "Sixteen Years After: The Squarest Battle of the War," *Detroit Weekly Free Press,* March 4, 1882, in Bound Volume 16, Record Group 55-B, LHAC, Tulane. Hereafter cited as "Sixteen Years After." The writer of this article is not identified.

35. Taylor, *Destruction and Reconstruction*, p. 81. "Sixteen Years After." "Taylor's Louisiana Brigade." Krick, *Conquering the Valley*, p. 411-412.

36. OR 12, pt. 1. p. 697. Kelly, *Port Republic*, p. 19.

37. Jones, *Lee's Tigers*, 88-89; Samuel D. Buck, *With the Old Confeds*, (Baltimore, 1925), p. 38.

38. OR 12, pt. 1, p. 692. "Taylor's Louisiana Brigade." Kelly, *Port Republic*, p. 20.

39. Krick, *Conquering the Valley*, pp. 426-428. "Sixteen Years After."

40. Krick, *Conquering the Valley*, pp. 428-429. Taylor, *Destruction and Reconstruction*, p. 81.

41. OR 12, pt. 1, p. 786. Taylor, *Destruction and Reconstruction*, p. 81. "Taylor's Louisiana Brigade." Krick, *Conquering the Valley*, p. 429, pp. 435-437.

42. OR 12, pt. 1, p. 700. Kelly, *Port Republic*, p. 21.

43. Taylor, *Destruction and Reconstruction*, p. 82.

44. OR 12, pt. 1, p. 787. Compiled Service Records, 6th Louisiana Infantry, File M320, Rolls 163-173. Bartlett, *Military Record of Louisiana*, p. 61. List of 6th Louisiana casualties at Port Republic, LHAC, Tulane. There is some inevitable and unresolvable conflict in various casualty lists for this battle, which the author has sought to sort out as best he can in his own list accompanying the text. Bartlett's list and the Tulane list of Port Republic also list a Pvt. A. Benito as killed in the battle, but no such name is found in the microfilmed service records at the National Archives. The Tulane list (but not Bartlett's) also includes a Pvt. C. White of Company G as killed, but service records do not confirm that. Pvt. John Modien, a native of Norway who enlisted in Company I in March 1862, is shown as killed on June 9, 1862, on the company's record roll at Tulane, but his name does not appear on Bartlett's list or the Tulane list of casualties at Port Republic. The stated birthplaces of the dead are based on the author's search of the regiment's compiled service records.

45. OR 12, pt. 1, p. 787, p. 690. Krick, *Conquering the Valley*, pp. 508-510.

46. OR 12, pt. 1, p. 803. Taylor, *Destruction and Reconstruction,* p. 82. Edward A. Moore, *The Story of a Canoneer under Stonewall Jackson*, (New York, 1907), p. 75. Krick, *Conquering the Valley*, 429-430.

47. Richmond *Whig*, June 18, 1862.

48. OR 12, pt. 1, p. 786, p. 715.

49. Jones, *Lee's Tigers*, pp. 91-92.

50. Ring to wife, June 14, 1862, from Camp Ashby, Va. LHAC, Tulane.

51. Parrish, *Richard Taylor*, p. 213. Concerning casualties, the 6th Louisiana had the most killed in the brigade, and the highest overall casualties among the units attacking the Coaling. However the 7th Louisiana, reflecting its desperate fight on the plain, had the highest overall casualties in the brigade—11 killed, 137 wounded, 24 missing, for a total of 172, according to Krick, nearly half of its strength.

52. Taylor, *Destruction and Reconstruction*, p. 82.

53. Ring diary, LHAC, Tulane. Taylor, *Destruction and Reconstruction*, p. 83.

Chapter Four – To the Peninsula: The Seven Days' Battle

1. Herron to Anne McCarthy, Feb. 13, 1862, LHAC, Tulane. Roanoke Island, a Confederate stronghold in North Carolina coastal waters, fell to a Federal amphibious assault on February 8, 1862, endangering Norfolk and opening a "back door" to Richmond.

2. George W. Cable, "New Orleans before the Capture," in *Battles and Leaders of the Civil War*, vol. 2, p. 15.

3. Winters, *The Civil War in Louisiana*, pp. 85-89.

4. Ibid, pp. 90-98.

5. Hubert to Letitia Bailey, from Rockingham County, Va., May 2, 1862, Hubert Papers, SCL-DU. The reference is to Maj. Gen. Mansfield Lovell, commander of the Confederate military department that included New Orleans. Hubert may have been able to overhear the Ewell remark cited because he had been detached to serve as an orderly at Taylor's brigade headquarters and thus was often in the presence of high ranking officers.

6. Isaac G. Seymour to William J. Seymour, May 2, 1862, Seymour papers, SCWC, Michigan. William J. Seymour, *The Civil War Memoirs of Captain William J. Seymour*, edited by Terry L. Jones, (Baton Rouge, 1991), pp. 3-4. Hereinafter cited as Seymour, *Memoirs*.

7. Ring to wife, June 14, 1862, LHAC, Tulane.

8. Hubert to Bailey, May 10, 1862, Hubert Papers, SCL-DU.

9. Winters, *The Civil War in Louisiana*, p. 132. The infamy of the Union commander in New Orleans must have made life uncomfortable for one 6th Louisiana soldier—Pvt. Benjamin R. Butler of Company C. One can just imagine the merciless ribbing he must have taken for sharing the hated name. According to his service record, Butler was appointed Sergeant Major of the regiment about July 15, 1862, and was discharged from the service on September 26 of that year on a surgeon's certificate of disability, owing to a gunshot wound in his thigh. The records do not state when or where Butler was wounded.

10. Taylor, *Destruction and Reconstruction*, pp. 85-87.

11. Stephen W. Sears, *To the Gates of Richmond*, (New York, 1992) p. 24

12. Clifford Dowdey, *The Seven Days: The Emergence of Lee*, (Boston, 1964) pp. 131-132. Freeman, *Lee's Lieutenants*, vol. 2, p. 244, p. 262. Jones, *Lee's Tigers*, pp. 93-96.

13. Freeman, *Lee's Lieutenants*, vol. 2, p. 468. Worsham, *One of Jackson's Foot Cavalry*, p. 54. Ring diary, LHAC, Tulane.

14. Taylor, *Destruction and Reconstruction*, p. 90. Parrish, *Richard Taylor*, p. 227. Parrish describes Taylor's ailment as an "attack of rheumatoid arthritis" which left his arms and legs "almost fully paralyzed."

15. Seymour to Sec. of War, June 29, 1861, in Letters Received by the Secretary of War, file M437, roll 5, National Archives. OR 11, pt. 1, p.621. Handerson, *Yankee in Gray*, p. 44.

16. Dowdey, *The Seven Days*, p. 196-197. Krick, *Conquering the Valley*, p. 287.

17. OR 11, vol. 2, pp. 498-499. Freeman, *Lee's Lieutenants*, p. 494-495. Henderson, *Stonewall Jackson*, vol. 2, pp. 9-11.

18. OR 11, pt. 2, pp. 834-835. Henderson, *Stonewall Jackson*, vol. 2, pp. 15-16. Dowdey, *Seven Days*, pp. 201-202. In his report, Jackson stated that "we distinctly heard" the sound of cannon announcing A.P. Hill's battle, but didn't explain his failure to come to Hill's aid. Brig. Gen. Isaac Trimble, in his report, "heard distinctly the volleys of artillery and musketry" coming from Mechanicsville and boldly added, "in my opinion we should have marched to the support of General Hill that evening." See OR 11, pt. 2, p. 553 and 614.

19. Sears, *To the Gates of Richmond*, pp. 206-209.

20. OR 11, pt. 1, pp. 54-55. OR 11, pt. 2, p. 272. Sears, *To the Gates of Richmond*, pp. 210-211.

21. OR 11, pt. 2, p. 605, p. 621. "Recollections of Gaines Mill," *Confederate Veteran*, vol. 7, p. 54.

22. Sears, *To the Gates of Richmond*, pp. 218-219, pp. 227-228.

23. Handerson, *Yankee in Gray*, pp. 44-45. Jones, *Lee's Tigers*, p. 102.

24. Handerson, *Yankee in Gray*, p. 45. Walshe, "Recollections of Gaines Mill." The Cold Harbor name caused considerable puzzlement then as now. It is nowhere near water, thus no harbor, nor was it cold, certainly not in June. It apparently derived from an old English term for an inn or tavern that was not heated. There was such a tavern at a crossroads called Old Cold Harbor—and to confuse things further—another one at a newer settlement called New Cold Harbor. Many contemporary accounts corrupted the name to "Coal Harbor" or "Cool Arbor." It would become notorious as the site of a costly Federal defeat on June 3, 1864.

25. OR 11, pt. 2, p. 224. OR 11, pt. 2, p. 492. Dowdey, *Seven Days*, p. 224. Sears, *To the Gates of Richmond*, pp. 213-215.

26. OR 11, pt. 2, p 492. Sears, *To the Gates of Richmond*, p. 213-215.

27. OR 11, pt. 2, pp. 836-837.

28. OR 11, pt. 2, p. 492, p. 605, p.837.

29. OR 11, pt. 2, p. 605. Walshe, "Recollections of Gaines' Mill."

Nisbet, *Four Years on the Firing Line*, p. 64.

30. Walshe, "Recollections of Gaines' Mill." Handerson, *Yankee in Gray*, p. 45, p. 96.

31. OR 11, pt. 2, p. 614. Handerson, *Yankee in Gray*, p. 96. Exactly which of Porter's troops the 6th Louisiana faced is a matter of some uncertainty. According to Robert E.L. Krick, historian at Richmond National Battlefield Park, the Louisiana Brigade attacked the right of Morell's division, probably in the area held by the brigade of Brig. Gen. Charles Griffin, composed of the 14th New York, 4th Michigan, 9th Massachusetts and 62nd Pennsylvania regiments. However, as Griffin's line weakened during the battle, some of McCall's Pennsylvania Reserves were fed into that position, and may have been there by the time the Louisiana Brigade attacked. The battlefield's detailed maps suggest the 3rd Pennsylvania Reserves was positioned near the point of Seymour's attack. Additionally, the position of the various Louisiana regiments in the brigade's line of battle is unknown.

32. Walshe, "Recollections of Gaines' Mill."

33. OR 11, pt. 2, p. 620. *The Commercial Bulletin*, New Orleans, July 30, 1862. Handerson, *Yankee in Gray*, p. 46. Handerson's account of Wheat's sudden and lonely death undercuts the well-told myth that Wheat cried out, "Bury me on the battlefield, boys!" as his last words. Seymour, too, fell without any legend-making utterance.

34. Handerson, *Yankee in Gray*, p. 45. Walshe, "Recollections of Gaines' Mill." Jones, *Lee's Tigers,* p. 104.

35. Walshe, "Recollections of Gaines' Mill

36. Handerson, *Yankee in Gray*, p. 46. Hood's Brigade was one of two in the division of Brig. Gen. W.H.C. Whiting, which joined Jackson's command in June after the Valley campaign ended. Besides three regiments from Texas, Hood's Brigade included the 18th Georgia and Hampton's Legion of South Carolina.

37. OR 11, pt. 2, p. 224-225. OR 11, pt. 1, pp. 55-56. Sears, *To the Gates of Richmond*, pp. 240-242. Dowdey, *Seven Days*, pp. 238-239.

38. OR 11, pt. 1, p. 225-226. OR 11, pt. 1, pp. 493-494. Dowdey, *Seven Days*, pp. 240-242.

39. OR 11, pt. 2, p. 41, p. 609. Besides Colonel Seymour, the 6th Louisiana men killed at Gaines' Mill (with their companies in parenthesis) were Sgt. Benjamin Stagg (C), Pvt. Otto Ludorf (G), Cpl. William F. Forkell (H) Pvt. John Cassidy (D), Pvts. Thomas O. Connor, Joseph Hale and, possibly, Michael Lyons, (K). Napier Bartlett's *Military Record of Louisiana* lists Pvt. M. Lyons as killed in the battle, but that is not confirmed in Lyons' compiled service records, which record him as wounded, and later deserting. Mortally wounded were Pvts. A.D. Cassidy (C) and Henry Shiller (G), who died not long after the battle, and Sgt. James K. McGuiness (B) who apparently died later, at an uncertain date. McGuinness was listed as wounded, but Company B records list him as killed at Gaines' Mill. Nearly all of the dead were immigrants—four from Ireland, three from Germany, one from Switzerland. Only Stagg was native of Louisiana.

40. OR 11, pt. 2, p. 605, p. 554.

41. Nisbet, *Four Years on the Firing Line,* p. 64.

42. Dowdey, *Seven Days*, p. 231. Sears, *To the Gates of Richmond*, p. 229.

43. Taylor, *Destruction and Reconstruction*, pp. 91-92.

44. *The Commercial Bulletin*, New Orleans, July 30, 1962. Colonel Seymour's body initially was transported to Lynchburg for burial there, and shortly after the war his remains were moved to Macon, Ga., where he had been a newspaper editor and mayor of the city. He is buried in Rose Hill Cemetery beside his wife and children.

45. Seymour, William. *The Civil War Memoirs of Capt. William J. Seymour*, edited by Terry L. Jones (Baton Rouge, 1991), p. 4. Hereinafter cited as Seymour, *Memoirs*.

46. Walshe, "Recollections of Gaines' Mill." The "Sergt. O'Reilly" mentioned appears to be Sgt. Edward O'Riley, Company C, who survived his wounds at Gaines' Mill but was killed September 19, 1864 at the third battle of Winchester.

47. *Confederate Veteran*, vol. 10, p. 124. Miss Hill died in 1902 and was buried in New Orleans' Evergreen Cemetery following a funeral cortege in which members of the regiment, including Blayney Walshe, marched in tribute. Curiously, regimental records show two Sam Hills in Company F of the Sixth Louisiana, a 40-year-old former engineer carried on the rolls as Samuel Hill, who was wounded at Chantilly on Sept. 1, 1862 and transferred later to the Engineers Dept. at Mobile, Ala., and a 45-year-old former sailor listed as Samuel W. Hill. It is unclear which was the nurse's brother—if, indeed, there were two Samuel Hills.

48. Compiled Service Records, 6th Louisiana, file M320, rolls 169, 170, 172. National Archives. The inferences regarding Offutt are based on letters in Offutt's service records, explained in greater detail in Chapter Seven.

49. Dowdey, *Seven Days*, p. 255. Taylor, *Destruction and Reconstruction*, p. 93.

50. OR 11, pt. 2, p. 493, p. 607. Taylor, *Destruction and Reconstruction*, p. 98.

51. OR 11, pt. 2, p. 494, p. 556. Dowdey, *Seven Days*, p. 268, p. 279. Debate continues even today over Jackson's delay in crossing Grapevine bridge. Frank Vandiver, in *Mighty Stonewall*, p. 312, cites an overlooked order from Lee to Stuart directing the cavalry to guard the Chickahominy against any Federal attempt to recross the river and ordering Stuart to advise Jackson similarly. Jackson acknowledged this order about 3 p.m., wrote Vandiver, who argued that the order provided Jackson good reason for staying put rather than crossing the river to aid Magruder.

52. OR 11, pt. 2, pp. 556-557, p. 495. Henderson, *Stonewall Jackson*, vol. 2, p. 49-55. Taylor, *Destruction and Reconstruction*, p. 100.

53. OR 11, pt 2, p. 496. Henderson, *Stonewall Jackson*, vol. 2, p. 60. Sears, *To the Gates of Richmond*, pp. 310-311. Memo to the author from Robert E.L. Krick, historian, Richmond National Battlefield Park.

54. OR 11, pt. 2, p. 496. Taylor, *Destruction and Reconstruction,* p. 101.

55. Henderson, *Stonewall Jackson*, p. 61. Daniel H. Hill, "McClellan's Change of Base and Malvern Hill," *Battles and Leaders of the Civil War*, vol. 2, p. 390-391. (Hereinafter cited as *B&L*.) Sears, *To the Gates of Richmond*, pp. 313-314.

56. "Down the Peninsula with Richard Ewell, Capt. Campbell Brown's Memoirs of the Seven Day's Battles," in *The Peninsula Campaign of 1862: Yorktown to the Seven Days,* edited by Terry L. Jones, Savas Woodbury Publishers (Campbell, CA., 1995) pp. 59-60. Hereinafter cited as Campbell Brown memoirs. Twenty-one-year old Capt. G. Campbell Brown served as assistant adjutant general to Ewell.

57. Sears, *To the Gates of Richmond*, pp. 311-312

58. OR 11, pt. 2, p. 496, p. 620. Henderson, *Stonewall Jackson*, vol. 2, p. 61. Campbell Brown memoirs, p. 60, p. 64.

59. Hill, "McClellan's Change of Base and Malvern Hill," *B & L*, vol. 2, p. 394.

60. OR 11, pt. 2, p. 620. Campbell Brown memoir, p. 65.

61. OR 11, pt. 2, p. 620. Handerson, *Yankee in Gray*, p. 49-50.

62. OR 11, pt. 2, p. 609, p. 620. Campbell Brown memoir, p. 65. Compiled Service Records, 6th Louisiana Infantry, record group 109, file M320, rolls 163-173. In his report, Stafford said nothing about silencing or nearly capturing a battery. While official returns recorded nine men of the 6th Louisiana killed at Malvern Hill, examination of service records finds 12 men killed or mortally wounded. The Irishmen killed or mortally wounded at Malvern Hill were Pvts. John Adams (F), Mathew Campbell, James Cullen and Michael McDonald (B), Andrew Finley (I), John Fleming (K) and John Sugrue (D). Lt. George W. Francis (H), an Englishman, Pvt. John Laggerton (H), a Swede, and Pvt. Zelestine Meyers (B), a German, were the other immigrants killed. The two American-born fatalities in the battle were Lt. Stephen D. McCaulay (C), a Louisiana native probably of Irish ancestry, and Texas-born Pvt. Perry Higginbotham (C).

63. Compiled service records of Nathanial G. Offutt, letter dated July 17, 1862, signed by Capt. H. Bain Ritchie and Lt. George P. Ring and others, file M320, roll 170, National Archives. The charges against Offutt and his departure from the regiment are detailed in Chapter Seven.

64. Hill, "McClellan's Change of Base and Malvern Hill," *B&L,* vol. 2, p. 394. Sears, *To the Gates of Richmond*, pp. 332-335.

65. OR 11, part 2, p. 497.

CHAPTER FIVE – Back to Northern Virginia: Second Manassas & Chantilly

1. Campbell Brown memoir, pp. 68-69. OR 11, pt. 2, p. 497, p. 607. Ring diary, LHAC, Tulane.

2. Ben Hubert to Letitia Bailey, July 11, 1862, in Ben Hubert Papers, SCL-DU.

3. Jones, *Lee's Tigers*, pp. 111-113. *SHSP*, vol. 10, pp. 260-261. The new 2nd Louisiana Brigade was placed under the command of Brig. Gen. William E. Starke in Jackson's old division, commanded by General Winder until he was killed August 9 at Cedar Mountain, and thereafter by Brig. Gen. William Taliaferro.

4. James B. Sheeran, *Confederate Chaplain: A War Journal*, edited by Joseph T. Durkin, (Milwaukee, 1960), p. IX, pp. 1-2.

5. Henderson, *Stonewall Jackson*, pp. 78-79. John J. Hennessy, *Return to Bull Run*, (New York, 1993), pp. 6-8.

6. Henderson, *Stonewall Jackson*, vol. 2, p. 80-83. Robert K. Krick, *Stonewall Jackson* at *Cedar Mountain*, (Chapel Hill, N.C., 1990) pp. 5-7.

7. OR 12, pt. 2, 181-185. Henderson, *Stonewall Jackson*, vol. 2, pp. 91-95. Hennessy, *Return to Bull Run*, p. 28. The August 9 clash was variously called the battle of Cedar Mountain, Cedar Run, or Slaughter Mountain, taking the name of a landowner whose home rested on the base of the mountain.

8. OR 12, pt. 2, pp. 226-228, p. 237. Krick, *Stonewall Jackson at Cedar Mountain*, p. 279. Bartlett, *Military Record of Louisiana*, p. 62. Compiled service records, 6th Louisiana Volunteers, file M320,

roll 168. Bartlett records the wounded 6th Louisiana private as P.M. Kelley. However, his service records show the wounded man was Henry R. Kelly and list his birthplace as England (though his name suggests Irish lineage). He was a 30-year-old painter from New Orleans. The 6th Louisiana record roll in Tulane's archives records that Kelly was "wounded at Slaughter Mountain, not since heard from." Manning commanded Company K, the Violet Guards.

9. OR 12, pt. 2, p. 135, pp. 184-185. Henderson, *Stonewall Jackson*, vol. 2, pp. 98-101.

10. OR 12, pt. 2, pp. 4-6.

11. OR 12, pt. 2, pp. 12-13. Henderson, *Stonewall Jackson*, vol. 2, pp. 116-125.

12. W. B. Taliaferro, "Jackson's Raid around Pope," *B&L*, vol. 2, p. 501.

13. Taliaferro, "Jackson's Raid." Henderson, *Stonewall Jackson*, vol. 2, pp. 125-129. Jubal A. Early, *Autobiographical Sketch and Narrative of the War Between the States*, (Baltimore, 1989 reprint), p. 114. Hereafter cited as Early, Memoirs.

14. Jones, *Lee's Tigers*, p. 108. Hennessy, *Return to Bull Run*, pp. 111-112. Douglas, *I Rode with Stonewall*, p. 135.

15. OR 12, pt. 2, pp. 708-709. Ring diary, LHAC, Tulane. Sheeran, *Confederate Chaplain*, p. 9.

16. Sheeran, *Confederate Chaplain*, pp. 9-10. Hennessy, *Return to Bull Run*, p. 112. Hennessy, citing a North Carolina soldier's account, reports that the locomotive was named "The President" and carried a picture of Lincoln on its steam dome.

17. Jones, *Lee's Tigers*, p. 116. Hennessy, *Return to Bull Run*, pp. 113. *Confederate Veteran*, vol. 18, p. 231.

18. OR 12, pt. 2, p. 643. Douglas, *I Rode with Stonewall*, pp. 135-136. Ring diary, LHAC, Tulane.

19. OR 12, pt. 2, pp. 450-451.

20. OR 12, pt. 2, pp. 450-451, p. 708, p. 717. Early, Memoirs, p. 115. Jones, *Lee's Tigers*, pp. 116-117.

21. OR 12, pt. 2, p. 717. Hennessy, *Return to Bull Run*, p. 131. Early, Memoirs, p. 115.

22. OR 12, pt. 2, p. 454. Early, Memoirs, p. 116. Ring diary, LHAC, Tulane.

23. OR 12, pt. 2, p. 454, p. 461-462, pp. 708-709. Hennessy, *Return to Bull Run*, p. 132.

24. OR 12, pt. 2, p. 644, p. 709. Early, Memoirs, p. 116. Hennessy, *Return to Bull Run*, pp. 132-133.

25. OR 12, pt. 2, p. 709. Early, Memoirs, pp. 116-117. Hennessy, *Return to Bull Run*, pp. 132-134.

26. OR 12, pt. 2, pp. 717-718.

27. OR12, pt. 2, 716. Hays' Brigade casualty list in Confederate States Army Casualties, Lists and Narrative Reports, 1861-65, file M836, roll 5, National Archives (hereinafter cited as CSAC, file M836.) The five 6th Louisiana Irishmen killed at Bristoe Station were Sgt. Michael J. O'Connor (F), Pvts. John Nolan and John Phillips (I), Thomas Pierce and William Little (K). The four Germans, all of Company G, were Sgt. John Weiss and Pvts. Bernard Mertlin, August Mayer and Albert Zang. Pvt. Peter Frazier (I), a transplanted Yankee born in Maine, also was killed. In the Bristoe battle, Confederate casualties totaled 132, while Federal losses exceeded 300, possibly 400, though an exact figure is not available.

28. OR 12, pt. 2, pp. 643-644. Hennessy, *Return to Bull Run*, pp. 129-130. Douglas, *I Rode with Stonewall*, p. 136.

29. Sheeran, *Confederate Chaplain*, pp. 11-12. If the Louisiana Tigers actually found liquor, they were the lucky exceptions that day. The stern Jackson, a confirmed teetotaler, ordered a cavalry officer to "spill all the liquor" in the warehouses, declaring that "I fear that liquor more than General Pope's army." Jackson knew that a night of hard drinking would put his men in no shape for the fighting sure to come soon. See Hennessy, *Return to Bull Run*, p. 130.

30. OR 12, pt. 2, p. 644. Jones, *Lee's Tigers*, pp. 117-118. Hennessy, *Return to Bull Run*, p. 138.

31. OR 12, pt. 2, p. 710, p. 718. Hennessy, *Return to Bull Run*, pp. 143-144, pp. 161-162.

32. OR 12, pt. 2, p. 710.

33. OR 12, pt. 2, p. 644-645, pp. 710-711; Jones, *Lee's Tigers*, pp.118-119. Hennessy, *Return to Bull Run*, pp. 168-188. Gibbons' four regiments, which would become known in the Federal army as the Iron Brigade, were reinforced during the August 28 fight at Groveton by two regiments of Brig. Gen. Abner Doubleday's brigade. King's other two brigades took no part in the evening battle.

34. OR 12, pt. 2, pp. 710-711. Ring diary, LHAC, Tulane. Ewell was disabled for months, returning to the army in the spring of 1863 a changed man and, according to contemporary witnesses and many historians, a less effective general. "He was never the same old ironsides again," Henry Kyd Douglas wrote in his memoirs.

35. OR 12, pt. 2, p. 645. Hennessy, *Return to Bull Run*, pp. 200-201.

36. OR 12, pt. 2, p. 711. Early, Memoirs, pp. 122-123.

37. Hennessy, *Return to Bull Run*, 209-214.

38. James Longstreet, "Our March against Pope," *B&L*, vol. 2, pp. 519-520.

39. OR 12, pt. 2, pp. 711-712, p. 718. Allen. C. Redwood, "Jackson's Foot-Cavalry at the Second Bull Run," *B&L*, vol. 2, p. 535. Redwood was a private in the 55th Virginia, a regiment in Field's Brigade of A.P. Hill's Light Division.

40. Hennessy, *Return to Bull Run*, pp. 245-247.

41. OR 12, pt. 2, p. 646. Freeman, *Lee's Lieutenants*, vol. 2, pp. 114-115. Hennessy, *Return to Bull Run*, pp.247-248.

42. OR 12, pt. 2, p. 439, p. 556, p. 646. Hennessy, *Return to Bull Run*, pp. 253-257.

43. OR 12, pt. 2, p. 712, p. 718. As is true of nearly all the engagements of the 1st Louisiana Brigade, there are no reports in the official records on the Second Manassas campaign by the various regimental commanders of the brigade.

44. OR 12, pt. 2, p. 556, p. 646.

45. Ring diary, LHAC, Tulane. Ring's estimate of 2 p.m. as the hour the brigade moved to aid Hill is at variance with both Early's and Forno's, who agreed the time was 3:30 p.m.

46. OR 12, pt. 2, pp. 670-671.

47. Hennessy, *Return to Bull Run*, pp. 259-268. Terry Jones, author of the best modern history of Hays' Brigade, also wrote that Forno's attack was against Cuvier Grover's Federal brigade. See Jones, *Lee's Tigers*, pp. 120-122.

48. OR 12, pt. 2, p. 646, 712.

49. OR 12, pt. 2, p. 718.

50. Ring diary, LHAC, Tulane. The emphasis on Monaghan's horse is in the original as underlining.

51. OR 12, pt. 2, p. 812. Hays' Brigade casualty list in CSAC, file M836, roll 5, National Archives. Bartlett, *Military Record of Louisiana*, p. 62. Compiled Service Records, 6th Louisiana Volunteers, record group 109, file M320, rolls 163-173. In OR 12, pt. 2, p. 560, the report of Surgeon Lafayette Guild, Medical Director of Lee's army, shows the 6th Louisiana with 17 dead and 36 wounded on the list of casualties "at Manassas Plains in August, 1862," but those figures appear to combine the regiment's casualties at Bristoe Station and at Groveton on August 29. The six Irishmen of the 6th Louisiana killed August 29 were Pvts. John Conley (H), Edward T. Harney (E), Edward Dillon, Henry Gleason and James McGovern (B), and Lt. Henry Healey (H), who was mortally wounded and clung to life until the following November 8. (Healy is listed as killed in action on the Hays' Brigade casualty list.) The seventh man killed was Arkansas-born Sgt. Samuel J. Leslie (E).

52. The regimental strength figures, in this and other instances, come from original muster rolls and inspection reports for the 6th Louisiana examined by the author in the National Archives. The 780 figure cited for the regiment's nominal strength at this time includes all men, present and absent, on the 6th Louisiana's rolls, including those who were sick or wounded, held as prisoners, serving elsewhere on detached duty, stragglers and those absent without leave.

53. OR 12, pt. 2, 713. The five Louisiana regiments suffered a total of 135 casualties on August 29, with 37 dead, 94 wounded and four missing. See OR 12, pt. 2, p. 812.

54. The undated, unsigned memorandum on the 1st Louisiana Brigade covering the period of August 16 to September 1, 1862, is in Reminiscences, Army of Northern Virginia, Box 24, section 55-B, LHAC, Tulane. It is a three-page handwritten document, apparently written after the war, whose penmanship is strikingly similar to that found in the letters of the 6th Louisiana's George P. Ring. Whether or not Ring actually wrote the document cannot be established for certain.

55. Henderson, *Stonewall Jackson*, vol. 2, pp. 170-171. Jones, *Lee's Tigers*, p. 124.

56. OR 12, pt. 2, p. 557. Freeman, *Lee's Lieutenants*, vol. 1, pp. 121-128. Henderson, *Stonewall Jackson*, vol. 2, pp. 171-181.

57. Hennessy, *Return to Bull Run*, 441.

58. Ring diary, LHAC, Tulane.

59. OR 12, pt. 2, p. 647. Hennessy, *Return to Bull Run*, 443.

60. Joseph W.A. Whitehorn, "A Beastly, Comfortless Conflict: The Battle of Chantilly," *Blue & Gray magazine*, April-May, 1987, pp. 17-18. Hennessy, *Return to Bull Run*, pp. 446-447.

61. OR 12, pt. 2, p. 714. Whitehorn, "A Beastly, Comfortless Conflict", pp. 16-17.

62. OR 12, pt. 2, p. 714. Robert Ross Smith, "Ox Hill: The Most Neglected Battle of the Civil War," in *Fairfax County and the War Between the States* (Fairfax, Va., 1987) pp. 47-48. Whitehorne, "A Beastly Comfortless Conflict," p. 17. Hennessy, *Return to Bull Run,* pp. 448-449.

63. Smith, "Ox Hill," pp. 47-48. Whitehorn, "A Beastly, Comfortless Conflict," pp. 20-21.

64. OR 12, pt. 2, p. 672. Smith, "Ox Hill," p. 48.

65. Smith, "Ox Hill," pp. 49-49.Whitehorne, "A Beastly, Comfortless Conflict," pp. 21-22.

66. Smith, "Ox Hill," p. 49. Whitehorne, "A Beastly, Comfortless Conflict," pp. 21, 46. It is possible, but not certain, that one of the Louisianians fired the shot that killed Stevens. In his most definitive study of the battle, Lt. Col. Robert Ross Smith wrote: "The shot that killed him [Stevens] may have come from Hays's Brigade—if so, it was probably fired by a man of the 8th Louisiana—but it seems more likely that the bullet came from a musket in the hands of a soldier of the 49th Georgia of Thomas's Brigade, which had just come up on Hays's Brigade's right to replace Gregg's Brigade along the Confederate front." See Smith, "Ox Hill," p. 51.

67. Undated and unsigned notes on Second Manassas and Chantilly, in Reminiscences, Army of Northern Virginia, LHAC, Tulane. Smith, "Ox Hill," p. 50.

68. OR 12, pt. 2, pp. 714-715. Smith, "Ox Hill," p. 50.

69. OR 12, pt. 2, pp. 714-715.

70. OR 12, pt. 2, p. 715. Early, Memoirs, p. 130.

71. Sheeran, *Confederate Chaplain*, pp. 22-23. Sheeran's account is second-hand. He was not present during the battle and reached Ox Hill only the day after. What he wrote in his diary reflects the accounts of the fighting he heard from his Louisiana men, who naturally may have sought to place the blame elsewhere. Even the partisan Sheeran wrote, "There were also two of the La. regiments that did not display their usual valor. But the 14th and the 5th La. manfully stood their ground...." The implication of this passage is that the 6th and 7th Louisiana broke for the rear under the assault.

72. Ring diary, LHAC, Tulane.

73. Longstreet, "Our March around Pope," *B&L,* vol. 2, pp. 521-522.

74. Buck, *With the Old Confeds*, p. 58.

75. OR 12, pt. 2, p. 813. Hays' Brigade casualty list in CSAC, file M836, roll 5, National Archives. Jones, *Lee's Tigers*, p. 126. The 6th Louisiana men killed were Cpl. Isaiah Curtis and Pvt. Charles Vincent (A), Pvts. Stephen Jones (B), Jesse L. Vannoy (C), James B. Williams (E), John Brassel (I), Phillip McCormick (D) and Cpl. Frederick Roose and Pvt. Dennis Harrigan (H). Five of the dead were immigrants: Irishmen Brassel, Harrigan and McCormick; Jones was Welsh and Roose was German.

76. The combined casualty total for the three days is taken from Hays' Brigade casualty list in CSAC, file M836, roll 5, National Archives.

Chapter Six – Raiding North: Bloody Sharpsburg

1. Muster rolls, 6th Louisiana Volunteers, National Archives. The figures are derived from examining the original muster rolls of the regiment, preserved at the National Archives in Washington.

2. Compiled service records, 6th Louisiana, record group 109, file M320, rolls 163, 165, 171, 172. The three Company G deserters at Knoxville, according to their service records, were Pvt. James Aboth, Cpl. L. Renz, and Sgt. A. Theobald, all German immigrants from New Orleans.

3. OR 5, p. 737-738.

4. OR 19, pt. 2, pp. 605-606.

5. OR 19 pt. 2, pp. 142-143.

6. OR 19, pt. 1, pp. 590-591.

7. James V. Murfin, *The Gleam of Bayonets* (New York, 1965) pp. 64-69.

8. Early, Memoirs, p.134.

9. OR 19, pt. 1, p. 966. Sheeran, *Confederate Chaplain,* pp. 23-24. Ring diary, LHAC, Tulane.

10. Sheeran, *Confederate Chaplain*, p. 24.

11. Ibid, p. 27. Compiled Service Records, file M320, roll 171. Riley's accidental death is recorded in his service records, but the circumstances of the tragedy are not explained. "Killed at the blowing up of a bridge at Frederick City, Md.," the muster roll report for September-October 1862 states. A later record says the date of the accident was September 8, and the bridge was over the Monocacy River. The Battle of Monocacy was fought July 9, 1864, during General Early's invasion of Maryland. See Chapter Fourteen.

12. Henderson, *Stonewall Jackson*, vol. 2, pp. 211-212.

13. OR 19, pt. 1, p. 953. Henderson, *Stonewall Jackson*, vol. 2, pp. 214-216.

14. OR 19, pt. 1, p. 953-954, p. 966. Early, Memoirs, p. 137.

15. Ring to wife, September 15, 1862, LHAC, Tulane.

16. OR 19, pt. 1, p. 955.

17. Henderson, *Stonewall Jackson*, vol. 2, pp. 235. Sheeran, *Confederate Chaplain*, pp. 31-32.

18. Ring to wife, September 15, 1862, LHAC, Tulane. Jones, *Lee's Tigers*, p. 128.

19. Ring to wife, September 15, 1862, LHAC, Tulane. Ring did not specify which company had only four men present, but it evidently was Company H, the Orleans Rifles. In a letter written three days after the battle at Sharpsburg, Ring told his wife that he commanded Company H as well as his own Company K in the battle, and Company H went into the fight with four men, three of whom were wounded.

20. OR 19, pt. 1, p. 967.

21. OR 19, pt. 1, p. 967, p. 978. The estimate that the 6th Louisiana had only 100 or so men ready for duty on September 16 is based on Ring's count of 110 cited in his letter from Harper's Ferry the day before. It is also reasonable in light of Hays' statement in the official records that the brigade, composed of five regiments, carried 550 men into the battle along Antietam Creek.

22. OR 19, pt. 1, pp. 217-218. Murfin, *The Gleam of Bayonets*, p. 208.

23. Stephen W.Sears, *Landscape Turned Red*, (New Haven, Conn., 1983) pp. 174-175. Murfin, *Gleam of Bayonets*, p. 211. Henderson, *Stonewall Jackson*, vol. 2, pp. 242-243.

24. OR 19, pt. 1, p. 218. Murfin, *The Gleam of Bayonets,* pp. 212-213.

25. OR 19, pt 1, p 218. Murfin, *The Gleam of Bayonets*, p. 213. Jones, *Lee's Tigers*, p. 129.

26. OR 19, pt. 1, p. 218, p. 967. Sears, *Landscape Turned Red*, pp.181-182.

27. OR 19, pt. 1, p. 218.

28. OR 19, pt. 1, p. 968, 978. Ring to wife, Sept. 20, 1862, LHAC, Tulane.

29. OR 19, pt. 1, p. 978-979. Sears, *Landscape Turned Red*, pp. 188-189. Jones, *Lee's Tigers,* pp. 129-130. Hartsuff's brigade was the Third Brigade of Hooker's Second Division, commanded by Brig. Gen. James B. Ricketts. Hartsuff was wounded in the foot early in the action of September 17. Unfortunately, neither he nor any of his regimental commanders filed reports on the battle, and Ricketts' brief report is vague and lacking of detail. Similarly, Hays' report is the only one in the official records from his brigade, as the regimental commanders filed no reports.

30. Ring to wife, September 20, 1862, LHAC, Tulane. Sears, *Landscape Turned Red*, p. 188.

31. Ring to wife, September 20, 1862, LHAC, Tulane. Ring diary. William A. Frassanito, *Antietam: The Photographic Legacy of America's Bloodiest Day* (New York, 1978), pp. 122-125. Through meticulous research, Frassanito has documented that a large white horse, frozen dead in a striking upright position, which was photographed near the East Woods on September 20, 1862, was almost certainly Strong's mount. Strong was buried on the battlefield, but later his remains were removed to Washington Confederate Cemetery in Hagerstown, Md.

32. Ring to wife, September 20, 1862, LHAC, Tulane. Compiled service records, 6th Louisiana Volunteers, record group 109, file M320, rolls 163-173, National Archives.

33. OR 19, pt. 1, pp. 978-979. Jones, *Lee's Tigers,* p. 130. Ring diary, LHAC, Tulane.

34. OR 19, pt. 1, p. 979. Ring diary, LHAC, Tulane.

35. OR 19, pt. 1, p. 979. Sears, *Landscape Turned Red*, p. 190. The Louisiana Brigade losses were 45 dead, 289 wounded and two missing, according to the return of casualties in Ewell's Division for the battle of September 17, 1862. The total slightly exceeds the 323 killed and wounded cited in Hays' report of the battle. See OR 19, pt. 1, p. 974. Hartsuff's brigade lost 81 killed, 497 wounded and 20 missing. See OR 19, pt. 1, p. 190.

36. OR 19, pt. 1, p. 974. Jones, *Lee's Tigers*, p. 130. Ring diary, LHAC, Tulane. The 6th Louisiana's 11 killed exceeded the fatalities of the other regiments of the brigade, except for the 7th Louisiana, which also had 11 killed. No other regiment had more than two officers killed. The 8th Louisiana, with seven killed and 96 wounded, had the most total casualties in the brigade at Sharpsburg. In addition to those mentioned, the 6th Louisiana's killed at Sharpsburg included Sgt. G.W. Joiner and Pvt. W.J. Johnson (A), Pvt. E. Slone (C), Pvt. William F. Mansel (D), Pvt. Nicholas Maguire (aka Magner) (I). Others mortally wounded who would die in coming weeks included Lt. Charles H. Smith and Cpl. Louis Heintz (G), Pvts. Augustus Cenas (E), Joseph Mecker (H), Pierre Oger (C) and Michael Sullivan (K).

37. Murfin, *The Gleam of Bayonets*, pp. 281-286. Sears, *Landscape Turned Red*, pp. 285-293.

38. OR 19, pt. 1, p. 200, pp. 810-813. Sears, *Landscape Turned Red*, pp. 295-296.

39. OR 19, pt. 1, p. 972, p. 979. Ring diary, LHUC, Tulane. Ring wrote to his wife on September 20 that he "had the pleasure of holding the command [of the regiment] until today, when two captains making their appearance, I gracefully retired to the line again."

Chapter Seven – A Winter and Spring of War: Fredericksburg

1. Ring diary, LHAC, Tulane. Early, Memoirs, p. 162. The bulk of the fighting at Shepherdstown on September 20 was done by A.P. Hill's division, with Early's Division in support. Though under some artillery fire, the Louisiana Brigade sustained no casualties in this engagement.

2. Jones, *Lee's Tigers*, p. 133. Jackson's Corps consisted of the divisions of Ewell (Early), A.P. Hill, D.H. Hill and Jackson (Taliaferro). Longstreet's First Corps included divisions led by Lafayette McLaws, Richard H. Anderson, George E. Pickett and John B. Hood.

3. Ring diary, LHAC, Tulane.

4. Compiled service records, 6th Louisiana, record group 109, file M320, roll 170, National Archives.

5. The letter, dated "Camp near Richmond, July 17, 1862", is found in Offutt's compiled service record, file M320, roll 170, National Archives.

6. The witnesses listed at the bottom of the letter were given as "The Line Officers of the Regiment;" Pvt. John Charles, Company K; Pvt. J. Connally, Company F; Pvt. William Burke, Co. F; Sgts. G. Hanna and August Pheil and Pvt. C. Richmond of Company C.

7. Letters Received by the Secretary of War, file M437, roll 44, National Archives. Compiled service records, 6th Louisiana, file M320, roll 170, National Archives.

8. Compiled service records, 6th Louisiana, file M320, rolls 167, 169, 170, 171. The Monaghan letter, dated December 31, 1862, is found in Romer's service records. Romer, a German-born former clerk from New Orleans, spent most of 1863 detailed to hospital duty until he deserted in October. He took the oath of allegiance to the U.S. in December 1863, confirming his commander's low opinion of him as a soldier.

9. Ring diary, LHAC, Tulane. Muster roll reports, 6th Louisiana Volunteers, National Archives.

10. Record of events, 6th Louisiana, file M861, roll 23, National Archives. Jones, *Lee's Tigers*, p. 139.

11. Early, Memoirs, 165. Ring diary, LHAC, Tulane.

12. Ring diary, LHAC, Tulane. Henderson, *Stonewall Jackson*, vol. 2, p. 302. Early, Memoirs, p. 166.

13. James Longstreet, "The Battle of Fredericksburg," *B&L*, vol. 3, pp. 72-73. Henderson, *Stonewall Jackson*, vol. 2, pp. 305-306.

14. OR 21, p. 663. Ring diary, LHAC, Tulane.

15. OR 21, pp. 91-93, pp. 511-512, 552-554, p. 561, pp. 674-675. William F. Smith, "Franklin's Left Grand Division," *B&L*, vol 3, p. 134-135. Compiled service records, 6th Louisiana, file M320, roll 171, National Archives. The soldier killed December 13 is listed under the name Henry Rosenberg in his service file at the National Archives, but his name is variously given as Rosenburgh, Rusenberger, Roughenburgh and other variations in the records.

16. OR 21, p. 555. James M. McPherson, *Battle Cry of Freedom*, (New York, 1988) pp. 571-572. Longstreet, "The Battle of Fredericksburg," pp. 79-85. Ring diary, LHAC, Tulane.

17. OR 21, pp. 1004-1005.

18. Jones, *Lee's Tigers*, p. 144. Ring diary, LHAC, Tulane. Sheeran, *Confederate Chaplain*, p. 37.

19. Sheeran, *Confederate Chaplain,* pp. 37-38.

20. Record of events, 6th Louisiana, file M861, roll 23, National Archives.

21. Ibid. Jones, *Lee's Tigers*, p.141.

22. OR 21, pp. 1097-1098.

23. OR 21, pp. 1098-1099.

24. Seymour, *Memoirs*, p. 44.

25. Sheeran, *Confederate Chaplain*, 41.

26. Seymour, *Memoirs,* pp. 102-103. The soldier who crossed the river probably was Pvt. George C. Russell of Company K. According to his service records, Russell was born in Albany, N.Y. and was a 28-year-old printer in New Orleans when he enlisted in the 6th Louisiana.

27. Ibid.

28. Sheeran, *Confederate Chaplain*, p. 39.

29. Seymour, *Memoirs*, p. 45.

30. Ibid., p. 47.

31. John Bigelow, Jr., *The Campaign of Chancellorsville* (New York, 1995 reprint edition), p. 134, p. 136, pp. 166-167. Ernest B. Furgurson, *Chancellorsville, 1863: The Souls of the Brave* (New York, 1992), pp. 63-64, p. 88.

32. Bigelow, *Chancellorsville,* p. 178, p. 190. Darius N. Couch, "The Chancellorsville Campaign," *Battles & Leaders,* vol. 3, pp.156-157.

33. OR 25, pt. 1, p. 1000. Seymour, *Memoirs*, p. 48. Furgurson, *Chancellorsville 1863*, pp. 97-98. Ring diary, LHAC, Tulane.

34. Seymour, *Memoirs*, p. 48. The author has been unable to determine the identity of the woman. There apparently were several women who served the regiment as laundresses. One was Mrs. Christopher Avenholtz, who appears on a roster of recruits from New Orleans dated March 31, 1862. She was the wife of a private in Company B, an immigrant from Amsterdam, who deserted in mid-1862. The Irish woman mentioned by Seymour cannot be traced.

35. Ring diary, LHAC, Tulane. *Mobile Advertiser & Register*, June 4, 1863.

36. Seymour, *Memoirs,* pp. 48-49.

37. OR 25, pt. 1, pp. 271-272. Bigelow, *Chancellorsville,* pp. 204-205. Ring diary, LHAC, Tulane. Ring recorded that the 6th Louisiana reached the riverside rifle pits about 7 a.m., and held out until about 9 a.m. when the Federals forced their way across in boats.

Bigelow states that the crossing by the boats began about 9 a.m. and was completed by 10 a.m.

38. James P. Sullivan, *An Irishman in the Iron Brigade: The Civil War Memoirs of James P. Sullivan*, edited by William Beaudot and Lance Herdegen, pp. 76-78. OR 25, pt. 1, pp. 266-267. Sullivan, a farmhand, was the son of Irish immigrant parents who moved to Wisconsin in the early 1840s, either shortly before or after he was born in 1843.

39. *Mobile Advertiser & Register*, June 4, 1863. The identity of "Chester" is unknown. In his report, Colonel Meredith stated that his brigade killed 30, wounded "a large number" and captured nearly 200 prisoners in landing on the Confederate side of the river. The numbers, as is often the case in such reports, appear to be somewhat inflated.

40. Seymour, *Memoirs*, p. 49.

41. Record of events, 6th Louisiana, file M861, Roll 23, National Archives.

42. Ring diary, LHAC, Tulane. Compiled Service Records, 6th Louisiana, file M320, rolls 163-173. Record of Events, 6th Louisiana, file M861, roll 23, National Archives. Hays' Brigade casualty

list in CSAC, file M836, roll 6, National Archives. *Mobile Advertiser & Register,* June 4, 1863. Besides Pvt. Godwin, the 6th Louisiana men killed April 29, 1863 included Pvts. J.H. Paxton and Adolph Reinfrank (D), John Smith (G), Lemuel Houston and Henry Stewart (H), and John Donohue (I). At least two more men died of wounds received April 29: Pvts. Michael Duffy, who died May 22, and Patrick Mathews, who died May 26, both of Company K. The service records of Pvt. Patrick Hanlon (F) contain a muster role notation for May-June 1863 stating that he was killed in Federicksburg April 29, but Hanlon is listed on Hays' Brigade casualty list as missing rather than killed. A later record, dated March 20, 1865 at Petersburg, reports Hanlon killed May 1, 1863.

43. Seymour, *Memoirs*, p. 50. Ring diary, LHAC, Tulane.

44. OR 25, pt. 1, p. 797. Bigelow, *Chancellorsville,* pp. 232-233.

45. OR 25, pt. 1, p. 839, 1000-1001. Bigelow, *Chancellorsville*, pp. 386-387. Jones, *Lee's Tigers,* p. 151. By this time, only Sedgwick's VI Corps remained south of the river at Fredericksburg, as Hooker had called two other corps—I and III— to join the fight at Chancellorsville. See OR 25, pt. 1, pp. 558.

46. Ring diary, LHAC, Tulane. Seymour, *Memoirs*, p. 51.

47. OR 25, pt. 1, p. 558, p. 798. OR 25, pt. 2, p. 365. Henderson, *Stonewall Jackson*, vol. 2, pp. 432-454. Bigelow, *Chancellorsville*, pp. 295-320.

48. OR 25, pt. 1, p. 559. Furgurson, *Chancellorsville 1863*, pp. 256.

49. OR 25, pt. 1, p. 839, p. 1001. Jones, *Lee's Tigers*, p. 151. Handerson, *Yankee in Gray,* p. 55. Ring diary, LHAC, Tulane. *Mobile Advertiser & Register*, June 4, 1863.

50. OR 25, pt. 1, 839, p. 1001. Ring diary, LHAC, Tulane. *Mobile Advertiser & Register*, June 4, 1863. Furgurson, *Chancellorsville 1863*, p. 261. Early, Memoirs, p. 207.

51. OR 25, pt. 1, p. 559, pp. 599-600, pp. 839-841. Early, Memoirs, pp. 206-207. The Union troops that advanced directly toward the 6th Louisiana's position at the base of Lee's Hill were mostly Vermont men led by Col. T.O. Seaver of the 3rd Vermont regiment. See OR 25, pt. 1, p. 602.

52. Seymour, *Memoirs*, pp. 52-53.

53. *Mobile Advertiser & Register,* June 4, 1863.

54. Seymour, *Memoirs*, p. 53. Ring diary, LHAC, Tulane. Hays' Brigade casualty list in CSAC, file M836, roll 6, National Archives. The three 6th Louisiana men killed on May 3 were Pvt. Antoine Desbrest (C), and Pvts. Lawrence Schofield and Max Rhomick (H).

55. OR 25, pt. 1, pp. 559-560, p. 1001. Early, Memoirs, p. 210. Furgurson, *Chancellorsville 1863*, p. 266-267.

56. Furgurson, *Chancellorsville 1863*, pp. 293-294. Bigelow, *Chancellorsville,* p. 406.

57. OR 25, pt. 1, p. 560, p. 1001. Furgurson, *Chancellorsville 1863*, p. 285, p. 289-291. Bigelow, *Chancellorsville,* p. 406.

58. Bigelow, *Chancellorsville,* p. 410. *Mobile Advertiser & Register*, June 4, 1863.

59. OR 25, pt. 1, p. 1002. *Mobile Advertiser & Register*, June 4, 1863.

60. OR 25, pt. 1, p. 600. Bigelow, *Chancellorsville,* pp. 413-414. Howe's first line was held by Brig. Gen. Thomas H. Neill's brigade plus two regiments from Grant's Vermont brigade, the 4th and 5th Vermont. Bigelow stated that Howe had 12 artillery pieces posted in the woods, but cites no source. National Park Service Historian Ray Brown, an authority on this battle, told the author he can confirm the presence of only one battery on Grant's line.

61. *Mobile Advertiser & Register*, June 4, 1863. "Chester's" newspaper account inaccurately named Marye's Heights as the site of this uphill attack, which occurred well to the rear of Marye's Heights, on the range of hills above Hazel Run ravine, over which the Plank Road ran west to Chancellorsville.

62. Seymour, *Memoirs*, p.53-54. *Mobile Advertiser & Register*, June 4, 1863.

63. Handerson, *Yankee in Gray*, p. 57. Jones, *Lee's Tigers,* p. 153.

64. OR 25, pt. 1, p. 597, p. 604, p. 610. *Mobile Advertiser & Register*, June 4, 1863. Bigelow, *Chancellorsville*, p. 414. Furgurson, *Chancellorsville 1863*, p. 297.

65. Handerson, *Yankee in Gray,* p. 57.

66. Early, Memoirs, pp. 228-229. Jones, *Lee's Tigers*, p. 155. Jones wrote that Early and Lee watched the Louisiana attack together, but this conflicts with Early's own account in his memoirs.

Early stated that he met with Lee before the attack and Lee, after hearing Early describe his plans, "then left me." Early, who watched the attack from the heights near the Telegraph Road opposite the Alum Springs Mill (Lee's Hill), made no mention of Lee being with him.

67. Handerson, *Yankee in Gray*, p. 57. *Mobile Advertiser & Register*, June 4, 1863.

68. *Mobile Advertiser & Register*, June 4, 1863.

69. OR 25, pt. 1, p. 605, p. 1002. Handerson, *Yankee in Gray*, p. 58. Jones, *Lee's Tigers*, 154; Furgurson, *Chancellorsville 1863*, p. 298. Seymour, *Memoirs*, p. 54. Colonel Grant, in his official report, claimed that the number of prisoners taken by his Vermont brigade was "at least 1,500," but in the subsequent withdrawal of the Federals to Scott's Ford on the Rappahannock river, many escaped in the darkness and "only about 400 were actually brought off." General Howe, in his report, cited "a large number of prisoners, among them 21 officers and nearly all of the men of the Eighth Louisiana Regiment."

70. OR 25, Pt. 1, p. 808. Hays' Brigade casualty list in CSAC, file M836, roll 6, National Archives. Jones, *Lee's Tigers*, p. 155. Muster rolls of the 6th Louisiana for April 30, 1863, showed an aggregate strength of 585 men, present and absent, but only 275 were recorded as present for duty. The six 6th Louisiana men killed May 4 were Pvts. Leon Petrie (C), Charles Reinhart (D), Richard White (D), Michael Casey (F), James Lewis (I) and Assistant Surgeon F. M. Traylor, a physician who had joined Company A as an infantryman in June 1861 and had only a month before been promoted to assistant surgeon of the regiment. Among the mortally wounded were Pvts. Frederick Wolff (G), who died May 8, Alois Young (G), who died May 14, and Patrick Donovan (I), who died May 29. Record of Events, 6th Louisiana Field and Staff, state the battles of May 3 and 4 resulted in 8 killed, 55 wounded and 21 missing in the 6th Louisiana. Though the official return of casualties shows 14 killed in the regiment during the fighting from April 29 through May 4, the author's study of service records finds at least 20, perhaps 21 men killed and mortally wounded at Second Fredericksburg, making it one of the costliest engagements of the war for the regiment.

71. *Mobile Advertiser & Register*, June 4, 1863.

72. Henderson, *Stonewall Jackson*, vol. 2, pp. 450-451, p. 470. Seymour, *Memoirs*, p. 56.

Chapter Eight —The Second Battle: Return to Winchester

1. Ring diary, LHAC, Tulane. *Mobile Advertiser & Register*, June 4, 1863.

2. OR 25, pt. 2, p. 840. Bigelow, *Chancellorsville*, p. 473, p. 475. The casualty figures cited are Bigelow's. Official returns show 1,581 killed and 8,700 wounded, totaling 10,281 on the Confederate side, for which no missing or captured were reported. See OR 25, pt. 1. p. 809. On the Union side, returns show 1,567 killed, 9,469 wounded and 5,699 missing/captured, totaling 16,735 for the battles at Chancellorsville and Fredericksburg, which were reported separately. See OR 25, pt. 1, p. 185, p. 191. Bigelow's slightly higher figures reflect his exhaustive study of the subject and are considered more complete.

3. OR 27, pt. 2, p. 305, p. 313.

4. Muster rolls, 6th Louisiana Volunteers, National Archives. Ring Diary, LHAC.

5. Ring diary, LHAC, Tulane. Early, Memoirs, p. 237.

6. OR 27, pt. 2, p. 305. Freeman, *Lee's Lieutenants*, vol. 3, pp. 1-19. Early, Memoirs, p. 237. Ring diary, LHAC, Tulane.

7. OR 27, pt. 2, p. 459. Ring diary, LHAC, Tulane. Buck diary, pp. 194-195. Seymour, *Memoirs*, pp. 58-59.

8. *Civil War Battles in Winchester and Frederick County, Virginia*, published by the Winchester-Frederick County Centennial Commission, (Winchester, 1961), from the foreword. Brandon H. Beck and Charles S. Grunder, *The Second Battle of Winchester, June 12-15, 1863* (Lynchburg, Va., 1989) p. 4.

9. Beck and Grunder, *The Second Battle of Winchester*, pp. 10-11. "Forward the Louisiana Brigade!", *Confederate Veteran*, Vol. 27 (1919), p. 449. The letter was written June 17, 1863, from Winchester by Capt. Samuel H. Adams of the 5th Louisiana.

10. OR 27, pt. 2, pp. 42-43.

11. OR 27, pt. 2, pp. 460-461. Early, Memoirs, pp. 241-243. Seymour, *Memoirs*, pp. 59-60. Ring diary, LHAC, Tulane.

12. OR 27, pt. 2, p. 46, p. 61-62, p. 461. Beck and Grunder, *The Second Battle of Winchester*, pp. 15-15. Freeman, *Lee's Lieutenants,* vol. 3, pp. 21-22.

13. OR 27, pt. 2, p. 60-61, p. 461. Early, Memoirs, p. 244-246. Seymour, *Memoirs*, p. 61.

14. Jones, *Lee's Tigers*, 159; Early, Memoirs, 246; Seymour, *Memoirs*, 61.

15. OR 27, pt. 2, p. 462, p. 477.

16. OR 27, pt. 2, p. 61, p. 462. pp. 477-478.

17. OR 27, pt. 2, pp. 477-478. Record of events, 6th Louisiana, file M861, roll 23, National Archives.

18. *Confederate Veteran*, vol. 12, p. 540.

19. OR 27, pt. 2, p. 61, p. 478. Seymour, *Memoirs*, pp. 61-62.

20. OR 27, pt. 2, p. 61, pp. 476-478.Jones, *Lee's Tigers*, pp.159-160.Seymour, *Memoirs*, pp. 61-62. "Forward the Louisiana Brigade!", *Confederate Veteran,* vol. 26 (1919), p. 449.

21. Harry Gilmor, *Four Years in the Saddle* (New York, 1866), pp. 89-90. Gilmor was mistaken in reporting that two Louisiana brigades made the charge; the 2nd Louisiana Brigade, attached to Johnson's Division, was demonstrating east of Winchester when Hays' Brigade attacked the forts.

22. OR 27, pt. 2, p. 478. Seymour, *Memoirs*, p. 62. The 6th Louisiana men who served as "volunteer cannoneers" probably were men from Company E, the Mercer Guards, commanded by Capt. John J. Rivera. This company had been detached for duty with the artillery for several weeks in 1862. In his report, Hays says the captured Union guns were "served by some of my men who had previously been for a short time in the artillery service." Terry Jones, in Lee's Tigers, (p. 160) identifies the 5th Louisiana men who helped fire the guns as the Orleans Cadets.

23. OR 27, pt. 2, p. 47, p. 441, p. 463, p. 478. Early, Memoirs, p. 249. Early stated in his report that 3,358 Federal prisoners were taken at Winchester.

24. OR 27, pt. 2, p. 464. Jones, *Lee's Tigers*, p. 161.

25. OR 27, pt 2, p. 451, p. 478. Ewell's report stated that General Early had recommended Orr for captain of cavalry, "he being desirous of entering that branch of the service, for which he is eminently qualified." However, no such promotion ever occurred, for reasons unknown.

26. OR 27, pt. 2, p. 442, pp. 463-464. Jones, *Lee's Tigers*, p. 163. Seymour, *Memoirs*, p. 63.

27. OR 27, pt. 2, p. 53, p. 442, p. 478. Record of events, 6th Louisiana Volunteers, file M861, roll 23, National Archives. Early's Division casualty list, CSAC, file M836, roll 7, National Archives. The return of casualties for Early's Division at Winchester (OR 27, pt. 2, p 474) shows seven killed and 36 wounded in the 6th Louisiana, but the 6th Louisiana's record of events file reports eight killed and 55 wounded. In addition to Cpl. Cahill, those killed at Second Winchester included Pvts. Bernard Cullen, James Keegan and John McClung (B) Pvt. Michael Gleason (E), Sgt. William Burke (H) and Pvt. Michael Kirwin (K), all Irish-born. The mortally wounded included Pvt. G. Grasser (K), who died July 25, 1863; Pvt. B.O. Scarborough (A), who died June 18, 1863 and Pvts. Isaac R. Scott (C) who died sometime in August 1863 and Ozemus Smith (C) whose date of death is not known. In addition, Pvt. James Mahon (B) probably was killed; he is so recorded on the 6th Louisiana's record roll book at Tulane, and the only entry in his service records in the National Archives says he "fell nobly" in battle, without details. He is not listed as killed or wounded on Early's casualty list. Early's list names a Pvt. T. J. Sibley (A) as killed, but the only Sibley in the regiment's service records is Pvt. Reddick W. Sibley, who was severely wounded and had his leg amputated after the battle; he may have been presumed mortally wounded by the officer reporting the regiment's casualties.

28. *Confederate Veteran*, vol. 12, pp. 495-496. In 1900, the two sisters were honored with a medal presented by three surviving officers of the 6th Louisiana—John Orr, John. J. Rivera and Blayney T. Walshe.

29. Seymour, *Memoirs*, p. 64

30.OR 27, pt. 2, p. 464-465. Early, Memoirs, pp. 253-256; Jones, *Lee's Tigers*, pp. 163-164; Seymour, *Memoirs*, p. 65.

31. Seymour, *Memoirs*, p. 64-66.

32. OR 27, pt. 2, pp. 464-465. Seymour, *Memoirs,* p. 67.

33. OR 27, pt. 2, p. 307. Record of events, 6th Louisiana, file M861, roll 23, National Archives.

Chapter Nine – The Turning Point: Gettysburg

1. OR 27, pt. 1, p. 61, p. 114.

2. OR 27, pt. 2, p. 467-468, p. 479, p. 637-638. Seymour, *Memoirs,* 70.

3. OR 27, pt. 2, p. 444, Freeman, *Lee's Lieutenants*, vol. 3, pp. 79-81. Harry W. Pfanz, *Gettysburg, Culp's Hill and Cemetery Hill* (Chapel Hill, 1993), pp. 21-22.

4. OR 27, pt. 2, p. 479. Seymour, *Memoirs*, p. 70.

5. Compiled service records, 6th Louisiana, file M320, roll 167, National Archives. The June 30, 1863 muster roll for the regiment showed an aggregate strength of 528 officers and men, present and absent, with 222 present for duty.

6. OR 27, pt. 2, p. 479; J. Warren Jackson to R. Stark Jackson, July 20, 1863, in David Boyd Papers, Louisiana and Lower Mississippi Valley Collection, Louisiana State University, Baton Rouge, as quoted in *Civil War Times Illustrated*, January/February 1991, p. 56.

7. OR 27, pt. 2, pp. 468-469. Pfanz, *Gettysburg*, p. 39-41.

8. OR 27, pt. 1, pp. 712-713; pt. 2, pp. 468-469; p. 479.

9. OR 27, pt. 2, p. 479. p. 721. Seymour, *Memoirs*, p. 71.

10. OR 27, pt. 2, p. 479; Seymour, *Memoirs*, 71; Jackson letter, *Civil War Times Illustrated,* January/February 1991, p. 56.

11. Record of events, 6th Louisiana, file M861, Roll 23, National Archives.

12. OR 27, pt. 2, p. 469. Early, Memoirs, p. 271. Jones, *Lee's Tigers,* pp. 168-169.

13. Early, Memoirs, pp. 269-271.

14. OR 27, pt. 2, p. 445, p. 469. Early, Memoirs, 269-271; Gilmor, *Four Years in the Saddle*, pp. 97-98. Pfanz, *Gettysburg*, pp. 72-77.

15. Seymour, *Memoirs*, p. 72.

16. OR 27, pt. 2, p. 445. Ewell, in defense of his decision, cited reasons for not making the attack, including the fact that he could not bring artillery to bear on Cemetery Hill, that "all the troops with me were jaded by twelve hours' marching and fighting" and that he was informed Johnson's Division, which was fresh, "was close to the town" and thus presumably worth waiting for. The false report of Federals on the York road, threatening his rear, delayed Johnson's arrival until "night was far advanced," making an attack impracticable, Ewell reported.

17. OR 27, pt. 2, 480. Early's Division casualty list in CSAC, file M836, roll 7, National Archives. The five 6th Louisiana men reported missing July 1 were Cpl. Edward Grady, Pvts. Thomas Cummings and H.P. Tracy (F) and Pvts. J.P. Rodgers and Patrick Ford (G).

18. OR 27, pt. 2, p. 470, p. 480.

19. Seymour, *Memoirs,* p. 73.

20. OR 27, pt 2, pp. 318-319, pp. 446-447, p. 470, p. 480. Pfanz, *Gettysburg*, pp. 120-122. Freeman, *Lee's Lieutenants*, vol. 3, p. 114-120.

21. Pfanz, *Gettysburg,* p. 127. Seymour, *Memoirs*, 73.

22. OR 27, pt 2, p. 446. Freeman, *Lee's Lieutenants*, vol. 3, pp. 115-118.

23. Seymour, *Memoirs,* p. 74. Pfanz, *Gettysburg,* p. 179-180. According to Pfanz, the "Boy Major" Latimer, who was only 20 years old, had 20 guns on Benner's Hill. Latimer was mortally wounded in the engagement and died a hero, highly praised by Ewell and others.

24. Seymour, *Memoirs*, 75; Jackson letter, *Civil War Times Illustrated*, January/February 1991, p. 57.

25. OR 27, pt. 2, p. 470, p. 480. Seymour, *Memoirs*, p. 75. Early reported that he ordered the attack "a little before dusk." Hays cited the time as "a little before 8 p.m."

26. OR 27, pt. 2, p. 480; Seymour, *Memoirs*, p. 75. As Harry W. Pfanz has noted, there are no lucid descriptions of the exact routes followed by Early's two brigades in the twilight attack. From his exhaustive study, Pfanz concluded that Hays' Brigade probably struck the 107th Ohio and 25th Ohio regiments on the left of Harris's brigade line. The ground covered by the Louisianians' attack no

longer resembles that of 1863, because of the construction of a modern public school building which changed the topography of the ground covered by the assault.

27. OR 27, pt. 1, p. 715. Pfanz, *Gettysburg*, pp. 242-245. Compiled service records, 6th Louisiana, file M320, roll 163, National Archives. The wounded Color Sgt. Bolger was captured after the battle and survived his severe wounds, but he was disabled and did not return to the regiment. Muster rolls for mid-1864 reported Bolger assigned to the Engineers' Corps.

28. Pfanz, *Gettysburg*, p. 242, pp. 244-249. Jones, *Lee's Tigers*, p. 172. Jackson letter, *Civil War Times Illustrated*, January/February 1991.

29. OR 27, pt. 2, p. 715. Pfanz, *Gettysburg*, p. 249.

30. OR 27, pt. 1, p. 747, p. 894; pt. 2, p. 480. Jones, *Lee's Tigers*, p. 173.

31. OR 27, pt. 1, p. 894. Pfanz, *Gettysburg*, p. 254, p. 268.

32. Gilmor, *Four Years in the Saddle*, pp. 98-99. Gilmor's story of the wild, shouting Irishman who sprang upon the gun is strikingly similar to the incident related by General Richard Taylor about the capture of the Coaling guns at Port Republic in June 1862. Taylor wrote of his Irishmen going "mad with cheering" with one of them "riding cockhorse on a gun." There is no way to document that these wild fellows were members of the 6th Louisiana's Irish clan, but the behavior certainly seems in character. The identity of the small captain is unknown, but Gilmor wrote that he survived his wound.

33. OR 27, pt. 2, p. 480.

34. OR 27, pt 2, pp. 480-481. Seymour, *Memoirs*, p. 75. Jones, *Lee's Tigers*, pp. 173-174.

35. Seymour, *Memoirs*, p. 76. Pfanz, *Gettysburg*, p. 263-264.

36. OR 27, pt. 1, p. 731, p. 740, p. 743. Pfanz, *Gettysburg*, p. 272.

37. OR 27, pt. 1, p. 457, p. 459. Pfanz, *Gettysburg*, pp. 273-275. While it is difficult to determine with certainty which Federal units struck Wiedrich's guns where the men of the 6th Louisiana probably were, the account related here relies on the interpretation of Harry W. Pfanz, whose exhaustive study of the fighting on Cemetery Hill and Culp's Hill stands as the most authoritative source. "Perhaps there were some men from Hays' Louisiana Brigade who, when at Wiedrich's battery, had seen Carroll's line in the dark distance and were influenced by it, but they were driven back primarily by units of the Eleventh Corps," according to Pfanz.

38. OR 27, pt. 2, p. 481; Seymour, *Memoirs*, p. 76.

39. Jones, *Lee's Tigers*, 175.

40. OR 27, pt. 2, p. 470, p. 556. Early, *Memoirs*, p. 274.

41. Freeman, *Robert E. Lee*, vol. 3, p. 102. Historical memo in record roll, 6th Louisiana Volunteer Regiment, LHAC, Tulane. Manning incorrectly remembered the date as July 1 rather than July 2.

42. OR 27, pt. 2, p. 447; Early, Memoirs, p. 278.

43. OR 27, pt. 2, p. 475. Early's Division casualty list in CSAC, file M836, roll 7, National Archives. Robert K. Krick, *The Gettysburg Death Roster* (Dayton, Ohio, 1993) p. 9. In his report, Hays reported somewhat lower casualties—21 killed, 119 wounded and 41 missing, but the figures reported for casualties in Early's Division are more complete. The five 6th Louisiana soldiers reported on Early's list as killed outright on July 2 were Sgt. Thomas Casey and Pvt. John Good (B), Captain Cormier and Pvt. J.D. Haines (C) and Pvt. John Carroll (F). Others mortally wounded were Cpl. Ulysses W. Fisher (C) and Pvt. William Murray (F). Sgt. Patrick McGuinn (B), another New Orleans Irishman, was listed as missing on Early's official returns, but he is shown as killed in action July 2 in Company B's record book. His compiled service record does not contain any official confirmation of his death, however. The Irish again dominated the list of the dead. Casey, Good, Carroll, Murray and McGuinn were Irish immigrants from New Orleans.

44. "A War Incident," unidentified newspaper clipping in Seymour family scrapbook, Seymour Papers, SCWC, Michigan.

45. OR 27, pt. 2, pp. 320-321, p. 481.

46. OR 27, pt. 2, p. 481. Early, Memoirs, p. 276. The bloodless nature of the third day at Gettysburg for the 6th Louisiana is shown in the regiment's casualty list for July 3, which records no men killed or wounded and only two—Pvts. James Mulholland and Alfred Renaud (C)— missing. (Neither would return to the regiment; Mulholland, a Pennsylvania native who joined as a drummer boy, apparently took the oath of allegiance, and Renaud, a French immigrant, committed the ultimate

Confederate sin by joining the U.S. 3rd Maryland cavalry regiment to win his release from Fort Delaware) The July 3 losses brought the regiment's total casualties for the three days to'five killed, 34 wounded and 16 missing (using officially reported figures), which made Gettysburg a much less bloody engagement for the regiment than such battles as Port Republic, Chantilly and Second Fredericksburg.

47. OR 27, pt. 1, p. 187, pt. 2, p. 346.

CHAPTER TEN – Autumn of Disaster: Rappahannock Station.

1. OR 27, pt. 2, pp. 471-472. Early, Memoirs, p. 276-279. Seymour, *Memoirs,* p. 79-80. Jones, *Lee's Tigers*, p. 176.

2. OR 27, pt. 1, p. 448. Sheeran, *Confederate Chaplain*, p. 50. Seymour, *Memoirs,* p. 80.

3. Record of Events, 6th Louisiana, File M861, Roll 23, National Archives; Seymour, *Memoirs*, p. 80. It was near Hagerstown on July 8 that Pvt. Richard Kelly (I) was mortally wounded, under circumstances that are somewhat mysterious. Hospital records in Kelly's service records show he died July 14, 1863, of a gunshot wound to the base of the skull at Seminary Hospital in Hagersown. A muster roll report for March/April 1864 states:

"Died at the hosp. at Williamsport, Md. on or about 12 July from a gunshot wound received on the 8th." Curiously, a record dated March 20, 1865 at Petersburg, Va., states that Kelly, a 26-year-old Irish immigrant and former New Orleans butcher, was "killed in the discharge of his duty by an assassin."

4. OR 27, pt. 1, pp. 83-84, pp. 91-92.

5. OR 27, pt. 2, pp. 448-449, p. 472. Early, *Memoirs*, p. 281-283; Foote, *The Civil War,* vol. 2, pp. 586-591; Seymour, *Memoirs*, pp. 80-81.

6. OR 27, pt. 2, pp. 472-473. Seymour, *Memoirs*, pp. 81-82. Record of events, 6th Louisiana, file M861, roll 23, National Archives.

7. Handerson, *Yankee in Gray*, p. 65. Seymour, *Memoirs,* pp. 81-82. John Orr to J.M. Wilson, Aug. 19, 1863, Army of Northern Virginia Papers, LHAC, Tulane. Muster rolls, 6th Louisiana, National Archives. Pvt. Adolph Hale soon had second-thoughts about rejoining the regiment. After rejoining from desertion on August 18, according to company muster rolls, he again deserted on August 27—this time apparently for good. As for Pvt. John Curry, who deserted from the hospital, a company officer wrote this of him in Petersburg in February 1865: "Joined Cavalry and since kild." Whether he actually joined the cavalry and was killed is unknown.

8. Record of events, 6th Louisiana, file M861, roll 23, National Archives. Seymour, *Memoirs*, pp. 83-86. Compiled service records, 6th Louisiana, file M320, rolls 164, 168, 172, National Archives. The muster rolls for the regiment show an aggregate of 517 officers and men, but more than 300 of them were absent for one reason or another—sick, detailed to other duty, on furlough, or absent without leave. Companies ranged in size from a mere six men present in Company E to 41 in Company B.

9. OR 29, pt. 1, p. 9. Freeman, *Lee's Lieutenants*, vol. 3, pp. 232-233. Early, Memoirs, pp. 303-304.

10. Record of events, 6th Louisiana, file M861, roll 23, National Archives.

11. OR 29, pt. 1, p. 250, p. 413. Freeman, *Lee's Lieutenants,* vol. 3. pp. 242-247. Seymour, *Memoirs*, pp. 86-88.

12. Seymour, *Memoirs,* p. 89. The unfortunate turncoat captured near Bristoe Station, Pvt. John Conley, was hardly the only 6th Louisiana man who became a galvanized Yankee. The author's search of compiled service records turned up no less than 20 men of the regiment who joined the U.S. Army to win their release from Federal prisons.

13. Compiled service records, 6th Louisiana, file M320, roll 164, National Archives. John Connolly's name is listed on various records as Conley, Conally, Conolly and Connelly. Seymour recorded his name as Connolly, and his court martial records give it as Conally, but his service records are filed under Conley, as they appear in the accompanying roster of the regiment. He is not to be confused with Pvt. John Conley of Company H, who was killed at Manassas on August 29, 1862, nor Pvt. John Conley of Company F, who was captured at Rappahannock Station and in the Wilderness. Such

name confusion is one of the perils of a reporting on regiment whose rolls are filled with common Irish names.

14. Record of events, 6th Louisiana, file M861, roll 23, National Archives. Seymour, Memoirs, pp. 89-90, pp.100-101.

15. OR 29, pt. 1, pp. 626-627. Freeman, *Lee's Lieutenants,* vol. 3, p. 265. Early, Memoirs, pp. 307. Seymour, *Memoirs,* pp. 90-91.

16. OR 29, pt. 1, pp. 619-620, pp. 626-627. Early, *Memoirs,* pp. 308-309.

17. OR 29, pt. 1, p. 11, p. 587.

18. OR 29, pt. 1, pp. 619-619, p. 627. Early, Memoirs, pp. 309-310. Seymour, *Memoirs,* p. 91.

19. OR 29, pt. 1, p. 619. Early, Memoirs, p. 310.

20. OR 29, pt. 1, pp. 575-575, p. 621, pp. 628-629. The three regiments led by Col. Godwin were the 6th, 54th and 57th North Carolina. Hays reported he had 800 to 900 men with him, and Godwin's regiments totaled about the same.

21. OR 29, pt. 1, pp. 621-622; Seymour, *Memoirs*, p. 92. Early, Memoirs, p. 313.

22. OR 29, pt. 1, pp. 587-588; pp. 592-593; pp. 595-596.

23. OR 29, pt. 1, pp. 598-600.

24. OR 29, pt. 1, pp. 595-600. Seymour, *Memoirs*, p. 93. Jeffry Wert, "Rappahannock Station", *Civil War Times Illustrated*, December 1976, pp. 5-8, pp. 40-46.

25. Seymour, *Memoirs,* pp. 93-94. Early, Memoirs, 314-315. Jones, *Lee's Tigers*, 183-184.

26. Lieutenant M. McNamara, "Lieutenant Charlie Pierce's Daring Attempts to Escape from Johnson's Island," *SHSP*, vol. 8 (1880), pp. 61-62. The identity of the author is unknown. The reference to Colonel Terry is to Lt. Col. Thomas M. Terry of the 7th Louisiana. In his diary, Captain Seymour wrote that among the captured were Colonels Penn of the 7th Louisiana and Godwin, commanding the North Carolina brigade, and Capt. A.L. Gusman, commanding the 8th Louisiana and Capt. John G. Angell commanding the 5th Louisiana. Seymour also reported that Monaghan and Manning swam the river to escape.

27. OR 29, pt. 1, p. 622, p. 628.

28. OR 29, pt. 1, pp. 628-629. Jones, *Lee's Tigers*, pp. 184-185. Compiled Service Records, 6th Louisiana, file M320, rolls 164, 170, 171, National Archives. The brigade's official return of casualties for Rappahannock Station do not show anyone killed in the 6th Louisiana, but regimental records list Sgt. Conway of Company F as killed Nov. 7 in the battle, as do Conway's service records on file at the National Archives. Another Irishman, Pvt. John Whelan of Company F, was wounded and captured at the battle and later died of his wounds, according to Whelan's service records.

29. OR 29, pt. 1, p. 589. Lt. Col. Charles Cormier, 1st Louisiana Regiment, to unknown, November 15, 1863, in Army of Northern Virginia papers, LHAC, Tulane University. Russell's figure on the number captured was low, as the actual number of prisoners neared 1,600. Hays reported 684 taken prisoner and Hoke's Brigade reported 906 captured. The 6th Louisiana's loss of 90 men was the smallest of any regiment in the brigade, and only half of the 7th Louisiana's loss of 180 men. See OR 29, pt. 1, p. 629.

30. OR 29, pt. 1, pp. 611-616. Early, Memoirs, p. 316. Jones, *Lee's Tigers*, p. 185.

31. Record of events, 6th Louisiana, file M861, roll 23, National Archives.

32. OR 29, pt. 1, pp. 830-840. Jones, *Lee's Tigers*, p. 187. Compiled service records, 6th Louisiana, file M320, roll 167, National Archives. Hanlon's service records show that he was absent sick from the regiment from September 1863 to early May 1864, on furlough part of that time in Columbus, Miss. His record of frequent absences from the regiment suggest that Hanlon never regained his health completely after his severe bayonet wounding at the first battle of Winchester, May 25, 1862.

33. OR 29, pt. 1, p. 13. Seymour, *Memoirs*, p. 95.

34. Record of events, 6th Louisiana, file M861, roll 23, National Archives. Hays' Brigade casualty list in CSAC, file M836, roll 6, National Archives. Among the Mine Run casualties was Irish-born Pvt. Daniel Corbett (I), who was severely wounded on the skirmish line November 29 and died of his wounds, complicated by pneumonia, at Gordonsville on March 9, 1864. Also wounded at Mine Run were Sgt. Thomas Flanagan (I), and Pvt. Allen S. Neathery (A), while Pvts. Marshall K. Burgoyne (D)

and Michael F. Welsh (F) and Dan Riordan (I) were captured, all on November 30. Monaghan reported that the Louisiana Brigade had two killed, seven wounded and three missing at Mine Run.

35. Record Group 109, War Department Collection of Confederate Records, Entry 183: Manuscript Rolls, No. 3315, National Archives.

36. Seymour, *Memoirs*, p. 100.

37. Ibid, pp. 100-101.

38. Ibid.

39. Ibid, pp. 101-102.

40. Record of events, 6th Louisiana, file M861, roll 23, National Archives.

41. Ibid.

42. Trahern memoir, VHS, p. 24.

43. Jones, *Lee's Tigers*, p. 191-192. Record of events, 6th Louisiana, file M861, roll 23, National Archives.

Chapter Eleven – The Overland Campaign: Wilderness & Spotsylvania

1. Gordon C. Rhea, *The Battle of the Wilderness, May 5-6, 1864* (Baton Rouge, La., 1994), p. 21, p. 34. Alexander S. Webb, "Through the Wilderness," *B&L*, vol. 4, pp. 152-153. According to Rhea, Meade's Army of the Potomac reported 99,438 men present for duty on April 30. When joined by the independent IX Corps, commanded by Maj. Gen. Ambrose Burnside and numbering more than 19,000, the Union force under Grant would swell to more than 118,000. Burnside's corps was guarding the Orange and Alexandria Railroad north of the Rappahannock River, and followed Meade's army as soon as it crossed the Rapidan on May 4 and 5.

2. OR 36, pt. 1, p. 1070. Rhea, *Wilderness*, pp. 25-27. E.M. Law, "From the Wilderness to Cold Harbor," *B&L*, vol. 4, p.118.

3. Law, *B&L*, vol. 4, pp. 118-119. Sheeran, *Confederate Chaplain*, p. 86.

4. Jones, *Lee's Tigers*, 193. Trahern memoir, VHS, p. 25. Trahern's recollection jibes quite closely with muster roll figures which showed 173 men present for duty as of April 30, 1864.

5. OR 36, pt. 1, p. 1070. Law, *B&L*, vol. 4, p. 121.

6. OR 36, pt. 1, p. 1070. Rhea, *Wilderness*, p. 123. Official reports from the Confederate side on the battles of the Wilderness and Spotsylvania are few and relatively scanty. Ewell's report is relied on extensively in the absence of any official reports by Early or by Hays, who was seriously wounded on May 10. As usual, there are no reports by the Louisiana Brigade's regimental commanders.

7. Webb, *B&L*, vol. 4, p. 154. Rhea, *Wilderness*, p. 102. The field took its name from the family that had most recently farmed it. In 1996, it looked much as it did in 1864, and is the focal point of a walking tour in the Wilderness Battlefield Park.

8. OR 36, pt. 1, p. 555, p. 590, p.1070, p. 1077. Seymour, *Memoirs*, pp. 107-108. Steere, *The Wilderness Campaign*, p. 149-165.

9. Seymour, *Memoirs*, p. 109. Steere, *The Wilderness Campaign*, p. 243-246. The brigade of Virginians led by John Pegram, a West Point graduate and veteran brigadier who had fought in the west, previously had been led by William "Extra Billy" Smith, who resigned after his indifferent performance at Gettysburg and went on to become governor of Virginia in 1864.

10. OR 36, pt. 1, p. 719. Seymour, *Memoirs*, p. 109. Rhea, *Wilderness*, pp. 181-183. Ring to wife, dated "Battle Field Wilderness, Va.," May 6, 1864, LHAC, Tulane. Trahern memoir, VHS, p. 25.

11. Steere, *The Wilderness Campaign*, pp. 245-249. Seymour, *Memoirs*, pp. 109-110. Jones, *Lee's Tigers*, pp. 197-198. Ring to wife, May 6, 1864, LHAC, Tulane. Casualty list of 6th Louisiana, Wilderness, May 5, in Archer Anderson Collection, Eleanor S. Brockenbrough Library, Museum of the Confederacy, Richmond. No after-action report was filed for Hays' Brigade at the Wilderness, and no official return of casualties exists. However, a handwritten casualty list for the regiment is contained in a fragment of a 6th Louisiana record/roll book discovered in the files of the Museum of the Confederacy. It contains names of the killed, wounded and missing for May 5, and several subsequent battles from May through July 1864. The four men listed as killed were Sgt. Michael Joyce (H) and Pvts. Nathaniel Bushnell (C), Thomas Hughes (I) and John Kingston (K). On May 6, one more man

was killed: Pvt. James McAdams (K). In his May 6 letter, Ring also reported that Major Manning "is missing and is supposed to be a prisoner." Manning would remain a prisoner at Fort Delaware, Del., and Hilton Head, S.C., for five months.

12. James I. Robertson Jr., "The Scourge of Elmira," in *Civil War History*, vol. 8, no. 2.

13. Steere, *The Wilderness Campaign*, p. 251.

14. OR 36, pt. 1, pp. 728-729. Seymour, *Memoirs*, p. 111. The time of the attack is taken from the battle report of Federal Brig. Gen. Truman Seymour. The Louisiana Brigade's Captain Seymour (the name similarity is coincidental) put the time of the Federal attack at 8 p.m., and said that it lasted until "half past nine o'clock."

15. OR 36, pt. 1, pp. 728-729.

16. OR 36, pt. 1, p. 728. Mertz, Gregory A."The Battle of the Wilderness." *Blue & Gray Magazine*, vol.12, issue 4, April 1995, p. 63.

17. Trahern memoir, VHS, pp. 25-26.

18. Freeman, *Lee's Lieutenants*, vol. 3, pp. 351-352. Rhea, *Wilderness*, 264-270.

19. OR 36, pt. 1, pp. 728-729, p.1071. Rhea, *Wilderness*, pp. 320-323. Pegram was succeeded in command by Col. John S. Hoffman, but returned to the army in the fall to command a division before being killed Feb. 6, 1865, at Hatcher's Run, Va., near Petersburg.

20. Ring to wife, May 6, 1864, LHAC, Tulane. The Company K soldier that Ring mentioned being killed as he wrote was Pvt. James McAdams, the only 6th Louisiana man killed on May 6. The only other casualty in the regiment that day was Pvt. Edward Lejeune (C), who was wounded. The two names are listed on the handwritten casualty list for the 6th Louisiana found in the Archer Anderson Collection at the Museum of the Confederacy.

21. Freeman, *Lee's Lieutenants*, vol. 3, pp. 360-366. Rhea, *Wilderness*, pp. 369-372.

22. OR 36, pt. 1, p. 1071, pp. 1077-1078. John B. Gordon, *Reminiscences of the Civil War*, (New York, 1903) pp. 243-261. Rhea, *Wilderness*, 416-424. In his memoirs, written 40 years after the war, Gordon asserted that General Lee arrived at Ewell's headquarters at 5:30 p.m. May 6, and when informed of Gordon's plan, immediately ordered the Georgian to attack. Other Confederate officers denied any such meeting occurred. For a discussion of this unresolved controversy, see Rhea, *Wilderness*, pp. 412-416. Hays' Louisianians did not participate in Gordon's flank attack, except for some skirmishing.

23. OR 36, pt. 1, p. 133. Rhea, *Wilderness*, pp. 435-436, p. 440. Seymour, *Memoirs*, p. 110.

24. Sheeran, *Confederate Chaplain*, p. 87. Trahern memoir, VHS, p. 26.

25. Rhea, *Wilderness*, pp. 438-441. David Herbert Donald, *Lincoln* (New York, 1995) p. 501.

26. OR 36, pt. 1, pp. 18-19, p. 1071. Freeman, *Lee's Lieutenants*, vol. 3, pp. 375-379.

27. Freeman, *Lee's Lieutenants*, vol. 3, pp. 380-383. Foote, *The Civil War*, vol. 3, pp. 191-196; Seymour, *Memoirs*, p. 118. Richard Anderson had begun the war as colonel of the 1st South Carolina infantry and risen to brigade commander and then division commander in Longstreet's Corps. He led the I Corps until October, when Longstreet returned to duty.

28. OR 36, pt. 1, p. 1071. Seymour, *Memoirs*, p. 118. The Ring letter quoted here was published May 28, 1864 in the *Daily Advertiser* of Montgomery, Ala., as part of a group of five letters headed "Extracts from a private letter of an officer in Hays' La. Brigade, 6th Reg." The first and fifth letters of this published collection are identical to the originals of Captain Ring's letters to his wife dated May 6 and May 15 which are found in Tulane University's LHAC. The three others letters published in this group also are undoubtedly Captain Ring's, though the originals are not in the Tulane collection. Ring's wife Virginia resided in Montgomery during this period of the war, and he had urged her to submit his letters to a newspaper for publication.

29. OR 36, pt. 2, pp. 974-975; OR 51, pt 2, pp. 902-903. Jones, *Lee's Tigers*, pp. 201-202. Freeman, *Lee's Lieutenants*, vol. 3, pp. 390-391.

30. OR 36, pt. 1, p. 1071. Seymour, *Memoirs*, pp. 119-120. Freeman, *Lee's Lieutenants*, vol. 3, pp. 393-394.

31. Seymour, *Memoirs*, pp. 119-120.

32. OR 36, pt. 1, p. 19. Foote, *The Civil War*, vol. 3, p. 203. William D. Matter, *If It Takes All Summer: The Battle of Spotsylvania* (Chapel Hill, 1988), p. 102.

33. Ring to wife, May 10, 1864, published in the *The Daily Advertiser*, Montgomery, Ala., May 28, 1864. This letter is the third in the group of five published by the Montgomery newspaper and attributed only to an officer of the 6th Louisiana, but there is no doubt it was written by Ring.

34. OR 36, pt. 1, pp. 667-668, p. 1072, p. 1078. Matter, If It Takes All Summer, pp. 149-151, pp. 161-167. Seymour, *Memoirs*, pp. 120-121; Gordon, *Reminiscences*, pp. 272-273. Upton reported capturing 1,000 to 1,200 Confederate prisoners while losing 1,000 of his men killed, wounded and captured. The Confederate line, Upton reported, was "completely broken and an opening had been made for the division which was to have supported our left, but it did not arrive." Upton was supposed to have been supported by the division of Brig. Gen. Gershom Mott, of Hancock's II Corps, but Mott failed to advance and was widely blamed for the failure of Upton's brilliantly executed attack.

35. OR 36, pt. 1, p. 1072. Jones, *Lee's Tigers*, p. 203. Seymour, *Memoirs*, p. 121. Ring to wife, May 12, 1864, published in *The Daily Advertiser*, Montgomery, Ala., May 28, 1864, as the fourth in a group of five letters attributed only to an officer of the 6th Louisiana.

36. Ulysses S. Grant, *Personal Memoirs of U.S. Grant*, edited by E.B. Long, (Cleveland, 1952), reprint edition by Da Capo Press (New York, 1982) pp. 418-421. Hereinafter cited as Grant, *Memoirs*.

37. Jones, *Lee's Tigers*, p. 204. Seymour, *Memoirs*, pp. 121-122.

38. OR 36, pt. 1, pp. 334-335, p. 1072. Freeman, *Lee's Lieutenants*, vol. 3, pp. 397-398. Matter, *If It Takes All Summer*, pp. 175-179.

39. OR 36, pt. 1, p. 1044. p. 1072, pp. 1079-1080, p. 1086. Seymour, *Memoirs*, pp. 122-123. Jones, *Lee's Tigers*, p. 204.

40. Seymour, *Memoirs*, pp. 122-123.

41. OR 36, pt. 1, pp. 334-335.

42. Seymour, *Memoirs*, p. 123. Pegram's Brigade at this time was commanded by Col. John Hoffman, and Gordon's Brigade was under Col. Clement Evans.

43. Seymour, *Memoirs*, p. 123; Jones, *Lee's Tigers*, p. 205.

44. Seymour, *Memoirs*, pp. 123-124.

45. OR 36, pt. 1, p. 335, p. 1072. Hancock reported taking nearly 4,000 Confederate prisoners and 20 cannon in the May 12 attack.

46. OR 36, pt. 1, p. 1080. William S. Dunlop, *Lee's Sharpshooters* (Little Rock, 1899), Morningside House reprint edition (Dayton, 1988) pp. 457-458. *The London Herald* article of May 25, 1864, headed "Battle of Spottsylvania Court House," is reprinted in an appendix to Dunlop's memoirs of the war. It is a detailed, lengthy account of the battle by an unnamed correspondent for the paper who was with Lee's army at the time.

47. *The London Herald*, May 25, 1864, reprinted in Dunlop, *Lee's Sharpshooters*, 460-461.

48. Seymour, *Memoirs*, p. 124; Matter, *If It Takes All Summer*, p. 199.

49. OR 36, pt. 1, pp. 335-336, p. 1044, p. 1072, p. 1082. Seymour, *Memoirs*, pp. 125-126. Gordon, *Reminiscences*, pp. 277-281, Matter, *If It Takes All Summer*, p. 199, pp. 202-205.

50. Matter, *If It Takes All Summer*, pp. 202-207.

51. Ring to wife, as published in the *Daily Advertiser* of Montgomery, Ala., May 28, 1864. This is the fourth of five letters published that day, all attributed to a 6th Louisiana officer, all written by Ring.

52. OR 36, pt. 1, pp. 336-337, p. 539, p. 669, pp. 1072-1073. Grant, *Memoirs*, pp. 422-423.

53. Ring to wife, Battle Field, Spotsylvania C.H., May 15, 1864, LHAC, Tulane. This letter, slightly edited from the original, makes up the fifth letter among the five published by the Montgomery *Daily Advertiser*, May 28, 1864.

54. Ring to wife, May 15, 1864, LHAC, Tulane. Seymour, *Memoirs*, p. 127.

55. Foote, *The Civil War*, vol. 3, pp. 221-223. Jones, *Lee's Tigers*, pp. 206-207. G. Norton Galloway, "Hand to Hand Fighting at Spotsylvania," *B&L*, vol. 4, pp. 170-174.

56. Casualties in the 6th Louisiana, May 12, 1864, handwritten fragment of record-roll book in Archer Anderson Collection, Museum of the Confederacy, Richmond. The mortally wounded 6th Louisiana men were Sgt. John Mulrooney (I) and Pvt. Michael Shay (K), two New Orleans Irishmen. Though it isn't known when he was shot, Pvt. A.H. Gilbert (A) was sent to a Richmond hospital on May 17 with a wound in his lungs, and died there May 26, another apparent fatality of the

Spotsylvania fighting. The service records of Pvt. James Graham (K) state that he was severely wounded at Spotsylvania May 12 and died in a Lynchburg hospital June 6, 1864, but the hand-written casualty list of the regiment found in the Museum of the Confederacy states that Graham was wounded May 16 "accidentally, by himself" and died afterward.

57. Jones, *Lee's Tigers*, p. 207. Sheeran, *Confederate Chaplain*, p. 88.

58. Jones, *Lee's Tigers*, p. 207.

59. OR 36, pt. 1, pp. 337-338. p. 1073, p. 1087. Freeman, *Lee's Lieutenants*, vol. 3, pp. 437-439.

60. OR 31, pt. 1, p. 4, p. 149. Matter, *If It Takes All Summer*, p. 348.

61. Ring to wife, May 15, 1864, LHAC, Tulane.

Chapter Twelve – The Gates of Washington: Monocacy

1. Record of events, 6th Louisiana, file M861, roll 23, National Archives. The record of events notes, which are taken from the muster rolls and usually provide at least brief accounts of the regiment's movements and actions, are little help for the period after April 1864. The records of the regiment for the period after May 1 were "destroyed by fire in Stanton, Virginia," according to the record of events notes. Exactly how that happened was not explained.

2. Freeman, *Lee's Lieutenants*, vol. 3, p. 508. Foote, *The Civil War,* vol. 3, pp. 291-297. 6th Louisiana casualty list in Archer Anderson Collection, Museum of the Confederacy, Richmond. The handwritten 6th Louisiana record book fragment lists Hanlon as wounded on June 2, and shows Capt. Charles M. Pilcher of the Orleans Rifles, Company H, as commanding the 6th Louisiana on June 3 during Grant's attack. It also records these other Cold Harbor casualties: Pvt. Samuel Jenkins, sharpshooter, (B) wounded June 1; Pvt. William Pugh (A) mortally wounded on June 3, (died in Chimborazo Hospital, Richmond, on June 12); Pvt. Philip Ursery, wounded June 3; Pvt. George Copeland (F) missing and "supposed killed" on June 3; Pvts. Henry Smith (G) and William Knox (I) wounded on June 3. Copeland's service records confirm he was killed on June 3.

3. OR 51, pt. 2, p.1008.

4. OR 36, pt. 3, p. 873-74. Seymour, *Memoirs,* p. 133. Jones, *Lee's Tigers*, p. 208. York was the only Polish-American to become a Confederate General. Pilcher's command of the regiment is inferred from the information in the handwritten record-book fragment in the Museum of the Confederacy, which had Pilcher in command June 3 at Cold Harbor. Hanlon's wound must not have been serious, however, for he was back in command of the regiment by early July.

5. OR 36, pt. 1, p. 1074. Freeman, *Lee's Lieutenants,* vol. 3, p. 498-499, p. 510. Ewell wanted to return to his corps command, but Lee concluded he was no longer up to that demanding job and had him appointed on June 14 to command of Richmond's defenses, a severe blow to the old soldier.

6. OR 37, pt. 1, pp. 94-97. Frank E. Vandiver, *Jubal's Raid: General Early's Famous Attack on Washington in 1864* (New York, 1960) pp. 7-9. Hunter had replaced the hapless General Sigel after the latter had been defeated at New Market, Va., on May 15 by a Confederate force commanded by Breckinridge, whose division was called to fight at Cold Harbor before being sent back to the valley against Sigel's successor.

7. OR 37, pt. 1, p. 346.

8. OR 37, pt. 1, pp. 99-101. Early, *Memoirs*, pp. 371-379. The three divisions in Early's Corps were commanded by the veteran Robert Rodes and two newly minted major generals—John Brown Gordon, who replaced the captured Edward Johnston, and boyish, 27-year old Stephen Dodson Ramseur, a North Carolinian who had been a brigadier under Rodes, who succeeded Early. The command structure of Ewell's old corps had been devastated in the month of fighting from the Wilderness to Cold Harbor, losing 10 of 16 general officers—four killed, four wounded and incapacitated from command, and two captured. See Freeman, *Lee's Lieutenants*, vol. 3, p. 513.

9. OR 37, pt. 1, p. 768. Early, *Memoirs*, pp. 381-382. Freeman, *Lee's Lieutenants,* vol. 3, pp. 557-559.

10. Early, *Memoirs*, pp. 380-384. Vandiver, *Jubal's Raid*, pp. 74-88. Worsham, *One of*

11. Early, *Memoirs*, p. 385, p. 388. Vandiver, *Jubal's Raid*, p. 107. Joseph Judge, *Season of Fire: The Confederate Strike on Washington* (Berryville, Va., 1994), pp. 150-151. Ricketts' division, the

Third Division of the VI Corps, numbering about 5,000 men, sailed from City Point, Va., Grant's supply base below Richmond on the James River, in several boats on July 6.

12. OR 37, pt. 1, pp. 193-196. Glenn H. Worthington, "The Battle of Monocacy," *Confederate Veteran*, vol. 36, p. 20. Judge, *Season of Fire*, pp. 168-169. Wallace, a Mexican War veteran who had fought at Shiloh and Fort Donelson in the western theater of the Civil War, commanded the U.S. Army's Middle Department, headquartered in Baltimore. Not all of Ricketts' division reached the battlefield. Wallace reported that those on the ground for the battle were the five regiments of Col. William S. Truex's First Brigade (14th New Jersey, 106th and 151st New York, 87th Pennsylvania and 10th Vermont) plus four regiments of Col. Matthew R. McClennan's Second brigade (110th and 126th Ohio, 138th Pennsylvania, and the 9th New York Heavy Artillery, fighting as infantry). Three of McClennan's regiments (6th Maryland, 122nd Ohio and 67th Pennsylvania) inexplicably halted eight miles from the battlefield at Monrovia. About 3,500 of Ricketts' 5,000 men were in the battle, according to Wallace's report. See OR 37, pt. 1, pp. 195-196.

13. Worsham, *One of Jackson's Foot Cavalry*, p. 151.

14. OR 37, pt. 1, p 196. Worthington, "The Battle of Monocacy," pp. 20-21. Vandiver, *Jubal's Raid,* pp. 197-108.

15. Early, *Memoirs*, p. 387. Vandiver, *Jubal's Raid,* pp.108-109.

16. OR 37, pt. 1, pp. 196-197. Worthington, "The Battle of Monocacy," pp. 21-22. Early, *Memoirs*, pp. 387-388. Vandiver, *Jubal's Raid*, p. 110. The Worthington house still stands on land owned by the Monocacy National Battlefield Park. The Thomas House, known as Araby, stands nearby, but it is privately owned and occupied. The battlefield retains much of its natural beauty but is marred by Interstate Highway 70, which slices directly over the ground where Gordon's Division clashed with Rickett's brigades.

17. OR 37, pt. 1, pp. 350-351. Gordon, *Reminiscences*, pp. 310-311.

18. OR 37, pt. 1, p. 351. Worthington, "The Battle of Monocacy," p. 22.

19. OR 37, pt. 1, p. 351. Gordon, *Reminiscences*, pp. 311-312.

20. OR 37, pt. 1, p. 351. Gordon, *Reminiscences*, p. 312. Worthington, "The Battle of Monocacy," p. 23.

21. OR 37, pt. 1, p. 352. Jones, *Lee's Tigers*, p. 212. Worthington, "The Battle of Monocacy," p. 23.

22. OR 37, pt. 1, p. 197, p. 202, pp. 351-352. Jones, *Lee's Tigers*, p. 212. In his report, Early stated that his entire loss at Monocacy, including cavalry, was between 600 and 700 men. But this surely understates the Confederate casualties, for Gordon alone reported losing 698 men from his division. While Gordon's men did the heavy fighting, additional losses must have been incurred by Ramseur and Rodes. Early's report brushed off the fighting at Monocacy in less than one paragraph.

23. Sheeran, *Confederate Chaplain*, p. 94.

24. Worthington, "The Battle of Monocacy," p. 23. Worthington spent years studying the battle that occurred on his father's farm and wrote extensively about it. His *Confederate Veteran* account reported the Confederate casualties at Monocacy as high as 275 killed and 435 wounded, totaling 710, quite close to Gordon's figure.

25. OR 37, pt. 1, p. 200, p. 349. Compiled service records, 6th Louisiana Volunteers, record group 109, file M320, rolls 163-173. Monocacy casualty list for the 6th Louisiana in record/roll book fragment, in Archer Anderson Collection, Museum of the Confederacy. The handwritten pages list the Monocacy killed as Lt. Michael Murray, who was commanding Companies A and F, Sgt. William Phair of Company F., and Sgt. Frederick Koesner of Company H. The mortally wounded were Pvts. Daniel Curry (K) and Joseph Higgins (I). Not on that list, but also killed, were Sgt. Michael J. Kennedy (H) and Pvt. James Richardson (H). Of the fatalities, all but Koesner were Irish. Privates Curry and Higgins are buried in marked graves in Mount Olivet Cemetery in Frederick, Md., Curry in grave no. 250 and Higgins in no. 269. They rest there along with Pvt. Michael Sullivan of Company K of the 6th Louisiana, who died April 22, 1863 and is interred in grave no. 196.

26. OR 37, pt. 1, p. 200, p. 202. The monument that Wallace proposed with his words of inscription was never erected. A monument erected on the 100th anniversary of the battle by the Maryland Civil War Centennial Commission is inscribed "The Battle that Saved Washington," which at least

preserves Wallace's thought. Why the monument designers did not use Wallace's more poignant quote is unknown. Regarding Union casualties, officially reported losses were 123 killed, 603 wounded, and 557 missing or captured, with more than 1,000 of the losses in Rickett's division.

27. OR 37, pt. 1, p. 348. Early, *Memoirs*, p. 389.

28. Gordon, *Reminiscences,* pp. 314-315. Early, *Memoirs*, pp. 390-394. Vandiver, *Jubal's Raid,* pp. 159-172. Early, in his memoirs written long after the war, claimed that he remained determined even after the July 11 council of war with his generals to attack Fort Stevens at daylight on July 12, but that during the night he learned that two Union corps had arrived in Washington. This conflicts with Gordon's assertion that there was not a dissenting voice against retreating when the generals met in council on the night of the 11th. This may be part of the long Early-Gordon conflict after the war, or simply Early's effort to portray fighting spirit after being criticized for not attacking Washington.

29. OR 37, pt. 1, pp. 348-349. "I am sorry I did not succeed in capturing Washington," Early reported to Lee on July 14. But he expressed satisfaction that "there was intense excitement and alarm in Washington and Baltimore and all over the North" and that his force was "very greatly exaggerated" in Northern accounts. Another bold objective of his raid on Washington—the release of Confederate prisoners at Point Lookout, in Maryland, which was to be accomplished by a cavalry expedition—had to be abandoned when Early retreated from the Federal capital.

Chapter Thirteen – Luck Runs Out: Third Winchester

1. Hotchkiss, *Make Me a Map*, pp. 215-216. The number of men in the regiment at this time is estimated based on the subsequent report of inspection taken Aug. 21, 1864, which showed 57 men present for duty in the 6th Louisiana.

2. Early, "Winchester, Fisher's Hill and Cedar Creek," *B&L*, vol. 4, p. 522.

3. Early, *Memoirs*, pp. 398-399.

4. Ring to wife, dated "Headquarters, York's Command, Martinsburg, Va.," July 27, 1864, LHAC, Tulane. Hotchkiss, *Make Me a Map*, pp. 217-218. Early, *Memoirs*, p. 399. Morning report of the 6th Louisiana, July 19, 1864, record-book fragment in Archer Anderson Collection, Museum of the Confederacy. The July 19 morning report shows eight officers and 44 men fit for duty. In addition to those 52, 12 men of the regiment were listed as sick or disabled, one in arrest, eight on extra duty, for a total of nine officers and 64 men, an aggregate of 73.

5. Ring to wife, July 27, 1864. Early, *Memoirs*, p. 399. Hotchkiss, *Make Me a Map*, p. 217.

6. OR 38, pt. 1, p. 286. Ring to wife, July 27, 1864. Early, *Memoirs*, p. 399.

7. Ring to wife, July 27, 1864.

8. OR 38, pt. 1, p. 286. Early, *Memoirs*, pp. 399-400. Jones, *Lee's Tigers*, p. 214. Sixth Louisiana record/roll book fragment, Archer Anderson Collection, Museum of the Confederacy, Richmond, Va. The record/roll book pages, handwritten by an unknown officer, state that the 6th Louisiana brought only 35 infantrymen into the engagement. It lists the killed as Sgt. Thomas Byrnes (B) and Pvt. Stephen W. Morris (A). Four of the five listed casualties were Irishmen—Sgt. Byrnes and Pvts. Patrick Flanagan and James Gallagher (B), and Richard Nolan (I), all wounded. Though he is unmentioned on that list, the service records of Pvt. Godfrey Estlow (K) show that he was severely wounded in the chest at Kernstown and died in a Mount Jackson, Va., hospital on September 9, 1864. There are no official returns of casualties in the OR for the Confederates at Kernstown. The estimate of 13 casualties in the Louisiana Brigade is from Jones' *Lee's Tigers*, which does not cite a source. The Official Records do not include any after-battle report from Early or any of his division commanders on the fight at Kernstown, which Early treats briefly in two pages of his memoirs.

9. OR 38, pt. 1, p. 286. Ring to wife, July 17, 1864, LHAC, Tulane. Early, *Memoirs*, p. 400-401.

10. Jeffry D. Wert, From *Winchester to Cedar Creek*, (Mechanicsburg, Pa., 1997) pp. 10-12, p. 22. Grant, *Memoirs*, pp. 468-471.

11. Wert, From *Winchester to Cedar Creek*, pp. 16-17.

12. OR 43, pt. 1, p. 1002. Wert, *From Winchester to Cedar Creek*, p. 26. Gordon, *Reminiscences*, p. 317.

13. Hotchkiss, *Make Me a Map*, pp. 220-224. Early, *Memoirs*, pp. 406-409.

14. Wert, *From Winchester to Cedar Creek,* pp. 32-27.

15. Early, *Memoirs*, p. 415. Compiled service records, 6th Louisiana Volunteers, file M320, roll 170, National Archives. Report of Inspector General, Aug. 19, 1864, record group 109, file M935, roll 10, National Archives. Monaghan's service record shows him absent at the fighting at Cold Harbor, Monocacy and Second Kernstown. The nature of his illness is not known, nor the exact date of his return to duty. The table of organization for Early's Army of the Valley for August 20, 1864, lists Monaghan in command of Hays' Brigade and Hanlon in command of the 6th Louisiana. See OR 43, pt. 1, p. 1002.

16. OR 43, pt. 1, p. 425. Hotchkiss, *Make Me a Map*, p. 225. Early, *Memoirs,* p. 409.

17. OR 43, pt. 1, p. 425. Early, *Memoirs*, p. 409. Hotchkiss, *Make Me a Map*, p. 224.

18. OR 43, pt. 1, p. 425. *Hotchkiss, Make Me a Map*, p. 224. Early, *Memoirs,* p. 409. Worsham, *One of Jackson's Foot Cavalry*, pp. 163-165.

19. Early, *Memoirs*, p. 409. Worsham, *One of Jackson's Foot Cavalry*, 163-165.

20. Monaghan's grave lies among those of 56 unknown Confederate dead and 106 Southern soldiers with marked graves, near a monument erected in 1870 by the Southern Soldiers Memorial Association. Shepherdstown, now in West Virginia, is only about three miles south of Sharpsburg, Md., where many of the Confederates buried there were killed in the 1862 battle.

21. Compiled service records, 6th Louisiana Volunteers, file M320, roll 167. In a postwar speech, one of Hanlon's comrades in the 6th Louisiana, Capt. Blayney T. Walshe, said that Hanlon "was shot through the body at the First Winchester, never fully recovered, and died shortly after the close of the war." See *Confederate Veteran*, vol. 6, p. 177.

22. OR 43, pt. 1, p. 609-610. Moore's inspection report also noted that on leaving Staunton in late June "the transportation of Lieutenant General Early's command was reduced so as to allow neither company nor field officers an ounce of baggage, except such as they could carry themselves or on their horses; hence records have been left behind and reports are irregular and incomplete." This may explain why the records of the 6th Louisiana, including muster rolls, are missing for the summer of 1864, and why they were lost at Staunton, as mentioned in company "record of events" notes for the period.

23. Inspection report, Hays and Stafford's brigades, Winchester, Va., August 19, 1864, record group 109, file M935, roll 10, National Archives.

24. Ibid.

25. Lonn, *Desertion in the Civil War*, pp. 7-10, pp. 19-20. For more on desertion in the Louisiana regiments, see appendixes in Jones' Lee's Tigers, pp. 233-254. Statistics on desertion are sketchy and highly suspect and it is difficult to directly compare one regiment to another. Only a name-by-name search of service records for each regiment could produce accurate statistics on how many men actually deserted. Some men listed as deserters at one point turned up later to have been prisoners, or killed, and some returned from desertion.

26. Inspection report, Hays' and Staffords' Brigades, Winchester, Va., August 19, 1864, record group 109, file M935, roll 10, National Archives.

27. Early, *Memoirs*, p. 415. Wert, *From Winchester to Cedar Creek*, pp. 40-41.

28. OR 43, pt. 1, p. 554. Early, *Memoirs*, p. 419. Wert, From *Winchester to Cedar Creek*, pp. 44-45. Ring to wife, September 21, 1864, LHAC, Tulane. Ring's letter, datelined "Line of battle near Strasburg," was written only two days after the Confederates' defeat at Third Winchester, is a vivid, highly detailed account covering 12 handwritten pages. It was written from Fisher's Hill.

29. Wert, *From Winchester to Cedar Creek*, pp. 48-51. Ring to wife, September 21, 1864.

30. OR 43, pt. 1, pp. 554-555. Early, *Memoirs,* p. 421. Wert, *From Winchester to Cedar Creek,* p. 53. In 1995, the Association for the Preservation of Civil War Sites, Inc., purchased 222 acres of the battlefield on which Gordon's Division fought, adjacent to Hackwood, an imposing house that still looms over the ground. The property is one of the few remaining unspoiled areas of the Third Winchester battle area, which has been overrun by commercial and residential development. The APCWS site lies along Redbud Road about a mile east of Interstate 81, but as of early 1998 was not yet open to visitors.

31. OR 43, pt. 1, p. 318. Ring to wife, September 21, 1864. Wert, *From Winchester to Cedar Creek,* p. 56.

32. OR 43, pt. 1, p. 318. Ring to wife, September 21, 1864.

33. Ring to wife, September 21, 1864. Seymour, *Memoirs*, pp. 139-140. Wert, *From Winchester to Cedar Creek*, pp. 53-55.

34. OR 43, pt. 1, p. 318, p. 555. Early, *Memoirs,* p. 422. Ring to wife, September 21, 1864.

35. Ring to wife, September 21, 1864. Wert, *From Winchester to Cedar Creek*, pp. 59-62. "We learned to our surprise and gratification that the Brigade immediately opposed to our Command was the 1st Louisiana Regulars, mostly made up in New Orleans," Ring wrote to his wife. There was no such unit on the battlefield, and it is impossible to know how such a rumor arose among the Confederate Louisianians, but Ring's letter makes it clear that it did, and it had an effect on their fighting mood. There were Federal regiments raised in New Orleans after the Union recaptured the city in April 1862, but none fought in Sheridan's army. It's true, however, that the XIX Corps, which opposed the Louisianians in this battle, had been shipped from New Orleans and diverted to duty defending Washington and later pursuing Early. Possibly this fact led to reports that these troops were Federals from New Orleans.

36. OR 43, pt. 1, p. 555. Ring to wife, September 21, 1864. Early, *Memoirs*, p. 424-425. Jones, *Lee's Tigers*, p. 216.

37. OR 43, pt. 1, p. 555. Early, *Memoirs*, pp. 424-425. Wert, *From Winchester to Cedar Creek,* pp. 83-92.

38. Seymour, *Memoirs*, p. 141. Ring to wife, September 21, 1864.

39. Ring to wife, September 21, 1864.

40. OR 43, pt. 1, p. 555. Ring to wife, September 21, 1964. Early, *Memoirs,* pp. 424-426. Jones, *Lee's Tigers,* pp. 215-216.

41. OR 43, pt. 1, p. 555, p. 557. Freeman, *Lee's Lieutenants*, vol. 3, p. 581. Wert, *From Winchester to Cedar Creek*, p. 103. The estimate of 1,000 casualties (mostly captured) among the Confederate cavalry is Freeman's. Officially, the cavalry reported 346 killed and wounded for the month of September, with no estimate for captured or missing. Freeman puts Early's losses at Winchester at nearly 40 percent of an estimated 12,000 men engaged.

42. OR 43, pt. 1, p. 118, p. 321. Wert, *From Winchester to Cedar Creek*, p. 103.

43. Ring to wife, September 21, 1864. Record of events, 6th Louisiana, file M861, roll 23, National Archives. The OR does not provide any official return of casualties for the Louisianians for the Third Winchester battle. A study of the 6th Louisiana's compiled service records in the National Archives provides this unofficial list of casualties: Killed: Lt. Edward O'Riley (C), a Louisiana native probably of Irish ancestry. Mortally wounded: Pvt. J. Arceneaux (G), who was shot in the stomach and died 11 days after the battle, and Pvt. O. Hearty (K), an Irish immigrant serving as a regimental teamster who was shot in the neck. The wounded included Pvt. John H. Murray (E), severely wounded in both thighs and disabled for the rest of the war, Pvt. John Shannon (E), Lt. Henry Long (B) severely wounded in the right arm and retired to the Invalid Corps five months later, and Pvt. Richard Nolan (I). Pvts. Martin Kelly (D) and George F. Singleton (H) were captured.

Chapter Fourteen – Valley of Humiliation: Fisher's Hill & Cedar Creek

1. Ring to wife, September 21, 1864.

2. Ibid.

3. Ibid.

4. OR 43, pt. 1, p 556. Early, *Memoirs*, p. 429. Wert, *From Winchester to Cedar Creek*, pp. 109-110.

5. Seymour, *Memoirs*, p. 143.

6. Early, *Memoirs*, p. 429. Wert, *From Winchester to Cedar Creek*, pp. 110-111.

7. OR 43, pt. 1, p. 363. Wert, *From Winchester to Cedar Creek*, pp.119-121.

8. OR 43, pt. 1, p. 363-364. Seymour, *Memoirs,* p. 144. Gordon, *Reminiscences*, p. 326. Wert, *From Winchester to Cedar Creek*, pp. 121-123. Early, *Memoirs*, pp. 429-430. Compiled service

records, 6th Louisiana, file M320, rolls 163-173. In addition to Nolan and Duncan, those captured at Fisher's Hill included Pvts. John Fay, James Gallagher and Mathew Hanley (B), William Arden (C), Alexander Reed (D), John Flynn (H) and Leon Dirr (K). Pvt. Robert W. Grinstead (B) was wounded and crippled, later retiring to the Invalid Corps.

9. OR 43, pt. 1, p. 556-557. Gordon, *Reminiscences*, p. 326. Gordon, whose animosity for Early is barely concealed in his war memoir, implicitly blamed his commanding general for the rout at Fisher's Hill. Though the Confederates were greatly outnumbered, "our position was such that in our stronghold we could have whipped General Sheridan had the weak point on our left been sufficiently protected," he wrote. Early's effort to rush infantry brigades to the collapsing left were made "too late," Gordon declared. In contrast to Early's complaint of "panic" among the infantry, Gordon commented, "It is not just to blame the troops" who saw the "hopelessness" of the situation and realized their only choice was retreat or capture.

10. OR 43, pt. 1, p. 124, pp. 557-558.

11. OR 43, pt. 1, p. 443. Wert, *From Winchester to Cedar Creek*, p. 144, pp. 158-159. In his burning of the valley, Sheridan was operating under direct instructions from Grant. He reported to Grant on October 7 that his men had burned over 2,000 barns filled with grain and implements and over 70 flour mills, had confiscated 4,000 head of livestock and killed 3,000 sheep for meat. The destruction, he said, encompassed the Luray Valley and Little Fort Valley as well as the main valley of the Shenandoah. The Valley, "from Winchester up to Staunton, 92 miles, will have but little in it for man or beast," Sheridan reported. See OR 43, pt. 1, pp. 30-31.

12. Ring's letter, dated September 26, 1864, and Lee's response, dated November 12, 1864, are found in Hanlon's Confederate service record, file M320, roll 167, National Archives. Ring apparently was the ranking officer present with the few men of the 6th Louisiana at the time he wrote this letter. Hanlon's service record shows him absent sick at this time, as he so stated in his brief note disavowing Ring's letter. Major Manning and Captain Rivera, captured in May, remained prisoners of war at this time. Ring was free-lancing, and it backfired, perhaps dooming Hanlon's chance to become a full colonel.

13. OR 43, pt. 1, pp. 558-559. Gordon, *Reminiscences*, p. 331. Seymour, *Memoirs*, p. 147. Lee greatly underestimated the odds against Early. Refusing to believe Early's estimates of Sheridan's strength, the Confederate commander wrote: "The enemy's force cannot be so greatly superior to yours. His effective infantry, I do not think, exceeds 12,000 men." Sheridan's infantry was probably three times as large as Lee's guess.

14. OR 43, pt. 1, p. 561. Hotchkiss, *Make Me a Map*, pp. 236-237. Theodore C. Mahr, *The Battle of Cedar Creek* (Lynchburg, Va., 1992), pp. 66-69. Ring to wife, October 14, 1864, LHAC, Tulane. In the October 13 fight at the Abram Stickley farm along Cedar Creek, which is detailed in Hotchkiss' diary and mentioned in Ring's letter, the Confederates lost 22 killed and 160 wounded. They killed 22 Union soldiers, wounded 110 and took 77 prisoners. Despite Ring's assertion that the Confederates could have routed the whole Union army, Early reported that "this was a position too strong to attack in front," so he returned to Fisher's Hill to see if Sheridan would advance against him.

15. Gordon, *Reminiscences*, pp. 333-334. Hotchkiss, *Make Me a Map*, p. 237. Robert G. Stephens Jr., *Intrepid Warrior: Clement Anselm Evans* (Dayton, Ohio, 1992), pp. 479-481. The peak from which Gordon, Evans and Hotchkiss viewed the Union camps at Cedar Creek is also called Three Top Mountain, the name Hotchkiss used in his journal. In a letter to his wife written on the day after climbing up to the mountain top, General Evans wrote: "We were able to locate precisely [the enemy's] cavalry, his artillery, his infantry and wagon train. We could see precisely where he had run his line of entrenchments and where they stopped. Even the house where Sheridan made Hd. Qrs. was pointed out. There all was, with the roads leading to it, the place where he could be best attacked, and how the lines could move, how far to go and what to do—just like a large map. I believe that we can utterly rout them, if we attack their left flank."

16. OR 43, pt. 1, p. 561. Early, *Memoirs*, 437-443. Hotchkiss, *Make Me a Map*, p. 238. Freeman, *Lee's Lieutenants*, vol. 3, p. 598. While Rosser's cavalry participated in the attack at Cedar Creek, another Confederate mounted division under Lomax was north of Front Royal to keep the Federal cavalry from threatening Gordon from the east.

17. Ring to wife, October 14, 1864. There is considerable uncertainty as to who commanded the unified Louisiana Brigade at this time, after General York was wounded at Winchester on September 19. The table of organization for Early's army at Cedar Creek in the official records (OR 43, pt. 1, pp. 564-565) lists no names of officers in charge of Hays' and Stafford's Brigades. In *Lee's Tigers*, the best account of the Louisiana brigades, historian Terry Jones is silent on the question. Jeffry Wert, in *From Winchester to Cedar Creek*, speculates that Col. Edmund Pendleton of the 15th Louisiana was in command of the brigade at the October 19 battle, but that supposition appears based on Pendleton's seniority rather than any specific evidence. Theodore Mahr, in *The Battle of Cedar Creek*, places Col. William R. Peck of the 9th Louisiana in command. Ring's letter, written only five days before the battle, reported Hanlon in charge of "Hays' & Staffords'" which the unified brigade was commonly called. His reference to "Capt. Prados" is to Louis Prados of the 8th Louisiana, who held the mostly honorary post of commander of the five regiments formerly in Hays' Brigade. Jed Hotchkiss' map for the battle labels the Louisiana Brigade "York," but the disabled brigadier was not present. In the absence of other evidence, Ring's statement placing Hanlon in command is the best historical record available.

18. Gordon, *Reminiscences*, pp. 336-337. Mahr, *The Battle of Cedar Creek*, pp. 101-102. Trahern memoir, VHS, p. 28. Trahern erred in placing the Union XI Corps at Cedar Creek. In addition to the XIX and the VIII Corps (Crook's Army of West Virginia) the other Union corps was Wright's VI Corps.

19. Gordon, *Reminiscences*, pp. 338-339. Mahr, *The Battle of Cedar Creek*, pp. 109-110. The dispositions of the brigades within each of three divisions led by Gordon is indicated in Jed Hotchkiss's map of the battlefield on Plate LXXXII (82) of the Official Military Atlas of the Civil War. There is some historical evidence suggesting that Gordon's attack force used two fords to cross the Shenandoah, namely, Bowman's Ford and a second crossing known as McInturff's Ford, which was several hundred yards upstream, near the mouth of Cedar Creek. The Louisianians may have crossed at McInturffs with Evans. However, official Confedererate sources and Jed Hotchkiss's maps show the crossing only at Bowman's Ford. See Mahr, *The Battle of Cedar Creek*, pp. 386-387.

20. Trahern memoir, VHS, p. 29. Samuel D. Buck, "Battle of Cedar Creek, Va., Oct. 19th, 1864," *SHSP* 30, p. 105.

21. OR 43, pt. 1, pp. 158-161, p. 403. Gordon, *Reminiscences*, pp. 339-340. Mahr, *The Battle of Cedar Creek*, pp. 127-128. Stephens, *Intrepid Warrior*, p. 487, p. 499. Stephens, who was Evans' grandson, said the unpublished report dated October 31, 1864, was among the general's letters, diaries and other papers found by family members long after the war. Evans' letters also indicate he saw a copy of General Gordon's official report on the battle, which also never was published.

22. Wert, *From Winchester to Cedar Creek*, pp. 178-180. Trahern memoir, VHS, p. 29.

23. OR 43, pt. 1, p. 158, pp. 284-285.

24. OR 43, pt. 1, p. 561. Gordon, *Reminiscences*, p. 340. Stephens, *Intrepid Warrior*, p. 499. Joseph W.A.Whitehorn, *The Battle of Belle Grove or Cedar Creek*, (Strasburg, Va., 1987) pp. 18-21.

25. In addition to Early's report as army commander, the official records contain only one Confederate report at division level, that of Brig. Gen. Bryan Grimes, writing for the mortally-wounded Ramseur. There are no reports from Evans, Pegram, Kershaw and Wharton. Of 17 brigade commanders, only three—two from Kershaw's Division and one from Ramseur's—had their reports published. Evans apparently saw a copy of Gordon's draft report, for he wrote this to his wife on November 5, 1864: "Maj. General Gordon's official report pays me high compliments, but what of those when the final report must go from Genl. Early who will do neither Gen. Gordon nor myself simple justice." By that time, Evans evidently suspected that Early intended to blame both his subordinate generals and his soldiers for the disastrous turn of the battle.

26. OR 43, pt. 1, pp. 158-159, 193-194. Wright in his report credited Getty's division with checking the Confederate advance, buying time for the Union army to reorganize and find a defensive line it could hold.

27. Trahern memoir, VHS, p. 29. It is not possible to say whether Trahern's account of the looting came from first-hand observation and participation, or from knowledge acquired after the war. His statement that "we killed much valuable time during our voluntary digression," however, seems to

suggest participation in the plundering by Trahern and his comrades. Evans, in his unpublished battle report, (Stephens, *Intrepid Warrior*, p. 501) seemed intent on rebutting Early's charge of widespread looting by writing that "there were remarkably few skulkers and plunderers" from his division, while "the pursuit was vigorous." However, there are many accounts by Confederates in the ranks of widespread looting. Samuel Buck of the 13th Virginia in Pegram's Division wrote long after the war that the Confederates could have won at Cedar Creek but "half of our army was unfortunately back pillaging the captured wagons, hunting for clothing and shoes, as many were almost naked and barefooted." See *SHSP* 30, p. 107 and Wert, *From Winchester to Cedar Creek*, pp. 217-218.

28. OR 43, pt. 1, p. 52-53. Wert, *From Winchester to Cedar Creek,* pp. 224-225. Hotchkiss map of Cedar Creek battlefield, Official Military Atlas, plate LXXXII (82). Hotchkiss' map shows "York," the Louisiana Brigade, between Terry's Virginians on the right and Evans' Georgians on the left, with a large gap of perhaps a quarter-mile between

29. OR 43, pt. 1, p. 53, p. 285, p. 562.Early, *Memoirs*, p. 447. Gordon, *Reminiscence*s, p. 346-347. Wert, *From Winchester to Cedar Creek*, pp. 226-227.

30. OR 43, pt. 1, p. 53, p. 562, pp. 599-600. Gordon, *Reminiscences*, p. 348. Trahern memoir, VHS, p. 30. Wert, *From Winchester to Cedar Creek*, pp. 229-234.

31. Trahern memoir, VHS, p. 30. Hotchkiss, *Make Me a Map*, p. 240.

32. OR 43, pt. 1, p. 137, pp. 560-564. In his report written two days after the battle, Early initially estimated his loss in killed and wounded at "not more than 700 or 800," with few prisoners lost, but this was too low. In his memoirs, he used the higher figures cited here. The Union casualties totaled 644 killed, 3430 wounded and 1,591 captured.

33. OR 43, pt. 1, p. 137, pp. 560-564. Stephens, *Intrepid Warrior*, p. 497.

34. Compiled service records, 6th Louisiana Volunteers, record group 109, file M320, rolls 163-173. The absence of all the 6th Louisiana's captains is established in examining a "List of officers absent, Hay's and Staffords' Brigades," in the inspection report dated Dec. 29, 1864. According to that report, the captains of the 6th Louisiana who were Union prisoners were Thomas Redmond, Co. B, (Rappahannock Station), Parnell Scott, Co. C. (Wilderness), David F. Buckner, Co. D, ("captured while crossing the Mississippi River last spring,"), John J. Rivera, Co. E, (Spotsylvania), Michael O'Connor, Co. F (Rappahannock Station), and Jeff Van Benthuysen, Co. G (Gettysburg). Absent wounded were Captains Blaney Walsh, Co. I, and George Ring, Co. K.

35. Examination of the compiled service records yields an unofficial casualty list for the 6th Louisiana at Cedar Creek. Killed: Sgt. Richard Carr (H). Mortally wounded: Pvt. John W. Coleman (K), who died November 7, 1864. Others wounded: Captain Ring (K), Lt. Joseph B. Bresnan (I), Pvt. John Walker (B). Captured: Pvts. William Coffey (B), Henry Smith and Leonard Pfister (G).

36. Inspection report, October 31, 1864, File M935, Roll 11, National Archives. Jones, *Lee's Tigers*, p. 219. The October 31 inspection report does not give numbers present from each of the former regiments, such as the 6th Louisiana. For the brigade, out of a nominal total of 3,135 officers and men, it showed 563 men present, 970 prisoners of war, 852 absent sick, and 389 absent without authority, which would have included deserters and stragglers and possibly some uncounted killed and wounded. This report lists Lt. Col. David Zable of the 14th Louisiana in command at the end of October, but he was succeeded in November by Col. William R. Peck of the 9th Louisiana.

37. OR 43, pt. 1 p. 584. Hotchkiss, *Make Me a Map*, p. 244, p. 247. Gordon, *Reminiscences*, pp. 373-374.

Chapter Fifteen – The Bitter End: Petersburg &Appomattox

1. Inspection report, York's command, Camp Stafford, Dinwiddie County, Va., December 29, 1864, record group 109, file M935, roll 11, National Archives. Jones, *Lee's Tigers*, p. 219.

2. OR 46, pt. 1, p. 61, pp. 383-384. Noah Andre Trudeau, *The Last Citadel* (Boston, 1991), pp. 4-5. In addition to the 80,000-man Army of the Potomac, Grant could also call upon the 41,000-man Army of the James posted nearby, giving the Union better than two-to-one odds against the Confederates at Petersburg.

3. Inspection report, York's command, December 29, 1864, File M935, roll 10, National Archives. Compiled service record of Edward Fitzgerald, file M320, roll 165.

4. Theodore H. Woodard to "Dear Sister," datelined "Camp Near Petersburg, Va., Jany. 18th, 1864," Louisiana Room Papers Collection, Eleanor S. Brockenbrough Library, Museum of the Confederacy, Richmond, Va. Though Woodard wrote 1864 rather than 1865 as the year in the letter's dateline, he must have simply forgotten that a new year had begun, for the 6th Louisiana was not anywhere near Petersburg in January 1865. The content of the letter shows it was written in 1865.

5. Ibid.

6. Gordon, *Reminiscences*, p. 377, pp. 381-82. Jones, *Lee's Tigers*, pp. 220-221.

7. OR 46, pt. 1, p. 253-254, pp. 390-391. Trudeau, *Last Citidel*, pp. 312-317. "The Battle of Hatcher's Run," *Atlanta Weekly Intelligencer*, April 12, 1865.

8. OR 46, pt. 1, p. 254, p. 390. *Atlanta Weekly Intelligencer*, April 12, 1865. Trudeau, *Last Citadel*, pp. 318-319. Chris Calkins, "The Battle of Hatcher's Run," manuscript, Petersburg National Military Park files.

9. OR 46, pt. 1, p. 392.

10. OR 46, pt. 1, p. 255, p. 392. *Atlanta Weekly Intelligencer*, April 12, 1865.

11. OR 46, pt. 1, pp. 391-392; Trudeau, *The Siege of Petersburg*, p. 35. There are no official casualty figures for the Confederates. The estimate of 1,000 is from Major Henry Kyd Douglas, who participated in the battle and said General Pegram died in his arms. See Douglas, *I Rode with Stonewall*, pp. 326-327. Union casualties at Hatcher's Run were 171 killed, 1181 wounded, 187 missing, total 1,539, mostly in Warren's V Corps. See OR 46, pt. 1, p. 69. The author's search of compiled service records confirmed only one Hatcher's Run casualty, Pvt. Porter of Company C, who was wounded in the right leg, sent to a hospital in Petersburg and captured there April 3. Long after the war, under a Louisiana program that awarded land grants to indigent war veterans and their widows, the widows of two men filed claims that they had been killed at Hatcher's Run—a Pvt. Patrick Kelly of Company A, and Pvt. James Normile of Company I. The only Patrick Kelly recorded in the 6th Louisiana's compiled service records at the National Archives was a Company H private who was captured at Rappahannock Station and was in Elmira, N.Y. as a prisoner at the time of the Hatcher's Run battle. Normile's record shows he deserted at Petersburg on February 18,1865 and took the oath of allegiance. Both claims thus appear to be false, as did many other such claims for 6th Louisiana men filed under the land-grant program.

12. William Miller Owen, *In Camp and Battle with the Washington Artillery of New Orleans* (Boston, 1885), pp. 362-363.

13. OR 46, pt. 1, pp. 381-382.

14. OR 46, pt. 2, p. 1258. Freeman, *Lee's Lieutenants*, vol. 3, p. 623-634. Trudeau, *The Siege of Petersburg*, p. 36. Jones, *Lee's Tigers*, p. 221. Brooks and Jones, *Lee's Foreign Legion*, p. 2-3.

15. Record roll, 6th Louisiana Volunteers, bound volumes in LHAC, Tulane.

16. OR 46, pt. 1, pp. 316-317.Freeman, *Lee's Lieutenants*, vol. 3, pp. 645-647. Gordon, *Reminiscences*, pp. 397-400. Douglas, *I Rode with Stonewall*, p. 328.

17. OR 46, pt. 1, pp. 316-317. Gordon, *Reminiscences*, p. 401-406. Freeman, *Lee's Lieutenants*, pp. 646-647. Trudeau, *Last Citadel*, pp. 334-337.

18. Gordon, *Reminiscences*, pp.401-405. Freeman, *Lee's Lieutenants*, vol. 3, pp. 646-647.

19. Bartlett, *Military Record of Louisiana*, p. 39. Jones, *Lee's Tigers*, p. 222.

20. Gordon, *Reminiscences*, p. 408. All the details, perhaps colored by passage of time, are from the general's memoirs, written nearly 40 years after the war.

21. OR 46, pt. 1, p. 317, p. 332. Gordon, *Reminiscences*, p. 410. In his report, Brig. Gen. Napoleon B. McLaughlen, commanding troops at Fort Stedman, wrote: "The enemy, aware of the recent order allowing deserters to bring in their arms, approached my picket line under that disguise, in small squads, and thus surprised the pickets, capturing them without any alarm being given."

22. "The Louisiana Troops in the Battle Near Petersburg," in *The Richmond Whig*, April 1, 1865. Gordon, *Reminiscences*, 410. Stephens, *Intrepid Warrior*, pp. 534-535. The lengthy quotation from *The Richmond Whig* is from an unsigned letter to the editor. General Evans' unpublished battle report, written on the day of the assault and found in his personal papers, said the troops penetrating Fort

Stedman were the division sharpshooters, the 13th and 31st Georgia regiments commanded by Col. J.H. Lowe, and "the Louisiana troops, Col. Waggaman commanding." This confirms that the 6th Louisiana men were among those who spearheaded the attack and penetrated Fort Stedman.

23. Bartlett, *Military Record of Louisiana*, 40.

24. OR 46, pt. 1, p. 317, pp. 331-332, p. 382. Gordon, *Reminiscences*, p. 410. Trudeau, *Last Citadel*, pp. 340-341.

25. OR 46, pt. 1, pp. 345-347. Gordon, *Reminiscences*, pp. 410-411. Trudeau, *Last Citadel,* pp. 345-349.

26. OR 46, pt. 1, p. 318, p. 348. Gordon, *Reminiscences*, pp. 411-412. Freeman, *Lee's Lieutenants*, vol. 3, pp. 650-651. Bartlett, *Military Record of Louisiana*, pp.40-41. Stephens, *Intrepid Warrior*, p. 535. Compiled service records, 6th Louisiana, file M320, rolls 164,167, 169, 173, National Archives. Sgt. Jenkins died in a Petersburg hospital on April 11, two days after Lee surrendered at Appomattox Court House. Bresnan and Husselby were captured in Confederate hospitals on April 3 and were transferred to Federal hospitals. Pvt. Coleman remained a prisoner at Point Lookout, Md., until released on June 24, 1865. Union IX Corps casualties in the March 25 attack totaled 72 killed, 450 wounded and 522 missing or captured, total 1,044. After the morning attack failed, the Union II Corps and VI Corps attacked along the line, on the theory that Lee had weakened other sectors to mass troops for the attack on the IX Corps area. Those Union attacks were repulsed with considerable loss—690 casualties in the II Corps, about 400 in the VI Corps.

27. OR 46, pt. 1, p. 1264.Freeman, *Lee's Lieutenants*, vol. 3, pp. 662-671. Grant, *Memoirs*, 530-535.

28. Bartlett, *Military Record of Louisiana,* p. 41. Jones, *Lee's Tigers,* p. 224. Gordon, *Reminiscences*, pp. 420-421. Stephens, *Intrepid Warrior*, pp. 540-542.

29. OR 46, pt. 1, p. 1265. Gordon, *Reminiscences,* 423. Freeman, *Lee's Lieutenants,* vol. 3, pp. 686-690. The number of men of the 6th Louisiana on the retreat is based on the official record of those who surrendered and were paroled at Appomattox Court House on April 9, which totaled 52, plus three more who were captured by Union cavalry in the days after the surrender. See *SHSP* 15, p. 4, pp. 230-234. One 6th Louisiana man was captured on the retreat. The service records of Pvt. Charles Devan, Company B, show he was captured at High Bridge, near Farmville, Va., on April 6. He was released from prison the following June 25.

30. OR 46, pt. 1, pp. 1265-1266. Freeman, *Lee's Lieutenants*, vol. 3, p. 707. Gordon, *Reminiscences*, pp. 429-430.

31. OR 46, pt. 1, p. 1266, p. 1303. Chris M. Calkins, *The Battles of Appomattox Station and Appomattox Court House* (Lynchburg, Va., 1987), p. 55.

32. OR 46, pt. 1, p. 1303. Calkins, *Appomattox Court House*, p. 56-57, p. 76. *SHSP* 15, p. 237. Fitzhugh Lee reported that his troopers numbered 2,400 men and Gordon's infantry 1,600 men. The official records do not contain any report from Gordon on the retreat to Appomattox Court House and the final battle there. The description of the troop positions and the movement of the line is from Calkins' study, the most detailed reconstruction of these final actions. Waggaman's statement on the strength of his brigade was given by him at the time of his parole and appears at the end of the list of names of 368 officers and men of the Louisiana Brigade who surrendered on April 9, in *SHSP* 15.

33. OR 46, pt. 1, p. 1303. Calkins, *Appomattox Court House,* p. 60, p. 76, p. 100-101. Gordon, *Reminiscences*, pp. 436-437.

34. Gordon, *Reminiscences*, pp. 437-438.

35. Bartlett, *Military Record of Louisiana,* pp. 43-44. Jones, *Lee's Tigers*, pp. 225-226. William Kaigler, "Concerning Last Charge at Appomattox," *Confederate Veteran,* November 1898, p. 524. It is not known whether the 6th Louisiana took any casualties in this final charge of their war, but it is possible that one man was killed. In 1899, a Leela Allen of New Orleans filed a widow's claim under Louisiana's land grant act claiming that her late husband, Pvt. Nathan Allen of Company C, 6th Louisiana, was killed on the 7th day of April 1865 in a battle at Appomattox, Va. She had two witnesses verify her claim. However, there is no record of a Nathan Allen in the 6th Louisiana records in the National Archives. There was a Pvt. Ethan Allen in Company D, but records say he was discharged af-

ter being wounded at Winchester, May 25, 1862. The author has found that many of the claims for benefits under the land-grant act were apparently false, in conflict with the soldier's service records.

36. *SHSP* 15, pp. 233-234. Compiled service records, 6th Louisiana, file M320, rolls 163-173.

37. Ibid.

38. Freeman, *Lee's Lieutenants*, vol. 3, pp. 746-747.

39. *SHSP* 15, pp. 230-234. The names on the *SHSP* list of those surrendered do not always conform to the spellings in the service records of 6th Louisiana soldiers. For example, the list contains a J.P. Bruce and a William Hall in Company E, but the men who surrendered at Appomattox were Pvts. Henry C. Hall and G. Paul Burce. The spellings have been corrected to conform with the compiled service records. In addition, three men of the 6th Louisiana not present at the parole but later captured and paroled under its terms were: Sgt. Andrew Kennedy and Pvt. James Donovan of Company B, and Pvt. Daniel Riordan of Company F. (There were two privates named Daniel Riordan in Company F, carried on the company rolls as No. 1 and No. 2.)

40. Army of Northern Virginia Papers, LHAC, Tulane.

41. Ibid.

Conclusion – Reflections on the Irish Rebels

1. Compiled service records, 6th Louisiana, record group 109, file M320, roll 170, National Archives.

2. Ibid, rolls 163-173.

3. *Adjutant General's Report*, State of Louisiana, 1890.

4. Jones, *Lee's Tigers*, pp. 233-247.

5. Historical Memorandum, Company E, 6th Louisiana record roll, LHAC, Tulane.

6. John Francis Maguire, *The Irish in America* (London, 1868; reprint edition, 1969) p. 546.

7. Ibid, pp. 546-547.

8. *The Daily True Delta*, New Orleans, August 4, 1861.

9. Maguire, *The Irish in America*, p. 550.

10. Ibid, pp. 576-577.

11. Grady McWhiney and Perry D. Jamieson, *Attack and Die*, (Tuscaloosa, Ala., 1982) p. 172.

12. Ibid, pp. 178-181. Many if not most Civil War historians disagree with McWhiney's and Jamieson's theories on the Celtic influence on the Confederacy's battle tactics. They are worth pondering, however, as a contributing factor in the collective personality of the Confederate fighter.

13. *Confederate Veteran*, vol. 19, p. 300. The exact date of original publication of this poem is not known. On republishing it, *Confederate Veteran* said only that it was "from the *Mobile Tribune* of 1863." By then, New Orleans' newspapers were under Federal control, which would explain by young Miss Bryant would have sent it out of state for publication in a loyal Confederate newspaper.

Bibliography

PRIMARY SOURCES:

Manuscripts

Duke University, Durham, N.C., Special Collections Library

Ben Hubert Papers: Letters of Ben Hubert.

University of Michigan, Ann Arbor, Mich., William M. Clements Library. Schoff Civil War Collection.

Isaac Gurdon Seymour Papers: Letters of Isaac Gurdon Seymour; Seymour Civil War scrapbook; Seymour photographs.

Museum of the Confederacy, Richmond, Va., Eleanor S. Brockenbrough Library.

From the Archer Anderson Collection: Record/Roll Book (fragment) of the 6th Louisiana Volunteers, May-August 1864.

From the Louisiana Room Papers Collection: Letters of Theodore Hoyt Woodard.

Tulane University, New Orleans, La., Howard-Tilton Memorial Library, Louisiana Historical Association Collection (LHAC)

Herron Family Correspondence: Letters of Nicholas Herron.

Ring Family Correspondence: Letters of George P. Ring. Diary of George P. Ring.

Record Roll, 6th Louisiana Volunteers, bound volume.

The Virginia Historical Society, Richmond Virginia.

Memoirs of William E. Trahern.

Antietam National Battlefield Park Library, Sharpsburg, Maryland.

6th Louisiana Infantry Regiment File: Letters of George Zeller, donated by Joyce Watkins, Tucson, AZ.

Fredericksburg & Spotsylvania National Military Park Library, Fredericksburg, Va.

6th Louisiana Infantry Regiment File: "Letter from the Sixth Louisiana," Mobile Advertiser & Register, June 4, 1863; Letter from "Volunteer, First Louisiana Brigade," Mobile Advertiser & Register, May 21, 1863; "Extracts from a Private Letter of an Officer in Hays' Louisiana Brigade, 6th Regiment," Daily Advertiser, Montgomery, Alabama, May 28, 1864.

Gettysburg National Battlefield Park Library

6th Louisiana Infantry Regiment File: List of Louisiana Soldiers Killed at Gettysburg.

Manassas National Battlefield Park Library

6th Louisiana Infantry Regiment File: Letter of Jeremiah Hogan.

National Archives, Washington, D.C.

Compiled Service Records, 6th Louisiana Volunteers, Record Group 109, File M320, Rolls 163-173.

Record of Events, 6th Louisiana Volunteers, Record Group 109, File M861, Roll 23.

Confederate States Army Casualties: Lists and Narrative Reports, 1861-65, Record Group 109, File M836.

Letters Received by Confederate Secretary of War, File M437.

State of Louisiana, Division of Archives, Records Management and History. Land Grant records, under Acts No. 96 of 1884, No. 116 of 1886 and No. 55 of 1896, Widows' Proofs and Soldiers' Proofs, 6th Louisiana Regiment.

Official Publications

United States War Department. *The War of Rebellion: A compilation of the Official Records of the Union and Confederate Armies,* 128 vols., Washington, D.C.: Government Printing Office, 1880-1901.

—*Atlas to Accompany the Official Records of the Union and Confederate Armies.* Washington, D.C.: Government Printing Office, 1891-1895.

Newspapers

Detroit *Free Press*
Montgomery (Ala.) *Daily Advertiser*
Mobile (Ala.) *Advertiser & Register*
The Commercial Bulletin, New Orleans, La.
New Orleans *Daily Picayune.*
New Orleans *Sunday Delta*
The Daily True Delta, New Orleans, La.
Richmond *Examiner*
Richmond Whig

Autobiographies, Diaries, Journals, Reminiscences and Unit Histories

Bartlett, Napier. *Military Record of Louisiana.* Baton Rouge, 1964.

Beaudot, William J.K. and Herdegen, Lance J., *An Irishman in the Iron Brigade: The Civil War Memoirs of James P. Sullivan.* Fordham University Press. New York. 1993.

Buck, Samuel D. *With the Old Confeds: Actual Experiences of a Captain in the Line.* H.E. Houck & Co. Baltimore. 1925.

Buck, Lucy Rebecca. *Sad Earth, Sweet Heaven: The Diary of Lucy Rebecca Buck.* Buck Publishing Co., Birmingham, Ala. 1992 edition.

Douglas, Henry Kyd. *I Rode with Stonewall.* University of North Carolina Press. Chapel Hill, N.C. 1940.

Early, Jubal A. *Jubal Early's Memoirs : Autobiographical Sketch and Narrative of the War Between the States.* Nautical & Aviation Publishing Co. of America. Baltimore, Md. 1989.

Gilmor, Harry. *Four Years in the Saddle.* Harper & Brothers. New York. 1866.

Gordon, John B. *Reminiscences of the Civil War.* Charles Scribner's Sons. New York. 1903. Reprint edition, Morningside House, Inc., Dayton, Ohio, 1988.

Jones, Terry L., editor. *The Civil War Memoirs of Captain William J. Seymour.* Louisiana State University Press. Baton Rouge, La. 1991.

Handerson, Henry E. *Yankee in Gray.* Western Reserve University Press. Cleveland, Ohio. 1962

Maguire, John Francis. *The Irish in America*. Longmans, Green and Co. London. 1868. Reprint edition, 1969, by Arno Press, Inc.

Moore, Edward A. *The Story of a Cannoneer under Stonewall Jackson*. New York, 1907. Reprint edition, 1983.

Nisbet, James Cooper. *Four Years on the Firing Line*. McCowat-Mercer Press. Jackson, Tenn. 1963.

Owen, William Miller. *In Camp and Battle with the Washington Artillery of New Orleans*. Ticknor and Company, Boston, 1885.

Sheeran, James B., *Confederate Chaplain: The War Journal of the Rev. James B. Sheeran, C.SS.R.*, edited by Joseph T. Durkin, Bruce Publishing Co. Milwaukee. 1960.

Stiles, Robert. *Four Years under Marse Robert*. Neale Publishing Co. New York, 1903.

Taylor, Richard. *Destruction and Reconstruction*. Bantam Books. New York, N.Y. 1992.

Worsham, John H. *One of Jackson's Foot Cavalry*. McCowat-Mercer Press. Jackson, Tenn. 1964.

Secondary Sources:

Books

Beck, Brandon H., and Grunder, Charles S., *The Second Battle of Winchester, June 12-15, 1863*. H.E. Howard, Inc. Lynchburg, Va. 1989.

Bergeron, Arthur W., Jr. *Guide to Louisiana Confederate Military Units, 1861-65*. Louisiana State University Press. Baton Rouge, La. 1989.

Booth, Andrew. *Records of Louisiana Confederate Soldiers and Louisiana Confederate Commands*, 3 vols., New Orleans, 1920.

Bigelow, John Jr. *Chancellorsville*. Smithmark Publishers, Inc., New York. 1995 reprint edition.

Calkins, Chris M. *The Battles of Appomattox Station and Appomattox Court House*, April *8-9, 1865* (Lynchburg, Va., 1987).

Davis, Burke. *They Called Him Stonewall*. Fairfax Press. New York, 1988.

Dowdey, Clifford. *The Seven Days: The Emergence of Lee*. Boston, 1964.

Dunlop, William S. *Lee's Sharpshooters*. Morningside House, Inc. Dayton, Ohio. 1988. Reprint of 1899 edition.

Foote, Shelby. *The Civil War: A Narrative*. Three volumes. Random House. New York. 1963.

Frassanito, William A. *Antietam: The Photographic Legacy of America's Bloodiest Day*. New York, 1978.

Freeman, Douglas Southall. *Lee's Lieutenants: A Study in Command*. Three volumes. Charles Scribner's Sons. New York, 1944.

Furgurson, Ernest B. *Chancellorsville 1863: The Souls of the Brave*. Alfred A. Knopf. New York. 1992.

Hale, Laura Virginia. *Four Valiant Years*. Shenandoah Publishing House, Strasburg, Va. 1973.

Henderson, G.F.R. *Stonewall Jackson and the American Civil War*, 2 vols. Blue and Gray Press. Secaucus, N.J. 1989 reprint edition.

Hennessy, John J. *Return to Bull Run*. Simon & Schuster. New York. 1993.

Hodge, Robert A. *A Death Roster of the Confederate General Hospital at Culpeper, Virginia*. Fredericksburg, Va., 1977.

Jones, Terry L. *Lee's Tigers: The Louisiana Infantry in the Army of Northern Virginia.* Louisiana State University Press. Baton Rouge, La. 1987.

Judge, Joseph. *Season of Fire: The Confederate Strike on Washington.* Rockbridge Publishing Co. Berryville, Va. 1994.

Krick, Robert K. *Stonewall Jackson at Cedar Mountain.* Chapel Hill, N.C.: University of North Carolina Press, 1990.

Krick, Robert K. *Conquering the Valley: Stonewall Jackson at Port Republic.* New York: William Morrow and Co., 1996.

Lonn, Ella. *Foreigners in the Confederacy.* University of North Carolina Press. Chapel Hill, N.C. 1940.

Lonn, Ella. *Desertion during the Civil War.* Appleton-Century-Crofts, Inc. Gloucester, Mass. 1966.

Mahr, Theodore C. *The Battle of Cedar Creek: Showdown in the Shenandoah* (Lynchburg, Va. 1992).

McWhiney, Grady and Jamieson, Perry D. *Attack and Die: Civil War Military Tactics and the Southern Heritage.* University of Alabama Press. Tuscaloosa, Ala. 1982.

Matter, William D. *If It Takes All Summer: The Battle of Spotsylvania.* University of North Carolina Press. Chapel Hill, N.C. 1988.

Moore, Alison. *The Louisiana Tigers, or The Two Louisiana Brigades in the Army of Northern Virginia, 1861-65.* Baton Rouge, 1961.

Murfin, James V. *The Gleam of Bayonets.* Bonanza Books, New York, 1965.

Niehaus, Earl F. *The Irish in New Orleans, 1800-1860.* Louisiana State University Press. Baton Rouge, La. 1965.

Parrish, T. Michael. *Richard Taylor: Soldier Prince of Dixie.* University of North Carolina Press, Chapel Hill, N.C. 1992.

Rhea, Gordon C. *The Battle of the Wilderness, May 5-6, 1864.* Louisiana State University Press, Baton Rouge, La. 1994

Sears, Stephen W. *Landscape Turned Red: The Battle of Antietam.* Ticknor & Fields. New York. 1983.

Sears, Stephen W. *To the Gates of Richmond.* Ticknor & Fields. New York. 1992.

Steere, Edward. *The Wilderness Campaign.* Stackpole Co. Harrisburg, Pa. 1960.

Stephens, Robert Grier Jr. *Intrepid Warrior: Clement Anselm Evans.* Morningside, Dayton, Ohio, 1992.

Tanner, Robert G. *Stonewall in the Valley.* Stackpole Books, Mechanicsburg, Pa. 1996.

Vandiver, Frank E. *Jubal's Raid: General Early's Famous Attack on Washington in 1864,* McGraw Hill Book Co., New York, 1960. Reprint edition by Olde Soldier Books, Gaithersburg, Md. 1988.

Vandiver, Frank E. *Mighty Stonewall.* McGraw Hill Book Co., New York, 1957.

Winters, John D. *The Civil War in Louisiana.* Louisiana State University Press. Baton Rouge, La. 1963.

Periodicals

Brown, G. Campbell. *The Peninsula Campaign of 1862: Yorktown to the Seven Days, Vol. 2,* edited by Terry L. Jones. Savas Woodbury Publishers. Campbell, CA. 1995.

Jones, Terry L., ed. "Going Back into the Union at Last—A Louisiana Tiger's Account of the Gettysburg Campaign." *Civil War Times Illustrated*, January/February 1991.

Harry W. Pfanz. "The Battle of Gettysburg," National Park Civil War Series. Eastern National Park & Monument Association, 1994.

Noah Andre Trudeau. "The Siege of Petersburg," National Park Civil War Series. Eastern National Park & Monument Association, 1995.

Frank E. Vandiver, ed., "A Collection of Louisiana Confederate Letters." *The Louisiana Historical Quarterly*, Vol. 26, No. 4, October 1943, 937-974.

Jeffry Wert, "Rappahannock Station." *Civil War Times Illustrated*, December 1976.

Battles and Leaders of the Civil War, four volumes.

Confederate Veteran, specific articles cited.

Southern Historical Society Papers, specific articles cited.

INDEX